FAMILY PROCEDURE RULES 2010

Related titles from Law Society Publishing:

Domestic Abuse
Jane Wilson

Elderly Client Handbook (4th edn)
General Editors: Caroline Bielanska and Martin Terrell, Consultant Editor: Gordon R. Ashton

Family Law Protocol (3rd edn)
The Law Society

Good Practice in Child Care Cases (2nd edn)
The Law Society

Related Family and Criminal Proceedings
General Editor: Ananda Hall

Resolution Family Disputes Handbook
General Editor: Andrew Greensmith

Resolution Family Law Handbook (2nd edn)
General Editor: Andrew Greensmith

Tax and Family Breakdown
Jason Lane

Titles from Law Society Publishing can be ordered from all good bookshops or direct (telephone 0870 850 1422, email lawsociety@prolog.uk.com or visit our online shop at www.lawsociety.org.uk/bookshop).

FAMILY PROCEDURE RULES 2010

A Guide to the New Law

Stephen Parker

The Law Society

*With love and thanks to Matthew and William
and in loving memory of Catherine Parker*

All rights reserved. No part of this publication may be reproduced in any material form, whether by photocopying, scanning, downloading onto computer or otherwise without the written permission of the Law Society except in accordance with the provisions of the Copyright, Designs and Patents Act 1988. Applications should be addressed in the first instance, in writing, to Law Society Publishing. Any unauthorised or restricted act in relation to this publication may result in civil proceedings and/or criminal prosecution.

The author has asserted the right under the Copyright, Designs and Patents Act 1988 to be identified as author of this work.

While all reasonable care has been taken in the preparation of this publication, neither the publisher nor the author can accept any responsibility for any loss occasioned to any person acting or refraining from action as a result of relying upon its contents.

The views expressed in this publication should be taken as those of the author only unless it is specifically indicated that the Law Society has given its endorsement.

© The Law Society 2011

ISBN–13: 978-1-907698-14-9

Crown copyright material is reproduced here with the permission of the Controller of HMSO.

Published in 2011 by the Law Society
113 Chancery Lane, London WC2A 1PL

Reprinted in 2011

Typeset by Columns Design XML Ltd, Reading
Printed by CPI Antony Rowe, Chippenham and Eastbourne

The paper used for the text pages of this book is FSC certified. FSC (the Forest Stewardship Council) is an international network to promote responsible management of the world's forests.

CONTENTS

Abbreviations		x
1	**A new procedural code for family proceedings**	**1**
1.1	Introduction	1
1.2	Modernisation of language	2
1.3	Streamlining of procedure and harmonisation with the CPR	3
1.4	A single unified code of practice	3
1.5	Alignment with all levels of court	4
1.6	The rules: a brief overview	5
2	**The key changes**	**9**
2.1	Modernisation of language and process	9
2.2	Matrimonial and civil partnership proceedings	11
2.3	Financial proceedings	14
2.4	Children proceedings	15
2.5	Family proceedings in magistrates' courts	17
2.6	Appeals	20
3	**The rules explained**	**22**
3.1	Introduction	22
3.2	Part 1: Overriding objective	22
3.3	Part 2: Interpretation	24
3.4	Part 3: Alternative dispute resolution	25
3.5	Part 4: Case management powers	27
3.6	Part 5: How to start proceedings	35
3.7	Part 6: Service	38
3.8	Part 7: Procedure for applications in matrimonial and civil partnership proceedings	43
3.9	Part 8: Procedure for miscellaneous applications	48
3.10	Part 9: Applications for financial remedy	49
3.11	Parts 10 and 11: Applications under Parts IV and IVA of the Family Law Act 1996	56
3.12	Part 12: Proceedings relating to children save in relation to parental order, adoption and placement proceedings	57

3.13	Part 13: Proceedings under section 54 of the Human Fertilisation and Embryology Act 2008	65
3.14	Part 14: Procedure for applications in adoption, placement and related proceedings	65
3.15	Part 15: Representation of protected parties	67
3.16	Part 16: Representation of children and reports in proceedings involving children	68
3.17	Part 17: Statements of truth	71
3.18	Part 18: Procedure for other applications	73
3.19	Part 19: Alternative procedure for applications	76
3.20	Part 20: Interim remedies and security for costs	78
3.21	Part 21: Miscellaneous rules about disclosure and inspection of documents	80
3.22	Part 22: Evidence	81
3.23	Part 23: Miscellaneous rules about evidence disclosure and inspection of documents	83
3.24	Part 24: Witnesses, depositions generally and taking of evidence in Member States of the EU	83
3.25	Part 25: Experts and assessors	84
3.26	Part 26: Change of solicitor	88
3.27	Part 27: Hearings and directions appointments	89
3.28	Part 28: Costs	92
3.29	Part 29: Miscellaneous	93
3.30	Part 30: Appeals	94
3.31	Part 31: Registration of orders under the Council Regulation, the Civil Partnership (Jurisdiction and Recognition of Judgments) Regulations 2005 and the Hague Convention 1996	96
3.32	Part 32: Registration and enforcement of orders	96
3.33	Part 33: Enforcement	97
3.34	Part 34: Reciprocal enforcement of maintenance orders	99
3.35	Part 35: Mediation Directive	100
3.36	Part 36: Transitional provisions	100
4	**Conclusions**	102

APPENDICES

1	**The Family Procedure Rules 2010**	105
	Part 1 Overriding objective	105
	Part 2 Application and interpretation of the rules	106
	Part 3 Alternative dispute resolution: the court's powers	114
	Part 4 General case management powers	115
	Part 5 Forms and start of proceedings	118
	Part 6 Service	118
	Part 7 Procedure for applications in matrimonial and civil partnership proceedings	131
	Part 8 Procedure for miscellaneous applications	146
	Part 9 Applications for a financial remedy	154
	Part 10 Applications under Part 4 of the Family Law Act 1996	174

Part 11 Applications under Part 4A of the Family Law Act 1996	178
Part 12 Proceedings relating to children except parental order proceedings and proceedings for applications in adoption, placement and related proceedings	183
Part 13 Proceedings under section 54 of the Human Fertilisation and Embryology Act 2008	223
Part 14 Procedure for applications in adoption, placement and related proceedings	230
Part 15 Representation of protected parties	247
Part 16 Representation of children and reports in proceedings involving children	249
Part 17 Statements of truth	261
Part 18 Procedure for other applications in proceedings	262
Part 19 Alternative procedure for applications	265
Part 20 Interim remedies and security for costs	267
Part 21 Miscellaneous rules about disclosure and inspection of documents	270
Part 22 Evidence	271
Part 23 Miscellaneous rules about evidence	276
Part 24 Witnesses, depositions generally and taking of evidence in member states of the European Union	278
Part 25 Experts and assessors	283
Part 26 Change of solicitor	286
Part 27 Hearings and directions appointments	288
Part 28 Costs	292
Part 29 Miscellaneous	294
Part 30 Appeals	298
Part 31 Registration of orders under the Council Regulation, the Civil Partnership (Jurisdiction and Recognition of Judgments) Regulations 2005 and under the Hague Convention 1996	303
Part 32 Registration and enforcement of orders	310
Part 33 Enforcement	319
Part 34 Reciprocal enforcement of maintenance orders	326
Part 35 Mediation Directive	343
Part 36 Transitional arrangements and pilot schemes	345
Glossary	345

2 **Practice Directions** 347

Practice Direction 2A – Functions of the court in the Family Procedure Rules 2010 and practice directions which may be performed by a single justice of the peace	347
Practice Direction 3A – Pre-application protocol for mediation information and assessment	355
Practice Direction 4A – Striking out a statement of case	359
Practice Direction 4B – Civil restraint orders	361
Practice Direction 5A – Forms	364
Practice Direction 6A – Service within the jurisdiction	374
Practice Direction 6B – Service out of the jurisdiction	381

Practice Direction 6C – Disclosure of addresses by government departments (amending PD of 13 February 1989)	390
Practice Direction 7A – Procedure for applications in matrimonial and civil partnership proceedings	394
Practice Direction 7B – Medical examinations on applications for annulment of a marriage	398
Practice Direction 7C – Polygamous marriages	398
Practice Direction 7D – Gender Recognition Act 2004	399
Practice Direction 9A – Application for a financial remedy	402
Practice Direction 10A – Part 4 of the Family Law Act 1996	407
Practice Direction 12A – Public law proceedings guide to case management	409
Practice Direction 12B – The revised private law programme	433
Practice Direction 12C – Service of application in certain proceedings relating to children	439
Practice Direction 12D – Inherent jurisdiction (including wardship) proceedings	445
Practice Direction 12E – Urgent business	448
Practice Direction 12F – International child abduction	450
Practice Direction 12G – Communication of information	460
Practice Direction 12H – Contribution orders	465
Practice Direction 12I – Applications for Reporting Restriction Orders	465
Practice Direction 12J – Residence and Contact Orders: Domestic Violence and Harm	466
Practice Direction 12K – Children Act 1989: Exclusion Requirement	471
Practice Direction 12L – Children Act 1989: Risk Assessments under Section 16A	471
Practice Direction 12M – Family Assistance Orders: Consultation	472
Practice Direction 12N – Enforcement of Children Act 1989 Contact Orders: Disclosure of Information to Officers of the National Probation Service (High Court and County Court)	472
Practice Direction 12O – Arrival of child in England by air	473
Practice Direction 12P – Removal from jurisdiction: Issue of passports	473
Practice Direction 14A – Who receives a copy of the application form for orders in proceedings	474
Practice Direction 14B – The First Directions Hearing – Adoptions with a foreign element	475
Practice Direction 14C – Reports by the adoption agency or local authority	475
Practice Direction 14D – Reports by a registered medical practitioner ('health reports')	484
Practice Direction 14E – Communication of information relating to proceedings	486
Practice Direction 14F – Disclosing information to an adopted adult	489
Practice Direction 15A – Protected parties	490

Practice Direction 16A – Representation of children	492
Practice Direction 17A – Statements of truth	500
Practice Direction 18A – Other applications in proceedings	504
Practice Direction 19A – Alternative procedure for applications	508
Practice Direction 20A – Interim remedies	510
Practice Direction 21A – Disclosure and inspection	515
Practice Direction 22A – Written evidence	515
Practice Direction 24A – Witnesses, depositions and taking of evidence in member states of the European Union	525
Practice Direction 25 – Experts and assessors in family proceedings	530
Practice Direction 26A – Change of solicitor	544
Practice Direction 27A – Family proceedings: Court bundles (Universal practice to be applied in all courts other than the family proceedings court)	545
Practice Direction 27B – Attendance of media representatives at hearings in family proceedings (High Court and county courts)	550
Practice Direction 27C – Attendance of media representatives at hearings in family proceedings (Family Proceedings Court)	553
Practice Direction 28A – Costs	556
Practice Direction 29A – Human Rights, joining the Crown	559
Practice Direction 29B – Human Rights Act 1998	559
Practice Direction 30A – Appeals	560
Practice Direction 31A – Registration of orders under the Council Regulation, the Civil Partnership (Jurisdiction and Recognition of Judgments) Regulations 2005 and under the 1996 Hague Convention	580
Practice Direction 33A – Enforcement of undertakings	584
Practice Direction 34A – Reciprocal enforcements of maintenance orders	585
Practice Direction 34B – Practice Note (Tracing Payers Overseas)	596
Practice Direction 35A – Mediation Directive	596
Practice Direction 36A – Transitional arrangements	597

ABBREVIATIONS

ADR	alternative dispute resolution
CA 1989	Children Act 1989
CAFCASS	Children and Family Court Advisory and Support Service
CE	cash equivalent
CMH	case management hearing
CPA 2004	Civil Partnership Act 2004
CPR 1998	Civil Procedure Rules 1998
CRO	civil restraint order
DPMCA 1978	Domestic Proceedings and Magistrates' Courts Act 1978
DWP	Department for Work and Pensions
FDR	family dispute resolution
FDRH	first dispute resolution hearing
FHDRA	First Hearing Dispute Resolution Appointment
FLA 1986	Family Law Act 1986
FLA 1996	Family Law Act 1996
FPR 1991	Family Proceedings Rules 1991
FPR 2010	Family Procedure Rules 2010
HFEA	Human Fertilisation and Embryology Authority
IRH	Issues Resolution Hearing
LSC	Legal Services Commission
MCA 1973	Matrimonial Causes Act 1973
MFPA 1984	Matrimonial and Family Proceedings Act 1984
PD	practice direction
PPF	Pension Protection Fund

1 A NEW PROCEDURAL CODE FOR FAMILY PROCEEDINGS

1.1 INTRODUCTION

1.1.1 A brief history

The Courts Act 2003, s.75 established a new power to make one set of simple and plainly expressed self-contained rules for all family proceedings so that the family justice system is accessible to all and both fair and efficient.

In order to achieve that end, Her Majesty's Courts Service and the Family Procedure Rules Committee have been charged since 2004 with delivering a new set of unified Family Procedure Rules for all tiers of court.

Initially, this resulted in the Family Procedure (Adoption) Rules 2005, SI 2005/2795.

Their next task was to complete the process for all family proceedings, which led to a consultation paper produced by the then Department for Constitutional Affairs (CP 19/06) dated 30 August 2006, the consultation to which closed on 1 December 2006.

The responses to that consultation were produced on 22 February 2008 by Her Majesty's Courts Service (CP(R) 19/06). The new Family Procedure Rules 2010, SI 2010/2955 (FPR 2010) were ultimately laid before Parliament on 17 December 2010 and came into operation on 6 April 2011.

1.1.2 Aims and scope of the rules

The rules 'provide a new code of procedure for family proceedings in the High Court, county courts and magistrates' courts, and replace existing rules of court for family proceedings' (FPR 2010, Explanatory note).

The significance of the new FPR 2010 (which extend to nearly 300 pages and which have been six years in the making) cannot be overstated both as to the extent of unification of all previous rules relating to family proceedings across all tiers of court and in respect of their dovetailing with the Civil Procedure Rules 1998, SI 1998/3132 (CPR).

The new rules also modernise many aspects of the current procedures and borrow extensively from the CPR in respect of a number of new powers which family practitioners are going to have to familiarise themselves with.

In essence, the new Family Procedure Rules replace all those rules currently governing the practice and procedure in family proceedings, including in particular the Family Proceedings Rules 1991, SI 1991/1247 (FPR 1991), the Family Proceedings Courts (Children Act 1989) Rules 1991, SI 1991/1395, the Family Proceedings Courts (Matrimonial Proceedings etc.) Rules 1991, SI 1991/1991 and the Family Procedure (Adoption) Rules 2005, SI 2005/2795, together with the sets of rules relating to reciprocal enforcement of maintenance orders, in particular the Magistrates' Courts (Reciprocal Enforcement of Maintenance Orders) Rules 1974, SI 1974/668.

The FPR 2010 accordingly provide for a single set of rules of court and codes of procedure for all family proceedings, be they proceedings in the High Court, county court or magistrates' court, based upon the model set out in the CPR. They also draw from attempts to forge a unified family court as first envisaged in the Finer Report of 1974.

Like the CPR, they are supplemented by dedicated practice directions (PDs) and forms, establishing a modern, consolidated comprehensive code of family procedure across all tiers of court and in relation to all types of proceedings.

Not only does this have the benefit of bringing together various procedural provisions into one single package but it enables further future amendments and updates to the rules to be made more simply and cohesively as opposed to the multitude of changes to a wide set of rules, guidance and forms as was the case in the past.

From the outset it must be recognised that the initial consultation documents set out four key objectives that the FPR 2010 intended to achieve:

- modernisation of language;
- streamlining of procedure and harmonisation with the CPR;
- a single, simply expressed unified code of practice and procedure similar to the CPR for all family proceedings;
- alignment in all levels of court.

1.2 MODERNISATION OF LANGUAGE

As the aims which led to the development and phraseology of the CPR included, notably, the reduction in complexity and modernisation of terminology, it was similarly recognised that the existing family proceedings rules contained what some regarded as outdated language.

The new rules therefore involve a fundamental review of language and style.

Thus, where appropriate, the new rules ditch what is perceived as outdated language in favour of their more modern equivalent.

Gone from the new rules are 'cause lists' and 'special procedure'. 'Permission' has replaced 'leave', 'without notice' replaces 'ex parte' and 'permission to apply to the court' replaces 'liberty to apply'.

It was also the intention to take out 'prayer', 'decree nisi' and 'decree absolute' but the costs of updating the court's own software proved prohibitive meaning that the terms remain for now.

In addition to modernising the general language of the rules, the opportunity has also been taken to introduce new terms to describe certain procedures and documents.

1.3 STREAMLINING OF PROCEDURE AND HARMONISATION WITH THE CPR

The Committee charged with reform felt that it was wholly unsatisfactory that the old Rules of the Supreme Court and County Court Rules which had been revoked for civil proceedings were still relied upon in family proceedings.

As far as possible, therefore, the new Family Procedure Rules have been harmonised with and modelled on the Civil Procedure Rules so that we have one set of simply expressed rules of court for all family proceedings supplemented by dedicated practice directions and forms.

1.4 A SINGLE UNIFIED CODE OF PRACTICE

The Courts Act 2003, s.75(5) sets out the objective that the new FPR should be made with a view to securing that:

(a) the family justice system is accessible, fair and efficient; and
(b) the rules are both simple and simply expressed.

It was widely recognised that the current rules governing practice and procedure within the family jurisdiction were a mishmash, contained as they were in a number of different statutory instruments, as listed in **1.1.2** above as well as the County Court Rules 1981, SI 1981/1687 and Rules of the Supreme Court 1965, SI 1965/1776.

The result was that in many cases the exact practice and procedure which needed to be applied in any given case could be difficult to locate, were sometimes outdated and, more importantly, out of line with that of the CPR which have widely been regarded as a success.

The time was thus ripe for change.

To further add to the family practitioner's woes there were a plethora of practice directions, protocols and other forms of guidance, many of which were often not followed or even known about!

Accordingly, as with the CPR, in order to achieve simplification and accessibility, the FPR 2010 will be accompanied and supported by a mandatory set of practice directions easily located and understandable so as to provide, at the fingertips of all court users, procedural guidance.

Furthermore, many of the longer provisions of the previous rules have been broken down into shorter rules for the sake of clarity.

The new FPR therefore establish a comprehensive code of family procedure replacing a large body of previously unconsolidated rules, forms for different courts and different types of proceedings and providing a new, single set of rules, which will apply to all levels of family courts.

Clearly, such transparency will be ever increasingly important given the gradual erosion of publicly funded services and the rise in numbers of litigants in person.

1.5 ALIGNMENT WITH ALL LEVELS OF COURT

Historically, the jurisdiction of magistrates' courts in family proceedings has been (and, to a large extent, still remains) different from the jurisdiction of the High Court and county court which resulted in the development of differing rules of court governing both practice and procedure.

The rules of court governing practice and procedure in family proceedings (with the exception of adoption proceedings) at High Court and county court level were, of course, contained in the Family Proceedings Rules 1991.

The Children Act 1989 (CA 1989) brought into existence the Family Proceedings Court, the rules of which mirrored to a large extent those regulating applications in the High Court and county court.

However, even then, the rules of court governing practice and procedure in family proceedings in the magistrates' court (excluding adoption proceedings) were contained in a plethora of statutory instruments, principally:

- the Magistrates' Courts Rules 1981, SI 1981/552;
- the Family Proceedings Courts (Matrimonial Proceedings etc.) Rules 1991, SI 1991/1991; and
- the Family Proceedings Courts (Children Act 1989) Rules 1991, SI 1991/1395.

The new rules now provide for an even closer alignment of practice and procedure between all three tiers of court as they govern both practice and procedure in all levels of family proceedings, be they progressing in the High Court, county court or magistrates' court (family proceedings court).

1.6 THE RULES: A BRIEF OVERVIEW

Parts 1 to 6 'provide for fundamental matters of general application and various preliminary matters' (FPR 2010, Explanatory note).

Like the CPR, the FPR 2010 open in Part 1 with a statement of their overriding objective which now encompasses all types of family proceedings.

As with the CPR, the overriding objective is to enable the court to deal with cases justly; but the particular nature of the issues raised in family proceedings is addressed by highlighting 'welfare issues', so that the key objective in the FPR 2010 is that of enabling the court to deal with cases justly, *having regard to any welfare issues involved* (a departure from their CPR equivalent).

Part 2 contains the provisions for interpreting and applying the rules including provision about the delegation of certain functions of a magistrates' court to a single justice, thus hopefully promoting the maximisation of the court's resources and in turn reducing delay.

The FPR 2010 go on in the next four parts to follow the structure of the CPR.

There is a family-specific modification by way of Part 3 which is devoted to the court's powers in relation to encouraging alternative dispute resolution and to adjourn for such purpose.

Case management may be described as 'a judicially controlled process guiding an application towards a specific objective in a way which is fair, just, humane and child centred and at a reasonable cost within a reasonable timescale'. Part 4 accordingly contains provisions for the exercise of those case management powers and encompasses the ability to require a party's legal representative to attend court, to hold a hearing or to receive evidence by phone or other method of direct oral communication.

Part 5 provides for all the forms which are to be used in family proceedings (many of which have changed) and how family proceedings are commenced.

Part 6 makes provision for service of documents in family proceedings including service abroad. Of particular note are new and detailed provisions for service on and by children and/or their guardians or legal representatives, including provision for all documents to be routinely served on the guardian, the Children and Family Court Advisory and Support Service (CAFCASS) or the local authority if they are preparing a report under CA 1989, s.7 or for the purposes of a special guardianship order or family assistance order.

Parts 7 to 14 'make provision for procedure for the key types of family proceedings' (FPR 2010, Explanatory note), including applications in matrimonial (including divorce) and civil partnership proceedings (Part 7), applications for a 'financial remedy' (Part 9) and most children proceedings (Part 12).

As with the CPR, the FPR 2010 provide for two standard 'generic' forms of procedure (Parts 18 and 19), but with the addition of certain specific dedicated provisions for the procedure in various specific proceedings contained within Parts 7 to 14, the two generic procedures being available for all other matters.

The 'Part 18 procedure' is the procedure to be used to commence proceedings:

- where there is no specific procedure prescribed;
- where an application is required within existing proceedings; and
- in relation to proceedings which have been concluded.

The 'Part 19 procedure' is for cases where the Part 18 procedure does not apply (for instance because a rule or practice direction prohibits its usage) and:

- there is no prescribed form for the application; or
- the applicant is seeking the court's decision on a matter which is unlikely to involve a substantial dispute of fact; or
- its use is necessitated by a rule or practice direction.

The dedicated procedural provisions for specific applications are as follows:

- Part 7 – The procedure for matrimonial and civil partnership proceedings.
- Part 8 – The procedure for various miscellaneous proceedings such as a gender recognition certificate, permission to apply for financial relief after overseas divorce and transfer of tenancy applications under Sched. 7 to the Family Law Act 1996 (FLA 1996).
- Part 9 – The procedure for applications for a financial remedy (formerly 'ancillary relief') but now also including proceedings under CA 1989, Sched.1.
- Parts 10 and 11 – The procedure for domestic violence and forced marriages.
- Part 12 – The procedure for children applications save for parental, adoption and placement orders.
- Part 13 – The procedure for applications for parental orders under the Human Fertilisation and Embryology Act 2008, s.54.
- Part 14 – The procedure for adoption and placement proceedings.

Parts 15 and 16 make provision corresponding to CPR Part 21 for the representation of, and other issues relating to, children and protected parties.

The plethora of guidance and practice directions relating to the separate representation of children has been distilled into one distinct part (Part 16). Although it is modelled on the previous rules, the child's representative is now called 'the children's guardian' (even in private law proceedings) as opposed to 'guardian ad litem'.

Part 16 and the accompanying practice direction also deal with the duties and appointment of a child's guardian as well as the various types of reporting and welfare officers who are appointed from time to time within the different types of children proceedings.

In particular, PD 16A, Part 3 sets out the duties of a children's guardian in specified proceedings and adoption as well as in private law cases. The duties of the children and family reporter are found in PD 16A, Part 6. PD 16A, Part 5 deals with reporting officers in adoption and Part 7 with parental orders in Human Fertilisation and

Embryology Authority (HFEA) cases. PD 16A, Part 8 covers risk assessments and contact enforcement. Thus, one only has to look in one place for the rules about the various roles a family court reporter may undertake in all levels of court and in any type of proceedings.

FPR 2010, Part 17 makes provision about statements of truth and when they are required to verify documents which mirrors that of CPR Part 22.

FPR 2010, Part 18 deals with the procedure for other applications in proceedings, such as applications seeking permission to bring proceedings.

Part 19 deals with the alternative procedure for applications, such as applications seeking an order to prevent disclosure of information to an adopted person pursuant to Adoption and Children Act 2002, s.60(3).

The remaining parts of the rules are of general application and contain procedural provisions mirroring (subject to various modifications) the comparable parts of the CPR.

Part 20 deals with interim remedies/injunctions and now helpfully lists the vast majority of pre-existing powers of the court to make interim orders as well as orders as to security for costs.

Contained within the accompanying PD 20A are detailed provisions in respect of search orders which are no doubt in response to the decision in *Imerman* v. *Imerman* [2010] EWCA Civ 908.

Disclosure and inspection of documents is dealt with in Part 21; evidence by Parts 22 to 24; experts and assessors by Part 25; change of solicitor by Part 26.

Part 27 deals with hearings and directions appointments and includes provisions relating to the giving of reasons in a magistrates' court.

In respect of the costs rules, which are contained in Part 28, the main costs provisions of the CPR (Parts 43, 44, 47 and 48) are applied to family proceedings with various modifications reflecting the fact that, as a general rule, the court will not normally make a costs order in proceedings for a financial remedy.

Part 29 contains miscellaneous provisions including those relating to withdrawal of proceedings, protection of personal details in proceedings, Human Rights Act 1998 issues and remedies raised within family proceedings, issues of jurisdiction concerning child maintenance, and matters such as court seals and required formalities to be included on all orders.

Part 30 deals with appeals and now applies to all appellate courts.

Parts 31, 32 and 34 cover procedure in relation to international recognition and enforcement of certain orders in family matters and reciprocal enforcement of maintenance orders.

In particular, Parts 31 and 32 deal with registration and enforcement of foreign orders (including Scottish or Northern Irish orders).

Part 33 applies certain parts of the CPR, with appropriate modifications, to the enforcement of orders generally in family proceedings made in the High Court and county courts including committal and other money orders as well as undertakings.

Part 34 deals with the reciprocal enforcement of maintenance orders.

Part 35 relates to the Mediation Directive (i.e. mediated cross-border disputes that are subject to Directive 2008/52/EC on certain aspects of mediation in civil and commercial matters).

Part 36 makes provision for transitional arrangements which mirrors that of Part 51 of the CPR.

There are also a number of detailed supplementary provisions which support many parts of the rules and are contained in practice directions.

2 THE KEY CHANGES

2.1 MODERNISATION OF LANGUAGE AND PROCESS

2.1.1 Language

Since the modernisation brought about by the Civil Procedure Rules it was clearly only a matter of time before the language contained in the Matrimonial Causes Act 1973 (MCA 1973) (cause and petition, to name but a few) would be viewed as increasingly out of synch with the modern world.

Accordingly, which for some will be a fundamental review of language and style, the new rules will remove what was previously perceived to be outdated terminology and put in place a more modern user-friendly plain-English style equivalent which mirrors that of the CPR.

Current term	*Proposed new term*
Dissolution order	Civil partnership order
Decree of divorce	Matrimonial order
Decree of nullity	Matrimonial order
Decree of judicial separation	Matrimonial order
Ancillary relief	Application for a financial order/remedy
Matrimonial cause	Proceedings for a matrimonial order
Petition	Application
Petitioner	Applicant
Party cited/co-respondent	Second respondent
Avoidance of disposition order	Avoidance of disposition order/order preventing a disposition
Maintenance pending suit	Maintenance pending suit/maintenance pending outcome of proceedings

Power to make a civil restraint order

The power to make a civil restraint order really is a major development and the effect is even more draconian than that of a section 91(14) bar under the CA 1989.

Civil restraint orders were primarily a weapon utilised within the civil jurisdiction to control an abuse of process.

A civil restraint order is an order restraining a party from:

(a) making any further applications in current proceedings (a limited civil restraint order);
(b) issuing any further applications or making certain applications in specified courts (an extended civil restraint order); or
(c) issuing any claim or making any application in specified courts (a general civil restraint order),

without permission of a judge.

Within the CPR (rule 3.3(7)) there is provision, where a court dismisses an application before it, to consider whether to make a civil restraint order, if the court considers that the application before it was totally without merit.

There is now contained within the FPR 2010 a provision similar to those in the Family Procedure (Adoption) Rules 2005, rule 16 and CPR Part 3 and the accompanying practice direction.

2.1.2 Process

Electronic service of documents

Under the previous rules, service by email was not permitted (FPR 1991, rules 10.2 and 10.3).

Furthermore, documents could only be served by fax where the party being served was represented by a solicitor who agreed to that form of service. Even then, to be effective, a hard copy of the document faxed had to also be sent by post.

In the twenty-first century this archaic approach to modes of service clearly needed revisiting.

Under CPR rule 6.2(1)(d) and para.4 of the accompanying practice direction, service by both email and fax is allowed, even on those not represented by a solicitor, provided there is written agreement to that effect. Neither is it necessary to follow this up with a hard copy by way of ordinary post.

The FPR 2010 replicate these provisions by introducing service by email, which clearly underpins the objective of modernisation.

However, given the personal and often sensitive nature of the proceedings and the perceived lack of security compared to other modes of service (a misguided perception, in the author's view), more stringent restrictions have been imposed on the use of electronic service in the FPR 2010 than in the CPR.

2.2 MATRIMONIAL AND CIVIL PARTNERSHIP PROCEEDINGS

2.2.1 Application by a respondent for a matrimonial or civil partnership order

Under the previous rules, respondents to a divorce petition could file a cross-petition which in turn could be met with an answer and so on which often created a duality of proceedings and degree of complexity which could be confusing to manage even when matters are subsequently compromised by way of cross-decrees.

Under the new rules, the aim of which is to manage claims conveniently and effectively, all applications, whether for a matrimonial or civil partnership order, made by a respondent will be treated as an application in the original proceedings reflective of the current practice in CPR Part 20 (Counterclaims and other additional claims).

Respondents in such circumstances will be subject to stricter time limits, as any such application must be made within 21 days of the date by which the respondent is to acknowledge service of the original application, unless permission of the court is sought and obtained for an extension of time.

2.2.2 Parties to proceedings – divorce cases involving allegations of adultery

Both Resolution's Code of Practice and the Law Society's Family Law Protocol recommend that, in a divorce petition based upon an allegation of adultery, solicitors should discourage their clients from naming the co-respondent, in order to foster a conciliatory approach and thus reduce any potential for further animosity.

The new rules by way of practice direction reinforce this. In the event that an applicant does choose to name the person with whom the respondent is alleged to have committed adultery, that person will be made a party automatically, as it is considered inappropriate to deny such a person named in proceedings the opportunity to refute those allegations.

2.2.3 Extending the special procedure to applications for the annulment of a marriage or a civil partnership

Under the current rules, undefended divorces and dissolution cases are dealt with under what is known as the 'special procedure' (FPR 1991, rule 2.24(3)) whereby the court will consider, on paper only, the petition, acknowledgement of service, the supporting affidavit and, if satisfied that the petitioner has proved his/her case, will issue a certificate of entitlement to the decree.

If the court is not so satisfied, a request for further information can be made or the case removed from the special procedure list and a hearing set.

Under those rules, the special procedure could not be used in cases of nullity, even when undefended.

The new rules, however, now provide that undefended nullity cases can be dealt with using the special procedure, unless the court, in the exercise of its discretion, considers that a hearing is necessary. (Note that the terms 'special procedure' and 'request for directions for trial' have been abandoned in favour of the more apt 'application for decree nisi/condition order'.)

This seems to be a positive development as one could argue that there appears little merit in having a hearing in an uncontested nullity case which unnecessarily adds to the costs of the proceedings, use of court time and distress to the parties, where the matter could quite easily be disposed of on paper, much in the same way as undefended divorce is conducted.

2.2.4 Statement of arrangements for children

In divorce, dissolution, nullity, or judicial separation proceedings, wherever there is a child of the family who is under the age of 16, or between 16 and 18 and receiving education or training at an educational or vocational establishment, the petition must be accompanied by a statement containing information about the arrangements to be made for such child(ren) in order to enable the court to fulfil its duty under the MCA 1973, s.41 or under the Civil Partnership Act 2004, s.63 (namely, whether the court needs to exercise its powers under CA 1989 and, if so, to what extent).

There has been some debate as to the relevance of some of the questions posed, bearing in mind that there is a clear overlap between the information provided by the form, the contents of the petition and the information contained within applications made pursuant to CA 1989, s.8.

For example, specific details of the accommodation in which the children reside (namely the number of rooms, etc.) may be of debatable relevance, as this may change over the course of time as the proceedings progress due to a future move.

In reality, what is required is sufficient information to enable the court to discharge its statutory function.

One of the aims of the Family Procedure Rules Committee was to decrease the amount of information which previously was often repeated in both petition and statement, thus reducing the length of the forms, saving time and reducing the amount of information required.

Accordingly, the new Statement (Form D8A) contains less repetition of information and has been simplified to include:

- details of the children's names, dates of birth and gender;
- whether any of the children have special health or educational needs;
- whether there are, or have previously been, any other court proceedings.

2.2.5 Statements of truth instead of affidavits

An affidavit is a written statement in the name of a person by whom it is voluntarily signed and sworn or affirmed which is intended to be used as his or her evidence in court.

To be given as evidence in family proceedings the affidavit must be sworn before one of the following:

- a judge or district judge;
- a justice of the peace;
- an officer of a court appointed by the judge for that purpose;
- a commissioner for oaths or any person authorised to take affidavits under the Commissioners for Oaths Acts 1889 and 1891.

An affidavit has been increasingly seen to be a document of a bygone age, particularly following the advent of the Civil Procedure Rules.

In practical terms, it meant that a person wishing to swear an affidavit must first identify and locate one of the above persons, then attend before them in person in order to be sworn to it.

This not only inconveniences parties and often puts them to expense, but also results in a delay in progressing matters.

One innovation of the CPR is rule 22 which introduced the statement of truth which must be made if a party wishes to rely on any matter as evidence.

This is a statement made by a party which asserts the truth as to the contents of his or her evidence (be it in an application or witness statement).

The clear benefit of statements of truth over affidavits is their simplicity in procedure and consequential reduction in delay.

Statements of truth have now been adopted in the FPR 2010 (albeit to a lesser extent than proposed in the consultation process). Again, this is a positive development. It removes the need for a document to be formally sworn, but without compromising the importance that the court places on verifying the truth of the evidence given.

A statement of truth must be signed by the party or their legal representative and a statement of truth verifying a witness statement must be signed by the witness.

The rules also provide, as with the CPR, that evidence submitted without such a statement of truth is inadmissible and that the court can order the verification of such evidence by way of the endorsement of such a statement of truth on it.

2.3 FINANCIAL PROCEEDINGS

2.3.1 Ancillary relief rules

Proceedings for ancillary relief are now no longer 'ancillary' to the divorce or dissolution proceedings to which they relate. The proceedings for divorce and a financial order are now separate and distinct entities.

An application will now commence all proceedings rather than the old 'notice of intention to proceed with an application'.

Accordingly, such proceedings will now be known as 'proceedings for a financial order' and the term 'financial remedy' will apply to all such related proceedings.

Rather more revolutionary is the fact that the ancillary relief procedure will now cover a wider range of financial proceedings rather than just divorce or dissolution, the emphasis being on early full and frank disclosure of the parties' respective financial positions and settlement.

In particular, the ancillary relief procedure will apply to the following proceedings:

- Applications under MCA 1973, s.27 or the Civil Partnership Act 2004, Sched.5, Part 9 (failure to maintain).
- Applications under the Matrimonial and Family Proceedings Act 1984, Part III or the Civil Partnership Act 2004, Sched.7 (financial provision following overseas divorce/dissolution).
- Applications under MCA 1973, s.35 or the Civil Partnership Act 2004, Sched.5, para.69 (alteration of maintenance agreement by court during lifetime of parties).
- Applications under CA 1989, Sched.1.

Other financial applications which do not involve such a generous ambit of discretion in determining their outcome will be dealt with using a procedure similar to that prescribed by Part 8 of the CPR, such as applications under the Married Women's Property Act 1882, s.17 and MCA 1973, s.36 (alteration of agreements by court after the death of one party).

The Pensions Act 2004 introduced the Pension Protection Fund (PPF) which is a compensation scheme for those whose occupational pension schemes cannot afford to cover liabilities due to an 'insolvency event'. FPR 2010, Part 9, Chapter 8 refines the procedure in relation to pension sharing and attachment orders having regard to the PPF. Chapter 9 of Part 9 goes on to introduce a procedure for applications for pension compensation sharing and attachment orders.

2.3.2 Making an application for a financial order

Section 28(3) of MCA 1973 prevents a party to the marriage, who has remarried, from applying for a financial provision order or a property adjustment order.

The previous rules provided for an application to be made either in the petition itself or answer or in Form A (FPR 1991, rule 2.53) which thus provided an important form of protection to a party to divorce or dissolution proceedings who might subsequently remarry or enter into a civil partnership and was thus a remedy routinely pleaded in the prayer.

The intention of the new rules was to separate matrimonial and civil partnership proceedings from their related financial proceedings, the application for a financial order remaining wholly separate from the divorce or civil partnership application.

At consultation stage it was therefore no longer possible to include an application for a financial order within the application for a matrimonial or civil partnership order.

This provided a real trap for the unwary, as a person who did not apply separately for a financial order before remarrying or entering into a civil partnership would lose their entitlement to apply for a financial order in the future, which might be ground for a possible claim in negligence against their legal adviser.

As a safeguard, the new application form for a divorce, nullity or dissolution order was to contain a prominent warning of the consequences of remarriage on a party's future right to apply for a financial order, although as a further precaution, one would have been well advised to amend any standard letters accordingly when sending such applications out to clients.

One further upshot of this was that parties would quite possibly be forced to issue applications for a financial order sooner than they might have normally anticipated if a remarriage or civil partnership was on the cards, or in the event that they might wish to protect their claim for backdated periodical payments.

At the time of writing it appears that a rethink took place prior to final implementation of the rules. The new Form D8 contains the old style 'prayer' in relation to financial orders and thus it appears that the protection provided by the previous rules remains.

2.4 CHILDREN PROCEEDINGS

2.4.1 Protocol for Judicial Case Management in Public Law Children Act cases and Private Law Programme

The Private Law Programme sets the guideline for a First Dispute Resolution Hearing (FDRH) to take place within four to six weeks with the aim of improving the resolution of private law family cases in a timely and effective manner.

The Protocol for Judicial Case Management in Public Law Children Act cases ('Public Law Protocol') sets a guideline of 40 weeks for the conclusion of care cases (now replaced by the Public Law Outline as from 1 April 2008).

With the aim of reducing the plethora of protocols and guidance to produce one set of coherent rules and guidance by way of practice directions in accordance with their CPR equivalent, the FPR 2010 in respect of children proceedings incorporate both sets of documents.

A further aim of the new rules is to strike a balance between the necessary flexibility required for individual cases and the underlying timetable for their speedier disposal through:

- the fixing of the final hearing at any point in the proceedings; and
- the varying of the timetable at any hearing.

This is achieved by robust case management powers similar to those contained in the CPR Parts 1, 3 and 29 which will apply to both private and public law Children Act cases.

Pivotal to this aim will be the usage of:

- Case Management Conferences (the objective being to consider case management directions and timetables).
- Pre-hearing reviews (the objective being to identify and narrow the issues and ensure an effective final hearing).
- Schedule of issues (a composite schedule of issues produced by the advocates at the end of an advocates' meeting prior to a Case Management Conference or pre-hearing review which should be agreed as far as possible and, where not agreed, should set out the parties' differing positions).

2.4.2 Forms for applications under the Children Act 1989

A wide range of changes to the existing forms is required to support the FPR 2010.

The new application forms which accompany the rules mirror their style and content on those of the Adoption and Children Act 2002. Not only does this achieve consistency, it also provides a more user-friendly style and simplification of language used.

Where possible, provision for more direct questions and 'tick box' responses are provided paving the way for online completion thus reducing the need to enter 'free text'.

There are now also separate forms for different Children Act applications, e.g. one separate form for care and supervision applications.

The new application forms also contain a much more comprehensive set of guidance notes and a list of documents that need to be attached, similar to that of Form E in applications for a financial order.

Due to the increasing importance attached by the court to the mediation process (see FPR 2010, Part 3) and the stated intention to place privately funded and unrepresented applicants in a similar position to publicly funded applicants undergoing a Community Legal Service funding code referral, the new forms include questions about the use of mediation before the court process is commenced.

Again, further questions are raised as to information on domestic violence in light of current thinking and the ongoing concerns on its under-reporting and consequential effects on the victim and children.

2.5 FAMILY PROCEEDINGS IN MAGISTRATES' COURTS

2.5.1 Aligning rules governing practice and procedure in the magistrates' courts with those of the High Court and county courts

The aim of the FPR 2010 is to align the rules across all jurisdictions wherever possible in order to achieve both simplicity and the ultimate aim of a single family court.

2.5.2 Single justice

The new rules also provide that certain functions of the court in relation to proceedings in a magistrates' court may be performed by a single justice of the peace, provided he or she is a member of the family panel thus maximising the usage of the court's resources (FPR 2010, rule 2.6(1) and PD 2A).

However, a single justice cannot make a decision at the final hearing of an application for a substantive order.

2.5.3 Financial proceedings in magistrates' courts

As part of the aim of the new rules to achieve unification of the court process, another revolutionary and welcome development is the application of the ancillary relief procedure to financial proceedings in the magistrates' court.

However, given the fact that such financial proceedings will not present quite the same complexities as their county court counterparts and thus not merit the same detailed disclosure, a simplified version of the ancillary relief procedure (detailed below) will apply as well as a separate and distinct Financial Statement (Form E2 as opposed to Form E1, the latter of which is to be used within financial proceedings within the county court):

1. Applicant files application (Form A2).
2. Court issues application with notice of first appointment and date for exchange of Financial Statement.
3. Applicant serves notice of first appointment on respondent.
4. Parties exchange Financial Statements (Form E2) on a date specified by the court.
5. The overriding objective will apply to the management of the case including what (if any) further disclosure should be ordered.

6. First appointment hearing – court decides whether further disclosure required and the future management of the case to final hearing.

However, it must be noted that much of the magistrates' court procedure is defined by statute (Magistrates' Courts Act 1980, ss.53–64) which the new rules cannot override or ignore (although the Lord Chief Justice can and, it is anticipated, will). In addition there is also an existing procedural code which is set out in the Magistrates' Courts Rules 1981.

Furthermore, proceedings under the enactments listed in the Magistrates' Courts Act 1980, s.65 are defined as 'family proceedings'. However, this definition does not include enforcement proceedings or proceedings for variation of periodical payments registered in the magistrates' court and thus such applications are not provided for in the rules as they lay outside the Rules Committee's terms of reference; accordingly, nothing in the FPR 2010 can apply to proceedings which are not formally defined as 'family proceedings' within the meaning of the Magistrates' Courts Act 1980, s.65. This also excludes applications under Trusts of Land and Appointment of Trustees Act 1996, s.14 and the Inheritance (Provision for Family and Dependants) Act 1975 as these too are not 'family proceedings'.

2.5.4 Procedural changes

Power to order disclosure against a non-party

CPR rule 31.17 provides for disclosure against a non-party as do rules 79 and 80 of the Family Procedure (Adoption) Rules 2005.

FPR 1991, r 2.62(7) gave the court power to order a non-party to attend court to produce documents. The power of discovery against a third party is now available in the magistrates' court (FPR 2010, Part 21).

Power to stay proceedings

Previously, a magistrates' court did not generally have the power to stay proceedings, unlike that in the county court, which is a particularly useful mechanism within the civil jurisdiction.

That has now been remedied by a general power to do so contained within the FPR 2010.

Power to issue a witness summons

Such power, previously available at county court level, is now available in the magistrates' court for all family proceedings.

Appointing, changing or removing a solicitor from the court record

Apart from that as provided for under the Family Procedure (Adoption) Rules 2005, Part 18, there was previously no specific provision with regard

This has now been remedied to provide a power similar to that contained in CPR Part 42 (change of solicitor) to all family proceedings courts.

Authentication of documents

Rule 9 of the Family Procedure (Adoption) Rules 2005, which provides for the authentication of documents by seal or stamp of the court, now applies to all family proceedings, whatever level of court.

Providing for evidence by way of affidavit

In line with the policy of harmonisation of the rules for family proceedings with the CPR, the use of affidavits in family proceedings has been curtailed, preference being given to statements of truth.

Provision of written reasons in the family proceedings courts

Rule 21(5) of the Family Proceedings Courts (Children Act 1989) Rules 1991 and rule 12(5) of the Family Proceedings Courts (Matrimonial Proceedings etc.) Rules 1991 required the justices' clerk to record in writing, in consultation with the bench, the reasons for the court's decision and any findings of fact before the court made an order or refused an application before it.

Thus, no order could be made without there being a written record of the court's reasons and findings of fact.

For all of us who regularly practise in this field of law, this is perhaps the most annoying, inconvenient and often frustrating aspect of advocacy within the family proceedings court.

Not only does one, after the conclusion of the case, have to wait for what often seems an indeterminate amount of time for the delivery of written reasons, but one also has to build into any time estimate given to the court, for the conduct of a contested hearing, provision for formulating and handing down such written judgment with reasons.

Indeed, even in cases proceeding by consent, written reasons for making an order have to be given. Such is the disdain for these provisions that many advocates took the lead in writing out the court's reasons for making the order sought themselves which are then handed to the magistrates to formally endorse.

This is in sharp contrast to the position at county court and High Court level which provided for greater flexibility.

At the higher levels of jurisdiction there is no duty to pre-record the reasons and findings in writing and judges (even deputies) are able to deliver judgments orally at one and the same time as making the order.

As a welcome compromise, therefore, the current procedure is adjusted to allow magistrates to announce their decision, and to provide the parties with the order and a summary of the reasons for their decision and, thereafter, full written reasons to be given by the end of the court day or whenever practicable. This, it is envisaged, will hopefully, to some extent, mitigate the previous regime and consequential delay and stress encountered.

It is also intended to develop standardised templates to aid the process.

2.6 APPEALS

2.6.1 Process of appeal

The rules regulating appeals from family proceedings courts were often complex and confusing having developed piecemeal over many years through a variety of different statutes such as CA 1989, s.94 and the Domestic Proceedings and Magistrates' Courts Act 1978 (DPMCA 1978), s.29 and necessitated commencement in a variety of ways such as:

- case stated (such application to be made within 21 days of the decision (Magistrates' Courts Act 1980, s.111(2)));
- notice of appeal (pursuant to CA 1989, s.94, such notice to be filed within 14 days (FPR 1991, rule 4.22(3)));
- notice of motion (under DPMCA 1978, s.29, such notice to be lodged within six weeks of the decision (FPR 1991, rule 8.2(2))).

The new rules sensibly, and not before time, to the undoubted relief of practitioners, provide for a single process of appeal from decisions of a magistrates' court in family proceedings by way of a single form of appeal notice.

This, of course, is consistent with making rules which are simple and easy to follow, which is more than can be said for their predecessors.

Again, as part of the process of harmonising the Family Proceedings Rules with the provisions of the Civil Procedure Rules, CPR Part 52 has been adjusted to apply to all family proceedings, as has been the case with Part 19 of the Family Procedure (Adoption) Rules 2005, and appeals from decisions of a family proceedings court by way of case stated have accordingly been abolished.

2.6.2 Route of appeal

Not only has the mode of appeal changed but so has the route.

Previously, all appeals from decisions in the family proceedings court had to be made to a High Court judge (no doubt much to their annoyance given the sheer volume of work done at family proceedings court level).

The rules now state that, quite sensibly in the author's view, all such appeals in the future shall be dealt with at county court level by a circuit judge. In other words, we now have a tier-based approach, as with the civil jurisdiction, with any final decision appealed to a court one level up from the decision being appealed against.

This again is clearly consistent with the longer-term objective of creating a single civil and family court.

3 THE RULES EXPLAINED

3.1 INTRODUCTION

The FPR 2010 are contained in 36 Parts covering different areas of procedure and different types of proceedings and to a large extent are modelled on the CPR subject to certain modifications.

The intention is for the FPR 2010 to be a self-contained code of rules, practice directions and forms, where possible and practicable, applying across all tiers of court.

Much of the detail of the procedure to be followed is contained in practice directions supplementing the different parts of the rules.

There are some substantive changes, such as the inclusion of strike-out provisions from the CPR and a wider requirement for permission to appeal.

3.2 PART 1: OVERRIDING OBJECTIVE

The overriding objective derives from CPR Part 1.

Just like the CPR, the new FPR 2010 set out at their very inception the overriding objective and guiding philosophy of the new rules so as to provide a 'compass' to guide courts and litigants and legal advisers as to the general course of the rules.

Perhaps the first thing to emphasise is FPR 2010, rule 1.1 which permeates the whole ethos of the FPR and is known as the 'overriding objective'. This repeats the overriding objective in ancillary relief proceedings which was contained in rule 2.51D of the FPR 1991. The objective is now extended to all family litigation.

The importance of this is also set out in FPR 2010, rule 1.3, which states that not only are the parties required to assist the court in furthering the 'overriding objective' but, through rule 1.4, the court itself is required to further the overriding objective by actively managing cases ('active case management').

3.2.1 What is the overriding objective?

The overriding objective requires all cases to be dealt with 'justly, having regard to any welfare issues' (FPR 2010, rule 1.1(1)).

It is important to observe that welfare issues are an additional requirement of the FPR 2010 as compared with the CPR. Given the nature of family litigation which, often as it does, involves the issue of children in respect of both children proceedings and financial applications, this is clearly an important and intentional additional gloss.

The reference to welfare is not limited to that of children and can include adults, particularly if they are vulnerable or otherwise lack capacity.

Dealing with a case justly includes the following:

- Ensuring that it is dealt with expeditiously and fairly.
- Dealing with the case in ways which are proportionate to the:
    - nature of the case;
    - importance of the case;
    - complexity of the issues.
- Ensuring that the parties are on equal footing (note the likely readjustment of any perceived imbalance where there is a litigant in person, in particular the preparation of a court bundle or draft order by a represented party even if the litigant is in fact the applicant).
- Saving expense (note this interrelates also with the issue of proportionality particularly when dealing with the appointment of experts).
- Allotting to it an appropriate share of the court's resources whilst taking into account the need to allot resources to other cases (again, the proportionality issue).

Active case management includes the following:

- Encouraging the parties to co-operate with each other in the conduct of the proceedings (each party clearly owes a duty to the court in ensuring that its orders are complied with and that the case is progressed).
- Identifying at an early stage:
    - the issues; and
    - who should be a party to the proceedings (particularly important when dealing with the question of adding a second respondent in divorce proceedings or the issue of joinder in a financial application).
- Deciding promptly which issues need full investigation at trial and which do not and the appropriate procedure to be followed. (This clearly points the way to more robust case management, particularly given the objective of dealing with cases in a manner which is proportionate as set out previously, bearing in mind court resources.)
- Deciding the order in which issues are to be resolved.
- Encouraging the parties to use an alternative dispute resolution procedure if the court considers that appropriate and facilitating the use of such procedure (notably mediation, conciliation and collaborative law practice).
- Helping the parties to settle the whole or part of the case. (Emphasising the proactive role of judges and possibly the adoption at more hearings of a family

dispute resolution (FDR) style approach where appropriate as well as adjourning for the purposes of alternative dispute resolution (ADR).)
- Fixing timetables or otherwise controlling the progress of the case. (Again this dovetails with the objective of ensuring cases are dealt with expeditiously.)
- Considering whether the likely benefits of taking a particular step justify the cost of taking it. (A cost/benefits analysis.)
- Dealing with as many aspects of the case as possible on the same occasion. (Emphasising the importance of utilising the court's resources and a focused approach to the case to achieve an expeditious conclusion within a predefined timeframe.)
- Dealing with the case without the parties needing to attend at court.
- Making use of technology (e.g. the giving of evidence by video link and other electronic means (FPR 2010, rule 22.3)).

The latter two points are increasingly important in the civil jurisdiction as many hearings take place by way of telephone hearings without requiring the formal attendance of the parties or, indeed, within the precincts of the court, thus saving substantial costs.

Whether or not this is going to be extensively used in children and financial proceedings, where at present the parties' attendance is required, remains to be seen, but as far as an FDA is concerned this may to a large extent be seen as a welcome option in an appropriate case.

- Giving directions to ensure that the trial of a case proceeds quickly and efficiently. (Again this links in with the objective of attempting to deal with as many issues as possible at any hearing listed, irrespective of its original purpose.)

3.3 PART 2: INTERPRETATION

This Part contains interpretation of terms used throughout the rules. A substantial part of the glossary of the previous rules has been altered and familiarity with the new terms and what they mean will be essential for the busy family practitioner.

Some terms will be more readily recognisable than others.

The main definitions include the following:

- **Alternative dispute resolution** – out of court resolution to include mediation.
- **Application form** – a document in which the applicant states his or her intention to seek an order other than in accordance with the Part 18 procedure.
- **Application notice** – an application in accordance with the Part 18 procedure.
- **Civil restraint order** – an order restraining a party from making:
    (a) any further applications in current proceedings (a limited civil restraint order);
    (b) certain applications at specified courts (an extended civil restraint order); or

(c) any applications in specified courts (a general civil restraint order).
- **Financial order** – this covers an avoidance of disposition order, and orders for periodical payments, lump sum, property adjustment and pension sharing.
- **Financial remedy** – not only does this cover a financial order (see above) but it includes a whole raft of financial provisions contained in a multitude of legislation including CA 1989, Sched.1.
- **Matrimonial order** – a decree of divorce, a decree of nullity or a decree of judicial separation.

3.4 PART 3: ALTERNATIVE DISPUTE RESOLUTION

These are new provisions intended to complement the overriding objective.

As part of the continual drive to encourage and facilitate mediation as a way of resolving disputes amicably, thus saving costs and recourse to the courts, the FPR 2010 set out the court's powers in dealing with ADR (including mediation).

This is backed up by the corresponding practice direction, PD 3A which by way of introduction states that:

> There is a general acknowledgement that an adversarial court process is not always best-suited to the resolution of family disputes, particularly private law disputes between parents relating to children, with such disputes often best resolved through discussion and agreement …(PD 3A, para.3.1)

> Parties will therefore be expected to explore the scope for resolving their dispute through mediation before embarking on the court process. (PD 3A, para.3.5)

> … all potential applicants for a court order in relevant family proceedings will be expected, before making their application, to have followed the steps set out in the Protocol. (PD 3A, para.4.1)

In essence, FPR 2010, rule 3.2 sets out the objective that the court must consider, at every stage in the proceedings, whether ADR is an appropriate mechanism which should be utilised in attempting to resolve matters.

Indeed, it is provided in FPR 2010, rule 3.3 that if it is felt that ADR is appropriate, then the court can direct that the proceedings be adjourned for such period or periods as is felt appropriate to enable the parties to obtain information and advice in respect of ADR and, indeed, for ADR to take place (the court cannot compel parties to undertake ADR). Note that this contrasts with the power of the civil court to order a general 'stay' so that it is likely that such adjournment will always be to a fixed date as opposed to an adjournment generally (but see the court's general case management powers to order a stay at **3.5** below).

Such directions can be given either by invitation of the parties themselves or of the court's own initiative.

It is worth noting that the power of the court to direct an adjournment for the purpose of ADR of its own initiative could mean, in an appropriate case, adjourning proceedings without the parties being present, as a paper exercise, without hearing representations, if the court feels that insufficient attempts have been made to negotiate matters or that other options have not been properly explored before instigating such proceedings.

If that is the case then note the important provisions provided by FPR 2010, rules 4.1(7) and 4.3(2)–(6).

Where such an adjournment is directed, the court will also set out the corresponding duty of the parties to keep the court informed of the outcome of such ADR referral or process.

It is to be expected that, as with the CPR, any order adjourning the proceedings for the purposes of ADR will provide a direction that by a specified date the applicant must advise the court as to whether or not ADR has been successful and, if so, whether a consent order can be filed, or whether a further adjournment is required due to ongoing mediation or, in the event that ADR has not been successful, what further directions are required, in order to bring about an expedited resolution of the proceedings by way of a hearing.

In the event that such information is not provided again, as with the civil jurisdiction, the court can give such directions as it considers appropriate in respect of the future management of the case. However, one would imagine that if the adjournment is to a fixed date, such directions will be given on that occasion rather than of the court's own initiative. We will have to wait and see.

The accompanying practice direction (PD 3A) incorporates within Annex A the ADR pre-action protocol which the court will normally expect an applicant to follow before bringing an application either in respect of financial proceedings or in relation to proceedings in respect of children.

In essence, this provides that as from 6 April 2011 anyone contemplating applying for an order in 'relevant family proceedings' (as defined in Annex B of the practice direction) should explore whether or not mediation might be an appropriate forum in which to resolve their dispute by attending (either together with, or separately from, the respondent) a Mediation Information and Assessment Meeting with a mediator to learn about mediation or other forms of ADR before embarking on court proceedings (PD 3A, para.4.1) unless they fall within any of the exemptions set out in Annex C (see below).

It should be noted that 'relevant family proceedings' do not include, for example, enforcement proceedings or proceedings pursuant to Matrimonial Causes Act 1973, s.37.

Furthermore, a Family Mediation Information and Assessment Form (Form FM1) will need to be completed and filed together with the application to confirm that such a meeting has taken place or, if not, why not, as the court now has the power to adjourn proceedings in order that this step is undertaken.

Whilst such attendance, of course, is not compulsory, non-compliance may result in costs sanctions, particularly if the court is of the view that such refusal to mediate is unreasonable.

Case law relevant to ADR within the CPR might well prove instructive on this point:

> The question whether a party has acted unreasonably in refusing ADR must be determined having regard to all the circumstances of the particular case ... in many cases no single factor will be decisive. (*Halsey* v. *Milton Keynes* [2004] 1 WLR 3002)

Furthermore, a refusal to attend a round-table meeting, for example, may also be met by a costs order (*Jarrom* v. *Sellars* [2007] EWHC 1366 (Ch), [2007] All ER (D) 202 (Apr)).

It has also been held that where a party who agreed to mediation adopted an unreasonable stance during the mediation process then they could be treated by the court as if they had unreasonably refused to mediate (*Earl of Malmesbury* v. *Strutt & Parker (a partnership)* [2008] EWHC 616 (QB)).

The exceptions to the requirement to attend a Mediation Information and Assessment Meeting are detailed in Annex C. These include such matters as: domestic abuse (but only where the police have been involved or an order has been sought in the last 12 months); urgency (but only where there is a risk to the life, liberty or physical safety of the applicant, their family or their home; or where any delay caused by mediation would cause a risk of significant harm to a child; significant risk of a miscarriage of justice, unreasonable hardship or irretrievable problems in dealing with the dispute (such as an irretrievable loss of significant evidence, e.g. 'post-*Imerman*' search orders)).

It does, however, seem odd that in a domestic violence case, for example, where an applicant has fled or is fleeing the home and has yet to issue FLA 1996, Part IV proceedings (or has no need of doing so because he or she is safe elsewhere) that they would now need to cross an apparent 'threshold' in order to bypass mediation (the alternative would be to go through the motions and secure confirmation from a mediator that the case is unsuitable, but this of course causes delay).

3.5 PART 4: CASE MANAGEMENT POWERS

The new rules (again in similar form to CPR Part 3) provide for extensive case management powers with the intention of regulating the proceedings before the court.

These powers are in addition to any other powers given to the court by any other rule, practice direction or other enactment.

They include:

- extending or shortening the time limit for compliance with any rule, practice direction or order (this can be granted retrospectively);
- making orders for disclosure and inspection (including specific disclosure);
- adjourning or bringing forward a hearing;
- requiring a party or legal representative to attend court;
- holding a hearing and receiving evidence by telephone (it is suggested that

telephone hearings may well become an increasingly useful feature in family proceedings much as they are with regard to their civil counterparts);
- staying the proceedings either generally or to a specified date (this might be particularly appropriate where matters are subject to ongoing mediation and negotiation and, as with the powers of adjournment set out previously under Part 3, there will no doubt be provision in the order as to keeping the court informed with regard to outcome prior to expiry of the stay, as currently under the CPR);
- directing a separate hearing of any issue (split trial);
- excluding an issue from consideration;
- directing a party to file and serve an estimate of costs (note that this can be ordered at any time and not merely, as currently required under the ancillary relief procedure, before a hearing);
- taking any other step or making any other order for the purposes of managing the case and furthering the overriding objective (this is an extremely wide clause which sweeps up everything else).

It will be clear from all this that there is a wide discretion to conduct proceedings in the manner most appropriate to the issues and available evidence, from a full hearing with witnesses at one end of the scale, to submissions on the basis of reading the evidence at the other.

One of the aims of the overriding objective is to use means which are proportionate to the importance, complexity and gravity of the issues before the court.

The relevant considerations will be:

I.   the sufficiency of the evidence to make the decision;
II. whether the evidence the applicant for a full trial proposes to adduce, and whether the opportunity for cross-examination is likely to effect the outcome;
III. the welfare of any child and the affect of further litigation;
IV. whether the delay will be so detrimental to a child's welfare that exceptionally there should not be a full hearing;
V.   the prospects of success of the application;
VI. whether justice requires a full investigation with oral evidence.

(*Re B (Minors) (Contact)* [1994] 2 FLR 1)

The court's case management powers also include the power of the court to make any order subject to conditions including the condition of paying a sum of money into court (FPR 2010, rule 4.1(4)(a)).

Such power is often used within the civil jurisdiction where the prospects of success of an application are considered marginal. This provision may provide some protection for a respondent should the applicant face a costs order which ultimately they might not be able to comply with.

How far this is going to be used in family proceedings, which of course are different in nature from their civil counterparts, remains to be seen, but it is a useful power to have in addition to perhaps those cases where the claimant has to provide an undertaking in damages and, subject to means, does provide more security. However, such an order should not be made unless the court is satisfied that in all the circumstances such a sanction is appropriate.

As far as other non-pecuniary conditions are concerned (e.g. strike-out), such conditions must be clear and precise and capable of being complied with. It is also worth noting that the court is not obliged to impose such an express sanction immediately but can do so at a later date if such non-compliance persists.

The court can also go on to specify the consequences of failure to comply with the condition which may well be to strike out the application.

Of particular importance also is FPR 2010, rule 4.1(5) which provides that in making any case management decision the court can take into account whether or not a party has complied with any pre-action protocol.

This is particularly important in this age of a 'cards on the table' approach and in encouraging parties to try and settle matters. In future, any failure to comply with such protocol can be visited by sanctions through the court's case management powers.

Again, similar to the CPR, the FPR 2010 give the court jurisdiction to exercise any of these case management powers of its own initiative, which again reinforces the overriding objective through 'active case management'.

When exercising such powers, the court must give any person likely to be affected by any order the opportunity of making representations and to specify the time by which such representations should be made.

Furthermore, where the court makes an order of its own initiative without hearing the parties (an 'own motion order'), the face of the order itself must contain a statement that any party affected by it may apply to have it set aside, varied or stayed within a specified period or, in the event that no period is specified, within seven days of service of the order upon them.

Therefore, if not happy, act quickly; one has an automatic right to do so.

As indicated earlier, an extremely important addition to the new FPR provides that where, on exercising a case management decision, the court strikes out a case or dismisses an application and considers that such application was totally without merit, then the court must record that fact on the face of the court file and consider whether it is appropriate to then go on and make a civil restraint order.

The court will only go on to make such an order if the records indicate that there have been two or more such applications which have been adjudged as being totally without merit.

This is an extremely important weapon in the court's armoury, particularly when faced with vexatious litigants in person, the guidance for which is set out in PD 4B.

What is clear is that the court should not consider such an order unless there have been *multiple* applications made which have been totally without merit.

A civil restraint order (CRO) consists of three distinct types of order:

- a limited civil restraint order;
- an extended civil restraint order;
- a general civil restraint order.

Each order is more draconian than the one before and the court will adopt a stepped approach in that if a lower grade order doesn't work the court must then go on to the next level (*R (Kumar)* v. *Secretary of State for Constitutional Affairs* [2006] EWCA Civ 990, [2007] 1 WLR 536; *Ferraro* v. *Halifax plc & Albert Dock Management Ltd* [2007] EWHC 2323 (QB)).

Thus when dealing with a vexatious litigant, the above restrictions should be imposed in order, progressively, if the litigant acts in breach of a restraint order, unless the court is of the opinion that such a CRO would not be sufficient or appropriate, e.g. where a litigant adopts a scattergun approach to litigation on a number of different grievances without necessarily exhibiting such an obsessive approach to a single topic that a limited CRO can appropriately be made against them (perhaps more of a rarity in family proceedings than in general civil proceedings).

This power does not apply however to Children Act proceedings where CA 1989, s.91(14) still applies.

3.5.1 Limited civil restraint order

This can be made either by a county court (including by a district judge) or by a High Court judge in circumstances where a party has made two or more applications which are totally without merit.

The effect of such an order is to restrain a person from making any further applications in the proceedings without first obtaining permission of the court.

Such an order is therefore limited to the particular proceedings in which it is made and will remain in force for the duration of the proceedings unless the court orders otherwise.

3.5.2 Extended civil restraint order

This can only be made by a High Court judge and applies where a party has persistently made applications which are totally devoid of merit.

The effect of such an order is to restrain a party from making applications in any court concerning any matter involving or relating to, or touching upon, or leading to, the proceedings in which the order is made without first seeking and obtaining the court's permission.

Such an order can be made for up to two years.

3.5.3 General civil restraint order

This order again can only be made by a High Court judge and is appropriate where a party persists in making applications which are totally without merit in circumstances where a limited or an extended civil restraint order would be insufficient or inappropriate.

The effect of this order is to restrain a party from making any application in any court without first obtaining the court's permission.

Such an order cannot last for more than two years and is an order of the last resort, only to be used where the lesser orders have been tried and have failed.

Any party may apply for such an order using the Part 18 procedure.

A party subject to such an order, when seeking permission to make an application, will need to apply in writing and provide at least seven days' notice to the other party, setting out the nature and grounds of the application and submitting to the court any response to the same from the other party.

Such applications will normally be determined without a hearing.

FPR 2010, rule 4.4 also provides a new power (similar to that contained in the CPR) to strike out a statement of case. It should be noted that this new power does not apply to private and public law proceedings under the Children Act 1989, the Human Fertilisation and Embryology Act 2008 and adoption and placement proceedings. The power arises in the following circumstances:

1. where the statement of case discloses no reasonable grounds for bringing or defending the application (contrast the CPR equivalent of no 'reasonable grounds' for bringing a claim);
2. where the statement of case is an abuse of the court process or otherwise likely to obstruct the disposal of the proceedings; or
3. where there has been a failure to comply with the rule, practice direction or court order.

Point 1 above deals with hopeless cases; however, if in doubt, the court can always direct the filing of further information on an 'unless' basis before exercising such a provision (i.e. unless the defaulting party complies with the provision within a set timescale the application will be struck out).

Some examples of where the court may conclude that the statement of case discloses no reasonable grounds for bringing or defending the application are contained in the accompanying PD 4A and include:

(a) those which set out no facts indicating what the application is about;
(b) those which are incoherent and make no sense;
(c) those which contain a coherent set of facts but those facts, even if true, do not disclose any legally recognisable application against the respondent.

An application which has no prospect of succeeding either in law or on the facts or cannot be justified because it is frivolous, scurrilous or ill-founded may also be struck out as an abuse of process.

An answer is liable to be struck out where it consists of a bare denial or otherwise sets out no coherent statement of facts. However, it is more than likely, in accordance with the overriding objective, that the court will allow the respondent time to file and serve a proper answer or to clarify it or file additional information in accordance with para.4.4 of PD 4A.

Such order can be made of the court's own initiative, or on application (under Part 18) and with or without a hearing. Any such application should be lodged as soon as possible.

In addition, where the court does strike out all or part of a party's statement of case, it can also go on to enter judgment.

The onus will be on the applicant to satisfy the court that there are no reasonable grounds for bringing or defending the application. In accordance with the overriding objective, all such strike-out applications should be made as soon as possible so as to cut short any 'hopeless' cases sooner rather than later.

Whilst such applications can be made without filing or serving any evidence in support, due to the draconian nature of such applications, it is invariably good practice to do so. (See in any event PD 18A, para.11.)

A court, however, will not simply strike out an application if the statement of case does present an arguable application but does so poorly.

The court will also not strike out a statement of case if it appears that the application is unlikely to succeed as the court must be satisfied that the application is bound to fail.

If an issue can only be determined by oral evidence at a hearing then the court should not strike out the application without first hearing that evidence.

Regarding point 2 above, abuse of the court's process has been defined as 'using that process for a purpose or in a way significantly different from its ordinary and proper use' (*Attorney General* v. *Barker* [2000] 1 FLR 759, DC). The court should adopt a broad merits-based approach when considering an application to strike out a claim on the basis that it is an abuse of process; an example of this might be a case where the claim could, and should, have been brought in previous proceedings (*Henderson* v. *Henderson*[1843–60] All ER Rep 378) or where a claimant is guilty of misconduct in relation to proceedings which is so serious that it would be an affront to the court to permit them to continue their claim (non-disclosure).

With regard to point 3 above, again an 'unless order' should normally be used in the first instance as any sanction imposed must be appropriate and proportionate in the circumstances. Courts should not abuse their case management powers by going to the extremes of striking out claims where a proportionate use of a more flexible power would be more appropriate.

Moreover, the activation of a sanction in an 'unless order', is a powerful weapon in a judge's case management armoury and should only be deployed where its consequences can be fully justified.

Having said that, there is no reason why the court cannot make serious, flagrant and dishonest breaches of a court order the subject of such an order.

However, the other sanctions that are available to the court and must bear consideration as alternatives include the following.

- **An adverse costs order** – the court may order that the defaulting party should pay the costs occasioned by the delay on an indemnity basis and summarily assess them.

  If the court is of the view that the fault lies with the solicitor, and not the party, the court may make a wasted costs order.

- **'Unless orders'** (see above) – in reality a court faced with a strike-out application is likely initially to make an 'unless order' as any sanction imposed must be proportionate to the breach.

  Moreover, any party applying to enforce an order, or to attach a sanction or both, must do so promptly, and provide an advance warning first, in accordance with the overriding objective.

  Any sanction embodied in an unless order will normally take effect without the need for any further order if the party to whom it is addressed fails to comply with it in any material respect. It is thus unnecessary for a party who seeks to rely on the other party's non-compliance with such order to make an application to the court for the sanction to be imposed. However, do note that an order which states that in the event of default the claim 'will be struck out' implies that another order has to be made by the court actually striking the claim out, whereas an order that states that the claim 'will' or 'shall be treated as struck out' does not require another order to validate it. This is now confirmed in PD 4A – Striking out a Statement of Case at para.2.6.

- **Conditional orders** – to further the overriding objective, an order may be made subject to conditions (including a payment into court) and may specify the consequences of failure to comply with them.

  The conditions must be clear and precise and capable of being complied with. The court is not obliged to impose an express sanction for failure to comply; however, it can do so at a later date, i.e. striking out all or part of a statement of case of a party who fails to comply, or preventing a party from subsequently taking part in the proceedings until the breach is remedied.

- **Impose a stay** – the court has specific power to stay an application until further order (PD 4A, para.3.3) and make provision that no application to lift the stay shall be heard until the applicant files such further information or documentation as specified by the court. This is particularly useful in circumstances where an application is ambiguous or does not make sense and provides the applicant an opportunity to rectify matters.

  If such an order is made, FPR 2010, rule 4.4(5) again makes provision for marking the court file 'totally without merit' and consideration being given to the making a civil restraint order in an appropriate case. However, this power is only available in the High Court or county court.

These new powers are extremely important for all practitioners to be aware of when faced with a recalcitrant litigant and is a clear improvement on the rather less productive 'penal notice' sanctions. A party in default must apply for relief from the sanction imposed under FPR 2010, rule 4.5 if they wish to escape its consequences.

FPR 2010, rule 4.5(1) makes important provisions with regard to obtaining such relief, the obligation being on the defaulter.

FPR 2010, rule 4.6(1) sets out a checklist which the court must systematically consider in determining such applications which largely mirror those in the CPR:

- the interests of the administration of justice;
- whether the application for relief was made promptly;
- whether the failure to comply was intentional;
- whether there was a good explanation for the failure;
- compliance with other rules and court orders;
- whether the failure to comply was caused by the party's legal representative;
- whether the trial date can still be met if relief is granted;
- the effect which failure to comply (or the granting of relief) would have on either side or a child whose interest the court considers relevant.

When hearing such applications, all the circumstances of the case must also be considered.

Practitioners will need to note that when making such applications, justification for the order sought will need to fall fairly and squarely within the above checklist in the evidence in support of the application.

The court will only grant such relief of its own initiative in exceptional cases as, normally, evidence will be required as to the rule 4.6 factors before the court's discretion can be exercised.

It is likely that the CPR case law will have some bearing in guiding the court in this process, although clearly there is a substantial difference in ethos between the two jurisdictions.

In particular, whilst the court has jurisdiction to extend time for compliance with an order after the time for its compliance has passed (even when there is 'an unless' order), that power will no doubt be exercised with caution; accordingly, it is always better to be proactive and avoid retrospective applications.

The true test, in practical terms, in determining such applications will be whether, notwithstanding that an unless order was a proper order to make for the purposes of furthering the overriding objective in the circumstances known at that time, it remains appropriate at the time of the application for relief, to allow the sanction to take effect. Clearly, the affected parties' art.6 rights under the European Convention on Human Rights (the right to a fair hearing) will be engaged in this process.

The question has to be whether the court's decision to maintain the sanction, with or without conditions, constitutes a legitimate aim, is proportionate in the circumstances and does not destroy the essence of a party's rights under art.6.

3.6 PART 5: HOW TO START PROCEEDINGS

Part 5 is derived from CPR Part 7. The previous rules made provision for family proceedings to be commenced in a variety of ways, e.g. petition, application and summons. As part of the goal in making the rules accessible and simple, proceedings are now commenced by an application.

All the forms required by the new rules are listed in PD 5A for ease of reference. The forms are designed to be as simple as possible. There is extensive use of tick boxes and there are accompanying guidance notes to assist in the completion of longer forms.

Note rule 5.1(2) which provides that any form may be varied by the court or a party if such variation is required by the circumstances of a particular case. This is quite interesting. Does this mean that information as provided by the form can be omitted or does it mean that information not formally provided by the form can be added and, if so, to what extent? The answer appears to be in rule 5.1(3) which prohibits the omission of information which otherwise must be given in the form itself.

Now for a brief summary of the main changes to some of the more common forms which may be encountered.

3.6.1 Application for a matrimonial order

Worthy of note is the new Application for a Matrimonial Order (Form D8) (although still called a petition). It is now comprised exclusively of boxes to fill in or tick, and presumably will spell the end for petitions typed from scratch. Its style and layout are uncluttered and it is very easy for people to fill out themselves without legal assistance (no bad thing considering the impending abolition of legal aid for divorce).

There are comprehensive notes for guidance which can be found at D8 (notes).

The following items are new: the dates of birth and gender of the parties and children are required to be stated, as are whether a statement of arrangements is attached, whether special assistance will be needed at court and whether the applicant is represented. On the other hand, it is no longer necessary to state whether the parties' names have changed since the marriage, or whether there have been child support proceedings.

The new style application also mentions the differences between civil and religious marriages for those persons who may have entered into two ceremonies.

Part 9 of the form is significant in so far as service details are concerned, as both parties can now give an address for service.

The particulars in support are now referred to as the 'statement of case'.

3.6.2 Statement of arrangements form

As previously highlighted, the statement of arrangements form for the children now has a statement of truth at the end.

In addition, there is now no duplication of the children's details which have already been given in the petition.

Having said that, the form contains the same basic information as before, but in a better format.

3.6.3 Answer

This is an entirely new form that clearly says on page 1: 'PLEASE TREAT THIS AS MY ANSWER TO THE PETITION'.

It also indicates that, if the respondent wishes to apply for a matrimonial order, then that should be done on his or her own application which will be issued within the existing case (FPR 2010, rule 7.14).

3.6.4 Form A (A1 in the family proceedings court)

The revised form reflects the new pension compensation attachment and sharing order provisions.

It also asks if the applicant has attended a mediation information/assessment meeting in line with the objectives set out in Part 3. Presumably, any covering letter issuing an application will need to deal with these requirements so as to avoid the possibility of an automatic adjournment.

3.6.5 Form E (comprising both Forms E1 and E2)

There are now two forms: Form E1, which applies to the county court and Form E2, which applies to financial proceedings within the magistrates' court.

In so far as changes to Form E itself are concerned, para.4.5 under the heading 'Details of any other circumstances that you consider could significantly affect the extent of the financial provision' now mentions:

1. Any agreement made between you and your spouse/civil partner before or after your marriage/civil partnership stating whether or not you rely upon the agreement giving your reasons (echoing the importance of the decision in *Rademacher v. Granatino* [2010] UKSC 42, [2010] WLR (D) 260).
2. Any plans to marry, form a civil partnership or live with a new partner.

The Form E notes for guidance have also been updated and are easy to read.

3.6.6 Form C1

The form for giving details of any alleged domestic violence and harm is now better set out in a tick box format with the ability to indicate whether such harm is to the applicant or a child.

The new form also asks about any FLA 1996 orders which have been sought.

There are now questions about the whereabouts of the children's passports which is a significant addition, especially in potential child abduction cases.

Section 5 of the form requires a party to indicate what type of contact that party would agree to (this of course assumes the person completing the form is the one with the children).

Section 7 asks what facilities are needed at court and includes such things as separate waiting rooms, exits and entrances, video links and advance viewing of the court, all of which are aimed at reassuring a nervous applicant or one who has faced domestic abuse or otherwise is in fear of the other party.

Finally, the application needs to be signed with a statement of truth.

Another innovation is that any person who receives an application can now comment upon the allegations on the same form, sign the statement of truth and send it to the court.

3.6.7 Form C2

The C2 is broadly the same as before with more information to be given about the parties; the important information on the front page is now kept to a minimum.

It is also now a requirement that the form is signed with a statement of truth.

3.6.8 Form C5

This is a new form and relates to an application concerning the registration of a child-minder or provider of day care (Childcare Act 2006, s.72).

The orders that can be made are:

1. Cancellation of the registration of the child-minder or provider of day care.
2. Variation of a requirement imposed on the child-minder or provider of day care.
3. Removal of a requirement, or imposition of an additional requirement, on the child-minder or provider of day care.

3.6.9 Form C8

Confidential address form – this stays the same (FPR 2010, rule 29.1).

3.6.10 Form C100

This new form relates to applications for a s.8 order and to vary, or discharge such order under CA 1989.

It allows for the names of three children on the first page and their basic details, including the names of the parents of each child.

All references to 'sex' have been changed to 'gender'.

There is also space for details for the parties' email addresses to be included and, thankfully, there is now no need to repeat the children's details throughout the form.

Details of all persons with parental responsibility and all social workers' details now need to be provided on one page.

Most important is the statement of truth that now needs to be signed at the end of the form.

3.6.11 Other forms

Other Children Act forms of note include the following:

- C63 – **Application for a declaration of parentage.** This form outlines the same method of application as before but the requirements are now encompassed in a form rather than FPR 1991, rule 3.13. An application can be made in any court (Family Law Act 1986 (FLA 1986), s.55A(1)).
- C64 – **Application for declaration of legitimation under FLA 1986, s.56(1)(b) and (2).** Such application can only be made in the High Court or county court.
- C65 – **Application as to declaration of an adoption effected overseas.** Such application (FLA 1986, s.57) can only be made in the High Court or county court.
- C66 – **Application for inherent jurisdiction order in relation to children.** Again, such application can only be made in the High Court or county court.

All the above forms must be signed with a statement of truth.

A full list of the revised forms is as follows and is set out in PD 5A (see **Appendix 2**).

3.7 PART 6: SERVICE

Part 6 of the FPR 2010 regulates service of documents and is derived from CPR Part 6.

It is worth mentioning at the outset that a new rule providing for service by an alternative method or at an alternative place based on the CPR is now included.

The accompanying PD 6A sets out a number of general provisions relating to service as follows:

- when service may be effected by document exchange;
- service by fax or email;
- applications for service by an alternative method or place of service;
- applications for an order to dispense with service;
- deemed service (this does not apply to applications for a matrimonial or civil partnership order (FPR 2010, rule 6.34));
- service on children and protected parties.

Specifically relating to applications for matrimonial and civil partnership orders, PD 6A deals with the following:

- service by court bailiff;

- service on children and protected parties.

There is no formal definition of 'service' in Part 6. However, the glossary to the FPR 2010 refers to 'steps required by rules of court to bring documents used in court proceedings to a person's attention'.

The rule itself, like many others in the FPR 2010, is broken down into various chapters in order to aid navigation.

PD 6C extends the Registrar's Direction of 26 April 1988 regarding the disclosure of addresses by government departments. PD 6C now also covers tracing of persons for the purposes of enforcing orders for financial provision, and tracing the whereabouts of a child or person with whom the child is said to be pursuant to the Child Abduction and Custody Act 1985. The practice direction then goes on to list the various bodies who can assist and what information will be required. The bodies include the Department for Work and Pensions (formerly DSS), the Office for National Statistics, the Home Office Identity and Passport Service (formerly UK Passport Agency) and the Ministry of Defence.

3.7.1 Chapter 2 (rules 6.3–6.22)

Chapter 2 regulates the service requirements of an application for a matrimonial order or civil partnership order which are largely unchanged.

In essence an application for a matrimonial order or civil partnership order must initially be served either by personal service (but not by the applicants themselves), first class post or document exchange (unless, in the latter case, the party or solicitor indicates that they are not prepared to accept service by such method (FPR 2010, rule 6.11)). (Note there is no provision for service of such by fax or email; query, however, whether or not one can effect service by way of email and then apply for an application for service by an alternative method.)

Service on the respondent must be effected at their usual or last known address.

The usual or last known address within rule 6.13(2) cannot include an address at which the respondent has never resided, nor an address at which the applicant merely believes the respondent to have resided. Instead, the serving party should have actual knowledge of that address or it should be knowledge that they could have acquired exercising reasonable diligence.

Where the applicant has reason to believe that the respondent is no longer residing at that usual or last known address then they must take reasonable steps to ascertain a current address.

Taking as a guide established principles from the CPR it may be surmised as follows:

- If an address for service is given then the application must be served at that address.
- If no address given then the application can be served at the last known address.
- If an address for service is given as a solicitor's address then one must serve the application on the solicitor. (It is worth noting that if a party nominates a

solicitor but that solicitor has not notified the applicant that they are authorised to accept service, then service will still be valid because the respondent will have provided an address for service at which service should be effected (rule 6.12).)
- If the solicitor confirms he is authorised to accept service then service must be effected on him (rule 6.11).
- However, the mere fact that a solicitor is acting does not mean he is instructed to accept service; do not infer – check first. There must be express authority to that effect.

There are also new rules which apply where the applicant has reason to believe that the address is an address where the respondent no longer resides. In that eventuality the applicant must take reasonable steps to ascertain the respondent's current address. If the applicant is unable to discover the correct address, then service can be effected at an alternative place or by an alternative method provided by the rules.

The other forms of service which one can have recourse to are as before; namely service by a court bailiff (Form D89) (rule 6.9 – note that the bailiff's endorsement of service will now be known as a certificate of service), deemed service (rule 6.16), service at an alternative place or by alternative method (previously 'substituted service') (rule 6.19) and dispensing with service (rule 6.20 – Form 13B).

In cases of service by court bailiff it is worth noting that the practice direction states that such requests will rarely be granted where the applicant is legally represented as it will normally be expected that in such circumstances service should be effected by a process server as opposed to a bailiff thus passing the burden of resources and costs from the court service to the solicitor (PD 6A, para.11.4). Thus, request the other side's representatives to acknowledge service of the papers (and then apply for deemed service) or request that they ensure that their client promptly files the acknowledgement (rule 6.15), utilising a costs threat as leverage.

Failing this, you will either have to resort to personal service, with all its consequential expenses, or seek to persuade the court that, notwithstanding that a solicitor is acting, bailiff service should nonetheless be authorised in accordance with the overriding objective and in the interests of saving expense. Good luck!

The previous express provision for substituted service of an application for a matrimonial or civil partnership order by way of advertisement has now been removed given the rarity of this mode of service.

FPR 2010, rule 6.19 in particular enables the court to make an order permitting service by an alternative method or at an alternative place retrospectively by an order deeming service on a particular date ('the court may order that steps already taken to bring the claim form to the attention of the respondent by an alternative method or at an alternative place is good service'). However, this is only likely to be allowed in exceptional cases, and indeed, not before any other method of service has been attempted first. The court, in such eventuality, will need to be convinced that reasonable steps have been taken to locate the respondent.

Applications for alternative service are specifically dealt with within PD 6A, which deals with both prospective and retrospective applications (at para.6).

Examples of service by such method and the evidential requirements of the same are also, most helpfully, set out in the practice direction and, for the more technologically minded amongst us, also include service by SMS text and voicemail.

Of particular note is rule 6.11 which provides that where a solicitor is acting for a respondent and has notified the applicant in writing that they are instructed to accept service, then the application must be served on that solicitor.

3.7.2 Chapter 3 (rules 6.23–6.39)

Chapter 3 regulates the service of documents in other proceedings in the UK (as opposed to the jurisdiction) and encompasses:

- personal service;
- first class post;
- leaving in a place specified;
- fax or other means of electronic communication.

Again, drawing an analogy from the CPR, where such documents are delivered to the recipient in a manner provided for by the rules, they will be deemed served whether or not the recipient actually received them. 'Last known address' is plain and unqualified and, on the face of it, it does not matter that the recipient is no longer there.

Of particular note is rule 6.23 which provides that such service may now be effected by fax or email. However, this rule does not apply to an application for a matrimonial or civil partnership order or documents in relation to adoption and parental order proceedings. The rules and the supporting PD 6A in relation to such service replicate the provisions of the CPR.

This authorises service by such means not only upon a solicitor instructed by a party to accept service by such means but also upon the party himself/herself, provided he/she has indicated in writing that he/she is willing to accept such service in advance of it being effected.

There must therefore be a specific written agreement to serve by email and/or fax.

Notwithstanding this, however, an email or fax number on the notepaper or on a statement of case or answer can be sufficient indication that the respondent is willing to accept service by such method although, in the case of an email address on the letterhead, it must be qualified by a statement that confirms that service by such method is accepted (which is the opposite to the scenario concerning service by fax).

The chances are that not many solicitors will rush to their stationers to change their letterhead on this one!

In addition, in so far as service by email is concerned, there is the additional requirement to ascertain from the recipient any limitations on their agreement to accept service by such method, e.g. format and size of attachments. Thus, it would be good practice for a party serving paperwork by such method to, in any event, telephone to check any such restrictive conditions.

Once service has been effected by such method there is no requirement to follow this up with a hard copy, which seems both sensible and environmentally friendly. Note also that confirmation of the date and time of completion of the transmission (be it email or fax) will be sufficient for the purposes of the certificate of service (FPR 2010, rule 6.37).

It is also worth noting that there are various provisions throughout the rules requiring documents to be served or sent to persons such as the children's guardian and CAFCASS officer. Where the children's guardian is to be so served, the intention is that the guardian shall be served at one and the same time as, and in addition to, the solicitor acting for the child; this is an important new provision (FPR 2010, rules 6.30(3), and 6.31(2), (3)).

Reference must also be made to the supplementary provisions relating to service on children pursuant to Part 12 (rule 6.33) which also provides for service on a CAFCASS officer and/or, as appropriate, a local authority, in addition to service on any guardian who has been appointed.

As far as service on children and protected parties is concerned, rule 6.14(7) makes provision as to how such an application must be served. A document so served in accordance with that rule must be endorsed with a notice in Form D5 as set out in the relevant practice direction (PD 6A, para.9.1).

3.7.3 Chapter 4 (rules 6.40–6.48)

Chapter 4 of Part 6 regulates service out of the jurisdiction and contains provisions to give effect to Council Regulation (EC) No. 1393/2007 on the service in the Member States of judicial and extra-judicial documents in civil and commercial matters ('the Service Regulation'), which assists service of family court documents across Europe. As before, this is supplemented by a practice direction (PD 6B, para.2 regulates service in Member States of the European Union and para.4 regulates service in Commonwealth states or British Overseas Territories).

The Service Regulation is annexed to the practice direction.

Paragraph 5.1 helpfully sets out the requisite periods within which a respondent must file an acknowledgement of service or answer to an application dependent upon where they reside.

3.8 PART 7: PROCEDURE FOR APPLICATIONS IN MATRIMONIAL AND CIVIL PARTNERSHIP PROCEEDINGS

Part 7 derives from Part II of FPR 1991 and regulates the procedure for applications for matrimonial and civil partnership orders. Again it is broken down into various chapters.

The procedure to be followed in matrimonial proceedings has remained largely unchanged since the introduction of the special procedure for undefended divorces over 35 years ago.

A number of changes are brought in by the rules with the aim of making the procedure more efficient, encouraging parties to resolve their differences and making the rules more accessible by eliminating some of the more 'outdated' terms.

Whilst the terms 'decree nisi', 'decree absolute', 'judicial separation' and 'answer' have been preserved following consultation (except in civil partnership proceedings where we have the terms 'conditional order', 'final order' and 'separation order'), the terms 'petition' and 'cross-petition' have been replaced by the singular term of 'application for a matrimonial order' or 'civil partnership order'.

3.8.1 Commencing and responding to proceedings

This is regulated by FPR 2010, rules 7.5–7.15.

An application for a matrimonial or civil partnership order must be made in the form set out in PD 5A (Form D8) and be accompanied by the documents specified within the form itself and completed in accordance with the detailed notes which accompany it.

There are separate practice directions, PD 7C and PD 7D, which deal with the specific requirements of polygamous marriages and the provision of gender recognition certificates under the Gender Recognition Act 2004.

The new rules differentiate between an opposed case (defended case), where an answer is filed opposing the grant of a matrimonial or civil partnership order, or the respondent has himself or herself filed an application for a matrimonial or civil partnership order, and unopposed cases (undefended case).

Note that this new definition now includes applications for a nullity order and therefore unopposed applications for nullity will be treated in the same way as applications for an unopposed divorce and wherever possible dealt with without a hearing. (See FPR 2010, rule 7.19 at **3.8.2** below.)

Also note that the detailed provisions relating to medical examinations in nullity proceedings have been removed from the rules and can now be found in a supporting PD 7B – Medical Examinations on Applications for Annulment of a Marriage.

In essence, where an application for annulment is based on incapacity to consummate, medical evidence will not normally be required in proceedings which are not defended and even in cases which are defended, such evidence will only be directed where it appears necessary to do so.

Any medical evidence that is directed must comply with the rules relating to experts generally as set out in FPR 2010, Part 25.

Rather surprisingly, the Statement of Reconciliation (Form D6) is still preserved by rule 7.6. This is a statutory requirement which the rules alone cannot change.

FPR 2010, rule 7.9 entitles an applicant to withdraw an application for a matrimonial order, at any time before it has been served, by giving written notice to the court. This is an improvement over the previous procedure whereby one had to file a notice of discontinuance and thereafter seek dismissal of the petition.

As before, the rules do not require a person with whom the respondent is alleged to have committed adultery to be named.

However, rule 7.10(2) provides that where an applicant alleges that the other party to the marriage has committed adultery with a person who is so named, then that named person will automatically be named as second respondent unless the court otherwise directs.

Rule 7.10(4) goes further and states that where an application for a matrimonial or civil partnership order alleges that the other party has formed an improper association with a named individual, then the court may also direct that that named person be made a second respondent.

It is clear from rule 7.10(5) that the court will usually direct party status unless the proceedings are not defended.

The clear emphasis and encouragement therefore is to lean away from naming such a party so as to avoid future delay and unnecessary complexity. Indeed, the practice direction supplementing this Part contains further dissuasion against naming alleged adulterers (PD 7A, para.2.1). Indeed, even in cases where 'an improper association' is alleged, such person should not be so named, unless it is likely that the proceedings will be defended.

Rule 7.12 sets out the procedure in so far as the respondent is concerned when receiving an application for a matrimonial or civil partnership order.

In essence, they must set out whether or not they intend to defend the proceedings.

Rule 7.12(8) provides that, where a respondent wishes to oppose the making of an order, he or she must file and serve an answer (Form D8B) within 21 days beginning with the date by which the acknowledgement of service is required to be filed. After that period, an application for extension of time will be needed, although dependent upon the extent of the delay, the court may well grant such an application of its own initiative. The form of answer is set out in PD 5A.

A respondent to proceedings who wishes to make an application himself or herself for a matrimonial order must now file his or her own application within the proceedings and can no longer issue a separate application (rule 7.14). (Note the abandonment of the terms 'cross-petition' 'reply' and 'supplemental petition' thus making for a simpler procedure.)

Amendments can be made to an application or answer at any time before the application for the decree nisi is made (rule 7.13).

3.8.2 Procedure for determining applications for a matrimonial or civil partnership order

This procedure is regulated by FPR 2010, rules 7.16–7.27.

Rule 7.15 sets out the procedural requirements when requests are made for further information as to the contents of an application or answer and is further supplemented by para.6 of the corresponding PD 7A which provides that before making such an application a written request for clarification should be sought first.

Such request, it is envisaged, will need to be in the format of a questionnaire in that it must be in a separate document or letter which is dated and signed, contain no other subject matter apart from the request, make clear on the face of it that it is a request for information pursuant to rule 7.15 and specify a date (which of course must be reasonable) by which a response should be provided.

Such request must be concise and confined to matters which are reasonably necessary and proportionate to enable the requesting party to prepare his or her own case or understand the other party's case.

The reply itself should also follow the same format, that is, it should be contained in a separate document or letter which must be dated and signed, contain no other subject matter and make clear that it is a reply to a rule 7.15 request.

The reply itself must repeat each request and provide the corresponding response to it (much in the same way as a financial questionnaire).

Any objections to providing a response or inability to respond must also be dealt with together with reasons which, the author suggests, should be dealt with in the response document itself for ease of reference.

Rule 7.16 sets out the general rule that hearings in relation to matrimonial and civil partnership proceedings will normally be heard in public subject to various exceptions contained in rule 7.16(3).

Rules 7.19 and 7.20 set out the procedure for applying for a decree nisi, judicial separation, separation order or conditional order which is almost identical to the previous procedural requirements including the necessity to use a supporting affidavit (the contents of which are as before (see rule 7.19(4)) save that it is now made clear that the document can be affirmed instead of sworn) as opposed to a statement of truth which was proposed during the consultation exercise. Note that this applies only to unopposed cases and can be made not only by the applicant to a matrimonial order but by the other party as well (after the time for filing an answer has expired), which is an innovation to the rules and one which applicants will need to be made fully aware of.

Thus the applicant is now no longer fully in control of the proceedings and the respondent can prevent delay and procrastination by applying himself or herself (rule 7.19(2)(b)).

If the information required to be provided by the initial application form is no longer correct, a supporting statement must be filed setting out the details of any changes.

If the court is not satisfied as to such entitlement it can request the provision of further information (to be verified by affidavit if necessary) or list the matter for a case management hearing. It is suggested that the provision of further information will be sought first.

If costs are applied for the court has two choices:

- if satisfied, certify the applicant is so entitled; or
- if not so satisfied, make no such direction.

Note there appears to be no provision for the listing of the issue as to costs to be determined on the occasion of the pronouncement of the matrimonial order. However, this seems to be preserved by rule 7.21(2).

Any party wishing to attend court for the purposes of opposing or applying for costs must now, not less than two days before the hearing, serve on the other party, written notice of their intention to do so thus filling a lacuna in the previous rules.

If such notice is not provided then the rules provide that the party is not entitled to be heard (rule 7.21(2)).

Accordingly, in cases where, for example, the costs of the proceedings are in dispute and an attendance is required to dispute the issue, solicitors will need to advise the other party accordingly.

If notice is not so given, then the question will be whether or not the court has discretion to proceed and determine any issue or whether an adjournment should be ordered so that effective notice can be given. Hopefully, good sense will prevail and a proportionate response given in line with the overriding objective.

In opposed cases, the court will list a case management hearing (CMH), the procedural considerations for which are dealt with in rule 7.22. Note, in particular, the footnote to rule 7.22 which draws attention to the court's powers to encourage the parties to use ADR in line with the ethos set out in Part 3.

It will be noted that these proceedings are much less complex than previously. The overriding objective and the expectation that the court will manage these cases at an initial CMH means that if an application is contested then the proceedings will be tightly controlled.

The provisions relating to disclosure and inspection in defended cases are supported by PD 7A, para.7, which sets out the duty of making a reasonable search for documents which are required to be disclosed. As with disclosure generally, what is reasonable will, of course, be measured in accordance with the individual facts of each case and the overriding principle of proportionality.

Disclosure is to be by way of list, which must comply with the requirements set out in PD 7A, para.7.3 and contain the statement which is set out in para.7.5.

Once disclosure is ordered there is a continuing duty of disclosure until the cessation of the proceedings. Any additional documents coming to light will need to be incorporated in a supplemental list.

The issue of privilege or other reasons for opposing such disclosure must be set out in the disclosure statement itself.

Hearings for the pronouncement of the decree, or final hearings in opposed cases, are to be held in public. Under FPR 2010, rule 7.16 such a hearing may only be held in private if:

- (a) publicity would defeat the object of the hearing;
- (b) it involves matters relating to national security;
- (c) it involves confidential information (including information relating to personal financial matters) and publicity would damage that confidentiality;
- (d) a private hearing is necessary to protect the interests of any child or protected party;
- (e) it is a hearing of an application made without notice and it would be unjust to any respondent for there to be a public hearing; or
- (f) the court considers this to be necessary, in the interests of justice.

The court may also order that the identity of any party or witness must not be disclosed if it considers non-disclosure necessary to protect the interests of that party or witness.

In so far as the arrangements for the children are concerned, the rules are identical, contained as they now are in rule 7.25, save that where a district judge makes a direction under MCA 1973, s.41(2), that a conditional order is not to be made final or, as the case may be, the decree nisi should not be made absolute, the rules provide that written reasons must be given including the exceptional circumstances warranting it.

Similarly, if the court fails to issue a certificate and gives directions under FPR 2010, rule 7.25(4), whether for further evidence, a CAFCASS report or indeed the parties' attendance, it must set out its reasons for doing so in writing.

3.8.3 Orders of the court

Orders of the court are regulated by FPR 2010, rules 7.28–7.36.

Rule 7.31 provides the procedure for applications to prevent the conditional order being made final or the decree nisi being made absolute.

Any such application must be made pursuant to the FPR 2010, Part 18 procedure. However, it is worth noting that pursuant to *Miller Smith* v. *Miller Smith (No. 2)*

[2009] EWHC 3623 whilst there is such a power, such power should only be exercised in special or exceptional circumstances.

Rule 7.32 sets out the procedure for the applicant when applying for a final order or decree absolute. The procedure is largely unchanged, including the provision for making an application where more than 12 months have expired since the decree or order was made (rule 7.32((3)).

In undefended cases, where expedition of the decree absolute or final order is required, the Part 18 procedure must be used.

Rule 7.33 sets out the procedure for applying for a final order or decree absolute by the spouse against whom such decree or order was made.

Note rules 7.34 and 7.35 which state that the precise time when the decree nisi was made absolute or the conditional order was made final must be set out on the face of the document.

3.9 PART 8: PROCEDURE FOR MISCELLANEOUS APPLICATIONS

As part of the drive for a unified set of procedures and unification of the rules, Part 8 sets out the procedural requirements for various types of applications, more particularly, applications under the Married Women's Property Act 1882, s.17 and their civil partnership equivalent, declarations of parentage and marital status pursuant to FLA 1986, ss.55 and 55A, applications for financial provision after an overseas divorce (which builds upon guidance set out in *Agbaje v. Akinnoye-Agbaje* [2010] UKSC 13) and applications for a transfer of tenancy order pursuant to FLA 1996, Sched.7.

This Part derives predominantly from Part III of FPR 1991 and rationalises the previous rules so that the various forms of relief available under the listed enactments shall generally follow what is known as 'the alternative procedure'.

The rules governing the procedure are set out in Part 19 save for Chapters 4 (applications under the Married Women's Property Act 1882) and 6 (applications for permission to apply for a financial remedy after an overseas divorce) which follow the Part 18 procedure.

3.9.1 Application for permission to apply for a financial remedy after overseas proceedings

Once permission has been granted to bring proceedings under Part III of the Matrimonial and Family Proceedings Act 1984 (MFPA 1984) and Sched.7 to the Civil Partnership Act 2004 (CPA 2004), the High Court may direct that the substantive application be dealt with in the principal registry of the Family Division (FPR 2010, rule 8.28).

Very often, the issue that requires High Court judge involvement is the initial application for permission to bring proceedings following overseas proceedings. Once permission is granted, the substantive application will now be dealt with procedurally in the same way as any other application for a financial remedy under FPR 2010, Part 9.

A problem regularly occurring under the previous rules is that where a pension sharing order is made in an overseas jurisdiction relating to a pension based in this jurisdiction, the pension provider in the UK would not recognise the foreign pension sharing order and therefore a reciprocal order would be necessary under MFPA 1984, Part III.

Such applications are normally made by consent.

The new rules now provide that where both the application for permission and substantive application proceed with the full co-operation of the parties, then the matter may be dealt with at county court level, if evidence of consent is filed with the application.

3.9.2 Transfer of tenancy under Schedule 7 to FLA 1986

Where a free-standing application for a transfer of tenancy under FLA 1996, Sched.7 is made, the Part 18 procedure must be followed unless the application is contained in an application for ancillary relief, in which case the Part 19 procedure will apply.

3.10 PART 9: APPLICATIONS FOR FINANCIAL REMEDY

Part 9 and the procedures set out within it (which are derived from FPR 1991, Part II) now apply to many more applications for a financial remedy that involve a wide ambit of discretion than previously, whether proceeding in the county court or family proceedings court.

This enables such proceedings to benefit from tighter case management, the more widespread use of Form Es and FDR appointments for the purposes of discussion and negotiation at which parties must use their best endeavours to reach agreement on matters at issue between them.

Part 9 is supported by PD 9A. This practice direction, however, does not apply to proceedings in the magistrates' court.

The pre-application protocol, which is annexed to the practice direction, outlines the steps that a party should take prior to commencing an application which the court will expect the parties to have complied with, any breach of which may be met by a costs sanction. The new rules clearly give the protocol more force than it had before.

The protocol is also different from the one produced by Resolution and the Family Law Panel.

The aim of the pre-application protocol, of course, is to assist the parties to resolve their differences or at least narrow the issues and to ensure that applications are resolved as speedily as possible without incurring unreasonable costs and in accordance with the overriding objective and in particular the maxim of proportionality.

Amongst other things, the protocol cautions against automatic pre-action disclosure so as to avoid excessive and uncontrolled costs and delay. Such pre-action disclosure is only to be encouraged where both parties agree and where disclosure is unlikely to be an issue.

Making an application to the court should not be regarded as a hostile step or last resort, rather as a way of commencing the court timetable and exerting control.

Furthermore, solicitors should consider from the outset and on an ongoing basis whether or not mediation or collaborative law should be suggested to clients as an alternative to solicitor negotiation or court-based litigation. This, of course, is now enshrined in FPR 2010, Part 3.

There is an emphasis in the protocol on a conciliatory approach. The tone of the initial pre-action letter and subsequent correspondence is important and should focus on the clarification of applications and the identification of issues and their resolution.

The protocol also sets out a number of uncontroversial principles which should be adhered to in accordance with, and supplemental to, the overriding objective:

> The needs of any children should be addressed and safeguarded. The procedures which it is appropriate to follow should be conducted with minimum distress to the parties and in a manner designed to promote as good a continuing relationship between the parties and any children affected as is possible in the circumstances.

Finally, full and frank disclosure of all material facts, documents and other relevant information is promoted (an ongoing duty which applies throughout the life of the proceedings), as is proportionality, avoiding trial by correspondence and discouraging protracted correspondence and correspondence which raises irrelevant issues or which may promote entrenched polarised or hostile positions. Practitioners should consider the impact their correspondence might have on the recipient and in particular the parties themselves. The instantaneousness of emails themselves in particular merits a 'government health warning'.

Returning to the rules themselves, rules 9.4–9.9 cover applications for a financial order (defined in rule 2.3) made within proceedings for a matrimonial order (MCA 1973, ss.27 and 35) and include applications pursuant to MCA 1973, s.37; MFPA 1984, Part III; CA 1989, Sched.1; and DPMCA 1978, Part 1 and interim orders, for example, maintenance pending suit and their respective civil partnership equivalents (rule 9.15(5)(b) and (7)(a)). These applications are to be made pursuant to the Part 18 procedure.

Following on from this, new to the procedure is the inclusion of a section specifically dealing with 'interim orders' at rule 9.7.

In so far as an application for an interim order is concerned, where such an application is made before a party has filed his or her financial statement, the evidence in support must explain why such an order is necessary and provide up-to-date information about the party's financial circumstances. Such applications can be made without notice.

Also worth a mention is the procedure for obtaining a corresponding order (the request for a periodical payments order at the same rate as an order for maintenance pending suit). This has been altered so that the procedure in Part 18 must be used, which in turn is based on CPR Part 23.

Any other application not listed will be covered by the procedure set out in Part 19 of the FPR 2010.

Rule 9.11 now specifically empowers the court to direct that a child should be separately represented on any application for a financial remedy relating to a child; this now also applies to the magistrates' court.

This may be particularly relevant in so far as applications under CA 1989, Sched.1 are concerned in light of the sentiments expressed in *Walker* v. *Jeffries*; *Re S (a child)* [2006] EWCA Civ 479 and *Morgan* v. *Hill* [2007] 1 FLR 1480 (CA).

The procedure set out in the old rules with regard to FDRs in so far as ancillary relief proceedings are concerned remains intact and is now set out in FPR 2010, rules 9.12–9.17. However, as indicated previously, this procedure now applies to many more types of financial proceedings than merely ancillary relief.

Within county court proceedings there is the newly named Form E1 which, although broadly the same as the previous version, has a better layout.

A newly devised Form E2 is to be used for financial proceedings within the magistrates' court.

The list of the various enclosures to Form E is also broadly the same as previously (rule 9.14(2)); however, the rule now provides for the Pension Protection Fund (PPF) information to be provided in addition to the usual documentation.

In addition to the requirements of rule 9.14(5) in relation to FDRs, the parties are under a duty to agree and file the following (PD 9A, para.4.1):

- an agreed case summary;
- a detailed schedule of assets; and
- a draft of the directions sought and, where relevant, the identity of any expert to be instructed.

Where the details of a proposed expert are not sent in advance of the First Directions Appointment (FDA) hearing, such details should be made available at the hearing itself.

The detailed provisions contained in PD 22A (Written Evidence) regulating the collation and pagination of documents are applicable to Forms E1 and E2.

In particular note the following:

1. Photocopies may be exhibited as long as the originals are made available for inspection by the other party before the hearing and by the court at the hearing.
2. Court documents must not be exhibited (they prove themselves).
3. Where an exhibit contains more than one document, a front page should be attached setting out a list of the documents contained in the exhibit. The list should contain the dates of the documents.
4. An exhibit with more than one document should be fastened securely in a way that does not hinder the reading of documents – and must *not* be stapled.
5. The pages in the bundle should be numbered consecutively in the bottom centre.
6. Every page should be legible; typed pages of illegible documents should be prefaced with 'a' when numbering.
7. Where affidavits/statements and exhibits have become numerous, they should be put in separate bundles and numbered consecutively throughout.
8. Where the service of exhibits or copies of exhibits is difficult or impracticable, the directions of the court should be sought for arrangements to bring the exhibits to the attention of the other parties and to the custody of those documents pending trial.

Although Form E has a schedule of documents comprising a list of documents attached, it should be noted it does not provide for the dates of the documents to be identified.

Any breach of the above provisions will be taken into account by the court when deciding whether or not to depart from the general rule on costs applicable to such proceedings, subject to an explanation given for any failure to comply (rule 9.15(6)).

Requests for information and responses to such financial questionnaires must now be verified by a statement of truth. PD 9A, para.5.2 provides that replies to such questionnaires need not be filed with the court unless directed otherwise.

Flexibility regarding service of an application for a financial remedy is now provided by the option for service by the applicant as opposed to the court (rule 9.12(2)).

Certificates of service must be filed to prove service of Form A, and also to substantiate the persons upon whom the application has been so served.

Also intact from the previous rules is the requirement that both parties must attend the FDA and the FDR appointments unless the court directs otherwise. It is also a requirement that costs estimates are to be provided at each hearing.

It may well be mooted that, in future, some FDAs may be more amenable to be conducted by way of a telephone hearing, particularly where it is unlikely to be conducted as an FDR. However, it is envisaged that, due to its nature, an effective FDR hearing will always require an attendance at court by the parties.

The court can also direct at the FDA that the case be adjourned if it considers that ADR is appropriate (rule 3.3).

As for FDR hearings generally and the conduct of the same, practitioners must take careful note of the provisions of paras.6.1–6.3 and 6.5 of PD 9A. Failure to do so may well be visited by a costs sanction (PD 9A, para.3.4).

In particular, note that the parties are expected to negotiate and consider all offers made and the legal representatives who attend such hearings are expected to have full knowledge of the case.

Furthermore, it is also worth noting and advising clients where relevant that anything said or any admission made at an FDR appointment will not be admissible in evidence, except at a trial of a person for an offence committed at the appointment or, in very exceptional circumstances, as indicated in *Re D (minors) (Conciliation: Disclosure of Information)* [1993] Fam 231.

Having said that, if a party has been deliberately untruthful, criminal proceedings can be brought against them under the Fraud Act 2006 as well as proceedings for perjury if they have made a false statement in a document which is confirmed by an affidavit.

As outlined in the introduction, rules 9.18–9.20 set out a new simplified procedure, with abbreviated timescales, for parties seeking to apply for a financial remedy in the family proceedings court. This reflects the fact that such courts do not have jurisdiction to make property adjustment or pensions orders and only a limited power to make orders for lump sum payments.

On issue of an application for an order, the court will fix a hearing date not less than four weeks and not more than eight weeks after the date of filing of the application and at the same time send a blank Financial Statement (Form E2) to both parties to complete.

Again, there is provision for the applicant to serve the application on the respondent.

It will be noted that this provides for a substantially shorter timescale than that of its county court equivalent (a 50 per cent reduction) and, unlike the position in the county court, it is the court that sends out a blank Financial Statement for completion by the parties rather than the onus being on the parties themselves to obtain this.

The Financial Statement itself must be exchanged not more than 14 days after the date of issue of the application which, again, is a substantial reduction in timescale when compared to that of the county court equivalent which, of course, requires for exchange not less than 35 days before the first appointment.

Rule 9.19 sets out those matters that must be dealt with by the first hearing.

On the occasion of the first hearing itself, the court has power to direct further evidence, set a date for further directions or list the matter for a final hearing (rule 9.20).

Whilst the duty to make open proposals is now contained in rule 9.28 and applies to all tiers of court, the requirement for filing and serving a full and accurate estimate as to costs (including sums paid on account of them) at each and every hearing as set out in rule 9.27 only applies to the High Court and county court. There is also no FDR-style procedure in the magistrates' court. Query therefore, where there is a dual jurisdiction (e.g. CA 1989, Sched.1 proceedings) whether there will be a temptation to issue proceedings in the county court so that parties can avail themselves of the facilities of an FDR appointment. Having said that, because of the jurisdictional restrictions in relation to magistrates when dealing with these types of applications the author does not perceive a significant problem in practice.

Rule 9.26 sets out the procedure in respect of dealing with consent orders which remains intact, namely: one application, two copies of the draft order, one endorsed with a statement signed by the respondent signifying their agreement and a statement of information in support of the consent order from both parties.

Generally, consent orders may be endorsed by the solicitors for the parties (if on the record) or the parties themselves, unless they contain undertakings, in which case there must be a signature from the person giving the undertaking.

However, when drafting a consent order with undertakings, due care and attention should be given to the provisions contained in FPR 2010, rule 12.33 (warning notices).

The rules make it clear that attendance by the parties on a consent order dealing with a financial application is not necessary, unless the court directs otherwise.

However, where an application proceeds by consent, both parties must certify in writing that they have read the other's statement of information (rule 9.26(2) and (3)) – an important addition in the author's view as this enables the court to be satisfied that the parties have knowledge of each other's means when agreeing to the terms sought, bearing in mind the obligation of full and frank disclosure and is an added layer of protection for those representing them. As a side note, attention is also drawn to PD 18A, para.12.

Rule 35.2 deals with applications for consent orders where the parties wish to have the content of a written mediation agreement, to which the Mediation Directive applies, converted into an agreed order.

Note also the provisions of rule 9.32 where the consent order makes provision for pension sharing.

Where a pension sharing order or pension sharing compensation order is agreed, and no application for a financial order has been served on the pension trustees or the board, and the information at Part C of Form P has not been provided, the party with pension rights must ask the pension trustees to provide the information at Section C of the Pension Enquiry Form (Form P) (Section C of Form P requires disclosure of such information as required pursuant to the Pensions on Divorce etc. (Provision of Information) Regulations 2000, SI 2000/1048).

Upon receipt of that information it must be sent to the other party.

Where the parties have agreed the terms of an order which includes provision for a pension attachment or pension compensation attachment order, and the trustees of the pension have not been served with the application, then the parties must serve on the trustees:

1. a copy of the application for a consent order;
2. a draft of the proposed order;
3. the information set out in rule 9.33 or rule 9.42 as the case might be.

No consent order can be made unless 21 days have passed since the date of service of the application for the consent order and no objection has been received *or* the court has considered an objection and in order to consider that objection directions have been given.

As with previous pension sharing and pension attachment orders, the body of the consent order must state that there is to be provision by way of pension sharing or pension attachment compensation orders and refer to the pension annex attached to the order.

There must be one annex for each pension that is to be shared/attached.

As far as pensions themselves are concerned, rule 9.30 places an obligation on the party concerned to obtain information relating to the valuation of the pension rights or benefits.

Dealing with pensions generally, there are now lengthy provisions (rules 9.38–9.45) concerning the formalities of pension orders and their implementation.

The rules in particular deal with pension compensation sharing and attachment orders and the requirement to file and serve a Pension Protection Fund Inquiry Form (rule 9.15(7)(d)). Note, also, the additional procedural requirements where the PPF becomes involved with the pension scheme (rules 9.37–9.45).

In essence, a member who receives notification that there is an assessment period in relation to that scheme or that the Board has assumed responsibility for that scheme, is now obliged to make available to the other spouse:

1. a copy of that notification;
2. a copy of the valuation summary.

Form E now requires all parties to provide 'cash equivalent' (CE) values for each pension and a valuation for the PPF or compensation entitlement for the PPF. If the CE is not available, then the member must attach a letter to the trustees or the Board or the Department for Work and Pensions (DWP) requesting that information.

When the CE information is received, a copy must be sent to the other party within seven days of receipt.

The addresses for the Pension Schemes Registry, Future Pensions Centre and the PPF can be found in the notes to Form E.

PPF payments are also mentioned in the Income section of Form E.

PD 9A, para.8.1 deals with the subsequent withdrawal of an application under MCA 1973, s.10(2) and CPA 2004, s.48(2). Effectively such notice of withdrawal must be signed and can be filed and served without requiring the court's permission. Once this has been done, a formal order dismissing or striking out the application is unnecessary.

Finally, note also para.9.2 of PD 9A which discourages the use of orders for financial provision for a child expressed as payable to the child direct as opposed to a party for the benefit of child.

3.11 PARTS 10 AND 11: APPLICATIONS UNDER PARTS IV AND IVA OF THE FAMILY LAW ACT 1996

Part 10 of FPR 2010 regulates the procedural requirements in respect of applications for an occupation order and/or a non-molestation order under Part IV of FLA 1996 and is based upon rules contained in Part III of FPR 1991 and the Family Proceedings Courts (Matrimonial Proceedings etc.) Rules 1991.

It also incorporates rules to support amendments to FLA 1996, Part IV brought about by the Domestic Violence, Crime and Victims Act 2004.

The procedural requirements are broadly the same as previously, save that the application for an occupation/non-molestation order must be supported by a witness statement rather than an affidavit.

An application for an occupation/non-molestation order in a magistrates' court may be made 'without notice' but only with permission of the court (rule 10.2(3)).

The certificate of service form has also been introduced to prove service of the application.

Worth noting are the provisions of rule 10.5 which provide that in the High Court and county court only, any hearing relating to an occupation order or non-molestation order will be heard in private unless the court directs otherwise.

However, if an ex parte non-molestation or occupation order with a power of arrest is made at a private hearing, the terms of the order and name of the respondent must be announced in open court at the earliest opportunity, either on that same day or on the following listed sitting day.

Furthermore, where a person is brought to court after arrest under a power of arrest, the press and public must be permitted to attend unless impracticable for security reasons.

Part 10 is supported by PD 10A and expands upon the rules relating to the admission of the media to such hearings; however, paras.4.1–7.1 (which relate to enforcement) do not apply in the magistrates' court.

Applications for an order under FLA 1996, Part IV by a minor must be made to the county court pursuant to FPR 2010, Part 18.

Finally, there is provision for information to be provided on an application for bail, which includes details of where the person applying would reside if bail is granted, any recognisance which can be offered, the grounds and any change of circumstances since any prior refusal of bail.

Part 11 of FPR 2010 similarly regulates applications under FLA 1996, Part IVA (inserted by the Forced Marriage (Civil Protection) Act 2007), more particularly by way of a forced marriage protection order. The provisions are based on the rules contained in the Family Proceedings (Amendment) Rules 2008, SI 2008/2446.

Under the FPR 2010, however, a separate part is devoted to the procedure under FLA 1996. However, although there is power to extend the jurisdiction to the magistrates' court, as of yet, the rules do not apply to proceedings in the magistrates' court.

Applications for permission to apply for a forced marriage protection order must follow the process set out in rule 11.3 and applications for a person to be joined or removed as a party to proceedings for a forced marriage protection order must follow the process in rule 11.6. As for the process for other applications in proceedings, although the Part 18 procedure is not to be followed, the application notice for Part 18 is to be used.

It is also perhaps worth mentioning that the provisions for withholding information in forced marriage applications are broader than before, as the previous position permitted the withholding of documents only, whereas rule 11.7 now provides for the withholding of any submissions made or evidence adduced.

Again, the proceedings will be heard in private unless the court directs otherwise.

3.12 PART 12: PROCEEDINGS RELATING TO CHILDREN SAVE IN RELATION TO PARENTAL ORDER, ADOPTION AND PLACEMENT PROCEEDINGS

Part 12 regulates the bulk of children proceedings in both the county court and magistrates' court.

It applies to private law proceedings, public law proceedings and emergency proceedings, wardship and Hague Convention applications.

It does not, however, include adoption and placement proceedings or proceedings under the Human Fertilisation and Embryology Act 2008.

This Part is derived from Parts IV, IVA, V and VI of the Family Proceedings Rules 1991 and Family Proceedings Courts (Children Act 1989) Rules 1991.

It is divided into seven chapters: interpretation and application; general rules; special provisions about public law proceedings; special provisions about private law proceedings; special provisions about inherent jurisdiction proceedings; proceedings under the Hague Conventions 1980 and 1996, European Convention and the Council Regulation and communication of information about proceedings relating to children.

It includes rules to support the Practice Direction of 13 February 2008 entitled 'Guide to Case Management in Public Law Proceedings' (incorporating the Public Law Outline) and also includes rules to support Part 1 of the Children and Adoption Act 2006.

PD 12A sets out the Public Law Proceedings Guide to Case Management (April 2010). PD 12B sets out the Revised Private Law Programme of 1 April 2010. The key elements of both practice directions must be followed and there should be no flexibility on the prescribed timescales.

Where a party requires permission before applying to bring a Children Act application then such application must be dealt with pursuant to the Part 18 procedure and not under this Part.

In so far as interpretation of the rules is concerned, particular mention ought to be made of the reference to 'Case Management Order' which refers to the case management document form of order as set out in PD 12A and 'interim order' which refers to both an interim care order and an interim supervision order.

Rule 12.3 sets out in detail, in tabular form, who the respective applicants and respondents are in so far as various proceedings are concerned under this Part and thus provides a useful checklist for practitioners.

The definition of 'public law proceedings' in rule 12.2 includes proceedings for:

(a) an order under CA 1989, s.39(3A) varying or discharging an interim care order in so far as it imposes an exclusion requirement on a person who is not entitled to apply for an order to be discharged; and
(b) an order under s.39(3B) of the 1989 Act varying or discharging an interim care order in so far as it confers a power of arrest attached to an exclusion requirement.

Provisions relating to the giving of notice of applications are now contained in a supplementary practice direction – PD 12C.

PD 12C in relation to service contains three tables: one specifying to whom documentation should be sent in certain types of proceedings (this also provides for service on CAFCASS as well); the second specifying the minimum number of days prior to a hearing or directions appointment when proceedings should be served; and the third setting out the non-parties to whom notice should be given of the proceedings/hearing/directions appointment.

By way of an additional note, any person who has foreign parental responsibility for a child and receives notice of any proceedings to which Part 12 applies, can apply to be joined as a party using the Part 18 procedure (rule 12.4(5)).

Rule 12.5 provides that where proceedings are issued, the court in private law proceedings will consider listing the matter for a First Hearing Dispute Resolution Appointment (FHDRA) (rule 12.31) and, as far as public law proceedings are concerned, a first appointment (rule 12.25).

PDs 12A and 12B in particular set out the details relating to the FHDRA and the first appointment.

In specified proceedings, a children's guardian will be appointed unless the court considers that such appointment is not necessary to safeguard the child's interests (rule 12.6).

In cases where a request for transfer of the proceedings from the magistrates' court to a county court is refused on paper, a party may make an application for an 'on notice' hearing using the Part 18 procedure for an order transferring the proceedings from the magistrates' court. Such application must be made to the county court not the magistrates' court that refused the allocation order.

Rule 12.12(2) and (4) lists the directions that the court may consider giving in so far as case progression is concerned, including the filing of any risk assessment by CAFCASS.

Where CAFCASS has filed a risk assessment (known as a 'Schedule 2 Letter') copies will be served by the court on each of the parties. Before doing so, however, the court must consider whether in order to prevent risk of harm to the child it is necessary for:

- information to be deleted from a copy of the risk assessment before that copy is served on a party; or
- service of a copy of the risk assessment (whether with information deleted from it or not) on a party should be delayed for a specified period and may give directions accordingly.

Particular attention must also be drawn to the guidance on fact-finding hearings contained in PD 12B.

A fact-finding hearing should only be ordered if the court takes the view that the case cannot properly be decided without such a hearing. Even if one is necessary it does not automatically follow that such a hearing needs to be separate from the substantive hearing (see *Re L, Re V, Re M & Re H (Contact: Domestic Violence)* [2000] 2 FLR 334; *Re C* [2009] EWCA Civ 994; *AA v. NA and Kab (Fact-Finding Hearing)* [2010] EWHC 1282 (Fam)).

The court can exercise any of these powers either upon application of the parties themselves or of its own initiative. Where the court does exercise such powers of its own initiative, then the procedure set out in rule 4.3(2)–(7) will apply, namely advising the parties of their right to make representations as to the effects of an order made in their absence.

Rule 12.13 provides that the court will normally always adjourn to a date rather than provide for a general adjournment in order to avoid any drift, particularly in cases concerning children. Whether the court will impose a general stay to encourage negotiation and mediation, as opposed to adjourning to a date under its general case management powers, is a moot point.

Rule 12.13 also reinforces the positive duty on the court to set a timetable for the case imposed by CA 1989, s.11(1).

Rule 12.14 also provides that unless the court directs otherwise, the parties themselves must attend any hearing.

Again, whether or not usage will be made of telephone hearings without requiring the parties' attendance remains to be seen, but much will depend upon the purposes of the hearing and whether matters can be progressed without requiring the parties' attendance.

At this stage the answers to these questions remain unknown and we will have to wait and see as to what transpires in practice.

Rule 12.16 sets out the procedure for making applications without notice.

An application in proceedings for a s.8 order and emergency proceedings can be made without notice as long as the application is filed at the same time or, if the application is made by telephone, the next business day.

In the magistrates' court, the application must be filed at the time when the application is made.

It will also be noted that there is an additional difference between the county court and magistrates' court procedures in that, in the county court, an application can be made without notice whereas, in the magistrates' court, permission of the court has to be sought first before bringing such an application.

Presumably permission will have to first be sought from the court clerk.

Rule 12.18 deals with the disclosure of the requisite report in special guardianship proceedings and rule 12.19 deals with the filing of additional evidence which applies to both special guardianship proceedings and applications for a s.8 order. Note the general restriction on filing evidence other than that specifically permitted by direction of the court which reinforces the court's duty in controlling evidence.

Of particular note is rule 12.19(3) which provides that where a party fails to comply with any directions dealing with the filing and service of witness statements and other documentation (including expert evidence), the defaulting party cannot seek to rely upon it unless the court directs. This, no doubt, will call into play the considerations required by the overriding objective of enabling the court to deal with cases justly, which will involve a balancing exercise between those who have complied with the rules and those who have not.

Rule 12.21(1) specifies that the court may give directions concerning the order of speeches although the rule itself is silent as to the 'normal' order for such speeches.

Chapter 3 of Part 12 sets out certain special provisions concerning public law proceedings.

In particular, rule 12.23 states that the court must set any timetable in accordance with the 'Timetable for the Child'.

This is further defined to provide that such timetable must take into account the dates of the significant steps in the life of the child who is the subject of the proceedings or which are otherwise appropriate for the child. A key objective is to avoid unnecessary delay and avoid any drift which would be detrimental to the child concerned.

As part of the overriding objective and active case management, rule 12.24 imposes upon the parties a duty to monitor compliance with the directions given by the court and to advise the court as to any failure to comply with such directions and any other delay in the proceedings irrespective of whether or not this might affect the timetable.

The new rules also preserve the usage of first appointments, Case Management Conferences and Issue Resolutions Hearings as well as advocates' meetings.

The matters which the court must have regard to at those various hearings are set out in PD 12A.

Advocates' meetings, in particular, will be required to discuss the provisions of the Case Management Order (the local authority taking the lead) in an attempt to agree this and then draft and submit it to the court prior to any Case Management Conference or Issue Resolutions Hearing (rule 12.26). (Note: rule 12.26(1) now says that the court 'will direct' a discussion between the advocates to discuss the Case Management Order and consider PD 12A; previously the wording was 'will consider'.)

The rules also now provide for the route the advocates must take when the Case Management Order is not agreed (rule 12.26(4)).

Note the word 'advocate' also includes a litigant in person (rule 12.26(6)) and where there is a litigant in person, the court will direct how that person is to take part in the advocates' discussions (rule 12.26(2)).

In passing, it is also worth bearing in mind the provisions of rule 12.28 which regulates the exclusion requirements pursuant to interim care orders and emergency protection orders. This is supplemented by PD 12K which deals with the practice of announcing such orders in open court if a power of arrest is attached.

Concerning applications for secure accommodation orders, rule 12.30 regulates the provision as to the circulation of copies of all written reports filed within those proceedings prior to the hearing.

Chapter 4 of Part 12 makes special provision in respect of private law proceedings, more particularly the filing and service of an answer to the application by the respondent, the listing of the FHDRA (which is directed by the Private Law Programme) and the procedure for making applications for the attachment of warning notices to contact orders as well as the filing and service of risk assessments by CAFCASS (unless it is necessary to withhold service or to serve an edited version in order to prevent harm to a child (rule 12.34)).

All parties as well as CAFCASS are required to attend the FHDRA.

Pursuant to rule 12.35, where an enforcement order is made, it is the duty of the applicant to arrange personal service of it upon the defaulting party, unless the court directs otherwise.

The various issues to be considered at the FHDRA are set out in PD 12B.

Where domestic violence and applications for contact and residence are concerned the previous practice direction relating to this issue (Residence and Contact Orders: Domestic Violence and Harm [2009] 2 FLR 1400) and the considerations as to fact-finding hearings are set out in PD 12J.

As before, when faced with issues of domestic violence the court must consider the nature of any allegation and the extent to which any domestic violence, if admitted or proved, will be relevant in deciding whether to make any order. If an order is made the court will need to consider what terms should be included and accordingly give directions to enable the factual and welfare issues to be determined expeditiously and fairly.

Upon the issue of an application CAFCASS will undertake an initial screening as to risk assessment pursuant to CA 1989, s.16A (see also PD 16A).

It should be noted that not every allegation of domestic violence will activate the court's attention but only such violence as alleged which, if proved, would be likely to affect the decision of the court and have an impact on the conduct and outcome of those proceedings. It is thus a matter of discretion for the judge whether to order a preliminary fact-finding hearing and it is permissible for them not to do so provided reasons are given (*Re C* [2009] EWCA Civ 994).

Moreover, a fact-finding hearing should only be ordered if the court can discern a real purpose for such a hearing. If such inquiry would not be purposeful then one should not be ordered (*AA v. NA and Kab (Fact-Finding Hearing)* [2010] EWHC 1282).

A fact-finding hearing itself is part of the process of trying a case and is not a separate exercise so that after determination of the facts at issue and adjournment of the case for disposal of the primary application it remains part-heard and should accordingly be relisted before the same judge (*Re B (Children)* [2008] 2 FLR 141).

Once a fact-finding determination has been made, particularly where there is a finding of domestic violence, the court has within its power the ability to direct that a party should seek advice or treatment as a precondition to an order for contact. The court should also attach a schedule to the judgment setting out exactly what findings have been made (*Re M (Allegations of Rape: Fact-Finding Hearing)* [2009] EWCA Civ 1385). What the court must not do is then go on to deal with the substantive application there and then (see *Re E (A Child)* [2009] EWCA Civ 1238). This has to await in essence what is the later disposal hearing.

In determining whether contact should take place the court will be guided by the principles originally enumerated in the seminal case of *Re L, Re V, Re M & Re H (Contact: Domestic Violence)* [2000] 2 FLR 334 in order to weigh the seriousness of the domestic violence, the risks involved and the impact on the child against the positive factors of contact, namely:

- the conduct of both parties to each other and the children;
- the effect the domestic violence which has been established has on the child and on the parent with whom the child is living;
- the extent to which the parent seeking the order is motivated by a desire to promote the best interests of the child or, conversely, is using the proceedings as a means of continuing a process of violence, intimidation or harassment against the other parent;
- the likely behaviour during contact of the parent seeking contact and the effect on the child of that behaviour;
- the capacity of the parent seeking contact to appreciate the effect of past violence and the potential for future violence on the other parent and the child;
- the attitude of the parent seeking the order to past violence, by that parent; and in particular whether that parent has the capacity to change and to behave appropriately.

PD 12M deals with the steps the court must undertake prior to making a family assistance order pursuant to CA 1989, s.16. Essentially the court must obtain the opinion of the CAFCASS officer or local authority to whom the order is directed as to whether such order is in the best interests of the child and if so how it should operate and over what duration.

PD 12N provides for disclosure to the National Probation Service in cases of applications for contact enforcement orders under CA 1989, s.11J or alleged breaches of the same. This practice direction only applies to proceedings in the High Court or county court.

Chapter 5 deals with special provisions in relation to the court's inherent jurisdiction (wardship proceedings) which must be commenced in the High Court and is supported by PD 12D which contains examples of where the inherent jurisdiction of the High Court in relation to children might be used. See PD 12D – Inherent Jurisdiction (Including Wardship) Proceedings at para.1.2 – a very useful guide!

PD 12P deals with the removal of a child who is a ward of court from the jurisdiction for holiday periods, which will normally be by way of a open ended order and the issue of passports for them without any restriction.

Chapter 6 deals with Hague Convention and child abduction proceedings.

In so far as child abduction proceedings are concerned, the rules support the Child Abduction and Custody Act 1985, giving effect to the main provisions of the 1980 Hague Convention on the Civil Aspects of International Child Abduction and the European Convention on Recognition and Enforcement of Decisions concerning Custody of Children and on the Restoration of Custody of Children.

The rules also support the articles dealing with children matters in Council Regulation (EC) No. 2201/2003 concerning jurisdiction and the recognition and enforcement of judgments in matrimonial matters and the matters of parental responsibility. However, the rules relating to recognition and enforcement under the Council Regulation are contained in Part 31.

The supporting practice direction (PD 12F) sets out in detail the procedure to be followed in both Convention and non-Convention cases and has been drafted with the aim of being more accessible to litigants in person (i.e. in a comprehensible plain-English style).

PD 12F also sets out, rather usefully, the procedure for the port alert scheme as well as the procedure whereby the Identity and Passport Service (IPS) may take action to prevent a UK passport or replacement passport from being issued and includes a draft letter.

It also deals with the Council Regulation in relation to enforcement of access orders more particularly in light of the decision of *Re G (A Minor)(Hague Convention: Access)* [1993] 1 FLR 669, the impact of which is set out in the accompanying annex and duplicates the Practice Note [1993] 1 FLR 804 which states that in the vast majority of such cases a separate application will be needed under CA 1989, s.8.

Part 6 of PD 12F provides ready access to the protocol concerning child abduction cases between the UK and Pakistan.

PD 12O relates to the disclosure of information concerning a child arriving in the UK by air in respect of applications for return orders.

Chapter 7 regulates the issues as to whom disclosure of information can be made to within children proceedings without making that party in contempt of court (rules 12.73 and 12.75) and is supplemented by PD 12G which again sets out a useful list of such persons in tabular form. It is important to note that rule 12.75 includes disclosure to a McKenzie Friend.

Rule 12.74 also reinforces the provision that no party may instruct an expert in relation to the proceedings without the court's permission, and where such an unauthorised instruction has been given, no evidence from that instruction can be adduced to the court without first seeking the court's permission.

PD 12E describes the procedure to be followed in respect of urgent (including out of hours) business, in the High Court Family Division and relates specifically to applications concerning children.

PD 12I deals with applications in the High Court for an order restricting publication of information relating to children and incapacitated adults by the media (reporting restrictions orders).

Such orders must not be granted where the person against whom the application is made is neither present or represented unless:

- the applicant has taken all practicable steps to notify the respondent; or
- there are compelling reasons why they should not be so notified.

Orders will only be made without such notice in exceptional circumstances.

3.13 PART 13: PROCEEDINGS UNDER SECTION 54 OF THE HUMAN FERTILISATION AND EMBRYOLOGY ACT 2008

This Part regulates applications under the Human Fertilisation and Embryology Act 2008 for a parental order.

Upon issue of proceedings, the court will set a date for the first directions hearing, appoint a parental order reporter and set a date for the hearing of the application.

Rule 13.9 deals with the various matters which must be considered at the first directions hearing, more particularly, the timetabling of filing the parental order report, statement of facts and any other evidence.

In some cases, directions may be given automatically upon issue of proceedings, thus dispensing with the need for a first directions hearing. Where this occurs, the procedure set out in rule 4.3(2)–(7) applies in respect of orders made of the court's own initiative. See, also, rule 13.9(4)(a) concerning the court's exercise of its case management powers of its own initiative at any stage in the proceedings.

3.14 PART 14: PROCEDURE FOR APPLICATIONS IN ADOPTION, PLACEMENT AND RELATED PROCEEDINGS

This Part regulates the procedure in adoption, placement and related proceedings; in essence, the general provisions contained within the Family Procedure (Adoption) Rules 2005 have been incorporated in their entirety in FPR 2010 save that rules 14.13 and 14.14, relating to confidential reports and communication of information relating to the proceedings, are additions.

This Part also applies to contact orders under the Adoption and Children Act 2002.

Again, rule 14.3 sets out a very useful table indicating the identity of the proposed applicants and respondents to various proceedings regulated by this Part. PD 14A helpfully sets out all those who must be given a copy of the form pursuant to rule 14.6(1)(b)(ii).

Rule 14.7 specifies that, unless the court directs otherwise, the first directions hearing in applications governed by this rule must be listed within four weeks of the date of issue of the application.

Rule 14.8 goes on to set out the various matters on which the court will consider giving directions at the first directions hearing. It is also a requirement that the parties or their legal representatives must attend the first directions hearing unless the court directs otherwise. Moreover, the court cannot make a placement order unless the legal representative for the applicant attends the final hearing (rule 14.16(9)).

As part of the court's duty of active case management, directions can be given at any stage in the proceedings and can be undertaken of the court's own initiative. To supplement this proactive approach, following on from the first directions hearing, the court will monitor compliance by the parties with the court's timetable and the directions given (rule 14.8(4), (5) and (7)).

PD 14B supplements rule 14.8(3) and deals with the additional requirements and considerations at first directions hearings where applications for an adoption order involve a foreign element.

In relation to parents' consent to a placement for adoption, or indeed the making of an adoption order itself, PD 5A details the requirements of the form of consent.

The matters to be covered in the suitability report or placement report pursuant to rule 14.11(3) are set out in Annexes A and B respectively of PD 14C.

The matters which need to be contained in the relevant health reports pursuant to rule 14.12(1) are set out in the annex to PD 14D.

Rule 14.14 sets out the circumstances in which disclosure of information in relation to the proceedings will not be regarded as a contempt of court and is supported by PD 14E which provides a useful list of who may disclose what to whom and for what purpose in tabular form.

Rule 14.18(1)(d) is supported by PD 14F which deals with information which may be disclosed to an adopted adult and the related procedure.

An adopted adult over 18 is entitled to obtain the following:

- the application form for an adoption order;
- the adoption order itself;
- any contact order made post adoption;
- any transcript or written reasons of the court's decision;
- any report prepared by a children's guardian, reporting officer, children and family reporter, local authority or adoption agency.

Such application is made on Form A64.

On the issue of applications for recovery orders under rule 14.20, it is worth noting that in the High Court and county court such applications can be made without notice. In the magistrates' court, however, such without notice orders can only be made following permission of the court.

Rule 14.21 allows the applicant to request the High Court, pursuant to its inherent jurisdiction, for directions on the necessity of giving to a father without parental responsibility notice of the applicant's intention to place a child for adoption. This, of course, will engage the usual arguments as to the European Convention on

Human Rights, arts.6 and 8 and the need to balance the subject child's interests against those of the biological father. One would expect that in most cases notice will be given unless the case provides an exception to the rule (e.g. conception as a result of rape or child placed at severe risk).

3.15 PART 15: REPRESENTATION OF PROTECTED PARTIES

This Part governs the appointment of the Official Solicitor and others to represent the interests of mentally incapable parties. It contains special provisions which apply in proceedings involving protected parties and is derived from CPR Part 21 and Part IX of the Family Proceedings Rules 1991.

'Litigation friend' is now to be used in place of 'next friend' and 'guardian ad litem'. It applies to all three levels of court.

Part 15 has been separated from the Part containing more detailed provisions relating to the representation of children (Part 16).

There is, of course, a presumption of capacity (Mental Capacity Act 2005, s.1) that no one should be treated as incapable of making decisions all of the time; the relevant test should be applied to each decision when it is to be (or was) made, because capacity may vary.

A protected party is 'a party, or an intended party who lacks capacity . . . to conduct the proceedings' (FPR 2010, rule 2.3).

Section 2(1) of the Mental Capacity Act 2005 provides that 'a person lacks capacity in relation to a matter if at the material time he is unable to make a decision for himself in relation to the matter because of an impairment of, or a disturbance in the functioning of, the mind or brain'.

Section 3 refers to a party's inability to make a decision which is based on whether they are able:

- (a) to understand the information relevant to the decision,
- (b) to retain that information,
- (c) to use or weigh that information as part of the process of making the decision, or
- (d) to communicate his decision (whether by talking, using sign language or any other means).

There is thus a two-stage test:

- Is there an impairment of, or disturbance in the functioning of, the person's mind or brain? (Diagnostic threshold.)
- Is that impairment or disturbance sufficient to render the person incapable of making that particular decision?

There must therefore be an assessment of capacity as well as a medical diagnosis of mental disorder.

The rule is concerned with whether the party lacks capacity and is now more issues based. A person may lack capacity for some purposes but not others and thus the test of capacity is decision specific as the impairment or disturbance may be permanent or temporary (*Masterman-Lister v. Brutton & Co and Jewell & Anor* [2002] EWCA Civ 1889).

This, of course, is a question of fact based upon the balance of probabilities but with a presumption of capacity. Often an expert's report will be required (see PD 25A, paras.2.6–2.9 dealing with experts in family proceedings in this instance) as well as evidence from those who know the individual concerned and, of course, from meeting that individual face to face.

A protected party must have a litigation friend to conduct proceedings on their behalf (rule 15.2).

Furthermore, a person may not, without the permission of the court, take any steps within the proceedings until a protected party has a litigation friend, and any step which is so taken will have no effect unless the court orders otherwise by way of ratification (rule 15.3(2) and (3)).

Any litigation friend appointed without a court order will need to sign and file a certificate of suitability in accordance with the provisions of para.3.1(b) of PD 15A together with an authority to act as well as an undertaking as to costs (rules 15.4(3)(c) and 15.5(3)).

The court can also appoint a litigation friend itself on an application made pursuant to the Part 18 procedure subject to receiving the evidence as set out in para.4.3 of PD 15A (FPR 2010, rule 15.6).

The duties of a litigation friend are set out in rule 15.4(3); in essence a litigation friend is required to fairly and competently conduct proceedings on behalf of the protected party; must have no interest in the proceedings adverse to that of the protected party; and all steps and decisions taken by him or her must be taken for the benefit of the protected party.

3.16 PART 16: REPRESENTATION OF CHILDREN AND REPORTS IN PROCEEDINGS INVOLVING CHILDREN

Part 16 of FPR 2010 and the supporting PD 16A contain special provisions in relation to the representation of children and the circumstances in which the court will make a child a party to family proceedings. The provisions apply to proceedings across all three levels of court involving children and incorporate rule 9.5 of FPR 1991. They are intended to reflect the current provision for the representation of children in FPR 1991 and the Family Procedure (Adoption) Rules 2005.

The term 'guardian ad litem' is now abolished and replaced by 'children's guardian'.

The other terms for CAFCASS officers, such as 'children and family reporter', remain unchanged.

These rules cover:

- the appointment of a children's guardian in specified proceedings and adoption proceedings;
- the appointment of a litigation friend;
- the appointment of a person to represent children in other proceedings (non-specified) (now to be known as a rule 16.2 children's guardian).

In non-specified proceedings the court *may* make a child a party if it is adjudged as being in the child's best interests so to do (rule 16.2).

PD 16A Part 4, paras.7.1–7.3 set out the matters which the court must take into consideration before making a child a party in private law proceedings, which no doubt will prove an extremely useful and readily accessible aide memoire.

An important change here is the fact that family proceedings courts can now appoint a children's guardian in private law cases.

The appointment of a guardian for a child in specified proceedings is dealt with in rule 16.3 and may be undertaken either by application or of the court's own initiative, the latter being the more normal course.

In essence the court *must* appoint a children's guardian unless satisfied that it is not necessary to do so in order to safeguard the interests of the child.

When making such an appointment the court will, of course, consider the appointment of anyone who has acted as guardian for the same child previously so as to provide continuity of representation (rule 16.3(4)).

Rule 16.5 states that a child who is a party to the proceedings but who is not the subject of those proceedings must have a litigation friend.

Rule 16.6 prescribes the circumstances in which a child is able to conduct proceedings without assistance from a guardian or litigation friend in non-specified proceedings.

In essence the court *must* appoint a children's guardian unless satisfied that it is not necessary to do so in order to safeguard the interests of the child.

This will apply where permission of the court has been obtained or the child's solicitor considers that, having regard to the child's level of understanding (irrespective of age), they are able to give instructions direct.

Chapter 5 of Part 16 sets out the requirements of a litigation friend when conducting proceedings on behalf of a child.

The corresponding PD 16A, Part 2 deals with their duties and the procedural requirements of their appointment either without a court order or by application pursuant to the Part 18 procedure.

Note the provisions of rule 16.8(3) which provides that any step taken in proceedings before a litigation friend is appointed will be of no effect unless the court directs otherwise.

Chapter 6 of Part 16 provides similarly in respect of a children's guardian in relation to specified proceedings.

Note, in particular, the powers and duties of the children's guardian contained in rule 16.20 whereby such guardian must act on behalf of the child with a view to safeguarding the child's interests. The guardian is also under a duty to provide assistance to the court.

Most of the duties of the children's guardian and provisions as to how they are exercised are now contained in the accompanying practice direction (PD 16A, Part 3) as opposed to within the body of the rules themselves.

In particular, a children's guardian appointed under rule 16.3 must contact or seek to interview such persons as the children's guardian thinks appropriate or as the court directs and obtain such professional assistance as is available which the guardian thinks appropriate or which the court directs to be obtained.

Either the guardian or their solicitor (but not both) must attend all directions hearings unless excused (this is a change from previously where the children's guardian had to attend, thus, where appropriate, freeing up a valuable resource provided the solicitor with conduct has full instructions or is able to obtain them over the telephone). They must advise the court as to competence, wishes and appropriate forum and timing for the proceedings, and of the range of options available. The advice may be given orally or in writing, but if given orally must be noted by the court (PD 16A, para.6.7).

Where the guardian decides to inspect local authority or adoption agency documents pursuant to CA 1989, s.42 or the Adoption and Children Act 2002, s.103 (which it is, of course, good practice to do), the guardian must bring to the attention of the court and the other parties (unless otherwise directed) any documents and records which may assist in the proper determination of the proceedings. For all those of us who represent guardians it is important to draw this duty of disclosure to their attention as well as to the attention of the local authorities.

Worthy of mention is the fact that PD 16A, para.6.8(a) provides that reports are to be filed according to the court's own timetable and not, as previously, not less than 14 days before the hearing (active case management).

Where the child subsequently instructs a solicitor direct or intends to conduct the proceedings himself or herself and is capable of doing so, the guardian must immediately inform the court (rule 16.21).

Chapter 7 sets out the requirements of a guardian appointed in non-specified proceedings pursuant to rule 16.4.

Applications for the appointment of a private law guardian must be made pursuant to FPR 2010, Part 18 and be supported by evidence.

It is to be noted that private law guardians are only to be appointed in cases which involve an issue of significant difficulty. Other options are to be considered first. The criteria set out at para.7.1 of PD 16A are in similar terms to the previous practice direction regulating the appointment of guardians, namely asking CAFCASS to carry out further work, making a referral to social services or obtaining expert evidence. PD 16A, para.7.2 gives guidance by way of examples which might justify the making of such an order.

Again, any step taken before a child has a children's guardian will be of no effect unless the court subsequently ratifies it (rule 16.23(3)).

The powers and duties of such a guardian and the exercise of those powers is again set out in PD 16A Part 4, Section 2.

The practice direction also goes on to set out the procedural requirements of being appointed either without a court order or pursuant to an application under the Part 18 procedure.

Rule 16.25 also, for the first time, sets out how to apply to remove a children's guardian in a private law case for which purpose the Part 18 procedure must be used. Evidence must also be filed in support.

Chapter 8 sets out the duties of a solicitor acting for a child.

Such solicitor must act in accordance with instructions relayed from the children's guardian unless the child's instructions conflict with those of the guardian and the child is able, having regard to their level of understanding, to give instructions direct.

Before the solicitor makes such a decision, however, the views of both the guardian and the court must be sought first (rule 16.29(3)).

Furthermore, when giving permission for a child to instruct a solicitor directly in private law proceedings, the court no longer has to discharge the children's guardian.

Note the provisions of rule 16.33 that any report from a children and family reporter appointed is confidential and the 'officer' (person preparing the report) may be questioned by a party about it, be it oral or written.

Chapters 9, 10 and 11 set out the duties of a reporting officer, children and family reporter and welfare officer and parental order reporter.

Again, provisions as to the exercise of their respective powers and duties are set out in PD 16A, Parts 5–7.

Finally, Part 8 of PD 16A sets out the duties, and how they should be exercised, of various officers of the service and local authority in the field of risk assessment pursuant to rule 12.34.

3.17 PART 17: STATEMENTS OF TRUTH

The benefit of using a statement of truth is to simplify the procedure and reduce the likelihood of delay without compromising the importance of statements being given truthfully. The rules provide for the possibility of contempt proceedings against a person who makes a false statement in a document verified by a statement of truth.

Part 17 itself is derived from CPR Part 22.

The following documents in particular must be verified by a statement of truth:

- a statement of case;
- a witness statement;
- an acknowledgement of service (in an application commenced using the Part 19 procedure);
- an expert's report (note the specific wording contained in PD 25A);
- a certificate of service;
- a statement of arrangements for the children of the family;
- a statement of information pursuant to rule 9.26(1)(b).

However, this list does not include an application for a matrimonial or civil partnership order or an answer to such an application. Nor does a statement of truth apply to any document which needs to be verified by an affidavit (e.g. Financial Statements Form E).

The various forms of statement of truth and who can sign them are set out in PD 17A and contained within the annex are some case-specific examples.

Moreover, if an applicant wishes to rely on the contents of an application form or notice as evidence, then it must be verified by a statement of truth. Although a failure to verify a party's statement of case by a statement of truth still means that it will remain effective unless struck out, that party will not be able to rely upon it as their evidence; there is also a danger that the other party will apply to have such a statement struck out (rule 17.3(3)). However, such application is likely to be met by an unless order in the first instance together with the usual costs sanctions (PD 17A, para.5.3).

Similar rules apply to witness evidence (rule 17.4).

Any person who has failed to verify a document with a statement of truth may find the court directing that it is inadmissible until such time as it is so verified (rule 17.5).

A litigation friend acting on behalf of a party must endorse any document requiring a statement of truth to the effect that they believe the facts stated in it to be true.

Attention must be drawn to para.3.8 of PD 17A in relation to a legal representative signing a statement of case or application notice on a client's behalf. The statement must refer to the client's belief, not their own.

Where so signed the legal representative's signature will be treated by the court as their statement that:

- the client has authorised them to do so;
- before signing they had explained to the client that by doing so they were confirming their client's belief that the facts contained within it were true; and
- they had informed the client as to the consequences of knowingly making a false statement.

Be warned!

As for contempt proceedings for dishonestly making a false statement in a document verified by a statement of truth, recourse may usefully be had to the case law applying to the CPR equivalent.

In order to be satisfied as to a contempt of court, four elements have to be established beyond reasonable doubt:

1. a false statement had been made;
2. it was made in a document verified by a statement of truth; and
3. it was so made without an honest belief in its truth; and
4. it has (or would have) interfered with the course of justice.

It is not the case that where there are discrepancies between a statement so verified and other evidence that a contempt of court will have arisen.

A person who makes a statement verified by a statement of truth is only guilty of contempt if the statement was false and they knew it to be so when it was made.

It has to be in the public interest for contempt proceedings to be brought, and the relevant factors are:

- that the case against the alleged contemnor is strong;
- that the false statement was significant in the proceedings;
- whether the alleged contemnor understood the likely effect of the statement;
- the use to which it would be put; and
- the deterrent effect of contempt proceedings.

See *Barnes v. Seabrook* [2010] EWHC 1849 (Admin).

3.18 PART 18: PROCEDURE FOR OTHER APPLICATIONS

Part 18, which is derived from CPR Part 23, replaces the previous reliance on RSC O.32 and CCR O.13 and is the standard way to commence proceedings, to make an application in the course of proceedings or after they have been concluded.

It contains rules governing applications:

1. within existing proceedings;
2. to commence proceedings (i.e. pre-action applications and applications for permission, save where prescribed elsewhere);
3. in connection with proceedings which have been concluded.

Applications are generally made by application notice (Form FP2) which replaces the use of summons and notice of applications although for Children Act proceedings there is a revised Form C2.

Addresses can be withheld by completing Form A65 or entering the serial number in adoption cases.

PD 18A reiterates the overriding objective and the parties' duties to further the same by emphasising that every application should be made as soon as it becomes apparent that it is necessary or desirable (PD 18A, para.4.6).

The following paragraphs of the practice direction deserve to be set out in full:

> 4.8 The parties must anticipate that at any hearing (including any directions hearing) the court may wish to review the conduct of the case as a whole and give any necessary directions. They should be ready to assist the court in doing so and to answer questions the court may ask for this purpose.
>
> 4.9 Where a date for a hearing has been fixed, a party who wishes to make an application at that hearing but does not have sufficient time to file an application notice should as soon as possible inform the court (if possible in writing) and, if possible, the other parties of the nature of the application and the reason for it. That party should then make the application orally at the hearing.

Paragraph 5.1 provides that an application may be made without service of an application notice only:

> (a) where there is exceptional urgency;
> (b) where the overriding objective is best furthered by doing so;
> (c) by consent of all parties;
> (d) with the permission of the court;
> (e) where paragraph 4.9 applies; or
> (f) where a court order, rule or practice direction permits.

From this it should be noted that to ensure that as many aspects of the case are dealt with at the same time such applications, wherever possible, should be made prior to any forthcoming hearing. However, nothing prevents a party from making an oral application if there is insufficient time available to file one.

Applications for permission to apply for an order under CA 1989, s.8 should be made under this Part.

Such applications can be dealt with without a hearing unless they are proceedings in the magistrates' court in which case the application must always be dealt with at a hearing (rule 18.9(3)).

However, if an application for permission is refused on paper then, upon the applicant's request, the court must list the application for an 'on notice' hearing.

The application notice must set out what order is sought and why and be verified by a statement of truth. A draft of the proposed order must also be submitted together with any written evidence to be relied on.

The application notice should also set out whether or not a hearing is requested or alternatively whether or not the matter can be dealt with without a hearing or by way of a telephone hearing (see further below).

Additional requirements in relation to application notices generally and certain specific types of applications are set out in PD 18A.

PD 18A, para.5.1 gives examples of when an application may be made without notice.

Notwithstanding any request made by the applicant for disposal on paper or at a hearing, upon receipt of an application there is power for the court to deal with the same without a hearing pursuant to the court's powers of active case management as well as directing the filing of additional evidence before considering the matter further.

If such a 'without notice' order is made then the order must, on the face of it, contain a statement of a party's right to make an application to have it set aside or to vary its terms within seven days of service (rules 18.10(3) and 18.11).

On an 'on notice' application service must be effected at least seven days before the hearing (14 days in cases of an application for an interim order) unless time is abridged (rule 18.8(4)). Informal notice should be given if the full seven days is not possible.

An important innovation in the new rules is in relation to the specific provision for telephone hearings, which is detailed in PD 18A, para.8 and will usually only arise where all parties consent to a hearing being undertaken by such method. If a hearing is to be conducted by telephone then no advocate is allowed to attend in person unless agreed by the other side. (Presumably this is to avoid any impression of unfairness.)

The applicant's legal adviser is responsible for arranging the conference call. Advocates are to be assembled on the telephone conference before the judge or bench is joined. An interesting experience for lay magistrates!

As for the conduct of hearings generally, the court may proceed in the absence of a party who has failed to attend or relist the application so as to afford the absent party an opportunity to attend.

Another practice which has been adopted from the CPR (albeit from the Small Claims Track) is that the parties are now able to agree for the court to dispose of an application based upon the written evidence only without a formal attendance at a hearing (rule 18.9(1)(b)). To take up this option the parties must inform the court in writing and confirm that all evidence that is being relied upon has been disclosed to each other. The court will then go on to decide the application on paper. Interestingly enough, no provision has been made, unlike in the CPR, for the court to furnish the parties with the reasons for any decision taken when adopting such a course.

Note also the provision relating to the county court and High Court that where an application is dismissed and the court considers that such application was totally without merit, the court order must record that fact on the face of the order and at the same time give consideration as to whether or not it is appropriate to make a civil restraint order (rule 18.13).

As indicated previously, this is a very important provision to control vexatious litigants and is an important part of the court's armoury in controlling the use of continual unmerited applications particularly in but not restricted to children's cases (rule 18.13).

3.19 PART 19: ALTERNATIVE PROCEDURE FOR APPLICATIONS

Part 19 mirrors very closely the procedure derived from CPR Part 8 and introduces an alternative simplified procedure for applications where Part 18 does not apply, there is no substantial dispute of fact or where there is no other form prescribed by the rules or practice directions in which an application can be made.

An appropriate application might be where an order or direction is sought which is unopposed by the parties before the commencement of proceedings.

Forced marriage applications and applications for permission to appeal will always fall to be dealt with under this Part.

Where an applicant uses the Part 19 procedure, the application form (Form FP1) referred to in PD 5A must be used.

Applications are commenced by an application verified by a statement of truth which must state:

- that the Part 19 procedure applies;
- what, if any, enactment it is made under;
- the question which the applicant wishes the court to decide;
- the order the applicant is seeking;
- the legal basis for the application.

At the same time as issuing the application the applicant must also file and serve any written evidence upon which he or she intends to rely.

The respondent must then file and serve an acknowledgement (Form FP5 referred to within PD 5A) together with written evidence within 14 days. Note that PD 19A indicates that such acknowledgement can be given in an informal document such as a letter as opposed to the prescribed form.

The acknowledgement must state whether or not the application is contested and, if the respondent seeks a different order from that set out in the application, what that order is.

If the respondent fails to file such an acknowledgement together with their written evidence then although they are not precluded from attending the hearing, they will be unable to play any part in it without the court's permission.

It should be noted that although a respondent must file and serve their written evidence when filing an acknowledgement, there is no provision for filing an answer to the application. The provision as to the filing of written evidence comes at an earlier stage, namely at the outset of the proceedings thus shortening the overall procedure.

Any written evidence not so filed and served in accordance with rule 19.7 cannot be later relied upon unless permission is granted by the court.

However, it is expected that the court will readily grant such permission as required on condition that any defect is remedied.

Although rule 19.7 sets out the timescales for filing and serving such written evidence; permission can be sought for an extension of time and to file additional evidence.

As far as extensions of time are concerned, the parties are able to agree these between themselves by consent provided that such consent is in writing.

Where the agreement relates to an extension of time in so far as the respondent is concerned, such written agreement must be filed at one and the same time as the acknowledgement itself (therefore be proactive and act quickly) and must not extend the time to more than 28 days after the date the service of the respondent's evidence is due. Any extension beyond this will require the court's permission and cannot therefore be done solely between the parties themselves, even by consent.

In so far as the applicant is concerned, again any extension must not extend the time beyond 28 days after the service of the respondent's evidence.

The corresponding CPR case law on such written agreements no doubt will prove instructive.

For example, in *Ian Thomas v. Home Office* [2006] EWCA Civ 1355, it was held that such written agreement of the parties did not have to be in a single document and could be constituted by an exchange of letters. An oral agreement that is later confirmed in writing by both sides is also within the concept of a written agreement. An oral agreement between two solicitors subsequently recorded in a letter sent by one solicitor to the other but not answered by the other, however, cannot be said to constitute a written agreement of the parties. What is required is a document or exchange of documents intended to constitute the agreement or to confirm or record the agreement. It will not be sufficient for one solicitor merely to communicate to a third party what has allegedly been agreed. Nor is it sufficient for each side to note their oral agreement, unless the notes are exchanged.

Thus, one must have:

- one document signed by both sides; or
- an exchange of documents whereby one party sets out the agreement and the other then expressly confirms that agreement.

The rules also provide for a respondent to contend that the Part 19 procedure should not be used on the grounds that there is a substantial dispute of fact, or the use of the procedure is not required or permitted by a rule or practice direction (rule 19.9).

The court also has power itself to direct that the application shall be treated as not having been issued under the Part 19 procedure if it is felt appropriate to do so, so as to enable the application to continue despite the fact that the Part 19 procedure may have been used incorrectly (rule 19.1(3)).

Upon receipt of any acknowledgement and written evidence (or after expiry of the period in which such acknowledgement should have been filed), the court will proceed to give directions as to the future management of the case either of its own motion or at a hearing fixed for such purpose. It may be useful therefore to try and agree directions and file them with the court so as to gain some control and input in the decision-making process.

On the occasion of the hearing the court can either dispose of the case (if relatively straightforward) or give case management directions.

3.20 PART 20: INTERIM REMEDIES AND SECURITY FOR COSTS

Part 20 derives from CPR Part 25, but unlike the majority of the new Family Procedure Rules, the remedies listed in rule 20.2 do not apply to family proceedings in the magistrates' court.

They also do not apply to the following:

- CA 1989, s.48 (discovery orders);
- CA 1989, s.50 (recovery orders);
- FLA 1986, s.33 (disclosure of a child's whereabouts);
- FLA 1986, s.34 (recovery order).

Of particular note is rule 20.2(1)(c)(v) which provides the court with the power to order 'the sale of relevant property which is of a perishable nature or for which for any good reason it is desirable to sell quickly'. In this eventuality an interim sale can be ordered, although the rules do not provide for an interim distribution. It is a moot point as to whether this reflects an extension of the court's powers in light of *Miller-Smith* v. *Miller-Smith* [2009] EWCA Civ 1297.

Remedies also worthy of mention include interim injunctions, freezing injunctions, interim declarations, search orders under s.7 of the Civil Procedure Act 1997 and orders for disclosure of documents or inspection of property against a non-party pursuant to the Supreme Court Act 1981, s.34 (now known as the Senior Court Act 1981) or the County Courts Act 1984, s.53.

However, the fact that a particular kind of interim remedy is not listed does not affect any power that the court may have to grant that remedy (rule 20.2(3)).

Obviously, only the High Court has jurisdiction to grant a 'search order' and 'freezing injunction'.

As for the requisite guidance on making an application, reference must be had to paras.2.1–2.4 of PD 20A. Particular note must also be taken of the need to file a draft of the order sought with the application notice including having available an electronic version for the usage of the court.

Paragraphs 3.1–3.4 of PD 20A set out the evidential requirements for applications for interim injunctions as well as for search orders and freezing injunctions.

Paragraph 6 of PD 20A sets out the detailed requirements of search orders in relation to the preservation of evidence and property.

An interim remedy may be applied for at any time, including even before the commencement of proceedings, provided the matter is urgent or it is otherwise desirable in the interests of justice. If such an interim remedy is granted before the instigation of proceedings the court will go on to give directions concerning the issue of the substantive application.

The Part 18 procedure must be used.

An interim remedy may also be applied for without notice if there are good reasons for doing so, but this must be set out in the supporting evidence (rule 20.4).

It should also be noted that, notwithstanding the move towards using statements of truth in family proceedings, applications for freezing orders and search orders must still be supported by affidavit evidence (PD 20A – Interim Remedies), although it is difficult to see the rationale for this apart from the draconian effect of such an order and the potential infringement of a party's art.8 rights (of the European Convention on Human Rights – the right to respect for private and family life).

Urgent applications and applications without notice are dealt with in para.4 of the practice direction and cover the procedural requirements of without notice applications dealt with at a hearing both after issue (para.4.3) and before issue (para.4.4) of such an application.

Note that unless essential, some notice, albeit informal, is better than none at all (para.4.3(c)).

Paragraph 4.5 deals with applications made outside normal business hours (urgent telephone applications) and para.5.1 deals with what an injunction order should contain which will include undertakings to:

- pay any damages which the respondent might sustain (this can also include a similar undertaking to a third party who might suffer loss as a result of the order); and
- where an order is obtained without notice, arrange service upon the respondent of the application notice, evidence in support and any order made; and
- where an order is obtained before the filing of an application, file and pay the appropriate fee; and
- where an order is made before the filing of an application, issue and pay the appropriate fee.

Finally, paras.8.1 and 8.2 of the practice direction make provision in respect of injunctions against third parties. Note, in particular, para.8.2 in respect of the duty to supply information requested by the third party and to do so promptly.

If the application is stayed, other than by way of an agreement between the parties, the interim injunction will be set aside unless the court orders otherwise.

A respondent to any application for an interim remedy may also apply for security for costs of the proceedings.

In so far as security for costs is concerned, such an application can only be made by a respondent and must be supported by written evidence.

The importance of the remedy lies in the fact that it protects the costs recovery position of the respondent in respect of a potentially 'dodgy' application.

The order as to security for costs will determine the amount of the security and direct the manner and time in which it must be given.

The conditions to be satisfied before making such an order are set out in rule 20.7(2). In essence, the court may make an order for security for costs if it is just to do so and:

- (a) the applicant is—
    - (i) resident out of the jurisdiction; but
    - (ii) not resident in a Brussels Contracting State, a Lugano Contracting State or a Regulation State, as defined in section 1(3) of the Civil Jurisdiction and Judgments Act 1982 or a Member State bound by the Council Regulation;
- (b) the applicant has changed address since the application was started with a view to evading the consequences of the litigation;
- (c) the applicant failed to give an address in the application form, or gave an incorrect address in that form;
- (d) the applicant has taken steps in relation to the applicant's assets that would make it difficult to enforce an order for costs against the applicant.

However, such provisions do not apply to the costs of proceedings under the Hague Convention.

3.21 PART 21: MISCELLANEOUS RULES ABOUT DISCLOSURE AND INSPECTION OF DOCUMENTS

This Part is based upon a compressed version of CPR Part 31 and is supported by PD 21A.

'Document' means anything in which information of any description is recorded.

'Copy' means anything on to which information recorded in the document has been copied, by whatever means and whether directly or indirectly. This is a wide description and encompasses information recorded electronically.

In proceedings, other than for a financial remedy, disclosure will now normally be by way of list (but only where directed) or questionnaire setting out the existence of documentation material to the proceedings which a party is aware of or which has been in their control. This is known as 'standard disclosure' – a term borrowed from the CPR.

This is contrasted with 'specific disclosure' which is where, pursuant to a court order, a party must disclose documents, or a class of documents, by carrying out a search and disclosing any documents located as a result of such search.

The results of such a search must also specify those documents that the respondent does not have in their control or claims the right to withhold (e.g. public interest immunity/privilege).

In so far as the duty itself is concerned, a reasonable search should be tailor made to the value and significance of the likely product of such a search. If the value of such evidence is not likely to be high, then a 'reasonable search' should be correspondingly limited (*Nichia Corporation* v. *Argos Ltd* [2007] EWCA Civ 741).

The extent of discovery thus has to be assessed on a case-by-case basis. The judge should consider the features of the case with a view to making an order tailored to achieving a just outcome, which includes limiting costs as far as possible (*Fiddes* v. *Channel 4 Television Corporation* [2010] EWCA Civ 516).

To that extent the court will be guided by the overriding objective.

The court will consider all of the circumstances of the case and in particular proportionality. The relevance of the documents requested will also be analysed by reference to the issues in dispute between the parties.

Note that within matrimonial and civil partnership proceedings the court may also order disclosure to clarify any matter in dispute.

Rule 21.2 makes provision for disclosure by a person who is not a party to the proceedings, application for which can be made with or without notice. However, an order may only be made where such disclosure is necessary in order to dispose fairly of the proceedings or to save costs. (Note that the terms 'inspection appointment' and 'production appointment' are no longer used.)

However, an order for disclosure cannot compel a person to produce a document which that person cannot be compelled to produce at a final hearing.

Furthermore, notwithstanding that the test set out in rule 21.2(3) is subsequently satisfied, there is still a residual discretion on the part of the court as to whether or not to make such an order. It is at this stage that broader considerations come into play, such as where the public interest lies and whether or not disclosure would infringe third-party rights in relation, for example, to privacy or confidentiality. In such circumstances, the court must conduct a careful balancing exercise (see rule 21.3).

In line with the principle of aligning procedures across all tiers of court, this rule will also apply to family proceedings in magistrates' courts which will no doubt be a welcome and long overdue addition to their powers.

3.22 PART 22: EVIDENCE

This rule derives from CPR Part 32.

Note that despite the increasing use of statements of truth, affidavits are still required in respect of contempt proceedings, and where otherwise specified.

There are also now detailed provisions for the standard format of witness statements and affidavits (see later).

Rule 22.1 sets out the court's powers to control evidence which includes power to give directions as to:

- the issues upon which evidence is required;
- the nature of the evidence required to decide those issues;
- the way in which such evidence is to be placed before the court.

The court also has the power to exclude evidence which would otherwise be admissible, although it is submitted that such a rule is ultra vires, particularly in so far as it appears to permit the exclusion of otherwise admissible evidence, unless, of course, such exclusion, as part of the court's powers to manage its own proceedings, relates to exclusion on the basis of the evidence being irrelevant to the issues before the court.

The normal rule is that a person's witness statement at a final hearing will stand as his or her evidence in chief save that, with permission of the court, the witness may be allowed to amplify upon it or give evidence in relation to new matters which have arisen since its service.

In cases where a party has failed to serve a witness statement in accordance with a direction from the court then such witness may not be called to give oral evidence at a hearing without permission.

The court also has the additional power of limiting the extent of cross-examination thus giving the court wide powers of controlling the proceedings before it.

At a final hearing, evidence will normally be presented to the court orally; at any other hearing, evidence is to be presented by written evidence verified by a statement of truth (note the wording of a statement of truth that needs to be contained in such a witness statement (see further PD 22A, para.6.4)).

There are, of course, exceptions to this rule, more notably public law Children Act proceedings, such as secure accommodation, interim care and supervision orders.

There is also a new power to use witness summaries in cases where a witness statement is unable to be obtained; however, its usage in family proceedings remains to be seen (rule 22.9). One potential example might be where an urgent application is pending and instructions can only be taken over the phone or on a brief attendance where full instructions cannot be taken (e.g. an application for an interim care order) or a draft statement has been prepared but not yet approved by the client or the client has failed to return a signed statement or a witness is currently out of the country or otherwise unavailable.

In so far as affidavit and witness statements are concerned, such documents must comply with the requirements set out in PD 22A as to:

- heading and format (paras.3.1–3.3);
- content (paras.4.1–4.5);

- exhibits (paras.9.1–13.4);
- jurat (paras.6.1–6.3).

Where a person is unable to read or sign a statement/affidavit, note the provisions of PD 22A, paras.7.1–7.4 and Annexes 1 and 2 in relation to the requirements of properly executed affidavits, affirmations and witness statements.

In essence, the person before whom the affidavit is sworn must certify in the jurat that the person has read the affidavit to the deponent and that they appeared to understand it and made their mark in that person's presence.

Note that where the maker makes more than one affidavit/statement with exhibits, the numbering of the exhibits should run consecutively throughout, and not start again with each new statement or affidavit.

These requirements are important because if they are not complied with the court may refuse to admit the evidence and may also refuse to allow the costs arising from its preparation. However, having said that, it seems unlikely that minor non-compliances will lead to the refusal to admit such evidence, particularly where litigants in person are concerned. Again, reference also must be had to the overriding objective and proportionality.

As for affidavits generally, pursuant to para.4.3 of PD 22A, the affidavit in particular must indicate which of the statements within it are made from the deponent's own knowledge and those which are matters of information or belief and, in relation to the latter, the source for such matters of information or belief.

PD 22A also provides extensive guidance on the use of video conferencing in the family courts which is set out in Annex 3.

Also worthy of note is the fact that witness statements may only be used for the purposes of the proceedings in which they are served.

Finally, note the provision as to service of a notice to admit facts which must be served no later than 21 days before the final hearing (rule 22.15).

3.23 PART 23: MISCELLANEOUS RULES ABOUT EVIDENCE

Part 23 is derived from CPR Part 33 and controls the use of hearsay, plans and photographs as evidence.

Note that in proceedings in a magistrates' court, it is the justice's clerk or the court who are responsible for keeping a note of the substance of the oral evidence given at hearings and direction appointments (rule 23.9).

3.24 PART 24: WITNESSES, DEPOSITIONS GENERALLY AND TAKING OF EVIDENCE IN MEMBER STATES OF THE EU

Part 24 is derived from CPR Part 34.

It contains provisions to support Council Regulation (EC) No.1206/2001 of 8 May 2001 on cooperation between the courts of the Member States on the taking of evidence in civil or commercial matters ('the Taking of Evidence Regulation').

The accompanying practice direction, PD 24A – 'Witnesses, Depositions and Taking of Evidence in the Member States of the European Union' has the Council Regulation annexed to it (Annex B).

The rule and related practice direction make extensive provisions for taking evidence by way of witness summons, deposition and letters of request.

As part of the process of modernisation of language 'conduct money' for a witness who has been summonsed is now more naturally described as 'travelling expenses and compensation for loss of time'.

Depositions, which were previously only provided for in connection with the Family Procedure (Adoption) Rules 2005, SI 2005/2795, are now generally available as a means of obtaining evidence (where appropriate) and are a more cost-effective, less combative, quicker and easier way to avoid the difficulties frequently encountered of getting all the necessary parties, witnesses and experts to court on any given day.

Very helpfully the practice direction itself also has a Draft Letter of Request set out within it which can be found in Annex A and in Annex C there is also a list of courts which are delegated to take such evidence pursuant to the Taking of Evidence Regulation.

3.25 PART 25: EXPERTS AND ASSESSORS

Part 25 is derived from CPR Part 35 and contains rules relating to the appointment and duties of an expert in family proceedings. It also contains a rule relating to the appointment of assessors (rule 25.14).

The practice direction supporting the rules (PD 25A) incorporates and supersedes the practice direction, 'Experts in Family Proceedings relating to children', which was issued simultaneously with the Public Law Outline.

Paragraphs 1–9 of PD 25A deal with the use of and the instruction of experts. Paragraph 10 deals with the appointment of assessors.

Paragraph 4 of the practice direction deals specifically with proceedings relating to children whereas para.5 deals with expert evidence in relation to non-children related proceedings.

A useful addition within the annex to PD 25A is suggested questions for inclusion within letters of instruction to experts. These include questions to child mental health professionals or paediatricians and adult psychiatrists and applied psychologists in Children Act proceedings.

Rule 25.1 imposes a duty to restrict expert evidence to what is reasonably required to resolve the proceedings, i.e. it must be relevant and necessary.

Rule 25.2(2) helpfully defines a 'single joint expert' for the purpose of the rules.

Rule 25.3 sets out that an expert's overriding duty is to the court. Any opinion provided must be wholly independent of the party instructing the expert and deal only with questions that are within the expert's field of skill and experience (expertise).

Rule 25.4 sets out the general rule in family proceedings that the court's permission is required before a party can rely on expert evidence. Such permission when sought should also deal with the field of expertise and the identity of the expert concerned.

Such application for permission to instruct an expert should be sought as soon as possible in order to avoid unnecessary delay and, of course, in furtherance of the overriding objective.

The court when granting such permission can also limit the amount of the expert's fees.

Once obtained the order should also be served upon the expert instructed.

Rule 25.5 provides that in the first instance expert evidence must be given by way of a written report, oral evidence only being given at a hearing where it is necessary to do so in the interests of justice. This, of course, accords with the overriding objective and the issue of proportionality and the saving of costs.

The content of the expert's report itself is set out in detail in PD 25A, para.3.3 and should be verified by a statement of truth in accordance with the wording set out in para.3.3(i).

The letter of instruction in the first instance must be by way of a jointly agreed letter; in default of such agreement it is possible for each party to provide their own instructions to the expert but such instructions must also be disclosed to the other party (rule 25.8(1), (3)).

Rule 25.6 provides that questions may be put to an expert for the purposes of clarification. These questions may only be put once and must be put within 10 days of service of the expert's report. The purpose of such questioning must be for clarification only, rather than by way of supplemental instructions, and a copy of the questions must be sent to the other parties.

Rule 25.7 permits the court to limit expert evidence to that of a single joint expert wherever possible (which will be the normal practice).

Rule 25.8 deals with the instructions to a single joint expert.

Rule 25.10 states that an expert's report must comply with PD 25A. The report must also contain a statement that the expert understands and has complied with his or her duty to the court.

Rule 25.12 sets out the procedure for discussions and joint statements where evidence from more than one expert is permitted in order to limit, wherever possible, the need for the experts to attend court to give oral evidence and thus save expense.

Such statements must deal with the issues upon which they agree and those on which they disagree together with a summary of their reasons for agreeing or disagreeing and what, if any, action needs to be taken to resolve any outstanding disagreement or question.

The practical arrangements for such discussions and meetings are set out in para.6.3 of the accompanying PD 25A. Adherence to this will be crucial but note the option of utilising telephone conferences or video links.

Note, in particular, that questions for the experts to address which repeat questions in the initial letter of instruction or which seek to rehearse cross-examination are to be discouraged. (The word used in the practice direction is the more forceful 'rejected'.)

The practice direction itself also imposes stringent timescales:

- Arrangements to be made for the experts' meeting (15 business days post experts' report).
- Formulation of an agenda (which may consist of a list of questions to be addressed) (five business days prior to the meeting).
- Agenda and/or list of questions to be sent to each expert (two business days before the meeting). (Note that only in exceptional circumstances should questions be added to the agenda less than two days before the meeting and under no circumstances should any question received on the day or during the meeting be accepted. Although this does not preclude questions arising during the meeting itself for the purposes of clarification, it is difficult to see how this is going to be adequately policed if the parties or experts themselves do not raise any objections!)
- The filing and service of a signed Statement of Agreement and Disagreement (five business days post meeting).
- Written notice of a party's position refusal to be bound by an agreement reached at an experts' meeting (10 business days post meeting, or, where an Issues Resolutions Hearing (IRH) is to be held, five business days before the IRH).

As to the appointment of a second expert generally the key issue will be: is the evidence required relevant to the core issues? Or, in the alternative, will there be an understandable sense of grievance for the applicant, judged objectively, were permission to be refused; or would there be more understandable sense of grievance for the respondent if permission were to be granted? (*Daniels* v. *Walker* [2000] EWCA Civ 508, [2000] 1 WLR 1382 and *Cosgrove and Anor* v. *Pattison and Anor* (unreported, 27 November 2000).)

In deciding whether to grant permission to adduce additional expert evidence, the court will exercise its discretion, taking into account the following factors:

- the nature of the issue or issues being addressed by the expert;
- the number of issues between the parties;
- the reason the new expert is wanted;
- the amount at stake and, if it is not purely money, the nature of the issues at stake and their importance;
- the effect of permitting one party to call further expert evidence on the conduct of the proceedings;
- the delay, if any, in making the application;
- any delay that the instructing and calling of a new expert will cause;
- any other special features of the case; and
- the overall justice to the parties in the context of the proceedings.

A party might also be permitted to adduce evidence from a further expert in circumstances where their original expert had modified their opinion.

However, a change of opinion does not, in itself, establish that further evidence is 'reasonably required' for the purposes of rule 25.1, since the change of opinion is not binding on the instructing party. However, further expert evidence may be permitted if it is apparent that the instructed expert has stepped outside their expertise or brief, or has displayed incompetence.

Rule 25.6, however, does not preclude a party from putting questions to their own expert. This, in any event, should be done as a prerequisite to an application for permission to rely on evidence from a second expert, since the answers to questions relating to a change of opinion might be important in determining whether the change raised questions as to whether the expert had stepped outside their expertise or brief or whether the competence of the expert is subject to challenge.

Focusing on the accompanying practice direction (PD 25A) itself, its stated aim is to encourage the early determination of the question as to whether or not expert evidence is required and, if it is, the questions and issues that such expertise needs to address. This will be determined by whether or not the court requires an opinion on a matter which lies outside its area of skill and expertise in order to determine the matter before it.

Moreover, even before the commencement of proceedings it is clear that the court will expect the guidance set out in the practice direction to be followed (PD 25A, para.2.3).

Paragraph 4 of the practice direction sets out the preliminary enquiries that must be made and responded to by a proposed expert to be instructed in proceedings relating to children prior to any hearing at which the permission to instruct such an expert is likely to be addressed. These requirements are essential and familiarity will be crucial as the court is likely to be policing this very closely. (It is suggested that template letters should be set up now and that practitioners should ensure an instructed expert can and does respond in good time prior to any hearing.)

This is further reinforced by the fact that by 11 am the business day before the hearing any party who proposes to seek permission of the court to instruct an expert at that hearing must file and serve a proposal of instruction together with a draft order detailing the various matters and directions set out in the practice direction at paras.4.3 and 4.4.

Once permission is granted the instructing party must within five business days after that hearing file and serve a letter of instruction which must comply with para.4.5 and thereafter keep the expert fully up to date by promptly providing a copy of any new document filed and an updated index.

PD 25A also sets out the procedure to be followed where the court is required to settle the letter of instruction itself in the event of a lack of consensus (para.4.6).

Where an expert or experts are required to attend court the provisions of PD 25A, paras.8.1 and 8.2 apply in so far as the practical arrangements are concerned.

Note, in particular, that all parties will need to focus their minds on the issues which the experts are asked to address and in cases where all the experts agree but a party nevertheless wishes to challenge their evidence, then that party must be prepared to set out his or her reasons for not accepting the agreed opinions.

As feedback is no doubt important to any expert instructed, PD 25a provides for the lead solicitor to inform the expert in writing of the outcome and the use made by the court of their opinion within 10 days of the final hearing. In the family proceedings court this requirement will be met by sending a copy of the written reasons for the court's decision.

3.26 PART 26: CHANGE OF SOLICITOR

Part 26 is derived from CPR Part 42 and contains provisions relating to a change of solicitor including provision for a change of solicitor for a children's guardian thus removing the previous reliance on RSC O.67 and CCR O.50.

Rule 26.2 provides for the requirement as to filing and service of a notice of change, whether it be in relation to a change in address for service generally, or in relation to the appointment of a new solicitor in place of one previously instructed, or the appointment of one by a party who was previously acting in person, or indeed a person who now wishes to act in person.

Rule 26.3 provides for the procedure to be followed where a solicitor wishes to apply to the court to cease acting and come off the court record as so acting.

Such application must be on notice and be supported by evidence as to the reasons. The application should be in accordance with the Part 18 procedure.

Rule 26.4 provides for a similar procedure where another party may apply to have a solicitor removed from the court record as acting.

It must be stressed, and this is highlighted by the accompanying PD 26A, that in circumstances where a solicitor has previously given an address for service, or there is a current Legal Services Commission (LSC) funding service, until the requirements of FPR 2010, Part 26 have been complied with, a solicitor will still remain on the court record as acting.

The requisite form of notice is set out in PD 5A.

3.27 PART 27: HEARINGS AND DIRECTIONS APPOINTMENTS

This important new addition to the rules aims to allow the justice or justices to announce a decision and give the parties a short explanation of that decision (rule 27.2). It also allows for the supply of a copy of the order and reasons for the court's decision by close of business on the day when the decision is announced, or, if that is not practicable, no later than 72 hours from the announcement of the decision itself.

Parties are expected to attend all hearings of which they have notice unless their attendance is excused (rule 27.3) because, for instance, the hearing is to be conducted by way of a telephone hearing.

Hearings may properly proceed in the absence of a party, provided that it is proved that the non-attending respondent received reasonable notice of the date of hearing or the court is satisfied that the circumstances justify proceeding without them.

In the case of a child party, the court may proceed in their absence where the child is represented by a guardian, or a solicitor who has the opportunity to make representations, including representations from the child himself/herself if he/she is of sufficient understanding (note, age is not mentioned as a relevant factor) (rule 27.4).

In the case of the non-appearance of an applicant the court may refuse the application or nevertheless proceed. These provisions, however, do not apply where the court is considering making a contact activity direction or order, or an enforcement order or compensation order under the various sections 11 of CA 1989 (separate provisions are set out for such hearings in FPR 2010, Part 12).

Of particular interest is rule 27.5 which provides for a party's right to set aside a judgment or order following the party's failure to attend (note that the latter rule does not applying to the magistrates' court).

In essence, where a party does not attend a hearing or directions appointment and an order is made against him or her, the party who has failed to attend may apply for the order to be set aside.

The onus is thus on the party who has failed to attend to demonstrate why it is that the judgment or order should be set aside.

Such application must, of course, be supported by evidence and, in particular, be mindful of the fact that the court may only grant such an application if the following conditions have been met:

- The party acted promptly once he/she became aware of the order.
- The party had a good reason for not attending.
- The party has a reasonable prospect of success at the hearing or directions appointment.

Case law relating to similar provisions contained within CPR rule 39.3(5) will no doubt prove of use.

In *Brazil v. Brazil* [2002] EWCA Civ 1135, Mummery LJ said this:

> There has been some debate before us, as there was before the judge, about what is or is not capable of being a 'good reason'. In my opinion the search for a definition or description of 'good reason' or for a set of criteria differentiating between good and bad reasons is unnecessary. I agree with Hart J that, although the court must be satisfied that the reason is an honest or genuine one, that by itself is not sufficient to make a reason for non-attendance a 'good reason'. The court has to examine all the evidence relevant to the defendant's non-attendance; ascertain from the evidence what, as a matter of fact, was the true 'reason' for non attendance; and, looking at the matter in the round, ask whether that reason is sufficient to entitle the applicant to invoke the discretion of the court to set aside the order. An over analytical approach to the issue is not appropriate, bearing in mind the duty of the court, when interpreting the rules and exercising any power given to it by the rules, to give effect to the overriding objective of enabling it to deal with cases justly. The perfectly ordinary English phrase 'good reason' . . . is a sufficiently clear expression of the standard of acceptability to be applied to enable a court to determine whether or not there is a good reason for non-attendance.

In *Estate Acquisition and Development Ltd v. Wiltshire* [2006] EWCA Civ 533 the Court of Appeal followed what Mummery LJ had said in *Brazil v. Brazil*. Dyson LJ added this:

> Moreover, [the rule] must be interpreted so as to comply with article 6 of the European Convention on Human Rights (right to a fair hearing). I refer to the judgment of Brooke LJ in *Goode v. Martin* [2001] EWCA Civ 1899, [2002] 1 WLR 1828 para 35. In my view, it is necessary to have both article 6 and the overriding objective in mind when interpreting and applying the phrase 'good reason'. It should not be overlooked that the power to set aside an order made in the absence of the applicant may only be exercised where all three of the conditions . . . are satisfied. In addition to the need to show a good reason for not attending, the applicant must have acted promptly and that he has a reasonable prospect of success. If the phrase 'good reason' is interpreted too strictly against an applicant, there is a danger that the interpretation will not give effect to the overriding objective and not comply with article 6.

However, rule 27.5 only contemplates a hearing or directions appointment in the absence of a party who has been served under the rules or in respect of whom service has been dispensed with and does not apply to judgments irregularly obtained in the sense of being obtained without service of the application in accordance with the rules (*Akram v. Adam* [2004] EWCA Civ 1601).

Thus, rule 27.5 only applies if the respondent has had notice of the hearing; if not then the court's discretion to set aside a judgment arises instead under FPR 2010, rules 4.7(b) and 4.1(3)(o).

Oddly, although rule 27.4, which permits these quasi default judgments to be made, applies to all tiers of court, rule 27.5, which empowers the court to set aside such judgments, where appropriate, does not apply to the magistrates' court. Whilst it is easy to imagine why it may be unwise to leave the application of such legal tests to lay magistrates, it seems that in cases of peremptory dismissal, or refusal of such an application by magistrates because a person has failed to attend a hearing, the only route of challenge may now be to appeal the order itself.

PD 27A incorporates the subsisting President's Direction of 27 July 2006 relating to court bundles which still omits cases proceeding in the family proceedings court. Note the threats in cases of non-compliance set out in *Re X & Y (Bundles)* [2008] 2 FLR 2053.

Rules 27.10 and 27.11 deal specifically with media access in private proceedings and generally provide that all hearings covered by the rules are to be held in private unless provided for otherwise by a rule, enactment or a direction.

For the purpose of the exercise of such discretion, hearings conducted for the purposes of judicially assisted conciliation or negotiation (e.g. FDRs, FHDRAs and IRHs) and proceedings for adoption and placement proceedings are excluded.

The court can also exclude the media of its own initiative or if representations are made by:

(a) a party to the proceedings;
(b) any witness in the proceedings;
(c) where appointed, any children's guardian;
(d) where appointed, an officer of the service or Welsh family proceedings officer, on behalf of the child the subject of the proceedings;
(e) the child, if of sufficient age and understanding.

Applications to exclude the media should normally be dealt with by way of oral submissions and advance notice given if it is known that the media are likely to attend any given hearing.

As for the exercise of such discretion in excluding duly accredited representatives of news agencies from private proceedings, see in particular rule 27.11(3).

In essence, exclusion is based upon the interests of any child, the safety of the parties or any witness, the orderly conduct of the proceedings or the impediment or prejudice of the administration of justice.

The rule is backed up by two practice directions. PD 27B deals with the attendance of the media in family proceedings in the High Court and county court. PD 27C deals with family proceedings in the family proceedings court.

Note in particular paras.5.2, 5.3 and 5.4 of both practice directions in respect of the exercise of the court's discretion in excluding the media.

3.28 PART 28: COSTS

This Part is derived from CPR Parts 43–47 and largely replicates the previous costs rules in FPR 1991 together with the ancillary relief costs rules introduced in 2006.

Note, however, the definition of 'financial remedy proceedings' excludes orders for maintenance pending suit, orders pending outcome of proceedings, interim periodical payments orders or indeed any other form of interim order.

Schedule 1 to CA 1989 is also not included in this definition and neither is an application pursuant to MCA 1973, s.27 or DPMCA 1978, Part 1 or their CPA 2004 equivalents.

Needless to say, CPR Part 47 (detailed assessment of costs) does not apply to family proceedings in the magistrates' court (rule 28.2(2)) – so no great changes there.

FPR 2010, rule 28.1 simply provides that the court may, at any time, make such order as to costs as it thinks just.

Worthy of note is the fact that the costs rules, applying to ancillary relief proceedings under which the general rule is that the court will not order one party to pay the costs of another party, have now been extended to all financial remedy proceedings (see in particular rule 28.3(4)–(7)).

Rule 28.3(6) and (7) sets out the circumstances where, within financial proceedings, it may be appropriate to make a costs order, which will normally be based upon a party's conduct before, or during, the proceedings themselves which the accompanying PD 28A refers to as 'litigation conduct'.

It is clear from the list of circumstances to which the court must have regard that, although conduct includes that prior to the initiation of the proceedings, it is primarily litigation conduct as opposed to marital conduct that is the focus of the rule and will include (rule 28.3(7)):

   (a) any failure by a party to comply with these rules, any order of the court or any practice direction which the court considers relevant;
   (b) any open offer to settle made by a party;
   (c) whether it was reasonable for a party to raise, pursue or contest a particular allegation or issue;
   (d) the manner in which a party has pursued or responded to the application or a particular allegation or issue;
   (e) any other aspect of a party's conduct in relation to proceedings which the court considers relevant; and
   (f) the financial effect on the parties of any costs order.

The factors to be considered are the same as before, save that the practice directions now have mandatory force and the pre-action protocols are contained within the practice directions.

It is also worthy of note that the rule refers to 'open offers' and, as the accompanying practice direction sets out, the court is not able to take into account any offers to settle that are expressed to be 'without prejudice' or 'without prejudice save as to costs' when it comes to deciding what, if any, costs order to make (PD 28A, para.4.3).

PD 28A also provides that when dealing with a party's conduct the court will also have regard to his or her obligation to assist the court in the furtherance of the overriding objective (which, of course, permeates all family proceedings before the court) and, more particularly, the ethos of proportionality (PD 28A, para.4.4).

If a party does wish to seek a costs order, notwithstanding the provisions of rule 28.3(5), then this should be made plain either in open correspondence or in a skeleton argument prior to the hearing itself and, in any event, where a summary assessment of costs is appropriate, then a statement of costs will need to be filed and served in Form N260 24 hours in advance of any hearing (PD 28A, para.4.5).

Also of note is the provision of rule 28.4 which states that where a wasted costs order is made against a legal representative in the magistrates' court, any appeal now lies to the Crown Court.

3.29 PART 29: MISCELLANEOUS

Part 29 is derived from Part X of FPR 1991 and contains rules governing a number of general or miscellaneous matters, including provisions previously contained in Part X of FPR 1991. It also includes rules drawn from CPR Part 40 relating to the drawing and service of orders.

It is now a rule that no party is required to disclose his or her address or contact details or those of a child unless directed to do so. However, those details must still be provided to the court.

The accompanying PD 29A contains guidance and the requisite procedural requirements where the court is considering joining the Crown within ongoing proceedings, where it is considering a declaration of incompatibility pursuant to the Human Rights Act 1998 or an order as to compensation pursuant to the Human Rights Act 1998, ss.7(1)(a) and 9(3).

PD 29B provides the necessary requirements as to the citation of authorities in the Human Rights Act cases and, in essence, the authorities cited must be an authoritative and complete report (e.g. HUDOC). It also confirms that any application for a declaration of incompatability under s.4 of the Act (or any issue which may lead to the court considering such a declaration) must be dealt with by a High Court judge.

Of particular note is rule 29.4 which outlines the procedure for withdrawing an application. Withdrawal of an application can only be made with permission of the court which must generally be sought by written request setting out the reasons which can be dealt with without the necessity of a hearing provided the other party has received notification of such intention and has been afforded an opportunity of responding to such a request (rule 29.4(6)).

Having said that, such a request for permission to withdraw may be made orally to the court if the parties are present.

The now common practice of arranging for a legal representative to draw up and agree the wording of an order is formalised in rule 29.11.

Rule 29.15 provides that a judgment or order takes effect from the day when it is given or made unless the court specifies a later date.

Finally, note the provision as to the 'slip rule' contained in rule 29.16.

The operation of the slip rule, however, is limited to accidental slips or omissions. Matters deliberately included by the parties in an order drawn up and sealed by the court do not constitute an accidental slip or omission within that rule (*Leo Pharma A/S and Anor v. Sandoz Ltd* [2010] EWHC 1911 (Pat)).

3.30 PART 30: APPEALS

Part 30 is derived from CPR Part 52 and Part VIII of FPR 1991.

This Part represents a significant shift in the procedure for appeals, and constrains a party's rights of appeal even further.

Part 30 and PD 30A apply to appeals in the High Court and the county court but not to detailed assessment decisions which are still governed by the CPR.

PD 30A usefully sets out in table format which court an appeal should be made to. As mentioned previously, an appeal from a decision made in the magistrates' court now lies to the circuit judge of the county court.

Pursuant to rule 30.3, it is now necessary to obtain permission to appeal from every decision of a district judge or costs judge (except in cases where a party's liberty is at stake, i.e. committal or secure accommodation). The procedure for seeking permission is set out in PD 30A. It should be noted that permission is still not required for an appeal against the decision of a district judge in the magistrates' court.

Permission should be by way of an oral application at the hearing at which the decision to appeal is made (rule 30.3).

An application may also be made to the appeal court if permission is not sought at the lower court or such permission, if sought, is rejected.

If the appeal court rejects the application for permission without a hearing the appellant can apply for one within seven days from service of the notice of rejection (see PD 30A, paras.3.14–3.16).

Permission is likely to be granted in cases where the appeal would have a real prospect of success or there is some other compelling reason why the appeal should be heard.

In addition to an applicant (rule 30.4), a respondent may also file and serve a notice of appeal (rule 30.5) – for the procedural requirements, see para.6 of PD 30A.

Appeals from circuit judges lie to the Court of Appeal and continue to be covered by CPR Part 52.

The general time limit for appeals is 21 days with a shorter period of seven days in the case of interim care orders or interim supervision orders (rule 30.4).

An application to vary the time limit for filing an appeal notice must be made to the court; the parties are unable extend the time limit by agreement.

As was previously the case, all appeals are to be in the form of a review, unless the court decides otherwise or any specific and applicable rule or practice direction provides for otherwise.

The appeal court has all the powers of the lower court.

In addition to what was discussed above in respect of the routes of appeal and the procedural requirements, it is worth noting that permission to appeal from a district judge in relation to a detailed assessment of costs now also requires leave as in the case of civil proceedings.

Furthermore, under the new rules and practice directions, the only way to challenge an order made by consent will now be by way of appeal which now provides greater certainty and clarity than was the case before (PD 30A, para.9.1).

All parties to an appeal must comply with PD 30A and set out the justification for the appeal in light of rule 30.12(3) and whether such appeal is on the basis of a point of law or a finding of fact.

An important stipulation in PD 30A is that where the advocate or the court from whom permission to appeal is sought considers that the judgment contains a material omission or inadequate reasons, before an appeal is launched, the lower court must be given the opportunity of considering matters, thus significantly restricting one's ability to use such omission as the basis for an appeal (PD 30A, paras.3.6, 3.8 and 3.9).

PD 30A, para.4.8 sets out the documents which the appellant needs to file with their appeal bundle (para.4.9) and notice (para.4.1) and paras.4.13–4.22 set out the procedural requirements of skeleton arguments.

All documents extraneous to the issues comprising the appeal must be excluded. Furthermore, where the appellant is represented a certificate should be incorporated to the effect that these provisions have been fully complied with.

As before, an appeal does not operate as a stay on the decision appealed against unless the court orders otherwise (rule 30.8).

Rule 30.10 empowers the appeal court to strike out the whole or part of an appeal, set aside a permission to appeal either in whole or in part or impose conditions or limit the issues on which an appeal may be brought, all of which again reinforces the court's wide powers of case management. Note also the cross-over with security for costs contained in FPR 2010, Part 20 and PD 20A.

Furthermore, if the appeal court strikes out, refuses permission or dismisses an appeal, the court must then go on to consider whether or not a civil restraint order should be made.

Rule 30.11 sets out in detail the powers of the appeal court and rule 30.12(3) sets out the circumstances in which the appeal court will allow an appeal.

Rule 30.13 sets out the requirements of the 'leap-frog' procedure.

In essence, if an appeal raises an important point of principle or practice or there are some other compelling reasons why the Court of Appeal should hear the appeal then the county court and High Court can be bypassed. However, this procedure does not apply to proceedings in the magistrates' court.

3.31 PART 31: REGISTRATION OF ORDERS UNDER THE COUNCIL REGULATION, THE CIVIL PARTNERSHIP (JURISDICTION AND RECOGNITION OF JUDGMENTS) REGULATIONS 2005 AND THE HAGUE CONVENTION 1996

Part 31 is derived from Part VII of FPR 1991 and contains rules to support the articles relating to the registration of orders under Council Regulation (EC) No. 2201/2003 of 27 November 2003 on jurisdiction and the recognition and enforcement of judgments in matrimonial matters and in matters of parental responsibility. It is supported by PD 31A.

It also makes provision for the recognition and registration of judgments to which the Civil Partnership (Jurisdiction and Recognition of Judgments) Regulations 2005, SI 2005/3334 apply.

Finally, provision is made for the recognition, non-recognition and registration of measures to which the 1996 Hague Convention applies.

Such applications must be made to the principal registry.

Rule 31.14 regulates applications for recognition of judgments only.

Appeals in respect of recognition and registration of judgments are dealt with following the procedure set out in the practice direction regulating appeals, namely PD 30A.

3.32 PART 32: REGISTRATION AND ENFORCEMENT OF ORDERS

Part 32 is derived from Part VII of FPR 1991 and contains rules relating to the registration of orders under the Maintenance Orders Act 1950 (Chapter 2), the Maintenance Orders Act 1958 (Chapter 3) and the registration and enforcement of custody orders under FLA 1986 (Chapter 4).

Although the general tenor of the rules is to unify all family proceedings, the provision in respect of proceedings in the magistrates' court pursuant to the

Maintenance Orders Act 1950 is contained in the rules made pursuant to s.144 of the Magistrates' Courts Act 1980.

FPR 2010, Part 18 procedure must be used in respect of applications for enforcement or the cancellation of the registration of a Scottish or Northern Irish order in the High Court.

Applications under FLA 1986, s.28(2) must be made in accordance with the Part 19 procedure (rule 32.28(3)).

Some administrative procedures which were contained in the previous rules are now contained in the accompanying practice direction (PD 32A).

3.33   PART 33: ENFORCEMENT

Part 33 is derived from Part VII of FPR 1991 and CPR Parts 70–74 and applies to applications for enforcement in the High Court and county court only of money orders. The reason for the omission of enforcement in the magistrates' court is due to the fact that such proceedings are not 'family proceedings' and are therefore outside the scope of the Family Procedures Rules Committee's terms of reference.

The new rules also now provide for what is known as a 'pay-up summons' (Form D50K).

This provides that an applicant who wishes to seek to enforce an order for the payment of money may either apply for an order specifying the method of enforcement or for an order for such method of enforcement as the court may consider appropriate (rule 33.3(2)). Where such an application is made, an order requiring the respondent to attend court to give information about his or her means will be made.

The rationale for this is to provide greater flexibility to the court and in particular assist the ever-increasing number of litigants in person who appear before it. Under the previous rules, it was the court's experience that quite often an applicant for enforcement had applied for a method of enforcement that would have been ineffective in the particular circumstances of the case leading to delay, increased costs, injustice and the potential increase in insecurity for any child adversely affected by the non-payment.

The application notice for enforcement of an order for the payment of money must be accompanied by a statement which must state the amount due under the order, how such sum has been arrived at and be verified by a statement of truth.

Chapter 2 deals with applications for committal by way of judgment summons.

Changes in terminology should also be noted arising from harmonisation with the CPR. The terms 'garnishee' and 'oral examination' are replaced by 'third party debt orders' (Chapter 7) and 'orders to obtain information' (Chapter 6).

However, in a departure from such harmonisation and unification, the rules provide that the relevant parts of the CPR are to apply to such proceedings (more particularly with third party debt orders) with various modifications rather than incorporating them with their 'family-specific' modifications as with the rest of the rules (rules 33.23 and 33.24).

This is also the case with charging orders in Chapter 8 (rule 33.25) where, with various modifications, CPR Part 73 will regulate the procedural requirements.

The author respectfully submits this is an area which has sustained the previous bad practice, rather than eradicating it, and surely would it not have been more in keeping with the ethos of simplifying the rules to set out in full the procedural requirements but with their proposed modifications? Now we have rules 33.24 and 33.25 which must be read together with CPR Parts 72 and 73.

The rules also strengthen the provisions regarding undertakings and in particular emphasise the consequences of non-compliance with a financial undertaking. (Note what was said earlier in respect of financial undertakings contained in consent orders made within applications for a financial remedy – see **3.10** above.)

In particular, the rules reflect the fact that an undertaking is as enforceable as a court order which is now backed up by a corresponding Practice Direction 33A – Enforcement of Undertakings (para.1.3).

Such an undertaking must have a warning notice endorsed on it setting out the consequences of breach by the person giving it with a statement to the effect that they understand what consequences might flow from not abiding by its provisions. The wording of both the notice and statement is set out in PD 33A and differs depending upon whether or not the undertaking is a financial undertaking or a non-financial undertaking.

3.33.1 Non-financial warning and undertaking

1. 'You may be sent to prison for contempt of court if you break the promises that you have given to the court.'
2. 'I understand the undertaking that I have given, and that if I break any of my promises to the court I may be sent to prison for contempt of court.'

3.33.2 Financial warning and undertaking

1. 'If you fail to pay any sum of money which you have promised the court that you would pay, a person entitled to enforce the undertaking may apply to the court for an order. If it is proved that you have had the means to pay the sum but you have refused or neglected to pay that sum, you may be sent to prison.'
2. 'I understand the undertaking that I have given, and that if I break my promise to the court to pay any sum of money, I may be sent to prison.'

A useful amendment to the rules is that such an undertaking need not be given personally before the court; it can be endorsed on a court copy of the undertaking or may be filed in a separate document such as a letter.

The rules explained 99

This might prove useful in FLA 1996 proceedings in respect of personal protection proceedings where matters are disposed of by way of an undertaking and thus may avoid attendance by the parties, or indeed their representatives, provided the court is satisfied that the applicant will be adequately protected by such an undertaking as opposed to an order (FLA 1996, ss.46(3) and (3A)).

A full explanation of the Debtors Act 1869 and its provisions in relation to the RSC and CCR is also given in PD 33A.

3.34 PART 34: RECIPROCAL ENFORCEMENT OF MAINTENANCE ORDERS

Part 34 is derived from Part VII of FPR 1991; the Magistrates' Courts (Reciprocal Enforcement of Maintenance Orders) Rules 1974, SI 1974/668; the Magistrates' Courts (Reciprocal Enforcement of Maintenance Orders) (Hague Convention Countries) Rules 1980, SI 1980/108; the Magistrates' Courts (Reciprocal Enforcement of Maintenance Orders) (Republic of Ireland) Rules 1975, SI 1975/286; and the Magistrates' Courts (Reciprocal Enforcement of Maintenance Orders) (United States of America) Rules 1995, SI 1995/2802.

Part 34 contains rules relating to the Maintenance Orders (Facilities for Enforcement) Act 1920 (Chapter 1); the enforcement of maintenance orders under Part 1 of the Maintenance Orders (Reciprocal Enforcement) Act 1972 (Chapter 2) and the enforcement of maintenance orders under the Civil Jurisdiction and Judgments Act 1982, Council Regulation (EC) No. 44/2001 of 22 December 2000 on jurisdiction and the recognition and enforcement of judgments in civil and commercial matters ('the Judgments Regulation') and the Lugano Convention 2007 (Chapter 3).

Note that the provisions in respect of confirmation of a provisional order varying a maintenance order under the Maintenance Orders (Reciprocal Enforcement) Act 1972 and consideration and notification of a variation of a maintenance order made by a magistrates' court under the 1972 Act are contained in the rules made under the Magistrates' Courts Act 1980. s.144.

The main rules are modified in relation to their application to the 1980 Hague Convention Countries, the Republic of Ireland and the USA respectively, such modifications being set out in full in annexes to PD 34A.

The rules have also been simplified, with provisions directed to court officials contained in PD 34A which also makes provision relating to payment of sums due under registered orders and the rules relating to applications generally.

Rule 34.38 sets out the requirements relating to the admissibility and authentication of documents used in proceedings within contracting states.

Such documentation includes a summary of the evidence given in court which is admissible as evidence of any fact stated within it to the same extent as oral evidence of that fact.

PD 34B deals with the procedure for tracing parties who reside in Australia, Canada, New Zealand and South Africa for the purposes of obtaining or enforcing maintenance orders pursuant to the Maintenance Orders (Facilities for Enforcement) Act 1920 or Part I of the Maintenance Orders (Reciprocal Enforcement) Act 1972.

Application is made on Form D312 (principal registry of the Family Division) or Form D85 (county court) and must be supported by a written undertaking that any address received in response to such an enquiry will not be disclosed or used except for the purposes of the proceedings.

3.35 PART 35: MEDIATION DIRECTIVE

This Part applies to mediated cross-border disputes that are subject to Directive 2008/52/EC which relates to certain aspects of mediation in civil and commercial matters, where one party may apply for a mediated settlement to be put into the terms of an order and the other party agrees.

This is supported by PD 35A.

Amongst other things, it contains provisions for mediation evidence to be disclosed or inspected or for witnesses to be called.

Any application for a consent order under rule 35.2 must be completed in English or accompanied by an English translation.

3.36 PART 36: TRANSITIONAL PROVISIONS

The new rules are to apply so far as practicable to applications and appeals made, but not disposed of, before the FPR 2010 came into force. However, where this is not practicable, the old rules will continue to apply.

The exception to this is that the overriding objective set out in Part 1 will apply come what may.

The detailed transitional provisions are contained in a supplementary practice direction (PD 36A), which sets out the circumstances where the old rules (FPR 1991) will normally apply and the circumstances where the new rules (FPR 2010) will apply.

In essence, where a step has been undertaken using forms or documentation under the old rules then, in the first instance, the case will proceed under the old rules.

In cases where a new step is taken in any existing proceedings on or after 6 April 2011, it is to be taken under the new FPR 2010.

However, notwithstanding this, the court has discretion as to how FPR 2010 are to apply and may disapply certain parts of their provisions pursuant to its case management powers although there is a general presumption that FPR 2010 will apply (PD 36A, para.4.4(3)).

If an application is issued prior to 6 April 2011 but listed after that date, the presumption is that the application will be decided having regard to the FPR 2010, and where the first occasion on which existing proceedings are before a court after 6 April 2011 is a hearing of a substantive issue, the general presumption is that the hearing will be conducted according to the FPR 2010.

An assessment of costs taking place after 6 April 2011 will be in accordance with FPR 2010, Part 28, but the presumption is that no costs for work undertaken prior to 6 April 2011 will be disallowed if they would have been allowed if assessed prior to that date. The question of whether to allow costs for work undertaken on or after 6 April 2011 will generally be considered in accordance with FPR 2010.

It must also be observed that whilst the relating practice direction dealing with experts and assessors (PD 25A) does not apply to proceedings issued before 6 April 2011, the court has a discretion to apply the guidance either wholly or in part (PD 25A, para.2.2)

There is also a useful glossary at the end of FPR 2010 setting out as a guide the various meanings of certain legal expressions used throughout the rules such as 'stay' and 'without prejudice'.

4 CONCLUSIONS

The rules come in one cohesive set which will be helpful to all those who practise in the field of family law.

It is difficult to predict the true extent of the impact of the new rules, save that a few observations may be made in so far as a number of new insertions are concerned, which can be gleaned from the impact their CPR equivalent has had in the civil courts.

First of all there is the overriding objective itself as contained in FPR 2010, rule 1 which all new cases before the court must have regard to. It refers to the rules as being a new procedural code. One consequence of this is that previously reported decisions on procedure may need to be reconsidered in light of the new regime. It is the author's belief that guidance will initially be had from case law on the various CPR equivalents to FPR 2010.

As the overriding objective applies to all family proceedings practitioners will need to adjust to the fact that this now includes matrimonial and civil partnership proceedings as well as those under Parts IV and IVA of the Family Law Act 1996.

There is then the new self-contained Part 3 with its emphasis on mediation which applies at every stage of the proceedings.

It is clear that many more cases than just children's cases are going to be affected by this and not only at the first hearing, but also on an ongoing basis throughout the life of the case and indeed even upon issue of proceedings.

It is envisaged that courts may well exercise their powers to adjourn for the purposes of ADR more readily than before, particularly if applications have been issued which are non-protocol compliant.

Indeed, many of the revised application forms (e.g. Forms A and A1) themselves require details as to what steps a party has, or has not, taken to avail themselves of ADR and will call for an explanation if such avenues have not been explored.

There is now an expectation that parties will have attended a mediator before coming to court. However, the protocol does not take away a party's right to issue an application notwithstanding the absence of Form FM1 signed by a mediator.

Although it is envisaged that court staff will advise parties of the protocol and it is expected that a Form FM1 will be filed, if the party insists on pressing ahead nonetheless without the form then the applicant will be allowed to issue proceedings.

However, the fact that no form is filed and the protocol has not been complied with will no doubt be raised with the parties by the judge at the first hearing and where appropriate, the following outcomes are possible:

- proceedings stayed to enable a referral to be made for a mediation information and assessment meeting;
- non-compliance being considered as a matter of conduct on the issue of costs; or
- the imposition of a sanction.

Part 4 will also have a dramatic impact, not least in the fact that telephone hearings are now made possible in all tiers of court. For applications and directions appointments not requiring the attendance of the parties, this will, in the author's opinion, prove a welcome option. However, given the requirements in family cases for parties to be present (certainly in children and financial applications) this may not have the same level of take-up as in civil proceedings.

There may be increased take-up of the court making orders of its own initiative in light of the court's expansive case management powers.

The court's powers of strike-out also bear comment as well as the ability to make civil restraint orders and corresponding applications for relief from sanctions.

Due to the increase in numbers of litigants in person and the emotions running through the veins of family cases, a fertile ground for developing case law in these particular areas is anticipated, and perhaps even more so than within the civil jurisdiction.

As for take-up of service by email under Part 6, it is possible the profession is likely to be slow to respond to this bearing in mind that service by fax itself is often not entertained as readily as perhaps it should be.

The provisions as to setting aside judgments contained in Part 27 may also see some fruitful litigation for the same reasons as applications for relief from sanctions as provided for in Part 4.

In conclusion it is the author's belief that the advent of one comprehensive set of rules as a 'catch all' provision can only be seen as a good thing as both litigants and practitioners alike will be assisted in knowing where they need to look to find what they need.

On a practical level, encouragement to parties to engage in ADR (previously mediation), and matters of strategic case planning such as attention to who should be a party at an early stage, the order in which issues should be resolved, dealing with multiple issues at one hearing if possible, dealing with matters without the attendance of the parties where possible and a general cost/benefit analysis on an issue-by-issue basis will all have an impact on family litigation in the future.

Appendix 1
FAMILY PROCEDURE RULES 2010

[SI 2010/2955]

PART 1 OVERRIDING OBJECTIVE

1.1 The overriding objective
(1) These rules are a new procedural code with the overriding objective of enabling the court to deal with cases justly, having regard to any welfare issues involved.
(2) Dealing with a case justly includes, so far as is practicable—
- (a) ensuring that it is dealt with expeditiously and fairly;
- (b) dealing with the case in ways which are proportionate to the nature, importance and complexity of the issues;
- (c) ensuring that the parties are on an equal footing;
- (d) saving expense; and
- (e) allotting to it an appropriate share of the court's resources, while taking into account the need to allot resources to other cases.

1.2 Application by the court of the overriding objective
The court must seek to give effect to the overriding objective when it—
- (a) exercises any power given to it by these rules; or
- (b) interprets any rule.

1.3 Duty of the parties
The parties are required to help the court to further the overriding objective.

1.4 Court's duty to manage cases
(1) The court must further the overriding objective by actively managing cases.
(2) Active case management includes—
- (a) encouraging the parties to co-operate with each other in the conduct of the proceedings;
- (b) identifying at an early stage—
  - (i) the issues; and
  - (ii) who should be a party to the proceedings;
- (c) deciding promptly—
  - (i) which issues need full investigation and hearing and which do not; and
  - (ii) the procedure to be followed in the case;
- (d) deciding the order in which issues are to be resolved;
- (e) encouraging the parties to use an alternative dispute resolution procedure if the court considers that appropriate and facilitating the use of such procedure;
- (f) helping the parties to settle the whole or part of the case;
- (g) fixing timetables or otherwise controlling the progress of the case;

- (h) considering whether the likely benefits of taking a particular step justify the cost of taking it;
- (i) dealing with as many aspects of the case as it can on the same occasion;
- (j) dealing with the case without the parties needing to attend at court;
- (k) making use of technology; and
- (l) giving directions to ensure that the case proceeds quickly and efficiently.

PART 2 APPLICATION AND INTERPRETATION OF THE RULES

2.1 Application of these Rules

(1) Unless the context otherwise requires, these rules apply to family proceedings in–

- (a) the High Court;
- (b) a county court; and
- (c) a magistrates' court.

(2) Nothing in these rules is to be construed as–

- (a) purporting to apply to proceedings in a magistrates' court which are not family proceedings within the meaning of section 65 of the Magistrates' Courts Act 1980 or
- (b) conferring upon a magistrate a function which a magistrate is not permitted by statute to perform.

2.2 The glossary

(1) The glossary at the end of these rules is a guide to the meaning of certain legal expressions used in the rules, but is not to be taken as giving those expressions any meaning in the rules which they do not have in the law generally.

(2) Subject to paragraph (3), words in these rules which are included in the glossary are followed by ['GL'].

(3) The word 'service', which appears frequently in the rules, is included in the glossary but is not followed by ['GL'].

2.3 Interpretation

(1) In these rules–

'the 1973 Act' means the Matrimonial Causes Act 1973;

'the 1978 Act' means the Domestic Proceedings and Magistrates' Courts Act 1978;

'the 1980 Hague Convention' means the Convention on the Civil Aspects of International Child Abduction which was signed at The Hague on 25 October 1980;

'the 1984 Act' means the Matrimonial and Family Proceedings Act 1984;

'the 1986 Act' means the Family Law Act 1986;

'the 1989 Act' means the Children Act 1989;

'the 1990 Act' means the Human Fertilisation and Embryology Act 1990;

'the 1991 Act' means the Child Support Act 1991;

'the 1996 Act' means the Family Law Act 1996;

'the 1996 Hague Convention' means the Convention on Jurisdiction, Applicable Law, Recognition, Enforcement and Co-Operation in Respect of Parental Responsibility and Measures for the Protection of Children;

'the 2002 Act' means the Adoption and Children Act 2002;

'the 2004 Act' means the Civil Partnership Act 2004;

'the 2005 Act' means the Mental Capacity Act 2005;

'the 2008 Act' means the Human Fertilisation and Embryology Act 2008;

'adoption proceedings' means proceedings for an adoption order under the 2002 Act;

'Allocation Order' means any order made by the Lord Chancellor under Part 1 of Schedule 11 to the 1989 Act;

'alternative dispute resolution' means methods of resolving a dispute, including mediation, other than through the normal court process;

'application form' means a document in which the applicant states his intention to seek a court order other than in accordance with the Part 18 procedure;

'application notice' means a document in which the applicant states his intention to seek a court order in accordance with the Part 18 procedure;

'Assembly' means the National Assembly for Wales;

'bank holiday' means a bank holiday under the Banking and Financial Dealings Act 1971–

(a) for the purpose of service of a document within the United Kingdom, in the part of the United Kingdom where service is to take place; and

(b) for all other purposes, in England and Wales.

'business day' means any day other than–

(a) a Saturday, Sunday, Christmas Day or Good Friday; or
(b) a bank holiday;

'care order' has the meaning assigned to it by section 31(11) of the 1989 Act;

'CCR' means the County Court Rules 1981, as they appear in Schedule 2 to the CPR;

'child' means a person under the age of 18 years who is the subject of the proceedings; except that–

(a) in adoption proceedings, it also includes a person who has attained the age of 18 years before the proceedings are concluded; and

(b) in proceedings brought under the Council Regulation, the 1980 Hague Convention or the European Convention, it means a person under the age of 16 years who is the subject of the proceedings;

'child of the family' has the meaning given to it by section 105(1) of the 1989 Act;

'children and family reporter' means an officer of the Service or a Welsh family proceedings officer who has been asked to prepare a welfare report under section 7(1)(a) of the 1989 Act or section 102(3)(b) of the 2002 Act;

'children's guardian' means–

(a) in relation to a child who is the subject of and a party to specified proceedings or proceedings to which Part 14 applies, the person appointed in accordance with rule 16.3(1); and

(b) in any other case, the person appointed in accordance with rule 16.4;

'civil partnership order' means one of the orders mentioned in section 37 of the 2004 Act;

'civil partnership proceedings' means proceedings for a civil partnership order;

'civil partnership proceedings county court' means a county court so designated by the Lord Chancellor under section 36A of the 1984 Act;

'civil restraint order' means an order restraining a party–

(a) from making any further applications in current proceedings (a limited civil restraint order);

(b) from making certain applications in specified courts (an extended civil restraint order); or

(c) from making any application in specified courts (a general civil restraint order);

'Commission' means the Child Maintenance and Enforcement Commission;

'consent order' means an order in the terms applied for to which the respondent agrees;

'contact order' has the meaning assigned to it by section 8(1) of the 1989 Act;

'the Council Regulation' means Council Regulation (EC) No 2201/2003 of 27 November 2003 on jurisdiction and the recognition and enforcement of judgments in matrimonial matters and in matters of parental responsibility;

'court' means, subject to any rule or other enactment which provides otherwise, the High Court, a county court or a magistrates' court;

(rule 2.5 relates to the power to perform functions of the court.)

'court of trial' means–

(a) in proceedings under the 1973 Act, a divorce county court designated by the Lord Chancellor as a court of trial pursuant to section 33(1) of the 1984 Act; or

(b) in proceedings under the 2004 Act, a civil partnership proceedings county court designated by the Lord Chancellor as a court of trial pursuant to section 36A(1)(b) of the 1984 Act; and

in proceedings under the 1973 Act pending in a divorce county court or proceedings under the 2004 Act pending in a civil partnership proceedings county court, the principal registry is treated as a court of trial having its place of sitting at the Royal Courts of Justice;

'court officer' means–

(a) in the High Court or in a county court, a member of court staff; and

(b) in a magistrates' court, the designated officer;

('designated officer' is defined in section 37(1) of the Courts Act 2003.)

'CPR' means the Civil Procedure Rules 1998;

'deputy' has the meaning given in section 16(2)(b) of the 2005 Act;

'designated county court' means a court designated as–

(a) a divorce county court;

(b) a civil partnership proceedings county court; or

(c) both a divorce county court and a civil partnership proceedings county court;

'detailed assessment proceedings' means the procedure by which the amount of costs is decided in accordance with Part 47 of the CPR;

'directions appointment' means a hearing for directions;

'district judge'–

(a) in relation to proceedings in the High Court, includes a district judge of the principal registry and in relation to proceedings in a county court, includes a district judge of the principal registry when the principal registry is treated as if it were a county court;

(b) in relation to proceedings in a district registry or a county court, means the district judge or one of the district judges of that registry or county court, as the case may be;

'district registry' means–

(a) in proceedings under the 1973 Act, any district registry having a divorce county court within its district;

(b) in proceedings under the 2004 Act, any district registry having a civil partnership proceedings county court within its district; and

(c) in any other case, any district registry having a designated county court within its district;

'divorce county court' means a county court so designated by the Lord Chancellor pursuant to section 33(1) of the 1984 Act, including the principal registry when it is treated as a divorce county court;

'the European Convention' means the European Convention on Recognition and Enforcement of Decisions concerning Custody of Children and on the Restoration of Custody of Children which was signed in Luxembourg on 20 May 1980;

'filing', in relation to a document, means delivering it, by post or otherwise, to the court office;

'financial order' means–

(a) an avoidance of disposition order;
(b) an order for maintenance pending suit;
(c) an order for maintenance pending outcome of proceedings;
(d) an order for periodical payments or lump sum provision as mentioned in section 21(1) of the 1973 Act, except an order under section 27(6) of that Act;
(e) an order for periodical payments or lump sum provision as mentioned in paragraph 2(1) of Schedule 5 to the 2004 Act, made under Part 1 of Schedule 5 to that Act;
(f) a property adjustment order;
(g) a variation order;
(h) a pension sharing order; or
(i) a pension compensation sharing order;

('variation order', 'pension compensation sharing order' and 'pension sharing order' are defined in rule 9.3.)

'financial remedy' means–

(a) a financial order;
(b) an order under Schedule 1 to the 1989 Act;
(c) an order under Part 3 of the 1984 Act;
(d) an order under Schedule 7 to the 2004 Act;
(e) an order under section 27 of the 1973 Act;
(f) an order under Part 9 of Schedule 5 to the 2004 Act;
(g) an order under section 35 of the 1973 Act;
(h) an order under paragraph 69 of Schedule 5 to the 2004 Act;
(i) an order under Part 1 of the 1978 Act;
(j) an order under Schedule 6 to the 2004 Act;
(k) an order under section 10(2) of the 1973 Act; or
(l) an order under section 48(2) of the 2004 Act;

'hearing' includes a directions appointment;

'hearsay' means a statement made, otherwise than by a person while giving oral evidence in proceedings, which is tendered as evidence of the matters stated, and references to hearsay include hearsay of whatever degree;

'inherent jurisdiction' means the High Court's power to make any order or determine any issue in respect of a child, including in wardship proceedings, where it would be just and equitable to do so unless restricted by legislation or case law;

(Practice Direction 12D (Inherent Jurisdiction (including Wardship Proceedings)) provides examples of inherent jurisdiction proceedings.)

'judge', in the High Court or a county court, means, unless the context requires otherwise, a judge, district judge or a person authorised to act as such;

'jurisdiction' means, unless the context requires otherwise, England and Wales and any part of the territorial waters of the United Kingdom adjoining England and Wales;

'justices' clerk' has the meaning assigned to it by section 27(1) of the Courts Act 2003;

'legal representative' means a–
(a) barrister;
(b) solicitor;
(c) solicitor's employee;
(d) manager of a body recognised under section 9 of the Administration of Justice Act 1985; or
(e) person who, for the purposes of the Legal Services Act 2007, is an authorised person in relation to an activity which constitutes the conduct of litigation (within the meaning of the Act),

who has been instructed to act for a party in relation to proceedings;

'litigation friend' has the meaning given–
(a) in relation to a protected party, by Part 15; and
(b) in relation to a child, by Part 16;

'matrimonial cause' means proceedings for a matrimonial order;

'matrimonial order' means–
(a) a decree of divorce made under section 1 of the 1973 Act;
(b) a decree of nullity made on one of the grounds set out in sections 11 or 12 of the 1973 Act;
(c) a decree of judicial separation made under section 17 of the 1973 Act;

'note' includes a record made by mechanical means;

'officer of the Service' has the meaning given by section 11(3) of the Criminal Justice and Court Services Act 2000;

'order' includes directions of the court;

'order for maintenance pending outcome of proceedings' means an order under paragraph 38 of Schedule 5 to the 2004 Act;

'order for maintenance pending suit' means an order under section 22 of the 1973 Act;

'parental order proceedings' has the meaning assigned to it by rule 13.1;

'parental responsibility' has the meaning assigned to it by section 3 of the 1989 Act;

'placement proceedings' means proceedings for the making, varying or revoking of a placement order under the 2002 Act;

'principal registry' means the principal registry of the Family Division of the High Court;

'proceedings' means, unless the context requires otherwise, family proceedings as defined in section 75(3) of the Courts Act 2003;

'professional acting in furtherance of the protection of children' includes–
(a) an officer of a local authority exercising child protection functions;
(b) a police officer who is–
  (i) exercising powers under section 46 of the Act of 1989; or
  (ii) serving in a child protection unit or a paedophile unit of a police force;
(c) any professional person attending a child protection conference or review in relation to a child who is the subject of the proceedings to which the information regarding the proceedings held in private relates; or
(d) an officer of the National Society for the Prevention of Cruelty to Children;

'professional legal adviser' means a–
(a) barrister;
(b) solicitor;
(c) solicitor's employee;
(d) manager of a body recognised under section 9 of the Administration of Justice Act 1985; or

(e) person who, for the purposes of the Legal Services Act 2007, is an authorised person in relation to an activity which constitutes the conduct of litigation (within the meaning of that Act),

who is providing advice to a party but is not instructed to represent that party in the proceedings;

'property adjustment order' means–

(a) in proceedings under the 1973 Act, any of the orders mentioned in section 21(2) of that Act;
(b) in proceedings under the 1984 Act, an order under section 17(1)(a)(ii) of that Act;
(c) in proceedings under Schedule 5 to the 2004 Act, any of the orders mentioned in paragraph 7(1); or
(d) in proceedings under Schedule 7 to the 2004 Act, an order for property adjustment under paragraph 9(2) or (3);

'protected party' means a party, or an intended party, who lacks capacity (within the meaning of the 2005 Act) to conduct proceedings;

'reporting officer' means an officer of the Service or a Welsh family proceedings officer appointed to witness the documents which signify a parent's or guardian's consent to the placing of the child for adoption or to the making of an adoption order or a section 84 order;

'risk assessment' has the meaning assigned to it by section 16A(3) of the 1989 Act;

'Royal Courts of Justice', in relation to matrimonial proceedings pending in a divorce county court or civil partnership proceedings pending in a civil partnership proceedings county court, means such place as may be specified in directions given by the Lord Chancellor pursuant to section 42(2)(a) of the 1984 Act;

'RSC' means the Rules of the Supreme Court 1965 as they appear in Schedule 1 to the CPR;

'section 8 order' has the meaning assigned to it by section 8(2) of the 1989 Act;

'section 84 order' means an order made by the High Court under section 84 of the 2002 Act giving parental responsibility prior to adoption abroad;

'section 89 order' means an order made by the High Court under section 89 of the 2002 Act–

(a) annulling a Convention adoption or Convention adoption order;
(b) providing for an overseas adoption or determination under section 91 of the 2002 Act to cease to be valid; or
(c) deciding the extent, if any, to which a determination under section 91 of the 2002 Act has been affected by a subsequent determination under that section;

'Service' has the meaning given by section 11 of the Criminal Justice and Court Services Act 2000;

'the Service Regulation' means Regulation (EC) No. 1393/2007 of the European Parliament and of the Council of 13 November 2007 on the service in the Member States of judicial and extrajudicial documents in civil or commercial matters (service of documents), and repealing Council Regulation (EC) No. 1348/2000, as amended from time to time and as applied by the Agreement made on 19 October 2005 between the European Community and the Kingdom of Denmark on the service of judicial and extrajudicial documents in civil and commercial matters;

'specified proceedings' has the meaning assigned to it by section 41(6) of the 1989 Act and rule 12.27;

'welfare officer' means a person who has been asked to prepare a report under section 7(1)(b) of the 1989 Act;

'Welsh family proceedings officer' has the meaning given by section 35(4) of the Children Act 2004.

(2) In these rules a reference to–

    (a)   an application for a matrimonial order or a civil partnership order is to be read as a reference to a petition for–

        (i)   a matrimonial order;

        (ii)   a decree of presumption of death and dissolution of marriage made under section 19 of the 1973 Act; or

        (iii)   a civil partnership order,

    and includes a petition by a respondent asking for such an order;

    (b)   'financial order' in matrimonial proceedings is to be read as a reference to 'ancillary relief';

    (c)   'matrimonial proceedings' is to be read as a reference to a matrimonial cause or proceedings for an application for a decree of presumption of death and dissolution of marriage made under section 19 of the 1973 Act.

(3) Where these rules apply the CPR, they apply the CPR as amended from time to time.

2.4 Modification of rules in application to serial numbers etc.

If a serial number has been assigned under rule 14.2 or the name or other contact details of a party is not being revealed in accordance with rule 29.1–

(a) any rule requiring any party to serve any document will not apply; and

(b) the court will give directions about serving any document on the other parties.

2.5 Power to perform functions conferred on the court by these rules and practice directions

(1) Where these rules or a practice direction provide for the court to perform any function then, except where any rule or practice direction, any other enactment or any directions made by the President of the Family Division under section 9 of the Courts and Legal Services Act 1990, provides otherwise, that function may be performed–

    (a)   in relation to proceedings in the High Court or in a district registry, by any judge or district judge of that Court including a district judge of the principal registry;

    (b)   in relation to proceedings in a county court, by any judge or district judge including a district judge of the principal registry when the principal registry is treated as if it were a county court; and

    (c)   in relation to proceedings in a magistrates' court–

        (i)   by any family proceedings court constituted in accordance with sections 66 and 67 of the Magistrates' Courts Act 1980; or

        (ii)   by a single justice of the peace who is a member of the family panel in accordance with Practice Direction 2A.

(The Justices' Clerks Rules 2005 make provision for a justices' clerk or assistant clerk to carry out certain functions of a single justice of the peace.)

(2) A deputy High Court judge and a district judge, including a district judge of the principal registry, may not try a claim for a declaration of incompatibility in accordance with section 4 of the Human Rights Act 1998.

2.6 Powers of the single justice to perform functions under the 1989 Act, the 1996 Act, the 2002 Act and the Childcare Act 2006

(1) A single justice who is a member of the family panel may perform the functions of a magistrates' court–

(a) where an application without notice is made under sections 10, 44(1), 48(9), 50(4) and 102(1) of the 1989 Act;
(b) subject to paragraph (2), under sections 11(3) or 38(1) of the 1989 Act;
(c) under sections 4(3)(b), 4A(3)(b), 4ZA(6)(b), 7, 34(3)(b), 41, 44(9)(b) and (11)(b)(iii), 48(4), 91(15) or (17) or paragraph 11(4) of Schedule 14 of the 1989 Act;
(d) in accordance with the Allocation Order;
(e) where an application without notice is made under section 41(2) of the 2002 Act (recovery orders);
(f) where an application without notice is made for an occupation order or a non molestation order under Part 4 of the 1996 Act; or
(g) where an application is made for a warrant under section 79 of the Childcare Act 2006;

(2) A single justice of the peace may make an order under section 11(3) or 38(1) of the 1989 Act where–
   (a) a previous such order has been made in the same proceedings;
   (b) the terms of the order sought are the same as those of the last such order made; and
   (c) a written request for such an order has been made and–
      (i) the other parties and any children's guardian consent to the request and they or their legal representatives have signed the request; or
      (ii) at least one of the other parties and any children's guardian consent to the request and they or their legal representatives have signed the request, and the remaining parties have not indicated that they either consent to or oppose the making of the order.

(3) The proceedings referred to in paragraph (1)(a), (c) and (d) are proceedings which are prescribed for the purposes of section 93(2)(i) of the 1989 Act.

2.7 Single justice's power to refer to a magistrates' court

Where a single justice–

(a) is performing the function of a magistrates' court in accordance with rules 2.5(1)(c)(ii) and 2.6(1) and (2); and
(b) considers, for whatever reason, that it is inappropriate to perform the function,

the single justice must refer the matter to a magistrates' court which may perform the function.

2.8 Court's discretion as to where it deals with cases

The court may deal with a case at any place that it considers appropriate.

2.9 Computation of time

(1) This rule shows how to calculate any period of time for doing any act which is specified–
   (a) by these rules;
   (b) by a practice direction; or
   (c) by a direction or order of the court.

(2) A period of time expressed as a number of days must be computed as clear days.
(3) In this rule 'clear days' means that in computing the numbers of days–
   (a) the day on which the period begins; and
   (b) if the end of the period is defined by reference to an event, the day on which that event occurs,

are not included.
(4) Where the specified period is 7 days or less and includes a day which is not a business day, that day does not count.
(5) When the period specified–
   (a) by these rules or a practice direction; or
   (b) by any direction or order of the court,

   for doing any act at the court office ends on a day on which the office is closed, that act will be in time if done on the next day on which the court office is open.

2.10 Dates for compliance to be calendar dates and to include time of day
(1) Where the court makes an order or gives a direction which imposes a time limit for doing any act, the last date for compliance must, wherever practicable–
   (a) be expressed as a calendar date; and
   (b) include the time of day by which the act must be done.
(2) Where the date by which an act must be done is inserted in any document, the date must, wherever practicable, be expressed as a calendar date.
(3) Where 'month' occurs in any order, direction or other document, it means a calendar month.

PART 3   ALTERNATIVE DISPUTE RESOLUTION: THE COURT'S POWERS

3.1 Scope of this Part
(1) This Part contains the court's powers to encourage the parties to use alternative dispute resolution and to facilitate its use.
(2) The powers in this Part are subject to any powers given to the court by any other rule or practice direction or by any other enactment or any powers it may otherwise have.

3.2 Court's duty to consider alternative dispute resolution
The court must consider, at every stage in proceedings, whether alternative dispute resolution is appropriate.

3.3 When the court will adjourn proceedings or a hearing in proceedings
(1) If the court considers that alternative dispute resolution is appropriate, the court may direct that the proceedings, or a hearing in the proceedings, be adjourned for such specified period as it considers appropriate–
   (a) to enable the parties to obtain information and advice about alternative dispute resolution; and
   (b) where the parties agree, to enable alternative dispute resolution to take place.
(2) The court may give directions under this rule on an application or of its own initiative.
(3) Where the court directs an adjournment under this rule, it will give directions about the timing and method by which the parties must tell the court if any of the issues in the proceedings have been resolved.
(4) If the parties do not tell the court if any of the issues have been resolved as directed under paragraph (3), the court will give such directions as to the management of the case as it considers appropriate.
(5) The court or court officer will–
   (a) record the making of an order under this rule; and
   (b) arrange for a copy of the order to be served as soon as practicable on the parties.

(6) Where the court proposes to exercise its powers of its own initiative, the procedure set out in rule 4.3(2) to (6) applies.

(By rule 4.1(7), any direction given under this rule may be varied or revoked.)

PART 4   GENERAL CASE MANAGEMENT POWERS

4.1   The court's general powers of management

(1) In this Part, 'statement of case' means the whole or part of, an application form or answer.
(2) The list of powers in this rule is in addition to any powers given to the court by any other rule or practice direction or by any other enactment or any powers it may otherwise have.
(3) Except where these rules provide otherwise, the court may–
  (a) extend or shorten the time for compliance with any rule, practice direction or court order (even if an application for extension is made after the time for compliance has expired);
  (b) make such order for disclosure and inspection, including specific disclosure of documents, as it thinks fit;
  (c) adjourn or bring forward a hearing;
  (d) require a party or a party's legal representative to attend the court;
  (e) hold a hearing and receive evidence by telephone or by using any other method of direct oral communication;
  (f) direct that part of any proceedings be dealt with as separate proceedings;
  (g) stay[GL] the whole or part of any proceedings or judgment either generally or until a specified date or event;
  (h) consolidate proceedings;
  (i) hear two or more applications on the same occasion;
  (j) direct a separate hearing of any issue;
  (k) decide the order in which issues are to be heard;
  (l) exclude an issue from consideration;
  (m) dismiss or give a decision on an application after a decision on a preliminary issue;
  (n) direct any party to file and serve an estimate of costs; and
  (o) take any other step or make any other order for the purpose of managing the case and furthering the overriding objective.

(Rule 21.1 explains what is meant by disclosure and inspection.)

(4) When the court makes an order, it may–
  (a) make it subject to conditions, including a condition to pay a sum of money into court; and
  (b) specify the consequence of failure to comply with the order or a condition.
(5) Where the court gives directions it will take into account whether or not a party has complied with any relevant pre-action protocol[GL].
(6) A power of the court under these rules to make an order includes a power to vary or revoke the order.
(7) Any provision in these rules–
  (a) requiring or permitting directions to be given by the court is to be taken as including provision for such directions to be varied or revoked; and
  (b) requiring or permitting a date to be set is to be taken as including provision for that date to be changed or cancelled.
(8) The court may not extend the period within which a section 89 order must be made.

4.2 Court officer's power to refer to the court

Where a step is to be taken by a court officer–

(a) the court officer may consult the court before taking that step;
(b) the step may be taken by the court instead of the court officer.

4.3 Court's power to make order of its own initiative

(1) Except where an enactment provides otherwise, the court may exercise its powers on an application or of its own initiative.

(Part 18 sets out the procedure for making an application.)

(2) Where the court proposes to make an order of its own initiative–

    (a) it may give any person likely to be affected by the order an opportunity to make representations; and
    (b) where it does so it must specify the time by and the manner in which the representations must be made.

(3) Where the court proposes–

    (a) to make an order of its own initiative; and
    (b) to hold a hearing to decide whether to make the order,

it must give each party likely to be affected by the order at least 5 days' notice of the hearing.

(4) The court may make an order of its own initiative without hearing the parties or giving them an opportunity to make representations.

(5) Where the court has made an order under paragraph (4)–

    (a) a party affected by the order may apply to have it set aside[GL], varied or stayed[GL]; and
    (b) the order must contain a statement of the right to make such an application.

(6) An application under paragraph (5)(a) must be made–

    (a) within such period as may be specified by the court; or
    (b) if the court does not specify a period, within 7 days beginning with the date on which the order was served on the party making the application.

(7) If the High Court or a county court of its own initiative strikes out a statement of case or dismisses an application (including an application for permission to appeal) and it considers that the application is totally without merit–

    (a) the court's order must record that fact; and
    (b) the court must at the same time consider whether it is appropriate to make a civil restraint order.

4.4 Power to strike out a statement of case

(1) Except in proceedings to which Parts 12 to 14 apply, the court may strike out[GL] a statement of case if it appears to the court–

    (a) that the statement of case discloses no reasonable grounds for bringing or defending the application;
    (b) that the statement of case is an abuse of the court's process or is otherwise likely to obstruct the just disposal of the proceedings;
    (c) that there has been a failure to comply with a rule, practice direction or court order; or
    (d) in relation to applications for matrimonial and civil partnership orders and answers to such applications, that the parties to the proceedings consent.

(2) When the court strikes out a statement of case it may make any consequential order it considers appropriate.
(3) Where–
   (a) the court has struck out an applicant's statement of case;
   (b) the applicant has been ordered to pay costs to the respondent; and
   (c) before paying those costs, the applicant starts another application against the same respondent, arising out of facts which are the same or substantially the same as those relating to the application in which the statement of case was struck out,

the court may, on the application of the respondent, stay[GL] that other application until the costs of the first application have been paid.
(4) Paragraph (1) does not limit any other power of the court to strike out[GL] a statement of case.
(5) If the High Court or a county court strikes out an applicant's statement of case and it considers that the application is totally without merit–
   (a) the court's order must record that fact; and
   (b) the court must at the same time consider whether it is appropriate to make a civil restraint order.

4.5 Sanctions have effect unless defaulting party obtains relief

(1) Where a party has failed to comply with a rule, practice direction or court order, any sanction for failure to comply imposed by the rule, practice direction or court order has effect unless the party in default applies for and obtains relief from the sanction.

(Rule 4.6 sets out the circumstances which the court may consider on an application to grant relief from a sanction.)

(2) Where the sanction is the payment of costs, the party in default may only obtain relief by appealing against the order for costs.
(3) Where a rule, practice direction or court order–
   (a) requires a party to do something within a specified time; and
   (b) specifies the consequence of failure to comply,

the time for doing the act in question may not be extended by agreement between the parties.

4.6 Relief from sanctions

(1) On an application for relief from any sanction imposed for a failure to comply with any rule, practice direction or court order the court will consider all the circumstances including–
   (a) the interests of the administration of justice;
   (b) whether the application for relief has been made promptly;
   (c) whether the failure to comply was intentional;
   (d) whether there is a good explanation for the failure;
   (e) the extent to which the party in default has complied with other rules, practice directions, court orders and any relevant pre-action protocol[GL];
   (f) whether the failure to comply was caused by the party or the party's legal representative;
   (g) whether the hearing date or the likely hearing date can still be met if relief is granted;
   (h) the effect which the failure to comply had on each party; and
   (i) the effect which the granting of relief would have on each party or a child whose interest the court considers relevant.
(2) An application for relief must be supported by evidence.

4.7 General power of the court to rectify matters where there has been an error of procedure

Where there has been an error of procedure such as a failure to comply with a rule or practice direction–

(a) the error does not invalidate any step taken in the proceedings unless the court so orders; and
(b) the court may make an order to remedy the error.

4.8 Power of the court to make civil restraint orders

Practice Direction 4B sets out–
(a) the circumstances in which the High Court or a county court has the power to make a civil restraint order against a party to proceedings;
(b) the procedure where a party applies for a civil restraint order against another party; and
(c) the consequences of the court making a civil restraint order.

PART 5 FORMS AND START OF PROCEEDINGS

5.1 Forms

(1) Subject to rule 14.10(2) and(3), the forms referred to in a practice direction, shall be used in the cases to which they apply.
(2) A form may be varied by the court or a party if the variation is required by the circumstances of a particular case.
(3) A form must not be varied so as to leave out any information or guidance which the form gives to the recipient.
(4) Where these rules require a form to be sent by the court or by a party for another party to use, it must be sent without any variation except such as is required by the circumstances of the particular case.

5.2 Documents to be attached to a form

Subject to any rule or practice direction, unless the court directs otherwise, a form must have attached to it any documents which, in the form, are–

(a) stated to be required; or
(b) referred to.

5.3 Proceedings are started by issue of application form

(1) Proceedings are started when a court officer issues an application at the request of the applicant.
(2) An application is issued on the date entered in the application form by the court officer.

(Rule 29.7 requires an application form to be authenticated with the stamp of the court when it is issued)

PART 6 SERVICE

CHAPTER 1 SCOPE OF THIS PART AND INTERPRETATION

6.1 Part 6 rules about service apply generally

This Part applies to the service of documents, except where–

(a) another Part, any other enactment or a practice direction makes a different provision; or
(b) the court directs otherwise.

6.2 Interpretation

In this Part 'solicitor' includes any person who, for the purposes of the Legal Services Act 2007, is an authorised person in relation to an activity which constitutes the conduct of litigation (within the meaning of that Act).

CHAPTER 2 SERVICE OF THE APPLICATION FOR A MATRIMONIAL ORDER OR CIVIL PARTNERSHIP ORDER IN THE JURISDICTION

6.3 Interpretation

In this Chapter, unless the context otherwise requires, a reference to an application–

(a) is a reference to an application for a matrimonial or civil partnership order; and
(b) includes an application by a respondent as referred to in rule 7.4.

(Part 7 deals with applications in matrimonial or civil partnership proceedings.)

6.4 Methods of service

An application may be served by any of the following methods–

(a) personal service in accordance with rule 6.7;
(b) first class post, or other service which provides for delivery on the next business day, in accordance with Practice Direction 6A; or
(c) where rule 6.11 applies, document exchange.

6.5 Who is to serve the application

(1) Subject to the provisions of this rule, an application may be served by–

    (a)   the applicant; or
    (b)   a court officer, if so requested by the applicant.

(2) A court officer will not serve the application if the party to be served is a child or protected party.
(3) An application must not be served personally by the applicant himself or herself.

(Rule 6.14 deals with service of the application on children and protected parties.)

6.6 Every respondent to be served

The application must be served on every respondent.

6.7 Personal service

An application is served personally on a respondent by leaving it with that respondent.

6.8 Service of application by the court

(1) Where the application is to be served by a court officer, the applicant must give the court officer an address at which the respondent is to be served in accordance with rule 6.4.
(2) Where the court officer has sent a notification of failure of service to the applicant in accordance with rule 6.21, the applicant may request the court officer to serve the document on the respondent at an alternative address.

6.9 Service by the bailiff

(1) An applicant may request that an application be served by a bailiff delivering a copy of the application to the respondent personally.
(2) The request must be made in accordance with Practice Direction 6A.

(3) Where the bailiff is unable to serve the application, the applicant may apply to the court for an order under rule 6.19 (service by an alternative method or at an alternative place).

(Practice Direction 6A contains provision about when a request under this rule is appropriate.)

(Rule 6.22 provides for notice of non-service by a bailiff.)

6.10 Where to serve the application – general provisions

(1) The application must be served within the jurisdiction except as provided for by Chapter 4 of this Part (service out of the jurisdiction).
(2) The applicant must include in the application an address at which the respondent may be served.
(3) Paragraph (2) does not apply where an order made by the court under rule 6.19 (service by an alternative method or at an alternative place) specifies the place or method of service of the application.

6.11 Service of the application on a solicitor within the jurisdiction or in any EEA state

(1) Where a solicitor acting for the respondent has notified the applicant in writing that the solicitor is instructed by the respondent to accept service of the application on behalf of the respondent at a business address within the jurisdiction, the application must be served at the business address of that solicitor.
(2) Subject to the provisions of Chapter 4 of this Part, where a solicitor acting for the respondent has notified the applicant in writing that the solicitor is instructed by the respondent to accept service of the application on behalf of the respondent at a business address within any EEA state, the application must be served at the business address of that solicitor.

('Solicitor' has the extended meaning set out in rule 6.2 and 'EEA state' is defined in Schedule 1 to the Interpretation Act 1978.)

6.12 Service of the application where the respondent gives an address at which the respondent may be served

Subject to rule 6.13, the respondent may be served with the application at an address within the jurisdiction which the respondent has given for the purpose of being served with the proceedings.

6.13 Service of the application where the respondent does not give an address at which the respondent may be served

(1) This rule applies where–
    (a) rule 6.11 (service of application on solicitor); and
    (b) rule 6.12 (respondent gives address at which respondent may be served),

do not apply and the applicant does not wish the application to be served personally under rule 6.7.

(2) Subject to paragraphs (3) to (5) the application must be served on the respondent at his usual or last known address.
(3) Where the applicant has reason to believe that the respondent no longer resides at his usual or last known address, the applicant must take reasonable steps to ascertain the current address of the respondent.
(4) Where, having taken the reasonable steps required by paragraph (3), the applicant–
    (a) ascertains the respondent's current address, the application must be served at that address; or

(b) is unable to ascertain the respondent's current address, the applicant must consider whether there is–

   (i) an alternative place where; or
   (ii) an alternative method by which,
   service may be effected.

(5) If, under paragraph (4)(b), there is such a place where or a method by which service could be effected, the applicant must make an application under rule 6.19.

6.14 Service of the application on children and protected parties

(1) Where the respondent is a child, the application form must be served on–

   (a) one of the child's parents or guardians; or
   (b) if there is no parent or guardian, an adult with whom the child resides or in whose care the child is.

(2) Where the respondent is a protected party, the application must be served on–

   (a) one of the following persons with authority in relation to the protected party–

      (i) the attorney under a registered enduring power of attorney;
      (ii) the donee of a lasting power of attorney; or
      (iii) the deputy appointed by the Court of Protection; or

   (b) if there is no such person, an adult with whom the protected party resides or in whose care the protected party is.

(3) Any reference in this Chapter to a respondent or party to be served includes the person to be served with the application form on behalf of a child or protected party under paragraph (1) or (2).

(4) The court may make an order permitting an application form to be served on a child or protected party, or on a person other than the person specified in paragraph (1) or (2).

(5) An application for an order under paragraph (4) may be made without notice.

(6) The court may order that, although an application form has been sent or given to someone other than the person specified in paragraph (1) or (2), it is to be treated as if it had been properly served.

(7) Where a document is served in accordance with this rule–

   (a) it must be endorsed with the notice set out in Practice Direction 6A; and
   (b) the person commencing the proceedings must file a witness statement by the person on whom the application form was served stating whether–

      (i) the contents of the application form; or
      (ii) the purpose and intention of the application,

   were communicated to the child or protected party and, if not, why not.

(8) Paragraph (7)(b) does not apply where the Official Solicitor is, as the case may be–

   (a) the litigation friend of the protected party; or
   (b) the litigation friend or children's guardian of the child.

6.15 Deemed service – receipt of acknowledgment of service

(1) Subject to paragraph (2), an application is deemed to be served if the acknowledgment of service, signed by the party served or the solicitor acting on that party's behalf, is returned to the court office.

(2) Where the signature on the acknowledgment of service purports to be that of the other party to the marriage or civil partnership, the applicant must prove that it is the signature of that party by–

   (a) giving oral evidence to that effect at the hearing; or

(b) if the application is undefended, confirming it to be so in the affidavit the applicant files under rule 7.19(4).

6.16 Deemed service by post or alternative service where no acknowledgment of service filed

(1) Subject to paragraph (2), if—

(a) an application has been served on a respondent by post or other service which provides for delivery on the next business day;
(b) no acknowledgment of service has been returned to the court office; and
(c) the court is satisfied that the respondent has received the application,

the district judge may direct that the application is deemed to be served.

(2) Where—

(a) the application alleges 2 years' separation and the respondent consents to a matrimonial or civil partnership order being granted; and
(b) none of the other facts mentioned in section 1(2) of the 1973 Act or section 44(5) of the 2004 Act, as the case may be, is alleged,

paragraph (1) applies only if—
(i) the court is satisfied that the respondent has received notice of the proceedings; and
(ii) the applicant produces a written statement, signed by the respondent, containing the respondent's consent to the grant of an order.

6.17 Proof of personal service where no acknowledgment of service filed

(1) This rule applies where—

(a) an application has been served on a respondent personally; and
(b) no acknowledgment of service has been returned to the court office.

(2) The person serving the application must file a certificate of service stating the date and time of personal service.

(Practice Direction 6A makes provision for a certificate of service by a bailiff.)

(3) If the respondent served was the other party to the marriage or civil partnership, the certificate of service must show the means by which the person serving the application knows the identity of the party served.

6.18 Proof of service by the court etc.

(1) Where a court officer serves an application by post, or other service which provides for delivery on the next business day, the court officer must note in the court records the date of—

(a) posting; or
(b) leaving with, delivering to or collection by the relevant service provider.

(2) A record made in accordance with paragraph (1) is evidence of the facts stated in it.
(3) This rule does not affect the operation of section 133 of the County Courts Act 1984.

(Section 133 of the County Courts Act 1984 provides that where a summons or other process issued from a county court is served by an officer of a court, service may be proved by a certificate in a prescribed form.)

6.19 Service of the application by an alternative method or at an alternative place

(1) Where it appears to the court that there is a good reason to authorise service by a method or at a place not otherwise permitted by this Part, the court may direct that service is effected by an alternative method or at an alternative place.

(2) On an application under this rule, the court may direct that steps already taken to bring the application form to the attention of the respondent by an alternative method or at an alternative place is good service.
(3) A direction under this rule must specify–

  (a) the method or place of service;
  (b) the date on which the application form is deemed served; and
  (c) the period for filing an acknowledgment of service or answer.

6.20 Power of the court to dispense with service of the application

(1) The court may dispense with service of the application where it is impracticable to serve the application by any method provided for by this Part.
(2) An application for an order to dispense with service may be made at any time and must be supported by evidence.
(3) The court may require the applicant to attend when it decides the application.

6.21 Notification of failure of service by the court

Where–

(a) the court serves the application by post or other service which provides for delivery on the next business day; and
(b) the application is returned to the court,

the court will send notification to the applicant that the application has been returned.

6.22 Notice of non-service by bailiff

Where–

(a) the bailiff is to serve an application; and
(b) the bailiff is unable to serve it on the respondent,

the court officer will send notification to the applicant.

CHAPTER 3 SERVICE OF DOCUMENTS OTHER THAN AN APPLICATION FOR A MATRIMONIAL ORDER OR CIVIL PARTNERSHIP ORDER IN THE UNITED KINGDOM

6.23 Method of service

A document may be served by any of the following methods–

(a) personal service, in accordance with rule 6.25;
(b) first class post, document exchange or other service which provides for delivery on the next business day, in accordance with Practice Direction 6A;
(c) leaving it at a place specified in rule 6.26; or
(d) fax or other means of electronic communication in accordance with Practice Direction 6A.

(Rule 6.35 provides for the court to permit service by an alternative method or at an alternative place.)

6.24 Who is to serve

(1) A party to proceedings will serve a document which that party has prepared, or which the court has prepared or issued on behalf of that party, except where–

  (a) a rule or practice direction provides that the court will serve the document; or
  (b) the court directs otherwise.

(2) Where a court officer is to serve a document, it is for the court to decide which method of service is to be used.
(3) Where the court officer is to serve a document prepared by a party, that party must provide a copy for the court and for each party to be served.

6.25 Personal service

(1) Where required by another Part, any other enactment, a practice direction or a court order, a document must be served personally.
(2) In other cases, a document may be served personally except where the party to be served has given an address for service under rule 6.26(2)(a).
(3) A document is served personally on an individual by leaving it with that individual.

6.26 Address for service

(1) A party to proceedings must give an address at which that party may be served with documents relating to those proceedings.
(2) Subject to paragraph (4), a party's address for service must be–
   (a) the business address either within the United Kingdom or any other EEA state of a solicitor acting for the party to be served; or
   (b) where there is no solicitor acting for the party to be served, an address within the United Kingdom at which the party resides or carries on business.

('EEA state' is defined in Schedule 1 to the Interpretation Act 1978.)

(3) Where there is no solicitor acting for the party to be served and the party does not have an address within the United Kingdom at which that party resides or carries on business, the party must, subject to paragraph (4), give an address for service within the United Kingdom.
(4) A party who–
   (a) has been served with an application for a matrimonial or civil partnership order outside the United Kingdom; and
   (b) apart from acknowledging service of the application, does not take part in the proceedings,

   need not give an address for service within the United Kingdom.
(5) Any document to be served in proceedings must be sent, or transmitted to, or left at, the party's address for service unless it is to be served personally or the court orders otherwise.
(6) Where, in accordance with Practice Direction 6A, a party indicates or is deemed to have indicated that they will accept service by fax, the fax number given by that party must be at the address for service.
(7) Where a party indicates in accordance with Practice Direction 6A, that they will accept service by electronic means other than fax, the e-mail address or electronic identification given by that party will be deemed to be at the address for service.
(8) This rule does not apply where an order made by the court under rule 6.35 (service by an alternative method or at an alternative place) specifies where a document may be served.

6.27 Change of address for service

Where the address for service of a party changes, that party must give notice in writing of the change, as soon as it has taken place, to the court and every other party.

6.28 Service of an application form commencing proceedings on children and protected parties

(1) This rule applies to the service of an application form commencing proceedings other than an application for a matrimonial or civil partnership order.

(2) An application form commencing proceedings which would otherwise be served on a child or protected party must be served–
  (a) where the respondent is a child, in accordance with rule 6.14(1); and
  (b) where the respondent is a protected party, in accordance with rule 6.14(2).

6.29 Service of other documents on or by children and protected parties where a litigation friend has been or will be appointed

(1) This rule applies to–
  (a) a protected party; or
  (b) a child to whom the provisions of rule 16.5 and Chapter 5 of Part 16 apply (litigation friends).
(2) An application for an order appointing a litigation friend where a protected party or child has no litigation friend must be served in accordance with rule 15.8 or rule 16.13 as the case may be.
(3) Any other document which would otherwise be served on or by a child or protected party must be served on or by the litigation friend conducting the proceedings on behalf of the child or protected party.

6.30 Service on or by children where a children's guardian has been or will be appointed under rule 16.4

(1) This rule applies to a child to whom the provisions of rule 16.4 and Chapter 7 apply.
(2) An application for an order appointing a children's guardian where a child has no children's guardian must be served in accordance with rule 16.26.
(3) Any other document which would otherwise be served on or by a child must be served on or by the children's guardian conducting the proceedings on behalf of the child.

6.31 Service on or by children where a children's guardian has been appointed under rule 16.3

(1) This rule applies where a children's guardian has been appointed for a child in accordance with rule 16.3.
(2) Any document which would otherwise be served on the child must be served on–
  (a) the solicitor appointed by the court in accordance with section 41(3) of the 1989 Act; and
  (b) the children's guardian.
(3) Any document which would otherwise be served by the child must be served by–
  (a) the solicitor appointed by the court in accordance with section 41(3) of the 1989 Act or by the children's guardian; or
  (b) if no solicitor has been appointed as mentioned in paragraph (a), the children's guardian.

6.32 Supplementary provisions relating to service on children and protected parties

(1) The court may direct that a document be served on a protected party or child or on some person other than a person upon whom it would be served under rules 6.28 to 6.31 above.
(2) The court may direct that, although a document has been sent or given to someone other than a person upon whom it should be served under rules 6.28 to 6.31 above, the document is to be treated as if it had been properly served.
(3) This rule and rules 6.28 to 6.31 do not apply where the court has made an order under rule 16.6 allowing a child to conduct proceedings without a children's guardian or litigation friend.

6.33 Supplementary provision relating to service on children

(1) This rule applies to proceedings to which Part 12 applies.
(2) Where a rule requires–
- (a) a document to be served on a party;
- (b) a party to be notified of any matter; or
- (c) a party to be supplied with a copy of a document,

in addition to the persons to be served in accordance with rules 6.28 to 6.32, the persons or bodies mentioned in paragraph (3) must be served, notified or supplied with a copy of a document, as applicable, unless the court directs otherwise.

(3) The persons or bodies referred to in paragraph (2) are–
- (a) such of the following who are appointed in the proceedings–
  - (i) the children's guardian (if the children's guardian is not otherwise to be served);
  - (ii) the welfare officer;
  - (iii) the children and family reporter;
  - (iv) the officer of the Service, Welsh family proceedings officer or local authority officer acting under a duty referred to in rule 16.38; and
- (b) a local authority preparing a report under section 14A(8) or (9) of the 1989 Act.

6.34 Deemed service

A document, other than an application for a matrimonial or civil partnership order, served in accordance with these rules or a practice direction is deemed to be served on the day shown in the following table–

Method of service	Deemed day of service
First class post (or other service which provides for delivery on the next business day)	The second day after it was posted, left with, delivered to or collected by the relevant service provider, provided that day is a business day; or, if not, the next business day after that day.
Document exchange	The second day after it was left with, delivered to or collected by the relevant service provider, provided that day is a business day; or, if not, the next business day after that day.
Delivering the document to or leaving it at a permitted address.	If it is delivered to or left at the permitted address on a business day before 4.30p.m., on that day; or in any other case, on the next business day after that day.
Fax.	If the transmission of the fax is completed on a business day before 4.30p.m., on that day; or, in any other case, the next business day after the day on which it was transmitted.
Other electronic method.	If the e-mail or other electronic transmission is sent on a business day before 4.30p.m., on that day; or in any other case, on the next business day after the day on which it was sent.
Personal service	If the document is served personally before 4.30p.m. on a business day, on that day; or, in any other case, on the next business day after that day.

(Practice Direction 6A contains examples of how the date of deemed service is calculated.)

6.35 Service by an alternative method or at an alternative place

Rule 6.19 applies to any document in proceedings as it applies to an application for a matrimonial or civil partnership order and reference to the respondent in that rule is modified accordingly.

6.36 Power to dispense with service

The court may dispense with the service of any document which is to be served in proceedings.

6.37 Certificate of service

(1) Where a rule, practice direction or court order requires a certificate of service, the certificate must state the details set out in the following table–

Method of service	Details to be certified
Personal service.	Date and time of personal service and method of identifying the person served.
First class post, document exchange or other service which provides for delivery on the next business day.	Date of posting, leaving with, delivering to or collection by the relevant service provider.
Delivery of document to or leaving it at a permitted place.	Date and time when the document was delivered to or left at the permitted place.
Fax.	Date and time of completion of transmission.
Other electronic method	Date and time of sending the email or other electronic transmission.
Alternative method or place permitted by court	As required by the court.

(2) An applicant who is required to file a certificate of service of an application form must do so at or before the earlier of–

    (a) the first directions appointment in; or
    (b) the hearing of,

the proceedings unless a rule or practice direction provides otherwise.

(Rule 17.2 requires a certificate of service to contain a statement of truth.)

6.38 Notification of outcome of service by the court

Where–
(a) a document to be served by a court officer is served by post or other service which provides for delivery on the next working day; and
(b) the document is returned to the court,

the court officer will send notification to the party who requested service that the document has been returned.

6.39 Notification of non-service by bailiff

Where–

(a) the bailiff is to serve a document; and
(b) the bailiff is unable to serve it,

the court officer must send notification to the party who requested service.

CHAPTER 4   SERVICE OUT OF THE JURISDICTION

6.40   Scope and interpretation

(1) This Chapter contains rules about–

    (a)   service of application forms and other documents out of the jurisdiction; and
    (b)   the procedure for service.

('Jurisdiction' is defined in rule 2.3.)

(2) In this Chapter–

    'application form' includes an application notice;

    'Commonwealth State' means a State listed in Schedule 3 to the British Nationality Act 1981; and

    'the Hague Convention' means the Convention on the service abroad of judicial and extra-judicial documents in civil or commercial matters signed at the Hague on November 15, 1965.

6.41   Permission to serve not required

Any document to be served for the purposes of these rules may be served out of the jurisdiction without the permission of the court.

6.42   Period for acknowledging service or responding to application where application is served out of the jurisdiction

(1) This rule applies where, under these rules, a party is required to file–

    (a)   an acknowledgment of service; or
    (b)   an answer to an application,

and sets out the time period for doing so where the application is served out of the jurisdiction.

(2) Where the applicant serves an application on a respondent in–

    (a)   Scotland or Northern Ireland; or
    (b)   a Member State or Hague Convention country within Europe,

the period for filing an acknowledgment of service or an answer to an application is 21 days after service of the application.

(3) Where the applicant serves an application on a respondent in a Hague Convention country outside Europe, the period for filing an acknowledgment of service or an answer to an application is 31 days after service of the application.

(4) Where the applicant serves an application on a respondent in a country not referred to in paragraphs (2) and (3), the period for filing an acknowledgment of service or an answer to an application is set out in Practice Direction 6B.

6.43   Method of service – general provisions

(1) This rule contains general provisions about the method of service of an application for a matrimonial or civil partnership order, or other document, on a party out of the jurisdiction.

Where service is to be effected on a party in Scotland or Northern Ireland

(2) Where a party serves an application form or other document on a party in Scotland or Northern Ireland, it must be served by a method permitted by Chapter 2 (and references to 'jurisdiction' in that Chapter are modified accordingly) or Chapter 3 of this Part and rule 6.26(5) applies.

Where service is to be effected on a respondent out of the United Kingdom

(3) Where the applicant wishes to serve an application form, or other document, on a respondent out of the United Kingdom, it may be served by any method–

    (a) provided for by–

        (i) rule 6.44 (service in accordance with the Service Regulation);
        (ii) rule 6.45 (service through foreign governments, judicial authorities and British Consular authorities); or

    (b) permitted by the law of the country in which it is to be served.

(4) Nothing in paragraph (3) or in any court order authorises or requires any person to do anything which is contrary to the law of the country where the application form, or other document, is to be served.

6.44 Service in accordance with the Service Regulation

(1) This rule applies where the applicant wishes to serve the application form, or other document, in accordance with the Service Regulation.

(2) The applicant must file–

    (a) the application form or other document;
    (b) any translation; and
    (c) any other documents required by the Service Regulation.

(3) When the applicant files the documents referred to in paragraph (2), the court officer will–

    (a) seal[GL], or otherwise authenticate with the stamp of the court, the copy of the application form; and
    (b) forward the documents to the Senior Master of the Queen's Bench Division.

(The Service Regulation is annexed to Practice Direction 6B.)

(Article 20(1) of the Service Regulation provides that the Regulation prevails over other provisions contained in any other agreement or arrangement concluded by Member States.)

6.45 Service through foreign governments, judicial authorities and British Consular authorities

(1) Where the applicant wishes to serve an application form, or other document, on a respondent in any country which is a party to the Hague Convention, it may be served–

    (a) through the authority designated under the Hague Convention in respect of that country; or
    (b) if the law of that country permits–

        (i) through the judicial authorities of that country; or
        (ii) through a British Consular authority in that country.

(2) Where the applicant wishes to serve an application form, or other document, on a respondent in any country which is not a party to the Hague Convention, it may be served, if the law of that country so permits–

    (a) through the government of that country, where that government is willing to serve it; or

(b) through a British Consular authority in that country.
(3) Where the applicant wishes to serve an application form, or other document, in–
- (a) any Commonwealth State which is not a party to the Hague Convention;
- (b) the Isle of Man or the Channel Islands; or
- (c) any British Overseas Territory,

the methods of service permitted by paragraphs (1)(b) and (2) are not available and the applicant or the applicant's agent must effect service on a respondent in accordance with rule 6.43 unless Practice Direction 6B provides otherwise.

(4) This rule does not apply where service is to be effected in accordance with the Service Regulation.

(A list of British overseas territories is reproduced in Practice Direction 6B.)

6.46 Procedure where service is to be through foreign governments, judicial authorities and British Consular authorities

(1) This rule applies where the applicant wishes to serve an application form, or other document, under rule 6.45(1) or (2).
(2) Where this rule applies, the applicant must file–
- (a) a request for service of the application form, or other document, by specifying one or more of the methods in rule 6.45(1) or (2);
- (b) a copy of the application form or other document;
- (c) any other documents or copies of documents required by Practice Direction 6B; and
- (d) any translation required under rule 6.47.

(3) When the applicant files the documents specified in paragraph (2), the court officer will–
- (a) seal[GL], or otherwise authenticate with the stamp of the court, the copy of the application form or other document; and
- (b) forward the documents to the Senior Master of the Queen's Bench Division.

(4) The Senior Master will send documents forwarded under this rule–
- (a) where the application form, or other document, is being served through the authority designated under the Hague Convention, to that authority; or
- (b) in any other case, to the Foreign and Commonwealth Office with a request that it arranges for the application form or other document to be served.

(5) An official certificate which–
- (a) states that the method requested under paragraph (2)(a) has been performed and the date of such performance;
- (b) states, where more than one method is requested under paragraph (2)(a), which method was used; and
- (c) is made by–
    - (i) a British Consular authority in the country where the method requested under paragraph (2)(a) was performed;
    - (ii) the government or judicial authorities in that country; or
    - (iii) the authority designated in respect of that country under the Hague Convention,

is evidence of the facts stated in the certificate.

(6) A document purporting to be an official certificate under paragraph (5) is to be treated as such a certificate, unless it is proved not to be.

6.47 Translation of application form or other document

(1) Except where paragraphs (4) and (5) apply, every copy of the application form, or other

document, filed under rule 6.45 (service through foreign governments, judicial authorities and British Consular authorities) must be accompanied by a translation of the application form or other document.
(2) The translation must be–
   (a) in the official language of the country in which it is to be served; or
   (b) if there is more than one official language of that country, in any official language which is appropriate to the place in the country where the application form or other document is to be served.
(3) Every translation filed under this rule must be accompanied by a statement by the person making it that it is a correct translation, and the statement must include that person's name, address and qualifications for making the translation.
(4) The applicant is not required to file a translation of the application form, or other document, filed under rule 6.45 where it is to be served in a country of which English is an official language.
(5) The applicant is not required to file a translation of the application form or other document filed under rule 6.45 where–
   (a) the person on whom the document is to be served is able to read and understand English; and
   (b) service of the document is to be effected directly on that person.

(This rule does not apply to service in accordance with the Service Regulation which contains its own provisions about the translation of documents.)

6.48 Undertaking to be responsible for expenses of the Foreign and Commonwealth Office

Every request for service filed under rule 6.46 (procedure where service is to be through foreign governments, judicial authorities etc.) must contain an undertaking by the person making the request–
(a) to be responsible for all expenses incurred by the Foreign and Commonwealth Office or foreign judicial authority; and
(b) to pay those expenses to the Foreign and Commonwealth Office or foreign judicial authority on being informed of the amount.

PART 7 PROCEDURE FOR APPLICATIONS IN MATRIMONIAL AND CIVIL PARTNERSHIP PROCEEDINGS

CHAPTER 1 APPLICATION AND INTERPRETATION

7.1 Application and interpretation

(1) The rules in this Part apply to matrimonial and civil partnership proceedings.
(2) The rules in this Part do not apply to magistrates' courts.
(3) In this Part–
   'defended case' means matrimonial proceedings or civil partnership proceedings in which–
   (a) an answer has been filed opposing the grant of a matrimonial or civil partnership order on the application, and has not been struck out; or
   (b) the respondent has filed an application for a matrimonial or civil partnership order in accordance with rule 7.14 and neither party's application has been disposed of; or
   (c) rule 7.12(11) applies, notice has been given of intention to rebut and that notice has not been withdrawn,

and in which no matrimonial or civil partnership order has been made; and

'undefended case' means matrimonial proceedings or civil partnership proceedings other than a defended case.

(4) In this Part–

(a) a reference to a conditional order is a reference to a civil partnership order (other than a separation order) which has not been made final; and

(b) a reference to a final order is a reference to a conditional order which has been made final.

7.2 District Registries

A reference in this Part to a registry for a place at which sittings of the High Court in matrimonial or civil partnership proceedings are authorised is a reference–

(a) to the district registry for that place;

(b) where the place has no district registry, such district registry as the Lord Chancellor may designate for the purpose; or

(c) if the place is not situated within the district of any district registry, the principal registry.

7.3 Principal Registry

(1) A provision of this Part which refers to–

(a) proceedings being started or heard in a divorce county court or a civil partnership proceedings county court; or

(b) the transfer of proceedings to or from such a court,

includes a reference to the principal registry when treated as such a court.

(2) Proceedings to which this Part applies which were started in the principal registry or have been transferred to it as if it were a county court are treated as pending–

(a) if the proceedings are matrimonial proceedings, in a divorce county court; and

(b) if the proceedings are civil partnership proceedings, in a civil partnership proceedings county court.

7.4 References to respondents

(1) Where a respondent makes an application for a matrimonial order or a civil partnership order, unless the context otherwise requires, the rules in this Part shall apply with necessary modifications as if the reference to a respondent is a reference to the applicant in the other party's application for a matrimonial order or a civil partnership order.

(2) Where a respondent makes an application for a matrimonial order, unless the context otherwise requires, the rules in this Part shall apply with necessary modifications as if the reference to a co-respondent is a reference to a party cited in the respondent's application for a matrimonial order.

CHAPTER 2 RULES ABOUT STARTING AND RESPONDING TO PROCEEDINGS

7.5 Starting proceedings

(1) Matrimonial proceedings may be started in any divorce county court.

(2) Civil partnership proceedings may be started in any civil partnership proceedings county court.

7.6 Statement of reconciliation

Where the applicant is legally represented, the legal representative must, unless the court directs otherwise, complete and file with the application a statement in the form for this purpose referred to in Practice Direction 5A, certifying whether the legal representative has discussed with the applicant the possibility of a reconciliation and given the applicant the names and addresses of persons qualified to help effect a reconciliation.

7.7 Limitation on applications in respect of same marriage or civil partnership

(1) Subject to paragraph (2), a person may not make more than one application for a matrimonial or civil partnership order in respect of the same marriage or civil partnership unless–

 (a) the first application has been dismissed or finally determined; or
 (b) the court gives permission.

(2) Where a person–

 (a) has, within one year of the date of the marriage or civil partnership, made an application for, as the case may be, a decree of judicial separation or an order for separation; and
 (b) then, after that one-year period has passed, wishes to apply for a decree of divorce or a dissolution order on the same facts as those mentioned in the first application,

that person does not need the court's permission to make the application referred to in sub-paragraph (b).

7.8 Service of application

(1) After an application for a matrimonial or civil partnership order has been issued by the court, a copy of it must be served on the respondent and on any co-respondent.

(Rule 6.4 provides for who may serve an application for a matrimonial or civil partnership order.)

(2) When the application is served on a respondent it must be accompanied by–

 (a) a form for acknowledging service;
 (b) a notice of proceedings; and
 (c) where applicable, a copy of the statement of arrangements for children.

7.9 Withdrawal of application before service

An application for a matrimonial or civil partnership order may be withdrawn at any time before it has been served by giving notice in writing to the court where the proceedings were started.

7.10 Who the parties are

(1) The parties to matrimonial proceedings or civil partnership proceedings are–

 (a) the parties to the marriage or civil partnership concerned; and
 (b) any other person who is to be a party in accordance with a provision of the rules in this Part.

(2) Subject to paragraph (3), where an application for a matrimonial order or an answer to such an application alleges that the other party to the marriage has committed adultery with a named person, that named person is to be the co-respondent.

(3) The named person referred to in paragraph (2) is not to be a co-respondent where–

 (a) the court so directs;
 (b) that person has died; or
 (c) unless the court directs otherwise–
  (i) that person is under 16 years of age; or

(ii) the other party to the marriage is alleged in the application or answer to have committed rape on the named person.

(4) Where an application for a matrimonial or civil partnership order or an answer alleges that the other party to the marriage or civil partnership has had an improper association with a named person, the court may direct that the named person is to be a party to the application, unless the named person has died.

(5) An application for directions under paragraph (3)(a) or (c) may be made without notice if the acknowledgment of service indicates that no party intends to defend the case.

7.11 Nullity: Interim and full gender recognition certificates

(1) Where the application is for–

(a) nullity of marriage under section 12(g) of, or paragraph 11(1)(e) of Schedule 1 to, the 1973 Act; or

(b) an order of nullity of civil partnership under section 50(1)(d) of the 2004 Act,

the court officer must send to the Secretary of State a notice in writing that the application has been made.

(2) Where a copy of an interim gender recognition certificate has been filed with the application, that certificate must be attached to the notice.

(3) Where no copy of an interim gender recognition certificate has been filed the notice must also state–

(a) in matrimonial proceedings–

(i) the names of the parties to the marriage and the date and place of the marriage, and.

(ii) the last address at which the parties to the marriage lived together as husband and wife;

(b) in civil partnership proceedings–

(i) the names of the parties to the civil partnership and the date on, and the place at which, the civil partnership was formed, and.

(ii) the last address at which the parties to the civil partnership lived together as civil partners of each other; and

(c) in either case, such further particulars as the court officer considers appropriate.

(4) Where–

(a) the application is for a decree of nullity of marriage under section 12(h) of the 1973 Act or for an order of nullity of civil partnership under section 50(1)(e) of the 2004 Act; and

(b) a full gender recognition certificate has been issued to the respondent,

the applicant must file a copy of that full certificate with the application unless the court, on an application made without notice, directs otherwise.

7.12 What the respondent and co-respondent should do on receiving the application

(1) The respondent, and any co-respondent, must file an acknowledgment of service within 7 days beginning with the date on which the application for a matrimonial or civil partnership order was served.

(2) This rule is subject to rule 6.42 (which specifies how the period for filing an acknowledgment of service is calculated where the application is served out of the jurisdiction).

(3) The acknowledgment of service must–

(a) subject to paragraph (4), be signed by the respondent or the respondent's legal

　　　　　　　representative or, as the case may be, the co respondent or the co respondent's legal representative;
　　(b)　　include the respondent's or, as the case may be, the co respondent's address for service; and
　　(c)　　where it is filed by the respondent, indicate whether or not the respondent intends to defend the case.
(4) Where paragraph (5) or (6) applies, the respondent must sign the acknowledgment of service personally.
(5) This paragraph applies where–
　　(a)　　the application for a matrimonial order alleges that the respondent has committed adultery; and
　　(b)　　the respondent admits the adultery.
(6) This paragraph applies where–
　　(a)　　the application for a matrimonial or civil partnership order alleges that the parties to the marriage or civil partnership concerned have been separated for more than 2 years; and
　　(b)　　the respondent consents to the making of the matrimonial or civil partnership order.
(7) Where the respondent does not agree with the proposals set out in the applicant's statement of arrangements for children, the respondent may file a statement of arrangements for children under section 41(1) of the 1973 Act or section 63(1) of the 2004 Act.
(8) A respondent who wishes to defend the case must file and serve an answer within 21 days beginning with the date by which the acknowledgment of service is required to be filed.
(9) An answer is not required where the respondent does not object to the making of the matrimonial or civil partnership order but objects to paying the costs of the application or to the applicant's statement of arrangements for children.
(10) A respondent may file an answer even if the intention to do so was not indicated in the acknowledgment of service.
(11) Where the application is for nullity of marriage under section 12(d) of the 1973 Act or for nullity of civil partnership under section 50(1)(b) of the 2004 Act and the respondent files an answer containing no more than a simple denial of the facts stated in the application, the respondent must, if intending to rebut the matters stated in the application, give notice to the court of that intention when filing the answer.
(12) A respondent to an application for a matrimonial or civil partnership order alleging 2 years' separation and the respondent's consent may–
　　(a)　　indicate consent to the making of the matrimonial or civil partnership order in writing at any time after service of the application, whether in the acknowledgment of service or otherwise;
　　(b)　　indicate lack of consent to the making of that order, or withdraw any such consent already given, by giving notice to the court.
(13) Where a respondent gives a notice under paragraph (12)(b) and no other relevant fact is alleged, the proceedings must be stayed[GL], and notice of the stay[GL] given to the parties by the court officer.
(14) In this rule, a 'relevant fact' is–
　　(a)　　in matrimonial proceedings, one of the facts mentioned in section (1)(2) of the 1973 Act; and
　　(b)　　in civil partnership proceedings, one of the facts mentioned in section 44(5) of the 2004 Act.
(The form of the answer is referred to in Practice Direction 5A.)

7.13 Amendments to the application and the answer

(1) Unless paragraph (2) applies–

  (a) a party making an application for a matrimonial or civil partnership order may amend the application at any time before an answer to it has been filed;

  (b) a party who has filed an answer may amend the answer.

(2) No amendment to an application for a matrimonial or civil partnership order or to an answer may be made under paragraph (1) if an application under rule 7.19(1) has been made in relation to the marriage or civil partnership concerned.

(3) Where an amendment is made under paragraph (1)–

  (a) if the document amended is the application–

   (i) it must be served in accordance with rule 7.8 (service of application); and

   (ii) rule 7.12 (what the respondent and co respondent should do) applies;

  (b) rule 7.10 (parties) applies; and

  (c) any person who becomes a co-respondent to the proceedings in accordance with rule 7.10 as a consequence of such an amendment must be served with the documents required to be served on a co-respondent with an application for a matrimonial or civil partnership order.

(4) Paragraphs (1) and (2) do not apply if the amendment is made–

  (a) with the written consent of all the other parties; or

  (b) with the permission of the court.

(5) Where the court gives permission for a party to amend that party's application for a matrimonial or civil partnership order or answer it may give directions as to–

  (a) the service of the amended application or answer and any accompanying documents;

  (b) the joining of any additional parties in accordance with rule 7.10; and

  (c) the extent to which rule 7.12 must be complied with in respect of any amended application.

(6) The court may direct that any person cease to be a party if, in consequence of any amendment made under this rule, that person–

  (a) no longer falls within rule 7.10(2) or(4); or

  (b) falls within rule 7.10(4) but it is no longer desirable for that person to be a party to the proceedings.

7.14 How the respondent can make an application

(1) A respondent who wishes to make an application for a matrimonial or civil partnership order must make the application for that order within 21 days beginning with the date by which the respondent's acknowledgment of service is required to be filed, unless the court gives permission to make the application after that time has passed.

(2) Where the respondent makes an application under this rule, that application is to be treated as an application in the same proceedings for the purposes of this Part.

7.15 Further information about the contents of the application and the answer

(1) The court may at any time order a party–

  (a) to clarify any matter which is in dispute in the proceedings; or

  (b) to give additional information in relation to any such matter,

  whether or not the matter is contained or referred to in the application for a matrimonial or civil partnership order or in the answer.

(2) Paragraph (1) is subject to any rule of law to the contrary.

(3) Where the court makes an order under paragraph (1), the party against whom it is made must—

(a) file the reply to the order made under paragraph (1); and
(b) serve a copy of it on each of the other parties,

within the time specified by the court.

(4) The court may direct that information provided by a party to another party (whether given voluntarily or following an order made under paragraph (1)) must not be used for any purpose except for the proceedings in which it is given.

CHAPTER 3 HOW THE COURT DETERMINES MATRIMONIAL AND CIVIL PARTNERSHIP PROCEEDINGS

7.16 General rule – hearing to be in public

(1) The general rule is that a hearing to which this Part applies is to be in public.
(2) The requirement for a hearing to be in public does not require the court to make special arrangements for accommodating members of the public.
(3) A hearing, or any part of it, may be in private if—

(a) publicity would defeat the object of the hearing;
(b) it involves matters relating to national security;
(c) it involves confidential information (including information relating to personal financial matters) and publicity would damage that confidentiality;
(d) a private hearing is necessary to protect the interests of any child or protected party;
(e) it is a hearing of an application made without notice and it would be unjust to any respondent for there to be a public hearing; or
(f) the court considers this to be necessary, in the interests of justice.

(4) A hearing of an application for rescission of an order by consent under rule 7.28 is, unless the court directs otherwise, to be in private.
(5) The court may order that the identity of any party or witness must not be disclosed if it considers non-disclosure necessary in order to protect the interests of that party or witness.

7.17 Exercise of jurisdiction in cases heard at place other than the court in which the case is proceeding

Where a defended case is to be heard at a place other than the court in which it is proceeding, a judge of that other court may exercise all the powers that would be exercisable by a judge of the court in which the case is proceeding.

7.18 Notice of hearing

The court officer will give notice to the parties—

(a) of the date, time and place of every hearing which is to take place in a case to which they are a party; and
(b) in the case of a hearing following a direction under rule 7.20(2)(a), of the fact that, unless the person wishes or the court requires, the person need not attend.

7.19 Applications for a decree nisi or a conditional order

(1) An application may be made to the court for it to consider the making of a decree nisi, a conditional order, a decree of judicial separation or a separation order in the proceedings—

(a) at any time after the time for filing the acknowledgment of service has expired, provided that no party has filed an acknowledgment of service indicating an intention to defend the case; and

(b) in any other case, at any time after the time for filing an answer to every application for a matrimonial or civil partnership order made in the proceedings has expired.

(2) An application under paragraph (1) may be made–

    (a) in a case within paragraph (1)(a), by the applicant; and

    (b) in any other case, by either party to the marriage or civil partnership in question.

(3) An application under this rule must, if the information which was required to be provided by the application form is no longer correct, be accompanied by a statement setting out particulars of the change.

(4) If neither party has filed an answer opposing the making of a decree nisi, a conditional order, a decree of judicial separation or a separation order on the other's application, then an application under this rule must be accompanied by an affidavit–

    (a) stating whether there have been any changes in the information given in the application or in any statement of arrangements for children;

    (b) confirming that, subject to any changes stated, the contents of the application and any statement of arrangements for children are true; and

    (c) where the acknowledgment of service has been signed by the other party, confirming that party's signature on the acknowledgment of service.

7.20 What the court will do on an application for a decree nisi, a conditional order, a decree of judicial separation or a separation order

(1) This rule applies where an application is made under rule 7.19.

(2) If at the relevant time the case is an undefended case, the court must–

    (a) if satisfied that the applicant is entitled to–

        (i) in matrimonial proceedings, a decree nisi or a decree of judicial separation (as the case may be); or

        (ii) in civil partnership proceedings, a conditional order or a separation order (as the case may be),

    so certify and direct that the application be listed before a district judge for the making of the decree or order at the next available date;

    (b) if not so satisfied, direct–

        (i) that any party to the proceedings provide such further information, or take such other steps, as the court may specify; or

        (ii) that the case be listed for a case management hearing.

(3) If the applicant has applied for costs, the court may, on making a direction under paragraph (2)(a)–

    (a) if satisfied that the applicant is entitled to an order for costs, so certify; or

    (b) if not so satisfied, make no direction about costs.

(4) If at the relevant time the case is a defended case, the court must direct that the case be listed for a case management hearing.

(5) The court may, when giving a direction under paragraph (2)(b), direct that the further information provided be verified by an affidavit.

(6) The court must not give directions under this rule unless at the relevant time it is satisfied–

    (a) that a copy of each application for a matrimonial or civil partnership order or

answer (including any amended application or answer) has been properly served on each party on whom it is required to be served; and
- (b) that –
  - (i) in matrimonial proceedings, the application for a decree nisi or a decree of judicial separation; or
  - (ii) in civil partnership proceedings, the application for a conditional order or separation order,

  was made at a time permitted by rule 7.19(1).
- (7) In this rule, 'the relevant time' means the time at which the court is considering an application made under rule 7.19(1).

7.21 Further provisions about costs

(1) Subject to paragraph (2), any party to matrimonial or civil partnership proceedings may be heard on any question as to costs at the hearing of the proceedings.

(2) In the case of a hearing following a direction under rule 7.20(2)(a), a party will not be heard unless that party has, not less than 2 days before the hearing, served on every other party written notice of that party's intention to attend the hearing and apply for, or oppose the making of, an order for costs.

7.22 What the court must do for the case management hearing

(1) This rule applies to a case in which the court has directed a case management hearing under rule 7.20.

(2) Where a hearing has been directed under rule 7.20(4) the court must–
  - (a) decide where the hearing in the case should take place;
  - (b) set a timetable for the filing and service of evidence;
  - (c) make such order for the disclosure and inspection of documents as it considers appropriate; and
  - (d) give directions as to the conduct of the final hearing and the attendance of witnesses.

(Rule 21.1 explains what is meant by disclosure and inspection.)

(3) Where a hearing has been directed under rule 7.20(2)(b)(ii), the court must–
  - (a) consider what further evidence is required properly to dispose of the proceedings and give directions about the filing and service of such evidence;
  - (b) consider whether any further information is required about the arrangements for the children of the family and give directions about the filing and service of such information;
  - (c) give directions for the further conduct of the proceedings, including–
    - (i) giving a direction that on compliance with any directions under sub-paragraph (a) or (b) a further application may be made under rule 7.19(1) for the proceedings to be dealt with under rule 7.20(2)(a); or
    - (ii) giving a direction that the case is not suitable for determination under that rule.

(4) Where the court gives a direction under paragraph (3)(c)(ii), it may also give directions under paragraph (2) or direct that the case be listed for a further hearing at which such directions will be given.

(5) Any party to proceedings which are not being dealt with under rule 7.20(2)(a) may apply to the court for further directions at any time.

(Part 3 sets out the court's powers to encourage the parties to use alternative dispute resolution and Part 4 sets out the court's general case management powers.)

7.23 Where proceedings under this Part may be heard

A case, other than one dealt with under rule 7.20(2)(a), may be heard, where it is proceeding in the court set out in column 1 of the following table–

(a) in matrimonial proceedings, at the place referred to in column 2;
(b) in civil partnership proceedings, at the place referred to in column 3.

	Matrimonial Proceedings	Civil Partnership Proceedings
A county court.	Any divorce county court designated as a court of trial.	Any civil partnership proceedings county court designated as a court of trial.
The principal registry when proceedings are treated as pending in a county court.	The Royal Courts of Justice.	The Royal Courts of Justice.
The High Court (including the principal registry other than when proceedings are treated as pending in a county court).	a) The Royal Courts of Justice. b) Any court at which sittings of the High Court in matrimonial proceedings are authorised.	a) The Royal Courts of Justice. b) Any court at which sittings of the High Court in civil partnership proceedings are authorised.

7.24 The circumstances in which proceedings may be transferred between courts

(1) A court may transfer the hearing of a case which is due to be heard in one court to another court of the same type at which hearings of those proceedings are permitted under rule 7.23.

(2) A court in which matrimonial or civil partnership proceedings are pending may order them, or an application made in the course of them–

    (a) if the proceedings are pending in the High Court, to be transferred from the registry in which they are pending to another district registry;

    (b) if the proceedings are matrimonial proceedings pending in a divorce county court, to be transferred from that county court to another divorce county court; and

    (c) if the proceedings are civil partnership proceedings pending in a civil partnership proceedings county court, to be transferred from that county court to another civil partnership proceedings county court.

(3) An order transferring the hearing of an application must not be made under paragraph (2) unless it would be more convenient than transferring the proceedings themselves.

(4) No transfer may be made under this rule or under section 38 or 39 of the 1984 Act (transfers between High Court and a county court) unless–

    (a) the parties consent to the transfer;

    (b) the court has held a hearing to determine whether a transfer should be ordered; or

    (c) the court has transferred a case without a hearing where neither party has, within 14 days of being notified in writing of the court's intention to make such an order, requested a hearing to determine whether a transfer should be ordered.

(5) Proceedings–
- (a) which are transferred from the High Court to a divorce county court or a civil partnership proceedings county court and are to continue after the transfer in the principal registry are to be treated as pending in a divorce or civil partnership proceedings county court (as the case may be); and
- (b) which are transferred from a divorce county court or a civil partnership proceedings county court to the High Court and are to continue after the transfer in the principal registry are no longer to be treated as pending in a divorce or civil partnership proceedings county court (as the case may be).

(6) Proceedings transferred from a divorce county court or a civil partnership proceedings county court to the High Court are to proceed in the registry nearest to the court from which they were transferred unless–
- (a) the order transferring the proceedings directs otherwise; or
- (b) the court subsequently orders.

7.25 The procedure for complying with section 41 of 1973 Act or section 63 of 2004 Act

(1) Before the court–
- (a) gives a direction under rule 7.20(2)(a); or
- (b) makes–
   - (i) in matrimonial proceedings, a decree nisi or decree of judicial separation; or
   - (ii) in civil partnership proceedings, a conditional order or a separation order,

it must consider the matters set out in paragraph (2).

(2) The matters referred to in paragraph (1) are–
- (a) whether there are any children of the family to whom section 41(1) of the 1973 Act or section 63(1) of the 2004 Act (as the case may be) applies; and
- (b) if there are such children, and no application is pending in relation to them under Part 1 or 2 of the 1989 Act, the matters set out in section 41(1)(b) of the 1973 Act or in section 63(1)(b) of the 2004 Act (as the case may be).

(3) Where the court is satisfied that–
- (a) there are no children of the family to whom–
   - (i) in matrimonial proceedings, section 41 of the 1973 Act applies; and
   - (ii) in civil partnership proceedings, section 63 of the 2004 Act applies; or
- (b) there are such children but the court need not exercise its powers under the 1989 Act or its power to give a relevant direction with respect to any of them,

it must give a certificate to that effect.

(4) Where the court does not issue a certificate under paragraph (3) it may direct that–
- (a) the parties, or any of them, must file further evidence relating to the arrangements for the children and may direct what specific matters must be dealt with in that evidence;
- (b) a welfare report on the children, or any of them, be prepared;
- (c) the parties, or any of them, attend a hearing for the court to consider the matter.

(5) Where the court makes a direction under paragraph (4) or a relevant direction, it must state in writing–
- (a) its reasons for doing so; and

(b) in the case of a relevant direction, the exceptional circumstances which make it desirable in the interests of the child that the court should make such a direction.

(6) Nothing in this rule affects the court's power to make an order under the 1989 Act or a relevant direction.

(7) The court officer must send the parties–
- (a) a copy of any certificate given under paragraph (3);
- (b) a copy of any direction made under paragraph (4);
- (c) a copy of any relevant direction; and
- (d) a copy of any statement under paragraph (5).

(8) In this rule–

'parties' means a party to the marriage or civil partnership concerned and any person who appears to the court to have the care of any child of the family; and

'relevant direction' means–
- (a) in matrimonial proceedings, a direction under section 41(2) of the 1973 Act;
- (b) in civil partnership proceedings, a direction under section 63(2) of the 2004 Act.

7.26 Medical examinations in proceedings for nullity of marriage

(1) Where the application is for a decree of nullity of marriage on the ground of incapacity to consummate or wilful refusal to do so, the court must determine whether medical examiners should be appointed to examine the parties or either of them.

(2) The court must only appoint medical examiners under paragraph (1) where it considers that it is necessary for the proper disposal of the case.

(3) The person to be examined must, in the presence of the medical examiner, sign a statement identifying that person as the party to whom the order for examination applies.

(4) The medical examiner must certify on the same statement that it was signed in his or her presence by the person who has been examined.

(5) The person who carries out the examination must prepare a report and file it with the court by the date directed by the court.

(6) Either party is entitled to see a copy of a report filed under paragraph (5).

7.27 Stay of proceedings

(1) Where–
- (a) the court is considering an application in accordance with rule 7.20 or gives directions under rule 7.22;
- (b) it appears to the court that there are proceedings continuing in any country outside England and Wales which are in respect of the marriage or civil partnership in question or which are capable of affecting its validity or subsistence; and
- (c) the court considers that the question whether the proceedings should be stayed[GL] under paragraph 9 of Schedule 1 to the Domicile and Matrimonial Proceedings Act 1973 or, for civil partnership proceedings, under rules made under sections 75 and 76 of the Courts Act 2003,

the court must give directions for the hearing of that question.

(2) Where at any time after the making of an application under this Part it appears to the court in matrimonial proceedings that, under Articles 16 to 19 of the Council Regulation, the court does not have jurisdiction to hear the application and is or may be required to stay[GL] the proceedings, the court will–
- (a) stay[GL] the proceedings; and

(b) fix a date for a hearing to determine the questions of jurisdiction and whether there should be a further stay[GL] or other order.

(3) The court must give reasons for its decision under Articles 16 to 19 of the Council Regulation and, where it makes a finding of fact, state such finding of fact.

(4) An order under Article 17 of the Council Regulation that the court has no jurisdiction over the proceedings will be recorded by the court or the court officer in writing.

(5) The court may, if all parties agree, deal with any question about the jurisdiction of the court without a hearing.

CHAPTER 4   COURT ORDERS

7.28   The circumstances in which an order may be set aside (rescission)

(1) The court must not hear an application by a respondent for–

    (a) the rescission of a decree of divorce under section 10(1) of the 1973 Act;

    (b) the rescission of a dissolution order under section 48(1) of the 2004 Act,

less than 14 days after service of the application.

(2) Either party to the marriage concerned may apply–

    (a) after the decree nisi has been made but before it has been made absolute; or

    (b) after a decree of judicial separation has been made,

for the rescission of the decree on the grounds that the parties are reconciled and both consent to the rescission.

(3) Either party to the civil partnership concerned may apply–

    (a) after a conditional order has been made but before it has been made final; or

    (b) after a separation order has been made,

for the rescission of the order on the grounds that the parties are reconciled and both consent to the rescission.

7.29   Applications under section 10(2) of 1973 Act or section 48(2) of 2004 Act

Where the court makes–

(a) in the case of divorce, a decree absolute following an application under section 10(2) of the 1973 Act; or

(b) in the case of dissolution, a final order following an application under section 48(2) of the 2004 Act,

it must make a written record of the reasons for deciding to make that decree absolute or final order.

7.30   Orders under section 10A(2) of the 1973 Act

(1) Where the court has made an order under section 10A(2) of the 1973 Act, the declaration referred to in that section must–

    (a) be made and signed by both parties to the marriage concerned;

    (b) give particulars of the proceedings in which the order was obtained;

    (c) confirm that the steps required to dissolve the marriage in accordance with the religious usages appropriate to the parties have been taken;

    (d) be accompanied by–

        (i) a certificate from a relevant religious authority that all such steps have been taken; or

        (ii) such other documents showing the relevant steps have been taken as the court may direct; and

(iii) be filed at the court either before or together with an application to make the decree nisi absolute,

under rule 7.32 or 7.33.

(2) Where the certificate referred to in paragraph (1)(d)(i) is not in English it must be accompanied by a translation of that certificate into English, certified by a notary public or authenticated by statement of truth.

(3) The court may direct that the declaration need not be accompanied by the material mentioned in paragraph (1)(d).

(4) In this rule a religious authority is 'relevant' if the party who made the application for the order under section 10A(2) of the 1973 Act considers that authority competent to confirm that the steps referred to in paragraph (1)(c) have been taken.

7.31 Applications to prevent decrees nisi being made absolute or conditional orders being made final

(1) This rule applies to an application under section 8 or 9 of the 1973 Act or under section 39 or 40 of the 2004 Act to prevent–

   (a) in the case of divorce or nullity of marriage, a decree nisi being made absolute; or

   (b) in the case of dissolution or nullity of civil partnership, a conditional order being made final.

(2) An application to which this rule applies must be made using the Part 18 procedure, subject to paragraphs (3) to (6) of this rule.

(3) The person making an application to which this rule applies must within 28 days of filing the application apply to the court to give directions for the hearing of the application.

(4) Where the person making an application to which this rule applies does not apply for directions under paragraph (3), then the person in whose favour the decree nisi or conditional order (as the case may be) was made may do so.

(5) Rule 7.22(2) applies to an application to which this rule applies as it applies to an application for a matrimonial or civil partnership order.

(6) Where an application to which this rule applies is made by the Queen's Proctor–

   (a) the Queen's Proctor may give written notice, to the court and to the party in whose favour the decree nisi or conditional order (as the case may be) was made, of the Queen's Proctor's intention to make an application to prevent the decree nisi being made absolute or the conditional order being made final; and

   (b) where the Queen's Proctor does so the application under paragraph (1) must be made within 21 days beginning with the date on which the notice is given.

7.32 Making decrees nisi absolute or conditional orders final by giving notice

(1) Unless rule 7.33 applies–

   (a) in matrimonial proceedings, a spouse in whose favour a decree nisi has been made may give notice to the court that he or she wishes the decree nisi to be made absolute; or

   (b) in civil partnership proceedings, a civil partner in whose favour a conditional order has been made may give notice to the court that he or she wishes the conditional order to be made final.

(2) Subject to paragraphs (3) and (4), where the court receives a notice under paragraph (1) it will make the decree nisi absolute or the conditional order final (as the case may be) if it is satisfied that–

   (a) no application for rescission of the decree nisi or the conditional order is pending;

(b) no appeal against the making of the decree nisi or the conditional order is pending;
(c) no order has been made by the court extending the time for bringing an appeal of the kind mentioned in sub-paragraph (b), or if such an order has been made, that the time so extended has expired;
(d) no application for an order of the kind mentioned in sub-paragraph (c) is pending;
(e) no application to prevent the decree nisi being made absolute or the conditional order being made final is pending;
(f) the court has complied with section 41(1) of the 1973 Act or section 63(1) of the 2004 Act, as the case may be, and has not given any direction under subsection (2) of either of those sections;
(g) the provisions of section 10(2) to (4) of the 1973 Act or section 48(2) to (4) of the 2004 Act do not apply or have been complied with;
(h) any order under section 10A(2) of the 1973 Act has been complied with; and
(i) where the decree nisi was made on the ground in section 12(g) of, or paragraph 11(1)(e) of Schedule 1 to, the 1973 Act, or the conditional order was made under section 50(1)(d) of the 2004 Act—
  (i) there is not pending a reference under section 8(5) of the Gender Recognition Act 2004 in respect of the application on which the interim gender recognition certificate to which the application relates was granted;
  (ii) that interim certificate has not been revoked under section 8(6)(b) of that Act; and
  (iii) no appeal is pending against an order under section 8(6)(a) of that Act.

(3) Where the notice is received more than 12 months after the making of the decree nisi or the conditional order, it must be accompanied by an explanation in writing stating—
(a) why the application has not been made earlier;
(b) whether the applicant and respondent have lived together since the decree nisi or the conditional order was made, and, if so, between what dates;
(c) if the applicant is female, whether she has given birth to a child since the decree nisi or the conditional order was made and whether it is alleged that the child is or may be a child of the family;
(d) if the respondent is female, whether the applicant has reason to believe that she has given birth to a child since the decree nisi or the conditional order was made and whether it is alleged that the child is or may be a child of the family.

(4) Where paragraph (3) applies, the court may—
(a) require the applicant to file an affidavit verifying the explanation; and
(b) make such order on the application as it thinks fit, but where it orders the decree nisi to be made absolute or the conditional order to be made final that order is not to take effect until the court is satisfied that none of the matters mentioned in paragraph (2)(a) to (i) applies.

7.33 Applications to make decrees nisi absolute or conditional orders final

(1) An application must be made—
(a) in matrimonial proceedings, for the decree nisi to be made absolute; or
(b) in civil partnership proceedings, for the conditional order to be made final,
where the conditions set out in paragraph (2) apply.

(2) The conditions referred to in paragraph (1) are—
(a) the Queen's Proctor gives notice to the court under rule 7.31(6)(a) and has not withdrawn that notice;

(b) there are other circumstances which ought to be brought to the attention of the court before the application is granted; or
(c) the application is made–
   (i) in matrimonial proceedings, by the spouse against whom the decree nisi was made; or
   (ii) in civil partnership proceedings, by the civil partner against whom the conditional order was made.

(3) An application under this rule to which paragraph (2)(a) applies must be–
   (a) made to a judge, but not a district judge; and
   (b) served on the Queen's Proctor.

(4) Where the court orders–
   (a) in matrimonial proceedings, a decree to be made absolute under this rule; or
   (b) in civil partnership proceedings, a conditional order to be made final under this rule,

that order is not to take effect until the court is satisfied about the matters mentioned in rule 7.32(2)(a) to (i).

7.34 What the court officer must do when a decree nisi is made absolute

In matrimonial proceedings, where a decree nisi is made absolute the court officer must–
(a) endorse that fact on the decree nisi together with the precise time at which the decree was made absolute; and
(b) send a certificate that a decree nisi has been made absolute to the applicant, the respondent, any co-respondent and any other party.

7.35 What the court officer must do when a conditional order is made final

Where a conditional order is made final the court officer must–
(a) endorse that fact on the conditional order together with the precise time at which the order was made final; and
(b) send the final order to the applicant, the respondent and any other party.

7.36 Records of decrees absolute and final orders

(1) A central index of decrees absolute and final orders must be kept under the control of the principal registry.
(2) Any person, on payment of the prescribed fee, may require a search to be made of that index and to be provided with a certificate showing the results of that search.
(3) Any person who requests it must, on payment of the prescribed fee, be issued with a copy of the decree absolute or final order.

PART 8   PROCEDURE FOR MISCELLANEOUS APPLICATIONS

CHAPTER 1   PROCEDURE

8.1 Procedure

Subject to rules 8.13 and 8.24, applications to which this Part applies must be made in accordance with the Part 19 procedure.

CHAPTER 2 APPLICATION FOR CORRECTED GENDER RECOGNITION CERTIFICATE

8.2 Scope of this Chapter

The rules in this Chapter apply to an application under section 6(1) of the Gender Recognition Act 2004 for the correction of a full gender recognition certificate issued under section 5(1) or 5A(1) of that Act.

8.3 Where to start proceedings

The application must be made to the court which issued the original certificate unless the court directs otherwise.

8.4 Who the parties are

Where the applicant is–

(a) the person to whom the original certificate was issued, the Secretary of State must be a respondent;
(b) the Secretary of State, the person to whom the original certificate was issued must be a respondent.

8.5 Delivery of copy certificate to Secretary of State

Where the court issues a corrected full gender recognition certificate, a court officer must send a copy of the corrected certificate to the Secretary of State.

CHAPTER 3 APPLICATION FOR ALTERATION OF MAINTENANCE AGREEMENT AFTER DEATH OF ONE PARTY

8.6 Scope of this Chapter

The rules in this Chapter apply to an application under section 36 of the 1973 Act or paragraph 73 of Schedule 5 to the 2004 Act to alter a maintenance agreement after the death of one of the parties.

8.7 Where to start proceedings

(1) The application may be made in the High Court or a county court.
(2) Where the application is made in a county court it must be made in the divorce county court or civil partnership proceedings county court for the district in which–

    (a) the deceased resided at the time of death; or
    (b) if the deceased did not reside in England and Wales at the time of death–

        (i) the respondent or one of the respondents resides or carries on business; or
        (ii) where the respondent is the personal representative of the deceased, the deceased's estate is situated; or

    (c) if neither (a) nor (b) applies–

        (i) the applicant resides or carries on business; or
        (ii) where the applicant is the personal representative of the deceased, the deceased's estate is situated.

8.8 Who the parties are

(1) Where the applicant is–

(a) the surviving party to the agreement, the personal representative of the deceased must be a respondent;
(b) the personal representative of the deceased, the surviving party to the agreement must be a respondent.

(2) The court may at any time direct that–
(a) any person be made a party to proceedings; or
(b) a party be removed.

8.9 Representative parties

(1) The court may, before or after the application has been filed at court, make an order appointing a person to represent any other person or persons in the application where the person or persons to be represented–
(a) are unborn;
(b) cannot be found;
(c) cannot easily be ascertained; or
(d) are a class of persons who have the same interest in an application and–
  (i) one or more members of that class are within sub-paragraphs (a), (b) or (c); or
  (ii) to appoint a representative would further the overriding objective.

(2) An application for an order under paragraph (1) may be made by–
(a) any person who seeks to be appointed under the order; or
(b) any party to the application.

(3) An application for an order under paragraph (1) must be served on–
(a) all parties to the application to alter the maintenance agreement, if that application has been filed at court;
(b) the person sought to be appointed, if that person is not the applicant or a party to the application; and
(c) any other person as directed by the court.

(4) The court's approval is required to settle proceedings in which a party is acting as a representative.

(5) The court may approve a settlement where it is satisfied that the settlement is for the benefit of all the represented persons.

(6) Unless the court directs otherwise, any order made on an application in which a party is acting as a representative–
(a) is binding on all persons represented in the proceedings; and
(b) may only be enforced by or against a person who is not a party with the permission of the court.

(7) An application may be brought by or against trustees, executors or administrators without adding as parties any persons who have a beneficial interest in the trust or estate and any order made on the application is binding on the beneficiaries unless the court orders otherwise.

8.10 Acknowledgment of service

(1) A respondent who is a personal representative of the deceased must file with the acknowledgment of service a statement setting out–
(a) full particulars of the value of the deceased's estate for probate after providing for the discharge of the funeral, testamentary and administration expenses, debts and liabilities (including inheritance tax and interest); and
(b) the people (including names, addresses and details of any persons under

disability) or classes of people beneficially interested in the estate and the value of their interests so far as ascertained.

(2) The respondent must file the acknowledgment of service and any statement required under this rule within 28 days beginning with the date on which the application is served.

8.11 Hearings may be in private

The court may decide to hear any application to which this Chapter applies in private.

CHAPTER 4   APPLICATION FOR QUESTION AS TO PROPERTY TO BE DECIDED IN SUMMARY WAY

8.12 Scope of this Chapter

The rules in this Chapter apply to an application under section 17 of the Married Women's Property Act 1882 or section 66 of the 2004 Act.

8.13 Procedure

Where an application for an order under section 17 of the Married Women's Property Act 1882 or section 66 of the 2004 Act is made in any proceedings for a financial order, the application must be made in accordance with the Part 18 procedure.

8.14 Where to start proceedings

(1) The application may be made in the High Court or a county court.
(2) Where the application is made in a county court it must be made in the court–

   (a) in which any matrimonial proceedings or civil partnership proceedings have been started or are intended to be started by the applicant or the respondent; or
   (b) in the absence of any such proceedings, for the district in which the applicant or respondent resides.

(3) The application may be made to the principal registry as if it were a county court if–

   (a) any matrimonial proceedings or civil partnership proceedings have been started there or are intended to be started there by the applicant or the respondent; and
   (b) those proceedings are or will be treated as pending in a divorce county court or civil partnership proceedings county court.

8.15 Mortgagees as parties

(1) Where particulars of a mortgage are provided with the application–

   (a) the applicant must serve a copy of the application on the mortgagee; and
   (b) the mortgagee may, within 14 days beginning with the date on which the application was received, file an acknowledgment of service and be heard on the application.

(2) The court must direct that a mortgagee be made a party to the proceedings where the mortgagee requests to be one.

8.16 Injunctions

(1) The court may grant an injunction[GL] only if the injunction[GL] is ancillary or incidental to the assistance sought by the applicant.
(2) Applications for injunctive relief must be made in accordance with the procedure in rule 20.4 (how to apply for an interim remedy) and the provisions of rule 20.5 (interim injunction[GL] to cease if application is stayed[GL]) apply.

8.17 Application of other rules

Rule 9.24 applies where the court has made an order for sale under section 17 of the Married Women's Property Act 1882 or section 66 of the 2004 Act.

CHAPTER 5   DECLARATIONS

8.18 Scope of this Chapter

The rules in this Chapter apply to applications made in accordance with—
(a) section 55 of the 1986 Act (declarations as to marital status) and section 58 of the 2004 Act (declarations as to civil partnership status);
(b) section 55A of the 1986 Act (declarations of parentage);
(c) section 56(1)(b) and (2) of the 1986 Act (declarations of legitimacy or legitimation); and
(d) section 57 of the 1986 Act (declarations as to adoptions effected overseas).

8.19 Where to start proceedings

The application may be made in the High Court or a county court and applications under section 55A of the 1986 Act may also be made in a magistrates' court.

8.20 Who the parties are

(1) In relation to the proceedings set out in column 1 of the following table, column 2 sets out who the respondents to those proceedings will be.

Proceedings	Respondent
Applications for declarations as to marital or civil partnership status.	The other party to the marriage or civil partnership in question or, where the applicant is a third party, both parties to the marriage or civil partnership.
Applications for declarations of parentage.	The person whose parentage is in issue or any person who is or is alleged to be the parent of the person whose parentage is in issue.
Applications for declarations of legitimacy or legitimation.	The applicant's father and mother or the survivor of them.
Applications for declarations as to adoption effected overseas.	The person(s) whom the applicant is claiming are or are not the applicant's adoptive parents.

(2) The applicant must include in his application particulars of every person whose interest may be affected by the proceedings and his relationship to the applicant.
(3) The acknowledgment of service filed under rule 19.5 must give details of any other persons the respondent considers should be made a party to the application or be given notice of the application.
(4) Upon receipt of the acknowledgment of service, the court must give directions as to any other persons who should be made a respondent to the application or be given notice of the proceedings.
(5) A person given notice of proceedings under paragraph (4) may, within 21 days beginning with the date on which the notice was served, apply to be joined as a party.
(6) No directions may be given as to the future management of the case under rule 19.9 until the expiry of the notice period in paragraph (5).

8.21 The role of the Attorney General

(1) The applicant must, except in the case of an application for a declaration of parentage, send a copy of the application and all accompanying documents to the Attorney General at least one month before making the application.
(2) The Attorney General may, when deciding whether to intervene in the proceedings, inspect any document filed at court relating to any family proceedings mentioned in the declaration proceedings.
(3) If the court is notified that the Attorney General wishes to intervene in the proceedings, a court officer must send the Attorney General a copy of any subsequent documents filed at court.
(4) The court must, when giving directions under rule 8.20(4), consider whether to ask the Attorney General to argue any question relating to the proceedings.
(5) If the court makes a request to the Attorney General under paragraph (4) and the Attorney General agrees to that request, the Attorney General must serve a summary of the argument on all parties to the proceedings.

8.22 Declarations of parentage

(1) If the applicant or the person whose parentage or parenthood is in issue, is known by a name other than that which appears in that person's birth certificate, that other name must also be stated in any order and declaration of parentage.
(2) A court officer must send a copy of a declaration of parentage and the application to the Registrar General within 21 days beginning with the date on which the declaration was made.

CHAPTER 6 APPLICATION FOR PERMISSION TO APPLY FOR A FINANCIAL REMEDY AFTER OVERSEAS PROCEEDINGS

8.23 Scope of this Chapter

Subject to rule 9.26(6), the rules in this Chapter apply to an application for permission to apply for a financial remedy under section 13 of the 1984 Act and paragraph 4 of Schedule 7 to the 2004 Act.

(Rule 9.26(6) enables the application for permission to apply for a financial remedy under section 13 of the 1984 Act or paragraph 4 of Schedule 7 to the 2004 Act to be heard at the same time as the application for a financial remedy under Part 3 of the 1984 Act or Schedule 7 to the 2004 Act where that application is an application for a consent order.)

8.24 Where and how to start proceedings

(1) Subject to paragraph (2), the application must be made in the principal registry.
(2) Where rule 9.26(6) applies, the application must be made in the court hearing the application for a financial remedy.

(Rule 9.5(2) specifies the court where the application for the consent order should be filed.)
(3) The application must be made in accordance with the Part 18 procedure.

8.25 Application to be made without notice

(1) The court may grant an application made without notice if it appears to the court that there are good reasons for not giving notice.
(2) If the applicant makes an application without giving notice, the applicant must state the reasons why notice has not been given.

8.26 Notification of hearing date

The court officer must–

(a) fix a date, time and place for the hearing of the application by a judge, but not a district judge; and
(b) give notice of the date of the hearing to the applicant.

8.27 Hearings to be in private unless the court directs otherwise

An application under this Chapter must be heard in private unless the court directs otherwise.

8.28 Direction that application be dealt with by a district judge of the principal registry

If the application is granted, the judge may direct that the application for a financial remedy under Part 3 of the 1984 Act or Schedule 7 to the 2004 Act may be heard by a district judge of the principal registry.

CHAPTER 7 APPLICATION FOR THE TRANSFER OF A TENANCY UNDER SECTION 53 OF, AND SCHEDULE 7 TO, THE 1996 ACT

8.29 Scope of this Chapter

This Chapter applies to an application for the transfer of a tenancy under section 53 of, and Schedule 7 to, the 1996 Act.

8.30 Where to start proceedings

(1) Subject to paragraph (2), the application may be made in the High Court or a county court.
(2) The application must be made to the court in which any divorce, judicial separation, nullity or civil partnership proceedings are pending between the parties.

8.31 Service of the application

(1) The court will serve a copy of the application on–
　　(a)　the respondent; and
　　(b)　the landlord (as defined by paragraph 1 of Schedule 7 to the 1996 Act),
　　unless the court directs that the applicant must do so.
(2) Where service is effected by the applicant, the applicant must file a certificate of service.

8.32 Who the parties are

The court will direct that a landlord be made a party to the proceedings where the landlord requests to be one.

8.33 Orders for disclosure

Any party may apply to the court under rule 21.2 for an order that any person must attend an appointment before the court and produce any documents that are specified or described in the order.

8.34 Injunctions

(1) The court may grant an injunction[GL] only if the injunction[GL] is ancillary or incidental to the assistance sought by the applicant.
(2) Applications for injunctive relief must be made in accordance with the procedure in rule 20.4 (how to apply for an interim remedy) and the provisions of rule 20.5 (interim injunction[GL] to cease if application is stayed[GL]) apply accordingly.

CHAPTER 8   APPLICATIONS FOR ORDERS PREVENTING AVOIDANCE UNDER SECTION 32L OF THE CHILD SUPPORT ACT 1991

8.35   Scope of this Chapter

Subject to rule 8.40, the rules in this Chapter apply to applications made under section 32L (1) and (2) of the 1991 Act.

8.36   Interpretation

In this Chapter–

'child support maintenance' has the meaning assigned to it in section 3(6) of the 1991 Act;

'reviewable disposition' has the meaning assigned to it in section 32L(5) of the 1991 Act.

8.37   Where to start proceedings

(1) The application must be made to the High Court and be filed in–

  (a)   the principal registry; or
  (b)   any district registry.

(2) The application may be heard by a judge but not a district judge except–

  (a)   a district judge of the principal registry of the Family Division; or
  (b)   a district judge in a district registry who is directed by a judge to hear the application.

(Section 32L(10)(a) of the 1991 Act defines 'court' for the purposes of section 32L as being the High Court only.)

8.38   Who the parties are

(1) The applicant to the proceedings is the Commission and the respondent is the person who has failed to pay child support maintenance.

(2) The court may at any time direct that–

  (a)   any person be made a party to proceedings; or
  (b)   a party be removed from the proceedings.

8.39   Service of the application

(1) The applicant must serve the application and a copy of the applicant's written evidence on–

  (a)   any respondent;
  (b)   the person in whose favour the reviewable disposition is alleged to have been made; and
  (c)   such other persons as the court directs.

(2) Where an application includes an application relating to land, the applicant must serve a copy of the application on any–

  (a)   mortgagee;
  (b)   trustee of a trust of land or settlement; and
  (c)   other person who has an interest in the land,

of whom particulars are given in the application.

(3) Any person served under paragraph (2) may make a request to the court in writing, within 14 days beginning with the date of service of the application, for a copy of the applicant's written evidence.

(4) Any person who–

(a) is served with copies of the application and the applicant's written evidence under paragraph (1); or
(b) receives a copy of the applicant's written evidence following a request under paragraph (3),

may, within 14 days beginning with the date of service or receipt, file a statement in answer.

(5) A statement in answer filed under paragraph (4) must be verified by a statement of truth.

8.40 Applications without notice

(1) This rule applies to an application under section 32L(1) of the 1991 Act.
(2) The court may grant an application made without notice if it appears to the court that there are good reasons for not giving notice.
(3) If the applicant makes an application without giving notice, the evidence in support of the application must state the reasons why notice has not been given.
(4) If the court grants an application under paragraph (2)–
   (a) the order must include a provision allowing any respondent to apply to the court for an order to be reconsidered as soon as just and convenient at a full hearing; and
   (b) the applicant must, as soon as reasonably practicable, serve upon each respondent a copy of the order and a copy of the written evidence in support of the application.

CHAPTER 9 APPLICATION FOR CONSENT TO MARRIAGE OF A CHILD OR TO REGISTRATION OF CIVIL PARTNERSHIP OF A CHILD

8.41 Scope of this Chapter

The rules in this Chapter apply to an application under–

(a) section 3 of the Marriage Act 1949; or
(b) paragraph 3, 4 or 10 of Schedule 2 to the 2004 Act.

8.42 Child acting without a children's guardian

The child may bring an application without a children's guardian, unless the court directs otherwise.

8.43 Who the respondents are

Where an application follows a refusal to give consent to–

(a) the marriage of a child; or
(b) a child registering as the civil partner of another person,

every person who has refused consent will be a respondent to the application.

PART 9 APPLICATIONS FOR A FINANCIAL REMEDY

CHAPTER 1 APPLICATION AND INTERPRETATION

9.1 Application

The rules in this Part apply to an application for a financial remedy.

('Financial remedy' and 'financial order' are defined in rule 2.3)

Family Procedure Rules 2010   155

9.2   Application of Magistrates' Courts Rules 1981

Unless the context otherwise requires, and subject to the rules in this Part, the following rules of the Magistrates' Courts Rules 1981 apply to proceedings in a magistrates' court which are family proceedings under section 65 of the Magistrates' Courts Act 1980–

(a)   rule 39(6) (method of making periodical payments);
(b)   rule 41 (revocation etc. of orders for periodical payments);
(c)   rule 43 (service of copy of order);
(d)   rule 44 (remission of sums due under order);
(e)   rule 45 (duty of designated officer to notify subsequent marriage or formation of civil partnership of person entitled to payments under a maintenance order);
(f)   rule 48 (to whom payments are to be made);
(g)   rule 49 (duty of designated officer to give receipt);
(h)   rule 51 (application for further time);
(i)   rule 62 (particulars relating to payment of lump sum under a magistrates' courts maintenance order etc. to be entered in register);
(j)   rule 66 (register of convictions, etc.);
(k)   rule 67 (proof of service, handwriting, etc.);
(l)   rule 68 (proof of proceedings); and
(m)   rule 69 (proof that magistrates' court maintenance orders, etc, have not been revoked, etc.).

9.3   Interpretation

(1)   In this Part–

'avoidance of disposition order' means–

(a)   in proceedings under the 1973 Act, an order under section 37(2)(b) or (c) of that Act;
(b)   in proceedings under the 1984 Act, an order under section 23(2)(b) or 23(3) of that Act;
(c)   in proceedings under Schedule 5 to the 2004 Act, an order under paragraph 74(3) or (4); or
(d)   in proceedings under Schedule 7 to the 2004 Act, an order under paragraph 15(3) or (4);

'the Board' means the Board of the Pension Protection Fund;

'FDR appointment' means a Financial Dispute Resolution appointment in accordance with rule 9.17;

'order preventing a disposition' means–

(a)   in proceedings under the 1973 Act, an order under section 37(2)(a) of that Act;
(b)   in proceedings under the 1984 Act, an order under section 23(2)(a) of that Act;
(c)   in proceedings under Schedule 5 to the 2004 Act, an order under paragraph 74(2); or
(d)   in proceedings under Schedule 7 to the 2004 Act, an order under paragraph 15(2);

'pension arrangement' means–

(a)   an occupational pension scheme;
(b)   a personal pension scheme;
(c)   shareable state scheme rights;
(d)   a retirement annuity contract;
(e)   an annuity or insurance policy purchased, or transferred, for the purpose of giving effect to rights under an occupational pension scheme or a personal pension scheme; and
(f)   an annuity purchased, or entered into, for the purpose of discharging liability in

respect of a pension credit under section 29(1)(b) of the Welfare Reform and Pensions Act 1999 or under corresponding Northern Ireland legislation;

'pension attachment order' means–

(a)   in proceedings under the 1973 Act, an order making provision under section 25B or 25C of that Act;
(b)   in proceedings under the 1984 Act, an order under section 17(1)(a)(i) of that Act making provision equivalent to an order referred to in paragraph (a);
(c)   in proceedings under Schedule 5 to the 2004 Act, an order making provision under paragraph 25 or paragraph 26; or
(d)   in proceedings under Schedule 7 to the 2004 Act, an order under paragraph 9(2) or (3) making provision equivalent to an order referred to in paragraph (c);

'pension compensation attachment order' means–

(a)   in proceedings under the 1973 Act, an order making provision under section 25F of that Act;
(b)   in proceedings under the 1984 Act, an order under section 17(1)(a)(i) of that Act making provision equivalent to an order referred in to paragraph (a);
(c)   in proceedings under Schedule 5 to the 2004 Act, an order under paragraph 34A; and
(d)   in proceedings under Schedule 7 to the 2004 Act, an order under paragraph 9(2) or (3) making provision equivalent to an order referred to in paragraph (c);

'pension compensation sharing order' means–

(a)   in proceedings under the 1973 Act, an order under section 24E of that Act;
(b)   in proceedings under the 1984 Act, an order under section 17(1)(c) of that Act;
(c)   in proceedings under Schedule 5 to the 2004 Act, an order under paragraph 19A; and
(d)   in proceedings under Schedule 7 to the 2004 Act, an order under paragraph 9(2) or (3) making provision equivalent to an order referred to in paragraph (c);

'pension sharing order' means–

(a)   in proceedings under the 1973 Act, an order making provision under section 24B of that Act;
(b)   in proceedings under the 1984 Act, an order under section 17(1)(b) of that Act;
(c)   in proceedings under Schedule 5 to the 2004 Act, an order under paragraph 15; or
(d)   in proceedings under Schedule 7 to the 2004 Act, an order under paragraph 9(2) or (3) making provision equivalent to an order referred to in paragraph (c);

'pension scheme' means, unless the context otherwise requires, a scheme for which the Board has assumed responsibility in accordance with Chapter 3 of Part 2 of the Pensions Act 2004 (pension protection) or any provision in force in Northern Ireland corresponding to that Chapter;

'PPF compensation' has the meaning given to it–

(a)   in proceedings under the 1973 Act, by section 21C of the 1973 Act;
(b)   in proceedings under the 1984 Act, by section 18(7) of the 1984 Act; and
(c)   in proceedings under the 2004 Act, by paragraph 19F of Schedule 5 to the 2004 Act;

'relevant valuation' means a valuation of pension rights or benefits as at a date not more than 12 months earlier than the date fixed for the first appointment which has been furnished or requested for the purposes of any of the following provisions–

(a)   the Pensions on Divorce etc (Provision of Information) Regulations 2000;
(b)   regulation 5 of and Schedule 2 to the Occupational Pension Schemes (Disclosure of Information) Regulations 1996 and regulation 11 of and Schedule 1 to the Occupational Pension Schemes (Transfer Value) Regulations 1996;

(c) section 93A or 94(1)(a) or (aa) of the Pension Schemes Act 1993;
(d) section 94(1)(b) of the Pension Schemes Act 1993 or paragraph 2(a) (or, where applicable, 2(b)) of Schedule 2 to the Personal Pension Schemes (Disclosure of Information) Regulations 1987;
(e) the Dissolution etc. (Pensions) Regulations 2005;

'variation order' means–
(a) in proceedings under the 1973 Act, an order under section 31 of that Act; or
(b) in proceedings under the 2004 Act, an order under Part 11 of Schedule 5 to that Act.

(2) References in this Part to a county court are to be construed, in relation to proceedings for a financial order, as references to a divorce county court or a civil partnership proceedings county court, as the case may be.

CHAPTER 2   PROCEDURE FOR APPLICATIONS

9.4   When an Application for a financial order may be made

An application for a financial order may be made–
(a) in an application for a matrimonial or civil partnership order; or
(b) at any time after an application for a matrimonial or civil partnership order has been made.

9.5   Where to start proceedings

(1) An application for a financial remedy must be filed–
   (a) if there are proceedings for a matrimonial order or a civil partnership order which are proceeding in a designated county court, in that court; or
   (b) if there are proceedings for a matrimonial order or a civil partnership order which are proceeding in the High Court, in the registry in which those proceedings are taking place.

(2) In any other case, in relation to the application set out in column 1 of the following table, column 2 sets out where the application must be filed.

Provision under which application is made	Court where application must be filed
Section 27 of the 1973 Act.	Divorce county court.
Part 9 of Schedule 5 to the 2004 Act.	Civil partnership proceedings county court.
Part 3 of the 1984 Act.	Principal Registry or, in relation to an application for a consent order, a divorce county court.
Schedule 7 to the 2004 Act.	Principal Registry or, in relation to an application for a consent order, a civil partnership proceedings county court.
Section 35 of the 1973 Act.	High Court, a divorce county court or a magistrates' court.
Paragraph 69 of Schedule 5 to the 2004 Act.	High Court, a civil partnership proceedings county court or a magistrates' court.

Provision under which application is made	Court where application must be filed
Schedule 1 to the 1989 Act.	High Court, designated county court or a magistrates' court.
Part 1 of the 1978 Act.	magistrates' court.
Schedule 6 to the 2004 Act.	magistrates' court.

(3) An application for a financial remedy under Part 3 of the 1984 Act or Schedule 7 to the 2004 Act which is proceeding in the High Court must be heard by a judge, but not a district judge, of that court unless a direction has been made that the application may be heard by a district judge of the principal registry.

(Rule 8.28 enables a judge to direct that an application for a financial remedy under Part 3 of the 1984 Act or Schedule 7 to the 2004 Act may be heard by a district judge of the principal registry.)

9.6 Application for an order preventing a disposition

(1) The Part 18 procedure applies to an application for an order preventing a disposition.
(2) An application for an order preventing a disposition may be made without notice to the respondent.

('Order preventing a disposition' is defined in rule 9.3.)

9.7 Application for interim orders

(1) A party may apply at any stage of the proceedings for–

    (a) an order for maintenance pending suit;
    (b) an order for maintenance pending outcome of proceedings;
    (c) an order for interim periodical payments;
    (d) an interim variation order; or
    (e) any other form of interim order.

(2) The Part 18 procedure applies to an application for an interim order.
(3) Where a party makes an application before filing a financial statement, the written evidence in support must–

    (a) explain why the order is necessary; and
    (b) give up to date information about that party's financial circumstances.

(4) Unless the respondent has filed a financial statement, the respondent must, at least 7 days before the court is to deal with the application, file a statement of his means and serve a copy on the applicant.
(5) An application for an order mentioned in paragraph (1)(e) may be made without notice.

9.8 Application for periodical payments order at same rate as an order for maintenance pending suit

(1) This rule applies where there are matrimonial proceedings and–

    (a) a decree nisi of divorce or nullity of marriage has been made;
    (b) at or after the date of the decree nisi an order for maintenance pending suit is in force; and
    (c) the spouse in whose favour the decree nisi was made has made an application for an order for periodical payments.

(2) The spouse in whose favour the decree nisi was made may apply, using the Part 18 procedure, for an order providing for payments at the same rate as those provided for by the order for maintenance pending suit.

9.9 **Application for periodical payments order at same rate as an order for maintenance pending outcome of proceedings**

(1) This rule applies where there are civil partnership proceedings and—

(a) a conditional order of dissolution or nullity of civil partnership has been made;
(b) at or after the date of the conditional order an order for maintenance pending outcome of proceedings is in force;
(c) the civil partner in whose favour the conditional order was made has made an application for an order for periodical payments.

(2) The civil partner in whose favour the conditional order was made may apply, using the Part 18 procedure, for an order providing for payments at the same rate as those provided for by, the order for maintenance pending the outcome of proceedings.

CHAPTER 3   APPLICATIONS FOR FINANCIAL REMEDIES FOR CHILDREN

9.10 **Application by parent, guardian etc for financial remedy in respect of children**

(1) The following people may apply for a financial remedy in respect of a child—

(a) a parent, guardian or special guardian of any child of the family;
(b) any person in whose favour a residence order has been made with respect to a child of the family, and any applicant for such an order;
(c) any other person who is entitled to apply for a residence order with respect to a child;
(d) a local authority, where an order has been made under section 31(1)(a) of the 1989 Act placing a child in its care;
(e) the Official Solicitor, if appointed the children's guardian of a child of the family under rule 16.24; and
(f) a child of the family who has been given permission to apply for a financial remedy.

(2) In this rule 'residence order' has the meaning given to it by section 8(1) of the 1989 Act.

9.11 **Children to be separately represented on certain applications**

(1) Where an application for a financial remedy includes an application for an order for a variation of settlement, the court must, unless it is satisfied that the proposed variation does not adversely affect the rights or interests of any child concerned, direct that the child be separately represented on the application.

(2) On any other application for a financial remedy the court may direct that the child be separately represented on the application.

(3) Where a direction is made under paragraph (1) or (2), the court may if the person to be appointed so consents, appoint—

(a) a person other than the Official Solicitor; or
(b) the Official Solicitor,

to be a children's guardian and rule 16.24(5) and (6) and rules 16.25 to 16.28 apply as appropriate to such an appointment.

CHAPTER 4   PROCEDURE IN THE HIGH COURT AND COUNTY COURT AFTER FILING AN APPLICATION

9.12 **Duties of the court and the applicant upon issuing an application**

(1) When an application under this Part is issued in the High Court or in a county court—

(a) the court will fix a first appointment not less than 12 weeks and not more than 16 weeks after the date of the filing of the application; and

(b) subject to paragraph (2), within 4 days beginning with the date on which the application was filed, a court officer will–
   (i) serve a copy of the application on the respondent; and
   (ii) give notice of the date of the first appointment to the applicant and the respondent.

(2) Where the applicant wishes to serve a copy of the application on the respondent and on filing the application so notifies the court–
   (a) paragraph (1)(b) does not apply;
   (b) a court officer will return to the applicant the copy of the application and the notice of the date of the first appointment; and
   (c) the applicant must,–
      (i) within 4 days beginning with the date on which the copy of the application is received from the court, serve the copy of the application and notice of the date of the first appointment on the respondent; and
      (ii) file a certificate of service at or before the first appointment.

(Rule 6.37 sets out what must be included in a certificate of service.)

(3) The date fixed under paragraph (1), or for any subsequent appointment, must not be cancelled except with the court's permission and, if cancelled, the court must immediately fix a new date.

9.13 Service of application on mortgagees, trustees etc

(1) Where an application for a financial remedy includes an application for an order for a variation of settlement, the applicant must serve copies of the application on–
   (a) the trustees of the settlement;
   (b) the settlor if living; and
   (c) such other persons as the court directs.

(2) In the case of an application for an avoidance of disposition order, the applicant must serve copies of the application on the person in whose favour the disposition is alleged to have been made.

(3) Where an application for a financial remedy includes an application relating to land, the applicant must serve a copy of the application on any mortgagee of whom particulars are given in the application.

(4) Any person served under paragraphs (1), (2) or (3) may make a request to the court in writing, within 14 days beginning with the date of service of the application, for a copy of the applicant's financial statement or any relevant part of that statement.

(5) Any person who–
   (a) is served with copies of the application in accordance with paragraphs (1), (2) or (3); or
   (b) receives a copy of a financial statement, or a relevant part of that statement, following an application made under paragraph (4),

   may within 14 days beginning with the date of service or receipt file a statement in answer.

(6) Where a copy of an application is served under paragraphs (1), (2) or (3), the applicant must file a certificate of service at or before the first appointment.

(7) A statement in answer filed under paragraph (5) must be verified by a statement of truth.

9.14 Procedure before the first appointment

(1) Not less than 35 days before the first appointment both parties must simultaneously exchange with each other and file with the court a financial statement in the form referred to in Practice Direction 5A.

(2) The financial statement must–
    (a)   be verified by an affidavit; and
    (b)   accompanied by the following documents only–
        (i)   any documents required by the financial statement;
        (ii)   any other documents necessary to explain or clarify any of the information contained in the financial statement; and
        (iii) any documents provided to the party producing the financial statement by a person responsible for a pension arrangement, either following a request under rule 9.30 or as part of a relevant valuation; and
        (iv) any notification or other document referred to in rule 9.37(2), (4) or (5) which has been received by the party producing the financial statement.

(3) Where a party was unavoidably prevented from sending any document required by the financial statement, that party must at the earliest opportunity–
    (a)   serve a copy of that document on the other party; and
    (b)   file a copy of that document with the court, together with a written explanation of the failure to send it with the financial statement.

(4) No disclosure or inspection of documents may be requested or given between the filing of the application for a financial remedy and the first appointment, except–
    (a)   copies sent with the financial statement, or in accordance with paragraph (3); or
    (b)   in accordance with paragraphs (5) and (6).

(Rule 21.1 explains what is meant by disclosure and inspection.)

(5) Not less than 14 days before the hearing of the first appointment, each party must file with the court and serve on the other party–
    (a)   a concise statement of the issues between the parties;
    (b)   a chronology;
    (c)   a questionnaire setting out by reference to the concise statement of issues any further information and documents requested from the other party or a statement that no information and documents are required; and
    (d)   a notice stating whether that party will be in a position at the first appointment to proceed on that occasion to a FDR appointment.

(6) Not less than 14 days before the hearing of the first appointment, the applicant must file with the court and serve on the respondent confirmation–
    (a)   of the names of all persons served in accordance with rule 9.13(1) to (3); and
    (b)   that there are no other persons who must be served in accordance with those paragraphs.

9.15 Duties of the court at the first appointment

(1) The first appointment must be conducted with the objective of defining the issues and saving costs.

(2) At the first appointment the court must determine–
    (a)   the extent to which any questions seeking information under rule 9.14(5)(c) must be answered; and
    (b)   what documents requested under rule 9.14(5)(c) must be produced,

and give directions for the production of such further documents as may be necessary.

(3) The court must give directions where appropriate about–
    (a)   the valuation of assets (including the joint instruction of joint experts);
    (b)   obtaining and exchanging expert evidence, if required;
    (c)   the evidence to be adduced by each party; and

(d) further chronologies or schedules to be filed by each party.

(4) If the court decides that a referral to a FDR appointment is appropriate it must direct that the case be referred to a FDR appointment.

(5) If the court decides that a referral to a FDR appointment is not appropriate it must direct one or more of the following–

    (a) that a further directions appointment be fixed;
    (b) that an appointment be fixed for the making of an interim order;
    (c) that the case be fixed for a final hearing and, where that direction is given, the court must determine the judicial level at which the case should be heard.

(By rule 3.3 the court may also direct that the case be adjourned if it considers that alternative dispute resolution is appropriate.)

(6) In considering whether to make a costs order under rule 28.3(5), the court must have particular regard to the extent to which each party has complied with the requirement to send documents with the financial statement and the explanation given for any failure to comply.

(7) The court may–

    (a) where an application for an interim order has been listed for consideration at the first appointment, make an interim order;
    (b) having regard to the contents of the notice filed by the parties under rule 9.14(5)(d), treat the appointment (or part of it) as a FDR appointment to which rule 9.17 applies;
    (c) in a case where a pension sharing order or a pension attachment order is requested, direct any party with pension rights to file and serve a Pension Inquiry Form, completed in full or in part as the court may direct; and
    (d) in a case where a pension compensation sharing order or a pension compensation attachment order is requested, direct any party with PPF compensation rights to file and serve a Pension Protection Fund Inquiry Form, completed in full or in part as the court may direct.

(8) Both parties must personally attend the first appointment unless the court directs otherwise.

9.16 After the first appointment

(1) Between the first appointment and the FDR appointment, a party is not entitled to the production of any further documents except–

    (a) in accordance with directions given under rule 9.15(2); or
    (b) with the permission of the court.

(2) At any stage–

    (a) a party may apply for further directions or a FDR appointment;
    (b) the court may give further directions or direct that parties attend a FDR appointment.

9.17 The FDR appointment

(1) The FDR appointment must be treated as a meeting held for the purposes of discussion and negotiation.

(2) The judge hearing the FDR appointment must have no further involvement with the application, other than to conduct any further FDR appointment or to make a consent order or a further directions order.

(3) Not less than 7 days before the FDR appointment, the applicant must file with the court details of all offers and proposals, and responses to them.

(4) Paragraph (3) includes any offers, proposals or responses made wholly or partly

without prejudice[GL], but paragraph (3) does not make any material admissible as evidence if, but for that paragraph, it would not be admissible.

(5) At the conclusion of the FDR appointment, any documents filed under paragraph (3), and any filed documents referring to them, must, at the request of the party who filed them, be returned to that party and not retained on the court file.

(6) Parties attending the FDR appointment must use their best endeavours to reach agreement on matters in issue between them.

(7) The FDR appointment may be adjourned from time to time.

(8) At the conclusion of the FDR appointment, the court may make an appropriate consent order.

(9) If the court does not make an appropriate consent order as mentioned in paragraph (8), the court must give directions for the future course of the proceedings including, where appropriate–

    (a)   the filing of evidence, including up to date information; and
    (b)   fixing a final hearing date.

(10) Both parties must personally attend the FDR appointment unless the court directs otherwise.

CHAPTER 5   PROCEDURE IN THE MAGISTRATES' COURT AFTER FILING AN APPLICATION

9.18   Duties of the court and the applicant upon filing an application

(1) When an application for an order under this Part is issued in a magistrates' court–

    (a)   the court will fix a first hearing date not less than 4 weeks and not more than 8 weeks after the date of the filing of the application; and
    (b)   subject to paragraph (2), within 4 days beginning with the date on which the application was filed, a court officer will–
        (i)   serve a copy of the application on the respondent;
        (ii)   give notice of the date of the first hearing to the applicant and the respondent; and
        (iii)   send a blank financial statement to both the applicant and the respondent.

(2) Where the applicant wishes to serve a copy of the application on the respondent and, on filing the application, so notifies the court–

    (a)   paragraph (1)(b) does not apply;
    (b)   a court officer will return to the applicant the copy of the application and the notice of the date of the first hearing; and
    (c)   the applicant must–
        (i)   within 4 days beginning with the date on which the copy of the application is received from the court, serve the copy of the application and notice of the date of the first hearing on the respondent;
        (ii)   send a blank financial statement to the respondent; and
        (iii)   file a certificate of service at or before the first hearing.

(3) The date fixed under paragraph (1), or for any other subsequent hearing or appointment must not be cancelled except with the court's permission and, if cancelled, the court must immediately fix a new date.

9.19   Procedure before the first hearing

(1) Not more than 14 days after the date of the issue of the application both parties must simultaneously exchange with each other and file with the court a financial statement referred to in Practice Direction 5A.

(2) The financial statement must–
   (a) be verified by an affidavit; and
   (b) contain the following documents only–
      (i) any documents required by the financial statement; and
      (ii) any other documents necessary to explain or clarify any of the information contained in the financial statement.
(3) Where a party was unavoidably prevented from sending any document required by the financial statement, that party must at the earliest opportunity–
   (a) serve a copy of that document on the other party; and
   (b) file a copy of that document with the court, together with a statement explaining the failure to send it with the financial statement.
(4) No disclosure or inspection of documents may be requested or given between the filing of the application for a financial remedy and the first hearing except copies sent with the financial statement or in accordance with paragraph (3).

(Rule 21.1 explains what is meant by disclosure and inspection.)

9.20 Power of the court to direct filing of evidence and set dates for further hearings

Unless the court is able to determine the application at the first hearing the court may direct that further evidence be filed and set a date for a directions hearing or appointment or final hearing.

9.21 Who the respondent is on an application under section 20 or section 20A of the 1978 Act or Part 6 of Schedule 6 to the 2004 Act

In relation to proceedings set out in column 1 of the following table, column 2 sets out who the respondents to those proceedings will be.

Proceedings	Respondent
Application under section 20 of the 1978 Act, except an application for variation of an order.	The other party to the marriage; and where the order to which the application relates requires periodical payments to be made to, or in respect of, a child who is 16 years of age or over, that child.
Application under paragraphs 30 to 34 of Schedule 6 to the 2004 Act, except an application for variation of an order.	The other party to the civil partnership; and where the order to which the application relates requires periodical payments to be made to, or in respect of, a child who is 16 years of age or over, that child.
Application for the revival of an order under section 20A of the 1978 Act or paragraph 40 of Schedule 6 to the 2004 Act.	The parties to the proceedings leading to the order which it is sought to have revived.

9.22 Proceedings by or against a person outside England and Wales for orders under section 20 of the 1978 Act or paragraphs 30 to 34 of Schedule 6 to the 2004 Act other than proceedings for variation of orders

(1) Subject to the provisions of this rule, the jurisdiction conferred on a court by virtue of

section 20 of the 1978 Act or paragraphs 30 to 34 of Schedule 6 to the 2004 Act is exercisable when proceedings are brought by or against a person residing outside England and Wales.

(2) Subject to paragraph (3), where the court is satisfied that the respondent has been outside England and Wales for the whole of the period beginning one month before the making of the application and ending with the date of the hearing, it may proceed with the application provided that–

    (a) the applicant provided the court with an address for service of the application and written notice of the hearing on the respondent; or

    (b) the court is satisfied that the respondent has been made aware of the application and of the time and place appointed for the hearing otherwise than by service of the application upon the respondent by the court; and

    (c) it is reasonable in all the circumstances to proceed in the absence of the respondent.

(3) The court must not make the order for which the application is made unless it is satisfied that–

    (a) during the period of 6 months immediately preceding the making of the application the respondent was continuously outside England and Wales, or was not in England and Wales on more than 30 days; and

    (b) having regard to any communication to the court in writing purporting to be from the respondent, it is reasonable in all the circumstances to do so.

(4) This rule does not apply in relation to proceedings to vary an order for periodical payments.

(Rules made under section 144 of the Magistrates' Courts Act 1980 make provision in respect of proceedings by or against a person outside England and Wales for variation of orders under section 20 of the 1978 Act or paragraphs 30 to 34 of Schedule 6 to the 2004 Act.)

9.23 Duty to make entries in the court's register

(1) Where the designated officer for the court receives notice of any direction made in the High Court or a county court under section 28 of the 1978 Act by virtue of which an order made by the court under that Act or the 2004 Act ceases to have effect, particulars of the direction must be entered in the court's register.

(2) Where–

    (a) in proceedings under the 1978 Act, the hearing of an application under section 2 of that Act is adjourned after the court has decided that it is satisfied of any ground mentioned in section 1; or

    (b) in proceedings under the 2004 Act, the hearing of an application under Part 1 of Schedule 6 to that Act is adjourned after the court has decided that it is satisfied of any ground mentioned in paragraph 1,

and the parties to the proceedings agree to the resumption of the hearing in accordance with section 31 of the 1978 Act by a court which includes justices who were not sitting when the hearing began, particulars of the agreement must be entered into the court's register.

CHAPTER 6 GENERAL PROCEDURE

9.24 Power to order delivery up of possession etc.

(1) This rule applies where the court has made an order under–

    (a) section 24A of the 1973 Act;

    (b) section 17(2) of the 1984 Act;

    (c) Part 3 of Schedule 5 to the 2004 Act; or

(d) paragraph 9(4) of Schedule 7 to the 2004 Act.

(2) When the court makes an order mentioned in paragraph (1), it may order any party to deliver up to the purchaser or any other person–

(a) possession of the land, including any interest in, or right over, land;
(b) receipt of rents or profits relating to it; or
(c) both.

9.25 Where proceedings may be heard

(1) Paragraph (2) applies to an application–

(a) for a financial order;
(b) under Part 3 of the 1984 Act; or
(c) under Schedule 7 to the 2004 Act.

(2) An application mentioned in paragraph (1) must be heard–

(a) where the case is proceeding in the county court, at any court of trial; and
(b) where the case is proceeding in the High Court–
   (i) at the Royal Courts of Justice; or
   (ii) in matrimonial or civil partnership proceedings, any court at which sittings of the High Court are authorised.

(3) An application for an order under–

(a) section 27 of the 1973 Act; or
(b) Part 9 of Schedule 5 to the 2004 Act,

must be heard in a court of trial or in the High Court.

(4) A court may transfer a case to another court exercising the same jurisdiction, either of its own initiative or on the application of one of the parties, if–

(a) the parties consent to the transfer;
(b) the court has held a hearing to determine whether a transfer should be ordered; or
(c) paragraph (5) applies.

(5) A court may transfer a case without a hearing if–

(a) the court has notified the parties in writing that it intends to order a transfer; and
(b) neither party has, within 14 days of the notification being sent, requested a hearing to determine whether a transfer should be ordered.

9.26 Applications for consent orders for financial remedy

(1) Subject to paragraph (5) and to rule 35.2, in relation to an application for a consent order–

(a) the applicant must file two copies of a draft of the order in the terms sought, one of which must be endorsed with a statement signed by the respondent to the application signifying agreement; and
(b) each party must file with the court and serve on the other party, a statement of information in the form referred to in Practice Direction 5A.

(2) Where each party's statement of information is contained in one form, it must be signed by both the applicant and respondent to certify that they have read the contents of the other party's statement.

(3) Where each party's statement of information is in a separate form, the form of each party must be signed by the other party to certify that they have read the contents of the statement contained in that form.

(4) Unless the court directs otherwise, the applicant and the respondent need not attend the hearing of an application for a consent order.
(5) Where all or any of the parties attend the hearing of an application for a financial remedy the court may–
   (a) dispense with the filing of a statement of information; and
   (b) give directions for the information which would otherwise be required to be given in such a statement in such a manner as it thinks fit.
(6) In relation to an application for a consent order under Part 3 of the 1984 Act or Schedule 7 to the 2004 Act, the application for permission to make the application may be heard at the same time as the application for a financial remedy if evidence of the respondent's consent to the order is filed with the application.

(The following rules contain provision in relation to applications for consent orders – rule 9.32 (pension sharing order), rule 9.34 (pension attachment order), rule 9.41 (pension compensation sharing orders) and rule 9.43 (pension compensation attachment orders.)

CHAPTER 7   ESTIMATES OF COSTS

9.27   Estimates of Costs

(1) Subject to paragraph (2), at every hearing or appointment each party must produce to the court an estimate of the costs incurred by that party up to the date of that hearing or appointment.
(2) Not less than 14 days before the date fixed for the final hearing of an application for a financial remedy, each party ('the filing party') must (unless the court directs otherwise) file with the court and serve on each other party a statement giving full particulars of all costs in respect of the proceedings which the filing party has incurred or expects to incur, to enable the court to take account of the parties' liabilities for costs when deciding what order (if any) to make for a financial remedy.
(3) This rule does not apply to magistrates' courts.

(Rule 28.3 makes provision for orders for costs in financial remedy proceedings.)

9.28   Duty to make open proposals

(1) Not less than 14 days before the date fixed for the final hearing of an application for a financial remedy, the applicant must (unless the court directs otherwise) file with the court and serve on the respondent an open statement which sets out concise details, including the amounts involved, of the orders which the applicant proposes to ask the court to make.
(2) Not more than 7 days after service of a statement under paragraph (1), the respondent must file with the court and serve on the applicant an open statement which sets out concise details, including the amounts involved, of the orders which the respondent proposes to ask the court to make.

CHAPTER 8   PENSIONS

9.29   Application and interpretation of this Chapter

(1) This Chapter applies
   (a) where an application for a financial remedy has been made; and
   (b) the applicant or respondent is the party with pension rights.
(2) In this Chapter–
   (a) in proceedings under the 1973 Act and the 1984 Act, all words and phrases defined in sections 25D(3) and (4) of the 1973 Act have the meaning assigned by those subsections;

(b) in proceedings under the 2004 Act—
  (i) all words and phrases defined in paragraphs 16(4) to (5) and 29 of Schedule 5 to that Act have the meanings assigned by those paragraphs; and
  (ii) 'the party with pension rights' has the meaning given to 'civil partner with pension rights' by paragraph 29 of Schedule 5 to the 2004 Act;
(c) all words and phrases defined in section 46 of the Welfare Reform and Pensions Act 1999 have the meanings assigned by that section.

9.30 What the party with pension rights must do when the court fixes a first appointment

(1) Where the court fixes a first appointment as required by rule 9.12(1)(a) the party with pension rights must request the person responsible for each pension arrangement under which the party has or is likely to have benefits to provide the information referred to in regulation 2(2) of the Pensions on Divorce etc (Provision of Information) Regulations 2000.

(The information referred to in regulation 2 of the Pensions on Divorce etc (Provision of Information) Regulations 2000 relates to the valuation of pension rights or benefits.)

(2) The party with pension rights must comply with paragraph (1) within 7 days beginning with the date on which that party receives notification of the date of the first appointment.
(3) Within 7 days beginning with the date on which the party with pension rights receives the information under paragraph (1) that party must send a copy of it to the other party, together with the name and address of the person responsible for each pension arrangement.
(4) A request under paragraph (1) need not be made where the party with pension rights is in possession of, or has requested, a relevant valuation of the pension rights or benefits accrued under the pension arrangement in question.

9.31 Applications for pension sharing orders

Where an application for a financial remedy includes an application for a pension sharing order, or where a request for such an order is added to an existing application for a financial remedy, the applicant must serve a copy of the application on the person responsible for the pension arrangement concerned.

9.32 Applications for consent orders for pension sharing

(1) This rule applies where—
  (a) the parties have agreed on the terms of an order and the agreement includes a pension sharing order;
  (b) service has not been effected under rule 9.31; and
  (c) the information referred to in paragraph (2) has not otherwise been provided.
(2) The party with pension rights must—
  (a) request the person responsible for the pension arrangement concerned to provide the information set out in Section C of the Pension Inquiry Form; and
  (b) on receipt, send a copy of the information referred to in sub-paragraph (a) to the other party.

9.33 Applications for pension attachment orders

(1) Where an application for a financial remedy includes an application for a pension attachment order, or where a request for such an order is added to an existing

application for a financial remedy, the applicant must serve a copy of the application on the person responsible for the pension arrangement concerned and must at the same time send–

   (a) an address to which any notice which the person responsible is required to serve on the applicant is to be sent;
   (b) an address to which any payment which the person responsible is required to make to the applicant is to be sent; and
   (c) where the address in sub-paragraph (b) is that of a bank, a building society or the Department of National Savings, sufficient details to enable the payment to be made into the account of the applicant.

(2) A person responsible for a pension arrangement who receives a copy of the application under paragraph (1) may, within 21 days beginning with the date of service of the application, request the party with the pension rights to provide that person with the information disclosed in the financial statement relating to the party's pension rights or benefits under that arrangement.

(3) If the person responsible for a pension arrangement makes a request under paragraph (2), the party with the pension rights must provide that person with a copy of the section of that party's financial statement that relates to that party's pension rights or benefits under that arrangement.

(4) The party with the pension rights must comply with paragraph (3)–

   (a) within the time limited for filing the financial statement by rule 9.14(1); or
   (b) within 21 days beginning with the date on which the person responsible for the pension arrangement makes the request,

whichever is the later.

(5) A person responsible for a pension arrangement who receives a copy of the section of a financial statement as required pursuant to paragraph (4) may, within 21 days beginning with the date on which that person receives it, send to the court, the applicant and the respondent a statement in answer.

(6) A person responsible for a pension arrangement who files a statement in answer pursuant to paragraph (5) will be entitled to be represented at the first appointment, or such other hearing as the court may direct, and the court must within 4 days, beginning with the date on which that person files the statement in answer, give the person notice of the date of the first appointment or other hearing as the case may be.

9.34 Applications for consent orders for pension attachment

(1) This rule applies where service has not been effected under rule 9.33(1).
(2) Where the parties have agreed on the terms of an order and the agreement includes a pension attachment order, then they must serve on the person responsible for the pension arrangement concerned–

   (a) a copy of the application for a consent order;
   (b) a draft of the proposed order, complying with rule 9.35; and
   (c) the particulars set out in rule 9.33(1).

(3) No consent order that includes a pension attachment order must be made unless either–

   (a) the person responsible for the pension arrangement has not made any objection within 21 days beginning with the date on which the application for a consent order was served on that person; or
   (b) the court has considered any such objection, and for the purpose of considering any objection the court may make such direction as it sees fit for the person responsible to attend before it or to furnish written details of the objection.

9.35 Pension sharing orders or pension attachment orders

An order for a financial remedy, whether by consent or not, which includes a pension sharing order or a pension attachment order, must–

(a) in the body of the order, state that there is to be provision by way of pension sharing or pension attachment in accordance with the annex or annexes to the order; and
(b) be accompanied by a pension sharing annex or a pension attachment annex as the case may require, and if provision is made in relation to more than one pension arrangement there must be one annex for each pension arrangement.

9.36 **Duty of the court upon making a pension sharing order or a pension attachment order**

(1) A court which varies or discharges a pension sharing order or a pension attachment order, must send, or direct one of the parties to send–
    (a) to the person responsible for the pension arrangement concerned; or
    (b) where the Board has assumed responsibility for the pension scheme or part of it, the Board;
the documents referred to in paragraph (4).
(2) A court which makes a pension sharing order or pension attachment order, must send, or direct one of the parties to send to the person responsible for the pension arrangement concerned, the documents referred to in paragraph (4).
(3) Where the Board has assumed responsibility for the pension scheme or part of it after the making of a pension sharing order or attachment order but before the documents have been sent to the person responsible for the pension arrangement in accordance with paragraph (2), the court which makes the pension sharing order or the pension attachment order, must send, or direct one of the parties to send to the Board the documents referred to in paragraph (4).
(4) The documents to be sent in accordance with paragraph (1) to (3) are–
    (a) in the case of–
        (i) proceedings under the 1973 Act, a copy of the decree of judicial separation;
        (ii) proceedings under Schedule 5 to the 2004 Act, a copy of the separation order;
        (iii) proceedings under Part 3 of the 1984 Act, a copy of the document of divorce, annulment or legal separation;
        (iv) proceedings under Schedule 7 to the 2004 Act, a copy of the document of dissolution, annulment or legal separation;
    (b) in the case of divorce or nullity of marriage, a copy of the decree absolute under rule 7.31 or 7.32; or
    (c) in the case of dissolution or nullity of civil partnership, a copy of the order making the conditional order final under rule 7.31 or 7.32; and
    (d) a copy of the pension sharing order or the pension attachment order, or as the case may be of the order varying or discharging that order, including any annex to that order relating to that pension arrangement but no other annex to that order.
(5) The documents referred to in paragraph (1) must be sent–
    (a) in proceedings under the 1973 Act and the 1984 Act, within 7 days beginning with the date on which–
        (i) the relevant pension sharing or pension attachment order is made; or
        (ii) the decree absolute of divorce or nullity or decree of judicial separation is made,
    whichever is the later; and
    (b) in proceedings under the 2004 Act, within 7 days beginning with the date on which–

(i) the relevant pension sharing or pension attachment order is made; or
(ii) the final order of dissolution or nullity or separation order is made,

whichever is the later.

9.37 Procedure where Pension Protection Fund becomes involved with the pension scheme

(1) This rule applies where–
   (a) rules 9.30 to 9.34 or 9.36 apply; and
   (b) the party with the pension rights ('the member') receives or has received notification in compliance with the Pension Protection Fund (Provision of Information) Regulations 2005 ('the 2005 Regulations')–
       (i) from the trustees or managers of a pension scheme, that there is an assessment period in relation to that scheme; or
       (ii) from the Board that it has assumed responsibility for the pension scheme or part of it.

(2) If the trustees or managers of the pension scheme notify or have notified the member that there is an assessment period in relation to that scheme, the member must send to the other party, all the information which the Board is required from time to time to provide to the member under the 2005 Regulations including–
   (a) a copy of the notification; and
   (b) a copy of the valuation summary,

   in accordance with paragraph (3).

(3) The member must send the information or any part of it referred to in paragraph (2)–
   (a) if available, when the member sends the information received under rule 9.30(1); or
   (b) otherwise, within 7 days of receipt.

(4) If the Board notifies the member that it has assumed responsibility for the pension scheme, or part of it, the member must–
   (a) send a copy of the notification to the other party within 7 days of receipt; and
   (b) comply with paragraph (5).

(5) Where paragraph (4) applies, the member must–
   (a) within 7 days of receipt of the notification, request the Board in writing to provide a forecast of the member's compensation entitlement as described in the 2005 Regulations; and
   (b) send a copy of the forecast of the member's compensation entitlement to the other party within 7 days of receipt.

(6) In this rule–
   (a) 'assessment period' means an assessment period within the meaning of Part 2 of the Pensions Act 2004; and
   (b) 'valuation summary' has the meaning assigned to it by the 2005 Regulations.

CHAPTER 9 PENSION PROTECTION FUND COMPENSATION

9.38 Application and interpretation of this Chapter

(1) This Chapter applies–
   (a) where an application for a financial remedy has been made; and
   (b) the applicant or respondent is, the party with compensation rights.

(2) In this Chapter 'party with compensation rights' –

(a) in proceedings under the 1973 Act and the 1984 Act, has the meaning given to it by section 25G(5) of the 1973 Act;
(b) in proceedings under the 2004 Act, has the meaning given to 'civil partner with compensation rights' by paragraph 37(1) of Schedule 5 to the 2004 Act.

9.39 What the party with compensation rights must do when the court fixes a first appointment

(1) Where the court fixes a first appointment as required by rule 9.12(1)(a) the party with compensation rights must request the Board to provide the information about the valuation of entitlement to PPF compensation referred to in regulations made by the Secretary of State under section 118 of the Pensions Act 2008.
(2) The party with compensation rights must comply with paragraph (1) within 7 days beginning with the date on which that party receives notification of the date of the first appointment.
(3) Within 7 days beginning with the date on which the party with compensation rights receives the information under paragraph (1) that party must send a copy of it to the other party, together with the name and address of the trustees or managers responsible for each pension scheme.
(4) Where the rights to PPF Compensation are derived from rights under more than one pension scheme, the party with compensation rights must comply with this rule in relation to each entitlement.

9.40 Applications for pension compensation sharing orders

Where an application for a financial remedy includes an application for a pension compensation sharing order or where a request for such an order is added to an existing application for a financial remedy, the applicant must serve a copy of the application on the Board.

9.41 Applications for consent orders for pension compensation sharing

(1) This rule applies where–
    (a) the parties have agreed on the terms of an order and the agreement includes a pension compensation sharing order;
    (b) service has not been effected under rule 9.40; and
    (c) the information referred to in paragraph (2) has not otherwise been provided.
(2) The party with compensation rights must–
    (a) request the Board to provide the information set out in Section C of the Pension Protection Fund Inquiry Form; and
    (b) on receipt, send a copy of the information referred to in sub-paragraph (a) to the other party.

9.42 Applications for pension compensation attachment orders

Where an application for a financial remedy includes an application for a pension compensation attachment order or where a request for such an order is added to an existing application for a financial remedy, the applicant must serve a copy of the application on the Board and must at the same time send–
(a) an address to which any notice which the Board is required to serve on the applicant is to be sent;
(b) an address to which any payment which the Board is required to make to the applicant is to be sent; and
(c) where the address in sub-paragraph (b) is that of a bank, a building society or the Department of National Savings, sufficient details to enable the payment to be made into the account of the applicant.

Family Procedure Rules 2010   173

9.43 Applications for consent orders for pension compensation attachment

(1) This rule applies where service has not been effected under rule 9.42.
(2) Where the parties have agreed on the terms of an order and the agreement includes a pension compensation attachment order, then they must serve on the Board–

    (a)   a copy of the application for a consent order;
    (b)   a draft of the proposed order, complying with rule 9.44; and
    (c)   the particulars set out in rule 9.42.

9.44 Pension compensation sharing orders or pension compensation attachment orders

An order for a financial remedy, whether by consent or not, which includes a pension compensation sharing order or a pension compensation attachment order, must–

(a) in the body of the order, state that there is to be provision by way of pension compensation sharing or pension compensation attachment in accordance with the annex or annexes to the order; and
(b) be accompanied by a pension compensation sharing annex or a pension compensation attachment annex as the case may require, and if provision is made in relation to entitlement to PPF compensation that derives from rights under more than one pension scheme there must be one annex for each such entitlement.

9.45 Duty of the court upon making a pension compensation sharing order or a pension compensation attachment order

(1) A court which makes, varies or discharges a pension compensation sharing order or a pension compensation attachment order, must send, or direct one of the parties to send, to the Board–

    (a)   in the case of–
        (i)   proceedings under Part 3 of the 1984 Act, a copy of the document of divorce, annulment or legal separation;
        (ii)   proceedings under Schedule 7 to the 2004 Act, a copy of the document of dissolution, annulment or legal separation;
    (b)   in the case of–
        (i)   divorce or nullity of marriage, a copy of the decree absolute under rule 7.32 or 7.33;
        (ii)   dissolution or nullity of civil partnership, a copy of the order making the conditional order final under rule 7.32 or 7.33;
    (c)   in the case of separation–
        (i)   in the matrimonial proceedings, a copy of the decree of judicial separation;
        (ii)   in civil partnership proceedings, a copy of the separation order; and
    (d)   a copy of the pension compensation sharing order or the pension compensation attachment order, or as the case may be of the order varying or discharging that order, including any annex to that order relating to that PPF compensation but no other annex to that order.

(2) The documents referred to in paragraph (1) must be sent–

    (a)   in proceedings under the 1973 Act and the 1984 Act, within 7 days beginning with the date on which–
        (i)   the relevant pension compensation sharing or pension compensation attachment order is made; or

(ii) the decree absolute of divorce or nullity or the decree of judicial separation is made,

whichever is the later; and

(b) in proceedings under the 2004 Act, within 7 days beginning with the date on which–

(i) the relevant pension compensation sharing or pension compensation attachment order is made; or
(ii) the final order of dissolution or nullity or separation order is made,

whichever is the later.

PART 10 APPLICATIONS UNDER PART 4 OF THE FAMILY LAW ACT 1996

10.1 Scope and interpretation of this Part

The rules in this Part apply to proceedings under Part 4 of the 1996 Act.

10.2 Applications for an occupation order or a non-molestation order

(1) An application for an occupation order or a non-molestation order must be supported by a witness statement.
(2) Subject to paragraph (3), an application for an occupation order or a non-molestation order may be made without notice.
(3) An application for an occupation order or a non-molestation order may, in a magistrates' court, be made with the permission of the court without notice in which case the applicant must file the application at the time when the application is made or as directed by the court.
(4) Where an application is made without notice, the witness statement in support of the application must state the reasons why notice has not been given.

(Section 45 of the 1996 Act sets out the criteria for making an order without notice.)

10.3 Service of the application

(1) In an application made on notice, the applicant must serve–

(a) a copy of the application together with any statement in support; and
(b) notice of any hearing or directions appointment set by the court,

on the respondent personally–

(i) not less than 2 days before the hearing; or
(ii) within such period as the court may direct.

(2) Where the applicant is acting in person, the applicant may request the court officer to serve the application on the respondent.
(3) In an application for an occupation order under section 33, 35 or 36 of the 1996 Act, the applicant must serve on the mortgagee and any landlord of the dwelling-house in question–

(a) a copy of the application; and
(b) notice of the right to make representations in writing or orally at any hearing.

(4) The applicant must file a certificate of service after serving the application.

(Rule 6.23 makes provision for the different methods of serving a document and rule 6.35 provides for the court to authorise service by an alternative method.)

10.4 Transfer of pending proceedings to another court

Subject to any enactment, where an application for an occupation order or a non-molestation order is pending, the court may transfer the proceedings to another court of its own initiative or on the application of either party.

10.5 Privacy

In the High Court and a county court, any hearing relating to an application for an occupation order or a non-molestation order will be in private unless the court directs otherwise.

10.6 Service of an order

(1) The applicant must, as soon as reasonably practicable, serve on the respondent personally–
  (a) a copy of the order; and
  (b) where the order is made without notice–
     (i) a copy of the application together with any statement supporting it; and
     (ii) in a magistrates' court, a copy of the record of the reasons for a decision.

(Rule 27.2(8) makes provision for the court officer to supply a copy of the reasons for the court's decision to the persons referred to in rule 27.2(9).)

(2) The court must serve the documents listed in paragraph (1) if–
  (a) an applicant, acting in person, so requests; or
  (b) the court made the order of its own initiative.

(3 In an application for an occupation order under section 33, 35 or 36 of the 1996 Act, the applicant must serve a copy of any order made on the mortgagee and any landlord of the dwelling-house in question.

10.7 Representations made by a mortgagee or landlord

The court may direct that a hearing be held in order to consider any representations made by a mortgagee or a landlord.

10.8 Applications to vary, extend or discharge an order

Rules 10.5 to 10.7 apply to applications to vary, extend or discharge an order.

10.9 Orders containing provisions to which a power of arrest is attached

Where the court makes an occupation order containing one or more provisions to which a power of arrest is attached ('relevant provisions')–

(a) each relevant provision must be set out in a separate paragraph in the order; and
(b) a paragraph containing a relevant provision must not include a provision of the order to which the power of arrest is not attached.

10.10 Service of an order on the officer for the time being in charge of a police station

(1) Where the court makes–
  (a) an occupation order to which a power of arrest is attached; or
  (b) a non-molestation order,

  a copy of the order must be delivered to the officer for the time being in charge of–
     (i) the police station for the applicant's address; or
     (ii) such other police station as the court may specify.

(2) A copy of the order delivered under paragraph (1) must be accompanied by a statement showing that the respondent has been served with the order or informed of its terms (whether by being present when the order was made or by telephone or otherwise).

(3) The documentation referred to in paragraphs (1) and (2) must be delivered by–
  (a) the applicant; or

(b) the court officer, where the order was served following a request under rule 10.6(2).

(4) Paragraph (5) applies where an order is made varying or discharging–

(a) a provision of an occupation order to which a power of arrest is attached; or
(b) a provision of a non-molestation order.

(5) The court officer must–

(a) immediately inform–

(i) the officer who received a copy of the order under paragraph (1); and
(ii) if the applicant's address has changed, the officer for the time being in charge of the police station for the new address; and

(b) deliver a copy of the order referred to in paragraph (4)(a) or (b) and the order referred to in paragraph (1) to any officer so informed.

10.11 Proceedings following arrest in a county court or the High Court

(1) This rule applies where a person is arrested pursuant to–

(a) a power of arrest attached to a provision of an occupation order; or
(b) a warrant of arrest issued on an application under section 47(8) of the 1996 Act.

(2) The court before which a person is brought following arrest may–

(a) determine whether the facts, and the circumstances which led to the arrest, amounted to disobedience of the order; or
(b) adjourn the proceedings.

(3) Where the proceedings are adjourned and the arrested person is released–

(a) unless the court directs otherwise, the matter must be dealt with within 14 days beginning with the date of arrest; and
(b) the arrested person must be given not less than 2 days' notice of the hearing.

(4) An application notice seeking the committal for contempt of court of the arrested person may be issued if the arrested person is not dealt with within the period mentioned in paragraph (3)(a).

(The powers of a county court and the High Court to remand in custody or on bail are contained in section 47 of and Schedule 5 to the Family Law Act 1996.)

(For proceedings following arrest in a magistrates' court see rules made under section 144 of the Magistrates' Courts Act 1980.)

10.12 Enforcement of an order in a county court

Rule 1 of Order 29 of the CCR (enforcement of judgment to do or abstain from doing any act) has effect as if, for paragraph (3), there were substituted the following–

'(3) At the time when the order is drawn up, the court officer will–

(a) where the order made is (or includes) a non-molestation order; or
(b) where the order made is an occupation order and the court so directs,

issue a copy of the order, indorsed with or incorporating a notice as to the consequences of disobedience, for service in accordance with paragraph (2).'.

(For enforcement of an order generally in a county court or the High Court see Part 33. For enforcement of an order in a magistrates' court see rules made under section 144 of the Magistrates' Courts Act 1980.)

10.13 Enforcement of an undertaking in a county court

(1) This rule applies to applications for the enforcement of undertakings by committal order in a county court.

(2) Rule 1A of Order 29 of the CCR (undertaking given by party) applies with the necessary modifications, where an application is made in a county court to commit a person for breach of an undertaking.

(For enforcement of an undertaking in a magistrates' court see rules made under section 144 of the Magistrates' Courts Act 1980.)

10.14 Power to adjourn the hearing for consideration of the penalty

The High Court or a county court may adjourn the hearing for consideration of the penalty to be imposed for any contempt of court found proved and such a hearing may be restored if the respondent does not comply with any conditions specified by the court.

(Rules made under section 144 of the Magistrates' Courts Act 1980 contain an equivalent power for magistrates' courts.)

10.15 Hospital orders or guardianship orders under the Mental Health Act 1983

(1) Where the High Court or a county court makes a hospital order under the Mental Health Act 1983 the court officer must–
   (a) send to the hospital any information which will be of assistance in dealing with the patient; and
   (b) inform the applicant when the respondent is being transferred to hospital.
(2) Where the High Court or a county court makes a guardianship order under the Mental Health Act 1983, the court officer must send any information which will be of assistance in dealing with the patient to–
   (a) the patient's guardian; and
   (b) where the guardian is a person other than the local services authority, the local services authority.

(Section 51 of the 1996 Act provides a magistrates' court with a power to make a hospital order or a guardianship order under the Mental Health Act 1983 and attention is drawn to rules made under section 144 of the Magistrates' Courts Act 1980.)

10.16 Transfer directions under section 48 of the Mental Health Act 1983

(1) Where a transfer direction given by the Secretary of State under section 48 of the Mental Health Act 1983 is in force in respect of a person remanded in custody by the High Court or a county court, the court officer must notify–
   (a) the governor of the prison to which that person was remanded; and
   (b) the hospital where that person is detained,
   of any committal hearing which that person is required to attend.
(2) The court officer must also give notice in writing of any further remand to the hospital where that person is detained.

(Rules made under section 144 of the Magistrates' Courts Act 1980 make provision for magistrates' courts.)

10.17 Recognizances

(1) Where, in accordance with paragraph 2(1)(b)(ii) of Schedule 5 to the 1996 Act, the High Court or a county court fixes the amount of any recognizance with a view to it being taken subsequently, the recognizance may be taken by–
   (a) a district judge;
   (b) a police officer of the rank of inspector or above or in charge of a police station; or
   (c) the governor or keeper of a prison where the arrested person is in custody.

(2) The person having custody of an applicant for bail must release that applicant if satisfied that the required recognizances have been taken.

(A magistrates' court has a similar power to require a recognizance under Part 6 of the Magistrates' Courts Act 1980. Section 119 of that Act provides a magistrates' court with a power to postpone the taking of a recognizance and rules made under section 144 of the Magistrates' Courts Act 1980 set out the people who may subsequently take the recognizance.)

PART 11   APPLICATIONS UNDER PART 4A OF THE FAMILY LAW ACT 1996

11.1   Scope and interpretation

(1) The rules in this Part apply to proceedings in the High Court or a county court under Part 4A of the 1996 Act.
(2) In this Part–

'a forced marriage protection order' means an order under section 63A of the 1996 Act; and

'the person who is the subject of the proceedings' means the person who will be protected by the forced marriage protection order applied for or being considered by the court of its own initiative, if that order is made, or who is being protected by such an order.

11.2   Applications

(1) An application for a forced marriage protection order may be made without notice.
(2) Where an application is made without notice, it must be supported by a sworn statement explaining why notice has not been given.
(3) An application for a forced marriage protection order made by an organisation must state–

(a) the name and address of the person submitting the application; and
(b) the position which that person holds in the organisation.

11.3   Permission to apply

(1) Where the permission of the court is required to apply for a forced marriage protection order, the person seeking permission must file–

(a) a Part 18 application notice setting out–

(i) the reasons for the application, for the making of which permission is sought ('the proposed application');
(ii) the applicant's connection with the person to be protected;
(iii) the applicant's knowledge of the circumstances of the person to be protected; and
(iv) the applicant's knowledge of the wishes and feelings of the person to be protected;

and

(b) a draft of the proposed application, together with sufficient copies for one to be served on each respondent and (if different) the person to be protected.

(2) As soon as practicable after receiving an application under paragraph (1), the court must–

(a) grant the application; or
(b) direct that a date be fixed for the hearing of the application and fix the date.

(3) The court officer must inform the following persons of the court's action under paragraph (2)–
   (a) the applicant;
   (b) the respondent;
   (c) (if different) the person to be protected; and
   (d) any other person directed by the court.
(4) Where permission is granted to apply for a forced marriage protection order, the application must proceed in accordance with rule 11.2.

11.4 Service of applications on notice

(1) Subject to paragraphs (3) and (4A), where an application is made on notice, the applicant must serve a copy of the application, together with the notice of proceedings, personally on–
   (a) the respondent;
   (b) the person who is the subject of the proceedings (if that person is neither the applicant nor a respondent); and
   (c) any other person directed by the court,

   not less than 2 days before the date on which the application will be heard.
(2) The court may abridge the period specified in paragraph (1).
(3) Service of the application must be effected by the court if the applicant so requests (this does not affect the court's power to order substituted service).
(4) Where the application is served on the person who is the subject of the proceedings, it must be accompanied by a notice informing that person–
   (a) how to apply to become a party to the proceedings; and
   (b) of that person's right to make representations in writing or orally at any hearing.
(5) Where the person who is the subject of proceedings is not the applicant and is–
   (a) a child;
   (b) a person, not being a party, who lacks or may lack capacity within the meaning of the 2005 Act; or
   (c) a protected party,

   the court will give the directions about the persons who are to be served with the application.
(6) Where an application is served by the applicant, the applicant must file a certificate of service stating the date and time of personal service.

11.5 Transfer of proceedings

Subject to any enactment, where proceedings to which this Part applies are pending, the court may transfer the proceedings to another court of its own initiative or on the application of a party or (if not a party) the person who is the subject of the proceedings.

11.6 Parties

(1) In proceedings under this Part, a person may file a Part 18 application notice for that person or another person to–
   (a) be joined as a party; or
   (b) cease to be a party.
(2) As soon as practicable after receiving an application under paragraph (1), the court must do one of the following–
   (a) in the case only of an application under paragraph (1)(a), grant the application;

(b) order that the application be considered at a hearing, and fix a date for the hearing; or
(c) invite written representations as to whether the application should be granted, to be filed within a specified period, and upon expiry of that period act under sub-paragraph (a) or (b) as it sees fit.

(3) The court officer must inform the following persons of the court's action under paragraph (2)–
   (a) the applicant under paragraph (1);
   (b) (if different) the applicant for the forced marriage protection order and the respondent to that application;
   (c) (if different) the person who is the subject of the proceedings; and
   (d) any other person directed by the court.

(4) The court may at any time direct–
   (a) that a person who would not otherwise be a respondent under these rules be joined as a party to the proceedings; or
   (b) that a party to the proceedings cease to be a party,

and such a direction may be made by the court of its own initiative as well as upon an application under paragraph (1).

(5) Where the court directs the addition or removal of a party, it may give consequential directions about–
   (a) service on a new party of a copy of the application for the forced marriage protection order and other relevant documents; and
   (b) the management of the proceedings.

11.7 Hearings and service of orders

(1) Any hearing relating to an application for a forced marriage protection order must be in private unless the court otherwise directs.

(2) The court may direct the withholding of any submissions made, or any evidence adduced, for or at any hearing in proceedings to which this Part applies–
   (a) in order to protect the person who is the subject of the proceedings or any other person; or
   (b) for any other good reason.

(3) The applicant must, as soon as reasonably practical, serve personally–
   (a) a copy of the order;
   (b) a copy of the record of the hearing; and
   (c) where the order is made without notice, a copy of the application together with any statement supporting it,

on the respondent, the person who is the subject of the proceedings (if neither the applicant nor a respondent), and any other person named in the order.

(4) The court must serve the documents listed in paragraph (3) if–
   (a) an applicant, acting in person, so requests; or
   (b) the court made the order of its own initiative.

11.8 Orders made by the court of its own initiative

(1) Where the court makes a forced marriage protection order of its own initiative under section 63C of the 1996 Act, it must set out in the order–
   (a) a summary of its reasons for making the order; and
   (b) the names of the persons who are to be served with the order.

(2) The court may order service of the order on–

(a) any of the parties to the current proceedings;
(b) (if different) the person who is the subject of the proceedings; and
(c) any other person whom the court considers should be served.

(3) The court must give directions as to how the order is to be served.

11.9 Representations in respect of orders

Where the court makes an order (whether under rule 11.7 or 11.8), it may direct that a hearing (or further hearing) be held in order to consider any representations made by any of the persons named in, or directed to be served with, the order.

11.10 Applications to vary, extend or discharge an order

Rules 11.7 and 11.9 apply to applications to vary, extend or discharge a forced marriage protection order.

11.11 Orders containing provisions to which a power of arrest is attached

Where the court makes a forced marriage protection order containing one or more provisions to which a power of arrest is attached ('relevant provision')–

(a) each relevant provision must be set out in a separate paragraph in the order; and
(b) a paragraph containing a relevant provision must not include a provision of the order to which the power of arrest is not attached.

11.12 Service where order contains a power of arrest

(1) This rule applies where the court makes a forced marriage protection order consisting of or including a relevant provision (which has the meaning given in rule 11.11).
(2) The following documents must be delivered to the officer for the time being in charge of any police station for the address of the person being protected by the order or of such other police station as the court may specify–

(a) the power of arrest form; and
(b) a statement showing that the respondents and any persons directed by the court to be served with the order have been so served or informed of its terms (whether by being present when the order was made or by telephone or otherwise).

(3) The documents referred to in paragraph (2) must be delivered by–

(a) the applicant, if the applicant is responsible for serving the order in accordance with rule 11.7(3); or
(b) the court officer, if the court is responsible for serving the order in accordance with rule 11.7(4) or a direction given under rule 11.8(3).

(4) Where an order is made varying, extending or discharging any of the relevant provisions, the court officer must–

(a) immediately inform the officer who received a copy of the power of arrest form under paragraph (2) and, if the address of the person who is the subject of the proceedings has changed, the officer for the time being in charge of the police station for the new address; and
(b) deliver a copy of the order, together with a copy of the order referred to in paragraph (1), to any officer so informed.

11.13 Application for issue of warrant for arrest

(1) An application under section 63J(2) of the 1996 Act for the issue of a warrant for the arrest of a person must be supported by a sworn statement.
(2) An application for the issue of a warrant for arrest made by a person who is neither the

person who is the subject of the proceedings nor (if different) the person who applied for the order, shall be treated, in the first instance, as an application for permission to apply for the warrant to be issued, and the court shall either–

(a) grant the application; or
(b) direct that a date be fixed for the hearing of the application and fix a date.

(3) The court officer must inform the following persons of the court's action under paragraph (2)–

(a) the person applying for the issue of the warrant;
(b) the person being protected by the order; and
(c) any other person directed by the court.

11.14 Proceedings following arrest

(1) This rule applies where a person is arrested pursuant to–

(a) a power of arrest attached to a provision of a forced marriage protection order; or
(b) a warrant of arrest issued on an application under section 63J(2) of the 1996 Act.

(2) The court before whom a person is brought following his arrest may–

(a) determine whether the facts and the circumstances which led to the arrest amounted to disobedience of the order; or
(b) adjourn the proceedings.

(3) Where the proceedings are adjourned, the arrested person may be released and–

(a) unless the court directs otherwise, be dealt with within 14 days of the day on which the person was arrested; and
(b) be given not less than 2 days' notice of the adjourned hearing.

(4) An application notice seeking the committal for contempt of court of the arrested person may be issued if the arrested person is not dealt with within the period mentioned in paragraph (3)(a).

(The powers of a county court and the High Court to remand in custody or on bail are contained in section 47 of and Schedule 5 to the 1996 Act.)

11.15 Enforcement of orders

(1) The following provisions apply, with the necessary modifications, to the enforcement of orders made under this Part–

(a) RSC Order 52, rule 7 (power to suspend execution of committal order);
(b) in a case where an application for an order of committal is made to the High Court, RSC Order 52, rule 2 (application to Divisional Court);
(c) CCR Order 29, rule 1 (enforcement of judgment to do or abstain from doing any act);
(d) CCR Order 29, rule 1A (undertaking given by party);
(e) CCR Order 29, rule 3 (discharge of person in custody).

(2) Rule 1 of Order 29 of the CCR (enforcement of judgment to do or abstain from doing any act) has effect as if, for paragraph (3), there were substituted the following–

'(3) At the time when the order is drawn up, the court officer will, where the order made is (or includes) a forced marriage protection order, issue a copy of the order, indorsed with or incorporating a notice as to the consequences of disobedience, for service in accordance with paragraph (2).'

(For enforcement of an order generally in a county court or the High Court see Part 33.)

11.16 Power to adjourn the hearing for consideration of the penalty

The court may adjourn the hearing for consideration of the penalty to be imposed for any contempt of court found proved and such hearing may be restored if the contemnor does not comply with any conditions specified by the court.

11.17 Hospital orders or guardianship orders under the Mental Health Act 1983

(1) Where the court makes a hospital order under the Mental Health Act 1983, the court officer must–

    (a) send to the hospital any information which will be of assistance in dealing with the patient; and

    (b) inform the persons directed by the court to be informed about when the patient is being transferred to hospital.

(2) Where the court makes a guardianship order under the Mental Health Act 1983, the court officer must send any information which will be of assistance in dealing with the patient to–

    (a) the patient's guardian; and

    (b) where the guardian is a person other than the local services authority, the local services authority.

11.18 Transfer directions under section 48 of the Mental Health Act 1983

(1) Where a transfer direction given by the Secretary of State under section 48 of the Mental Health Act 1983 is in force in respect of a person remanded in custody by the court, the court officer must notify–

    (a) the governor of the prison to which that person was remanded; and

    (b) the hospital where that person is detained,

of any committal hearing which that person is required to attend.

(2) The court officer must also give notice in writing of any further remand to the hospital where that person is detained.

11.19 Recognizances

(1) Where, in accordance with paragraph 2(1)(b)(ii) of Schedule 5 to the 1996 Act, the court fixes the amount of any recognizance with a view to it being taken subsequently, the recognizance may be taken by–

    (a) a district judge;

    (b) a police officer of the rank of inspector or above or in charge of a police station; or

    (c) the governor or keeper of a prison where the arrested person is in the custody of that governor or keeper.

(2) The person having custody of an applicant for bail must release him if satisfied that the required recognizances have been taken.

PART 12 PROCEEDINGS RELATING TO CHILDREN EXCEPT PARENTAL ORDER PROCEEDINGS AND PROCEEDINGS FOR APPLICATIONS IN ADOPTION, PLACEMENT AND RELATED PROCEEDINGS

CHAPTER 1 INTERPRETATION AND APPLICATION OF THIS PART

12.1 Application of this Part

(1) The rules in this Part apply to–

(a) emergency proceedings;
(b) private law proceedings;
(c) public law proceedings;
(d) proceedings relating to the exercise of the court's inherent jurisdiction (other than applications for the court's permission to start such proceedings);
(e) proceedings relating to child abduction and the recognition and enforcement of decisions relating to custody under the European Convention;
(f) proceedings relating to the Council Regulation or the 1996 Hague Convention in respect of children; and
(g) any other proceedings which may be referred to in a practice direction.

(Part 18 sets out the procedure for making an application for permission to bring proceedings.)

(Part 31 sets out the procedure for making applications for recognition and enforcement of judgments under the Council Regulation or the 1996 Hague Convention.)

(2) The rules in Chapter 7 of this Part also apply to family proceedings which are not within paragraph (1) but which otherwise relate wholly or mainly to the maintenance or upbringing of a minor.

12.2 Interpretation

In this Part–

'the 2006 Act' means the Childcare Act 2006;

'advocate' means a person exercising a right of audience as a representative of, or on behalf of, a party;

'care proceedings' means proceedings for a care order under section 31(1)(a) of the 1989 Act;

'Case Management Order' means an order in the form referred to in Practice Direction 12A which may contain such of the provisions listed in that practice direction as may be appropriate to the proceedings;

'child assessment order' has the meaning assigned to it by section 43(2) of the 1989 Act;

'contact activity condition' has the meaning assigned to it by section 11C(2) of the 1989 Act;

'contact activity direction' has the meaning assigned to it by section 11A(3) of the 1989 Act;

'contribution order' has the meaning assigned to it by paragraph 23(2) of Schedule 2 to the 1989 Act;

'education supervision order' has the meaning assigned to it by section 36(2) of the 1989 Act;

'emergency proceedings' means proceedings for–

(a) the disclosure of information as to the whereabouts of a child under section 33 of the 1986 Act;
(b) an order authorising the taking charge of and delivery of a child under section 34 of the 1986 Act;
(c) an emergency protection order;
(d) an order under section 44(9)(b) of the 1989 Act varying a direction in an emergency protection order given under section 44(6) of that Act;
(e) an order under section 45(5) of the 1989 Act extending the period during which an emergency protection order is to have effect;
(f) an order under section 45(8) of the 1989 Act discharging an emergency protection order;
(g) an order under section 45(8A) of the 1989 Act varying or discharging an

emergency protection order in so far as it imposes an exclusion requirement on a person who is not entitled to apply for the order to be discharged;

(h) an order under section 45(8B) of the 1989 Act varying or discharging an emergency protection order in so far as it confers a power of arrest attached to an exclusion requirement;

(i) warrants under sections 48(9) and 102(1) of the 1989 Act and under section 79 of the 2006 Act; or

(j) a recovery order under section 50 of the 1989 Act;

'emergency protection order' means an order under section 44 of the 1989 Act;

'enforcement order' has the meaning assigned to it by section 11J(2) of the 1989 Act;

'financial compensation order' means an order made under section 11O(2) of the 1989 Act;

'interim order' means an interim care order or an interim supervision order referred to in section 38(1) of the 1989 Act;

'private law proceedings' means proceedings for–

(a) a section 8 order except a residence order under section 8 of the 1989 Act relating to a child who is the subject of a care order;

(b) a parental responsibility order under sections 4(1)(c), 4ZA(1)(c) or 4A(1)(b) of the 1989 Act or an order terminating parental responsibility under sections 4(2A), 4ZA(5) or 4A(3) of that Act;

(c) an order appointing a child's guardian under section 5(1) of the 1989 Act or an order terminating the appointment under section 6(7) of that Act;

(d) an order giving permission to change a child's surname or remove a child from the United Kingdom under sections 13(1) or 14C(3) of the 1989 Act;

(e) a special guardianship order except where that order relates to a child who is subject of a care order;

(f) an order varying or discharging such an order under section 14D of the 1989 Act;

(g) an enforcement order;

(h) a financial compensation order;

(i) an order under paragraph 9 of Schedule A1 to the 1989 Act following a breach of an enforcement order;

(j) an order under Part 2 of Schedule A1 to the 1989 Act revoking or amending an enforcement order; or

(k) an order that a warning notice be attached to a contact order;

'public law proceedings' means proceedings for–

(a) a residence order under section 8 of the 1989 Act relating to a child who is the subject of a care order;

(b) a special guardianship order relating to a child who is the subject of a care order;

(c) a secure accommodation order under section 25 of the 1989 Act;

(d) a care order, or the discharge of such an order under section 39(1) of the 1989 Act;

(e) an order giving permission to change a child's surname or remove a child from the United Kingdom under section 33(7) of the 1989 Act;

(f) a supervision order under section 31(1)(b) of the 1989 Act, the discharge or variation of such an order under section 39(2) of that Act, or the extension or further extension of such an order under paragraph 6(3) of Schedule 3 to that Act;

(g) an order making provision regarding contact under section 34(2) to (4) of the 1989 Act or an order varying or discharging such an order under section 34(9) of that Act;

(h) an education supervision order, the extension of an education supervision

order under paragraph 15(2) of Schedule 3 to the 1989 Act, or the discharge of such an order under paragraph 17(1) of Schedule 3 to that Act;
(i) an order varying directions made with an interim care order or interim supervision order under section 38(8)(b) of the 1989 Act;
(j) an order under section 39(3) of the 1989 Act varying a supervision order in so far as it affects a person with whom the child is living but who is not entitled to apply for the order to be discharged;
(k) an order under section 39(3A) of the 1989 Act varying or discharging an interim care order in so far as it imposes an exclusion requirement on a person who is not entitled to apply for the order to be discharged;
(l) an order under section 39(3B) of the 1989 Act varying or discharging an interim care order in so far as it confers a power of arrest attached to an exclusion requirement;
(m) the substitution of a supervision order for a care order under section 39(4) of the 1989 Act;
(n) a child assessment order, or the variation or discharge of such an order under section 43(12) of the 1989 Act;
(o) an order permitting the local authority to arrange for any child in its care to live outside England and Wales under paragraph 19(1) of Schedule 2 to the 1989 Act;
(p) a contribution order, or revocation of such an order under paragraph 23(8) of Schedule 2 to the 1989 Act;
(q) an appeal under paragraph 8(1) of Schedule 8 to the 1989 Act;

'special guardianship order' has the meaning assigned to it by section 14A(1) of the 1989 Act;

'supervision order' has the meaning assigned to it by section 31(11) of the 1989 Act;

'supervision proceedings' means proceedings for a supervision order under section 31(1)(b) of the 1989 Act;

'warning notice' means a notice attached to an order pursuant to section 8(2) of the Children and Adoption Act 2006.

(The 1980 Hague Convention, the 1996 Hague Convention, the Council Regulation, and the European Convention are defined in rule 2.3.)

CHAPTER 2   GENERAL RULES

12.3   Who the parties are

(1) In relation to the proceedings set out in column 1 of the following table, column 2 sets out who may make the application and column 3 sets out who the respondents to those proceedings will be.

Proceedings for	Applicants	Respondents
A parental responsibility order (section 4(1)(c), 4ZA(1)(c), or section 4A(1)(b) of the 1989 Act).	The child's father; the step parent; or the child's parent (being a woman who is a parent by virtue of section 43 of the Human Fertilisation and Embryology Act 2008 and who is not a person to whom section 1(3) of the Family Law Reform Act 1987(18) applies) (sections 4(1)(c), 4ZA(1)(c) and 4A(1)(b) of the 1989 Act).	Every person whom the applicant believes to have parental responsibility for the child; where the child is the subject of a care order, every person whom the applicant believes to have had parental responsibility immediately prior to the making of the care order; in the case of an application to extend, vary or discharge an order, the parties to the proceedings leading to the order which it is sought to have extended, varied or discharged; in the case of specified proceedings, the child.
An order terminating a parental responsibility order or agreement (section 4(2A), 4ZA(5) or section 4A(3) of the 1989 Act.	Any person who has parental responsibility for the child; or with the court's permission, the child (section 4(3), 4ZA(6) and section 4A(3) of the 1989 Act).	As above.
An order appointing a guardian (section 5(1) of the 1989 Act).	An individual who wishes to be appointed as guardian (section 5(1) of the 1989 Act).	As above.
An order terminating the appointment of a guardian (section 6(7) of the 1989 Act).	Any person who has parental responsibility for the child; or with the court's permission, the child (section 6(7) of the 1989 Act).	As above.
A section 8 order.	Any person who is entitled to apply for a section 8 order with respect to the child (section 10(4) to (7) of the 1989 Act); or with the court's permission, any person (section10(2)(b) of the 1989 Act).	As above.

Proceedings for	Applicants	Respondents
An enforcement order (section 11J of the 1989 Act).	A person who is, for the purposes of the contact order, a person with whom the child concerned lives or is to live; any person whose contact with the child concerned is provided for in the contact order; any individual subject to a condition under section 11(7)(b) of the 1989 Act or a contact activity condition imposed by a contact order; or with the court's permission, the child (section 11J(5) of the 1989 Act).	The person the applicant alleges has failed to comply with the contact order.
A financial compensation order (section 11O of the 1989 Act).	Any person who is, for the purposes of the contact order, a person with whom the child concerned lives or is to live; any person whose contact with the child concerned is provided for in the contact order; any individual subject to a condition under section 11(7)(b) of the 1989 Act or a contact activity condition imposed by a contact order; or with the court's permission, the child (section 11O(6) of the 1989 Act).	The person the applicant alleges has failed to comply with the contact order.
An order permitting the child's name to be changed or the removal of the child from the United Kingdom (section 13(1), 14C(3) or 33(7) of the 1989 Act).	Any person (section 13(1), 14C(3), 33(7) of the 1989 Act).	As for a parental responsibility order.

Proceedings for	Applicants	Respondents
A special guardianship order (section 14A of the 1989 Act).	Any guardian of the child; any individual in whose favour a residence order is in force with respect to the child; any individual listed in subsection (5)(b) or (c) of section 10 (as read with subsection (10) of that section) of the 1989 Act; a local authority foster parent with whom the child has lived for a period of at least one year immediately preceding the application; or any person with the court's permission (section 14A(3) of the 1989 Act) (more than one such individual can apply jointly (section 14A(3) and (5) of that Act)).	As above, and if a care order is in force with respect to the child, the child.
Variation or discharge of a special guardianship order (section 14D of the 1989 Act).	The special guardian (or any of them, if there is more than one); any individual in whose favour a residence order is in force with respect to the child; the local authority designated in a care order with respect to the child; any individual within section 14D(1)(d) of the 1989 Act who has parental responsibility for the child; the child, any parent or guardian of the child and any step-parent of the child who has acquired, and has not lost, parental responsibility by virtue of section 4A of that Act with the court's permission; or any individual within section 14D(1)(d) of that Act who immediately before the making of the special guardianship order had, but no longer has, parental responsibility for the child with the court's permission.	As above.

Proceedings for	Applicants	Respondents
A secure accommodation order (section 25 section of the 1989 Act).	The local authority which is looking after the child; or the Health Authority, Primary Care Trust, National Health Service Trust established under section 25 of the National Health Service Act 2006 or section 18(1) of the National Health Service (Wales) Act 2006, National Health Service Foundation Trust or any local authority providing accommodation for the child (unless the child is looked after by a local authority).	As above.
A care or supervision order (section 31 of the 1989 Act).	Any local authority; the National Society for the Prevention of Cruelty to Children and any of its officers (section 31(1) of the 1989 Act); or any authorised person.	As above.
An order varying directions made with an interim care or interim supervision order (section 38(8)(b) of the 1989 Act).	The parties to proceedings in which directions are given under section 38(6) of the 1989 Act; or any person named in such a direction.	As above.
An order discharging a care order (section 39(1) of the 1989 Act).	Any person who has parental responsibility for the child the child; or the local authority designated by the order (section 39(1) of the 1989 Act).	As above
An order varying or discharging an interim care order in so far as it imposes an exclusion requirement (section 39(3A) of the 1989 Act).	A person to whom the exclusion requirement in the interim care order applies who is not entitled to apply for the order to be discharged (section 39(3A) of the 1989 Act).	As above.

Proceedings for	Applicants	Respondents
An order varying or discharging an interim care order in so far as it confers a power of arrest attached to an exclusion requirement (section 39(3B) of the 1989 Act).	Any person entitled to apply for the discharge of the interim care order in so far as it imposes the exclusion requirement (section 39(3B) of the 1989 Act).	As above.
An order substituting a supervision order for a care order (section 39(4) of the 1989 Act).	Any person entitled to apply for a care order to be discharged under section 39(1) (section 39(4) of the 1989 Act).	As above.
A child assessment order (section 43(1) of the 1989 Act).	Any local authority; the National Society for the Prevention of Cruelty to Children and any of its officers; or any person authorised by order of the Secretary of State to bring the proceedings and any officer of a body who is so authorised (section 43(1) and (13) of the 1989 Act).	As above.
An order varying or discharging a child assessment order (section 43(12) of the 1989 Act).	The applicant for an order that has been made under section 43(1) of the 1989 Act; or the persons referred to in section 43(11) of the 1989 Act (section 43(12) of that Act).	As above.
An emergency protection order (section 44(1) of the 1989 Act).	Any person (section 44(1) of the 1989 Act).	As for a parental responsibility order.
An order extending the period during which an emergency protection order is to have effect (section 45(4) of the 1989 Act).	Any person who– has parental responsibility for a child as the result of an emergency protection order; and is entitled to apply for a care order with respect to the child (section 45(4) of the 1989 Act).	As above.

Proceedings for	Applicants	Respondents
An order discharging an emergency protection order (section 45(8) of the 1989 Act).	The child; a parent of the child; any person who is not a parent of the child but who has parental responsibility for the child; or any person with whom the child was living before the making of the emergency protection order (section 45(8) of the 1989 Act).	As above.
An order varying or discharging an emergency protection order in so far as it imposes the exclusion requirement (section 45(8A) of the 1989 Act).	A person to whom the exclusion requirement in the emergency protection order applies who is not entitled to apply for the emergency protection order to be discharged (section 45(8A) of the 1989 Act).	As above.
An order varying or discharging an emergency protection order in so far as it confers a power of arrest attached to an exclusion requirement (section 45(8B) of the 1989 Act).	Any person entitled to apply for the discharge of the emergency protection order in so far as it imposes the exclusion requirement (section 45(8B) of the 1989 Act).	As above.
An emergency protection order by the police (section 46(7) of the 1989 Act).	The officer designated for the purposes of section 46(3)(e) of the 1989 Act (section 46(7) of the 1989 Act).	As above.
A warrant authorising a constable to assist in exercise of certain powers to search for children and inspect premises (section 48 of the 1989 Act).	Any person attempting to exercise powers under an emergency protection order who has been or is likely to be prevented from doing so by being refused entry to the premises concerned or refused access to the child concerned (section 48(9) of the 1989 Act).	As above.

Proceedings for	Applicants	Respondents
A warrant authorising a constable to assist in exercise of certain powers to search for children and inspect premises (section 102 of the 1989 Act).	Any person attempting to exercise powers under the enactments mentioned in section 102(6) of the 1989 Act who has been or is likely to be prevented from doing so by being refused entry to the premises concerned or refused access to the child concerned (section 102(1) of that Act).	As above.
An order revoking an enforcement order (paragraph 4 of Schedule A1 to the 1989 Act).	The person subject to the enforcement order.	The person who was the applicant for the enforcement order; and, where the child was a party to the proceedings in which the enforcement order was made, the child.
An order amending an enforcement order (paragraphs 5 to 7 of Schedule A1 to the 1989 Act).	The person subject to the enforcement order.	The person who was the applicant for the enforcement order. (Rule 12.33 makes provision about applications under paragraph 5 of Schedule A1 to the 1989 Act.)
An order following breach of an enforcement order (paragraph 9 of Schedule A1 to the 1989 Act).	Any person who is, for the purposes of the contact order, the person with whom the child lives or is to live; any person whose contact with the child concerned is provided for in the contact order; any individual subject to a condition under section 11(7)(b) of the 1989 Act or a contact activity condition imposed by a contact order; or with the court's permission, the child (paragraph 9 of Schedule A1 to the 1989 Act).	The person the applicant alleges has failed to comply with the unpaid work requirement imposed by an enforcement order; and where the child was a party to the proceedings in which the enforcement order was made, the child.

Proceedings for	Applicants	Respondents
An order permitting the local authority to arrange for any child in its care to live outside England and Wales (Schedule 2, paragraph 19(1), to the 1989 Act).	The local authority (Schedule 2, paragraph 19(1), to the 1989 Act).	As for a parental responsibility order.
A contribution order (Schedule 2, paragraph 23(1), to the 1989 Act).	The local authority (Schedule 2, paragraph 23(1), to the 1989 Act).	As above and the contributor.
An order revoking a contribution order (Schedule 2, paragraph 23(8), to the 1989 Act).	The contributor; or the local authority.	As above.
An order relating to contact with the child in care and any named person (section 34(2) of the 1989 Act) or permitting the local authority to refuse contact (section 34(4) of that Act).	The local authority; or the child (section 34(2) or 34(4) of the 1989 Act).	As above; and the person whose contact with the child is the subject of the application.
An order relating to contact with the child in care (section 34(3) of the 1989 Act).	The child's parents; any guardian or special guardian of the child; any person who by virtue of section 4A of the 1989 Act has parental responsibility for the child; a person in whose favour there was a residence order in force with respect to the child immediately before the care order was made; a person who by virtue of an order made in the exercise of the High Court's inherent jurisdiction with respect to children had care of the child immediately before the care order was made (section 34(3)(a) of the 1989 Act); or with the court's permission, any person (section 34(3)(b) of that Act).	As above; and the person whose contact with the child is the subject of the application.

Proceedings for	Applicants	Respondents
An order varying or discharging an order for contact with a child in care under section 34 (section 34((9) of the 1989 Act).	The local authority; the child; or any person named in the order (section 34(9) of the 1989 Act).	As above; and the person whose contact with the child is the subject of the application.
An education supervision order (section 36 of the 1989 Act).	Any local authority (section 36(1) of the 1989 Act).	As above; and the child.
An order varying or discharging a supervision order (section 39(2) of the 1989 Act).	Any person who has parental responsibility for the child; the child; or the supervisor (section 39(2) of the 1989 Act).	As above; and the supervisor.
An order varying a supervision order in so far as it affects the person with whom the child is living (section 39(3) of the 1989 Act).	The person with whom the child is living who is not entitled to apply for the order to be discharged (section 39(3) of the 1989 Act).	As above; and the supervisor.
An order varying a direction under section 44(6) of the 1989 Act in an emergency protection order (section 44(9)(b) of that Act).	The parties to the application for the emergency protection order in respect of which it is sought to vary the directions; the children's guardian; the local authority in whose area the child is ordinarily resident; or any person who is named in the directions.	As above, and the parties to the application for the order in respect of which it is sought to vary the directions; any person who was caring for the child prior to the making of the order; and any person whose contact with the child is affected by the direction which it is sought to have varied.
A recovery order (section 50 of the 1989 Act).	Any person who has parental responsibility for the child by virtue of a care order or an emergency protection order; or where the child is in police protection the officer designated for the purposes of section 46(3)(e) of the 1989 Act (section 50(4) of the 1989 Act).	As above; and the person whom the applicant alleges to have effected or to have been or to be responsible for the taking or keeping of the child.

Proceedings for	Applicants	Respondents
An order discharging an education supervision order (Schedule 3, paragraph 17(1), to the 1989 Act).	The child concerned; a parent of the child; or the local authority concerned (Schedule 3, paragraph 17(1), to the 1989 Act).	As above; and the local authority concerned; and the child.
An order extending an education supervision order (Schedule 3, paragraph, 15(2), to the 1989 Act).	The local authority in whose favour the education supervision order was made (Schedule 3, paragraph 15(2), to the 1989 Act).	As above; and the child.
An appeal under paragraph (8) of Schedule 8 to the 1989 Act.	A person aggrieved by the matters listed in paragraph 8(1) of Schedule 8 to the 1989 Act.	The appropriate local authority.
An order for the disclosure of information as to the whereabouts of a child under section 33 of the 1986 Act.	Any person with a legitimate interest in proceedings for an order under Part 1 of the 1986 Act; or a person who has registered an order made elsewhere in the United Kingdom or a specified dependent territory.	Any person alleged to have information as to the whereabouts of the child.
An order authorising the taking charge of and delivery of a child under section 34 of the 1986 Act.	The person to whom the child is to be given up under section 34(1) of the 1986 Act.	As above; and the person who is required to give up the child in accordance with section 34(1) of the 1986 Act.
An order relating to the exercise of the court's inherent jurisdiction (including wardship proceedings).	A local authority (with the court's permission); any person with a genuine interest in or relation to the child; or the child (wardship proceedings only).	The parent or guardian of the child; any other person who has an interest in or relationship to the child; and the child (wardship proceedings only and with the court's permission as described at rule 12.37).

Proceedings for	Applicants	Respondents
A warrant under section 79 of the 2006 Act authorising any constable to assist Her Majesty's Chief Inspector for Education, Children's Services and Skills in the exercise of powers conferred on him by section 77 of the 2006 Act.	Her Majesty's Chief Inspector for Education, Children's Services and Skills.	Any person preventing or likely to prevent Her Majesty's Chief Inspector for Education, Children's Services and Skills from exercising powers conferred on him by section 77 of the 2006 Act.
An order in respect of a child under the 1980 Hague Convention.	Any person, institution or body who claims that a child has been removed or retained in breach of rights of custody or claims that there has been a breach of rights of access in relation to the child.	The person alleged to have brought the child into the United Kingdom; the person with whom the child is alleged to be; any parent or guardian of the child who is within the United Kingdom and is not otherwise a party; any person in whose favour a decision relating to custody has been made if that person is not otherwise a party; and any other person who appears to the court to have sufficient interest in the welfare of the child.
An order concerning the recognition and enforcement of decisions relating to custody under the European Convention.	Any person who has a court order giving that person rights of custody in relation to the child.	As above.
An application for the High Court to request transfer of jurisdiction under Article 15 of the Council Regulation or Article 9 of the 1996 Hague Convention (rule 12.65).	Any person with sufficient interest in the welfare of the child and who would be entitled to make a proposed application in relation to that child, or who intends to seek the permission of the court to make such application if the transfer is agreed.	As directed by the court in accordance with rule 12.65.

Proceedings for	Applicants	Respondents
An application under rule 12.71 for a declaration as to the existence, or extent, of parental responsibility under Article 16 of the 1996 Convention.	Any interested person including a person who holds, or claims to hold, parental responsibility for the child under the law of another State which subsists in accordance with Article 16 of the 1996 Hague Convention following the child becoming habitually resident in a territorial unit of the United Kingdom.	Every person whom the applicant believes to have parental responsibility for the child; any person whom the applicant believes to hold parental responsibility for the child under the law of another State which subsists in accordance with Article 16 of the 1996 Hague Convention following the child becoming habitually resident in a territorial unit of the United Kingdom; and where the child is the subject of a care order, every person whom the applicant believes to have had parental responsibility immediately prior to the making of the care order.
A warning notice.	The person who is, for the purposes of the contact order, the person with whom the child concerned lives or is to live; the person whose contact with the child concerned is provided for in the contact order; any individual subject to a condition under section 11(7)(b) of the 1989 Act or a contact activity condition imposed by the contact order; or with the court's permission, the child.	Any person who was a party to the proceedings in which the contact order was made. (Rule 12.33 makes provision about applications for warning notices).

(2) The court will direct that a person with parental responsibility be made a party to proceedings where that person requests to be one.

(3) Subject to rule 16.2, the court may at any time direct that–

    (a)   any person or body be made a party to proceedings; or

    (b)   a party be removed.

(4) If the court makes a direction for the addition or removal of a party under this rule, it may give consequential directions about–

    (a)   the service of a copy of the application form or other relevant documents on the new party;

    (b)   the management of the proceedings.

(5) In this rule–

'a local authority foster parent' has the meaning assigned to it by section 23(3) of the 1989 Act; and

'care home', 'independent hospital', 'local authority' and 'Primary Care Trust' have the meanings assigned to them by section 105 of the 1989 Act.

(Part 16 contains the rules relating to the representation of children.)

12.4 Notice of proceedings to person with foreign parental responsibility

(1) This rule applies where a child is subject to proceedings to which this Part applies and–
   (a) a person holds or is believed to hold parental responsibility for the child under the law of another State which subsists in accordance with Article 16 of the 1996 Hague Convention following the child becoming habitually resident in a territorial unit of the United Kingdom; and
   (b) that person is not otherwise required to be joined as a respondent under rule 12.3.
(2) The applicant shall give notice of the proceedings to any person to whom the applicant believes paragraph (1) applies in any case in which a person whom the applicant believed to have parental responsibility under the 1989 Act would be a respondent to those proceedings in accordance with rule 12.3.
(3) The applicant and every respondent to the proceedings shall provide such details as they possess as to the identity and whereabouts of any person they believe to hold parental responsibility for the child in accordance with paragraph (1) to the court officer, upon making, or responding to the application as appropriate.
(4) Where the existence of a person who is believed to have parental responsibility for the child in accordance with paragraph (1) only becomes apparent to a party at a later date during the proceedings, that party must notify the court officer of those details at the earliest opportunity.
(5) Where a person to whom paragraph (1) applies receives notice of proceedings, that person may apply to the court to be joined as a party using the Part 18 procedure.

12.5 What the court will do when the application has been issued

When the proceedings have been issued the court will consider–
(a) setting a date for–
   (i) a directions appointment;
   (ii) in private law proceedings, a First Hearing Dispute Resolution Appointment;
   (iii) in care and supervision proceedings and in so far as practicable other public law proceedings, the First Appointment; or
   (iv) the hearing of the application or an application for an interim order,

   and if the court sets a date it will do so in accordance with rule 12.13 and Practice Directions 12A and 12B;
(b) giving any of the directions listed in rule 12.12 or, where Chapter 6, section 1 applies, rule 12.48; and
(c) doing anything else which is set out in Practice Directions 12A or 12B or any other practice direction.

(Practice Directions 12A and 12B supplementing this Part set out details relating to the First Hearing Dispute Resolution Appointment and the First Appointment.)

12.6 Children's guardian, solicitor and reports under section 7 of the 1989 Act

As soon as practicable after the issue of proceedings or the transfer of the proceedings to the court, the court will–
(a) in specified proceedings, appoint a children's guardian under rule 16.3(1) unless–

(i) such an appointment has already been made by the court which made the transfer and is subsisting; or
(ii) the court considers that such an appointment is not necessary to safeguard the interests of the child;
(b) where section 41(3) of the 1989 Act applies, consider whether a solicitor should be appointed to represent the child, and if so, appoint a solicitor accordingly;
(c) consider whether to ask an officer of the service or a Welsh family proceedings officer for advice relating to the welfare of the child;
(d) consider whether a report relating to the welfare of the child is required, and if so, request such a report in accordance with section 7 of the 1989 Act.

(Part 16 sets out the rules relating to representation of children.)

12.7 What a court officer will do

(1) As soon as practicable after the issue of proceedings the court officer will return to the applicant the copies of the application together with the forms referred to in Practice Direction 5A.
(2) As soon as practicable after the issue of proceedings or the transfer of proceedings to the court or at any other stage in the proceedings the court officer will–
   (a) give notice of any hearing set by the court to the applicant; and
   (b) do anything else set out in Practice Directions 12A or 12B or any other practice direction.

12.8 Service of the application

The applicant will serve–
(a) the application together with the documents referred to in Practice Direction 12C on the persons referred to and within the time specified in that Practice Direction; and
(b) notice of any hearing set by the court on the persons referred to in Practice Direction 12C at the same time as serving the application.

12.9 Request for transfer from magistrates' court to county court or to another magistrates' court

(1) In accordance with the Allocation Order, a magistrates' court may order proceedings before the court (or any part of them) to be transferred to another magistrates' court or to a county court.
(2) Where any request to transfer proceedings to another magistrates' court or to a county court is refused, the court officer will send a copy of the written record of the reasons for refusing the transfer to the parties.

12.10 Procedure following refusal of magistrates' court to order transfer

(1) Where a request under rule 12.9 to transfer proceedings to a county court in accordance with the provisions of the Allocation Order is refused, a party to the proceedings may apply to a county court for an order transferring proceedings from the magistrates' court.
(2) Such an application must be made in accordance with Part 18 and the Allocation Order.

12.11 Transfer of proceedings from one court to another court

Where proceedings are transferred from one court to another court in accordance with the provisions of the Allocation Order, the court officer from the transferring court will notify the parties of any order transferring the proceedings.

12.12 Directions

(1) This rule does not apply to proceedings under Chapter 6 of this Part.

(2) At any stage in the proceedings, the court may give directions about the conduct of the proceedings including–
   (a) the management of the case;
   (b) the timetable for steps to be taken between the giving of directions and the final hearing;
   (c) the joining of a child or other person as a party to the proceedings in accordance with rules 12.3(2) and (3);
   (d) the attendance of the child;
   (e) the appointment of a children's guardian or of a solicitor under section 41(3) of the 1989 Act;
   (f) the appointment of a litigation friend;
   (g) the service of documents;
   (h) the filing of evidence including experts' reports; and
   (i) the exercise by an officer of the Service, Welsh family proceedings officer or local authority officer of any duty referred to in rule 16.38(1).
(3) Paragraph (4) applies where–
   (a) an officer of the Service or a Welsh family proceedings officer has filed a report or a risk assessment as a result of exercising a duty referred to in rule 16.38(1)(a); or
   (b) a local authority officer has filed a report as a result of exercising a duty referred to in rule 16.38(1)(b).
(4) The court may–
   (a) give directions setting a date for a hearing at which that report or risk assessment will be considered; and
   (b) direct that the officer who prepared the report or risk assessment attend any such hearing.
(5) The court may exercise the powers in paragraphs (2) and (4) on an application or of its own initiative.
(6) Where the court proposes to exercise its powers of its own initiative the procedure set out in rule 4.3(2) to (6) applies.
(7) Directions of a court which are still in force immediately prior to the transfer of proceedings to another court will continue to apply following the transfer subject to–
   (a) any changes of terminology which are required to apply those directions to the court to which the proceedings are transferred; and
   (b) any variation or revocation of the direction.
(8) The court or court officer will–
   (a) take a note of the giving, variation or revocation of a direction under this rule; and
   (b) as soon as practicable serve a copy of the note on every party.

(Rule 12.48 provides for directions in proceedings under the 1980 Hague Convention and the European Convention.)

12.13 Setting dates for hearings and setting or confirming the timetable and date for the final hearing

(1) At the–
   (a) transfer to a court of proceedings;
   (b) postponement or adjournment of any hearing; or
   (c) conclusion of any hearing at which the proceedings are not finally determined,
   the court will set a date for the proceedings to come before the court again for the purposes of giving directions or for such other purposes as the court directs.

(2) At any hearing the court may—
- (a) confirm a date for the final hearing or the week within which the final hearing is to begin (where a date or period for the final hearing has already been set);
- (b) set a timetable for the final hearing unless a timetable has already been fixed, or the court considers that it would be inappropriate to do so; or
- (c) set a date for the final hearing or a period within which the final hearing of the application is to take place.

(3) The court officer will notify the parties of—
- (a) the date of a hearing fixed in accordance with paragraph (1);
- (b) the timetable for the final hearing; and
- (c) the date of the final hearing or the period in which it will take place.

(4) Where the date referred to in paragraph (1) is set at the transfer of proceedings, the date will be as soon as possible after the transfer.

(5) The requirement in paragraph (1) to set a date for the proceedings to come before the court again is satisfied by the court setting or confirming a date for the final hearing.

12.14 Attendance at hearings

(1) This rule does not apply to proceedings under Chapter 6 of this Part except for proceedings for a declaration under rule 12.71.

(2) Unless the court directs otherwise and subject to paragraph (3), the persons who must attend a hearing are—
- (a) any party to the proceedings;
- (b) any litigation friend for any party or legal representative instructed to act on that party's behalf; and
- (c) any other person directed by the court or required by Practice Directions 12A or 12B or any other practice direction to attend.

(3) Proceedings or any part of them will take place in the absence of a child who is a party to the proceedings if—
- (a) the court considers it in the interests of the child, having regard to the matters to be discussed or the evidence likely to be given; and
- (b) the child is represented by a children's guardian or solicitor.

(4) When considering the interests of the child under paragraph (3) the court will give—
- (a) the children's guardian;
- (b) the solicitor for the child; and
- (c) the child, if of sufficient understanding,

an opportunity to make representations.

(5) Subject to paragraph (6), where at the time and place appointed for a hearing, the applicant appears but one or more of the respondents do not, the court may proceed with the hearing.

(6) The court will not begin to hear an application in the absence of a respondent unless the court is satisfied that—
- (a) the respondent received reasonable notice of the date of the hearing; or
- (b) the circumstances of the case justify proceeding with the hearing.

(7) Where, at the time and place appointed for a hearing one or more of the respondents appear but the applicant does not, the court may—
- (a) refuse the application; or
- (b) if sufficient evidence has previously been received, proceed in the absence of the applicant.

(8) Where at the time and place appointed for a hearing neither the applicant nor any respondent appears, the court may refuse the application.
(9) Paragraphs (5) to (8) do not apply to a hearing where the court–
  (a) is considering–
    (i) whether to make a contact activity direction or to attach a contact activity condition to a contact order; or
    (ii) an application for a financial compensation order, an enforcement order or an order under paragraph 9 of Schedule A1 to the 1989 Act following a breach of an enforcement order; and
  (b) has yet to obtain sufficient evidence from, or in relation to, the person who may be the subject of the direction, condition or order to enable it to determine the matter.
(10) Nothing in this rule affects the provisions of Article 18 of the Council Regulation in cases to which that provision applies.

(The Council Regulation makes provision in Article 18 for the court to stay proceedings where the respondent is habitually resident in another Member State of the European Union and has not been adequately served with the proceedings as required by that provision.)

12.15 Steps taken by the parties

If–
(a) the parties or any children's guardian agree proposals for the management of the proceedings (including a proposed date for the final hearing or a period within which the final hearing is to take place); and
(b) the court considers that the proposals are suitable,

it may approve them without a hearing and give directions in the terms proposed.

12.16 Applications without notice

(1) This rule applies to–
  (a) proceedings for a section 8 order;
  (b) emergency proceedings; and
  (c) proceedings relating to the exercise of the court's inherent jurisdiction (other than an application for the court's permission to start such proceedings and proceedings for collection, location and passport orders where Chapter 6 applies).
(2) An application in proceedings referred to in paragraph (1) may, in the High Court or a county court, be made without notice in which case the applicant must file the application–
  (a) where the application is made by telephone, the next business day after the making of the application; or
  (b) in any other case, at the time when the application is made.
(3) An application in proceedings referred to in paragraph (1)(a) or (b) may, in a magistrates' court, be made with the permission of the court, without notice, in which case the applicant must file the application at the time when the application is made or as directed by the court.
(4) Where–
  (a) a section 8 order;
  (b) an emergency protection order;
  (c) an order for the disclosure of information as to the whereabouts of a child under section 33 of the 1986 Act; or

(d) an order authorising the taking charge of and delivery of a child under section 34 of the 1986 Act,

is made without notice, the applicant must serve a copy of the application on each respondent within 48 hours after the order is made.

(5) Within 48 hours after the making of an order without notice, the applicant must serve a copy of the order on–

(a) the parties, unless the court directs otherwise;
(b) any person who has actual care of the child or who had such care immediately prior to the making of the order; and
(c) in the case of an emergency protection order and a recovery order, the local authority in whose area the child lives or is found.

(6) Where the court refuses to make an order on an application without notice it may direct that the application is made on notice in which case the application will proceed in accordance with rules 12.13 to 12.15.
(7) Where the hearing takes place outside the hours during which the court office is normally open, the court or court officer will take a note of the proceedings.

(Practice Direction 12E (Urgent Business) provides further details of the procedure for out of hours applications. See also Practice Direction 12D (Inherent Jurisdiction (including Wardship Proceedings)).)

(Rule 12.47 provides for without-notice applications in proceedings under Chapter 6, section 1 of this Part, (proceedings under the 1980 Hague Convention and the European Convention).)

12.17 Investigation under section 37 of the 1989 Act

(1) This rule applies where a direction is given to an appropriate authority by the court under section 37(1) of the 1989 Act.
(2) On giving the direction the court may adjourn the proceedings.
(3) As soon as practicable after the direction is given the court will record the direction.
(4) As soon as practicable after the direction is given the court officer will–

(a) serve the direction on–
  (i) the parties to the proceedings in which the direction is given; and
  (ii) the appropriate authority where it is not a party;
(b) serve any documentary evidence directed by the court on the appropriate authority.

(5) Where a local authority informs the court of any of the matters set out in section 37(3)(a) to (c) of the 1989 Act it will do so in writing.
(6) Unless the court directs otherwise, the court officer will serve a copy of any report to the court under section 37 of the 1989 Act on the parties.

(Section 37 of the 1989 Act refers to the appropriate authority and section 37(5) of that Act sets out which authority should be named in a particular case.)

12.18 Disclosure of a report under section 14A(8) or (9) of the 1989 Act

(1) In proceedings for a special guardianship order, the local authority must file the report under section 14A(8) or (9) of the 1989 Act within the timetable fixed by the court.
(2) The court will consider whether to give a direction that the report under section 14A(8) or (9) of the 1989 Act be disclosed to each party to the proceedings.
(3) Before giving a direction for the report to be disclosed, the court must consider whether any information should be deleted from the report.
(4) The court may direct that the report must not be disclosed to a party.

(5) The court officer must serve a copy of the report in accordance with any direction under paragraph (2).
(6) In paragraph (3), information includes information which a party has declined to reveal under rule 29.1(1).

12.19 Additional evidence

(1) This rule applies to proceedings for a section 8 order or a special guardianship order.
(2) Unless the court directs otherwise, a party must not–
   (a) file or serve any document other than in accordance with these rules or any practice direction;
   (b) in completing a form prescribed by these rules or any practice direction, give information or make a statement which is not required or authorised by that form; or
   (c) file or serve at a hearing–
      (i) any witness statement of the substance of the oral evidence which the party intends to adduce; or
      (ii) any copy of any document (including any experts' report) which the party intends to rely on.
(3) Where a party fails to comply with the requirements of this rule in relation to any witness statement or other document, the party cannot seek to rely on that statement or other document unless the court directs otherwise.

12.20 Expert evidence–examination of child

(1) No person may cause the child to be medically or psychiatrically examined, or otherwise assessed, for the purpose of preparation of expert evidence for use in the proceedings without the court's permission.
(2) Where the court's permission has not been given under paragraph (1), no evidence arising out of an examination or assessment referred to in that paragraph may be adduced without the court's permission.

12.21 Hearings

(1) The court may give directions about the order of speeches and the evidence at a hearing.
(2) Subject to any directions given under paragraph (1), the parties and the children's guardian must adduce their evidence at a hearing in the following order–
   (a) the applicant;
   (b) any party with parental responsibility for the child;
   (c) other respondents;
   (d) the children's guardian;
   (e) the child, if the child is a party to proceedings and there is no children's guardian.

CHAPTER 3 SPECIAL PROVISIONS ABOUT PUBLIC LAW PROCEEDINGS

12.22 Application of rules 12.23 to 12.26

Rules 12.23 to 12.26 apply to care and supervision proceedings and in so far as practicable other public law proceedings.

12.23 Timetable for the Child

(1) The court will set the timetable for the proceedings in accordance with the Timetable for the Child.

(2) The 'Timetable for the Child' means the timetable set by the court in accordance with its duties under section 1 and 32 of the 1989 Act and will–

(a) take into account dates of the significant steps in the life of the child who is the subject of the proceedings; and
(b) be appropriate for that child.

12.24 Directions

The court will direct the parties to–

(a) monitor compliance with the court's directions; and
(b) tell the court or court officer about–
   (i) any failure to comply with a direction of the court; and
   (ii) any other delay in the proceedings.

12.25 First Appointment, Case Management Conference and Issues Resolution Hearing

(1) The court may set the date for the First Appointment, Case Management Conference and Issues Resolution Hearing at the times and in the circumstances referred to in Practice Direction 12A.
(2) The matters which the court will consider at the hearings referred to in paragraph (1) are set out in Practice Direction 12A.

12.26 Discussion between advocates

(1) When setting a date for a Case Management Conference or an Issues Resolution Hearing the court will direct a discussion between the parties' advocates to–

(a) discuss the provisions of a draft of the Case Management Order; and
(b) consider any other matter set out in Practice Direction 12A.

(2) Where there is a litigant in person the court will give directions about how that person may take part in the discussions between the parties' advocates.
(3) The court will direct that following a discussion between advocates they must prepare or amend a draft of the Case Management Order for the court to consider.
(4) Where it is not possible for the advocates to agree the terms of a draft of the Case Management Order, the advocates should specify on a draft of the Case Management Order or on a separate document if more practicable–

(a) those provisions on which they agree; and
(b) those provisions on which they disagree.

(5) Unless the court directs otherwise–

(a) any discussion between advocates must take place no later than 2 days; and
(b) a draft of the Case Management Order must be filed with the court no later than 1 day,

before the Case Management Conference or the Issues Resolution Hearing whichever may be appropriate.

(6) For the purposes of this rule 'advocate' includes a litigant in person.

12.27 Matters prescribed for the purposes of the Act

(1) Proceedings for an order under any of the following provisions of the 1989 Act–

(a) a secure accommodation order under section 25;
(b) an order giving permission to change a child's surname or remove a child from the United Kingdom under section 33(7);

(c) an order permitting the local authority to arrange for any child in its care to live outside England and Wales under paragraph 19(1) of Schedule 2;
(d) the extension or further extension of a supervision order under paragraph 6(3) of Schedule 3;
(e) appeals against the determination of proceedings of a kind set out in sub-paragraphs (a) to (d);

are specified for the purposes of section 41 of that Act in accordance with section 41(6)(i) of that Act.

(2) The persons listed as applicants in the table set out in rule 12.3 to proceedings for the variation of directions made with interim care or interim supervision orders under section 38(8) of the 1989 Act are the prescribed class of persons for the purposes of that section.
(3) The persons listed as applicants in the table set out in rule 12.3 to proceedings for the variation of a direction made under section 44(6) of the 1989 Act in an emergency protection order are the prescribed class of persons for the purposes of section 44(9) of that Act.

12.28 Exclusion requirements: interim care orders and emergency protection orders

(1) This rule applies where the court includes an exclusion requirement in an interim care order or an emergency protection order.
(2) The applicant for an interim care order or emergency protection order must–
  (a) prepare a separate statement of the evidence in support of the application for an exclusion requirement;
  (b) serve the statement personally on the relevant person with a copy of the order containing the exclusion requirement (and of any power of arrest which is attached to it);
  (c) inform the relevant person of that person's right to apply to vary or discharge the exclusion requirement.
(3) Where a power of arrest is attached to an exclusion requirement in an interim care order or an emergency protection order, the applicant will deliver–
  (a) a copy of the order; and
  (b) a statement showing that the relevant person has been served with the order or informed of its terms (whether by being present when the order was made or by telephone or otherwise),

to the officer for the time being in charge of the police station for the area in which the dwelling-house in which the child lives is situated (or such other police station as the court may specify).

(4) Rules 10.6(2) and 10.10 to 10.17 will apply, with the necessary modifications, for the service, variation, discharge and enforcement of any exclusion requirement to which a power of arrest is attached as they apply to an order made on an application under Part 4 of the 1996 Act.
(5) The relevant person must serve the parties to the proceedings with any application which that person makes for the variation or discharge of the exclusion requirement.
(6) Where an exclusion requirement ceases to have effect whether–
  (a) as a result of the removal of a child under section 38A(10) or 44A(10) of the 1989 Act;
  (b) because of the discharge of the interim care order or emergency protection order; or
  (c) otherwise,

the applicant must inform–
  (i) the relevant person;

(ii) the parties to the proceedings;
(iii) any officer to whom a copy of the order was delivered under paragraph (3); and
(iv) (where necessary) the court.
(7) Where the court includes an exclusion requirement in an interim care order or an emergency protection order of its own motion, paragraph (2) will apply with the omission of any reference to the statement of the evidence.
(8) In this rule, 'the relevant person' has the meaning assigned to it by sections 38A(2) and 44A(2) of the 1989 Act.

12.29 Notification of consent

(1) Consent for the purposes of the following provisions of the 1989 Act–
  (a) section 16(3);
  (b) section 38A(2)(b)(ii) or 44A(2)(b)(ii); or
  (c) paragraph 19(3)(c) or (d) of Schedule 2,
must be given either–
  (i) orally to the court; or
  (ii) in writing to the court signed by the person giving consent.
(2) Any written consent for the purposes of section 38A(2) or 44A(2) of the 1989 Act must include a statement that the person giving consent–
  (a) is able and willing to give to the child the care which it would be reasonable to expect a parent to give; and
  (b) understands that the giving of consent could lead to the exclusion of the relevant person from the dwelling-house in which the child lives.

12.30 Proceedings for secure accommodation orders: copies of reports

In proceedings under section 25 of the 1989 Act, the court will, if practicable, arrange for copies of all written reports filed in the case to be made available before the hearing to–
(a) the applicant;
(b) the parent or guardian of the child to whom the application relates;
(c) any legal representative of the child;
(d) the children's guardian; and
(e) the child, unless the court directs otherwise,

and copies of the reports may, if the court considers it desirable, be shown to any person who is entitled to notice of any hearing in accordance with Practice Direction 12C.

CHAPTER 4 SPECIAL PROVISIONS ABOUT PRIVATE LAW PROCEEDINGS

12.31 The First Hearing Dispute Resolution Appointment

(1) The court may set a date for the First Hearing Dispute Resolution Appointment after the proceedings have been issued.
(2) The court officer will give notice of any of the dates so fixed to the parties.

(Provisions relating to the timing of and issues to be considered at the First Hearing Dispute Resolution Appointment are contained in Practice Direction 12B.)

12.32 Answer

A respondent must file and serve on the parties an answer to the application for an order in private law proceedings within 14 days beginning with the date on which the application is served.

12.33 Applications for warning notices or applications to amend enforcement orders by reason of change of residence

(1) This rule applies in relation to an application to the High Court or a county court for–
- (a) a warning notice to be attached to a contact order; or
- (b) an order under paragraph 5 of Schedule A1 to the 1989 Act to amend an enforcement order by reason of change of residence.

(2) The application must be made without notice.

(3) The court may deal with the application without a hearing.

(4) If the court decides to deal with the application at a hearing, rules 12.5, 12.7 and 12.8 will apply.

12.34 Service of a risk assessment

(1) Where an officer of the Service or a Welsh family proceedings officer has filed a risk assessment with the court, subject to paragraph (2), the court officer will as soon as practicable serve copies of the risk assessment on each party.

(2) Before serving the risk assessment, the court must consider whether, in order to prevent a risk of harm to the child, it is necessary for–
- (a) information to be deleted from a copy of the risk assessment before that copy is served on a party; or
- (b) service of a copy of the risk assessment (whether with information deleted from it or not) on a party to be delayed for a specified period,

and may make directions accordingly.

12.35 Service of enforcement orders or orders amending or revoking enforcement orders

(1) Paragraphs (2) and (3) apply where the High Court or a county court makes–
- (a) an enforcement order; or
- (b) an order under paragraph 9(2) of Schedule A1 to the 1989 Act (enforcement order made following a breach of an enforcement order).

(2) As soon as practicable after an order has been made, a copy of it must be served by the court officer on–
- (a) the parties, except the person against whom the order is made;
- (b) the officer of the Service or the Welsh family proceedings officer who is to comply with a request under section 11M of the 1989 Act to monitor compliance with the order; and
- (c) the responsible officer.

(3) Unless the court directs otherwise, the applicant must serve a copy of the order personally on the person against whom the order is made.

(4) The court officer must send a copy of an order made under paragraph 4, 5, 6 or 7 of Schedule A1 to the 1989 Act (revocation or amendment of an enforcement order) to–
- (a) the parties;
- (b) the officer of the Service or the Welsh family proceedings officer who is to comply with a request under section 11M of the 1989 Act to monitor compliance with the order;
- (c) the responsible officer; and
- (d) in the case of an order under paragraph 5 of Schedule A1 to the 1989 Act (amendment of enforcement order by reason of change of residence), the responsible officer in the former local justice area.

(5) In this rule, 'responsible officer' has the meaning given in paragraph 8(8) of Schedule A1 to the 1989 Act.

CHAPTER 5 SPECIAL PROVISIONS ABOUT INHERENT JURISDICTION PROCEEDINGS

12.36 Where to start proceedings

(1) An application for proceedings under the Inherent Jurisdiction of the court must be started in the High Court.
(2) Wardship proceedings, except applications for an order that a child be made or cease to be a ward of court, may be transferred to the county court unless the issues of fact or law make them more suitable for hearing in the High Court.

(The question of suitability for hearing in the High Court is explained in Practice Direction 12D (Inherent Jurisdiction (including Wardship Proceedings)).)

12.37 Child as respondent to wardship proceedings

(1) A child who is the subject of wardship proceedings must not be made a respondent to those proceedings unless the court gives permission following an application under paragraph (2).
(2) Where nobody other than the child would be a suitable respondent to wardship proceedings, the applicant may apply without notice for permission to make the wardship application–

　(a)　without notice; or
　(b)　with the child as the respondent.

12.38 Registration requirements

The court officer will send a copy of every application for a child to be made a ward of court to the principal registry for recording in the register of wards.

12.39 Notice of child's whereabouts

(1) Every respondent, other than a child, must file with the acknowledgment of service a notice stating–

　(a)　the respondent's address; and
　(b)　either–
　　(i)　the whereabouts of the child; or
　　(ii)　that the respondent is unaware of the child's whereabouts if that is the case.

(2) Unless the court directs otherwise, the respondent must serve a copy of that notice on the applicant.
(3) Every respondent other than a child must immediately notify the court in writing of–

　(a)　any subsequent changes of address; or
　(b)　any change in the child's whereabouts,

　and, unless the court directs otherwise, serve a copy of that notice on the applicant.
(4) In this rule a reference to the whereabouts of a child is a reference to–

　(a)　the address at which the child is living;
　(b)　the person with whom the child is living; and
　(c)　any other information relevant to where the child may be found.

12.40 Enforcement of orders in wardship proceedings

The High Court may secure compliance with any direction relating to a ward of court by an order addressed to the tipstaff.

(The role of the tipstaff is explained in Practice Direction 12D (Inherent Jurisdiction (including Wardship Proceedings)).)

12.41 Child ceasing to be ward of court

(1) A child who, by virtue of section 41(2) of the Senior Courts Act 1981, automatically becomes a ward of court on the making of a wardship application will cease to be a ward on the determination of the application unless the court orders that the child be made a ward of court.
(2) Nothing in paragraph (1) affects the power of the court under section 41(3) of the Senior Courts Act 1981 to order that any child cease to be a ward of court.

12.42 Adoption of a child who is a ward of court

An application for permission–

(a) to start proceedings to adopt a child who is a ward of court;
(b) to place such a child for adoption with parental consent; or
(c) to start proceedings for a placement order in relation to such a child,

may be made without notice in accordance with Part 18.

CHAPTER 6 PROCEEDINGS UNDER THE 1980 HAGUE CONVENTION, THE EUROPEAN CONVENTION, THE COUNCIL REGULATION, AND THE 1996 HAGUE CONVENTION

12.43 Scope

This Chapter applies to –

(a) proceedings relating to children under the 1980 Hague Convention or the European Convention; and
(b) applications relating to the Council Regulation or the 1996 Hague Convention in respect of children.

SECTION 1
Proceedings under the 1980 Hague Convention or the European Convention

12.44 Interpretation

In this section–

'the 1985 Act' means the Child Abduction and Custody Act 1985;

'Central Authority' means, in relation to England and Wales, the Lord Chancellor;

'Contracting State' has the meaning given in–

(a) section 2 of the 1985 Act in relation to the 1980 Hague Convention; and
(b) section 13 of the 1985 Act in relation to the European Convention; and

'decision relating to custody' has the same meaning as in the European Convention.

('the 1980 Hague Convention' and the 'the European Convention' are defined in rule 2.3)

12.45 Where to start proceedings

Every application under the 1980 Hague Convention or the European Convention must be–

(a) made in the High Court and issued in the principal registry; and
(b) heard by a Judge of the High Court unless the application is–

(i) to join a respondent; or
(ii) to dispense with service or extend the time for acknowledging service.

12.46 Evidence in support of application

Where the party making an application under this section does not produce the documents referred to in Practice Direction 12F, the court may–

(a) fix a time within which the documents are to be produced;
(b) accept equivalent documents; or
(c) dispense with production of the documents if the court considers it has sufficient information.

12.47 Without-notice applications

(1) This rule applies to applications–

(a) commencing or in proceedings under this section;
(b) for interim directions under section 5 or 19 of the 1985 Act;
(c) for the disclosure of information about the child and for safeguarding the child's welfare, under rule 12.57;
(d) for the disclosure of relevant information as to where the child is, under section 24A of the 1985 Act; or
(e) for a collection order, location order or passport order.

(2) Applications under this rule may be made without notice, in which case the applicant must file the application–

(a) where the application is made by telephone, the next business day after the making of the application; or
(b) in any other case, at the time when the application is made.

(3) Where an order is made without notice, the applicant must serve a copy of the order on the other parties as soon as practicable after the making of the order, unless the court otherwise directs.

(4) Where the court refuses to make an order on an application without notice, it may direct that the application is made on notice.

(5) Where any hearing takes place outside the hours during which the court office is usually open–

(a) if the hearing takes place by telephone, the applicant's solicitors will, if practicable, arrange for the hearing to be recorded; and
(b) in all other cases, the court or court officer will take a note of the proceedings.

(Practice Direction 12E (Urgent Business) provides further details of the procedure for out of hours applications. See also Practice Direction 12D (Inherent Jurisdiction (including Wardship Proceedings)).)

12.48 Directions

(1) As soon as practicable after an application to which this section applies has been made, the court may give directions as to the following matters, among others–

(a) whether service of the application may be dispensed with;
(b) whether the proceedings should be transferred to another court under rule 12.54;
(c) expedition of the proceedings or any part of the proceedings (and any direction for expedition may specify a date by which the court must issue its final judgment in the proceedings or a specified part of the proceedings);
(d) the steps to be taken in the proceedings and the time by which each step is to be taken;

(e) whether the child or any other person should be made a party to the proceedings;
(f) if the child is not made a party to the proceedings, the manner in which the child's wishes and feelings are to be ascertained, having regard to the child's age and maturity and in particular whether an officer of the Service or a Welsh family proceedings officer should report to the court for that purpose;
(g) where the child is made a party to the proceedings, the appointment of a children's guardian for that child unless a children's guardian has already been appointed;
(h) the attendance of the child or any other person before the court;
(i) the appointment of a litigation friend for a child or for any protected party, unless a litigation friend has already been appointed;
(j) the service of documents;
(k) the filing of evidence including expert evidence; and
(l) whether the parties and their representatives should meet at any stage of the proceedings and the purpose of such a meeting.

(Rule 16.2 provides for when the court may make the child a party to the proceedings and rule 16.4 for the appointment of a children's guardian for the child who is made a party. Rule 16.5 (without prejudice to rule 16.6) requires a child who is a party to the proceedings but not the subject of those proceedings to have a litigation friend.)

(2) Directions of a court which are in force immediately prior to the transfer of proceedings to another court under rule 12.54 will continue to apply following the transfer subject to–
   (a) any changes of terminology which are required to apply those directions to the court to which the proceedings are transferred; and
   (b) any variation or revocation of the directions.
(3) The court or court officer will–
   (a) take a note of the giving, variation or revocation of directions under this rule; and
   (b) as soon as practicable serve a copy of the directions order on every party.

12.49 Answer

(1) Subject to paragraph (2) and to any directions given under rule 12.48, a respondent must file and serve on the parties an answer to the application within 7 days beginning with the date on which the application is served.
(2) The court may direct a longer period for service where the respondent has been made a party solely on one of the following grounds–
   (a) a decision relating to custody has been made in the respondent's favour; or
   (b) the respondent appears to the court to have sufficient interest in the welfare of the child.

12.50 Filing and serving written evidence

(1) The respondent to an application to which this section applies may file and serve with the answer a statement verified by a statement of truth, together with any further evidence on which the respondent intends to rely.
(2) The applicant may, within 7 days beginning with the date on which the respondent's evidence was served under paragraph (1), file and serve a statement in reply verified by a statement of truth, together with any further evidence on which the applicant intends to rely.

12.51 Adjournment

The court will not adjourn the hearing of an application to which this section applies for more than 21 days at at any one time.

12.52 Stay of proceedings upon notification of wrongful removal etc.

(1) In this rule and in rule 12.53–

    (a) 'relevant authority' means –

        (i) the High Court;
        (ii) a county court;
        (iii) a magistrates' court;
        (iv) the Court of Session;
        (v) a sheriff court;
        (vi) a children's hearing within the meaning of section 93 of the Children (Scotland) Act 1995;
        (vii) the High Court in Northern Ireland;
        (viii) a county court in Northern Ireland;
        (ix) a court of summary jurisdiction in Northern Ireland;
        (x) the Royal Court of Jersey;
        (xi) a court of summary jurisdiction in Jersey;
        (xii) the High Court of Justice of the Isle of Man;
        (xiii) a court of summary jurisdiction in the Isle of Man; or
        (xiv) the Secretary of State; and

    (b) 'rights of custody' has the same meaning as in the 1980 Hague Convention.

(2) Where a party to proceedings under the 1980 Hague Convention knows that an application relating to the merits of rights of custody is pending in or before a relevant authority, that party must file within the proceedings under the 1980 Hague Convention a concise statement of the nature of that application, including the relevant authority in or before which it is pending.

(3) On receipt of a statement filed in accordance with paragraph (2) above, a court officer will notify the relegant authority in or before which the application is pending and will subsequently notify the relevant authority of the result of the proceedings.

(4) On receipt by the relevant authority of a notification under paragraph (3) from the High Court or equivalent notification from the Court of Session, the High Court in Northern Ireland or the High Court of Justice of the Isle of Man–

    (a) all further proceedings in the action will be stayed[GL] unless and until the proceedings under the 1980 Hague Convention in the High Court, Court of Session, the High Court in Northern Ireland or the High Court of Justice of the Isle of Man are dismissed; and

    (b) the parties to the action will be notified by the court officer of the stay[GL] and dismissal.

12.53 Stay of proceedings where application made under s.16 of the 1985 Act (registration of decisions under the European Convention)

(1) A person who–

    (a) is a party to–

        (i) proceedings under section 16 of the 1985 Act; or
        (ii) proceedings as a result of which a decision relating to custody has been registered under section 16 of the 1985 Act; and

    (b) knows that an application is pending under–

        (i) section 20(2) of the 1985 Act;

(ii) Article 21(2) of the Child Abduction and Custody (Jersey) Law 2005; or
(iii) section 42(2) of the Child Custody Act 1987 (an Act of Tynwald),

must file within the proceedings under section 16 of the 1985 Act a concise statement of the nature of the pending application.
(2) On receipt of a statement filed in accordance with paragraph (1) above, a court officer will notify the relevant authority in or before which the application is pending and will subsequently notify the relevant authority of the result of the proceedings.
(3) On receipt by the relevant authority of a notification under paragraph (2) from the High Court or equivalent notification from the Court of Session, the High Court in Northern Ireland or the High Court of Justice of the Isle of Man, the court officer will notify the parties to the action.

12.54 Transfer of proceedings

(1) At any stage in proceedings under the 1985 Act the court may–

(a) of its own initiative; or
(b) on the application of a party with a minimum of two days' notice;

order that the proceedings be transferred to a court listed in paragraph (4).
(2) Where the court makes an order for transfer under paragraph (1)–

(a) the court will state its reasons on the face of the order;
(b) a court officer will send a copy of the order, the application and the accompanying documents (if any) and any evidence to the court to which the proceedings are transferred; and
(c) the costs of the proceedings both before and after the transfer will be at the discretion of the court to which the proceedings are transferred.

(3) Where proceedings are transferred to the High Court from a court listed in paragraph (4), a court officer will notify the parties of the transfer and the proceedings will continue as if they had been commenced in the High Court.
(4) The listed courts are the Court of Session, the High Court in Northern Ireland, the Royal Court of Jersey or the High Court of Justice of the Isle of Man.

12.55 Revocation and variation of registered decisions

(1) This rule applies to decisions which–

(a) have been registered under section 16 of the 1985 Act; and
(b) are subsequently varied or revoked by an authority in the Contracting State in which they were made.

(2) The court will, on cancelling the registration of a decision which has been revoked, notify–

(a) the person appearing to the court to have care of the child;
(b) the person on whose behalf the application for registration of the decision was made; and
(c) any other party to the application.

(3) The court will, on being informed of the variation of a decision, notify–

(a) the party appearing to the court to have care of the child; and
(b) any party to the application for registration of the decision;

and any such person may apply to make representations to the court before the registration is varied.
(4) Any person appearing to the court to have an interest in the proceedings may apply for the registration of a decision for the cancellation or variation of the decision referred to in paragraph (1).

12.56 The central index of decisions registered under the 1985 Act

A central index of decisions registered under section 16 of the 1985 Act, together with any variation of those decisions made under section 17 of that Act, will be kept by the principal registry.

12.57 Disclosure of information in proceedings under the European Convention

At any stage in proceedings under the European Convention the court may, if it has reason to believe that any person may have relevant information about the child who is the subject of those proceedings, order that person to disclose such information and may for that purpose order that the person attend before it or file affidavit[GL] evidence.

SECTION 2
Applications relating to the Council Regulation and the 1996 Hague Convention

12.58 Interpretation

(1) In this section –

'Central Authority' means, in relation to England and Wales, the Lord Chancellor;

'Contracting State' means a State party to the 1996 Hague Convention;

'judgment' has the meaning given in Article 2(4) of the Council Regulation;

'Member State' means a Member State bound by the Council Regulation or a country which has subsequently adopted the Council Regulation;

'parental responsibility' has the meaning given in–

(a) Article 2(7) of the Council Regulation in relation to proceedings under that Regulation; and

(b) Article 1(2) of the 1996 Hague Convention in relation to proceedings under that Convention; and

'seised' has the meaning given in Article 16 of the Council Regulation.

(2) In rules 12.59 to 12.70, references to the court of another member State or Contracting State include authorities within the meaning of 'court' in Article 2(1) of the Council Regulation, and authorities of Contracting States which have jurisdiction to take measures directed to the protection of the person or property of the child within the meaning of the 1996 Hague Convention.

12.59 Procedure under Article 11(6) of the Council Regulation where the court makes a non-return order under Article 13 of the 1980 Hague Convention

(1) Where the court makes an order for the non-return of a child under Article 13 of the 1980 Hague Convention, it must immediately transmit the documents referred to in Article 11(6) of the Council Regulation–

(a) directly to the court with jurisdiction or the central authority in the Member State where the child was habitually resident immediately before the wrongful removal to, or wrongful retention in, England and Wales; or

(b) to the Central Authority for England and Wales for onward transmission to the court with jurisdiction or the central authority in the other Member State mentioned in sub-paragraph (a).

(2) The documents required by paragraph (1) must be transmitted by a method which, in the case of direct transmission to the court with jurisdiction in the other Member State, ensures and, in any other case, will not prevent, their receipt by that court within one month of the date of the non-return order.

12.60 Procedure under Article 11(7) of the Council Regulation where the court receives a non-return order made under Article 13 of the 1980 Hague Convention by a court in another Member State

(1) This rule applies where the court receives an order made by a court in another Member State for the non-return of a child.
(2) In this rule, the order for non-return of the child and the papers transmitted with that order from the court in the other Member State are referred to as 'the non-return order'.
(3) Where, at the time of receipt of the non-return order, the court is already seised of a question of parental responsibility in relation to the child, –

    (a) the court officer shall immediately –

        (i) serve copies of the non-return order on each party to the proceedings in which a question of parental responsibility in relation to the child is at issue; and

        (ii) where the non-return order was received directly from the court or the central authority in the other Member State, transmit to the Central Authority for England and Wales a copy of the non-return order.

    (b) the court shall immediately invite the parties to the 1980 Hague Convention proceedings to file written submissions in respect of the question of custody by a specified date, or to attend a hearing to consider the future conduct of the proceedings in the light of the non-return order.

(4) Where, at the time of receipt of the non-return order, the court is not already seised of the question of parental responsibility in relation to the child, it shall immediately–

    (a) open a court file in respect of the child and assign a court reference to the file;
    (b) serve a copy of the non-return order on each party to the proceedings before the court in the Member State which made that order;
    (c) invite each party to file, within 3 months of notification to that party of receipt of the non-return order, submissions in the form of–

        (i) an application for an order under–

            (aa) the 1989 Act; or
            (bb) (in the High Court only) an application under the inherent jurisdiction in respect of the child; or

        (ii) where permission is required to make an application for the order in question, an application for that permission;

    (d) where the non-return order was received directly from the court or central authority in the other Member State, transmit to the Central Authority for England and Wales a copy of the non-return order.

(5) In a case to which paragraph (4) applies where no application is filed within the 3 month period provided for by paragraph (4)(c) the court must close its file in respect of the child.

(Enforcement of a subsequent judgment requiring the return of the child, made under Article 11(8) by a court examining custody of the child under Article 11(7), is dealt with in Part 31 below.)

12.61 Transfer of proceedings under Article 15 of the Council Regulation or under Article 8 of the 1996 Hague Convention

(1) Where the court is considering the transfer of proceedings to the court of another Member State or Contracting State under rules 12.62 to 12.64 it will–

    (a) fix a date for a hearing for the court to consider the question of transfer; and
    (b) give directions as to the manner in which the parties may make representations.

(2) The court may, with the consent of all parties, deal with the question of transfer without a hearing.
(3) Directions which are in force immediately prior to the transfer of proceedings to a court in another Member State or Contracting State under rules 12.62 to 12.64 will continue to apply until the court in that other State accepts jurisdiction in accordance with the provisions of the Council Regulation or the 1996 Hague Convention (as appropriate), subject to any variation or revocation of the directions.
(4) The court or court officer will–
- (a) take a note of the giving, variation or revocation of directions under this rule; and
- (b) as soon as practicable serve a copy of the directions order on every party.

(5) A register of all applications and requests for transfer of jurisdiction to or from another Member State or Contracting State will be kept by the principal registry.

12.62 Application by a party for transfer of the proceedings

(1) A party may apply to the court under Article 15(1) of the Council Regulation or under Article 8(1) of the 1996 Hague Convention–
- (a) to stay[GL] the proceedings or a specified part of the proceedings and to invite the parties to introduce a request before a court of another Member State or Contracting State; or
- (b) to make a request to a court of another Member State or another Contracting State to assume jurisdiction for the proceedings, or a specified part of the proceedings.

(2) An application under paragraph (1) must be made–
- (a) to the court in which the relevant parental responsibility proceedings are pending; and
- (b) using the Part 18 procedure.

(3) The applicant must file the application notice and serve it on the respondents–
- (a) where the application is also made under Article 11 of the Council Regulation, not less than 5 days, and.
- (b) in any other case, not less than 42 days,

before the hearing of the application.

12.63 Application by a court of another Member State or another Contracting State for transfer of the proceedings

(1) This rule applies where a court of another Member State or another Contracting State makes an application under Article 15(2)(c) of the Council Regulation or under Article 9 of the 1996 Hague Convention that the court having jurisdiction in relation to the proceedings transfer the proceedings or a specific part of the proceedings to the applicant court.
(2) When the court receives the application, the court officer will–
- (a) as soon as practicable, notify the Central Authority for England and Wales of the application; and
- (b) serve the application, and notice of the hearing on all other parties in England and Wales not less than 5 days before the hearing of the application.

12.64 Exercise by the court of its own initiative of powers to seek to transfer the proceedings

(1) The court having jurisdiction in relation to the proceedings may exercise its powers of

its own initiative under Article 15 of the Council Regulation or Article 8 of the 1996 Hague Convention in relation to the proceedings or a specified part of the proceedings.
(2) Where the court proposes to exercise its powers, the court officer will give the parties not less than 5 days' notice of the hearing.

12.65 Application to High Court to make request under Article 15 of the Council Regulation or Article 9 of the 1996 Hague Convention to request transfer of jurisdiction

(1) An application for the court to request transfer of jurisdiction in a matter concerning a child from another Member State or another Contracting State under Article 15 of the Council Regulation, or Article 9 of the 1996 Hague Convention (as the case may be) must be made to the principal registry and heard in the High Court.
(2) An application must be made without notice to any other person and the court may give directions about joining any other party to the application.
(3) Where there is agreement between the court and the court or competent authority to which the request under paragraph (1) is made to transfer the matter to the courts of England and Wales, the court will consider with that other court or competent authority the specific timing and conditions for the transfer.
(4) Upon receipt of agreement to transfer jurisdiction from the court or other competent authority in the Member State, or Contracting State to which the request has been made, the court officer will serve on the applicant a notice that jurisdiction has been accepted by the courts of England and Wales.
(5) The applicant must attach the notice referred to in paragraph (3) to any subsequent application in relation to the child.
(6) Nothing in this rule requires an application with respect to a child commenced following a transfer of jurisdiction to be made to or heard in the High Court.
(7) Upon allocation, the court to which the proceedings are allocated must immediately fix a directions hearing to consider the future conduct of the case.

12.66 Procedure where the court receives a request from the authorities of another Member State or Contracting State to assume jurisdiction in a matter concerning a child

(1) Where any court other than the High Court receives a request to assume jurisdiction in a matter concerning a child from a court or other authority which has jurisdiction in another Member State or Contracting State, that court must immediately refer the request to a Judge of the High Court for a decision regarding acceptance of jurisdiction to be made.
(2) Upon the High Court agreeing to the request under paragraph (1), the court officer will notify the parties to the proceedings before the other Member State or Contracting State of that decision, and the case must be allocated as if the application had been made in England and Wales.
(3) Upon allocation, the court to which the proceedings are allocated must immediately fix a directions hearing to consider the future conduct of the case.
(4) The court officer will serve notice of the directions hearing on all parties to the proceedings in the other Member State or Contracting State no later than 5 days before the date of that hearing.

12.67 Service of the court's order or request relating to transfer of jurisdiction under the Council Regulation or the 1996 Hague Convention

The court officer will serve an order or request relating to transfer of jurisdiction on all parties, the Central Authority of the other Member State or Contracting State, and the Central Authority for England and Wales.

12.68 Questions as to the court's jurisdiction or whether the proceedings should be stayed

(1) If at any time after issue of the application it appears to the court that under any of Articles 16 to 18 of the Council Regulation it does not or may not have jurisdiction to hear an application, or that under Article 19 of the Council Regulation or Article 13 of the 1996 Hague Convention it is or may be required to stay[GL] the proceedings or to decline jurisdiction, the court must–

    (a) stay[GL] the proceedings; and
    (b) fix a date for a hearing to determine jurisdiction or whether there should be a stay[GL] or other order.

(2) The court officer will serve notice of the hearing referred to at paragraph (1)(b) on the parties to the proceedings.

(3) The court must, in writing–

    (a) give reasons for its decision under paragraph (1); and
    (b) where it makes a finding of fact, state such finding.

(4) The court may with the consent of all the parties deal with any question as to the jurisdiction of the court, or as to whether the proceedings should be stayed[GL], without a hearing.

12.69 Request for consultation as to contemplated placement of child in England and Wales

(1) This rule applies to a request made –

    (a) under Article 56 of the Council Regulation, by a court in another Member State; or
    (b) under Article 33 of the 1996 Hague Convention by a court in another Contracting State.

for consultation on or consent to the contemplated placement of a child in England and Wales.

(2) Where the court receives a request directly from a court in another Member State or Contracting State, the court shall, as soon as practicable after receipt of the request, notify the Central Authority for England and Wales of the request and take the appropriate action under paragraph (4).

(3) Where it appears to the court officer that no proceedings relating to the child are pending before a court in England and Wales, the court officer must inform the Central Authority for England and Wales of that fact and forward to the Central Authority all documents relating to the request sent by the court in the other Member State or Contracting State.

(4) Where the court receives a request forwarded by the Central Authority for England and Wales, the court must, as soon as practicable after receipt of the request, either–

    (a) where proceedings relating to the child are pending before the court, fix a directions hearing; or
    (b) where proceedings relating to the child are pending before another court in England and Wales, send a copy of the request to that court.

12.70 Request made by court in England and Wales for consultation as to contemplated placement of child in another Member State or Contracting State

(1) This rule applies where the court is contemplating the placement of a child in another Member State under Article 56 of the Council Regulation or another Contracting State under Article 33 of the 1996 Hague Convention, and proposes to send a request for

consultation with or for the consent of the central authority or other authority having jurisdiction in the other State in relation to the contemplated placement.
(2) In this rule, a reference to 'the request' includes a reference to a report prepared for purposes of Article 33 of the 1996 Hague Convention where the request is made under that Convention.
(3) Where the court sends the request directly to the central authority or other authority having jurisdiction in the other State, it shall at the same time send a copy of the request to the Central Authority for England and Wales.
(4) The court may send the request to the Central Authority for England and Wales for onward transmission to the central authority or other authority having jurisdiction in the other Member State.
(5) The court should give consideration to the documents which should accompany the request.

(See Chapters 1 to 3 of this Part generally, for the procedure governing applications for an order under paragraph 19(1) of Schedule 2 to the 1989 Act permitting a local authority to arrange for any child in its care to live outside England and Wales.)

(Part 14 sets out the procedure governing applications for an order under section 84 (giving parental responsibility prior to adoption abroad) of the Adoption and Children Act 2002.)

12.71 Application for a declaration as to the extent, or existence, of parental responsibility in relation to a child under Article 16 of the 1996 Hague Convention

(1) Any interested person may apply for a declaration–
   (a) that a person has, or does not have, parental responsibility for a child; or
   (b) as to the extent of a person's parental responsibility for a child,

where the question arises by virtue of the application of Article 16 of the 1996 Hague Convention.
(2) An application for a declaration as to the extent, or existence of a person's parental responsibility for a child by virtue of Article 16 of the 1996 Hague Convention must be made in the principal registry and heard in the High Court.
(3) An application for a declaration referred to in paragraph (1) may not be made where the question raised is otherwise capable of resolution in any other family proceedings in respect of the child.

CHAPTER 7 COMMUNICATION OF INFORMATION: PROCEEDINGS RELATING TO CHILDREN

12.72 Interpretation

(1) In this Chapter 'independent reviewing officer' means a person appointed in respect of a child in accordance with regulation 2A of the Review of Children's Cases Regulations 1991, or regulation 3 of the Review of Children's Cases (Wales) Regulations 2007.

12.73 Communication of information: general

(1) For the purposes of the law relating to contempt of court, information relating to proceedings held in private (whether or not contained in a document filed with the court) may be communicated–
   (a) where the communication is to–
      (i) a party;
      (ii) the legal representative of a party;
      (iii) a professional legal adviser;
      (iv) an officer of the service or a Welsh family proceedings officer;

(v) the welfare officer;
(vi) the Legal Services Commission;
(vii) an expert whose instruction by a party has been authorised by the court for the purposes of the proceedings;
(viii) a professional acting in furtherance of the protection of children;
(ix) an independent reviewing officer appointed in respect of a child who is, or has been, subject to proceedings to which this rule applies;

(b) where the court gives permission; or
(c) subject to any direction of the court, in accordance with rule 12.75 and Practice Direction 12G.

(2) Nothing in this Chapter permits the communication to the public at large, or any section of the public, of any information relating to the proceedings.
(3) Nothing in rule 12.75 and Practice Direction 12G permits the disclosure of an unapproved draft judgment handed down by any court.

12.74 Instruction of experts

(1) No party may instruct an expert for any purpose relating to proceedings, including to give evidence in those proceedings, without the permission of the court.
(2) Where the permission of the court has not been given under paragraph (1), no evidence arising out of an unauthorised instruction may be introduced without permission of the court.

12.75 Communication of information for purposes connected with the proceedings

(1) A party or the legal representative of a party, on behalf of and upon the instructions of that party, may communicate information relating to the proceedings to any person where necessary to enable that party–

(a) by confidential discussion, to obtain support, advice or assistance in the conduct of the proceedings;
(b) to engage in mediation or other forms of alternative dispute resolution;
(c) to make and pursue a complaint against a person or body concerned in the proceedings; or
(d) to make and pursue a complaint regarding the law, policy or procedure relating to a category of proceedings to which this Part applies.

(2) Where information is communicated to any person in accordance with paragraph (1)(a) of this rule, no further communication by that person is permitted.
(3) When information relating to the proceedings is communicated to any person in accordance with paragraphs (1)(b),(c) or (d) of this rule–

(a) the recipient may communicate that information to a further recipient, provided that–
 (i) the party who initially communicated the information consents to that further communication; and
 (ii) the further communication is made only for the purpose or purposes for which the party made the initial communication; and
(b) the information may be successively communicated to and by further recipients on as many occasions as may be necessary to fulfil the purpose for which the information was initially communicated, provided that on each such occasion the conditions in sub-paragraph (a) are met.

PART 13 PROCEEDINGS UNDER SECTION 54 OF THE HUMAN FERTILISATION AND EMBRYOLOGY ACT 2008

13.1 Interpretation and application

(1) A reference in this Part to the 2002 Act is a reference to that Act as applied with modifications by the Human Fertilisation and Embryology (Parental Order) Regulations 2010.

(2) In this Part–

'the other parent' means any person who is a parent of the child but is not one of the applicants or the woman who carried the child (including any man who is the father by virtue of section 35 or 36 of the 2008 Act or any woman who is a parent by virtue of section 42 or 43 of that Act);

'parental order' means an order under section 54 of the 2008 Act;

'parental order proceedings' means proceedings for the making of a parental order under the 2008 Act or an order under any provision of the 2002 Act;

'parental order reporter' means an officer of the service or a Welsh family proceedings officer appointed to act on behalf of a child who is the subject of parental order proceedings;

'provision for contact' means a contact order under section 8 or 34 of the 1989 Act.

(3) Except where the contrary intention appears, the rules in this Part apply to parental order proceedings.

13.2 Application of Part 12

Rules 12.9 to 12.11, 12.19 and 12.21 apply as appropriate, with any necessary modifications, to parental order proceedings.

13.3 Who the parties are

(1) An application for a parental order may be made by such of the following who satisfy the conditions set out in section 54(1) of the 2008 Act–

    (a) a husband and wife;
    (b) civil partners of each other; or
    (c) two persons who are living as partners in an enduring family relationship and are not within the prohibited degrees of relationship in relation to each other.

(2) The respondents to an application for a parental order are–

    (a) the woman who carried the child;
    (b) the other parent (if any);
    (c) any person in whose favour there is provision for contact; and
    (d) any other person or body with parental responsibility for the child at the date of the application.

(3) The court will direct that a person with parental responsibility for the child be made a party to proceedings where that person requests to be one.

(4) The court may at any time direct that–

    (a) any other person or body be made a respondent to the proceedings; or
    (b) a respondent be removed from the proceedings.

(5) If the court makes a direction for the addition or removal of a party, it may give consequential directions about–

    (a) serving a copy of the application form on any new respondent;
    (b) serving relevant documents on the new party; and
    (c) the management of the proceedings.

13.4 Notice of proceedings to person with foreign parental responsibility

(1) This rule applies where a child is subject to proceedings to which this Part applies and at the date of the application–

    (a) a person holds or is believed to hold parental responsibility for the child under the law of another State which subsists in accordance with Article 16 of the 1996 Hague Convention following the child becoming habitually resident in a territorial unit of the United Kingdom; and

    (b) that person is not otherwise required to be joined as a respondent under rule 13.3.

(2) The applicant shall give notice of the proceedings to any person to whom the applicant believes paragraph (1) applies.

(3) The applicant and every respondent to the proceedings shall provide such details as they possess as to the identity and whereabouts of any person they believe to hold parental responsibility for the child in accordance with paragraph (1) to the court officer, upon making, or responding to the application as appropriate.

(4) Where the existence of such a person only becomes apparent to a party at a later date during the proceedings, that party must notify the court officer of those details at the earliest opportunity.

(5) Where a person to whom paragraph (1) applies receives notice of proceedings, that person may apply to the court to be joined as a party using the Part 18 procedure.

13.5 What the court or a court officer will do when the application has been issued

(1) As soon as practicable after the issue of proceedings–

    (a) the court will–

        (i) if section 48(1) of the 2002 Act applies (restrictions on making parental orders), consider whether it is proper to hear the application;

        (ii) subject to paragraph (2), set a date for the first directions hearing;

        (iii) appoint a parental order reporter; and

        (iv) set a date for the hearing of the application; and

    (b) a court officer will–

        (i) return to the applicants the copies of the application together with any other documents the applicant is required to serve; and

        (ii) send a certified copy of the entry in the register of live births to the parental order reporter.

(2) Where it considers it appropriate the court may, instead of setting a date for a first directions appointment, give the directions provided for in rule 13.9.

13.6 Service of the application and other documents

(1) The applicants must, within 14 days before the hearing or first directions hearing, serve on the respondents–

    (a) the application;

    (b) a form for acknowledging service; and

    (c) a notice of proceedings.

(2) The applicants must serve a notice of proceedings on any local authority or voluntary organisation that has at any time provided accommodation for the child.

13.7 Acknowledgement

Within 7 days of the service of an application for a parental order, each respondent must file an acknowledgment of service and serve it on all the other parties.

13.8 Date for first directions hearing

Unless the court directs otherwise, the first directions hearing must be within 4 weeks beginning with the date on which the application is issued.

13.9 The first directions hearing

(1) At the first directions hearing in the proceedings the court will–

    (a) fix a timetable for the filing of–

        (i) any report from a parental order reporter;
        (ii) if a statement of facts has been filed, any amended statement of facts; and
        (iii) any other evidence;

    (b) give directions relating to the report of the parental order reporter and other evidence;

    (c) consider whether any other person should be a party to the proceedings and, if so, give directions in accordance with rule 13.3(3) or (4) joining that person as a party;

    (d) give directions relating to the appointment of a litigation friend for any protected party unless a litigation friend has already been appointed;

    (e) consider whether the case needs to be transferred to another court and, if so, give directions to transfer the proceedings to another court in accordance with the Allocation Order;

    (f) give directions about–

        (i) tracing the other parent or the woman who carried the child;
        (ii) service of documents;
        (iii) subject to paragraph (2), disclosure as soon as possible of information and evidence to the parties; and
        (iv) the final hearing.

(2) Rule 13.12 (reports of the parental order reporter and disclosure to parties) applies to any direction given under paragraph (1)(f)(iii) as it applies to a direction given under rule 13.12(1).

(3) The parties or their legal representatives must attend the first directions hearing unless the court directs otherwise.

(4) Directions may also be given at any stage in the proceedings–

    (a) of the court's own initiative; or
    (b) on the application of a party or the parental order reporter.

(5) Where the court proposes to exercise its powers in paragraph (1) of its own initiative the procedure set out in rule 4.3(2) to (7) applies.

(6) For the purposes of giving directions or for such purposes as the court directs–

    (a) the court may set a date for a further directions hearing or other hearing; and
    (b) the court officer will give notice of any date so fixed to the parties and to the parental order reporter.

(7) Directions of a court which are still in force immediately prior to the transfer of proceedings to another court shall continue to apply following the transfer subject to–

    (a) any changes of terminology which are required to apply those directions to the court to which the proceedings are transferred; and
    (b) any variation or revocation of the direction.

(8) The court or court officer will–

    (a) take a note of the giving, variation or revocation of a direction under this rule; and
    (b) as soon as practicable serve a copy of the note on every party.

(9) After the first directions hearing the court will monitor compliance by the parties with the court's timetable and directions.

13.10 Where the agreement of the other parent or the woman who carried the child is not required

(1) This rule applies where the agreement of the other parent or the woman who carried the child to the making of the parental order is not required as the person in question cannot be found or is incapable of giving agreement.
(2) The applicants must–

    (a) state that the agreement is not required in the application form, or at any later stage by filing a written note with the court;

    (b) file a statement of facts setting out a summary of the history of the case and any other facts to satisfy the court that the other parent or the woman who carried the child cannot be found or is incapable of giving agreement.

(3) On receipt of the application form or written note–

    (a) a court officer will–

        (i) unless the other parent or the woman who carried the child cannot be found, inform the other parent or the woman who carried the child that their agreement is not required;

        (ii) send a copy of the statement of facts filed in accordance with paragraph (2)(b) to–

            (aa) the other parent unless the other parent cannot be found;

            (bb) the woman who carried the child unless the woman cannot be found; and

            (cc) the parental order reporter; and

    (b) if the applicants consider that the other parent or the woman who carried the child is incapable of giving agreement the court will consider whether to–

        (i) appoint a litigation friend for the other parent or the woman who carried the child under rule 15.6(1) or

        (ii) give directions for an application to be made under rule 15.6(3),

    unless a litigation friend is already appointed for the other parent or the woman who carried the child.

13.11 Agreement

(1) Unless the court directs otherwise, the agreement of the other parent or the woman who carried the child to the making of the parental order may be given in the form referred to in Practice Direction 5A or a form to the like effect.
(2) Any form of agreement executed in Scotland must be witnessed by a Justice of the Peace or a Sheriff.
(3) Any form of agreement executed in Northern Ireland must be witnessed by a Justice of the Peace.
(4) Any form of agreement executed outside the United Kingdom must be witnessed by–

    (a) any person for the time being authorised by law in the place where the document is executed to administer an oath for any judicial or other legal purpose;

    (b) a British Consular officer;

    (c) a notary public; or

    (d) if the person executing the document is serving in any of the regular armed forces of the Crown, an officer holding a commission in any of those forces.

13.12 Reports of the parental order reporter and disclosure to the parties

(1) The court will consider whether to give a direction that a confidential report of the parental order reporter be disclosed to each party to the proceedings.
(2) Before giving such a direction the court will consider whether any information should be deleted including information which discloses the particulars referred to in rule 29.1(1) where a party has given notice under rule 29.1(2) (disclosure of personal details).
(3) The court may direct that the report shall not be disclosed to a party.

13.13 Notice of final hearing

A court officer will give notice to the parties and to the parental order reporter–

(a) of the date and place where the application will be heard; and
(b) of the fact that, unless the person wishes or the court requires, the person need not attend.

13.14 The final hearing

(1) Any person who has been given notice in accordance with rule 13.13 may attend the final hearing and be heard on the question of whether an order should be made.
(2) The court may direct that any person must attend a final hearing.

13.15 Proof of identity of the child

(1) Unless the contrary is shown, the child referred to in the application will be deemed to be the child referred to in the form of agreement to the making of the parental order where the conditions in paragraph (2) apply.
(2) The conditions are–

    (a) the application identifies the child by reference to a full certified copy of an entry in the registers of live-births;
    (b) the form of agreement identifies the child by reference to a full certified copy of an entry in the registers of live-births attached to the form; and
    (c) the copy of the entry in the registers of live-births referred to in sub-paragraph (a) is the same or relates to the same entry in the registers of live-births as the copy of the entry in the registers of live-births attached to the form of agreement.

(3) Where the precise date of the child's birth is not proved to the satisfaction of the court, the court will determine the probable date of birth.
(4) The probable date of the child's birth may be specified in the parental order as the date of the child's birth.
(5) Where the child's place of birth cannot be proved to the satisfaction of the court–

    (a) the child may be treated as having been born in the registration district of the court where it is probable that the child may have been born in–

        (i) the United Kingdom;
        (ii) the Channel Islands; or
        (iii) the Isle of Man; or

    (b) in any other case, the particulars of the country of birth may be omitted from the parental order.

13.16 Disclosing information to an adult who was subject to a parental order

(1) Subject to paragraph (2), the person who is subject to the parental order has the right to receive from the court which made the parental order a copy of the following–

(a) the application form for a parental order (but not the documents attached to that form);
(b) the parental order and any other orders relating to the parental order proceedings;
(c) a transcript of the court's decision; and
(d) a report made to the court by the parental order reporter.

(2) The court will not provide a copy of a document or order referred to in paragraph (1) unless the person making the request has completed the certificate relating to counselling in the form for that purpose referred to in Practice Direction 5A.
(3) This rule does not apply to a person under the age of 18 years.

13.17 Application for recovery orders

(1) An application for any of the orders referred to in section 41(2) of the 2002 Act (recovery orders) may–

    (a) in the High Court or a county court, be made without notice in which case the applicant must file the application–

        (i) where the application is made by telephone, the next business day after the making of the application; or
        (ii) in any other case, at the time when the application is made; and

    (b) in a magistrates' court, be made, with the permission of the court, without notice in which case the applicant must file the application at the time when the application is made or as directed by the court.

(2) Where the court refuses to make an order on an application without notice it may direct that the application is made on notice in which case the application shall proceed in accordance with rules 13.1 to 13.14.

(3) The respondents to an application under this rule are–

    (a) in a case where parental order proceedings are pending, all parties to those proceedings;
    (b) any person having parental responsibility for the child;
    (c) any person in whose favour there is provision for contact;
    (d) any person who was caring for the child immediately prior to the making of the application; and
    (e) any person whom the applicant alleges to have effected, or to have been or to be responsible for, the taking or keeping of the child.

13.18 Keeping of registers, custody, inspection and disclosure of documents and information

(1) Such part of the register kept in a family proceedings court in pursuance of rules made under the Magistrates' Courts Act 1980 as relates to parental order proceedings, must be kept in a separate book and the book must not contain particulars of any other proceedings.

(2) All documents relating to parental order proceedings and related proceedings under the 2002 Act including, in a family proceedings court, the book kept in accordance with paragraph (1), must, while they are in the custody of the court, be kept in a place of special security.

(3) Any person who obtains any information in the course of, or relating to, parental order proceedings must treat that information as confidential and must only disclose it if–

    (a) the disclosure is necessary for the proper exercise of that person's duties; or
    (b) the information is requested by–

        (i) a court or public authority (whether in Great Britain or not) having power to determine parental order proceedings and related matters, for

the purpose of that court or authority discharging its duties relating to those proceedings and matters; or
(ii) a person who is authorised in writing by the Secretary of State to obtain the information for the purposes of research.

13.19 Documents held by the court not to be inspected or copied without the court's permission

Subject to the provisions of these rules, any practice direction or any direction given by the court–
(a) no document or order held by the court in parental order proceedings and related proceedings under the 2002 Act will be open to inspection by any person; and
(b) no copy of any such document or order, or of an extract from any such document or order, shall be taken by or given to any person.

13.20 Orders

(1) A parental order takes effect from the date when it is made, or such later date as the court may specify.
(2) In proceedings in Wales a party may request that an order be drawn up in Welsh as well as English.

13.21 Copies of orders

(1) Within 7 days beginning with the date on which the final order was made in proceedings, or such shorter time as the court may direct, a court officer will send–
  (a) a copy of the order to the applicant;
  (b) a copy, which is sealed[GL], authenticated with the stamp of the court or certified as a true copy of a parental order, to the Registrar General;
  (c) a notice of the making or refusal of–
    (i) the final order; or
    (ii) an order quashing or revoking a parental order or allowing an appeal against an order in proceedings,
  to every respondent and, with the permission of the court, any other person.
(2) The court officer will also send notice of the making of a parental order to–
  (a) any court in Great Britain which appears to the court officer to have made any such order as is referred to in section 46(2) of the 2002 Act (order relating to parental responsibility for, and maintenance of, the child); and
  (b) the principal registry, if it appears to the court officer that a parental responsibility agreement has been recorded at the principal registry.
(3) A copy of any final order may be sent to any other person with the permission of the court.
(4) The court officer will send a copy of any order made during the course of the proceedings to all the parties to those proceedings unless the court directs otherwise.
(5) If an order has been drawn up in Welsh as well as in English in accordance with rule 13.20(2), any reference in this rule to sending an order is to be taken as a reference to sending both the Welsh and English orders.

13.22 Amendment and revocation of orders

(1) This rule applies to an application under paragraph 4 of Schedule 1 to the 2002 Act (amendment of a parental order and revocation of direction).
(2) If the application is made in a family proceedings court it must be made to a family

proceedings court for the same local justice area as the family proceedings court which made the parental order, by delivering it or sending it by post to the designated officer of the court.
(3) Subject to paragraph (4), an application may be made without serving a copy of the application notice.
(4) The court may direct that an application notice be served on such persons as it thinks fit.
(5) Where the court makes an order granting the application, a proper officer shall send the Registrar General a notice–

    (a)   specifying the amendments; or
    (b)   informing the Registrar General of the revocation,

giving sufficient particulars of the order to enable the Registrar General to identify the case.

PART 14 PROCEDURE FOR APPLICATIONS IN ADOPTION, PLACEMENT AND RELATED PROCEEDINGS

14.1 Application of this Part and interpretation
(1) The rules in this Part apply to the following proceedings–

    (a)   adoption proceedings;
    (b)   placement proceedings; and
    (c)   proceedings for–

        (i)   the making of a contact order under section 26 of the 2002 Act;
        (ii)   the variation or revocation of a contact order under section 27 of the 2002 Act;
        (iii)   an order giving permission to change a child's surname or remove a child from the United Kingdom under section 28(2) and (3) of the 2002 Act;
        (iv)   a section 84 order;
        (v)   a section 88 direction;
        (vi)   a section 89 order; or
        (vii)   any other order that may be referred to in a practice direction.

(2) In this Part–

'Central Authority' means–

    (a)   in relation to England, the Secretary of State; and
    (b)   in relation to Wales, the Welsh Ministers;

'Convention adoption order' means an adoption order under the 2002 Act which, by virtue of regulations under section 1 of the Adoption (Intercountry Aspects) Act 1999 (regulations giving effect to the Convention on Protection of Children and Co-operation in Respect of Intercountry Adoption, concluded at the Hague on 29th May 1993), is made as a Convention adoption order;

'guardian' means–

    (a)   a guardian (other than the guardian of the estate of a child) appointed in accordance with section 5 of the 1989 Act; and
    (b)   a special guardian within the meaning of section 14A of the 1989 Act;

'provision for contact' means a contact order under section 8 or 34 of the 1989 Act or a contact order under section 26 of the 2002 Act;

'section 88 direction' means a direction given by the High Court under section 88 of the 2002 Act that section 67(3) of that Act (status conferred by adoption) does not apply or does not apply to any extent specified in the direction.

14.2 **Application for a serial number**

(1) This rule applies to any application in proceedings by a person who intends to adopt the child.
(2) If, before the proceedings have started, the applicant requests a court officer to assign a serial number to identify the applicant in connection with the proceedings in order for the applicant's identity to be kept confidential in those proceedings, a serial number will be so assigned.
(3) The court may at any time direct that a serial number identifying the applicant in the proceedings referred to in paragraph (2) must be removed.
(4) If a serial number has been assigned to a person under paragraph (2)–
   (a) the court officer will ensure that any application form or application notice sent in accordance with these rules does not contain information which discloses, or is likely to disclose, the identity of that person to any other party to that application who is not already aware of that person's identity; and
   (b) the proceedings on the application will be conducted with a view to securing that the applicant is not seen by or made known to any party who is not already aware of the applicant's identity except with the applicant's consent.

14.3 **Who the parties are**

(1) In relation to the proceedings set out in column 1 of the following table, column 2 sets out who the application may be made by and column 3 sets out who the respondents to those proceedings will be.

Proceedings for	*Applicants*	*Respondents*
An adoption order (section 46 of the 2002 Act).	The prospective adopters (sections 50 and 51 of the 2002 Act).	Each parent who has parental responsibility for the child unless that parent has given notice under section 20(4)(a) of the 2002 Act (statement of wish not to be informed of any application for an adoption order) which has effect; any guardian of the child unless that guardian has given notice under section 20(4)(a) of the 2002 Act (statement of wish not to be informed of any application for an adoption order) which has effect; any person in whose favour there is provision for contact; any adoption agency having parental responsibility for the child under section 25 of the 2002 Act;

Proceedings for	Applicants	Respondents
		any adoption agency which has taken part at any stage in the arrangements for adoption of the child; any local authority to whom notice under section 44 of the 2002 Act (notice of intention to adopt or apply for a section 84 order) has been given; any local authority or voluntary organisation which has parental responsibility for, is looking after or is caring for, the child; and the child where– – permission has been granted to a parent or guardian to oppose the making of the adoption order (section 47(3) or 47(5) of the 2002 Act); – the child opposes the making of an adoption order; – a children and family reporter recommends that it

Proceedings for	Applicants	Respondents
		is in the best interests of the child to be a party to the proceedings and that recommendation is accepted by the court; – the child is already an adopted child; – any party to the proceedings or the child is opposed to the arrangements for allowing any person contact with the child, or a person not being allowed contact with the child after the making of the adoption order; – the application is for a Convention adoption order or a section 84 order; – the child has been brought into the United Kingdom in the circumstances where section 83(1) of the 2002 Act applies (restriction on bringing children in); – the application is for an adoption order other than a Convention adoption order and the prospective adopters intend the child to live in a country or territory outside the British Islands after the making of the adoption order; or – the prospective adopters are relatives of the child.
A section 84 order.	The prospective adopters asking for parental responsibility prior to adoption abroad.	As for an adoption order.

Proceedings for	Applicants	Respondents
A placement order (section 21 of the 2002 Act).	A local authority (section 22 of the 2002 Act).	Each parent who has parental responsibility for the child: any guardian of the child; any person in whose favour an order under the 1989 Act is in force in relation to the child; any adoption agency or voluntary organisation which has parental responsibility for, is looking after, or is caring for, the child; the child; and the parties or any persons who are or have been parties to proceedings for a care order in respect of the child where those proceedings have led to the application for the placement order.
An order varying a placement order (section 23 of the 2002 Act).	The joint application of the local authority authorised by the placement order to place the child for adoption and the local authority which is to be substituted for that authority (section 23 of the 2002 Act).	The parties to the proceedings leading to the placement order which it is sought to have varied except the child who was the subject of those proceedings; and any person in whose favour there is provision for contact.
An order revoking a placement order (section 24 of the 2002 Act).	The child; the local authority authorised to place the child for adoption; or where the child is not placed for adoption by the authority, any other person who has the permission of the court to apply (section 24 of the 2002 Act).	The parties to the proceedings leading to the placement order which it is sought to have revoked; and any person in whose favour there is provision for contact.

Proceedings for	Applicants	Respondents
A contact order (section 26 of the 2002 Act).	The child; the adoption agency; any parent, guardian or relative; any person in whose favour there was provision for contact under the 1989 Act which ceased to have effect on an adoption agency being authorised to place a child for adoption, or placing a child for adoption who is less than six weeks old (section 26(1) of the 2002 Act); a person in whose favour there was a residence order in force immediately before the adoption agency was authorised to place the child for adoption or placed the child for adoption at a time when the child was less than six weeks old; a person who by virtue of an order made in the exercise of the High Court's inherent jurisdiction with respect to children had care of the child immediately before that time; or any person who has the permission of the court to make the application (section 26 of the 2002 Act).	The adoption agency authorised to place the child for adoption or which has placed the child for adoption; the person with whom the child lives or is to live; each parent with parental responsibility for the child; any guardian of the child; and the child where– – the adoption agency authorised to place the child for adoption or which has placed the child for adoption or a parent with parental responsibility for the child opposes the making of the contact order under section 26 of the 2002 Act; – the child opposes the making of the contact order under section 26 of the 2002 Act; – existing provision for contact is to be revoked; – relatives of the child do not agree to the arrangements for allowing any person contact with the child, or a person not being allowed contact with the child; or – the child is suffering or is at risk of suffering harm within the meaning of the 1989 Act.
An order varying or revoking a contact order (section 27 of the 2002 Act).	The child; the adoption agency; or any person named in the contact order (section 27(1) of the 2002 Act).	The parties to the proceedings leading to the contact order which it is sought to have varied or revoked; and any person named in the contact order.

Proceedings for	Applicants	Respondents
An order permitting the child's name to be changed or the removal of the child from the United Kingdom (section 28(2) and (3) of the 2002 Act).	Any person including the adoption agency or the local authority authorised to place, or which has placed, the child for adoption (section 28(2) of the 2002 Act).	The parties to proceedings leading to any placement order; the adoption agency authorised to place the child for adoption or which has placed the child for adoption; any prospective adopters with whom the child is living; each parent with parental responsibility for the child; and any guardian of the child.
A section 88 direction.	The adopted child; the adopters; any parent; or any other person.	The adopters; the parents; the adoption agency; the local authority to whom notice under section 44 of the 2002 Act (notice of intention to apply for a section 84 order) has been given; and the Attorney-General.
A section 89 order.	The adopters; the adopted person; any parent; the relevant Central Authority; the adoption agency; the local authority to whom notice under section 44 of the 2002 Act (notice of intention to adopt or apply for a section 84 order) has been given; the Secretary of State for the Home Department; or any other person.	The adopters; the parents; the adoption agency; and the local authority to whom notice under section 44 of the 2002 Act (notice of intention to adopt or apply for a section 84 order) has been given.

(2) The court may at any time direct that a child, who is not already a respondent to proceedings, be made a respondent to proceedings where–

    (a)   the child–

        (i)   wishes to make an application; or

        (ii)   has evidence to give to the court or a legal submission to make which has not been given or made by any other party; or

    (b)   there are other special circumstances.

(3) The court may at any time direct that–

    (a)   any other person or body be made a respondent to proceedings; or

(b) a party be removed.
(4) If the court makes a direction for the addition or removal of a party, it may give consequential directions about–
   (a) serving a copy of the application form on any new respondent;
   (b) serving relevant documents on the new party; and
   (c) the management of the proceedings.

14.4 Notice of proceedings to person with foreign parental responsibility

(1) This rule applies where a child is subject to proceedings to which this Part applies and–
   (a) a parent of the child holds or is believed to hold parental responsibility for the child under the law of another State which subsists in accordance with Article 16 of the 1996 Hague Convention following the child becoming habitually resident in a territorial unit of the United Kingdom; and
   (b) that parent is not otherwise required to be joined as a respondent under rule 14.3.
(2) The applicant shall give notice of the proceedings to any parent to whom the applicant believes paragraph (1) applies in any case in which a person who was a parent with parental responsibility under the 1989 Act would be a respondent to the proceedings in accordance with rule 14.3.
(3) The applicant and every respondent to the proceedings shall provide such details as they possess as to the identity and whereabouts of any parent they believe to hold parental responsibility for the child in accordance with paragraph (1) to the court officer, upon making, or responding to the application as appropriate.
(4) Where the existence of such a parent only becomes apparent to a party at a later date during the proceedings, that party must notify the court officer of those details at the earliest opportunity.
(5) Where a parent to whom paragraph (1) applies receives notice of proceedings, that parent may apply to the court to be joined as a party using the Part 18 procedure.

14.5 Who is to serve

(1) The general rules about service in Part 6 are subject to this rule.
(2) In proceedings to which this Part applies, a document which has been issued or prepared by a court officer will be served by the court officer except where–
   (a) a practice direction provides otherwise; or
   (b) the court directs otherwise.
(3) Where a court officer is to serve a document, it is for the court to decide which of the methods of service specified in rule 6.23 is to be used.

14.6 What the court or a court officer will do when the application has been issued

(1) As soon as practicable after the application has been issued in proceedings–
   (a) the court will–
      (i) if section 48(1) of the 2002 Act (restrictions on making adoption orders) applies, consider whether it is proper to hear the application;
      (ii) subject to paragraph (4), set a date for the first directions hearing;
      (iii) appoint a children's guardian in accordance with rule 16.3(1);
      (iv) appoint a reporting officer in accordance with rule 16.30;
      (v) consider whether a report relating to the welfare of the child is required, and if so, request such a report in accordance with rule 16.33;
      (vi) set a date for the hearing of the application; and
      (vii) do anything else that may be set out in a practice direction; and

(b) a court officer will—

 (i) subject to receiving confirmation in accordance with paragraph (2)(b)(ii), give notice of any directions hearing set by the court to the parties and to any children's guardian, reporting officer or children and family reporter;

 (ii) serve a copy of the application form (but, subject to sub-paragraphs (iii) and (iv), not the documents attached to it) on the persons referred to in Practice Direction 14A;

 (iii) send a copy of the certified copy of the entry in the register of live-births or Adopted Children Register and any health report attached to an application for an adoption order to—

  (aa) any children's guardian, reporting officer or children and family reporter; and

  (bb) the local authority to whom notice under section 44 of the 2002 Act (notice of intention to adopt or apply for a section 84 order) has been given;

 (iv) if notice under rule 14.9(2) has been given (request to dispense with consent of parent or guardian), in accordance with that rule inform the parent or guardian of the request and send a copy of the statement of facts to—

  (aa) the parent or guardian;

  (bb) any children's guardian, reporting officer or children and family reporter;

  (cc) any local authority to whom notice under section 44 of the 2002 Act (notice of intention to adopt or apply for a section 84 order) has been given; and

  (dd) any adoption agency which has placed the child for adoption; and

 (v) do anything else that may be set out in a practice direction.

(2) In addition to the matters referred to in paragraph (1), as soon as practicable after an application for an adoption order or a section 84 order has been issued the court or the court officer will—

(a) where the child is not placed for adoption by an adoption agency—

 (i) ask either the Service or the Assembly to file any relevant form of consent to an adoption order or a section 84 order; and

 (ii) ask the local authority to prepare a report on the suitability of the prospective adopters if one has not already been prepared; and

(b) where the child is placed for adoption by an adoption agency, ask the adoption agency to—

 (i) file any relevant form of consent to—

  (aa) the child being placed for adoption;

  (bb) an adoption order;

  (cc) a future adoption order under section 20 of the 2002 Act; or

  (dd) a section 84 order;

 (ii) confirm whether a statement has been made under section 20(4)(a) of the 2002 Act (statement of wish not to be informed of any application for an adoption order) and if so, to file that statement;

 (iii) file any statement made under section 20(4)(b) of the 2002 Act (withdrawal of wish not to be informed of any application for an adoption order) as soon as it is received by the adoption agency; and

(iv) prepare a report on the suitability of the prospective adopters if one has not already been prepared.

(3) In addition to the matters referred to in paragraph (1), as soon as practicable after an application for a placement order has been issued–

    (a) the court will consider whether a report giving the local authority's reasons for placing the child for adoption is required, and if so, will direct the local authority to prepare such a report; and

    (b) the court or the court officer will ask either the Service or the Assembly to file any form of consent to the child being placed for adoption.

(4) Where it considers it appropriate the court may, instead of setting a date for a first directions hearing, give the directions provided for by rule 14.8.

14.7 Date for first directions hearing

Unless the court directs otherwise, the first directions hearing must be within 4 weeks beginning with the date on which the application is issued.

14.8 The first directions hearing

(1) At the first directions hearing in the proceedings the court will–

    (a) fix a timetable for the filing of–

        (i) any report relating to the suitability of the applicants to adopt a child;
        (ii) any report from the local authority;
        (iii) any report from a children's guardian, reporting officer or children and family reporter;
        (iv) if a statement of facts has been filed, any amended statement of facts;
        (v) any other evidence, and.
        (vi) give directions relating to the reports and other evidence;

    (b) consider whether the child or any other person should be a party to the proceedings and, if so, give directions in accordance with rule 14.3(2) or (3) joining that child or person as a party;

    (c) give directions relating to the appointment of a litigation friend for any protected party or child who is a party to, but not the subject of, proceedings unless a litigation friend has already been appointed;

    (d) consider whether the case needs to be transferred to another court and, if so, give directions to transfer the proceedings to another court in accordance with any order made by the Lord Chancellor under Part 1 of Schedule 11 to the 1989 Act;

    (e) give directions about–

        (i) tracing parents or any other person the court considers to be relevant to the proceedings;
        (ii) service of documents;
        (iii) subject to paragraph (2), disclosure as soon as possible of information and evidence to the parties; and
        (iv) the final hearing.

(By rule 3.3 the court may also direct that the case be adjourned if it considers that alternative dispute resolution is appropriate.)

(2) Rule 14.13(2) applies to any direction given under paragraph (1)(e)(iii) as it applies to a direction given under rule 14.13(1).

(3) In addition to the matters referred to in paragraph (1), the court will give any of the directions listed in Practice Direction 14B in proceedings for–

    (a) a Convention adoption order;

(b) a section 84 order;
(c) a section 88 direction;
(d) a section 89 order; or
(e) an adoption order where section 83(1) of the 2002 Act applies (restriction on bringing children in).

(4) The parties or their legal representatives must attend the first directions hearing unless the court directs otherwise.

(5) Directions may also be given at any stage in the proceedings–

(a) of the court's own initiative; or
(b) on the application of a party or any children's guardian or, where the direction concerns a report by a reporting officer or children and family reporter, the reporting officer or children and family reporter.

(6) For the purposes of giving directions or for such purposes as the court directs–

(a) the court may set a date for a further directions hearing or other hearing; and
(b) the court officer will give notice of any date so fixed to the parties and to any children's guardian, reporting officer or children and family reporter.

(7) After the first directions hearing the court will monitor compliance by the parties with the court's timetable and directions.

14.9 Requesting the court to dispense with the consent of any parent or guardian

(1) This rule applies where the applicant wants to ask the court to dispense with the consent of any parent or guardian of a child to–

(a) the child being placed for adoption;
(b) the making of an adoption order except a Convention adoption order; or
(c) the making of a section 84 order.

(2) The applicant requesting the court to dispense with the consent must–

(a) give notice of the request in the application form or at any later stage by filing a written request setting out the reasons for the request; and
(b) file a statement of facts setting out a summary of the history of the case and any other facts to satisfy the court that–

(i) the parent or guardian cannot be found or is incapable of giving consent; or
(ii) the welfare of the child requires the consent to be dispensed with.

(3) If a serial number has been assigned to the applicant under rule 14.2, the statement of facts supplied under paragraph (2)(b) must be framed so that it does not disclose the identity of the applicant.

(4) On receipt of the notice of the request–

(a) a court officer will–

(i) inform the parent or guardian of the request unless the parent or guardian cannot be found; and
(ii) send a copy of the statement of facts filed in accordance with paragraph (2)(b) to–

(aa) the parent or guardian unless the parent or guardian cannot be found;
(bb) any children's guardian, reporting officer or children and family reporter;
(cc) any local authority to whom notice under section 44 of the 2002 Act (notice of intention to adopt or apply for a section 84 order) has been given; and

     (dd) any adoption agency which has placed the child for adoption; and
 (b) if the applicant considers that the parent or guardian is incapable of giving consent, the court will consider whether to–
   (i) appoint a litigation friend for the parent or guardian under rule 15.6(1); or
   (ii) give directions for an application to be made under rule 15.6(3),
   (iii) unless a litigation friend is already appointed for that parent or guardian.

14.10 Consent

(1) Consent of any parent or guardian of a child–
 (a) under section 19 of the 2002 Act, to the child being placed for adoption; and
 (b) under section 20 of the 2002 Act, to the making of a future adoption order,

must be given in the form referred to in Practice Direction 5A or a form to the like effect.

(2) Subject to paragraph (3), consent–
 (a) to the making of an adoption order; or
 (b) to the making of a section 84 order,

may be given in the form referred to in Practice Direction 5A or a form to the like effect or otherwise as the court directs.

(3) Any consent to a Convention adoption order must be in a form which complies with the internal law relating to adoption of the Convention country of which the child is habitually resident.

(4) Any form of consent executed in Scotland must be witnessed by a Justice of the Peace or a Sheriff.

(5) Any form of consent executed in Northern Ireland must be witnessed by a Justice of the Peace.

(6) Any form of consent executed outside the United Kingdom must be witnessed by–
 (a) any person for the time being authorised by law in the place where the document is executed to administer an oath for any judicial or other legal purpose;
 (b) a British Consular officer;
 (c) a notary public; or
 (d) if the person executing the document is serving in any of the regular armed forces of the Crown, an officer holding a commission in any of those forces.

14.11 Reports by the adoption agency or local authority

(1) The adoption agency or local authority must file the report on the suitability of the applicant to adopt a child within the timetable fixed by the court.

(2) A local authority that is directed to prepare a report on the placement of the child for adoption must file that report within the timetable fixed by the court.

(3) The reports must cover the matters specified in Practice Direction 14C.

(4) The court may at any stage request a further report or ask the adoption agency or local authority to assist the court in any other manner.

(5) A court officer will send a copy of any report referred to in this rule to any children's guardian, reporting officer or children and family reporter.

(6) A report to the court under this rule is confidential.

14.12 Health reports

(1) Reports by a registered medical practitioner ('health reports') made not more than 3 months earlier on the health of the child and of each applicant must be attached to an application for an adoption order or a section 84 order except where–

(a) the child was placed for adoption with the applicant by an adoption agency;
(b) the applicant or one of the applicants is a parent of the child; or
(c) the applicant is the partner of a parent of the child.

(2) Health reports must contain the matters set out in Practice Direction 14D.
(3) A health report is confidential.

14.13 Confidential reports to the court and disclosure to the parties

(1) The court will consider whether to give a direction that a confidential report be disclosed to each party to the proceedings.
(2) Before giving such a direction the court will consider whether any information should be deleted including information which–

    (a) discloses, or is likely to disclose, the identity of a person who has been assigned a serial number under rule 14.2(2); or
    (b) discloses the particulars referred to in rule 29.1(1) where a party has given notice under rule 29.1(2) (disclosure of personal details).

(3) The court may direct that the report will not be disclosed to a party.

14.14 Communication of information relating to proceedings

For the purposes of the law relating to contempt of court, information (whether or not it is recorded in any form) relating to proceedings held in private may be communicated–

(a) where the court gives permission;
(b) unless the court directs otherwise, in accordance with Practice Direction 14E; or
(c) where the communication is to–

    (i) a party;
    (ii) the legal representative of a party;
    (iii) a professional legal adviser;
    (iv) an officer of the service or a Welsh family proceedings officer;
    (v) a welfare officer;
    (vi) the Legal Services Commission;
    (vii) an expert whose instruction by a party has been authorised by the court for the purposes of the proceedings; or
    (viii) a professional acting in furtherance of the protection of children.

14.15 Notice of final hearing

A court officer will give notice to the parties, any children's guardian, reporting officer or children and family reporter and to any other person to whom a practice direction may require such notice to be given–

(a) of the date and place where the application will be heard; and
(b) of the fact that, unless the person wishes or the court requires, the person need not attend.

14.16 The final hearing

(1) Any person who has been given notice in accordance with rule 14.15 may attend the final hearing and, subject to paragraph (2), be heard on the question of whether an order should be made.
(2) A person whose application for the permission of the court to oppose the making of an adoption order under section 47(3) or (5) of the 2002 Act has been refused is not entitled to be heard on the question of whether an order should be made.
(3) Any member or employee of a party which is a local authority, adoption agency or other body may address the court at the final hearing if authorised to do so.
(4) The court may direct that any person must attend a final hearing.

(5) Paragraphs (6) and (7) apply to–
  (a) an adoption order;
  (b) a section 84 order; or
  (c) a section 89 order.
(6) Subject to paragraphs (7) and (8), the court cannot make an order unless the applicant and the child personally attend the final hearing.
(7) The court may direct that the applicant or the child need not attend the final hearing.
(8) In a case of adoption by a couple under section 50 of the 2002 Act, the court may make an adoption order after personal attendance of one only of the applicants if there are special circumstances.
(9) The court cannot make a placement order unless a legal representative of the applicant attends the final hearing.

14.17 Proof of identity of the child

(1) Unless the contrary is shown, the child referred to in the application will be deemed to be the child referred to in the form of consent–
  (a) to the child being placed for adoption;
  (b) to the making of an adoption order; or
  (c) to the making of a section 84 order,

where the conditions in paragraph (2) apply.
(2) The conditions are–
  (a) the application identifies the child by reference to a full certified copy of an entry in the registers of live-births;
  (b) the form of consent identifies the child by reference to a full certified copy of an entry in the registers of live-births attached to the form; and
  (c) the copy of the entry in the registers of live-births referred to in sub-paragraph (a) is the same or relates to the same entry in the registers of live-births as the copy of the entry in the registers of live-births attached to the form of consent.
(3) Where the child is already an adopted child paragraph (2) will have effect as if for the references to the registers of live-births there were substituted references to the Adopted Children Register.
(4) Subject to paragraph (7), where the precise date of the child's birth is not proved to the satisfaction of the court, the court will determine the probable date of birth.
(5) The probable date of the child's birth may be specified in the placement order, adoption order or section 84 order as the date of the child's birth.
(6) Subject to paragraph (7), where the child's place of birth cannot be proved to the satisfaction of the court–
  (a) the child may be treated as having been born in the registration district of the court where it is probable that the child may have been born in–
    (i) the United Kingdom;
    (ii) the Channel Islands; or
    (iii) the Isle of Man; or
  (b) in any other case, the particulars of the country of birth may be omitted from the placement order, adoption order or section 84 order.
(7) A placement order identifying the probable date and place of birth of the child will be sufficient proof of the date and place of birth of the child in adoption proceedings and proceedings for a section 84 order.

14.18 Disclosing information to an adopted adult

(1) The adopted person has the right, on request, to receive from the court which made the adoption order a copy of the following–

(a) the application form for an adoption order (but not the documents attached to that form);
(b) the adoption order and any other orders relating to the adoption proceedings;
(c) orders allowing any person contact with the child after the adoption order was made; and
(d) any other document or order referred to in Practice Direction 14F.

(2) The court will remove any protected information from any copy of a document or order referred to in paragraph (1) before the copies are given to the adopted person.
(3) This rule does not apply to an adopted person under the age of 18 years.
(4) In this rule 'protected information' means information which would be protected information under section 57(3) of the 2002 Act if the adoption agency gave the information and not the court.

14.19 Translation of documents

(1) Where a translation of any document is required for the purposes of proceedings for a Convention adoption order the translation must–
(a) unless the court directs otherwise, be provided by the applicant; and
(b) be signed by the translator to certify that the translation is accurate.

(2) This rule does not apply where the document is to be served in accordance with the Service Regulation.

14.20 Application for recovery orders

(1) An application for any of the orders referred to in section 41(2) of the 2002 Act (recovery orders) may–
(a) in the High Court or a county court, be made without notice in which case the applicant must file the application–
(i) where the application is made by telephone, the next business day after the making of the application; or
(ii) in any other case, at the time when the application is made; and
(b) in a magistrates' court, be made, with the permission of the court, without notice in which case the applicant must file the application at the time when the application is made or as directed by the court.

(2) Where the court refuses to make an order on an application without notice it may direct that the application is made on notice in which case the application will proceed in accordance with rules 14.1 to 14.17.

(3) The respondents to an application under this rule are–
(a) in a case where–
(i) placement proceedings;
(ii) adoption proceedings; or
(iii) proceedings for a section 84 order,

are pending, all parties to those proceedings;

(b) any adoption agency authorised to place the child for adoption or which has placed the child for adoption;
(c) any local authority to whom notice under section 44 of the 2002 Act (notice of intention to adopt or apply for a section 84 order) has been given;
(d) any person having parental responsibility for the child;
(e) any person in whose favour there is provision for contact;
(f) any person who was caring for the child immediately prior to the making of the application; and

(g) any person whom the applicant alleges to have effected, or to have been or to be responsible for, the taking or keeping of the child.

14.21 Inherent jurisdiction and fathers without parental responsibility

Where no proceedings have started an adoption agency or local authority may ask the High Court for directions on the need to give a father without parental responsibility notice of the intention to place a child for adoption.

14.22 Timing of applications for section 89 order

An application for a section 89 order must be made within 2 years beginning with the date on which–
(a) the Convention adoption or Convention adoption order; or
(b) the overseas adoption or determination under section 91 of the 2002 Act,

to which it relates was made.

14.23 Custody of documents

All documents relating to proceedings under the 2002 Act must, while they are in the custody of the court, be kept in a place of special security.

14.24 Documents held by the court not to be inspected or copied without the court's permission

Subject to the provisions of these rules, any practice direction or any direction given by the court–
(a) no document or order held by the court in proceedings under the 2002 Act will be open to inspection by any person; and
(b) no copy of any such document or order, or of an extract from any such document or order, will be taken by or given to any person.

14.25 Orders

(1) An order takes effect from the date when it is made, or such later date as the court may specify.
(2) In proceedings in Wales a party may request that an order be drawn up in Welsh as well as English.

14.26 Copies of orders

(1) Within 7 days beginning with the date on which the final order was made in proceedings, or such shorter time as the court may direct, a court officer will send–
  (a) a copy of the order to the applicant;
  (b) a copy, which is sealed[GL], authenticated with the stamp of the court or certified as a true copy, of–
    (i) an adoption order;
    (ii) a section 89 order; or
    (iii) an order quashing or revoking an adoption order or allowing an appeal against an adoption order,
    to the Registrar General;
  (c) a copy of a Convention adoption order to the relevant Central Authority;
  (d) a copy of a section 89 order relating to a Convention adoption order or a Convention adoption to the–
    (i) relevant Central Authority;

(ii) adopters;
(iii) adoption agency; and
(iv) local authority;

(e) unless the court directs otherwise, a copy of a contact order under section 26 of the 2002 Act or a variation or revocation of a contact order under section 27 of the 2002 Act to the–

(i) person with whom the child is living;
(ii) adoption agency; and
(iii) local authority; and

(f) a notice of the making or refusal of–

(i) the final order; or
(ii) an order quashing or revoking an adoption order or allowing an appeal against an order in proceedings,

to every respondent and, with the permission of the court, any other person.

(2) The court officer will also send notice of the making of an adoption order or a section 84 order to–

(a) any court in Great Britain which appears to the court officer to have made any such order as is referred to in section 46(2) of the 2002 Act (order relating to parental responsibility for, and maintenance of, the child); and
(b) the principal registry, if it appears to the court officer that a parental responsibility agreement has been recorded at the principal registry.

(3) A copy of any final order may be sent to any other person with the permission of the court.

(4) The court officer will send a copy of any order made during the course of the proceedings to the following persons or bodies, unless the court directs otherwise–

(a) all the parties to those proceedings;
(b) any children and family reporter appointed in those proceedings;
(c) any adoption agency or local authority which has prepared a report on the suitability of an applicant to adopt a child;
(d) any local authority which has prepared a report on placement for adoption.

(5) If an order has been drawn up in Welsh as well as English in accordance with rule 14.25(2) any reference in this rule to sending an order is to be taken as a reference to sending both the Welsh and English orders.

14.27 Amendment and revocation of orders

(1) Subject to paragraph (2), an application under–

(a) section 55 of the 2002 Act (revocation of adoptions on legitimation); or
(b) paragraph 4 of Schedule 1 to the 2002 Act (amendment of adoption order and revocation of direction),

may be made without serving a copy of the application notice.

(2) The court may direct that an application notice be served on such persons as it thinks fit.
(3) Where the court makes an order granting the application, a court officer will send the Registrar General a notice–

(a) specifying the amendments; or
(b) informing the Registrar General of the revocation,

giving sufficient particulars of the order to enable the Registrar General to identify the case.

14.28 Keeping registers in the family proceedings court

(1) A magistrates' court officer will keep a register in which there will be entered a minute or memorandum of every adjudication of the court in proceedings to which this Part applies.

(2) The register may be stored in electronic form on the court computer system and entries in the register will include, where relevant, the following particulars–

   (a)   the name and address of the applicant;
   (b)   the name of the child including, in adoption proceedings, the name of the child prior to, and after, adoption;
   (c)   the age and sex of the child;
   (d)   the nature of the application; and
   (e)   the minute of adjudication.

(3) The part of the register relating to adoption proceedings will be kept separately to any other part of the register and will–

   (a)   not contain particulars of any other proceedings; and
   (b)   be kept by the court in a place of special security.

PART 15   REPRESENTATION OF PROTECTED PARTIES

15.1   Application of this Part

This Part contains special provisions which apply in proceedings involving protected parties.

15.2   Requirement for litigation friend in proceedings

A protected party must have a litigation friend to conduct proceedings on that party's behalf.

15.3   Stage of proceedings at which a litigation friend becomes necessary

(1) A person may not without the permission of the court take any step in proceedings except–

   (a)   filing an application form; or
   (b)   applying for the appointment of a litigation friend under rule 15.6,

   until the protected party has a litigation friend.

(2) If during proceedings a party lacks capacity (within the meaning of the 2005 Act) to continue to conduct proceedings, no party may take any step in proceedings without the permission of the court until the protected party has a litigation friend.

(3) Any step taken before a protected party has a litigation friend has no effect unless the court orders otherwise.

15.4   Who may be a litigation friend for a protected party without a court order

(1) This rule does not apply if the court has appointed a person to be a litigation friend.

(2) A person with authority as a deputy to conduct the proceedings in the name of a protected party or on that party's behalf is entitled to be the litigation friend of the protected party in any proceedings to which that person's authority extends.

(3) If there is no person with authority as a deputy to conduct the proceedings in the name of a protected party or on that party's behalf, a person may act as a litigation friend if that person–

   (a)   can fairly and competently conduct proceedings on behalf of the protected party;
   (b)   has no interest adverse to that of the protected party; and
   (c)   subject to paragraph (4), undertakes to pay any costs which the protected party may be ordered to pay in relation to the proceedings, subject to any right that person may have to be repaid from the assets of the protected party.

(4) Paragraph (3)(c) does not apply to the Official Solicitor.

('deputy' is defined in rule 2.3.)

15.5 How a person becomes a litigation friend without a court order

(1) If the court has not appointed a litigation friend, a person who wishes to act as a litigation friend must follow the procedure set out in this rule.

(2) A person with authority as a deputy to conduct the proceedings in the name of a protected party or on that party's behalf must file an official copy[GL] of the order, declaration or other document which confers that person's authority to act.

(3) Any other person must file a certificate of suitability stating that that person satisfies the conditions specified in rule 15.4(3).

(4) A person who is to act as a litigation friend must file–

    (a) the document conferring that person's authority to act; or
    (b) the certificate of suitability,

at the time when that person first takes a step in the proceedings on behalf of the protected party.

(5) A court officer will send the certificate of suitability to every person on whom, in accordance with rule 6.28, the application form should be served.

(6) This rule does not apply to the Official Solicitor.

15.6 How a person becomes a litigation friend by court order

(1) The court may, if the person to be appointed so consents, make an order appointing–

    (a) a person other than the Official Solicitor; or
    (b) the Official Solicitor,

as a litigation friend.

(2) An order appointing a litigation friend may be made by the court of its own initiative or on the application of–

    (a) a person who wishes to be a litigation friend; or
    (b) a party to the proceedings.

(3) The court may at any time direct that a party make an application for an order under paragraph (2).

(4) An application for an order appointing a litigation friend must be supported by evidence.

(5) Unless the court directs otherwise, a person appointed under this rule to be a litigation friend for a protected party will be treated as a party for the purpose of any provision in these rules requiring a document to be served on, or sent to, or notice to be given to, a party to the proceedings.

(6) Subject to rule 15.4(4), the court may not appoint a litigation friend under this rule unless it is satisfied that the person to be appointed complies with the conditions specified in rule 15.4(3).

15.7 Court's power to change litigation friend and to prevent person acting as litigation friend

(1) The court may–

    (a) direct that a person may not act as a litigation friend;
    (b) terminate a litigation friend's appointment; or
    (c) appoint a new litigation friend in substitution for an existing one.

(2) An application for an order or direction under paragraph (1) must be supported by evidence.

(3) Subject to rule 15.4(4), the court may not appoint a litigation friend under this rule unless it is satisfied that the person to be appointed complies with the conditions specified in rule 15.4(3).

15.8 Appointment of litigation friend by court order – supplementary

(1) A copy of the application for an order under rule 15.6 or 15.7 must be sent by a court officer to–

    (a) every person on whom, in accordance with rule 6.28, the application form should be served; and

    (b) unless the court directs otherwise, the protected party.

(2) A copy of an application for an order under rule 15.7 must also be sent to–

    (a) the person who is the litigation friend, or who is purporting to act as the litigation friend when the application is made; and

    (b) the person, if not the applicant, who it is proposed should be the litigation friend.

15.9 Procedure where appointment of litigation friend comes to an end

(1) When a party ceases to be a protected party, the litigation friend's appointment continues until it is brought to an end by a court order.

(2) An application for an order under paragraph (1) may be made by–

    (a) the former protected party;

    (b) the litigation friend; or

    (c) a party.

(3) On the making of an order under paragraph (1), the court officer will send a notice to the other parties stating that the appointment of the protected party's litigation friend to act has ended.

PART 16 REPRESENTATION OF CHILDREN AND REPORTS IN PROCEEDINGS INVOLVING CHILDREN

CHAPTER 1 APPLICATION OF THIS PART

16.1 Application of this Part

This Part–

(a) sets out when the court will make a child a party in family proceedings; and

(b) contains special provisions which apply in proceedings involving children.

CHAPTER 2 CHILD AS PARTY IN FAMILY PROCEEDINGS

16.2 When the court may make a child a party to proceedings

(1) The court may make a child a party to proceedings if it considers it is in the best interests of the child to do so.

(2) This rule does not apply to a child who is the subject of proceedings–

    (a) which are specified proceedings; or

    (b) to which Part 14 applies.

(The Practice Direction 16A sets out the matters which the court will take into consideration before making a child a party under this rule.)

CHAPTER 3 WHEN A CHILDREN'S GUARDIAN OR LITIGATION FRIEND WILL BE APPOINTED

16.3 Appointment of a children's guardian in specified proceedings or proceedings to which Part 14 applies

(1) Unless it is satisfied that it is not necessary to do so to safeguard the interests of the child, the court must appoint a children's guardian for a child who is–

(a) the subject of; and
(b) a party to,

proceedings–
(i) which are specified proceedings; or
(ii) to which Part 14 applies.

(Rules 12.6 and 14.6 set out the point in the proceedings when the court will appoint a children's guardian in specified proceedings and proceedings to which Part 14 applies respectively.)

(2) At any stage in the proceedings–

(a) a party may apply, without notice to the other parties unless the court directs otherwise, for the appointment of a children's guardian; or
(b) the court may of its own initiative appoint a children's guardian.

(3) Where the court refuses an application under paragraph (2)(a) it will give reasons for the refusal and the court or a court officer will–

(a) record the refusal and the reasons for it; and
(b) as soon as practicable, notify the parties and either the Service or the Assembly of a decision not to appoint a children's guardian.

(4) When appointing a children's guardian the court will consider the appointment of anyone who has previously acted as a children's guardian of the same child.

(5) Where the court appoints a children's guardian in accordance with this rule, the provisions of Chapter 6 of this Part apply.

16.4 Appointment of a children's guardian in proceedings not being specified proceedings or proceedings to which Part 14 applies

(1) Without prejudice to rule 8.42 or 16.6, the court must appoint a children's guardian for a child who is the subject of proceedings, which are not proceedings of a type referred to in rule 16.3(1), if–

(a) the child is an applicant in the proceedings;
(b) a provision in these rules provides for the child to be a party to the proceedings; or
(c) the court has made the child a party in accordance with rule16.2.

(2) The provisions of Chapter 7 of this Part apply where the appointment of a children's guardian is required in accordance with paragraph (1).

('children's guardian' is defined in rule 2.3.)

16.5 Requirement for a litigation friend

(1) Without prejudice to rule 16.6, where a child is–

(a) a party to proceedings; but
(b) not the subject of those proceedings,

the child must have a litigation friend to conduct proceedings on the child's behalf.

(2) The provisions of Chapter 5 of this Part apply where a litigation friend is required in accordance with paragraph (1).

CHAPTER 4 WHERE A CHILDREN'S GUARDIAN OR LITIGATION FRIEND IS NOT REQUIRED

16.6 Circumstances in which a child does not need a children's guardian or litigation friend

(1) Subject to paragraph (2), a child may conduct proceedings without a children's guardian or litigation friend where the proceedings are proceedings–

(a) under the 1989 Act;
(b) to which Part 11 (applications under Part 4A of the Family Law Act 1996) or Part 14 (applications in adoption, placement and related proceedings) of these rules apply; or
(c) relating to the exercise of the court's inherent jurisdiction with respect to children,

and one of the conditions set out in paragraph (3) is satisfied.

(2) Paragraph (1) does not apply where the child is the subject of and a party to proceedings–
  (a) which are specified proceedings; or
  (b) to which Part 14 applies.
(3) The conditions referred to in paragraph (1) are that either–
  (a) the child has obtained the court's permission; or
  (b) a solicitor–
    (i) considers that the child is able, having regard to the child's understanding, to give instructions in relation to the proceedings; and
    (ii) has accepted instructions from that child to act for that child in the proceedings and, if the proceedings have begun, the solicitor is already acting.
(4) An application for permission under paragraph (3)(a) may be made by the child without notice.
(5) Where a child–
  (a) has a litigation friend or children's guardian in proceedings to which this rule applies; and
  (b) wishes to conduct the remaining stages of the proceedings without the litigation friend or children's guardian,

the child may apply to the court, on notice to the litigation friend or children's guardian, for permission for that purpose and for the removal of the litigation friend or children's guardian.

(6) The court will grant an application under paragraph (3)(a) or (5) if it considers that the child has sufficient understanding to conduct the proceedings concerned or proposed without a litigation friend or children's guardian.
(7) In exercising its powers under paragraph (6) the court may require the litigation friend or children's guardian to take such part in the proceedings as the court directs.
(8) The court may revoke any permission granted under paragraph (3)(a) where it considers that the child does not have sufficient understanding to participate as a party in the proceedings concerned without a litigation friend or children's guardian.
(9) Where a solicitor is acting for a child in proceedings without a litigation friend or children's guardian by virtue of paragraph (3)(b) and either of the conditions specified in paragraph (3)(b)(i) or (ii) cease to be fulfilled, the solicitor must inform the court immediately.
(10) Where–
  (a) the court revokes any permission under paragraph (8); or
  (b) either of the conditions specified in paragraph (3)(b)(i) or (ii) is no longer fulfilled,

the court may, if it considers it necessary in order to protect the interests of the child concerned, appoint a person to be that child's litigation friend or children's guardian.

CHAPTER 5   LITIGATION FRIEND

16.7   Application of this Chapter

This Chapter applies where a child must have a litigation friend to conduct proceedings on the child's behalf in accordance with rule 16.5.

16.8   Stage of proceedings at which a litigation friend becomes necessary
(1) This rule does not apply in relation to a child who is conducting proceedings without a litigation friend in accordance with rule 16.6.
(2) A person may not without the permission of the court take any step in proceedings except–

   (a)   filing an application form; or
   (b)   applying for the appointment of a litigation friend under rule 16.11,

   until the child has a litigation friend.
(3) Any step taken before a child has a litigation friend has no effect unless the court orders otherwise.

16.9   Who may be a litigation friend for a child without a court order
(1) This rule does not apply if the court has appointed a person to be a litigation friend.
(2) A person may act as a litigation friend if that person–

   (a)   can fairly and competently conduct proceedings on behalf of the child;
   (b)   has no interest adverse to that of the child; and
   (c)   subject to paragraph (3), undertakes to pay any costs which the child may be ordered to pay in relation to the proceedings, subject to any right that person may have to be repaid from the assets of the child.

(3) Paragraph (2)(c) does not apply to the Official Solicitor, an officer of the Service or a Welsh family proceedings officer.

16.10   How a person becomes a litigation friend without a court order
(1) If the court has not appointed a litigation friend, a person who wishes to act as such must file a certificate of suitability stating that that person satisfies the conditions specified in rule 16.9(2).
(2) The certificate of suitability must be filed at the time when the person who wishes to act as litigation friend first takes a step in the proceedings on behalf of the child.
(3) A court officer will send the certificate of suitability to every person on whom, in accordance with rule 6.28, the application form should be served.
(4) This rule does not apply to the Official Solicitor, an officer of the Service or a Welsh family proceedings officer.

16.11   Appointment of litigation friend by the court
(1) The court may, if the person to be appointed consents, make an order appointing as a litigation friend–

   (a)   the Official Solicitor;
   (b)   an officer of the Service or a Welsh family proceedings officer; or
   (c)   some other person.

(2) An order appointing a litigation friend may be made by the court of its own initiative or on the application of–

   (a)   a person who wishes to be a litigation friend; or
   (b)   a party to the proceedings.

(3) The court may at any time direct that a party make an application for an order under paragraph (2).
(4) An application for an order appointing a litigation friend must be supported by evidence.
(5) Unless the court directs otherwise, a person appointed under this rule to be a litigation friend for a child will be treated as a party for the purpose of any provision in these rules requiring a document to be served on, or sent to, or notice to be given to, a party to the proceedings.
(6) Subject to rule 16.9(3), the court may not appoint a litigation friend under this rule unless it is satisfied that the person to be appointed complies with the conditions specified in rule 16.9(2).
(7) This rule is without prejudice to rule 16.6.

16.12 Court's power to change litigation friend and to prevent person acting as litigation friend

(1) The court may–
   (a) direct that a person may not act as a litigation friend;
   (b) terminate a litigation friend's appointment; or
   (c) appoint a new litigation friend in substitution for an existing one.
(2) An application for an order or direction under paragraph (1) must be supported by evidence.
(3) Subject to rule 16.9(3), the court may not appoint a litigation friend under this rule unless it is satisfied that the person to be appointed complies with the conditions specified in rule 16.9(2).

16.13 Appointment of litigation friend by court order – supplementary

(1) A copy of the application for an order under rule 16.11 or 16.12 must be sent by a court officer to every person on whom, in accordance with rule 6.28, the application form should be served.
(2) A copy of an application for an order under rule 16.12 must also be sent to–
   (a) the person who is the litigation friend, or who is purporting to act as the litigation friend when the application is made; and
   (b) the person, if not the applicant, who it is proposed should be the litigation friend.

16.14 Powers and duties of litigation friend

(1) The litigation friend–
   (a) has the powers and duties set out in Practice Direction 16A; and
   (b) must exercise those powers and duties in accordance with Practice Direction 16A.
(2) Where the litigation friend is an officer of the Service or a Welsh family proceedings officer, rule 16.20 applies as it applies to a children's guardian appointed in accordance with Chapter 6.

16.15 Procedure where appointment of litigation friend comes to an end

(1) When a child who is not a protected party reaches the age of 18, a litigation friend's appointment comes to an end.
(2) A court officer will send a notice to the other parties stating that the appointment of the child's litigation friend to act has ended.

CHAPTER 6   CHILDREN'S GUARDIAN APPOINTED UNDER RULE 16.3

16.16   Application of this Chapter

This Chapter applies where the court must appoint a children's guardian in accordance with rule 16.3.

16.17   Who may be a children's guardian

Where the court is appointing a children's guardian under rule 16.3 it will appoint an officer of the Service or a Welsh family proceedings officer.

16.18   What the court or a court officer will do once the court has made a decision about appointing a children's guardian

(1) Where the court appoints a children's guardian under rule 16.3 a court officer will record the appointment and, as soon as practicable, will–

    (a)   inform the parties and either the Service or the Assembly; and

    (b)   unless it has already been sent, send the children's guardian a copy of the application and copies of any document filed with the court in the proceedings.

(2) A court officer has a continuing duty to send the children's guardian a copy of any other document filed with the court during the course of the proceedings.

16.19   Termination of the appointment of the children's guardian

(1) The appointment of a children's guardian under rule 16.3 continues for such time as is specified in the appointment or until terminated by the court.

(2) When terminating an appointment in accordance with paragraph (1), the court will give reasons for doing so, a note of which will be taken by the court or a court officer.

16.20   Powers and duties of the children's guardian

(1) The children's guardian is to act on behalf of the child upon the hearing of any application in proceedings to which this Chapter applies with the duty of safeguarding the interests of the child.

(2) The children's guardian must also provide the court with such other assistance as it may require.

(3) The children's guardian, when carrying out duties in relation to specified proceedings, other than placement proceedings, must have regard to the principle set out in section 1(2) and the matters set out in section 1(3)(a) to (f) of the 1989 Act as if for the word 'court' in that section there were substituted the words 'children's guardian'.

(4) The children's guardian, when carrying out duties in relation to proceedings to which Part 14 applies, must have regard to the principle set out in section 1(3) and the matters set out in section 1(4)(a) to (f) of the 2002 Act as if for the word 'court' in that section there were substituted the words 'children's guardian'.

(5) The children's guardian's duties must be exercised in accordance with Practice Direction 16A.

(6) A report to the court by the children's guardian is confidential.

16.21   Where the child instructs a solicitor or conducts proceedings on the child's own behalf

(1) Where it appears to the children's guardian that the child–

    (a)   is instructing a solicitor direct; or

    (b)   intends to conduct and is capable of conducting the proceedings on that child's own behalf,

    the children's guardian must inform the court of that fact.

(2) Where paragraph (1) applies the children's guardian–
- (a) must perform such additional duties as the court may direct;
- (b) must take such part in the proceedings as the court may direct; and
- (c) may, with the permission of the court, have legal representation in the conduct of those duties.

CHAPTER 7   CHILDREN'S GUARDIAN APPOINTED UNDER RULE 16.4

16.22   Application of this Chapter

This Chapter applies where the court must appoint a children's guardian under rule 16.4.

16.23   Stage of proceedings at which a children's guardian becomes necessary

(1) This rule does not apply in relation to a child who is conducting proceedings without a children's guardian in accordance with rule 16.6.
(2) A person may not without the permission of the court take any step in proceedings except–
- (a) filing an application form; or
- (b) applying for the appointment of a children's guardian under rule 16.24,

until the child has a children's guardian.
(3) Any step taken before a child has a children's guardian has no effect unless the court orders otherwise.

16.24   Appointment of a children's guardian

(1) The court may make an order appointing as a children's guardian, an officer of the Service or a Welsh family proceedings officer or, if the person to be appointed consents –
- (a) a person other than the Official Solicitor; or
- (b) the Official Solicitor.

(2) An order appointing a children's guardian may be made by the court of its own initiative or on the application of–
- (a) a person who wishes to be a children's guardian; or
- (b) a party to the proceedings.

(3) The court may at any time direct that a party make an application for an order under paragraph (2).
(4) An application for an order appointing a children's guardian must be supported by evidence.
(5) The court may not appoint a children's guardian under this rule unless it is satisfied that that person–
- (a) can fairly and competently conduct proceedings on behalf of the child;
- (b) has no interest adverse to that of the child; and
- (c) subject to paragraph (6), undertakes to pay any costs which the child may be ordered to pay in relation to the proceedings, subject to any right that person may have to be repaid from the assets of the child.

(6) Paragraph (5)(c) does not apply to the Official Solicitor, an officer of the Service or a Welsh family proceedings officer.
(7) This rule is without prejudice to rule 16.6 and rule 9.11.

(Rule 9.11 provides for a child to be separately represented in certain applications for a financial remedy.)

16.25 Court's power to change children's guardian and to prevent person acting as children's guardian

(1) The court may–
   (a) direct that a person may not act as a children's guardian;
   (b) terminate the appointment of a children's guardian; or
   (c) appoint a new children's guardian in substitution for an existing one.
(2) An application for an order or direction under paragraph (1) must be supported by evidence.
(3) Subject to rule 16.24(6), the court may not appoint a children's guardian under this rule unless it is satisfied that the person to be appointed complies with the conditions specified in rule 16.24(5).

16.26 Appointment of children's guardian by court order – supplementary

(1) A copy of the application for an order under rule 16.24 or 16.25 must be sent by a court officer to every person on whom, in accordance with rule 6.28, the application form should be served.
(2) A copy of an application for an order under rule 16.25 must also be sent to–
   (a) the person who is the children's guardian, or who is purporting to act as the children's guardian when the application is made; and
   (b) the person, if not the applicant, who it is proposed should be the children's guardian.

16.27 Powers and duties of children's guardian

(1) The children's guardian–
   (a) has the powers and duties set out in Practice Direction 16A; and
   (b) must exercise those powers and duties in accordance with Practice Direction 16A.
(2) Where the children's guardian is an officer of the Service or a Welsh family proceedings officer, rule 16.20 applies to a children's guardian appointed in accordance with this Chapter as it applies to a children's guardian appointed in accordance with Chapter 6.

16.28 Procedure where appointment of children's guardian comes to an end

(1) When a child reaches the age of 18, the appointment of a children's guardian comes to an end.
(2) A court officer will send a notice to the other parties stating that the appointment of the child's children's guardian to act has ended.

CHAPTER 8   DUTIES OF SOLICITOR ACTING FOR THE CHILD

16.29 Solicitor for child

(1) Subject to paragraphs (2) and (4), a solicitor appointed–
   (a) under section 41(3) of the 1989 Act; or
   (b) by the children's guardian in accordance with the Practice Direction 16A,

   must represent the child in accordance with instructions received from the children's guardian.
(2) If a solicitor appointed as mentioned in paragraph (1) considers, having taken into account the matters referred to in paragraph (3), that the child–
   (a) wishes to give instructions which conflict with those of the children's guardian; and

(b) is able, having regard to the child's understanding, to give such instructions on the child's own behalf,

the solicitor must conduct the proceedings in accordance with instructions received from the child.

(3) The matters the solicitor must take into account for the purposes of paragraph (2) are–

(a) the views of the children's guardian; and
(b) any direction given by the court to the children's guardian concerning the part to be taken by the children's guardian in the proceedings.

(4) Where–

(a) no children's guardian has been appointed; and
(b) the condition in section 41(4)(b) of the 1989 Act is satisfied,

a solicitor appointed under section 41(3) of the 1989 Act must represent the child in accordance with instructions received from the child.

(5) Where a solicitor appointed as mentioned in paragraph (1) receives no instructions under paragraphs (1), (2) or (4), the solicitor must represent the child in furtherance of the best interests of the child.

(6) A solicitor appointed under section 41(3) of the 1989 Act or by the children's guardian in accordance with Practice Direction 16A must serve documents, and accept service of documents, on behalf of the child in accordance with rule 6.31 and, where the child has not been served separately and has sufficient understanding, advise the child of the contents of any document so served.

(7) Where the child wishes an appointment of a solicitor–

(a) under section 41(3) of the 1989 Act; or
(b) by the children's guardian in accordance with the Practice Direction 16A,

to be terminated–

(i) the child may apply to the court for an order terminating the appointment; and
(ii) the solicitor and the children's guardian will be given an opportunity to make representations.

(8) Where the children's guardian wishes an appointment of a solicitor under section 41(3) of the 1989 Act to be terminated–

(a) the children's guardian may apply to the court for an order terminating the appointment; and
(b) the solicitor and, if of sufficient understanding, the child, will be given an opportunity to make representations.

(9) When terminating an appointment in accordance with paragraph (7) or (8), the court will give its reasons for so doing, a note of which will be taken by the court or a court officer.

(10) The court or a court officer will record the appointment under section 41(3) of the 1989 Act or the refusal to make the appointment.

CHAPTER 9   REPORTING OFFICER

16.30   When the court appoints a reporting officer

In proceedings to which Part 14 applies, the court will appoint a reporting officer where–

(a) it appears that a parent or guardian of the child is willing to consent to the placing of the child for adoption, to the making of an adoption order or to a section 84 order; and
(b) that parent or guardian is in England or Wales.

16.31 Appointment of the same reporting officer in respect of two or more parents or guardians

The same person may be appointed as the reporting officer for two or more parents or guardians of the child.

16.32 The duties of the reporting officer

(1) The reporting officer must witness the signature by a parent or guardian on the document in which consent is given to–

    (a) the placing of the child for adoption;
    (b) the making of an adoption order; or
    (c) the making of a section 84 order.

(2) The reporting officer must carry out such other duties as are set out in Practice Direction 16A.

(3) A report to the court by the reporting officer is confidential.

(4) The reporting officer's duties must be exercised in accordance with Practice Direction 16A.

CHAPTER 10   CHILDREN AND FAMILY REPORTER AND WELFARE OFFICER

16.33 Request by court for a welfare report in respect of the child

(1) Where the court is considering an application for an order in proceedings, the court may ask–

    (a) in proceedings to which Parts 12 and 14 apply, a children and family reporter; or
    (b) in proceedings to which Part 12 applies, a welfare officer,

to prepare a report on matters relating to the welfare of the child, and, in this rule, the person preparing the report is called 'the officer'.

(2) It is the duty of the officer to–

    (a) comply with any request for a report under this rule; and
    (b) provide the court with such other assistance as it may require.

(3) A report to the court under this rule is confidential.

(4) The officer, when carrying out duties in relation to proceedings under the 1989 Act, must have regard to the principle set out in section 1(2) and the matters set out in section 1(3)(a) to (f) of that Act as if for the word 'court' in that section there were substituted the words 'children and family reporter' or 'welfare officer' as the case may be.

(5) A party may question the officer about oral or written advice tendered by that officer to the court.

(6) The court officer will notify the officer of a direction given at a hearing at which–

    (a) the officer is not present; and
    (b) the welfare report is considered.

(7) The officer's duties must be exercised in accordance with Practice Direction 16A.

('children and family reporter' and 'welfare officer' are defined in rule 2.3)

CHAPTER 11   PARENTAL ORDER REPORTER

16.34 When the court appoints a parental order reporter

In proceedings to which Part 13 applies, the court will appoint a parental order reporter in accordance with rule 13.5.

16.35 **Powers and duties of the parental order reporter**

(1) The parental order reporter is to act on behalf of the child upon the hearing of any application in proceedings to which Part 13 applies with the duty of safeguarding the interests of the child.
(2) The parental order reporter must–
    (a) investigate the matters set out in sections 54(1) to (8) of the 2008 Act;
    (b) so far as the parental order reporter considers necessary, investigate any matter contained in the application form or other matter which appears relevant to the making of the parental order; and
    (c) advise the court on whether there is any reason under section 1 of the 2002 Act (as applied with modifications by the Human Fertilisation and Embryology (Parental Orders) Regulations 2010) to refuse the parental order.
(3) The parental order reporter must also provide the court with such other assistance as it may require.
(4) The parental order reporter's duties must be exercised in accordance with Practice Direction 16A.
(5) A report to the court by the parental order reporter is confidential.

CHAPTER 12 SUPPLEMENTARY APPOINTMENT PROVISIONS

16.36 **Persons who may not be appointed as children's guardian, reporting officer or children and family reporter**

(1) In adoption proceedings or proceedings for a section 84 order or a section 89 order, no person may be appointed as a children's guardian, reporting officer or children and family reporter who–
    (a) is a member, officer or servant of a local authority which is a party to the proceedings;
    (b) is, or has been, a member, officer or servant of a local authority or voluntary organisation who has been directly concerned in that capacity in arrangements relating to the care, accommodation or welfare of the child during the 5 years prior to the start of the proceedings; or
    (c) is a serving probation officer who has, in that capacity, been previously concerned with the child or the child's family.
(2) In placement proceedings, a person described in paragraph (1)(b) or (c) may not be appointed as a children's guardian, reporting officer or children and family reporter.

16.37 **Appointment of the same person as children's guardian, reporting officer and children and family reporter**

The same person may be appointed to act as one or more of the following–

(a) the children's guardian;
(b) the reporting officer; and
(c) the children and family reporter.

CHAPTER 13 OFFICERS OF THE SERVICE, WELSH FAMILY PROCEEDINGS OFFICERS AND LOCAL AUTHORITY OFFICERS: FURTHER DUTIES

16.38 **Officers of the Service, Welsh family proceedings officers and local authority officers acting under certain duties**

(1) This rule applies when–

(a) an officer of the Service or a Welsh family proceedings officer is acting under a duty in accordance with–
- (i) section 11E(7) of the 1989 Act (providing the court with information as to the making of a contact activity direction or a contact activity condition);
- (ii) section 11G(2) of the 1989 Act (monitoring compliance with a contact activity direction or a contact activity condition);
- (iii) section 11H(2) of the 1989 Act (monitoring compliance with a contact order);
- (iv) section 11L(5) of the 1989 Act (providing the court with information as to the making of an enforcement order);
- (v) section 11M(1) of the 1989 Act (monitoring compliance with an enforcement order);
- (vi) section 16(6) of the 1989 Act (providing a report to the court in accordance with a direction in a family assistance order); and
- (vii) section 16A of the 1989 Act (making a risk assessment); and

(b) a local authority officer is acting under a duty in accordance with section 16(6) of the 1989 Act (providing a report to the court in accordance with a direction in a family assistance order).

(2) In this rule,–
- (a) 'contact activity direction', 'contact activity condition' and 'enforcement order' have the meanings given in rule 12.2; and
- (b) references to 'the officer' are to the officer of the Service, Welsh family proceedings officer or local authority officer referred to in paragraph (1).

(3) In exercising the duties referred to in paragraph (1), the officer must have regard to the principle set out in section 1(2) of the 1989 Act and the matters set out in section 1(3)(a) to (f) of the 1989 Act as if for the word 'court' in that section there were substituted the words 'officer of the Service, Welsh family proceedings officer or local authority officer'.

(4) The officer's duties referred to in paragraph (1) must be exercised in accordance with Practice Direction 16A.

CHAPTER 14   ENFORCEMENT ORDERS AND FINANCIAL COMPENSATION ORDERS: PERSONS NOTIFIED

16.39   Application for enforcement orders and financial compensation orders: duties of the person notified

(1) This rule applies where a person who was the child's children's guardian, litigation friend or legal representative in the proceedings in which a contact order was made has been notified of an application for an enforcement order or for a financial compensation order as required by Practice Direction 12C.

(2) The person who has been notified of the application must–
- (a) consider whether it is in the best interests of the child for the child to be made a party to the proceedings for an enforcement order or a financial compensation order (as applicable); and
- (b) before the date fixed for the first hearing in the case notify the court, orally or in writing, of the opinion reached on the question, together with the reasons for this opinion.

(3) In this rule, 'enforcement order' and 'financial compensation order' have the meanings given in rule 12.2.

PART 17   STATEMENTS OF TRUTH

17.1   Interpretation

In this Part 'statement of case' has the meaning given to it in Part 4 except that a statement of case does not include an application for a matrimonial order or a civil partnership order or an answer to such an application.

(Rule 4.1 defines 'statement of case' for the purposes of Part 4.)

17.2   Documents to be verified by a statement of truth

(1) Subject to paragraph (9), the following documents must be verified by a statement of truth–

    (a)   a statement of case;
    (b)   a witness statement;
    (c)   an acknowledgement of service in a claim begun by the Part 19 procedure;
    (d)   a certificate of service;
    (e)   a statement of arrangements for children;
    (f)   a statement of information filed under rule 9.26(1)(b); and
    (g)   any other document where a rule or practice direction requires it.

(2) Where a statement of case is amended, the amendments must be verified by a statement of truth unless the court orders otherwise.

(3) If an applicant wishes to rely on matters set out in the application form or application notice as evidence, the application form or notice must be verified by a statement of truth.

(4) Subject to paragraph (5), a statement of truth is a statement that–

    (a)   the party putting forward the document;
    (b)   in the case of a witness statement, the maker of the witness statement; or
    (c)   in the case of a certificate of service, the person who signs the certificate,

believes the facts stated in the document are true.

(5) If a party is conducting proceedings with a litigation friend, the statement of truth in–

    (a)   a statement of case; or
    (b)   an application notice,

is a statement that the litigation friend believes the facts stated in the document being verified are true.

(6) The statement of truth must be signed by–

    (a)   in the case of a statement of case–

        (i)   the party or litigation friend; or
        (ii)   the legal representative on behalf of the party or litigation friend; and

    (b)   in the case of a witness statement or statement of arrangements for children, the maker of the statement.

(7) A statement of truth, which is not contained in the document which it verifies, must clearly identify that document.

(8) A statement of truth in a statement of case may be made by–

    (a)   a person who is not a party; or
    (b)   by two parties jointly,

where this is permitted by a practice direction.

(9) An application that does not contain a statement of facts need not be verified by a statement of truth.

(Practice Direction 17A sets out the form of statement of truth.)

17.3 Failure to verify a statement of case

(1) If a party fails to verify that party's statement of case by a statement of truth–
   (a) the statement of case shall remain effective unless struck out; but.
   (b) the party may not rely on the statement of case as evidence of any of the matters set out in it.
(2) The court may strike out[GL] a statement of case which is not verified by a statement of truth.
(3) Any party may apply for an order under paragraph (2).

17.4 Failure to verify a witness statement

If the maker of a witness statement fails to verify the witness statement by a statement of truth, the court may direct that it shall not be admissible as evidence.

17.5 Power of the court to require a document to be verified

(1) The court may order a person who has failed to verify a document in accordance with rule 17.2 to verify the document.
(2) Any party may apply for an order under paragraph (1).

17.6 False statements

(1) Proceedings for contempt of court may be brought against a person who makes, or causes to be made, a false statement in a document verified by a statement of truth without an honest belief in its truth.
(2) Proceedings under this rule may be brought only–
   (a) by the Attorney General; or
   (b) with the permission of the court.
(3) This rule does not apply to proceedings in a magistrates' court.

PART 18 PROCEDURE FOR OTHER APPLICATIONS IN PROCEEDINGS

18.1 Types of application for which Part 18 procedure may be followed

(1) The Part 18 procedure is the procedure set out in this Part.
(2) An applicant may use the Part 18 procedure if the application is made–
   (a) in the course of existing proceedings;
   (b) to start proceedings except where some other Part of these rules prescribes the procedure to start proceedings; or
   (c) in connection with proceedings which have been concluded.
(3) Paragraph (2) does not apply–
   (a) to applications where any other rule in any other Part of these rules sets out the procedure for that type of application;
   (b) if a practice direction provides that the Part 18 procedure may not be used in relation to the type of application in question.

18.2 Applications for permission to start proceedings

An application for permission to start proceedings must be made to the court where the proceedings will be started if permission is granted.

18.3 Respondents to applications under this Part

(1) The following persons are to be respondents to an application under this Part–

    (a) where there are existing proceedings or the proceedings have been concluded–

        (i) the parties to those proceedings; and

        (ii) if the proceedings are proceedings under Part 11, the person who is the subject of those proceedings;

    (b) where there are no existing proceedings–

        (i) if notice has been given under section 44 of the 2002 Act (notice of intention to adopt or apply for an order under section 84 of that Act), the local authority to whom notice has been given; and

        (ii) if an application is made for permission to apply for an order in proceedings, any person who will be a party to the proceedings brought if permission is granted; and

    (c) any other person as the court may direct.

18.4 Application notice to be filed

(1) Subject to paragraph (2), the applicant must file an application notice.

(2) An applicant may make an application without filing an application notice if–

    (a) this is permitted by a rule or practice direction; or

    (b) the court dispenses with the requirement for an application notice.

18.5 Notice of an application

(1) Subject to paragraph (2), a copy of the application notice must be served on–

    (a) each respondent;

    (b) in relation to proceedings under Part 11, the person who is, or, in the case of an application to start proceedings, it is intended will be, the subject of the proceedings; and

    (c) in relation to proceedings under Parts 12 and 14, the children's guardian (if any).

(2) An application may be made without serving a copy of the application notice if this is permitted by–

    (a) a rule;

    (b) a practice direction; or

    (c) the court.

(Rule 18.8 deals with service of a copy of the application notice.)

18.6 Time when an application is made

When an application must be made within a specified time, it is so made if the court receives the application notice within that time.

18.7 What an application notice must include

(1) An application notice must state–

    (a) what order the applicant is seeking; and

    (b) briefly, why the applicant is seeking the order.

(2) A draft of the order sought must be attached to the application notice.

(Part 17 requires an application notice to be verified by a statement of truth if the applicant wishes to rely on matters set out in his application as evidence.)

18.8 Service of a copy of an application notice

(1) Subject to rule 2.4, a copy of the application notice must be served in accordance with the provisions of Part 6–
  (a) as soon as practicable after it is filed; and
  (b) in any event–
    (i) where the application is for an interim order under rule 9.7 at least 14 days; and
    (ii) in any other case, at least 7 days;
  before the court is to deal with the application.
(2) The applicant must, when filing the application notice, file a copy of any written evidence in support.
(3) If a copy of an application notice is served by a court officer it must be accompanied by–
  (a) a notice of the date and place where the application will be heard;
  (b) a copy of any witness statement in support; and
  (c) a copy of the draft order which the applicant has attached to the application.
(4) If–
  (a) an application notice is served; but
  (b) the period of notice is shorter than the period required by these rules or a practice direction,
  the court may direct that, in the circumstances of the case, sufficient notice has been given and hear the application.
(5) This rule does not require written evidence–
  (a) to be filed if it has already been filed; or
  (b) to be served on a party on whom it has already been served.

18.9 Applications which may be dealt with without a hearing

(1) The court may deal with an application without a hearing if–
  (a) the court does not consider that a hearing would be appropriate; or
  (b) the parties agree as to the terms of the order sought or the parties agree that the court should dispose of the application without a hearing and the court does not consider that a hearing would be appropriate.
(2) Where–
  (a) an application is made for permission to make an application in proceedings under the 1989 Act; and
  (b) the court refuses the application without a hearing in accordance with paragraph (1)(a),
  the court must, at the request of the applicant, re-list the application and fix a date for a hearing.
(3) Paragraph (2) does not apply to magistrates' courts.

18.10 Service of application notice following court order where application made without notice

(1) This rule applies where the court has disposed of an application which it permitted to be made without service of a copy of the application notice.
(2) Where the court makes an order, whether granting or dismissing the application, a copy of the application notice and any evidence in support must unless the court orders otherwise, be served with the order on–
  (a) all the parties in proceedings; and

(b) in relation to proceedings under Part 11, the person who is, or, in the case of an application to start proceedings, it is intended will be, the subject of the proceedings.

(3) The order must contain a statement of the right to make an application to set aside[GL] or vary the order under rule 18.11.

18.11 Application to set aside or vary order made without notice

(1) A person who was not served with a copy of the application notice before an order was made under rule 18.10 may apply to have the order set aside[GL] or varied.
(2) An application under this rule must be made within 7 days beginning with the date on which the order was served on the person making the application.

18.12 Power of the court to proceed in the absence of a party

(1) Where the applicant or any respondent fails to attend the hearing of an application, the court may proceed in the absence of that person.
(2) Where–
   (a) the applicant or any respondent fails to attend the hearing of an application; and
   (b) the court makes an order at the hearing,

the court may, on application or of its own initiative, re-list the application.
(3) Paragraph (2) does not apply to magistrates' courts.

18.13 Dismissal of totally without merit applications

If the High Court or a county court dismisses an application (including an application for permission to appeal) and it considers that the application is totally without merit–

(a) the court's order must record that fact; and
(b) the court must at the same time consider whether it is appropriate to make a civil restraint order.

PART 19   ALTERNATIVE PROCEDURE FOR APPLICATIONS

19.1 Types of application for which Part 19 procedure may be followed

(1) The Part 19 procedure is the procedure set out in this Part.
(2) An applicant may use the Part 19 procedure where the Part 18 procedure does not apply and–
   (a) there is no form prescribed by a rule or referred to in Practice Direction 5A in which to make the application;
   (b) the applicant seeks the court's decision on a question which is unlikely to involve a substantial dispute of fact; or
   (c) paragraph (5) applies.
(3) The court may at any stage direct that the application is to continue as if the applicant had not used the Part 19 procedure and, if it does so, the court may give any directions it considers appropriate.
(4) Paragraph (2) does not apply if a practice direction provides that the Part 19 procedure may not be used in relation to the type of application in question.
(5) A rule or practice direction may, in relation to a specified type of proceedings–
   (a) require or permit the use of the Part 19 procedure; and
   (b) disapply or modify any of the rules set out in this Part as they apply to those proceedings.

19.2 Applications for which the Part 19 procedure must be followed

(1) The Part 19 procedure must be used in an application made in accordance with–

    (a) section 60(3) of the 2002 Act (order to prevent disclosure of information to an adopted person);

    (b) section 79(4) of the 2002 Act (order for Registrar General to give any information referred to in section 79(3) of the 2002 Act); and

    (c) rule 14.21 (directions of High Court regarding fathers without parental responsibility).

(2) The respondent to an application made in accordance with paragraph (1)(b) is the Registrar General.

19.3 Contents of the application

Where the applicant uses the Part 19 procedure, the application must state–
(a) that this Part applies;
(b) either–

    (i) the question which the applicant wants the court to decide; or

    (ii) the order which the applicant is seeking and the legal basis of the application for that order;

(c) if the application is being made under an enactment, what that enactment is;
(d) if the applicant is applying in a representative capacity, what that capacity is; and
(e) if the respondent appears or is to appear in a representative capacity, what that capacity is.

(Part 17 requires a statement of case to be verified by a statement of truth.)

19.4 Issue of application without naming respondents

(1) A practice direction may set out circumstances in which an application may be issued under this Part without naming a respondent.

(2) The practice direction may set out those cases in which an application for permission must be made by application notice before the application is issued.

(3) The application for permission–

    (a) need not be served on any other person; and

    (b) must be accompanied by a copy of the application which the applicant proposes to issue.

(4) Where the court gives permission, it will give directions about the future management of the application.

19.5 Acknowledgment of service

(1) Subject to paragraph (2), each respondent must–

    (a) file an acknowledgment of service within 14 days beginning with the date on which the application is served; and

    (b) serve the acknowledgment of service on the applicant and any other party.

(2) If the application is to be served out of the jurisdiction, the respondent must file and serve an acknowledgment of service within the period set out in Practice Direction 6B.

(3) The acknowledgment of service must–

    (a) state whether the respondent contests the application;

    (b) state, if the respondent seeks a different order from that set out in the application, what that order is; and

    (c) be signed by the respondent or the respondent's legal representative.

19.6 Consequence of not filing an acknowledgment of service

(1) This rule applies where–
   (a) the respondent has failed to file an acknowledgment of service; and
   (b) the time period for doing so has expired.
(2) The respondent may attend the hearing of the application but may not take part in the hearing unless the court gives permission.

19.7 Filing and serving written evidence

(1) The applicant must, when filing the application, file the written evidence on which the applicant intends to rely.
(2) The applicant's evidence must be served on the respondent with the application.
(3) A respondent who wishes to rely on written evidence must file it when filing the acknowledgment of service.
(4) A respondent who files written evidence must also, at the same time, serve a copy of that evidence on the other parties.
(5) Within 14 days beginning with the date on which a respondent's evidence was served on the applicant, the applicant may file further written evidence in reply.
(6) An applicant who files further written evidence must also, within the same time limit, serve a copy of that evidence on the other parties.

19.8 Evidence – general

(1) No written evidence may be relied on at the hearing of the application unless–
   (a) it has been served in accordance with rule 19.7; or
   (b) the court gives permission.
(2) The court may require or permit a party to give oral evidence at the hearing.
(3) The court may give directions requiring the attendance for cross-examination[GL] of a witness who has given written evidence.

(Rule 22.1 contains a general power for the court to control evidence.)

19.9 Procedure where respondent objects to use of the Part 19 procedure

(1) A respondent who contends that the Part 19 procedure should not be used because–
   (a) there is a substantial dispute of fact; and
   (b) the use of the Part 19 procedure is not required or permitted by a rule or practice direction,

   must state the reasons for that contention when filing the acknowledgment of service.
(2) When the court receives the acknowledgment of service and any written evidence, it will give directions as to the future management of the case.

(Rule 19.7 requires a respondent who wishes to rely on written evidence to file it when filing the acknowledgment of service.)

(Rule 19.1(3) allows the court to make an order that the application continue as if the applicant had not used the Part 19 procedure.)

PART 20   INTERIM REMEDIES AND SECURITY FOR COSTS

CHAPTER 1   INTERIM REMEDIES

20.1 Scope of this Part

The rules in this Part do not apply to proceedings in a magistrates' court.

20.2 Orders for interim remedies

(1) The court may grant the following interim remedies–

- (a) an interim injunction[GL];
- (b) an interim declaration;
- (c) an order–
    - (i) for the detention, custody or preservation of relevant property;
    - (ii) for the inspection of relevant property;
    - (iii) for the taking of a sample of relevant property;
    - (iv) for the carrying out of an experiment on or with relevant property;
    - (v) for the sale of relevant property which is of a perishable nature or which for any other good reason it is desirable to sell quickly; and
    - (vi) for the payment of income from relevant property until an application is decided;
- (d) an order authorising a person to enter any land or building in the possession of a party to the proceedings for the purposes of carrying out an order under sub-paragraph (c);
- (e) an order under section 4 of the Torts (Interference with Goods) Act 1977 to deliver up goods;
- (f) an order (referred to as a 'freezing injunction[GL]')–
    - (i) restraining a party from removing from the jurisdiction assets located there; or
    - (ii) restraining a party from dealing with any assets whether located within the jurisdiction or not;
- (g) an order directing a party to provide information about the location of relevant property or assets or to provide information about relevant property or assets which are or may be the subject of an application for a freezing injunction[GL];
- (h) an order (referred to as a 'search order') under section 7 of the Civil Procedure Act 1997 (order requiring a party to admit another party to premises for the purpose of preserving evidence etc.);
- (i) an order under section 34 of the Senior Courts Act 1981 or section 53 of the County Courts Act 1984 (order in certain proceedings for disclosure of documents or inspection of property against a non-party);
- (j) an order for a specified fund to be paid into court or otherwise secured, where there is a dispute over a party's right to the fund;
- (k) an order permitting a party seeking to recover personal property to pay money into court pending the outcome of the proceedings and directing that, if money is paid into court, the property must be given up to that party;
- (l) an order directing a party to prepare and file accounts relating to the dispute;
- (m) an order directing any account to be taken or inquiry to be made by the court.

(2) In paragraph (1)(c) and(g), 'relevant property' means property (including land) which is the subject of an application or as to which any question may arise on an application.

(3) The fact that a particular kind of interim remedy is not listed in paragraph (1) does not affect any power that the court may have to grant that remedy.

20.3 Time when an order for an interim remedy may be made

(1) An order for an interim remedy may be made at any time, including–

- (a) before proceedings are started; and
- (b) after judgment has been given.

(Rule 5.3 provides that proceedings are started when the court issues an application form.)

(2) However–

(a) paragraph (1) is subject to any rule, practice direction or other enactment which provides otherwise; and
(b) the court may grant an interim remedy before an application has been started only if–
   (i) the matter is urgent; or
   (ii) it is otherwise desirable to do so in the interests of justice.
(3) Where the court grants an interim remedy before an application has been started, it will give directions requiring an application to be started.
(4) The court need not direct that an application be started where the application is made under section 33 of the Senior Courts Act 1981 or section 52 of the County Courts Act 1984 (order for disclosure, inspection etc. before starting an application).

20.4 How to apply for an interim remedy

(1) The court may grant an interim remedy on an application made without notice if it appears to the court that there are good reasons for not giving notice.
(2) An application for an interim remedy must be supported by evidence, unless the court orders otherwise.
(3) If the applicant makes an application without giving notice, the evidence in support of the application must state the reasons why notice has not been given.

(Part 4 lists general case-management powers of the court.)

(Part 18 contains general rules about making an application.)

20.5 Interim injunction to cease if application is stayed

If–
(a) the court has granted an interim injunction[GL] other than a freezing injunction[GL]; and
(b) the application is stayed[GL] other than by agreement between the parties,

the interim injunction[GL] will be set aside[GL] unless the court orders that it should continue to have effect even though the application is stayed[GL].

CHAPTER 2   SECURITY FOR COSTS

20.6 Security for costs

(1) A respondent to any application may apply under this Chapter of this Part for security for costs of the proceedings.

(Part 4 provides for the court to order payment of sums into court in other circumstances.)

(2) An application for security for costs must be supported by written evidence.
(3) Where the court makes an order for security for costs, it will–
   (a) determine the amount of security; and
   (b) direct–
      (i) the manner in which; and
      (ii) the time within which,
      the security must be given.

20.7 Conditions to be satisfied

(1) The court may make an order for security for costs under rule 20.6 if–
   (a) it is satisfied, having regard to all the circumstances of the case, that it is just to make such an order; and
   (b) either–

(i) one or more of the conditions in paragraph (2) applies; or
(ii) an enactment permits the court to require security for costs.

(2) The conditions are—

(a) the applicant is—

(i) resident out of the jurisdiction; but
(ii) not resident in a Brussels Contracting State, a Lugano Contracting State or a Regulation State, as defined in section 1(3) of the Civil Jurisdiction and Judgments Act 1982 or a Member State bound by the Council Regulation;

(b) the applicant has changed address since the application was started with a view to evading the consequences of the litigation;
(c) the applicant failed to give an address in the application form, or gave an incorrect address in that form;
(d) the applicant has taken steps in relation to the applicant's assets that would make it difficult to enforce an order for costs against the applicant.

(3) The court may not make an order for security for costs under rule 20.6 in relation to the costs of proceedings under the 1980 Hague Convention.

(Rule 4.4 allows the court to strike out[GL] a statement of case.)

20.8 Security for costs of an appeal

The court may order security for costs of an appeal against—

(a) an appellant;
(b) a respondent who also appeals,

on the same grounds as it may order security for costs against an applicant under this Part.

PART 21 MISCELLANEOUS RULES ABOUT DISCLOSURE AND INSPECTION OF DOCUMENTS

21.1 Interpretation

(1) A party discloses a document by stating that the document exists or has existed.
(2) Inspection of a document occurs when a party is permitted to inspect a document disclosed by another person.
(3) For the purposes of disclosure and inspection—

(a) 'document' means anything in which information of any description is recorded; and
(b) 'copy' in relation to a document, means anything onto which information recorded in the document has been copied, by whatever means and whether directly or indirectly.

21.2 Orders for disclosure against a person not a party

(1) This rule applies where an application is made to the court under any Act for disclosure by a person who is not a party to the proceedings.
(2) The application—

(a) may be made without notice; and
(b) must be supported by evidence.

(3) The court may make an order under this rule only where disclosure is necessary in order to dispose fairly of the proceedings or to save costs.
(4) An order under this rule must—

(a) specify the documents or the classes of documents which the respondent must disclose; and
(b) require the respondent, when making disclosure, to specify any of those documents–
   (i) which are no longer in the respondent's control; or
   (ii) in respect of which the respondent claims a right or duty to withhold inspection.

(5) Such an order may–
   (a) require the respondent to indicate what has happened to any documents which are no longer in the respondent's control; and
   (b) specify the time and place for disclosure and inspection.

(6) An order under this rule must not compel a person to produce any document which that person could not be compelled to produce at the final hearing.

(7) This rule does not limit any other power which the court may have to order disclosure against a person who is not a party to proceedings.

(Rule 35.3 contains provisions in relation to the disclosure and inspection of evidence arising out of mediation of cross-border disputes.)

21.3 Claim to withhold inspection or disclosure of a document

(1) A person may apply, without notice, for an order permitting that person to withhold disclosure of a document on the ground that disclosure would damage the public interest.

(2) Unless the court otherwise orders, an order of the court under paragraph (1)–
   (a) must not be served on any other person; and
   (b) must not be open to inspection by any other person.

(3) A person who wishes to claim a right or a duty to withhold inspection of a document, or part of a document, must state in writing–
   (a) the right or duty claimed; and
   (b) the grounds on which that right or duty is claimed.

(4) The statement referred to in paragraph (3) must be made to the person wishing to inspect the document.

(5) A party may apply to the court to decide whether a claim made under paragraph (3) should be upheld.

(6) Where the court is deciding an application under paragraph (1) or (5) it may–
   (a) require the person seeking to withhold disclosure or inspection of a document to produce that document to the court; and
   (b) invite any person, whether or not a party, to make representations.

(7) An application under paragraph (1) or (5) must be supported by evidence.

(8) This Part does not affect any rule of law which permits or requires a document to be withheld from disclosure or inspection on the ground that its disclosure or inspection would damage the public interest.

PART 22   EVIDENCE

CHAPTER 1   GENERAL RULES

22.1 Power of court to control evidence

(1) The court may control the evidence by giving directions as to–

(a) the issues on which it requires evidence;
(b) the nature of the evidence which it requires to decide those issues; and
(c) the way in which the evidence is to be placed before the court.

(2) The court may use its power under this rule to exclude evidence that would otherwise be admissible.
(3) The court may permit a party to adduce evidence, or to seek to rely on a document, in respect of which that party has failed to comply with the requirements of this Part.
(4) The court may limit cross-examination[GL].

22.2 Evidence of witnesses – general rule

(1) The general rule is that any fact which needs to be proved by the evidence of witnesses is to be proved–

   (a) at the final hearing, by their oral evidence; and
   (b) at any other hearing, by their evidence in writing.

(2) The general rule does not apply–

   (a) to proceedings under Part 12 for secure accommodation orders, interim care orders or interim supervision orders; or
   (b) where an enactment, any of these rules, a practice direction or a court order provides to the contrary.

(Section 45(7) of the Children Act 1989 (emergency protection orders) is an example of an enactment which makes provision relating to the evidence that a court may take into account when hearing an application.)

22.3 Evidence by video link or other means

The court may allow a witness to give evidence through a video link or by other means.

22.4 Witness statements

(1) A witness statement is a written statement signed by a person which contains the evidence which that person would be allowed to give orally.
(2) A witness statement must comply with the requirements set out in the Practice Direction 22A.

(Part 17 requires a witness statement to be verified by a statement of truth.)

22.5 Service of witness statements for use at the final hearing

(1) The court may give directions as to service on the other parties of any witness statement of the oral evidence on which a party intends to rely in relation to any issues of fact to be decided at the final hearing.
(2) The court may give directions as to–

   (a) the order in which witness statements are to be served; and
   (b) whether or not the witness statements are to be filed.

(3) Where the court directs that a court officer is to serve a witness statement on the other parties, any reference in this Chapter to a party serving a witness statement is to be read as including a reference to a court officer serving the statement.

22.6 Use at the final hearing of witness statements which have been served

(1) If a party–

   (a) has served a witness statement; and
   (b) wishes to rely at the final hearing on the evidence of the witness who made the statement,

that party must call the witness to give oral evidence unless the court directs otherwise or the party puts the statement in as hearsay evidence.

(Part 23 (miscellaneous rules about evidence) contains provisions about hearsay evidence.)

(2) The witness statement of a witness called to give oral evidence under paragraph (1) is to stand as the evidence in chief[GL] of that witness unless the court directs otherwise.

(3) A witness giving oral evidence at the final hearing may with the permission of the court–

(a) amplify his witness statement; and
(b) give evidence in relation to new matters which have arisen since the witness statement was served on the other parties.

(4) The court will give permission under paragraph (3) only if it considers that there is good reason not to confine the evidence of the witness to the contents of the witness statement.

(5) If a party who has served a witness statement does not–

(a) call the witness to give evidence at the final hearing; or
(b) put the witness statement in as hearsay evidence,

any other party may put the witness statement in as hearsay evidence.

22.7 Evidence at hearings other than the final hearing

(1) Subject to paragraph (2), the general rule is that evidence at hearings other than the final hearing is to be by witness statement unless the court, any other rule, a practice direction or any other enactment requires otherwise.

(2) At hearings other than the final hearing, a party may rely on the matters set out in that party's–

(a) application form;
(b) application notice; or
(c) answer,

if the application form, application notice or answer, as the case may be, is verified by a statement of truth.

22.8 Order for cross-examination

(1) Where, at a hearing other than the final hearing, evidence is given in writing, any party may apply to the court for permission to cross-examine[GL] the person giving the evidence.

(2) If the court gives permission under paragraph (1) but the person in question does not attend, that person's evidence may not be used unless the court directs otherwise.

(Rules 35.3 and 35.4 contain rules in relation to evidence arising out of mediation of cross-border disputes.)

22.9 Witness summaries

(1) A party who–

(a) is required to serve a witness statement for use at any hearing; but.
(b) is unable to obtain one,

may apply, without notice, for permission to serve a witness summary instead.

(2) A witness summary is a summary of–

(a) the evidence, if known, which would otherwise be included in a witness statement; or
(b) if the evidence is not known, the matters about which the party serving the witness summary proposes to question the witness.

(3) Unless the court directs otherwise, a witness summary must include the name and address of the intended witness.
(4) Unless the court directs otherwise, a witness summary must be served within the period in which a witness statement would have had to be served.
(5) Where a party serves a witness summary, so far as practicable rules 22.4(2) (form of witness statements), 22.5 (service of witness statements for use at the final hearing) and 22.6(3) (amplifying witness statements) apply to the summary.

22.10 Consequence of failure to serve witness statement

If a witness statement for use at the final hearing is not served in respect of an intended witness within the time specified by the court, then the witness may not be called to give oral evidence unless the court gives permission.

22.11 Cross-examination on a witness statement

A witness who is called to give evidence at the final hearing may be cross-examined[GL] on the witness statement, whether or not the statement or any part of it was referred to during the witness's evidence in chief[GL].

22.12 Affidavit evidence

(1) Evidence must be given by affidavit[GL] instead of or in addition to a witness statement if this is required by the court, a provision contained in any other rule, a practice direction or any other enactment.
(2) In relation to proceedings which are pending or treated as pending in a divorce county court or civil partnership county court, section 58(1)(c) of the County Courts Act 1984, shall have effect as if after paragraph (c) there were inserted–

'or

    (d)   a district judge of the principal registry; or
    (e)   any officer of the principal registry authorised by the President under section 2 of the Commissioner for Oaths Act 1889; or
    (f)   any clerk in the Central Office of the Royal Courts of Justice authorised to take affidavits[GL] for the purposes of proceedings in the Supreme Court.'.

(Rule 7.3 sets out when proceedings are treated as pending in a divorce county court or civil partnership proceedings county court.)

22.13 Form of affidavit

An affidavit[GL] must comply with the requirements set out in the Practice Direction 22A.

22.14 Affidavit made outside the jurisdiction

A person may make an affidavit [GL] outside the jurisdiction in accordance with–
(a) this Part; or
(b) the law of the place where the affidavit[GL] is made.

22.15 Notice to admit facts

(1) A party may serve notice on another party requiring the other party to admit the facts, or the part of the case of the serving party, specified in the notice.
(2) A notice to admit facts must be served no later than 21 days before the final hearing.
(3) Where the other party makes any admission in answer to the notice, the admission may be used against that party only–
    (a)   in the proceedings in which the notice to admit is served; and
    (b)   by the party who served the notice.

(4) The court may allow a party to amend or withdraw any admission made by that party on such terms as it thinks just.

22.16 Notice to admit or produce documents

(1) A party to whom a document is disclosed is deemed to admit the authenticity of that document unless notice is served by that party that the party wishes the document to be proved at the final hearing.
(2) A notice to prove a document must be served–
   (a) by the latest date for serving witness statements; or
   (b) within 7 days beginning with the date of service of the document, whichever is later.

22.17 Notarial acts and instruments

A notarial act or instrument may be received in evidence without further proof as duly authenticated in accordance with the requirements of law unless the contrary is proved.

CHAPTER 2 RULES APPLYING ONLY TO PARTICULAR PROCEEDINGS

22.18 Scope of this Chapter

This Chapter of this Part applies to affidavits[GL] and affirmations as it applies to witness statements.

22.19 Availability of witness statements for inspection during the final hearing

(1) This rule applies to proceedings under Part 7 (matrimonial and civil partnership proceedings).
(2) A witness statement which stands as evidence in chief[GL] is open to inspection during the course of the final hearing unless the court directs otherwise.
(3) Any person may ask for a direction that a witness statement is not open to inspection.
(4) The court will not make a direction under paragraph (2) unless it is satisfied that a witness statement should not be open to inspection because of–
   (a) the interests of justice;
   (b) the public interest;
   (c) the nature of any expert medical evidence in the statement;
   (d) the nature of any confidential information (including information relating to personal financial matters) in the statement; or
   (e) the need to protect the interests of any child or protected party.
(5) The court may exclude from inspection words or passages in the witness statement.

22.20 Use of witness statements for other purposes

(1) This rule applies to proceedings under Part 7 (matrimonial and civil partnership proceedings) or Part 9 (financial remedies).
(2) Except as provided by this rule, a witness statement may be used only for the purpose of the proceedings in which it is served.
(3) Paragraph (2) does not apply if and to the extent that–
   (a) the court gives permission for some other use; or
   (b) the witness statement has been put in evidence at a hearing held in public.

PART 23 MISCELLANEOUS RULES ABOUT EVIDENCE

23.1 Scope and interpretation of this Part

Rules 23.2 to 23.6 apply to evidence to which the Children (Admissibility of Hearsay Evidence) Order 1993 does not apply.

23.2 Notice of intention to rely on hearsay evidence

(1) Where a party intends to rely on hearsay evidence at the final hearing and either–

    (a)   that evidence is to be given by a witness giving oral evidence; or

    (b)   that evidence is contained in a witness statement of a person who is not being called to give oral evidence,

that party complies with section 2(1)(a) of the Civil Evidence Act 1995 by serving a witness statement on the other parties in accordance with the court's directions.

(2) Where paragraph (1)(b) applies, the party intending to rely on the hearsay evidence must, when serving the witness statement–

    (a)   inform the other parties that the witness is not being called to give oral evidence; and

    (b)   give the reason why the witness will not be called.

(3) In all other cases where a party intends to rely on hearsay evidence at the final hearing, that party complies with section 2(1)(a) of the Civil Evidence Act 1995 by serving a notice on the other parties which–

    (a)   identifies the hearsay evidence;

    (b)   states that the party serving the notice proposes to rely on the hearsay evidence at the final hearing; and

    (c)   gives the reason why the witness will not be called.

(4) The party proposing to rely on the hearsay evidence must–

    (a)   serve the notice no later than the latest date for serving witness statements; and

    (b)   if the hearsay evidence is to be in a document, supply a copy to any party who requests it.

23.3 Circumstances in which notice of intention to rely on hearsay evidence is not required

Section 2(1) of the Civil Evidence Act 1995 (duty to give notice of intention to rely on hearsay evidence) does not apply–

(a) to evidence at hearings other than final hearings;

(b) to an affidavit[GL] or witness statement which is to be used at the final hearing but which does not contain hearsay evidence; or

(c) where the requirement is excluded by a practice direction.

23.4 Power to call witness for cross-examination on hearsay evidence

(1) Where a party–

    (a)   proposes to rely on hearsay evidence; and

    (b)   does not propose to call the person who made the original statement to give oral evidence,

the court may, on the application of any other party, permit that party to call the maker of the statement to be cross-examined[GL] on the contents of the statement.

(2) An application for permission to cross-examine[GL] under this rule must be made within 14 days beginning with the date on which a notice of intention to rely on the hearsay evidence was served on the applicant.

(Rules 35.3 and 35.4 contain rules in relation to evidence arising out of mediation of cross-border disputes.)

23.5 Credibility

(1) Where a party proposes to rely on hearsay evidence, but–
   (a) does not propose to call the person who made the original statement to give oral evidence; and
   (b) another party wishes to call evidence to attack the credibility of the person who made the statement,

   the party who so wishes must give notice of that intention to the party who proposes to give the hearsay statement in evidence.
(2) A party must give notice under paragraph (1) within 14 days after the date on which a hearsay notice relating to the hearsay evidence was served on that party.

23.6 Use of plans, photographs and models etc as evidence

(1) This rule applies to–
   (a) evidence (such as a plan, photograph or model) which is not–
      (i) contained in a witness statement, affidavit[GL] or expert's report;
      (ii) to be given orally at the final hearing; or
      (iii) evidence of which prior notice must be given under rule 23.2; and
   (b) documents which may be received in evidence without further proof under section 9 of the Civil Evidence Act 1995.
(2) Except as provided below, section 2(1)(a) of the Civil Evidence Act 1995 (notice of proposal to adduce hearsay evidence) does not apply to evidence falling within paragraph (1).
(3) Such evidence is not receivable at the final hearing unless the party intending to rely on it (in this rule, 'the party') has–
   (a) served it or, in the case of a model, a photograph of it with an invitation to inspect the original, on the other party in accordance with this rule; or
   (b) complied with such directions as the court may give for serving the evidence on, or for giving notice under section 2(1)(a) of the Civil Evidence Act 1995 in respect of the evidence to, the other party.
(4) Where the party intends to use the evidence as evidence of any fact then, except where paragraph (6) applies, the party must serve the evidence not later than the latest date for serving witness statements.
(5) The party must serve the evidence at least 21 days before the hearing at which the party proposes to rely on it if–
   (a) there are not to be witness statements; or
   (b) the party intends to put in the evidence solely in order to disprove an allegation made in a witness statement.
(6) Where the evidence forms part of expert evidence, the party must serve the evidence when the expert's report is served on the other party.
(7) Where the evidence is being produced to the court for any reason other than as part of factual or expert evidence, the party must serve the evidence at least 21 days before the hearing at which the party proposes to rely on it.
(8) Where the court directs a party to give notice that the party intends to put in the evidence, the court may direct that every other party be given an opportunity to inspect it and to agree to its admission without further proof.

23.7 Evidence of finding on question of foreign law

(1) This rule sets out the procedure which must be followed by a party (in this rule, 'the party') who intends to put in evidence a finding on a question of foreign law by virtue of section 4(2) of the Civil Evidence Act 1972.
(2) The party must give any other party notice of that intention.
(3) The party must give the notice–
 (a) if there are to be witness statements, not later than the latest date for serving them; or
 (b) otherwise, not less than 21 days before the hearing at which the party proposes to put the finding in evidence.
(4) The notice must–
 (a) specify the question on which the finding was made; and
 (b) enclose a copy of a document where it is reported or recorded.

23.8 Evidence of consent of trustee to act

In proceedings to which Part 9 (financial remedies) applies, a document purporting to contain the written consent of a person to act as trustee and to bear that person's signature verified by some other person is evidence of such consent.

23.9 Note of oral evidence in magistrates' courts

In proceedings in a magistrates' court, the justices' clerk or the court shall keep a note of the substance of the oral evidence given at a directions appointment or at a hearing of any proceedings.

PART 24 WITNESSES, DEPOSITIONS GENERALLY AND TAKING OF EVIDENCE IN MEMBER STATES OF THE EUROPEAN UNION

CHAPTER 1 WITNESSES AND DEPOSITIONS

24.1 Scope of this Chapter

(1) This Chapter provides–
 (a) for the circumstances in which a person may be required to attend court to give evidence or to produce a document; and
 (b) for a party to obtain evidence before a hearing to be used at the hearing.
(2) This Chapter, apart from rule 24.10(2) to (4), does not apply to proceedings in a magistrates' court.

(Rules 34.16 to 34.21 and 34.24 of the CPR apply to incoming requests for evidence.)

24.2 Witness summonses

(1) A witness summons is a document issued by the court requiring a witness to–
 (a) attend court to give evidence; or
 (b) produce documents to the court.
(2) A witness summons must be in the form set out in Practice Direction 24A.
(3) There must be a separate witness summons for each witness.
(4) A witness summons may require a witness to produce documents to the court either–
 (a) on the date fixed for a hearing; or
 (b) on such date as the court may direct.

(5) The only documents that a summons under this rule can require a person to produce before a hearing are documents which that person could be required to produce at the hearing.

(Rules 35.3 and 35.4 contain rules in relation to evidence arising out of mediation of cross-border disputes.)

24.3 Issue of a witness summons

(1) A witness summons is issued on the date entered on the summons by the court.
(2) A party must obtain permission from the court where that party wishes to–
    (a) have a summons issued less than 7 days before the date of the final hearing;
    (b) have a summons issued for a witness to attend court to give evidence or to produce documents on any date except the date fixed for the final hearing; or
    (c) have a summons issued for a witness to attend court to give evidence or to produce documents at any hearing except the final hearing.
(3) A witness summons must be issued by–
    (a) the court where the case is proceeding; or
    (b) the court where the hearing in question will be held.
(4) The court may set aside[GL] or vary a witness summons issued under this rule.

24.4 Time for serving a witness summons

(1) The general rule is that a witness summons is binding if it is served at least 7 days before the date on which the witness is required to attend before the court.
(2) The court may direct that a witness summons is binding although it is served less than 7 days before the date on which the witness is required to attend before the court.
(3) A witness summons which is–
    (a) served in accordance with this rule; and
    (b) requires the witness to attend court to give evidence,

is binding until the conclusion of the hearing at which the attendance of the witness is required.

(Rules 35.3 and 35.4 contain rules in relation to evidence arising out of mediation of cross-border disputes.)

24.5 Who is to serve a witness summons

(1) Subject to paragraph (2), a witness summons is to be served by the party on whose behalf it is issued unless that party indicates in writing, when asking the court to issue the summons, that that party wishes the court to serve it instead.
(2) In proceedings to which Part 14 (procedure for applications in adoption, placement and related proceedings) applies, a witness summons is to be served by the court unless the court directs otherwise.
(3) Where the court is to serve the witness summons, the party on whose behalf it is issued must deposit, in the court office, the money to be paid or offered to the witness under rule 24.6.

24.6 Right of witness to travelling expenses and compensation for loss of time

At the time of service of a witness summons the witness must be offered or paid–

(a) a sum reasonably sufficient to cover the expenses of the witness in travelling to and from the court; and
(b) such sum by way of compensation for loss of time as may be specified in Practice Direction 24A.

24.7 Evidence by deposition

(1) A party may apply for an order for a person to be examined before the hearing takes place.
(2) A person from whom evidence is to be obtained following an order under this rule is referred to as a 'deponent' and the evidence is referred to as a 'deposition'.
(3) An order under this rule is for a deponent to be examined on oath before–
   (a) a judge;
   (b) an examiner of the court; or
   (c) such other person as the court appoints.

(Rule 24.14 makes provision for the appointment of examiners of the court.)

(4) The order may require the production of any document which the court considers is necessary for the purposes of the examination.
(5) The order must state the date, time and place of the examination.
(6) At the time of service of the order the deponent must be offered or paid–
   (a) a sum reasonably sufficient to cover the expenses of the deponent in travelling to and from the place of examination; and
   (b) such sum by way of compensation for loss of time as may be specified in Practice Direction 24A.
(7) Where the court makes an order for a deposition to be taken, it may also order the party who obtained the order to serve a witness statement or witness summary in relation to the evidence to be given by the person to be examined.

(Part 22 (evidence) contains the general rules about witness statements and witness summaries.)

(Rules 35.3 and 35.4 contain rules in relation to evidence arising out of mediation of cross-border disputes.)

24.8 Conduct of examination

(1) Subject to any directions contained in the order for examination, the examination must be conducted in the same way as if the witness were giving evidence at a final hearing.
(2) If all the parties are present, the examiner may conduct the examination of a person not named in the order for examination if all the parties and the person to be examined consent.
(3) In defended proceedings under Part 7 (matrimonial and civil partnership proceedings), the examiner may conduct the examination in private if of the view that it is appropriate to do so.
(4) Save in proceedings to which paragraph (3) applies, the examiner will conduct the examination in private unless of the view that it is not appropriate to do so.
(5) The examiner must ensure that the evidence given by the witness is recorded in full.
(6) The examiner must send a copy of the deposition–
   (a) to the person who obtained the order for the examination of the witness; and
   (b) to the court where the case is proceeding.
(7) The court will give directions as to service of the deposition on the other party.

24.9 Enforcing attendance of witness

(1) If a person served with an order to attend before an examiner–
   (a) fails to attend; or
   (b) refuses to be sworn for the purpose of the examination or to answer any lawful question or produce any document at the examination,

a certificate of that person's failure or refusal, signed by the examiner, must be filed by the party requiring the deposition.
(2) On the certificate being filed, the party requiring the deposition may apply to the court for an order requiring that person to attend or to be sworn or to answer any question or produce any document, as the case may be.
(3) An application for an order under this rule may be made without notice.
(4) The court may order the person against whom an order is made under this rule to pay any costs resulting from that person's failure or refusal.

(Rules 35.3 and 35.4 contain rules in relation to evidence arising out of mediation of cross-border disputes. Rule 35.4(1)(d) relates specifically to this rule.)

24.10 Use of deposition at a hearing

(1) A deposition ordered under rule 24.7 may be given in evidence at a hearing unless the court orders otherwise.
(2) A party intending to put in evidence a deposition at a hearing must file notice of intention to do so on the court and the court will give directions about serving the notice on every other party.
(3) The party must file the notice at least 21 days before the day fixed for the hearing.
(4) The court may require a deponent to attend the hearing and give evidence orally.
(5) Where a deposition is given in evidence at the final hearing, it is treated as if it were a witness statement for the purposes of rule 22.19 (availability of witness statements for inspection).

(Rules 35.3 and 35.4 contain rules in relation to evidence arising out of mediation of cross-border disputes. Rule 35.4(1)(e) relates specifically to this rule.)

24.11 Restrictions on subsequent use of deposition taken for the purpose of any hearing except the final hearing

(1) This rule applies to proceedings under Part 7 (matrimonial and civil partnership proceedings) or Part 9 (financial remedies).
(2) Where the court orders a party to be examined about that party's or any other assets for the purpose of any hearing except the final hearing, the deposition may be used only for the purpose of the proceedings in which the order was made.
(3) However it may be used for some other purpose–
    (a) by the party who was examined;
    (b) if the party who was examined agrees; or
    (c) if the court gives permission.

24.12 Where a person to be examined is out of the jurisdiction – letter of request

(1) This rule applies where a party wishes to take a deposition from a person who is–
    (a) out of the jurisdiction; and
    (b) not in a Regulation State within the meaning of Chapter 2 of this Part.
(2) The High Court may order the issue of a letter of request to the judicial authorities of the country in which the proposed deponent is.
(3) A letter of request is a request to a judicial authority to take the evidence of that person, or arrange for it to be taken.
(4) The High Court may make an order under this rule in relation to county court proceedings.
(5) If the government of a country allows a person appointed by the High Court to examine a person in that country, the High Court may make an order appointing a special examiner for that purpose.
(6) A person may be examined under this rule on oath or affirmation or in accordance with any procedure permitted in the country in which the examination is to take place.

(7) If the High Court makes an order for the issue of a letter of request, the party who sought the order must file–
   (a) the following documents and, except where paragraph (8) applies, a translation of them–
      (i) a draft letter of request;
      (ii) a statement of the issues relevant to the proceedings; and
      (iii) a list of questions or the subject matter of questions to be put to the person to be examined; and
   (b) an undertaking to be responsible for the Secretary of State's expenses.
(8) There is no need to file a translation if–
   (a) English is one of the official languages of the country where the examination is to take place; or
   (b) a practice direction has specified that country as a country where no translation is necessary.

(Rules 35.3 and 35.4 contain rules in relation to evidence arising out of mediation of cross-border disputes. Rule 35.4(1)(f) relates specifically to this rule.)

24.13 Fees and expenses of examiner of the court

(1) An examiner of the court may charge a fee for the examination.
(2) The examiner need not send the deposition to the court unless the fee is paid.
(3) The examiner's fees and expenses must be paid by the party who obtained the order for examination.
(4) If the fees and expenses due to an examiner are not paid within a reasonable time, the examiner may report that fact to the court.
(5) The court may order the party who obtained the order for examination to deposit in the court office a specified sum in respect of the examiner's fees and, where it does so, the examiner will not be asked to act until the sum has been deposited.
(6) An order under this rule does not affect any decision as to the party who is ultimately to bear the costs of the examination.

24.14 Examiners of the court

(1) The Lord Chancellor will appoint persons to be examiners of the court.
(2) The persons appointed must be barristers or solicitor-advocates who have been practising for a period of not less than 3 years.
(3) The Lord Chancellor may revoke an appointment at any time.

CHAPTER 2   TAKING OF EVIDENCE – MEMBER STATES OF THE EUROPEAN UNION

24.15 Interpretation

In this Chapter–

'designated court' has the meaning given in Practice Direction 24A;

'Regulation State' has the same meaning as 'Member State' in the Taking of Evidence Regulation, that is all Member States except Denmark;

'the Taking of Evidence Regulation' means Council Regulation (EC) No. 1206/2001 of 28 May 2001 on co-operation between the courts of the Member States in the taking of evidence in civil or commercial matters.

24.16 Where a person to be examined is in another Regulation State

(1) This rule applies where a party wishes to take a deposition from a person who is–

(a) outside the jurisdiction; and
(b) in a Regulation State.

(2) The court may order the issue of a request to a designated court ('the requested court') in the Regulation State in which the proposed deponent is.

(3) If the court makes an order for the issue of a request, the party who sought the order must file–

(a) a draft Form A as set out in the annex to the Taking of Evidence Regulation (request for the taking of evidence);
(b) except where paragraph (4) applies, a translation of the form;
(c) an undertaking to be responsible for costs sought by the requested court in relation to–
   (i) fees paid to experts and interpreters; and
   (ii) where requested by that party, the use of special procedures or communications technology; and
(d) an undertaking to be responsible for the court's expenses.

(4) There is no need to file a translation if–

(a) English is one of the official languages of the Regulation State where the examination is to take place; or
(b) the Regulation State has indicated, in accordance with the Taking of Evidence Regulation, that English is a language which it will accept.

(5) Where article 17 of the Taking of Evidence Regulation (direct taking of evidence by the requested court) allows evidence to be taken directly in another Regulation State, the court may make an order for the submission of a request in accordance with that article.

(6) If the court makes an order for the submission of a request under paragraph (5), the party who sought the order must file–

(a) a draft Form I as set out in the annex to the Taking of Evidence Regulation (request for direct taking of evidence);
(b) except where paragraph (4) applies, a translation of the form; and
(c) an undertaking to be responsible for the court's expenses.

PART 25   EXPERTS AND ASSESSORS

25.1   Duty to restrict expert evidence

Expert evidence will be restricted to that which is reasonably required to resolve the proceedings.

25.2   Interpretation

(1) A reference to an 'expert' in this Part–

(a) is a reference to a person who has been instructed to give or prepare expert evidence for the purpose of family proceedings; and
(b) does not include–
   (i) a person who is within a prescribed description for the purposes of section 94(1) of the 2002 Act (persons who may prepare a report for any person about the suitability of a child for adoption or of a person to adopt a child or about the adoption, or placement for adoption, of a child); or
   (ii) an officer of the Service or a Welsh family proceedings officer when acting in that capacity.

(Regulation 3 of the Restriction on the Preparation of Adoption Reports Regulations 2005 (S.I. 2005/1711) sets out which persons are within a prescribed description for the purposes of section 94(1) of the 2002 Act.)

(2) 'Single joint expert' means an expert instructed to prepare a report for the court on behalf of two or more of the parties (including the applicant) to the proceedings.

25.3 Experts – overriding duty to the court

(1) It is the duty of experts to help the court on matters within their expertise.
(2) This duty overrides any obligation to the person from whom experts have received instructions or by whom they are paid.

25.4 Court's power to restrict expert evidence

(1) No party may call an expert or put in evidence an expert's report without the court's permission.
(2) When parties apply for permission they must identify–
   (a) the field in which the expert evidence is required; and
   (b) where practicable, the name of the proposed expert.
(3) If permission is granted it will be in relation only to the expert named or the field identified under paragraph(2).
(4) The court may limit the amount of a party's expert's fees and expenses that may be recovered from any other party.

25.5 General requirement for expert evidence to be given in a written report

(1) Expert evidence is to be given in a written report unless the court directs otherwise.
(2) The court will not direct an expert to attend a hearing unless it is necessary to do so in the interests of justice.

25.6 Written questions to experts

(1) A party may put written questions about an expert's report (which must be proportionate) to–
   (a) an expert instructed by another party; or
   (b) a single joint expert appointed under rule 25.7.
(2) Written questions under paragraph (1)–
   (a) may be put once only;
   (b) must be put within 10 days beginning with the date on which the expert's report was served; and
   (c) must be for the purpose only of clarification of the report,
   unless in any case–
   (i) the court directs otherwise; or
   (ii) a practice direction provides otherwise.
(3) An expert's answers to questions put in accordance with paragraph (1) are treated as part of the expert's report.
(4) Where–
   (a) a party has put a written question to an expert instructed by another party; and
   (b) the expert does not answer that question,
   the court may make use of one or both of the following orders in relation to the party who instructed the expert–
   (i) that the party may not rely on the evidence of that expert; or
   (ii) that the party may not recover the fees and expenses of that expert from any other party.

25.7 Court's power to direct that evidence is to be given by a single joint expert

(1) Where two or more parties wish to submit expert evidence on a particular issue, the court may direct that the evidence on that issue is to be given by a single joint expert.
(2) Where the parties who wish to submit the evidence ('the relevant parties') cannot agree who should be the single joint expert, the court may–

    (a) select the expert from a list prepared or identified by the instructing parties; or
    (b) direct that the expert be selected in such other manner as the court may direct.

25.8 Instructions to a single joint expert

(1) Where the court gives a direction under rule 25.7(1) for a single joint expert to be used, the instructions are to be contained in a jointly agreed letter unless the court directs otherwise.
(2) Where the instructions are to be contained in a jointly agreed letter, in default of agreement the instructions may be determined by the court on the written request of any relevant party copied to the other relevant parties.
(3) Where the court permits the relevant parties to give separate instructions to a single joint expert, each instructing party must, when giving instructions to the expert, at the same time send a copy of the instructions to the other relevant parties.
(4) The court may give directions about–

    (a) the payment of the expert's fees and expenses; and
    (b) any inspection, examination or assessments which the expert wishes to carry out.

(5) The court may, before an expert is instructed, limit the amount that can be paid by way of fees and expenses to the expert.
(6) Unless the court directs otherwise, the relevant parties are jointly and severally liable for the payment of the expert's fees and expenses.

25.9 Power of court to direct a party to provide information

(1) Subject to paragraph (2), where a party has access to information which is not reasonably available to another party, the court may direct the party who has access to the information to prepare, file and serve a document recording the information.
(2) In proceedings under Part 14 (procedure for applications in adoption, placement and related proceedings),–

    (a) the court may direct the party with access to the information to prepare and file a document recording the information; and
    (b) a court officer will send a copy of that document to the other party.

25.10 Contents of report

(1) An expert's report must comply with the requirements set out in Practice Direction 25A.
(2) At the end of an expert's report there must be a statement that the expert understands and has complied with their duty to the court.
(3) The instructions to the expert are not privileged against disclosure.

(Rule 21.1 explains what is meant by disclosure.)

25.11 Use by one party of expert's report disclosed by another

Where a party has disclosed an expert's report, any party may use that expert's report as evidence at any relevant hearing.

25.12 Discussions between experts

(1) The court may, at any stage, direct a discussion between experts for the purpose of requiring the experts to–

(a) identify and discuss the expert issues in the proceedings; and
(b) where possible, reach an agreed opinion on those issues.
(2) The court may specify the issues which the experts must discuss.
(3) The court may direct that following a discussion between the experts they must prepare a statement for the court setting out those issues on which–
(a) they agree; and
(b) they disagree,

with a summary of their reasons for disagreeing.

25.13 Expert's right to ask court for directions
(1) Experts may file written requests for directions for the purpose of assisting them in carrying out their functions.
(2) Experts must, unless the court directs otherwise, provide copies of the proposed request for directions under paragraph (1)–
(a) to the party instructing them, at least 7 days before they file the requests; and
(b) to all other parties, at least 4 days before they file them.
(3) The court, when it gives directions, may also direct that a party be served with a copy of the directions.

25.14 Assessors
(1) This rule applies where the court appoints one or more persons under section 70 of the Senior Courts Act 1981 or section 63 of the County Courts Act 1984 as an assessor
(2) An assessor will assist the court in dealing with a matter in which the assessor has skill and experience.
(3) The assessor will take such part in the proceedings as the court may direct and in particular the court may direct an assessor to–
(a) prepare a report for the court on any matter at issue in the proceedings; and
(b) attend the whole or any part of the hearing to advise the court on any such matter.
(4) If the assessor prepares a report for the court before the hearing has begun–
(a) the court will send a copy to each of the parties; and
(b) the parties may use it at the hearing.
(5) Unless the court directs otherwise, an assessor will be paid at the daily rate payable for the time being to a fee-paid deputy district judge of the principal registry and an assessor's fees will form part of the costs of the proceedings.
(6) The court may order any party to deposit in the court office a specified sum in respect of an assessor's fees and, where it does so, the assessor will not be asked to act until the sum has been deposited.
(7) Paragraphs (5) and (6) do not apply where the remuneration of the assessor is to be paid out of money provided by Parliament.

PART 26   CHANGE OF SOLICITOR

26.1 Solicitor acting for a party
Where the address for service of a party is the business address of that party's solicitor, the solicitor will be considered to be acting for that party until the provisions of this Part have been complied with.

(Part 6 contains provisions about the address for service.)

26.2 Change of solicitor – duty to give notice

(1) This rule applies where–
- (a) a party for whom a solicitor is acting wants to change solicitor;
- (b) a party, after having conducted the application in person, appoints a solicitor to act for that party (except where the solicitor is appointed only to act as an advocate for a hearing); or
- (c) a party, after having conducted the application by a solicitor, intends to act in person.

(2) Where this rule applies, the party or the party's solicitor (where one is acting) must–
- (a) serve notice of the change on–
  - (i) every other party; and
  - (ii) where paragraph (1)(a) or (c) applies, the former solicitor; and
- (b) file notice of the change.

(3) Except where a serial number has been assigned under rule 14.2 or the name or address of a party is not being revealed in accordance with rule 29.1, the notice must state the party's new address for service.

(4) The notice filed at court must state that notice has been served as required by paragraph (2)(a) or, where rule 2.4 applies, in accordance with the court's directions given under that rule.

(5) Subject to paragraph (6), where a party has changed solicitor or intends to act in person, the former solicitor will be considered to be the party's solicitor unless and until–
- (a) notice is filed and served in accordance with paragraph (2)(a) or, where rule 2.4 applies, in accordance with the court's directions given under that rule; or
- (b) the court makes an order under rule 26.3 and the order is served as required by paragraph (3) of that rule.

(6) Where the certificate of a LSC funded client or an assisted person (in this rule 'C') is revoked or discharged–
- (a) the solicitor who acted for C will cease to be the solicitor acting in the case as soon as the retainer is determined under regulation 4 of the Community Legal Service (Costs) Regulations 2000; and
- (b) if C wishes to continue–
  - (i) where C appoints a solicitor to act on C's behalf, paragraph (2) will apply as if C had previously conducted the application in person; and
  - (ii) where C wants to act in person, C must give an address for service, in accordance with rule 6.26, unless the court directs otherwise.

(7) In this rule–

'assisted person' means an assisted person within the statutory provisions relating to legal aid;

'certificate' means a certificate issued under the Funding Code (approved under section 9 of the Access to Justice Act 1999); and

'LSC funded client' means an individual who receives services funded by the Legal Services Commission as part of the Community Legal Service within the meaning of Part 1 of the Access to Justice Act 1999.

26.3 Order that a solicitor has ceased to act

(1) A solicitor may apply for an order declaring that that solicitor has ceased to be the solicitor acting for–
- (a) a party; or

        (b)   a children's guardian.
(2) Where an application is made under this rule–
        (a)   notice of the application must be given to the party, or children's guardian, for whom the solicitor is acting, unless the court directs otherwise; and
        (b)   the application must be supported by evidence.
(3) Where the court makes an order declaring that a solicitor has ceased to act, a court officer will serve a copy of the order on–
        (a)   every party to the proceedings; and
        (b)   where applicable, a children's guardian.

26.4   Removal of solicitor who has ceased to act on application of another party
(1) Where–
        (a)   a solicitor who has acted for a party–
                (i)   has died;
                (ii)   has become bankrupt;
                (iii)   has ceased to practise; or
                (iv)   cannot be found; and
        (b)   the party has not given notice of a change of solicitor or notice of intention to act in person as required by rule26.2(2),

any other party may apply for an order declaring that the solicitor has ceased to be the solicitor acting for the other party in the case.
(2) Where an application is made under this rule, notice of the application must be given to the party to whose solicitor the application relates unless the court directs otherwise.
(3) Where the court makes an order made under this rule, a court officer will serve a copy of the order on every other party to the proceedings.

PART 27   HEARINGS AND DIRECTIONS APPOINTMENTS

27.1   Application of this Part

This Part is subject to any enactment, any provision in these rules or a practice direction.

(Rule 27.4(7) makes additional provision in relation to requirements to stay proceedings where the respondent does not appear and a relevant European regulation or international convention applies)

27.2   Reasons for a decision of the magistrates' courts
(1) This rule applies to proceedings in a magistrates' court.
(2) After a hearing, the court will make its decision as soon as is practicable.
(3) The court must give written reasons for its decision.
(4) Paragraphs (5) and (6) apply where the functions of the court are being performed by–
        (a)   two or three lay justices; or
        (b)   by a single lay justice in accordance with these rules and Practice Direction 2A.
(5) The justices' clerk must, before the court makes an order or refuses an application or request, make notes of–
        (a)   the names of the justice or justices constituting the court by which the decision is made; and
        (b)   in consultation with the justice or justices, the reasons for the court's decision.
(6) The justices' clerk must make a written record of the reasons for the court's decision.

(7) When making an order or refusing an application, the court, or one of the justices constituting the court by which the decision is made, will announce its decision and–
   (a)   the reasons for that decision; or
   (b)   a short explanation of that decision.
(8) Subject to any other rule or practice direction, the court officer will supply a copy of the order and the reasons for the court's decision to the persons referred to in paragraph (9)–
   (a)   by close of business on the day when the court announces its decision; or
   (b)   where that time is not practicable and the proceedings are on notice, no later than 72 hours from the time when the court announced its decision.
(9) The persons referred to in paragraph (8) are–
   (a)   the parties (unless the court directs otherwise);
   (b)   any person who has actual care of a child who is the subject of proceedings, or who had such care immediately prior to the making of the order;
   (c)   in the case of an emergency protection order and a recovery order, the local authority in whose area the child lives or is found;
   (d)   in proceedings to which Part 14 applies–
      (i)   an adoption agency or local authority which has prepared a report on the suitability of the applicant to adopt a child;
      (ii)   a local authority which has prepared a report on the placement of the child for adoption;
   (e)   any other person who has requested a copy if the court is satisfied that it is required in connection with an appeal or possible appeal.
(10) In this rule, 'lay justice' means a justice of the peace who is not a District Judge (Magistrates' Courts).

(Rule 12.16(5) provides for the applicant to serve a section 8 order and an order in emergency proceedings made without notice within 48 hours after the making of the order. Rule 10.6(1) provides for the applicant to serve the order in proceedings under Part 4 of the 1996 Act. Rule 4.1(3)(a) permits the court to extend or shorten the time limit for compliance with any rule. Rule 6.33 provides for other persons to be supplied with copy documents under paragraph (8).)

27.3   Attendance at hearing or directions appointment

Unless the court directs otherwise, a party shall attend a hearing or directions appointment of which that party has been given notice.

27.4   Proceedings in the absence of a party

(1) Proceedings or any part of them shall take place in the absence of any party, including a party who is a child, if–
   (a)   the court considers it in the interests of the party, having regard to the matters to be discussed or the evidence likely to be given; and
   (b)   the party is represented by a children's guardian or solicitor,

   and when considering the interests of a child under sub-paragraph (a) the court shall give the children's guardian, the solicitor for the child and, if of sufficient understanding and the court thinks it appropriate, the child, an opportunity to make representations.
(2) Subject to paragraph (3), where at the time and place appointed for a hearing or directions appointment the applicant appears but one or more of the respondents do not, the court may proceed with the hearing or appointment.
(3) The court shall not begin to hear an application in the absence of a respondent unless–

(a) it is proved to the satisfaction of the court that the respondent received reasonable notice of the date of the hearing; or
(b) the court is satisfied that the circumstances of the case justify proceeding with the hearing.

(4) Where, at the time and place appointed for a hearing or directions appointment, one or more of the respondents appear but the applicant does not, the court may refuse the application or, if sufficient evidence has previously been received, proceed in the absence of the applicant.
(5) Where, at the time and place appointed for a hearing or directions appointment, neither the applicant nor any respondent appears, the court may refuse the application.
(6) Paragraphs (2) to (5) do not apply to a hearing to which paragraphs (5) to (8) of rule 12.14 do not apply by virtue of paragraph (9) of that rule.
(7) Nothing in this rule affects any provision of a European regulation or international convention by which the United Kingdom is bound which requires a court to stay proceedings where a respondent in another State has not been adequately served with proceedings in accordance with the requirements of that regulation or convention.

27.5 Application to set aside judgment or order following failure to attend

(1) Where a party does not attend a hearing or directions appointment and the court gives judgment or makes an order against him, the party who failed to attend may apply for the judgment or order to be set aside[GL].
(2) An application under paragraph (1) must be supported by evidence.
(3) Where an application is made under paragraph (1), the court may grant the application only if the applicant–
(a) acted promptly on finding out that the court had exercised its power to enter judgment or make an order against the applicant;
(b) had a good reason for not attending the hearing or directions appointment; and
(c) has a reasonable prospect of success at the hearing or directions appointment.
(4) This rule does not apply to magistrates' courts.

27.6 Court bundles and place of filing of documents and bundles

(1) The provisions of Practice Direction 27A must be followed for the preparation of court bundles and for other related matters in respect of hearings and directions appointments.
(2) Paragraph (3) applies where the file of any family proceedings has been sent from one designated county court or registry to another for the purpose of a hearing or for some other purpose.
(3) A document needed for the purpose for which the proceedings have been sent to the other court or registry must be filed in that court or registry.

(Practice Direction 27A (Family Proceedings: Court Bundles (Universal Practice to be applied in All Courts other than the Family Proceedings Courts)) does not apply to magistrates' courts.)

27.7 Representation of companies or other corporations

A company or other corporation may be represented at a hearing or directions appointment by an employee if–
(a) the employee has been authorised by the company or corporation to appear at the hearing or directions appointment on its behalf; and
(b) the court gives permission.

27.8 **Impounded documents**

(1) Documents impounded by order of the court must not be released from the custody of the court except in compliance with–

 (a) a court order; or
 (b) a written request made by a Law Officer or the Director of Public Prosecutions.

(2) A document released from the custody of the court under paragraph (1)(b) must be released into the custody of the person who requested it.

(3) Documents impounded by order of the court, while in the custody of the court, may not be inspected except by a person authorised to do so by a court order.

27.9 **Official shorthand note etc of proceedings**

(1) Unless the judge directs otherwise, an official shorthand note will be taken at the hearing in open court of proceedings pending in the High Court.

(2) An official shorthand note may be taken of any other proceedings before a judge if directions for the taking of such a note are given by the Lord Chancellor.

(3) The shorthand writer will sign the note and certify it to be a correct shorthand note of the proceedings and will retain the note unless directed by the district judge to forward it to the court.

(4) On being so directed, the shorthand writer will furnish the court with a transcript of the whole or such part of the shorthand note as may be directed.

(5) Any party, any person who has intervened in the proceedings, the Queen's Proctor or, where a declaration of parentage has been made under section 55A of the 1986 Act, the Registrar General is entitled to require from the shorthand writer a transcript of the shorthand note, and the shorthand writer will, at the request of any person so entitled, supply that person with a transcript of the whole or any part of the note on payment of the shorthand writer's charges authorised by any scheme in force providing for the taking of official shorthand notes of legal proceedings.

(6) Save as permitted by this rule, the shorthand writer will not, without the permission of the court, furnish the shorthand note or a transcript of the whole or any part of it to anyone.

(7) In these rules, references to a shorthand note include references to a record of the proceedings made by mechanical means and in relation to such a record references to the shorthand writer include the person responsible for transcribing the record.

27.10 **Hearings in private**

(1) Proceedings to which these rules apply will be held in private, except–

 (a) where these rules or any other enactment provide otherwise;
 (b) subject to any enactment, where the court directs otherwise.

(2) For the purposes of these rules, a reference to proceedings held 'in private' means proceedings at which the general public have no right to be present.

27.11 **Attendance at private hearings**

(1) This rule applies when proceedings are held in private, except in relation to–

 (a) hearings conducted for the purpose of judicially assisted conciliation or negotiation;
 (b) proceedings to which the following provisions apply–
  (i) Part 13 (proceedings under section 54 of the Human Fertilisation and Embryology Act 2008);
  (ii) Part 14 (procedure for applications in adoption, placement and related proceedings); and

(iii) any proceedings identified in a practice direction as being excepted from this rule.

(2) When this rule applies, no person shall be present during any hearing other than–
   (a) an officer of the court;
   (b) a party to the proceedings;
   (c) a litigation friend for any party, or legal representative instructed to act on that party's behalf;
   (d) an officer of the service or Welsh family proceedings officer;
   (e) a witness;
   (f) duly accredited representatives of news gathering and reporting organisations; and
   (g) any other person whom the court permits to be present.

(3) At any stage of the proceedings the court may direct that persons within paragraph (2)(f) shall not attend the proceedings or any part of them, where satisfied that–
   (a) this is necessary–
      (i) in the interests of any child concerned in, or connected with, the proceedings;
      (ii) for the safety or protection of a party, a witness in the proceedings, or a person connected with such a party or witness; or
      (iii) for the orderly conduct of the proceedings; or
   (b) justice will otherwise be impeded or prejudiced.

(4) The court may exercise the power in paragraph (3) of its own initiative or pursuant to representations made by any of the persons listed in paragraph (5), and in either case having given to any person within paragraph (2)(f) who is in attendance an opportunity to make representations.

(5) At any stage of the proceedings, the following persons may make representations to the court regarding restricting the attendance of persons within paragraph (2)(f) in accordance with paragraph (3)–
   (a) a party to the proceedings;
   (b) any witness in the proceedings;
   (c) where appointed, any children's guardian;
   (d) where appointed, an officer of the service or Welsh family proceedings officer, on behalf of the child the subject of the proceedings;
   (e) the child, if of sufficient age and understanding.

(6) This rule does not affect any power of the court to direct that witnesses shall be excluded until they are called for examination.

(7) In this rule 'duly accredited' refers to accreditation in accordance with any administrative scheme for the time being approved for the purposes of this rule by the Lord Chancellor.

PART 28   COSTS

28.1   Costs

The court may at any time make such order as to costs as it thinks just.

28.2   Application of other rules

(1) Subject to rule 28.3 and to paragraph (2), Parts 43, 44 (except rules 44.3(2) and (3), 44.9 to 44.12C, 44.13(1A) and (1B) and 44.18 to 20), 47 and 48 and rule 45.6 of the CPR apply to costs in proceedings, with the following modifications–

(a) in rule 43.2(1)(c)(ii), 'district judge' includes a district judge of the principal registry;
(b) in rule 48.7(1) after 'section 51(6) of the Senior Courts Act 1981' insert 'or section 145A of the Magistrates' Courts Act 1980';
(c) in accordance with any provisions in Practice Direction 28A; and
(d) any other necessary modifications.
(2) Part 47 and rules 44.3C and 45.6 of the CPR do not apply to proceedings in a magistrates' court.

28.3 Costs in financial remedy proceedings

(1) This rule applies in relation to financial remedy proceedings.
(2) Rule 44.3(1), (4) and (5) of the CPR do not apply to financial remedy proceedings.
(3) Rule 44.3(6) to (9) of the CPR apply to an order made under this rule as they apply to an order made under rule 44.3 of the CPR.
(4) In this rule–
   (a) 'costs' has the same meaning as in rule 43.2(1)(a) of the CPR; and
   (b) 'financial remedy proceedings' means proceedings for–
      (i) a financial order except an order for maintenance pending suit, an order for maintenance pending outcome of proceedings, an interim periodical payments order or any other form of interim order for the purposes of rule 9.7(1)(a), (b), (c) and (e);
      (ii) an order under Part 3 of the 1984 Act;
      (iii) an order under Schedule 7 to the 2004 Act;
      (iv) an order under section 10(2) of the 1973 Act;
      (v) an order under section 48(2) of the 2004 Act.
(5) Subject to paragraph (6), the general rule in financial remedy proceedings is that the court will not make an order requiring one party to pay the costs of another party.
(6) The court may make an order requiring one party to pay the costs of another party at any stage of the proceedings where it considers it appropriate to do so because of the conduct of a party in relation to the proceedings (whether before or during them).
(7) In deciding what order (if any) to make under paragraph (6), the court must have regard to–
   (a) any failure by a party to comply with these rules, any order of the court or any practice direction which the court considers relevant;
   (b) any open offer to settle made by a party;
   (c) whether it was reasonable for a party to raise, pursue or contest a particular allegation or issue;
   (d) the manner in which a party has pursued or responded to the application or a particular allegation or issue;
   (e) any other aspect of a party's conduct in relation to proceedings which the court considers relevant; and
   (f) the financial effect on the parties of any costs order.
(8) No offer to settle which is not an open offer to settle is admissible at any stage of the proceedings, except as provided by rule 9.17.

28.4 Wasted costs orders in the magistrates' court: appeals

A legal or other representative against whom a wasted costs order is made in the magistrates' court may appeal to the Crown Court.

PART 29 MISCELLANEOUS

29.1 Personal details

(1) Unless the court directs otherwise, a party is not required to reveal–

- (a) the party's home address or other contact details;
- (b) the address or other contact details of any child;
- (c) the name of a person with whom the child is living, if that person is not the applicant; or
- (d) in relation to an application under section 28(2) of the 2002 Act (application for permission to change the child's surname), the proposed new surname of the child.

(2) Where a party does not wish to reveal any of the particulars in paragraph (1), that party must give notice of those particulars to the court and the particulars will not be revealed to any person unless the court directs otherwise.

(3) Where a party changes home address during the course of proceedings, that party must give notice of the change to the court.

29.2 Disclosure of information under the 1991 Act

Where the Commission requires a person mentioned in regulation 3(1), 4(2) or 6(2)(a) of the Child Support Information Regulations 2008 to furnish information or evidence for a purpose mentioned in regulation 4(1) of those Regulations, nothing in these rules will–

(a) prevent that person from furnishing the information or evidence sought; or
(b) require that person to seek permission of the court before doing so.

29.3 Method of giving notice

(1) Unless directed otherwise, a notice which is required by these rules to be given to a person must be given–

- (a) in writing; and
- (b) in a manner in which service may be effected in accordance with Part 6.

(2) Rule 6.33 applies to a notice which is required by these rules to be given to a child as it applies to a document which is to be served on a child.

29.4 Withdrawal of applications in proceedings

(1) This rule applies to applications in proceedings–

- (a) under Part 7;
- (b) under Parts 10 to 14 or under any other Part where the application relates to the welfare or upbringing of a child or;
- (c) where either of the parties is a protected party.

(2) Where this rule applies, an application may only be withdrawn with the permission of the court.

(3) Subject to paragraph (4), a person seeking permission to withdraw an application must file a written request for permission setting out the reasons for the request.

(4) The request under paragraph (3) may be made orally to the court if the parties are present.

(5) A court officer will notify the other parties of a written request.

(6) The court may deal with a written request under paragraph (3) without a hearing if the other parties, and any other persons directed by the court, have had an opportunity to make written representations to the court about the request.

29.5 The Human Rights Act 1998

(1) In this rule–

'the 1998 Act' means the Human Rights Act 1998;

'Convention right' has the same meaning as in the 1998 Act; and

'declaration of incompatibility' means a declaration of incompatibility under section 4 of the 1998 Act.

(2) A party who seeks to rely on any provision of or right arising under the 1998 Act or seeks a remedy available under that Act must inform the court in that party's application or otherwise in writing specifying–

    (a) the Convention right which it is alleged has been infringed and details of the alleged infringement; and

    (b) the relief sought and whether this includes a declaration of incompatibility.

(3) The High Court may not make a declaration of incompatibility unless 21 days' notice, or such other period of notice as the court directs, has been given to the Crown.

(4) Where notice has been given to the Crown, a Minister, or other person permitted by the 1998 Act, will be joined as a party on giving notice to the court.

(5) Where a claim is made under section 7(1) of the 1998 Act (claim that public authority acted unlawfully) in respect of a judicial act–

    (a) that claim must be set out in the application form or the appeal notice; and

    (b) notice must be given to the Crown.

(6) Where paragraph (4) applies and the appropriate person (as defined in section 9(5) of the 1998 Act) has not applied within 21 days, or such other period as the court directs, beginning with the date on which the notice to be joined as a party was served, the court may join the appropriate person as a party.

(7) On any application concerning a committal order, if the court ordering the release of the person concludes that that person's Convention rights have been infringed by the making of the order to which the application or appeal relates, the judgment or order should so state, but if the court does not do so, that failure will not prevent another court from deciding the matter.

(8) Where by reason of a rule, practice direction or court order the Crown is permitted or required–

    (a) to make a witness statement;

    (b) to swear an affidavit[GL];

    (c) to verify a document by a statement of truth; or

    (d) to discharge any other procedural obligation,

that function will be performed by an appropriate officer acting on behalf of the Crown, and the court may if necessary nominate an appropriate officer.

(Practice Direction 29A (Human Rights – Joining the Crown) makes provision for the notices mentioned in this rule.)

29.6 Documents in proceedings concerning gender recognition

(1) This rule applies to all documents in proceedings brought under–

    (a) section 12(g) or (h) of, or paragraph 11(1)(e) of Schedule 1 to, the 1973 Act; or

    (b) the Gender Recognition Act 2004.

(2) Documents to which this rule applies must, while they are in the custody of the court, be kept in a place of special security.

29.7 Stamping or sealing court documents

(1) A court officer must, when issuing the following documents, seal[GL], or otherwise authenticate them with the stamp of the court–

    (a)   the application form;
    (b)   an order; and
    (c)   any other document which a rule or practice direction requires the court officer to seal[GL] or stamp.

(2) The court officer may place the seal[GL] or the stamp on the document–

    (a)   by hand; or
    (b)   by printing a facsimile of the seal[GL] on the document whether electronically or otherwise.

(3) A document purporting to bear the court's seal[GL] or stamp will be admissible in evidence without further proof.

29.8 Applications for relief which is precluded by the 1991 Act

(1) This rule applies where an application is made for an order which, in the opinion of the court, it would be prevented from making under section 8 or 9 of the 1991 Act and in this rule, 'the matter' means the question of whether or not the court would be so prevented.
(2) The court will consider the matter without holding a hearing.
(3) Where the court officer receives the opinion of the court, as mentioned in paragraph (1), the court officer must send a notice to the applicant of that opinion.
(4) Paragraphs (5) to (11) apply where the court officer sends a notice under paragraph (3).
(5) Subject to paragraph (6), no requirement of these rules apply except the requirements–

    (a)   of this rule;
    (b)   as to service of the application by the court officer; and
    (c)   as to any procedural step to be taken following the making of an application of the type in question.

(6) The court may direct that the requirements of these rules apply, or apply to such extent or with such modifications as are set out in the direction.
(7) If the applicant informs the court officer, within 14 days of the date of the notice, that the applicant wishes to persist with the application, the court will give appropriate directions for the matter to be heard and determined and may provide for the hearing to be without notice.
(8) Where directions are given in accordance with paragraph (7), the court officer must–

    (a)   inform the applicant of the directions;
    (b)   send a copy of the application to the other parties;
    (c)   if the hearing is to be without notice, inform the other parties briefly–

        (i)   of the nature and effect of the notice given to the applicant under paragraph (3);
        (ii)   that the matter is being resolved without a hearing on notice; and
        (iii)   that they will be notified of the result; and

    (d)   if the hearing is to be on notice, inform the other parties of–

        (i)   the circumstances which led to the directions being given; and
        (ii)   the directions.

(9) If the applicant does not inform the court officer as mentioned in paragraph (7), the application shall be treated as having been withdrawn.
(10) Where–

(a) the matter is heard in accordance with directions given under paragraph (7); and
(b) the court determines that it would be prevented, under section 8 or 9 of the 1991 Act, from making the order sought by the applicant,

the court will dismiss the application.

(11) Where the court dismisses the application–
(a) the court must give its reasons in writing; and
(b) the court officer must send a copy of the reasons to the parties.

29.9 Modification of rule 29.8 where the application is not freestanding

(1) Where the court officer sends a notice under rule 29.8(3) in relation to an application which is contained in another document ('the document') which contains material extrinsic to the application–
(a) subject to paragraph (2), the document will be treated as if it did not contain the application in respect of which the notice was served; and
(b) the court officer, when sending copies of the documents to the respondents under any provision of these rules, must attach–
(i) a copy of the notice under rule 29.8(3); and
(ii) a notice informing the respondents of the effect of paragraph (1)(a).

(2) If the court determines that it is not prevented by section 8 or 9 of the 1991 Act from making the order sought by the application, the court–
(a) must direct that the document shall be treated as if it contained the application; and
(b) may give such directions as it considers appropriate for the subsequent conduct of the proceedings.

29.10 Standard requirements

(1) Every judgment or order must state the name and judicial title of the person who made it.
(2) Every judgment or order must–
(a) bear the date on which it is given or made; and
(b) be sealed[GL] by the court.

29.11 Drawing up and filing of judgments and orders

(1) Except as provided by a rule or a practice direction, every judgment or order will be drawn up by the court unless–
(a) the court orders a party to draw it up;
(b) a party, with the permission of the court, agrees to draw it up; or
(c) the court dispenses with the need to draw it up.

(2) The court may direct that–
(a) a judgment or an order drawn up by a party must be checked by the court before it is sealed[GL]; or
(b) before a judgment or an order is drawn up by the court, the parties must file an agreed statement of its terms.

(3) Where a judgment or an order is to be drawn up by a party–
(a) that party must file it no later than 7 days after the date on which the court ordered or gave permission for the order to be drawn up so that it can be sealed by the court; and

(b) if that party fails to file it within that period, any other party may draw it up and file it.

29.12 Copies of orders made in open court

A copy of an order made in open court will be issued to any person who requests it on payment of the prescribed fee.

29.13 Service of judgments and orders

(1) The court officer must, unless the court directs otherwise, serve a copy of a judgment or an order made in family proceedings to every party affected by it.
(2) Where a judgment or an order has been drawn up by a party and is to be served by the court officer the party who drew it up must file a copy to be retained at court and sufficient copies for service on all the parties.
(3) A party in whose favour an order is made need not prove that a copy of the order has reached a party to whom it is required to be sent under this rule.
(4) This rule does not affect the operation of any rule or enactment which requires an order to be served in a particular way.

29.14 Power to require judgment or order to be served on a party as well as the party's solicitor

Where the party on whom a judgment or order is served is acting by a solicitor, the court may order the judgment or order to be served on the party as well as on the party's solicitor.

29.15 When judgment or order takes effect

A judgment or order takes effect from the day when it is given or made, or such later date as the court may specify.

29.16 Correction of errors in judgments and orders

(1) The court may at any time correct an accidental slip or omission in a judgment or order.
(2) A party may apply for a correction without notice.

PART 30   APPEALS

30.1 Scope and interpretation

(1) The rules in this Part apply to appeals to–
   (a) the High Court; and
   (b) a county court.
(2) This Part does not apply to an appeal in detailed assessment proceedings against a decision of an authorised court officer.

(Rules 47.20 to 47.23 of the CPR deal with appeals against a decision of an authorised court officer in detailed assessment proceedings.)

(3) In this Part–
   'appeal court' means the court to which an appeal is made;
   'appeal notice' means an appellant's or respondent's notice;
   'appellant' means a person who brings or seeks to bring an appeal;
   'lower court' means the court from which, or the person from whom, the appeal lies; and
   'respondent' means–

(a) a person other than the appellant who was a party to the proceedings in the lower court and who is affected by the appeal; and
(b) a person who is permitted by the appeal court to be a party to the appeal.

(4) This Part is subject to any rule, enactment or practice direction which sets out special provisions with regard to any particular category of appeal.

30.2 Parties to comply with the practice direction

All parties to an appeal must comply with Practice Direction 30A.

30.3 Permission

(1) An appellant or respondent requires permission to appeal—
 (a) against a decision in proceedings where the decision appealed against was made by a district judge or a costs judge, unless paragraph (2) applies; or
 (b) as provided by Practice Direction 30A.
(2) Permission to appeal is not required where the appeal is against—
 (a) a committal order; or
 (b) a secure accommodation order under section 25 of the 1989 Act.
(3) An application for permission to appeal may be made—
 (a) to the lower court at the hearing at which the decision to be appealed was made; or
 (b) to the appeal court in an appeal notice.

(Rule 30.4 sets out the time limits for filing an appellant's notice at the appeal court. Rule 30.5 sets out the time limits for filing a respondent's notice at the appeal court. Any application for permission to appeal to the appeal court must be made in the appeal notice (see rules 30.4(1) and 30.5(3).)

(4) Where the lower court refuses an application for permission to appeal, a further application for permission to appeal may be made to the appeal court.
(5) Where the appeal court, without a hearing, refuses permission to appeal, the person seeking permission may request the decision to be reconsidered at a hearing.
(6) A request under paragraph (5) must be filed within 7 days beginning with the date on which the notice that permission has been refused was served.
(7) Permission to appeal may be given only where—
 (a) the court considers that the appeal would have a real prospect of success; or
 (b) there is some other compelling reason why the appeal should be heard.
(8) An order giving permission may—
 (a) limit the issues to be heard; and
 (b) be made subject to conditions.
(9) In this rule 'costs judge' means a taxing master of the Senior Courts.

30.4 Appellant's notice

(1) Where the appellant seeks permission from the appeal court it must be requested in the appellant's notice.
(2) Subject to paragraph (3), the appellant must file the appellant's notice at the appeal court within—
 (a) such period as may be directed by the lower court (which may be longer or shorter than the period referred to in sub-paragraph (b)); or
 (b) where the court makes no such direction, 21 days after the date of the decision of the lower court against which the appellant wishes to appeal.

(3) Where the appeal is against an order under section 38(1) of the 1989 Act, the appellant must file the appellant's notice within 7 days beginning with the date of the decision of the lower court.
(4) Unless the appeal court orders otherwise, an appellant's notice must be served on each respondent and the persons referred to in paragraph (5)–

    (a) as soon as practicable; and
    (b) in any event not later than 7 days,

after it is filed.
(5) The persons referred to in paragraph (4) are–

    (a) any children's guardian, welfare officer, or children and family reporter;
    (b) a local authority who has prepared a report under section 14A(8) or (9) of the 1989 Act;
    (c) an adoption agency or local authority which has prepared a report on the suitability of the applicant to adopt a child;
    (d) a local authority which has prepared a report on the placement of the child for adoption; and
    (e) where the appeal is from a magistrates' court, the court officer.

30.5 Respondent's notice

(1) A respondent may file and serve a respondent's notice.
(2) A respondent who–

    (a) is seeking permission to appeal from the appeal court; or
    (b) wishes to ask the appeal court to uphold the order of the lower court for reasons different from or additional to those given by the lower court,

must file a respondent's notice.
(3) Where the respondent seeks permission from the appeal court it must be requested in the respondent's notice.
(4) A respondent's notice must be filed within–

    (a) such period as may be directed by the lower court; or
    (b) where the court makes no such direction, 14 days beginning with the date referred to in paragraph (5).

(5) The date referred to in paragraph (4) is–

    (a) the date on which the respondent is served with the appellant's notice where–

        (i) permission to appeal was given by the lower court; or
        (ii) permission to appeal is not required;

    (b) the date on which the respondent is served with notification that the appeal court has given the appellant permission to appeal; or
    (c) the date on which the respondent is served with notification that the application for permission to appeal and the appeal itself are to be heard together.

(6) Unless the appeal court orders otherwise, a respondent's notice must be served on the appellant, any other respondent and the persons referred to in rule 30.4(5)–

    (a) as soon as practicable; and
    (b) in any event not later than 7 days,

after it is filed.
(7) Where there is an appeal against an order under section 38(1) of the 1989 Act–

    (a) a respondent may not, in that appeal, bring an appeal from the order or ask the appeal court to uphold the order of the lower court for reasons different from or additional to those given by the lower court; and
    (b) paragraphs (2) and (3) do not apply.

30.6 Grounds of appeal

The appeal notice must state the grounds of appeal.

30.7 Variation of time

(1) An application to vary the time limit for filing an appeal notice must be made to the appeal court.
(2) The parties may not agree to extend any date or time limit set by–
- (a) these rules;
- (b) Practice Direction 30A; or
- (c) an order of the appeal court or the lower court.

(Rule 4.1(3)(a) provides that the court may extend or shorten the time for compliance with a rule, practice direction or court order (even if an application for extension is made after the time for compliance has expired).)

(Rule 4.1(3)(c) provides that the court may adjourn or bring forward a hearing.)

30.8 Stay

Unless the appeal court or the lower court orders otherwise, an appeal does not operate as a stay[GL] of any order or decision of the lower court.

30.9 Amendment of appeal notice

An appeal notice may not be amended without the permission of the appeal court.

30.10 Striking out appeal notices and setting aside or imposing conditions on permission to appeal

(1) The appeal court may–
- (a) strike out[GL] the whole or part of an appeal notice;
- (b) set aside[GL] permission to appeal in whole or in part;
- (c) impose or vary conditions upon which an appeal may be brought.

(2) The court will only exercise its powers under paragraph (1) where there is a compelling reason for doing so.
(3) Where a party was present at the hearing at which permission was given that party may not subsequently apply for an order that the court exercise its powers under paragraphs (1)(b) or (1)(c).

30.11 Appeal court's powers

(1) In relation to an appeal the appeal court has all the powers of the lower court.

(Rule 30.1(4) provides that this Part is subject to any enactment that sets out special provisions with regard to any particular category of appeal.)

(2) The appeal court has power to–
- (a) affirm, set aside[GL] or vary any order or judgment made or given by the lower court;
- (b) refer any application or issue for determination by the lower court;
- (c) order a new hearing;
- (d) make orders for the payment of interest;
- (e) make a costs order.

(3) The appeal court may exercise its powers in relation to the whole or part of an order of the lower court.

(Rule 4.1 contains general rules about the court's case management powers.)

(4) If the appeal court–
- (a) refuses an application for permission to appeal;
- (b) strikes out an appellant's notice; or
- (c) dismisses an appeal,

and it considers that the application, the appellant's notice or the appeal is totally without merit, the provisions of paragraph (5) must be complied with.

(5) Where paragraph (4) applies–
- (a) the court's order must record the fact that it considers the application, the appellant's notice or the appeal to be totally without merit; and
- (b) the court must at the same time consider whether it is appropriate to make a civil restraint order.

30.12 Hearing of appeals

(1) Every appeal will be limited to a review of the decision of the lower court unless–
- (a) an enactment or practice direction makes different provision for a particular category of appeal; or
- (b) the court considers that in the circumstances of an individual appeal it would be in the interests of justice to hold a re-hearing.

(2) Unless it orders otherwise, the appeal court will not receive–
- (a) oral evidence; or
- (b) evidence which was not before the lower court.

(3) The appeal court will allow an appeal where the decision of the lower court was–
- (a) wrong; or
- (b) unjust because of a serious procedural or other irregularity in the proceedings in the lower court.

(4) The appeal court may draw any inference of fact which it considers justified on the evidence.

(5) At the hearing of the appeal a party may not rely on a matter not contained in that party's appeal notice unless the appeal court gives permission.

30.13 Assignment of appeals to the Court of Appeal

(1) Where the court from or to which an appeal is made or from which permission to appeal is sought ('the relevant court') considers that–
- (a) an appeal which is to be heard by a county court or the High Court would raise an important point of principle or practice; or
- (b) there is some other compelling reason for the Court of Appeal to hear it,

the relevant court may order the appeal to be transferred to the Court of Appeal.

(2) This rule does not apply to proceedings in a magistrates' court.

30.14 Reopening of final appeals

(1) The High Court will not reopen a final determination of any appeal unless–
- (a) it is necessary to do so in order to avoid real injustice;
- (b) the circumstances are exceptional and make it appropriate to reopen the appeal; and
- (c) there is no alternative effective remedy.

(2) In paragraphs (1), (3), (4) and (6), 'appeal' includes an application for permission to appeal.

(3) This rule does not apply to appeals to a county court.

(4) Permission is needed to make an application under this rule to reopen a final determination of an appeal.
(5) There is no right to an oral hearing of an application for permission unless, exceptionally, the judge so directs.
(6) The judge will not grant permission without directing the application to be served on the other party to the original appeal and giving that party an opportunity to make representations.
(7) There is no right of appeal or review from the decision of the judge on the application for permission, which is final.
(8) The procedure for making an application for permission is set out in Practice Direction 30A.

PART 31 REGISTRATION OF ORDERS UNDER THE COUNCIL REGULATION, THE CIVIL PARTNERSHIP (JURISDICTION AND RECOGNITION OF JUDGMENTS) REGULATIONS 2005 AND UNDER THE HAGUE CONVENTION 1996

31.1 Scope

This Part applies to proceedings for the recognition, non-recognition and registration of–

(a) judgments to which the Council Regulation applies;
(b) measures to which the 1996 Hague Convention applies; and
(c) judgments to which the Jurisdiction and Recognition of Judgments Regulations apply, and which relate to dissolution or annulment of overseas relationships entitled to be treated as a civil partnership, or legal separation of the same.

31.2 Interpretation

(1) In this Part–

    (a) 'judgment' is to be construed–

        (i) in accordance with the definition in Article 2(4) of the Council Regulation where it applies;
        (ii) in accordance with regulation 6 of the Jurisdiction and Recognition of Judgments Regulations where those Regulations apply; or
        (iii) as meaning any measure taken by an authority with jurisdiction under Chapter II of the 1996 Hague Convention where that Convention applies;

    (b) 'the Jurisdiction and Recognition of Judgments Regulations' means the Civil Partnership (Jurisdiction and Recognition of Judgments) Regulations 2005;
    (c) 'Member State' means–

        (i) where registration, recognition or non-recognition is sought of a judgment under the Council Regulation, a Member State of the European Union which is bound by that Regulation or a country which has subsequently adopted it;
        (ii) where recognition is sought of a judgment to which the Jurisdiction and Recognition of Judgments Regulations apply, a Member State of the European Union to which Part II of those Regulations applies;

    (d) 'Contracting State' means a State, other than a Member State within the meaning of (c) above, in relation to which the 1996 Hague Convention is in force as between that State and the United Kingdom; and
    (e) 'parental responsibility'–

(i) where the Council Regulation applies, has the meaning given in Article 2(7) of that Regulation; and
(ii) where the 1996 Hague Convention applies, has the meaning given in Article 1(2) of that Convention.

(2) References in this Part to registration are to the registration of a judgment in accordance with the provisions of this Part.

31.3 Where to start proceedings

(1) Every application under this Part, except for an application under rule 31.18 for a certified copy of a judgment, or under rule 31.20 for rectification of a certificate issued under Articles 41 or 42, must be made to the principal registry.

(2) Nothing in this rule prevents the determination of an issue of recognition as an incidental question by any court in proceedings, in accordance with Article 21(4) of the Council Regulation.

(3) Notwithstanding paragraph (1), where recognition of a judgment is raised as an incidental question in proceedings under the 1996 Hague Convention or the Jurisdiction and Recognition of Judgments Regulations the court hearing those proceedings may determine the question of recognition.

31.4 Application for registration, recognition or non-recognition of a judgment

(1) Any interested person may apply to the court for an order that the judgment be registered, recognised or not recognised.

(2) Except for an application under rule 31.7, an application for registration, recognition or non-recognition must be—
 (a) made to a district judge of the principal registry; and
 (b) in the form, and supported by the documents and the information required by a practice direction.

31.5 Documents – supplementary

(1) Except as regards a copy of a judgment required by Article 37(1)(a) of the Council Regulation, where the person making an application under this Part does not produce the documents required by rule 31.4(2)(b) the court may—
 (a) fix a time within which the documents are to be produced;
 (b) accept equivalent documents; or
 (c) dispense with production of the documents if the court considers it has sufficient information.

(2) This rule does not apply to applications under rule 31.7.

31.6 Directions

(1) As soon as practicable after an application under this Part has been made, the court may (subject to the requirements of the Council Regulation) give such directions as it considers appropriate, including as regards the following matters—
 (a) whether service of the application may be dispensed with;
 (b) expedition of the proceedings or any part of the proceedings (and any direction for expedition may specify a date by which the court must give its decision);
 (c) the steps to be taken in the proceedings and the time by which each step is to be taken;
 (d) the service of documents; and
 (e) the filing of evidence.

(2) The court or court officer will—
 (a) record the giving, variation or revocation of directions under this rule; and

(b) as soon as practicable serve a copy of the directions order on every party.

31.7 Recognition and enforcement under the Council Regulation of a judgment given in another Member State relating to rights of access or under Article 11(8) for the return of the child to that State

(1) This rule applies where a judgment has been given in another Member State–

    (a) relating to rights of access: or.

    (b) under Article 11(8) of the Council Regulation for the return of a child to that State,

which has been certified, in accordance with Article 41(2) or 42(2) as the case may be, by the judge in the court of origin.

(2) An application for recognition or enforcement of the judgment must be–

    (a) made in writing to a district judge of the principal registry; and

    (b) accompanied by a copy of the certificate issued by the judge in the court of origin.

(3) The application may be made without notice.

(4) Rules 31.5 and 31.8 to 31.17 do not apply to an application made under this rule.

(5) Nothing in this rule shall prevent a holder of parental responsibility from seeking recognition and enforcement of a judgment in accordance with the provisions of rules 31.8 to 31.17.

31.8 Registration for enforcement or order for non-recognition of a judgment

(1) This rule applies where an application is made for an order that a judgment given in another Member State, or a Contracting State, should be registered, or should not be recognised, except where rule 31.7 applies.

(2) Where the application is made for an order that the judgment should be registered–

    (a) upon receipt of the application, and subject to any direction given by the court under rule 31.6, the court officer will serve the application on the person against whom registration is sought;

    (b) the court will not accept submissions from either the person against whom registration is sought or any child in relation to whom the judgment was given.

(3) Where the application is for an order that the judgment should not be recognised–

    (a) upon receipt of the application, and subject to any direction given by the court under rule 31.6, the court officer will serve the application on the person in whose favour judgment was given;

    (b) the person in whose favour the judgment was given must file an answer to the application and serve it on the applicant–

        (i) within 1 month of service of the application; or

        (ii) if the applicant is habitually resident in another Member State, within two months of service of the application.

(4) In cases to which the 1996 Hague Convention applies and the Council Regulation does not apply, the court may extend the time set out in subparagraph (3)(b)(ii) on account of distance.

(5) The person in whose favour the judgment was given may request recognition or registration of the judgment in their answer, and in that event must comply with 31.4(2)(b), to the extent that such documents, information and evidence are not already contained in the application for non-recognition.

(6) If, in a case to which the Council Regulation applies, the person in whose favour the judgment was given fails to file an answer as required by paragraph (3), the court will act in accordance with the provisions of Article 18 of the Council Regulation.

(7) If, in a case to which the 1996 Hague Convention applies and the Service Regulation does not, the person in whose favour the judgment was given fails to file a answer as required by paragraph (3)–

(a) where the Hague Convention of 15th November 1965 on the service abroad of judicial and extrajudicial documents in civil or commercial matters applies, the court shall apply Article 15 of that Convention; and

(b) in all other cases, the court will not consider the application unless–

(i) it is proved to the satisfaction of the court that the person in whose favour judgment was given was served with the application within a reasonable period of time to arrange his or her response; or

(ii) the court is satisfied that the circumstances of the case justify proceeding with consideration of the application.

(8) In a case to which the Jurisdiction and Recognition of Judgments Regulations apply, if the person in whose favour judgment was given fails to file an answer as required by paragraph (3), the court will apply the Service Regulation where that regulation applies, and if it does not–

(a) where the Hague Convention of 15th November 1965 on the service abroad of judicial and extrajudicial documents in civil or commercial matters applies, the court shall apply Article 15 of that Convention; and

(b) in all other cases, the court will apply the provisions of paragraph (7)(b).

31.9 Stay of recognition proceedings by reason of an appeal

Where recognition or non-recognition of a judgment given in another Member State or Contracting State is sought, or is raised as an incidental question in other proceedings, the court may stay the proceedings–

(a) if an ordinary appeal against the judgment has been lodged; or
(b) if the judgment was given in the Republic of Ireland, if enforcement of the judgment is suspended there by reason of an appeal.

31.10 Effect of refusal of application for a decision that a judgment should not be recognised

Where the court refuses an application for a decision that a judgment should not be recognised, the court may–

(a) direct that the decision to refuse the application is to be treated as a decision that the judgment be recognised; or

(b) treat the answer under paragraph (3)(b) of rule 31.8 as an application that the judgment be registered for enforcement if paragraph (5) of that rule is complied with and order that the judgment be registered for enforcement in accordance with rule 31.11.

31.11 Notification of the court's decision on an application for registration or non-recognition

(1) Where the court has–

(a) made an order on an application for an order that a judgment should be registered for enforcement; or

(b) refused an application that a judgment should not be recognised and ordered under rule 31.10 that the judgment be registered for enforcement,

the court officer will as soon as practicable take the appropriate action under paragraph (2) or (3).

(2) If the court refuses the application for the judgment to be registered for enforcement, the

court officer will serve the order on the applicant and the person against whom judgment was given in the state of origin.

(3) If the court orders that the judgment should be registered for enforcement, the court officer will–

    (a)   register the judgment in the central index of judgments kept by the principal registry;

    (b)   confirm on the order that the judgment has been registered; and

    (c)   serve on the parties the court's order endorsed with the court officer's confirmation that the judgment has been registered.

(4) A sealed order of the court endorsed in accordance with paragraph (3)(b) will constitute notification that the judgment has been registered under Article 28(2) of the Council Regulation or under Article 26 of the 1996 Hague Convention, as the case may be, and in this Part 'notice of registration' means a sealed order so endorsed.

(5) The notice of registration must state–

    (a)   full particulars of the judgment registered and the order for registration;

    (b)   the name of the party making the application and his address for service within the jurisdiction;

    (c)   the right of the person against whom judgment was given to appeal against the order for registration; and

    (d)   the period within which an appeal against the order for registration may be made.

31.12 Effect of registration under rule 31.11

Registration of a judgment under rule 31.11 will serve for the purpose of Article 21(3) of the Council Regulation, Article 24 of the 1996 Hague Convention, or regulation 7 of the Jurisdiction and Recognition of Judgments Regulations (as the case may be) as a decision that the judgment is recognised.

31.13 The central index of judgments registered under rule 31.11

The central index of judgments registered under rule 31.11 will be kept by the principal registry.

31.14 Decision on recognition of a judgment only

(1) Where an application is made seeking recognition of a judgment only, the provisions of rules 31.8 and 31.9 apply to that application as they do to an application for registration for enforcement.

(2) Where the court orders that the judgment should be recognised, the court officer will serve a copy of the order on each party as soon as practicable.

(3) A sealed order of the court will constitute notification that the judgment has been recognised under Article 21(3) of the Council Regulation, Article 24 of the 1996 Hague convention or regulation 7 of the Jurisdiction and Recognition of Judgments Regulations, as the case may be.

(4) The sealed order shall indicate–

    (a)   full particulars of the judgment recognised;

    (b)   the name of the party making the application and his address for service within the jurisdiction;

    (c)   the right of the person against whom judgment was given to appeal against the order for recognition; and

    (d)   the period within which an appeal against the order for recognition may be made.

31.15 Appeal against the court's decision under rules 31.10, 31.11 or 31.14

(1) An appeal against the court's decision under rules31.10, 31.11or 31.14 must be made to a judge of the High Court–

    (a) within one month of the date of service of the notice of registration; or

    (b) if the party bringing the appeal is habitually resident in another Member State, or a Contracting State, within two months of the date of service.

(2) The court may not extend time for an appeal on account of distance unless the matter is one to which the 1996 Hague Convention applies and the Council Regulation does not apply.

(3) If, in a case to which the 1996 Hague Convention applies and the Service Regulation does not, the appeal is brought by the applicant for a declaration of enforceability or registration and the respondent fails to appear–

    (a) where the Hague Convention of 15th November 1965 on the service abroad of judicial and extrajudicial documents in civil or commercial matters applies, the court shall apply Article 15 of that Convention; and

    (b) in all other cases, the court will not consider the appeal unless–

        (i) it is proved to the satisfaction of the court that the respondent was served with notice of the appeal within a reasonable period of time to arrange his or her response; or

        (ii) the court is satisfied that the circumstances of the case justify proceeding with consideration of the appeal.

(4) This rule is subject to rule 31.16.

(The procedure for applications under rule 31.15 is set out in Practice Direction 30A (Appeals).)

31.16 Stay of enforcement where appeal pending in state of origin

(1) A party against whom enforcement is sought of a judgment which has been registered under rule 31.11 may apply to the court with which an appeal is lodged under rule 31.15 for the proceedings to be stayed where–

    (a) that party has lodged an ordinary appeal in the Member State or Contracting State of origin; or

    (b) the time for such an appeal has not yet expired.

(2) Where an application for a stay is filed in the circumstances described in paragraph (1)(b), the court may specify the time within which an appeal must be lodged.

31.17 Enforcement of judgments registered under rule 31.11

(1) The court will not enforce a judgment registered under rule 31.11 until after–

    (a) the expiration of any applicable period under rules 31.15 or 31.16; or

    (b) if that period has been extended by the court, the expiration of the period so extended.

(2) A party applying to the court for the enforcement of a registered judgment must produce to the court a certificate of service of–

    (a) the notice of registration of the judgment; and

    (b) any order made by the court in relation to the judgment.

(Service out of the jurisdiction, including service in accordance with the Service Regulation, is dealt with in chapter 4 of Part 6 and in Practice Direction 6B.)

31.18 Request for a certificate or a certified copy of a judgment

(1) An application for a certified copy of a judgment, or for a certificate under Articles 39, 41 or 42 of the Council Regulation, must be made to the court which made the order or judgment in respect of which certification is sought and without giving notice to any other party.

(2) The application must be made in the form, and supported by the documents and information required by a practice direction.

(3) The certified copy of the judgment will be an office copy sealed with the seal of the court and signed by the district judge, or by the court where the application is made to the Magistrates' Court. It will be issued with a certified copy of any order which has varied any of the terms of the original order.

(4) Where the application is made for the purposes of applying for recognition or recognition and enforcement of the order in another Contracting State, the court must indicate on the certified copy of the judgment the grounds on which it based its jurisdiction to make the order, for the purposes of Article 23(2)(a) of the 1996 Hague Convention.

31.19 Certificates issued in England and Wales under Articles 41 and 42 of the Council Regulation

The court officer will serve–

(a) a certificate issued under Article 41 or 42; or
(b) a certificate rectified under rule 31.20,

on all parties and will transmit a copy to the Central Authority for England and Wales.

31.20 Rectification of certificate issued under Article 41 or 42 of the Council Regulation

(1) Where there is an error in a certificate issued under Article 41 or 42, an application to rectify that error must be made to the court which issued the certificate.

(2) A rectification under paragraph (1) may be made–

   (a) by the court of its own initiative; or
   (b) on application by–
      (i) any party to the proceedings; or
      (ii) the court or Central Authority of another Member State.

(3) An application under paragraph (2)(b) may be made without notice being served on any other party.

31.21 Authentic instruments and agreements under Article 46 of the Council Regulation

This Chapter applies to an authentic instrument and an agreement to which Article 46 of the Council Regulation applies as it applies to a judgment.

31.22 Application for provisional, including protective measures.

An application for provisional, including protective, measures under Article 20 of the Council Regulation or Articles 11 or 12 of the 1996 Hague Convention may be made notwithstanding that the time for appealing against an order for registration of a judgment has not expired or that a final determination of any issue relating to enforcement of the judgment is pending.

PART 32 REGISTRATION AND ENFORCEMENT OF ORDERS

CHAPTER 1 SCOPE AND INTERPRETATION OF THIS PART

32.1 Scope and interpretation

(1) This Part contains rules about the registration and enforcement of maintenance orders and custody orders.
(2) In this Part–
'the 1950 Act' means the Maintenance Orders Act 1950;
'the 1958 Act' means the Maintenance Orders Act 1958.
(3) Chapter 2 of this Part relates to–
- (a) the registration of a maintenance order, made in the High Court or a county court, in a court in Scotland or Northern Ireland in accordance with the 1950 Act; and
- (b) the registration of a maintenance order, made in Scotland or Northern Ireland, in the High Court in accordance with the 1950 Act.

(Provision in respect of proceedings in the magistrates' court under the 1950 Act is in rules made under section 144 of the Magistrates' Courts Act 1980).

(4) Chapter 3 of this Part contains rules to be applied in the High Court or a county court in relation–
- (a) The registration of a maintenance order, made in the High Court or a county court, in a magistrates' court in accordance with the 1958 Act; and
- (b) The registration of a maintenance order, made in a magistrates' court, in the High Court in accordance with the 1958 Act.

(Provision in respect of proceedings in the magistrates' court under the 1958 Act is in rules made under section 144 of the Magistrates' Courts Act 1980).

(5) Chapter 4 of this Part relates to the registration and enforcement of custody orders in accordance with the 1986 Act.

CHAPTER 2 REGISTRATION ETC. OF ORDERS UNDER THE 1950 ACT

SECTION 1
Interpretation of this Chapter

32.2 Interpretation

In this Chapter–
'the clerk of the Court of Session' means the deputy principal clerk in charge of the petition department of the Court of Session;

'county court order' means a maintenance order made in a county court;

'High Court order' means a maintenance order made in the High Court;

'maintenance order' means a maintenance order to which section 16 of the 1950 Act applies;

'Northern Irish order' means a maintenance order made by the Court of Judicature of Northern Ireland;

'the register' means the register kept for the purposes of the 1950 Act;

'the registrar in Northern Ireland' means the chief registrar of the Queen's Bench Division (Matrimonial) of the High Court of Justice in Northern Ireland;

'registration' means registration under Part 2 of the 1950 Act and 'registered' is to be construed accordingly; and

'Scottish Order' means a maintenance order made by the Court of Session.

SECTION 2
Registration etc of High Court and county court orders

32.3 Registration of a High Court order

(1) An application for the registration of a High Court order may be made by sending to a court officer at the court which made the order–

- (a) a certified copy of the order; and
- (b) a statement which–
    - (i) contains the address in the United Kingdom, and the occupation, of the person liable to make payments under the order;
    - (ii) contains the date on which the order was served on the person liable to make payments, or, if the order has not been served, the reason why service has not been effected;
    - (iii) contains the reason why it is convenient for the order to be enforced in Scotland or Northern Ireland, as the case may be;
    - (iv) contains the amount of any arrears due to the applicant under the order;
    - (v) confirms that the order is not already registered; and
    - (vi) is verified by a statement of truth.

(2) If it appears to the court that–

- (a) the person liable to make payments under the order resides in Scotland or Northern Ireland; and
- (b) it is convenient for the order to be enforced there,

the court officer will send the documents filed under paragraph (1) to the clerk of the Court of Session or to the registrar in Northern Ireland, as the case may be.

(3) On receipt of a notice of the registration of a High Court order in the Court of Session or the Court of Judicature of Northern Ireland, the court officer (who is the prescribed officer for the purposes of section 17(4) of the 1950 Act) will–

- (a) enter particulars of the notice of registration in the register;
- (b) note the fact of registration in the court records; and
- (c) send particulars of the notice to the principal registry.

32.4 Notice of Variation etc. of a High Court order

(1) This rule applies where a High Court order, which is registered in the Court of Session or the Court of Judicature of Northern Ireland, is discharged or varied.

(2) A court officer in the court where the order was discharged or varied will send a certified copy of that order to the clerk of the Court of Session or the registrar in Northern Ireland, as the case may be.

32.5 Cancellation of registration of a High Court order

(1) This rule applies where–

- (a) the registration of a High Court order registered in the Court of Session or the Court of Judicature of Northern Ireland is cancelled under section 24(1) of the 1950 Act; and
- (b) notice of the cancellation is given to a court officer in the court in which the order was made (who is the prescribed officer for the purposes of section 24(3)(a) of the 1950 Act).

(2) On receipt of a notice of cancellation of registration, the court officer will enter particulars of the notice in Part 1 of the register.

32.6 Application of this Chapter to a county court order

Rules 32.3 to 32.5 apply to an application to register a county court order as if–
(a) references to a High Court order were references to a county court order;
(b) where the order is to be registered in Scotland, references to the Court of Session and the clerk of the Court of Session were references to the sheriff court and the sheriff-clerk of the sheriff court respectively; and
(c) where the order is to be registered in Northern Ireland, references to the Court of Judicature of Northern Ireland and the registrar of Northern Ireland were references to the court of summary jurisdiction and the clerk of the court of summary jurisdiction respectively.

SECTION 3
Registration etc. of Scottish and Northern Irish orders

32.7 Registration of Scottish and Northern Irish orders

On receipt of a certified copy of a Scottish order or a Northern Irish order for registration, a court officer in the principal registry (who is the prescribed officer for the purposes of section 17(2) of the 1950 Act) will–

(a) enter particulars of the order in Part 2 of the register;
(b) notify the clerk of the Court of Session or the registrar in Northern Ireland, as the case may be, that the order has been registered; and
(c) file the certified copy of the order and any statutory declaration, affidavit[GL] or statement as to the amount of any arrears due under the order.

32.8 Application to adduce evidence before High Court

The Part 18 procedure applies to an application by a person liable to make payments under a Scottish order registered in the High Court to adduce before that court any evidence on which that person would be entitled to rely in any proceedings brought before the court by which the order was made for the variation or discharge of the order.

32.9 Notice of variation etc. of Scottish and Northern Irish orders

(1) This rule applies where–

    (a) a Scottish order or a Northern Irish order, which is registered in the High Court, is discharged or varied; and
    (b) notice of the discharge or variation is given to a court officer in the High Court (who is the prescribed officer for the purposes of section 23(1)(a) of the 1950 Act).

(2) On receipt of a notice of discharge or variation, the court officer will enter particulars of the notice in Part 2 of the register.

32.10 Cancellation of registration of Scottish and Northern Irish orders

(1) The Part 18 procedure applies to an application for the cancellation of the registration of a Scottish order or a Northern Irish order in the High Court.
(2) The application must be made without notice to the person liable to make payments under the order.
(3) If the registration of the order is cancelled, the court officer will–

    (a) note the cancellation in Part II of the register; and

(b) send written notice of the cancellation to–
   (i) the clerk of the Court of Session or the registrar in Northern Ireland, as the case may be; and
   (ii) the court officer in any magistrates' court in which the order has been registered in accordance with section 2(5) of the 1958 Act.

32.11 Enforcement

(1) The Part 18 procedure applies to an application for or with respect to the enforcement of a Scottish order or a Northern Irish order registered in the High Court.
(2) The application may be made without notice to the person liable to make payments under the order.

32.12 Inspection of register and copies of order

Any person–
(a) who is entitled to receive, or liable to make, payments under a maintenance order made by the High Court, the Court of Session or the Court of Judicature of Northern Ireland; or
(b) with the permission of the court,

may–
(i) inspect the register; or
(ii) request a copy of any order registered in the High Court under Part 2 of the 1950 Act and any statutory declaration, affidavit[GL] or statement filed with the order.

CHAPTER 3 REGISTRATION OF MAINTENANCE ORDERS UNDER THE 1958 ACT

32.13 Interpretation

In this Chapter 'the register' means the register kept for the purposes of the 1958 Act.

32.14 Registration of orders – prescribed period

The prescribed period for the purpose of section 2(2) of the 1958 Act is 14 days.

(Section 2(2) sets out the period during which an order, which is to be registered in a magistrates' court, may not be enforced)

32.15 Application for registration of a maintenance order in a magistrates' court

(1) An application under section 2(1) of the 1958 Act may be made by sending to the court officer at the court which made the order–
   (a) a certified copy of the maintenance order; and
   (b) two copies of the application.
(2) When, on the grant of an application, the court officer sends the certified copy of the maintenance order to the magistrates' court in accordance with section 2(2), the court officer must–
   (a) note on the order that the application for registration has been granted; and
   (b) send to the magistrates' court a copy of the application for registration of the order.
(3) On receiving notice that the magistrates' court has registered the order, the court officer must enter particulars of the registration in the court records.

32.16 Registration in a magistrates' court of an order registered in the High Court

(1) This rule applies where–
- (a) a maintenance order is registered in the High Court in accordance with section 17(4) of the 1950 Act; and
- (b) the court officer receives notice that the magistrates' court has registered the order in accordance with section 2(5) of the 1958 Act.

(2) The court officer must enter particulars of the registration in Part II of the register.

32.17 Registration in the High Court of a magistrates' court order

(1) This rule applies where a court officer receives a certified copy of a magistrates' court order for registration in accordance with section 2(4)(c) of the 1958 Act.
(2) The court officer must register the order in the High Court by–
- (a) filing the copy of the order; and
- (b) entering particulars in–
    - (i) the register; or
    - (ii) if the order is received in a district registry, the cause book or cause card.

(3) The court officer must notify the magistrates' court that the order has been registered.

32.18 Registration in the High Court of an order registered in a magistrates' court

(1) This rule applies where–
- (a) an order has been registered in the magistrates' court in accordance with section 17(4) of the 1950 Act; and
- (b) a sheriff court in Scotland or a magistrates' court in Northern Ireland has–
    - (i) made an order for the registration of that order in the High Court; and
    - (ii) sent a certified copy of the maintenance order to the court officer of the High Court in accordance with section 2(4)(c) of the 1958 Act.

(2) The court officer must register the order in the High Court by–
- (a) filing the copy of the order; and
- (b) entering particulars in the register.

(3) The court officer must notify–
- (a) the court which made the order; and
- (b) the magistrates' court in which the order was registered in accordance with section 17(4) of the 1950 Act,

that the order has been registered in the High Court.

32.19 Variation or discharge of an order registered in a magistrates' court

(1) This rule applies where a maintenance order is registered in a magistrates' court under Part 1 of the 1958 Act.
(2) If the court which made the order makes an order varying or discharging that order the court officer must send a certified copy of the order of variation or discharge to the magistrates' court.
(3) If the court officer receives from the magistrates' court a certified copy of an order varying the maintenance order the court officer must–
- (a) file the copy of the order; and
- (b) enter the particulars of the variation in the place where the details required by rule 32.15(3) were entered.

32.20 Variation or discharge of an order registered in the High Court

(1) This rule applies where a maintenance order is registered in the High Court under Part 1 of the 1958 Act.
(2) If the court officer receives from the magistrates' court a certified copy of an order varying or discharging the maintenance order the court officer must–
    (a) file the copy of the order;
    (b) enter the particulars of the variation or discharge in–
        (i) the register; or
        (ii) if the order is received in a district registry, the cause book or cause card; and
    (c) send notice of the variation or discharge to the court officer of a county court–
        (i) who has notified the court officer of enforcement proceedings in that court relating to the maintenance order; or
        (ii) to whom a payment is to be made under an attachment of earnings order made by the High Court for the enforcement of the registered order.

32.21 Cancellation of registration – orders registered in the High Court

(1) This rule applies where an order is registered in the High Court.
(2) A person giving notice under section 5(1) of the 1958 Act must give the notice to the court officer.
(3) The court officer must take the steps mentioned in paragraph (4) if–
    (a) notice is given under section 5 of the 1958 Act; and
    (b) the court officer is satisfied, by a witness statement by the person entitled to receive payments under the order that no enforcement proceedings in relation to the order, that were started before the giving of the notice, remain in force.
(4) The court officer must, if satisfied as mentioned in paragraph (3)–
    (a) cancel the registration by entering particulars of the notice in the register or cause book (or cause card) as the case may be; and
    (b) send notice of the cancellation to–
        (i) the court which made the order; and
        (ii) where applicable, to the magistrates' court in which the order was registered in accordance with section 17(4) of the 1950 Act.
(5) Where the cancellation results from a notice given under section 5(1) of the 1958 Act, the court officer must state that fact in the notice of cancellation sent in accordance with paragraph (4)(b).
(6) If notice is received from a magistrates' court that the registration in that court under the 1958 Act of an order registered in the High Court in accordance with section 17(4) of the 1950 Act has been cancelled, the court officer must note the cancellation in Part II of the register.

32.22 Cancellation of registration – orders registered in a magistrates' court

(1) Where the court gives notice under section 5(2) of the 1958 Act, the court officer must endorse the notice on the certified copy of the order of variation or discharge sent to the magistrates' court in accordance with rule 32.19(2).
(2) Where notice is received from a magistrates' court that registration of an order made by the High Court or a county court under Part 1 of the 1958 Act has been cancelled, the court officer must enter particulars of the cancellation in the place where the details required by rule 32.15(3) were entered.

CHAPTER 4 REGISTRATION AND ENFORCEMENT OF CUSTODY ORDERS UNDER THE 1986 ACT

32.23 Interpretation

In this Chapter–

'appropriate court' means, in relation to–
- (a) Scotland, the Court of Session;
- (b) Northern Ireland, the High Court in Northern Ireland; and
- (c) a specified dependent territory, the corresponding court in that territory;

'appropriate officer' means, in relation to–
- (a) the Court of Session, the Deputy Principal Clerk of Session;
- (b) the High Court in Northern Ireland, the Master (Care and Protection) of that court; and
- (c) the appropriate court in a specified dependent territory, the corresponding officer of that court;

'Part 1 order' means an order under Part 1 of the 1986 Act;

'the register' means the register kept for the purposes of Part 1 of the 1986 Act; and

'specified dependent territory' means a dependent territory specified in column 1 of Schedule 1 to the Family Law Act 1986 (Specified Dependent Territories) Order 1991.

32.24 Prescribed officer and functions of the court

(1) The prescribed officer for the purposes of sections 27(4) and 28(1) of the 1986 Act is the family proceedings department manager of the principal registry.

(2) The function of the court under sections 27(3) and 28(1) of the 1986 Act shall be performed by a court officer.

32.25 Application for the registration of an order made by the High Court or a county court

(1) An application under section 27 of the 1986 Act for the registration of an order made in the High Court or a county court may be made by sending to a court officer at the court which made the order–
- (a) a certified copy of the order;
- (b) a copy of any order which has varied the terms of the original order;
- (c) a statement which–
    - (i) contains the name and address of the applicant and the applicant's interest under the order;
    - (ii) contains–
        - (aa) the name and date of birth of the child in respect of whom the order was made;
        - (bb) the whereabouts or suspected whereabouts of the child; and
        - (cc) the name of any person with whom the child is alleged to be;
    - (iii) contains the name and address of any other person who has an interest under the order and states whether the order has been served on that person;
    - (iv) states in which of the jurisdictions of Scotland, Northern Ireland or a specified dependent territory the order is to be registered;
    - (v) states that to the best of the applicant's information and belief, the order is in force;
    - (vi) states whether, and if so where, the order is already registered;

(vii) gives details of any order known to the applicant which affects the child and is in force in the jurisdiction in which the order is to be registered;
(viii) annexes any document relevant to the application; and
(ix) is verified by a statement of truth; and
(d) a copy of the statement referred to in paragraph (c).
(2) On receipt of the documents referred to in paragraph (1), the court officer will, subject to paragraph (4)–
(a) keep the original statement and send the other documents to the appropriate officer;
(b) record in the court records the fact that the documents have been sent to the appropriate officer; and
(c) file a copy of the documents.
(3) On receipt of a notice that the document has been registered in the appropriate court the court officer will record that fact in the court records.
(4) The court officer will not send the documents to the appropriate officer if it appears to the court officer that–
(a) the order is no longer in force; or
(b) the child has reached the age of 16.
(5) Where paragraph (4) applies–
(a) the court officer must, within 14 days of the decision, notify the applicant of the decision of the court officer in paragraph (4) and the reasons for it; and
(b) the applicant may apply to a judge, but not a district judge, in private for an order that the documents be sent to the appropriate court.

32.26 Registration of orders made in Scotland, Northern Ireland or a specified dependent territory

(1) This rule applies where the prescribed officer receives, for registration, a certified copy of an order made in Scotland, Northern Ireland or a specified dependent territory.
(2) The prescribed officer will–
(a) enter in the register–
(i) the name and address of the applicant and the applicant's interest under the order;
(ii) the name and date of birth of the child and the date the child will attain the age of 16;
(iii) the whereabouts or suspected whereabouts of the child; and
(iv) the terms of the order, its date and the court which made it;
(b) file the certified copy and accompanying documents; and
(c) notify–
(i) the court which sent the order; and
(ii) the applicant,
that the order has been registered.

32.27 Revocation and variation of an order made in the High Court or a county court

(1) Where a Part 1 order, registered in an appropriate court, is varied or revoked, the court officer of the court making the order of variation or revocation will–
(a) send a certified copy of the order of variation or revocation to–
(i) the appropriate officer; and
(ii) if a different court, the court which made the Part 1 order;

(b) record in the court records the fact that a copy of the order has been sent; and
(c) file a copy of the order.

(2) On receipt of notice from the appropriate court that its register has been amended, this fact will be recorded by the court officer of–

(a) the court which made the order of variation or revocation; and
(b) if different, the court which made the Part 1 order.

32.28 Registration of varied, revoked or recalled orders made in Scotland, Northern Ireland or a specified dependent territory

(1) This rule applies where the prescribed officer receives a certified copy of an order made in Scotland, Northern Ireland or a specified dependent territory which varies, revokes or recalls a registered Part 1 order.
(2) The prescribed officer shall enter particulars of the variation, revocation or recall in the register and give notice of the entry to–

(a) the court which sent the certified copy;
(b) if different, the court which made the Part 1 order;
(c) the applicant for registration; and
(d) if different, the applicant for the variation, revocation of recall of the order.

(3) An application under section 28(2) of the 1986 Act must be made in accordance with the Part 19 procedure.
(4) The applicant for the Part 1 order, if not the applicant under section 28(2) of the 1986 Act, must be made a defendant to the application.
(5) Where the court cancels a registration under section 28(2) of the 1986 Act, the court officer will amend the register and give notice of the amendment to the court which made the Part 1 order.

32.29 Interim directions

The following persons will be made parties to an application for interim directions under section 29 of the 1986 Act–

(a) the parties to the proceedings for enforcement; and
(b) if not a party to those proceedings, the applicant for the Part 1 order.

32.30 Staying and dismissal of enforcement proceedings

(1) The following persons will be made parties to an application under section 30(1) or 31(1) of the 1986 Act–

(a) the parties to the proceedings for enforcement which are sought to be stayed[GL]; and
(b) if not a party to those proceedings, the applicant for the Part 1 order.

(2) Where the court makes an order under section 30(2) or (3) or section 31(3) of the 1986 Act, the court officer will amend the register and give notice of the amendment to–

(a) the court which made the Part 1 order; and
(b) the applicants for–
    (i) registration;
    (ii) enforcement; and
    (iii) stay[GL] or dismissal of the enforcement proceedings.

32.31 Particulars of other proceedings

A party to proceedings for or relating to a Part 1 order who knows of other proceedings which relate to the child concerned (including proceedings out of the jurisdiction and concluded proceedings) must file a witness statement which–

(a) states in which jurisdiction and court the other proceedings were begun;
(b) states the nature and current state of the proceedings and the relief claimed or granted;
(c) sets out the names of the parties to the proceedings and their relationship to the child;
(d) if applicable and if known, states the reasons why relief claimed in the proceedings for or relating to the Part 1 order was not claimed in the other proceedings; and
(e) is verified by a statement of truth.

32.32 Inspection of register

The following persons may inspect any entry in the register relating to a Part 1 order and may request copies of the order any document relating to it–

(a) the applicant for registration of the Part 1 order;
(b) a person who, to the satisfaction of a district judge, has an interest under the Part 1 order; and
(c) a person who obtains the permission of a district judge.

PART 33   ENFORCEMENT

CHAPTER 1   GENERAL RULES

33.1 Application

(1) The rules in this Part apply to an application made in the High Court and a county court to enforce an order made in family proceedings.
(2) Part 50 of, and Schedules 1 and 2 to, the CPR apply, as far as they are relevant and with necessary modification (including the modifications referred to in rule 33.7), to an application made in the High Court and a county court to enforce an order made in family proceedings.

SECTION 1
Enforcement of orders for the payment of money

33.2 Application of the Civil Procedure Rules

Part 70 of the CPR applies to proceedings under this Section as if–

(a) in rule 70.1, in paragraph (2)(d), 'but does not include a judgment or order for the payment of money into court' is omitted; and
(b) rule 70.5 is omitted.

33.3 How to apply

(1) Except where a rule or practice direction otherwise requires, an application for an order to enforce an order for the payment of money must be made in a notice of application accompanied by a statement which must–
   (a) state the amount due under the order, showing how that amount is arrived at; and
   (b) be verified by a statement of truth.
(2) The notice of application may either–
   (a) apply for an order specifying the method of enforcement; or
   (b) apply for an order for such method of enforcement as the court may consider appropriate.
(3) If an application is made under paragraph (2)(b), an order to attend court will be issued and rule 71.2 (6) and (7) of the CPR will apply as if the application had been made under that rule.

33.4 Transfer of orders

(1) This rule applies to an application for the transfer–
  (a) to the High Court of an order made in a designated county court; and
  (b) to a designated county court of an order made in the High Court.
(2) The application must be–
  (a) made without notice; and
  (b) accompanied by a statement which complies with rule 33.3(1).
(3) The transfer will have effect upon the filing of the application.
(4) Where an order is transferred from a designated county court to the High Court–
  (a) it will have the same force and effect; and
  (b) the same proceedings may be taken on it,
  as if it were an order of the High Court.
(5) This rule does not apply to the transfer of orders for periodical payments or for the recovery of arrears of periodical payments.

SECTION 2
Committal and injunction

33.5 General rule – committal hearings to be in public

(1) The general rule is that proceedings in the High Court for an order of committal will be heard in public.
(2) An order of committal may be heard in private where this is permitted by rule 6 of Order 52 of the RSC (cases in which a court may sit in private).

33.6 Proceedings in the principal registry treated as pending in a designated county court

(1) This rule applies where an order for the warrant of committal of any person to prison has been made or issued in proceedings which are–
  (a) in the principal registry; and
  (b) treated as pending in a designated county court or a county court.
(2) The person subject to the order will, wherever located, be treated for the purposes of section 122 of the County Courts Act 1984 as being out of the jurisdiction of the principal registry.
(3) Where–
  (a) a committal is for failure to comply with the terms of an injunction[GL]; or
  (b) an order or warrant for the arrest or committal of any person is made or issued in proceedings under Part 4 of the 1996 Act in the principal registry which are treated as pending in a county court,
  the order or warrant may, if the court so directs, be executed by the tipstaff within any county court.

33.7 Specific modifications of the CCR

(1) CCR Order 29, rule 1 (committal for breach of an order or undertaking) applies to–
  (a) section 8 orders, except those referred to in paragraph (2)(a); and
  (b) orders under the following sections of the 1989 Act–
    (i) section 14A (special guardianship orders);
    (ii) section 14B(2)(b) (granting of permission on making a special guardianship order to remove a child from the United Kingdom);

(iii) section 14C(3)(b) (granting of permission to remove from the United Kingdom a child who is subject to a special guardianship order); and
(iv) section 14D (variation or discharge of a special guardianship order),

as if paragraph (3) of that rule were substituted by the following paragraph–

'(3) In the case of a section 8 order (within the meaning of section 8(2) of the Children Act 1989) or an order under section 14A, 14B(2)(b), 14C(3)(b) or 14D of the Children Act 1989 enforceable by committal order under paragraph (1), the judge or the district judge may, on the application of the person entitled to enforce the order, direct that the proper officer issue a copy of the order, endorsed with or incorporating a notice as to the consequences of disobedience, for service in accordance with paragraph (2), and no copy of the order shall be issued with any such notice endorsed or incorporated save in accordance with such a direction.'.

(2) CCR Order 29, rule 1 applies to–
  (a) contact orders to which a notice has been attached under section 11I of the 1989 Act or under section 8(2) of the Children and Adoption Act 2006;
  (b) orders under section 11J of the 1989 Act (enforcement orders); and
  (c) orders under paragraph 9 of Schedule A1 to the 1989 Act (orders following breach of enforcement orders),

as if paragraph (3) were omitted.

33.8 Section 118 County Courts Act 1984 and the tipstaff

For the purposes of section 118 of the County Courts Act 1984 in its application to the hearing of family proceedings at the Royal Courts of Justice or the principal registry, the tipstaff is deemed to be an officer of the court.

CHAPTER 2   COMMITTAL BY WAY OF JUDGMENT SUMMONS

33.9 Interpretation

In this Chapter, unless the context requires otherwise–

'order' means an order made in family proceedings for the payment of money;

'judgment creditor' means a person entitled to enforce an order under section 5 of the Debtors Act 1869;

'debtor' means a person liable under an order; and

'judgment summons' means a summons under section 5 of the Debtor's Act 1869 requiring a debtor to attend court.

33.10 Application
(1) An application for the issue of a judgment summons may be made–
  (a) in the case of an order of the High Court–
    (i) where the order was made in matrimonial proceedings, to the principal registry, a district registry or a divorce county court, whichever in the opinion of the judgment creditor is most convenient;
    (ii) where the order was made in civil partnership proceedings, to the principal registry, a district registry or a civil partnership proceedings county court, whichever in the opinion of the judgment creditor is the most convenient; and
    (iii) in any other case, to the principal registry, a district registry or a designated county court, whichever in the opinion of the judgment creditor is most convenient;

(b) in the case of an order of a divorce county court, to whichever divorce county court is in the opinion of the judgment creditor most convenient; and
(c) in the case of an order of a civil partnership proceedings county court, to whichever civil partnership proceedings county court is in the opinion of the judgment creditor most convenient,

having regard (in any case) to the place where the debtor resides or carries on business and irrespective of the court or registry in which the order was made.

(2) An application must be accompanied by a statement which–
   (a) complies with rule 33.3(1);
   (b) contains all the evidence on which the judgment creditor intends to rely; and
   (c) has exhibited to it a copy of the order.

33.11 Judgment summons

(1) If the debtor is in default under an order of committal made on a previous judgment summons in respect of the same order, a judgment summons must not be issued without the court's permission.
(2) A judgment summons must–
   (a) be accompanied by the statement referred to in rule 33.10(2) and
   (b) be served on the debtor personally not less than 14 days before the hearing.
(3) A debtor served with the judgment summons under paragraph (2)(b) must be paid or offered a sum reasonably sufficient to cover the expenses of travelling to and from the court at which the debtor is summoned to appear.

33.12 Successive judgment summonses

Subject to rule 33.11(1), successive judgment summonses may be issued even if the debtor has ceased to reside or carry on business at the address stated in the application for the issue of a judgment summons since the issue of the original judgment summons.

33.13 Requirement for personal service

In proceedings for committal by way of judgment summons, the following documents must be served personally on the debtor–

(a) where the court has summonsed the debtor to attend and the debtor has failed to do so, the notice of the date and time fixed for the adjourned hearing; and
(b) copies of the judgment summons and the documents mentioned in rule 33.10(2).

33.14 Committal on application for judgment summons

(1) No person may be committed on an application for a judgment summons unless–
   (a) where the proceedings are in the High Court, the debtor has failed to attend both the hearing that the debtor was summonsed to attend and the adjourned hearing;
   (b) where the proceedings are in a county court, an order is made under section 110(2) of the County Courts Act 1984; or
   (c) the judgment creditor proves that the debtor–
      (i) has, or has had, since the date of the order the means to pay the sum in respect of which the debtor has made default; and
      (ii) has refused or neglected, or refuses or neglects, to pay that sum.
(2) The debtor may not be compelled to give evidence.

33.15 Orders for the benefit of different persons

Where an applicant has obtained one or more orders in the same application but for the benefit of different persons–

(a) where the judgment creditor is a child, the applicant may apply for the issue of a judgment summons in respect of those orders on behalf of the judgment creditor without seeking permission to act as the child's litigation friend; and

(b) only one judgment summons need be issued in respect of those orders.

33.16 Hearing of judgment summons

(1) On the hearing of the judgment summons the court may–

    (a) where the order is for lump sum provision or costs; or

    (b) where the order is an order for maintenance pending suit, an order for maintenance pending outcome of proceedings or an order for other periodical payments and it appears to the court that the order would have been varied or suspended if the debtor had made an application for that purpose,

make a new order for payment of the amount due under the original order, together with the costs of the judgment summons, either at a specified time or by instalments.

(2) If the court makes an order of committal, it may direct its execution to be suspended on terms that the debtor pays to the judgment creditor–

    (a) the amount due;

    (b) the costs of the judgment summons; and

    (c) any sums accruing due under the original order,

either at a specified time or by instalments.

(3) All payments under a new order or an order of committal must be made to the judgment creditor unless the court directs otherwise.

(4) Where an order of committal is suspended on such terms as are mentioned in paragraph (2)–

    (a) all payments made under the suspended order will be deemed to be made–

        (i) first, in or towards the discharge of any sums from time to time accruing due under the original order; and

        (ii) secondly, in or towards the discharge of a debt in respect of which the judgment summons was issued and the costs of the summons; and

    (b) the suspended order must not be executed until the judgment creditor has filed a statement of default on the part of the debtor.

33.17 Special provisions as to judgment summonses in the High Court

(1) The court may summons witnesses to give evidence to prove the means of the debtor and may issue a witness summons for that purpose.

(2) Where the debtor appears at the hearing, the court may direct that the travelling expenses paid to the debtor be allowed as expenses of a witness.

(3) Where the debtor appears at the hearing and no order of committal is made, the court may allow the debtor's proper costs including compensation for any loss of earnings.

(4) When the court makes–

    (a) a new order; or

    (b) an order of committal,

a court officer must send notice of the order to the debtor and, if the original order was made in another court, to that court.

(5) An order of committal must be directed–

    (a) where the order is to be executed by the tipstaff, to the tipstaff; or

(b) where the order is to be executed by a deputy tipstaff, to the county court within the district of which the debtor is to be found.

33.18 Special provisions as to judgment summonses in designated county courts

(1) Rules 1, 2, 3(2), 5, 7(3) and 9(2) of Order 28 of the CCR (which deal with the issue of a judgment summons in a county court and the subsequent procedure) do not apply to judgment summons issued in a designated county court.
(2) Rule 9(1) of Order 28 of the CCR (notification of order on judgment of High Court) applies to such a summons as if for the words 'the High Court' there were substituted the words–
   (a) 'any other court' where they first appear; and
   (b) 'that other court' where they next appear.
(3) Rule 7(1) and (2) of Order 28 of the CCR (suspension of a committal order) apply to such a summons subject to rule 33.16(2) and (3).

CHAPTER 3   ATTACHMENT OF EARNINGS

33.19 Proceedings in the Principal Registry

The Attachment of Earnings Act 1971 and Order 27 of the CCR (attachment of earnings) apply to the enforcement of an order made in family proceedings in the principal registry which are treated as pending in a designated county court as if they were an order made by such a court.

CHAPTER 4   WARRANT OF EXECUTION

33.20 Applications to vary existing orders

Where an application is pending for a variation of–
(a) a financial order;
(b) an order under section 27 of the 1973 Act; or
(c) an order under Part 9 of Schedule 5 to the 2004 Act,

no warrant of execution may be issued to enforce payment of any sum due under those orders, except with the permission of the district judge.

33.21 Section 103 County Courts Act 1984

Where a warrant of execution has been issued to enforce an order made in family proceedings pending in the principal registry which are treated as pending in a designated county court, the goods and chattels against which the warrant has been issued must, wherever they are located, be treated for the purposes of section 103 of the County Courts Act 1984 as being out of the jurisdiction of the principal registry.

CHAPTER 5   COURT'S POWER TO APPOINT A RECEIVER

33.22 Application of the CPR

Part 69 of the CPR applies to proceedings under this Part.

CHAPTER 6   ORDERS TO OBTAIN INFORMATION FROM JUDGMENT DEBTORS

33.23 Application of the CPR

Part 71 of the CPR applies to proceedings under this Part.

CHAPTER 7 THIRD PARTY DEBT ORDERS

33.24 Application of the CPR

(1) Part 72 of the CPR applies to proceedings under this Part with the following modifications.
(2) In rule 72.4–
  (a) in paragraph (1), for 'a judge' there is substituted 'the court'; and
  (b) in paragraph (2), for 'judge' there is substituted 'court'.
(3) In rule 72.7, in paragraph (2)(a), after 'the Royal Courts of Justice' insert ', or the principal registry'.
(4) Rule 72.10 is omitted.

CHAPTER 8 CHARGING ORDER, STOP ORDER, STOP NOTICE

33.25 Application of the CPR

(1) Part 73 of the CPR applies to proceedings under this Part with the following modifications.
(2) In rule 73.1, paragraph (2), sub-paragraphs (b) and (c) are omitted.
(3) For rule 73.2, there is substituted 'This Section applies to an application by a judgment creditor for a charging order under section 1 of the 1979 Act.'.
(4) In rule 73.3, paragraph (2), sub-paragraphs (b) and (c) are omitted.
(5) In rule 73.4–
  (a) in paragraph (1), for 'a judge' there is substituted 'the court,'; and
  (b) in paragraph (2), for 'judge' there is substituted 'court'.
(6) In rule 73.9, in the parenthesis after paragraph (1)–
  (a) 'and regulation 51.4 of the 1992 Regulations' is omitted;
  (b) for 'provides' there is substituted 'provide', and
  (c) ', or (where the 1992 Regulations apply) of the authority,' is omitted.
(7) In rule 73.10–
  (a) in paragraph (1), for 'a claim' there is substituted 'an application';
  (b) in paragraph (2) and the parenthesis following it, for 'A claim' each time it appears there is substituted 'An application';
  (c) in paragraph (3), for 'claimant' there is substituted 'applicant';
  (d) in paragraph (4), for 'claim form' there is substituted 'application'; and
  (e) in paragraph (5), for 'claimants'' there is substituted 'applicant's'.
(8) In rule 73.11, 'funds in court or' is omitted.
(9) In rule 73.12–
  (a) paragraph (1)(a) is omitted;
  (b) in paragraph (1)(b) 'other than securities held in court' is omitted;
  (c) in paragraph (2), in sub-paragraph (b), for 'claim form' there is substituted 'application notice'; and
  (d) in paragraph (3)–
    (i) 'or claim form' is omitted; and
    (ii) for sub-paragraph (b) there is substituted 'the person specified in rule 73.5(1)(d)'.
(10) Rule 73.13 is omitted.
(11) In rule 73.14, in paragraph (1), 'other than securities held in court' is omitted.
(12) In rule 73.16–
  (a) in paragraph (a) for '; and' there is substituted '.'; and

(b) paragraph (b) is omitted.

PART 34 RECIPROCAL ENFORCEMENT OF MAINTENANCE ORDERS

34.1 Scope and interpretation of this Part

(1) This Part contains rules about the reciprocal enforcement of maintenance orders.

(2) In this Part—

'the 1920 Act' means the Maintenance Orders (Facilities for Enforcement) Act 1920;

'the 1972 Act' means the Maintenance Orders (Reciprocal Enforcement) Act 1972;

'the 1982 Act' means the Civil Jurisdiction and Judgments Act 1982;

'the 1988 Convention' means the Convention on jurisdiction and the enforcement of judgments in civil and commercial matters done at Lugano on 16th September 1988;

'the Judgments Regulation' means Council Regulation (EC) No. 44/2001 of 22nd December 2000 on jurisdiction and the recognition and enforcement of judgments in civil and commercial matters; and

'the Lugano Convention' means the Convention on jurisdiction and the recognition and enforcement of judgments in civil and commercial matters, between the European Community and the Republic of Iceland, the Kingdom of Norway, the Swiss Confederation and the Kingdom of Denmark signed on behalf of the European Community on 30th October 2007.

(3) Chapter 1 of this Part relates to the enforcement of maintenance orders in accordance with the 1920 Act.

(4) Chapter 2 of this Part relates to the enforcement of maintenance orders in accordance with Part 1 of the 1972 Act.

(5) Chapter 3 of this Part relates to the enforcement of maintenance orders in accordance with—

(a) the 1982 Act;
(b) the Judgments Regulation; and
(c) the Lugano Convention.

34.2 Meaning of prescribed officer in a magistrates' court

(1) For the purposes of the 1920 Act, the prescribed officer in relation to a magistrates' court is the designated officer for that court.

(2) For the purposes of Part 1 of the 1972 Act and section 5(2) of the 1982 Act, the prescribed officer in relation to a magistrates' court is the justices' clerk for the local justice area in which the court is situated.

34.3 Registration of maintenance orders in magistrates' courts in England and Wales

Where a magistrates' court is required by any of the enactments referred to in rule 34.1(2) to register a foreign order the court officer must—

(a) enter and sign a memorandum of the order in the register kept in accordance with rules made under section 144 of the Magistrates' Courts Act 1980; and

(b) state on the memorandum the statutory provision under which the order is registered.

CHAPTER 1 ENFORCEMENT OF MAINTENANCE ORDERS UNDER THE MAINTENANCE ORDERS (FACILITIES FOR ENFORCEMENT) ACT 1920

34.4 Interpretation

(1) In this Chapter–

'payer', in relation to a maintenance order, means the person liable to make the payments for which the order provides; and

'reciprocating country' means a country or territory to which the 1920 Act extends.

(2) In this Chapter, an expression defined in the 1920 Act has the meaning given to it in that Act.

34.5 Confirmation of provisional orders made in a reciprocating country

(1) This rule applies where, in accordance with section 4(1) of the 1920 Act, the court officer receives a provisional maintenance order.
(2) The court must fix the date, time and place for a hearing.
(3) The court officer must register the order in accordance with rule 34.3.
(4) The court officer must serve on the payer–

   (a) certified copies of the provisional order and accompanying documents; and
   (b) a notice–

       (i) specifying the time and date fixed for the hearing; and
       (ii) stating that the payer may attend to show cause why the order should not be confirmed.

(5) The court officer must inform–

   (a) the court which made the provisional order; and
   (b) the Lord Chancellor,

   whether the court confirms, with or without modification, or decides not to confirm, the order.

34.6 Payment of sums due under registered orders

Where an order made by a reciprocating country is registered in a magistrates' court, the court must order payments due to be made to the court officer.

(Practice Direction 34A contains further provisions relating to the payment of sums due under registered orders.)

34.7 Enforcement of sums due under registered orders

(1) This rule applies to–

   (a) an order made in a reciprocating country which is registered in a magistrates' court; and
   (b) a provisional order made in a reciprocating country which has been confirmed by a magistrates' court.

(2) The court officer must–

   (a) collect the monies due under the order in the same way as for a magistrates' court maintenance order; and
   (b) send the monies collected to–

       (i) the court in the reciprocating country which made the order; or
       (ii) such other person or authority as that court or the Lord Chancellor may from time to time direct.

(3) The court officer may take proceedings in that officer's own name for enforcing payment of monies due under the order.

34.8 Prescribed notice for the taking of further evidence

(1) This rule applies where a court in a reciprocating country has sent a provisional order to a magistrates' court for the purpose of taking further evidence.
(2) The court officer must send a notice to the person who applied for the provisional order specifying–
   (a) the further evidence required; and
   (b) the time and place fixed for taking the evidence.

34.9 Transmission of maintenance orders made in a reciprocating country to the High Court

A maintenance order to be sent by the Lord Chancellor to the High Court in accordance with section 1(1) of the 1920 Act will be–

(a) sent to the senior district judge who will register it in the register kept for the purpose of the 1920 Act; and
(b) filed in the principal registry.

34.10 Transmission of maintenance orders made in the High Court to a reciprocating country

(1) This rule applies to maintenance orders made in the High Court.
(2) An application for a maintenance order to be sent to a reciprocating country under section 2 of the 1920 Act must be made in accordance with this rule.
(3) The application must be made to a district judge in the principal registry unless paragraph (4) applies.
(4) If the order was made in the course of proceedings in a district registry, the application may be made to a district judge in that district registry.
(5) The application must be–
   (a) accompanied by a certified copy of the order; and
   (b) supported by a record of the sworn written evidence.
(6) The written evidence must give–
   (a) the applicant's reason for believing that the payer resides in the reciprocating country;
   (b) such information as the applicant has as to the whereabouts of the payer; and
   (c) such other information as may be set out in Practice Direction 34A.

34.11 Inspection of the register in the High Court

(1) A person may inspect the register and request copies of a registered order and any document filed with it if the district judge is satisfied that that person is entitled to, or liable to make, payments under a maintenance order made in–
   (a) the High Court; or
   (b) a court in a reciprocating country.
(2) The right to inspect the register referred to in paragraph (1) may be exercised by–
   (a) a solicitor acting on behalf of the person entitled to, or liable to make, the payments referred to in that paragraph; or
   (b) with the permission of the district judge, any other person.

CHAPTER 2 ENFORCEMENT OF MAINTENANCE ORDERS UNDER PART 1 OF THE 1972 ACT

34.12 Interpretation

(1) In this Chapter–
- (a) 'reciprocating country' means a country to which Part 1 of the 1972 Act extends; and
- (b) 'relevant court in the reciprocating country' means, as the case may be–
  - (i) the court which made the order which has been sent to England and Wales for confirmation;
  - (ii) the court which made the order which has been registered in a court in England and Wales;
  - (iii) the court to which an order made in England and Wales has been sent for registration; or
  - (iv) the court to which a provisional order made in England and Wales has been sent for confirmation.

(2) In this Chapter, an expression defined in the 1972 Act has the meaning given to it in that Act.

(3) In this Chapter, 'Hague Convention Countries' means the countries listed in Schedule 1 to the Reciprocal Enforcement of Maintenance Orders (Hague Convention Countries) Order 1973.

34.13 Scope

(1) Section 1 of this Chapter contains rules relating to the reciprocal enforcement of maintenance orders under Part 1 of the 1972 Act.

(2) Section 2 of this Chapter modifies the rules contained in Section 1 of this Chapter in their application to–
- (a) the Republic of Ireland;
- (b) the Hague Convention Countries; and
- (c) the United States of America.

(Practice Direction 34A sets out in full the rules for the Republic of Ireland, the Hague Convention Countries and the United States of America as modified by Section 2 of this Chapter.)

SECTION 1
Reciprocal enforcement of maintenance orders under Part 1 of the 1972 Act

34.14 Application for transmission of maintenance order to reciprocating country

An application for a maintenance order to be sent to a reciprocating country under section 2 of the 1972 Act must be made in accordance with Practice Direction 34A.

34.15 Certification of evidence given on provisional orders

A document setting out or summarising evidence is authenticated by a court in England and Wales by a certificate signed, as the case may be, by–

(a) one of the justices; or
(b) the District Judge (Magistrates' Courts),

before whom that evidence was given.

(Section 3(5)(b), 5(4) and 9(5) of the 1972 Act require a document to be authenticated by the court.)

34.16 Confirmation of a provisional order made in a reciprocating country

(1) This rule applies to proceedings for the confirmation of a provisional order made in a reciprocating country.
(2) Paragraph (3) applies on receipt by the court of–
   (a)   a certified copy of the order; and
   (b)   the documents required by the 1972 Act to accompany the order.
(3) On receipt of the documents referred to in paragraph (2)–
   (a)   the court must fix the date, time and place for a hearing or a directions appointment; and
   (b)   the court officer must send to the payer notice of the date, time and place fixed together with a copy of the order and accompanying documents.
(4) The date fixed for the hearing must be not less than 21 days beginning with the date on which the court officer sent the documents to the payer in accordance with paragraph (2).
(5) The court officer will send to the relevant court in the reciprocating country a certified copy of any order confirming or refusing to confirm the provisional order.
(6) This rule does not apply to the confirmation of a provisional order made in a reciprocating country varying a maintenance order to which sections 5(5) or 9(6) of the 1972 Act applies.

(Section 5(5) and 7 of the 1972 Act provide for proceedings for the confirmation of a provisional order.)

(Provision in respect of confirmation of a provisional order varying a maintenance order under the 1972 Act is in rules made under section 144 of the Magistrates' Courts Act 1980).

(Rule 34.22 provides for the transmission of documents to a court in a reciprocating country.)

34.17 Consideration of revocation of a provisional order made by a magistrates' court

(1) This rule applies where–
   (a)   a magistrates' court has made a provisional order by virtue of section 3 of the 1972 Act;
   (b)   before the order is confirmed, evidence is taken by the court or received by it as set out in section 5(9) of the 1972 Act; and
   (c)   on consideration of the evidence the court considers that the order ought not to have been made.

(Section 5(9) of the 1972 Act provides that a magistrates' court may revoke a provisional order made by it, before the order has been confirmed in a reciprocating country, if it receives new evidence.)

(2) The court officer must serve on the person who applied for the provisional order ('the applicant') a notice which must–
   (a)   set out the evidence taken or received by the court;
   (b)   inform the applicant that the court considers that the order ought not to have been made; and
   (c)   inform the applicant that the applicant may–
      (i)   make representations in relation to that evidence either orally or in writing; and

(ii) adduce further evidence.
(3) If an applicant wishes to adduce further evidence–
- (a) the applicant must notify the court officer at the court which made the order;
- (b) the court will fix a date for the hearing of the evidence; and
- (c) the court officer will notify the applicant in writing of the date fixed.

34.18 Notification of variation or revocation of a maintenance order by the High Court or a county court

(1) This rule applies where–
- (a) a maintenance order has been sent to a reciprocating country in pursuance of section 2 of the 1972 Act; and
- (b) the court makes an order, not being a provisional order, varying or revoking that order.

(2) The court officer must send a certified copy of the order of variation or revocation to the relevant court in the reciprocating country.

(Rule 34.22 provides for the transmission of documents to a court in a reciprocating country.)

34.19 Notification of confirmation or revocation of a maintenance order by a magistrates' court

(1) This rule applies where a magistrates' court makes an order–
- (a) not being a provisional order, revoking a maintenance order to which section 5 of the 1972 Act applies;
- (b) under section 9 of the 1972 Act, revoking a registered order; or
- (c) under section 7(2) of the 1972 Act, confirming an order to which section 7 of that Act applies.

(2) The court officer must send written notice of the making, revocation or confirmation of the order, as appropriate, to the relevant court in the reciprocating country.

(3) This rule does not apply to a provisional order varying a maintenance order to which sections 5 or 9 of the 1972 Act apply.

(Section 5 of the 1972 Act applies to a provisional order made by a magistrates' court in accordance with section 3 of that Act which has been confirmed by a court in a reciprocating country.)

(Provision in respect of notification of variation of a maintenance order by a magistrates' court under the 1972 Act is made in rules made under section 144 of the Magistrates' Courts Act 1980.)

(Rule 34.22 provides for the transmission of documents to a court in a reciprocating country.)

34.20 Taking of evidence for court in reciprocating country

(1) This rule applies where a request is made by or on behalf of a court in a reciprocating country for the taking of evidence for the purpose of proceedings relating to a maintenance order to which Part 1 of the 1972 Act applies.

(Section 14 of the 1972 Act makes provision for the taking of evidence needed for the purpose of certain proceedings.)

(2) The High Court has power to take the evidence where–
- (a) the request for evidence relates to a maintenance order made by a superior court in the United Kingdom; and

    (b)   the witness resides in England and Wales.
(3) The county court has power to take the evidence where–
    (a)   the request for evidence relates to a maintenance order made by a county court; and
    (b)   the maintenance order has not been registered in a magistrates' court under the 1958 Act.
(4) The following magistrates' courts have power to take the evidence, that is–
    (a)   where the proceedings in the reciprocating country relate to a maintenance order made by a magistrates' court, the court which made the order;
    (b)   where the proceedings relate to an order which is registered in a magistrates' court, the court in which the order is registered; and
    (c)   a magistrates' court to which the Secretary of State sends the request to take evidence.
(5) A magistrates' court not mentioned in paragraph (4) has power to take the evidence if the magistrates' court which would otherwise have that power consents because the evidence could be taken more conveniently.
(6) The evidence is to be taken in accordance with Part 22.

34.21 Request for the taking of evidence by a court in a reciprocating country

(1) This rule applies where a request is made by a magistrates' court for the taking of evidence in a reciprocating country in accordance with section 14(5) of the 1972 Act.
(2) The request must be made in writing to the court in the reciprocating country.

(Rule 34.22 provides for the transmission of documents to a court in a reciprocating country.)

34.22 Transmission of documents

(1) This rule applies to any document, including a notice or request, which is required to be sent to a court in a reciprocating country by–
    (a)   Part 1 of the 1972 Act; or
    (b)   Section 1 of Chapter 2 of this Part of these rules.
(2) The document must be sent to the Lord Chancellor for transmission to the court in the reciprocating country.

34.23 Method of payment under registered orders

(1) Where an order is registered in a magistrates' court in accordance with section 6(3) of the 1972 Act, the court must order that the payment of sums due under the order be made–
    (a)   to the court officer for the registering court; and
    (b)   at such time and place as the court officer directs.

(Section 6(3) of the 1972 Act makes provision for the registration of maintenance orders made in a reciprocating country.)

(2) Where the court orders payments to be made to the court officer, whether in accordance with paragraph (1) or otherwise, the court officer must send the payments–
    (a)   by post to either–
        (i)   the court which made the order; or
        (ii)   such other person or authority as that court, or the Lord Chancellor, directs; or

(b) if the court which made the order is a country or territory specified in the Practice Direction 34A–
  (i) to the Crown Agents for Overseas Governments and Administrations for transmission to the person to whom they are due; or
  (ii) as the Lord Chancellor directs.

(Practice Direction 34A contains further provisions relating to the payment of sums due under registered orders.)

34.24 Enforcement of payments under registered orders

(1) This rule applies where a court has ordered periodical payments under a registered maintenance order to be made to the court officer.
(2) The court officer must take reasonable steps to notify the payee of the means of enforcement available.
(3) Paragraph (4) applies where periodical payments due under a registered order are in arrears.
(4) The court officer, on that officer's own initiative–
  (a) may; or
  (b) if the sums due are more than 4 weeks in arrears, must,

proceed in that officer's own name for the recovery of the sums due unless of the view that it is unreasonable to do so.

34.25 Notification of registration and cancellation

(1) The court officer must send written notice to the Lord Chancellor of the due registration of orders registered in accordance with section 6(3), 7(5), or 10(4) of the 1972 Act.
(2) The court officer must, when registering an order in accordance with section 6(3), 7(5), 9(10), 10(4) or (5) or 23(3) of the 1972 Act, send written notice to the payer stating–
  (a) that the order has been registered;
  (b) that payments under the order should be made to the court officer; and
  (c) the hours during which and the place at which the payments should be made.
(3) The court officer must, when cancelling the registration of an order in accordance with section 10(1) of the 1972 Act, send written notice of the cancellation to the payer.

SECTION 2
Modification of rules in Section 1 of this Chapter

SUB-SECTION 1
REPUBLIC OF IRELAND

34.26 Application of Section 1 of this Chapter to the Republic of Ireland

(1) In relation to the Republic of Ireland, Section 1 of this Chapter has effect as modified by this rule.
(2) A reference in this rule and in any rule which has effect in relation to the Republic of Ireland by virtue of this rule to–
  (a) the 1972 Act is a reference to the 1972 Act as modified by Schedule 2 to the Reciprocal Enforcement of Maintenance Orders (Republic of Ireland) Order 1993; and
  (b) a section under the 1972 Act is a reference to the section so numbered in the 1972 Act as so modified.
(3) A reference to a reciprocating country in rule 34.12(1) and Section 1 of this Chapter is a reference to the Republic of Ireland.

(4) In the words in brackets at the end of rule 34.15 (certification of evidence given on provisional orders), for the sections mentioned substitute 'section 3(5)(b) or 5(3)'.
(5) Rules 34.16 (confirmation of provisional orders) and 34.21 (request for the taking of evidence by a court in a reciprocating country) do not apply.
(6) For rule 34.17 (consideration of revocation of a provisional order made by a magistrates' court) substitute–

> '34.17 **Consideration of confirmation of a provisional order made by a magistrates' court**
>
> (1) This rule applies where–
>> (a) a magistrates' court has made a provisional order by virtue of section 3 of the 1972 Act;
>> (b) the payer has made representations or adduced evidence to the court; and
>> (c) the court has fixed a date for the hearing at which it will consider confirmation of the order.
>
> (2) The court officer must serve on the applicant for the provisional order–
>> (a) a copy of the representations or evidence; and
>> (b) written notice of the date fixed for the hearing.'.

(7) For rules 34.18 and 34.19 (notification of variation or revocation) substitute–

> '34.18 **Notification of variation or revocation of a maintenance order by the High Court**
>
> Where the High Court makes an order varying or revoking an order to which section 5 of the 1972 Act applies the court officer must send–
>
> (a) a certified copy of the order of variation or revocation; and
> (b) a statement as to the service on the payer of the documents mentioned in section 5(3) of the 1972 Act,
>
> to the court in the Republic of Ireland.
>
> (Rule 34.22 provides for the transmission of documents to a court in a reciprocating country.)
>
> 34.19 **Notification of revocation of a maintenance order by a magistrates' court**
>
> Where a magistrates' court makes an order revoking an order to which section 5 of the 1972 Act applies, the court officer must send written notice of the making of the order to the Lord Chancellor.
>
> (Section 5 of the 1972 Act applies to a maintenance order sent to the Republic of Ireland in accordance with section 2 of that Act and a provisional order made by a magistrates' court in accordance with section 3 of that Act which has been confirmed by such a court.)
>
> (Provision in respect of notification of variation of a maintenance order by magistrates' court under the 1972 Act is made in rules made under section 144 of the Magistrates' Courts Act 1980.)'.

(8) For rule 34.23(2) (method of payment under registered orders), substitute–

> '(2) Where the court orders payment to be made to the court officer, the court officer must send the payments by post–
>> (a) to the payee under the order; or

(b) where a public authority has been authorised by the payee to receive the payments, to that public authority.'.

(9) For rule 34.24 (enforcement of payments under registered orders), substitute–

'**34.24 Enforcement of payments under registered orders**

(1) This rule applies where periodical payments under a registered order are in arrears.
(2) The court officer must, on the written request of the payee, proceed in that officer's own name for the recovery of the sums due unless of the view that it is unreasonable to do so.
(3) If the sums due are more than 4 weeks in arrears the court officer must give the payee notice in writing of that fact stating the particulars of the arrears.'.

(10) For rule 34.25 (notification of registration and cancellation) substitute–

'**34.25 Notification of registration and cancellation**

The court officer must send written notice to–

(a) the Lord Chancellor, on the due registration of an order under section 6(3) or 10(4) of the 1972 Act; and
(b) to the payer under the order, on–
 (i) the registration of an order under section 10(4) of the 1972 Act; or
 (ii) the cancellation of the registration of an order under section 10(1) of that Act.'.

(11) After rule 34.25 insert–

'**34.25A Other notices under section 6 of the 1972 Act**

(1) A notice required under section 6(6) or (10) of the 1972 Act must be in the form referred to in a practice direction.
(2) Where a magistrates' court sets aside the registration of an order following an appeal under section 6(7) of the 1972 Act, the court officer must send written notice of the court's decision to the payee.

(Section 6(6) of the 1972 Act provides for notice of registration in a United Kingdom court of a maintenance order made in the Republic of Ireland, and section 6(10) of that Act for notice that a maintenance order made in the Republic of Ireland has not been registered in a United Kingdom court.)'

SUB-SECTION 2
HAGUE CONVENTION COUNTRIES

34.27 Application of Section 1 of this Chapter to the Hague Convention Countries

(1) In relation to the Hague Convention Countries, Section 1 of this Chapter has effect as modified by this rule.
(2) A reference in this rule, and in any rule which has effect in relation to the Hague Convention Countries by virtue of this rule to–
 (a) the 1972 Act is a reference to the 1972 Act as modified by Schedule 2 to the Reciprocal Enforcement of Maintenance Orders (Hague Convention Countries) Order 1993; and
 (b) a section under the 1972 Act is a reference to the section so numbered in the 1972 Act as so modified.
(3) A reference to a reciprocating country in rule 34.12(1) and Section 1 of this Chapter is a reference to a Hague Convention Country.

(4) Rules 34.15 (certification of evidence given on provisional orders), 34.16 (confirmation of provisional orders), 34.19 (notification of confirmation or revocation of a maintenance order by a magistrates' court) and 34.21 (request for the taking of evidence by a court in a reciprocating country) do not apply.
(5) For rule 34.17 (consideration of revocation of a provisional order made by a magistrates' court) substitute–

> '34.17 **Consideration of revocation of a maintenance order made by a magistrates' court**
>
> (1) This rule applies where–
>> (a) an application has been made to a magistrates' court by a payee for the revocation of an order to which section 5 of the 1972 Act applies; and
>> (b) the payer resides in a Hague Convention Country.
>
> (2) The court officer must serve on the payee, by post, a copy of any representations or evidence adduced by or on behalf of the payer.
>
> (Provision relating to consideration of variation of a maintenance order made by a magistrates' court to which section 5 of the 1972 Act applies is made in rules made under section 144 of the Magistrates' Courts Act 1980.)'.

(6) For rule 34.18 (notification of variation or revocation of a maintenance order by the High Court or county court) substitute–

> '34.18 **Notification of variation or revocation of a maintenance order by the High Court or a county court**
>
> (1) This rule applies if the High Court or a county court makes an order varying or revoking a maintenance order to which section 5 of the 1972 Act applies.
>
> (2) If the time for appealing has expired without an appeal having been entered, the court officer will send to the Lord Chancellor–
>> (a) the documents required by section 5(8) of the 1972 Act; and
>> (b) a certificate signed by the district judge stating that the order of variation or revocation is enforceable and no longer subject to the ordinary forms of review.
>
> (3) A party who enters an appeal against the order of variation or revocation must, at the same time, give written notice to the court officer.'.

(7) For rule 34.23(2) (method of payment under registered orders) substitute–

> '(2) Where the court orders payment to be made to the court officer, the court officer must send the payments by post to the payee under the order.'.

(8) For rule 34.25 (notification of registration and cancellation) substitute–

> '34.25 **Notification of registration and cancellation**
>
> The court officer must send written notice to–
>> (a) the Lord Chancellor, on the due registration of an order under section 10(4) of the 1972 Act; and
>> (b) the payer under the order, on–
>>> (i) the registration of an order under section 10(4) of the 1972 Act; or
>>> (ii) the cancellation of the registration of an order under section 10(1) of the 1972 Act.'.

(9) After rule 34.25 insert–

'34.25A   General provisions as to notices

(1)   A notice to a payer of the registration of an order in a magistrates' court in accordance with section 6(3) of the 1972 Act must be in the form referred to in a practice direction.

(Section 6(8) of the 1972 Act requires notice of registration to be given to the payer.)

(2)   If the court sets aside the registration of a maintenance order following an appeal under section 6(9) of the 1972 Act, the court officer must send written notice of the decision to the Lord Chancellor.

(3)   A notice to a payee that the court officer has refused to register an order must be in the form referred to in a practice direction.

(Section 6(11) of the 1972 Act requires notice of refusal of registration to be given to the payee.)

(4)   Where, under any provision of Part 1 of the 1972 Act, a court officer serves a notice on a payer who resides in a Hague Convention Country, the court officer must send to the Lord Chancellor a certificate of service.'.

SUB-SECTION 3
UNITED STATES OF AMERICA

34.28   Application of Section 1 of this Chapter to the United States of America

(1)   In relation to the United States of America, Section 1 of this Chapter has effect as modified by this rule.

(2)   A reference in this rule and in any rule which has effect in relation to the United States of America by virtue of this rule to–

(a)   the 1972 Act is a reference to the 1972 Act as modified by Schedule 1 to the Reciprocal Enforcement of Maintenance Orders (United States of America) Order 2007; and

(b)   a section under the 1972 Act is a reference to the section so numbered in the 1972 Act as so modified.

(3)   A reference to a reciprocating country in rule 34.12(1) and Section 1 of this Chapter is a reference to the United States of America.

(4)   Rules 34.15 (certification of evidence given on provisional orders), 34.16 (confirmation of provisional orders), 34.19 (notification of confirmation or revocation of a maintenance order made by a magistrates' court) and 34.21 (request for the taking of evidence in a reciprocating country) do not apply.

(5)   For rule 34.17 (consideration of revocation of a provisional order made by a magistrates' court) substitute–

'34.17   Consideration of revocation of a maintenance order made by a magistrates' court

(1)   This rule applies where–

(a)   an application has been made to a magistrates' court by a payee for the revocation of an order to which section 5 of the 1972 Act applies; and

(b)   the payer resides in the United States of America.

(2)   The court officer must serve on the payee by post a copy of any representations or evidence adduced by or on behalf of the payer.

(Provision relating to consideration of variation of a maintenance order made by a magistrates' court to which section 5 of the 1972 Act applies is made in rules made under section 144 of the Magistrates' Courts Act 1980.)'.

(6)   For rule 34.18 (notification of variation or revocation), substitute–

'34.18 Notification of variation or revocation

If the High Court or a county court makes an order varying or revoking a maintenance order to which section 5 of the 1972 Act applies, the court officer will send to the Lord Chancellor the documents required by section 5(7) of that Act.'.

(7) For 34.23(2)(method of payment under registered orders) substitute–

'(2) Where the court orders payment to be made to the court officer, the court officer must send the payments by post to the payee under the order.'.

(8) For rule 34.25 (notification of registration and cancellation) substitute–

'34.25 Notification of registration and cancellation

The court officer must send written notice to–

(a) the Lord Chancellor, on the due registration of an order under section 10(4) of the 1972 Act; or
(b) the payer under the order, on–
    (i) the registration of an order under section 10(4) of the 1972 Act; or
    (ii) the cancellation of the registration of an order under section 10(1) of that Act.'.

CHAPTER 3 ENFORCEMENT OF MAINTENANCE ORDERS UNDER THE CIVIL JURISDICTION AND JUDGMENTS ACT 1982, THE JUDGMENTS REGULATION AND THE LUGANO CONVENTION

SECTION 1
Registration and Enforcement in a Magistrates' Court of Maintenance Orders made in a Contracting State to the 1968 Convention, a Contracting State to the 1988 Convention, a Regulation State or a State bound by the Lugano Convention

34.29 Interpretation

In this Section–

(a) an expression defined in the 1982 Act has the meaning given to it in that Act; and
(b) 'the 1958 Act' means the Maintenance Orders Act 1958.

34.30 Registration of maintenance orders

(1) In this rule, 'assets to which the 1958 Act applies' means assets against which, after registration in the High Court, the maintenance order could be enforced under Part 1 of the 1958 Act.

(2) This rule applies where the court officer for a magistrates' court receives–

(a) an application under Article 31 of the 1968 Convention for the enforcement of a maintenance order made in a Contracting State other than the United Kingdom;
(b) an application under Article 31 of the 1988 Convention for the enforcement of a maintenance order made in a State bound by the 1988 Convention other than a Member State of the European Union;
(c) an application under Article 38 of the Judgments Regulation for the enforcement of a maintenance order made in a Regulation State other than the United Kingdom; or
(d) an application under Article 38 of the Lugano Convention for the enforcement

of a maintenance order made in a State bound by the Lugano Convention other than a Member State of the European Union.

(3) The court officer must–
   (a) take such steps as appear appropriate for ascertaining whether the payer resides within the local justice area for which the court acts; and
   (b) consider any available information as to the nature and location of the payer's assets.

(4) If the court officer is satisfied that the payer–
   (a) does not reside within the local justice area for which the court acts; and
   (b) does not have assets to which the 1958 Act applies,

the court officer must refuse the application and return the application to the Lord Chancellor stating the information the court officer has as to the whereabouts of the payer and the nature and location of the payer's assets.

(5) If the court officer is satisfied that the payer–
   (a) does not reside within the local justice area for which the court acts; but
   (b) has assets to which the 1958 Act applies,

then either–
   (i) the court officer must register the order; or
   (ii) if the court officer believes that the payer is residing within the local justice area in which another magistrates' court acts, the court officer may refuse the application and return the documents to the Lord Chancellor with the information referred to in paragraph (4) above.

(6) Except where paragraphs (4) or (5) apply, the court officer must register the order unless–
   (a) in the case of an application under Article 31 of the 1968 Convention, Articles 27 or 28 of that Convention apply; and
   (b) in the case of an application under Article 31 of the 1988 Convention, Articles 27 or 28 of that Convention apply.

(7) If the court officer refuses to register an order to which this rule relates the court officer must notify the applicant.

(8) If the court officer registers an order the court officer must send written notice of that fact to–
   (a) the Lord Chancellor;
   (b) the payer; and
   (c) the applicant.

(9) If the court officer considers that it would be appropriate for all or part of a registered order to be enforced in the High Court the court officer must notify the applicant–
   (a) that the court officer so considers it appropriate; and
   (b) that the applicant may apply under the 1958 Act for the order to be registered in the High Court.

34.31 Appeal from a decision relating to registration

(1) This rule applies to an appeal under–
   (a) Article 36 or Article 40 of the 1968 Convention;
   (b) Article 36 or Article 40 of the 1988 Convention;
   (c) Article 43 of the Judgments Regulation; or
   (d) Article 43 of the Lugano Convention.

(2) The appeal must be to the magistrates' court–

(a) in which the order is registered; or
(b) in which the application for registration has been refused,

as the case may be.

34.32 Payment of sums due under a registered order

(1) Where an order is registered in accordance with section 5(3) of the 1982 Act or Article 38 of the Judgments Regulation or Article 38 of the Lugano Convention, the court must order that payment of sums due under the order be made–

(a) to the court officer for the registering court; and
(b) at such time and place as the court officer directs.

(2) Where the court orders payments to be made to the court officer, whether in accordance with paragraph (1) or otherwise, the court officer must send the payments by post either–

(a) to the court which made the order; or
(b) to such other person or authority as that court, or the Lord Chancellor, directs.

(Practice Direction 34A contains further provisions relating to the payment of sums due under registered orders.)

34.33 Enforcement of payments under registered orders

(1) This rule applies where a court has ordered periodical payments under a registered maintenance order to be made to the court officer for a magistrates' court.
(2) The court officer must take reasonable steps to notify the payee of the means of enforcement available.
(3) Paragraph (4) applies where periodical payments due under a registered order are in arrears.
(4) The court officer, on that officer's own initiative–

(a) may; or
(b) if the sums due are more than 4 weeks in arrears, must,

proceed in that officer's own name for the recovery of the sums due unless of the view that it is unreasonable to do so.

34.34 Variation and revocation of registered orders

(1) This rule applies where the court officer for a registering court receives notice that a registered maintenance order has been varied or revoked by a competent court in a Contracting State to the 1968 Convention, a Contracting State to the 1988 Convention (other than a Member State of the European Union), a Regulation State or a State bound by the Lugano Convention, other than a Member State of the European Union.
(2) The court officer for the registering court must–

(a) register the order of variation or revocation; and
(b) send notice of the registration by post to the payer and payee under the order.

34.35 Transfer of registered order

(1) This rule applies where the court officer for the court where an order is registered considers that the payer is residing within the local justice area in England and Wales for which another magistrates' court acts.
(2) Subject to paragraph (4), the court officer must transfer the order to the other court by sending to that court–

(a) the information and documents relating to the registration;
(b) a certificate of arrears, if applicable, signed by the court officer;

- (c) a statement giving such information as the court officer possesses as to the whereabouts of the payer and the nature and location of the payer's assets; and
- (d) any other relevant documents which the court officer has relating to the case.

(3) The information and documents referred to in paragraph (2)(a) are those required, as appropriate, under–

- (a) Articles 46 and 47 of the 1968 Convention;
- (b) Articles 46 and 47 of the 1988 Convention;
- (c) Article 53 of the Judgments Regulation; or
- (d) Article 53 of the Lugano Convention.

(4) If an application is pending in the registering court for the registration of the whole or part of the order in the High Court under Part 1 of the 1958 Act, the court officer must not transfer the order, or the part to which the application relates, under paragraph (2).

(5) The court officer must give notice of the transfer of an order to–

- (a) the payee; and
- (b) the Lord Chancellor.

(6) If an order is transferred, the court officer for the court to which it is transferred must register the order.

34.36 Cancellation of registered orders

(1) Where the court officer for the registering court–

- (a) has no reason to transfer a registered order under rule 34.35; and
- (b) considers that the payer under the registered order is not residing within the local justice area for which the court acts and has no assets to which the 1958 Act applies,

the court officer must cancel the registration of the order.

(2) The court officer must–

- (a) give notice of cancellation to the payee; and
- (b) send the information and documents relating to the registration and the other documents referred to in rule 34.35(2) to the Lord Chancellor.

SECTION 2
Reciprocal enforcement in a Contracting State or Regulation State of Orders of a court in England and Wales

34.37 Application in a magistrates' court for a maintenance order, or revocation of a maintenance order, to which the 1982 Act, the Judgments Regulations or the Lugano Convention applies

(1) This rule applies where a person applies to a magistrates' court for a maintenance order, or for the revocation of a maintenance order, in relation to which the court has jurisdiction by virtue of the 1982 Act, the Judgments Regulation or the Lugano Convention, and the respondent is outside the United Kingdom.

(2) On the making of the application the court officer shall send the following documents to the Lord Chancellor–

- (a) notice of the proceedings, including a statement of the grounds of the application;
- (b) a statement signed by the court officer giving such information as he has regarding the whereabouts of, and information to assist in identifying, the respondent; and
- (c) where available, a photograph of the respondent.

(3) In considering whether or not to make a maintenance order pursuant to an application to which paragraph (1) applies, where the respondent does not appear and is not represented at the hearing the court shall take into account any written representations made and any evidence given by the respondent under these rules.

(Part 27 makes provision relating to attendance at hearings and directions appointments.)

(Part 9 makes provision for applications relating to financial remedies including those under Schedule 1 to the 1989 Act, Part 1 of the 1978 Act, and Schedule 6 to the 2004 Act.)

(Rules made under section 144 of the Magistrates' Courts Act 1980 make provision for applications to vary maintenance orders made in magistrates' courts.)

34.38 Admissibility of Documents

(1) This rule applies to a document, referred to in paragraph (2) and authenticated in accordance with paragraph (3), which comprises, records or summarises evidence given in, or information relating to, proceedings in a court in another part of the UK , another Contracting State to the 1968 Convention or the 1988 Convention, Regulation State or State bound by the Lugano Convention, and any reference in this rule to 'the court', without more, is a reference to that court.

(2) The documents referred to at paragraph (1) are documents which purport to–

    (a)   set out or summarise evidence given in the court;

    (b)   have been received in evidence the court;

    (c)   set out or summarise evidence taken in the court for the purpose of proceedings in a court in England and Wales to which the 1982 Act applies; or

    (d)   record information relating to payments made under an order of the court.

(3) A document to which paragraph (1) applies shall, in any proceedings in a magistrates' court in England and Wales relating to a maintenance order to which the 1982 Act applies, be admissible as evidence of any fact stated in it to the same extent as oral evidence of that fact is admissible in those proceedings.

(4) A document to which paragraph (1) applies shall be deemed to be authenticated–

    (a)   in relation to the documents listed at paragraph 2(a) or (c), if the document purports to be–

        (i)   certified by the judge or official before whom the evidence was given or taken; or

        (ii)   the original document recording or summarising the evidence, or a true copy of that document;

    (b)   in relation to a document listed at paragraph (2)(b), if the document purports to be certified by a judge or official of the court to be, or to be a true copy of, the document received in evidence; and

    (c)   in relation to the document listed at paragraph (2)(d), if the document purports to be certified by a judge or official of the court as a true record of the payments made under the order.

(5) It shall not be necessary in any proceedings in which evidence is to be received under this rule to prove the signature or official position of the person appearing to have given the certificate referred to in paragraph (4).

(6) Nothing in this rule shall prejudice the admission in evidence of any document which is admissible in evidence apart from this rule.

(7) Any request by a magistrates' court in England and Wales for the taking or providing of evidence by a court in another part of the United Kingdom or in another Contracting State to the 1968 Convention or the 1988 Convention or the Lugano Convention (other than a Member State of the European Union) for the purpose of proceedings to which the 1982 Act applies shall be communicated in writing to the court in question.

(Chapter 2 of Part 24 makes provision for taking of evidence by a court in another Regulation State).

34.39 Enforcement of orders of a magistrates' court

(1) This rule applies to applications to a magistrates' court under–

    (a)   section 12 of the 1982 Act;
    (b)   article 54 of the Judgments Regulation; or
    (c)   article 54 of the Lugano Convention.

(2) A person who wishes to enforce in a Contracting State to the 1968 Convention, a Contracting State to the 1988 Convention (other than a Member State of the European Union), a Regulation State or a State bound by the Lugano Convention (other than a Member State of the European Union) a maintenance order obtained in a magistrates' court must apply for a certified copy of the order.

(3) An application under this rule must be made in writing to the court officer and must specify–

    (a)   the names of the parties to the proceedings;
    (b)   the date, or approximate date, of the proceedings in which the maintenance order was made and the nature of those proceedings;
    (c)   the Contracting State or Regulation State in which the application for recognition or enforcement has been made or is to be made; and
    (d)   the postal address of the applicant.

(4) The court officer must, on receipt of the application, send a copy of the order to the applicant certified in accordance with a practice direction.

(5) Paragraph (6) applies where–

    (a)   a maintenance order is registered in a magistrates' court in England and Wales; and
    (b)   a person wishes to obtain a certificate giving details of any payments made or arrears accrued under the order while it has been registered, for the purposes of an application made or to be made in connection with that order in–

        (i)   another Contracting State to the 1968 Convention;
        (ii)   another Contracting State to the 1988 Convention (other than a Member State of the European Union);
        (iii)   another Regulation State;
        (iv)   another State bound by the Lugano Convention (other than a Member State of the European Union); or
        (v)   another part of the United Kingdom.

(6) The person wishing to obtain the certificate referred to in paragraph (5) may make a written application to the court officer for the registering court.

(7) On receipt of an application under paragraph (6) the court officer must send to the applicant a certificate giving the information requested.

(Rule 74.12 (application for certified copy of a judgment) and 74.13 (evidence in support) of the CPR apply in relation to the application for a certified copy of a judgment obtained in the High Court or a county court.)

PART 35   MEDIATION DIRECTIVE

35.1 Scope and Interpretation

(1) This Part applies to mediated cross-border disputes that are subject to Directive 2008/52/EC of the European Parliament and of the Council of 21 May 2008 on certain aspects of mediation in civil and commercial matters ('the Mediation Directive').

(2) In this Part–

'cross-border dispute' has the meaning given by article 2 of the Mediation Directive;

'mediation' has the meaning given by article 3(a) of the Mediation Directive;

'mediation administrator' means a person involved in the administration of the mediation process;

'mediation evidence' means evidence regarding information arising out of or in connection with a mediation process;

'mediator' has the meaning given by article 3(b) of the Mediation Directive; and

'relevant dispute' means a cross-border dispute that is subject to the Mediation Directive.

35.2 Relevant disputes: applications for consent orders in respect of financial remedies

(1) This rule applies in relation to proceedings for a financial remedy where the applicant, with the explicit consent of the respondent, wishes to make an application that the content of a written agreement resulting from mediation of a relevant dispute be made enforceable by being made the subject of a consent order.

(2) The court will not include in a consent order any matter which is contrary to the law of England and Wales or which is not enforceable under that law.

(3) The applicant must file two copies of a draft of the order in the terms sought.

(4) Subject to paragraph (5), the application must be supported by evidence of the explicit consent of the respondent.

(5) Where the respondent has written to the court consenting to the making of the order sought, the respondent is deemed to have given explicit consent to the order and paragraph (4) does not apply.

(6) Paragraphs (1)(b) and (2) to (6) of rule 9.26 apply to an application to which this rule applies.

35.3 Mediation evidence: disclosure and inspection

(1) Where a party to proceedings seeks disclosure or inspection of mediation evidence that is in the control of a mediator or mediation administrator, that party must first obtain the court's permission to seek the disclosure or inspection, by an application made in accordance with Part 18.

(2) The mediator or mediation administrator who has control of the mediation evidence must be named as a respondent to the application and must be served with a copy of the application notice.

(3) Evidence in support of the application must include evidence that–

(a) all parties to the mediation agree to the disclosure or inspection of the mediation evidence;

(b) disclosure or inspection of the mediation evidence is necessary for overriding considerations of public policy, in accordance with article 7(1)(a) of the Mediation Directive; or

(c) the disclosure of the content of an agreement resulting from mediation is necessary to implement or enforce that agreement.

(4) Where this rule applies, Parts 21 to 24 apply to the extent they are consistent with this rule.

35.4 Mediation evidence: witnesses and depositions

(1) This rule applies where a party wishes to obtain mediation evidence from a mediator or mediation administrator by–

(a) a witness summons;

(b)　　cross-examination with permission of the court under rule 22.8 or 23.4;
　　　(c)　　an order under rule 24.7 (evidence by deposition);
　　　(d)　　an order under rule 24.9 (enforcing attendance of witness);
　　　(e)　　an order under rule 24.10(4) (deponent's evidence to be given orally); or
　　　(f)　　an order under rule 24.12 (order for the issue of a letter of request).
(2) When applying for a witness summons, permission under rule 22.8 or 23.4 or order under rule 24.7, 24.9, 24.10(4) or 24.12, the party must provide the court with evidence that–
　　　(a)　　all parties to the mediation agree to the obtaining of the mediation evidence;
　　　(b)　　obtaining the mediation evidence is necessary for overriding considerations of public policy in accordance with article 7(1)(a) of the Mediation Directive; or
　　　(c)　　the disclosure of the content of an agreement resulting from mediation is necessary to implement or enforce that agreement.
(3) When considering a request for a witness summons, permission under rule 22.8 or 23.4 or order under rule 24.7, 24.9, 24.10(4) or 24.12, the court may invite any person, whether or not a party, to make representations.
(4) Where this rule applies, Parts 21 to 24 apply to the extent they are consistent with this rule.

PART 36　TRANSITIONAL ARRANGEMENTS AND PILOT SCHEMES

36.1　Transitional provisions

Practice Direction 36A shall make provision for the extent to which these rules shall apply to proceedings started before the day on which they come into force.

36.2　Pilot schemes

Practice directions may modify or disapply any provision of these rules–

(a) for specified periods; and
(b) in relation to proceedings in specified courts,

during the operation of pilot schemes for assessing the use of new practices and procedures in connection with proceedings.

GLOSSARY

Scope

This glossary is a guide to the meaning of certain legal expressions as used in these rules, but it does not give the expressions any meaning in the rules which they do not otherwise have in the law.

Expression	Meaning
Affidavit	A written, sworn, statement of evidence.
Cross-examination	Questioning of a witness by a party other than the party who called the witness.
Evidence in chief	The evidence given by a witness for the party who called him.

Expression	Meaning
Injunction	A court order prohibiting a person from doing something or requiring a person to do something.
Official copy	A copy of an official document, supplied and marked as such by the office which issued the original.
Pre-action protocol	Statements of best practice about pre-action conduct which have been approved by the President of the Family Division and which are annexed to a Practice Direction.
Privilege	The right of a party to refuse to disclose a document or produce a document or to refuse to answer questions on the ground of some special interest recognised by law.
Seal	A seal is a mark which the court puts on document to indicate that the document has been issued by the court.
Service	Steps required by rules of court to bring documents used in court proceedings to a person's attention.
Set aside	Cancelling a judgment or order or a step taken by a party in the proceedings.
Stay	A stay imposes a halt on proceedings, apart from the taking of any steps allowed by the rules or the terms of the stay. Proceedings can be continued if a stay is lifted.
Strike out	Striking out means the court ordering written material to be deleted so that it may no longer be relied upon.
Without prejudice	Negotiations with a view to settlement are usually conducted 'without prejudice' which means that the circumstances in which the content of those negotiations may be revealed to the court are very restricted.

Appendix 2
PRACTICE DIRECTIONS

PRACTICE DIRECTION 2A – FUNCTIONS OF THE COURT IN THE FAMILY PROCEDURE RULES 2010 AND PRACTICE DIRECTIONS WHICH MAY BE PERFORMED BY A SINGLE JUSTICE OF THE PEACE

This Practice Direction supplementing the Family Procedure Rules 2010 is made by the President of the Family Division under the powers delegated to him by the Lord Chief Justice under Schedule 2, Part 1, paragraph 2(2) of the Constitutional Reform Act 2005, and is approved by the Parliamentary Under Secretary of State, by authority of the Lord Chancellor.

This Practice Direction comes into force on 6th April 2011

This Practice Direction supplements FPR Part 2, rule 2.5(1)(c)(ii) (Power to perform functions conferred on the court by these rules and practice directions)

1.1 Where the FPR or a practice direction provide for the court to perform any function, that function may be performed by a single justice of the peace who is a member of a family panel except that such a justice cannot perform the functions listed in:

(a) column 2 of Table 1 in accordance with the rules listed in column 1; and
(b) column 2 of Table 2 in accordance with the paragraph of the practice direction listed in column 1.

1.2 For the avoidance of doubt, unless a rule, practice direction or other enactment provides otherwise, a single justice cannot make the decision of a magistrates' court at the final hearing of an application for a substantive order. For example, a single justice cannot make a residence order on notice, placement order, adoption or care order. However, a single justice can discharge the functions of a family proceedings court under the statutory provisions listed in rule 2.6 of the FPR.

Table 1

Rule	Nature of function
4.1(3)(g)	Stay the whole or part of any proceedings or judgment either generally or until a specified date or event.
4.1(3)(l)	Exclude an issue from consideration.
4.1(3)(m)	Dismiss or give a decision on an application after a decision on a preliminary issue.
4.1(4)(a)	When the court makes an order, making that order subject to conditions.
4.1(6)	Varying and revoking an order (other than directions which the court has made).
4.3(1)	Ability of the court to make orders (other than directions) of its own initiative.

Rule	Nature of function
4.4, 4.5 and 4.6	All the powers of a magistrates' court under these rules (power to strike out statement of case, sanctions have effect unless defaulting party obtains relief from sanctions).
8.20(4)	A direction that a child should be made a respondent to the application for a declaration of parentage under section 55A of the Family Law Act 1986, except where the parties consent to the child being made a respondent.
9.11(2)	Direction that a child be separately represented on an application.
9.22	All the powers of a magistrates' court under this rule (relating to proceedings by or against a person outside England and Wales for variation or revocation of orders under section 20 of the 1978 Act or paragraphs 30 to 34 of Schedule 6 to the 2004 Act).
12.3(2)	Where the person with parental responsibility is a child, a direction for that child be made a party, except where the parties consent to that child being made a party.
12.3(3)	Direction that a child be made a party to proceedings or that a child who is a party be removed, except where the parties consent to the child being made a party or to the removal of that party.
12.3(4)	Consequential directions following the addition or removal of a party except where a single justice is able to make such a direction under rule 12.3(2) and (3).
12.61(1) and (2)	Considering the transfer of proceedings to the court of another member state, directions in relation to the manner in which parties may make representations and power to deal with question of transfer without a hearing with the consent of parties.
12.64(1)	Exercising court's powers under Article 15 of the Council Regulation or Article 8 of the 1996 Hague Convention.
12.68(1)	Staying the proceedings.
12.68(3)	Giving reasons for the court's decision, making a finding of fact and stating a finding of fact where such a finding has been made.
12.70(1)	Contemplating the placement of a child in another member state.
12.70(3)	Sending request directly to the central authority or other authority having jurisdiction in the other Member State.
12.70(4)	Sending request to Central Authority for England and Wales for onward transmission.
12.70(5)	Considering the documents which should accompany the request.
13.3(3)	Where the person with parental responsibility is a child, a direction for that child be made a party, except where the parties consent to that child being made a party.
13.3(4)	Direction that a child be made a party to proceedings or that a child who is a party be removed, except where the parties consent to the child being made a party or to the removal of that party.
13.3(5)	Consequential directions following the addition or removal of a party except where a single justice is able to make such a direction under rule 13.3(3) and (4).

Practice Directions 349

Rule	Nature of function
13.9(7)	Variation or revocation of direction following transfer, except where a single justice would be able to make the direction in question under rule 13.9(1).
13.15(3)	Determination of the probable date of the child's birth.
13.20(1)	Specifying a later date by which a parental order takes effect.
14.3(2)	Direction that a child be made a respondent, except where the parties consent to the child being made a respondent.
14.3(3)(b)	Direction that a child who is a party be removed, except where the parties consent to the child being made a respondent.
14.3(4)	Consequential directions following the addition or removal of a party except where a single justice is able to make such a direction under rule 14.3(2) and (3)
14.8(3)	Any of the directions listed in PD14B in proceedings for– (a) a Convention adoption order (b) a section 84 order (c) a section 88 direction (d) a section 89 order; or (e) an adoption order where section 83(1) of the 2002 Act applies (restriction on bringing children in)
14.16(8)	Making an adoption order under section 50 of the 2002 Act after personal attendance of one only of the applicants if there are special circumstances.
14.16(9)	Not making a placement order unless the legal representative of the applicant attends the final hearing.
14.17(4)	Determination of the probable date of the child's birth.
14.25(1)	Specifying a later date by which an order takes effect.
15.3(1)	Permission to a person to take steps before the protected party has a litigation friend.
15.3(2)	Permission to a party to take steps (where during proceedings a person lacks capacity to continue to conduct proceedings) before the protected party has a litigation friend.
15.3(3)	Making an order that a step taken before a protected party has a litigation friend has effect.
15.6(1)	Making an order appointing a person as a litigation friend.
15.6(6)	Court may not appoint a litigation friend unless it is satisfied that the person complies with the conditions in rule 15.4(3).
15.7	Direction that a person may not act as a litigation friend, termination of an appointment, appointment of a litigation friend in substitution for an existing one.
16.2	Power of court to make a child a party to proceedings if it considers it is in the best interests of the child to do so.
16.6(3)(a)	Permission to a child to conduct proceedings without a children's guardian or litigation friend.
16.6(6)	Power of the court to grant an application under paragraph (3)(a) or (5) if the court considers that the child has sufficient understanding to conduct the proceedings.

Rule	Nature of function
16.6(7)	Power of the court to require the litigation friend or children's guardian to take such part in proceedings (referred to in paragraph (6)) as the court directs.
16.6(8)	Power of the court to revoke permission granted under paragraph (3) in specified circumstances.
16.6(10)	Power of the court, in specified circumstances, to appoint a person to be the child's litigation friend or children's guardian.
16.8(2)	Permission to a person to take steps before the child has a litigation friend.
16.8(3)	Making an order that a step taken before the child has a litigation friend has effect.
16.11(1)	Making an order appointing a person as a litigation friend.
16.12	Direction that a person may not act as a litigation friend, termination of an appointment, appointment of a litigation friend in substitution for an existing one.
16.23(2)	Permission to a person to take steps before the child has a children's guardian.
18.3(1)(c)	Direction that a child be a respondent to an application under Part 18.
18.9(1)(a)	Power of court to deal with a Part 18 application without a hearing.
18.12	Power of the court to proceed in absence of a party, except where a single justice has the power to make the relevant order applied for.
19.8(2)	The court's power to require or permit a party to give oral evidence at the hearing.
21.3	Power of court relating to withholding inspection or disclosure of a document.
22.1(2) to (4)	Power to exclude evidence that would otherwise be admissible, power to permit a party to adduce evidence, or to seek to rely on a document, in respect of which that party has failed to comply with requirements of Part 22 and power to limit cross examination.
22.6	Court's powers relating to use at final hearing of witness statements which have been served.
22.12	Power of court to require evidence by affidavit instead of or in addition to a witness statement.
22.15(4)	Permission for a party to amend or withdraw any admission made by that party on such terms as the court thinks just.
22.20(3)(a)	Permission for a witness statement in proceedings in the magistrates' court under Part 9 to be used for a purpose other than the proceedings in which it is served.
24.16(2)	Ordering the issue of a request to a designated court.
24.16(5)	Order for the submission of a request under article 17 of the Taking of Evidence Regulation.

Rule	Nature of function
27.10(1)(b)	Direction that proceedings to which the Rules apply will not be held in private, expect that a single justice may give such a direction in relation to a hearing which that single justice is conducting.
27.11(2)(g)	Power of the court to permit any other person to be present during any hearing, except that a single justice may give such permission in relation to a hearing which that single justice is conducting.
27.11(3)	Direction that persons within rule 27.11(2)(f) shall not attend the proceedings or any part of them.
Part 28	Powers of the court to make costs orders including wasted costs orders under section 145A of the Magistrates' Courts Act 1980.
29.8(1)	Court's opinion that it would be prevented b section 8 or 9 of the Child Support Act 1991 from making an order.
29.8(2)	Court's consideration of the matter without a hearing.
29.8(10)	Power of the court to determine that it would be prevented by sections 8 or 9 of the 1991 Act from making an order, and to dismiss the application.
29.8(11)	The court must give written reasons for its decision.
29.9(2)	Direction that the document will be treated as if it contained the application and directions as the court considers appropriate as to the subsequent conduct of the proceedings.
29.13(1)	Direction for a court officer not to serve a copy of an order (other than directions that the single justice has made) to every party affected by it.
29.15	Specifying alternative date for an order to take effect, except an order which the single justice has made.
29.16	Correcting an accidental slip or omission in an order, except where that order was made by a single justice.
Part 30	Any power of the magistrates' court (where it is the lower court) to grant or refuse permission to appeal except where a single justice has the power to make the order which is subject to the appeal.
31.9	Power for court to stay the proceedings.

Table 2

Practice Direction: Family Assistance Orders dated 3 September 2007 – Paragraphs 2, 3, and 5	Under paragraph 2 the court must have obtained the opinion of the appropriate officer about whether it would be in the best interests of the child in question for a family assistance order to be made and, if so, how the family assistance order could operate and for what period. Under paragraph 3 the court decides on the category of officer required to be made available under the family assistance order. Under paragraph 5 the court must give to the person it proposes to name in the order an opportunity to comment.
Public Law Proceedings Guide to Case Management: 6th April 2010 – Paragraphs 8.1 to 8.5	Under paragraphs 8.1 to 8.5 determination by the court of issues as to whether an adult party or intended party to proceedings lacks capacity.
Practice Direction: Residence and Contact Orders: Domestic Violence and Harm: 14 January 2009 – Paragraphs 17, 18, 21 to 23, 28 and 29	Under paragraph 17 the court will consider whether a child who is the subject of an application should be made a party to proceedings. Under paragraph 18 the court will consider whether an interim order for residence or contact is in the best interests of the child. Under paragraphs 21–23, 27, 28 and 29 determinations of the court at fact finding hearings, in cases where a finding of domestic violence is made consideration of the conduct of the parents and where there has been a finding of domestic violence court directions or conditions on orders.
Practice Direction: Attendance of Media Representatives at Hearings in Family Proceedings dated 6 April 2009	Generally – court's discretion to exclude media representatives from attending hearings or part of hearings for 'relevant proceedings' as defined in rule 1 of the Family Proceedings Courts (Children Act 1989) Rules 1991 (other than where a Single Justice or Justice's Clerk is conducting the hearing)

PD 14B – The First Directions Hearing – adoptions with a Foreign Element – Paragraph 2	Under paragraph 2 the court's consideration of:
	(a) whether the requirements of the Adoption and Children Act 2002 and the Adoptions with a Foreign Element Regulations 2005 (SI 2005/392) appear to have been complied with and, if not, consider whether or not it is appropriate to transfer the case to the High Court;
	(b) whether all relevant documents are translated into English and, if not, fix a timetable for translating any outstanding documents;
	(c) whether the applicant needs to file an affidavit setting out the full details of the circumstances in which the child was brought to the United Kingdom, of the attitude of the parents to the application and confirming compliance with the requirements of The Adoptions with a Foreign Element Regulations 2005; and
	(d) give directions about:
	  (i) the production of the child's passport and visa;
	  (ii) the need for the Official Solicitor and a representative of the Home office to attend future hearings; and
	  (iii) personal service on the parents (via the Central Authority in the case of an application for a Convention Adoption Order) including information about the role of the Official Solicitor and availability of legal aid to be represented within the proceedings; and
	(e) consider fixing a further directions no later than 6 weeks after the date of the first directions appointment and timetable a date by which the Official Solicitor should file an interim report in advance of that further appointment.

PD 15A – Protected Parties – Paragraph 4.2(b)	Under paragraph 4.2 (b) court directions on service on protected party.

PD16A – Representation of Children – Paragraphs 6.8 and 7.5	Under paragraph 6.8 the children's guardian must – (a) unless the court otherwise directs, file a written report advising on the interests of the child in accordance with the timetable set by the court; and (b) in proceedings to which Part 14 applies, where practicable, notify any person the joining of whom as a party to those proceedings would be likely, in the opinion of the children's guardian, to safeguard the interests of the child, of the court's power to join that person as a party under rule 14.3 and must inform the court (i) of any notification; (ii) of anyone whom the child's guardian attempted to notify under this paragraph but was unable to contact; and (iii) of anyone whom the children's guardian believes may wish to be joined to the proceedings Under paragraph 7.5 the court may, at the same time as deciding whether to join the child as a party, consider whether the proceedings should be transferred to another court taking into account the provisions of Part 3 of the Allocation and Transfer of Proceedings Order 2008.
PD18A – Other Applications in Proceedings Paragraphs 4.1 to 4.4(a)	Under paragraph 4.1 on receipt of an application notice containing a request for a hearing, unless the court considers that the application is suitable for consideration without a hearing, the court officer will, if serving a copy of the application notice, notify the applicant of the time and date fixed for the hearing of the application. Under paragraph 4.2 on receipt of an application notice containing a request that the application be dealt with without a hearing, the court will decide whether the application is suitable for consideration without a hearing. Under paragraph 4.3 where the court considers that the application is suitable for consideration without a hearing but is not satisfied that it has sufficient material to decide the application immediately it may give directions for the filing of evidence and will inform the applicant and the respondent(s) of its decision. Under paragraph 4.4 (a) where the court does not consider that the application is suitable for consideration without a hearing it may give directions as to the filing of evidence.

PD22A – Written Evidence Paragraphs 1.6, 14.1 and 14.2	Under paragraph 1.6 the court may give a direction under rule 22.12 that evidence shall be given by affidavit instead of or in addition to a witness statement on its own initiative; or after any party has applied to the court for such a direction. Under paragraph 14.1 where an affidavit, a witness statement or an exhibit to either an affidavit or a witness statement does not comply with Part 22 or PD 22A in relation to its form, the court may refuse to admit it as evidence and may refuse to allow the costs arising from its preparation. Under paragraph 14.2 permission to file a defective affidavit or witness statement or to use a defective exhibit may be obtained from the court where the case is proceeding.
PD 24A – Witnesses, Depositions and Taking of Evidence in Member States of the European Union – Paragraph 9.1 and 9.6	Under paragraph 9.1 where a person wishes to take a deposition from a person in another Regulation State, the court where proceedings are taking place may order the issue of a request to the designated court in the Regulation State (rule 24.16(2)). The form of request is prescribed as Form A in the Taking of Evidence Regulation. Under paragraph 9.6 Article 17 permits the court where proceedings are taking place to take evidence directly from a deponent in another Regulation State if the conditions of the article are satisfied. Direct taking of evidence can only take place of evidence is given voluntarily without the need for coercive measures. Rule 24.16(5) provides for the court to make an order for the submission of a request to take evidence directly. The form of request is Form I annexed to the Taking of Evidence Regulation and rule 24.16(6) makes provision for a draft of this form to be filed by the a party seeking the order. An application for an order under rule 24.16(5) should be by application notice in accordance with Part 18.

PRACTICE DIRECTION 3A – PRE-APPLICATION PROTOCOL FOR MEDIATION INFORMATION AND ASSESSMENT

This Practice Direction supplementing the Family Procedure Rules 2010 is made by the President of the Family Division under the powers delegated to him by the Lord Chief Justice under Schedule 2, Part 1 paragraph 2(2) of the Constitutional Reform Act 2005. and is approved by the Parliamentary Under Secretary of State, by authority of the Lord Chancellor.

This Practice Direction comes into force on 6th April 2011

This Practice Direction supplements FPR Part 3

1. **Introduction**

1.1 This Practice Direction applies where a person is considering applying for an order in family proceedings of a type specified in Annex B (referred to in this Direction as 'relevant family proceedings').

1.2 Terms used in this Practice Direction and the accompanying Pre-action Protocol have the same meaning as in the FPR.

1.3 This Practice Direction is supplemented by the following Annexes:

   (i) Annex A: The Pre-application Protocol ('the Protocol'), which sets out steps which the court will normally expect an applicant to follow before an application is made to the court in relevant family proceedings;

   (ii) Annex B: Proceedings which are 'relevant family proceedings' for the purposes of this Practice Direction; and

   (iii) Annex C: Circumstances in which attendance at a Mediation Information and Assessment Meeting is not expected.

2. **Aims**

2.1 The purpose of this Practice Direction and the accompanying Protocol is to:

   (a) supplement the court's powers in Part 3 of the FPR to encourage and facilitate the use of alternative dispute resolution;

   (b) set out good practice to be followed by any person who is considering making an application to court for an order in relevant family proceedings; and

   (c) ensure, as far as possible, that all parties have considered mediation as an alternative means of resolving their disputes.

3. **Rationale**

3.1 There is a general acknowledgement that an adversarial court process is not always best suited to the resolution of family disputes, particularly private law disputes between parents relating to children, with such disputes often best resolved through discussion and agreement, where that can be managed safely and appropriately.

3.2 Litigants who seek public funding for certain types of family proceedings are (subject to some exceptions) already required to attend a meeting with a mediator as a precondition of receiving public funding.

3.3 There is growing recognition of the benefits of early information and advice about mediation and of the need for those wishing to make an application to court, whether publicly-funded or otherwise, to consider alternative means of resolving their disputes, as appropriate.

3.4 In private law proceedings relating to children, the court is actively involved in helping parties to explore ways of resolving their dispute. The Private Law Programme, set out in Practice Direction 12B, provides for a first hearing dispute resolution appointment ('FHDRA'), at which the judge, legal advisor or magistrates, accompanied by an officer from Cafcass (the Children and Famliy Court Advisory and Support Service), will discuss with parties both the nature of their dispute and whether it could be resolved by mediation or other alternative means and can give the parties information about services which may be available to assist them. The court should also have information obtained through safeguarding checks carried out by Cafcass, to ensure that any agreement between the parties, or any dispute resolution process selected, is in the interests of the child and safe for all concerned.

3.5 Against that background, it is likely to save court time and expense if the parties take steps to resolve their dispute without pursuing court proceedings. Parties will therefore be expected to explore the scope for resolving their dispute through mediation before embarking on the court process.

4. The Pre-application Protocol

4.1 To encourage this approach, all potential applicants for a court order in relevant family proceedings will be expected, before making their application, to have followed the steps set out in the Protocol. This requires a potential applicant except in certain specified circumstances, to consider with a mediator whether the dispute may be capable of being resolved through mediation. The court will expect all applicants to have compiled with the Protocol before commencing proceedings and (except where any of the circumstances in Annex C applies) will expect any respondent to have attended a Mediation Information and Assessment Meeting, if invited to do so. If court proceedings are taken, the court will wish to know at the first hearing whether mediation has been considered by the parties. In considering the conduct of any relevant family proceedings, the court will take into account any failure to comply with the Protocol and may refer the parties to a meeting with a mediator before the proceedings continue further.

4.2 Nothing in the Protocol is to be read as affecting the operation of the Private Law Programme, set out in Practice Direction 12B, or the role of the court at the first hearing in any relevant family proceedings.

ANNEX A – THE PRE-APPLICATION PROTOCOL

1. This Protocol applies where a person ('the applicant') is considering making an application to the court for an order in relevant family proceedings.
2. Before an applicant makes an application to the court for an order in relevant family proceedings, the applicant (or the applicant's legal representative) should contact a family mediator to arrange for the applicant to attend an information meeting about family mediation and other forms of alternative dispute resolution (referred to in this Protocol as 'a Mediation Information and Assessment Meeting').
3. An applicant is not expected to attend a Mediation Information and Assessment Meeting where any of the circumstances set out in Annex C applies.
4. Information on how to find a family mediator may be obtained from local family courts, from the Community Legal Advice Helpline – CLA Direct (0845 345 4345) or at www.direct.gov.uk.
5. The applicant (or the applicant's legal representative) should provide the mediator with contact details for the other party or parties to the dispute ('the respondent(s)'), so that the mediator can contact the respondent(s) to discuss that party's willingness and availability to attend a Mediation Information and Assessment Meeting.
6. The applicant should then attend a Mediation Information and Assessment Meeting arranged by the mediator. If the parties are willing to attend together. the meeting may be conducted jointly, but where necessary separate meetings may be held. If the applicant and respondent(s) do not attend a joint meeting, the mediator will invite the respondent(s) to a separate meeting unless any of the circumstances set out in Annex C applies.
7. A mediator who arranges a Mediation Information and Assessment Meeting with one or more parties to a dispute should consider with the party or parties concerned whether public funding may be available to meet the cost of the meeting and any subsequent mediation. Where none of the parties is eligible for, or wishes to seek, public funding, any charge made by the mediator for the Mediation Information and Assessment Meeting will be the responsibility of the party or parties attending, in accordance with any agreement made with the mediator.
8. If the applicant then makes an application to the court in respect of the dispute, the applicant should at the same time file a completed Family Mediation Information and Assessment Form (Form FM1) confirming attendance at a Mediation Information and Assessment Meeting or giving the reasons for not attending.
9. The Form FM1, must be completed and signed by the mediator, and countersigned by the applicant or the applicant's legal representative, where either

(a) the applicant has attended a Mediation Information and Assessment Meeting; or

(b) the applicant has not attended a Mediation Information and Assessment Meeting and

   (i) the mediator is satisfied that mediation is not suitable because another party to the dispute is unwilling to attend a Mediation Information and Assessment Meeting and consider mediation;

   (ii) the mediator determines that the case is not suitable for a Mediation Information and Assessment Meeting; or

   (iii) a mediator has made a determination within the previous four months that the case is not suitable for a Mediation Information and Assessment Meeting or for mediation.

10. In all other circumstances, the Form FM1 must be completed and signed by the applicant or the applicant's legal representative.
11. The form may be obtained from magistrates' courts, county courts or the High Court or from www.direct.gov.uk.

ANNEX B – PROCEEDINGS WHICH ARE 'RELEVANT FAMILY PROCEEDINGS' FOR THE PURPOSES OF THIS PRACTICE DIRECTION

1. Private law proceedings relating to children, except:

   - proceedings for an enforcement order, a financial compensation order or an order under paragraph 9 or Part 2 of Schedule A1 to the Children Act 1989;
   - any other proceedings for enforcement of an order made in private law proceedings; or
   - where emergency proceedings have been brought in respect of the same child(ren) and have not been determined.

   ('Private law proceedings' and 'emergency proceedings' are defined in Rule 12.2)

2. Proceedings for a financial remedy, except:

   - Proceedings for an avoidance of disposition order or an order preventing a disposition;
   - Proceedings for enforcement of any order made in financial remedy proceedings.

   ('Financial remedy' is defined in Rule 2.3(1) and 'avoidance of disposition order' and 'order preventing a disposition' are defined in Rule 9.3(1))

ANNEX C – A PERSON CONSIDERING MAKING AN APPLICATION TO THE COURT IN RELEVANT FAMILY PROCEEDINGS IS NOT EXPECTED TO ATTEND A MEDIATION INFORMATION AND ASSESSMENT MEETING BEFORE DOING SO IF ANY OF THE FOLLOWING CIRCUMSTANCES APPLIES:

1. The mediator is satisfied that mediation is not suitable because another party to the dispute is unwilling to attend a Mediation Information and Assessment Meeting and consider mediation.
2. The mediator determines that the case is not suitable for a Mediation Information and Assessment Meeting.
3. A mediator has made a determination within the previous four months that the case is not suitable for a Mediation Information and Assessment Meeting or for mediation.
4. Domestic abuse

Any party has, to the applicant's knowledge, made an allegation of domestic Violence against another party and this has resulted in a police investigation or the issuing of civil proceedings for the protection of any party within the last 12 months.
5. Bankruptcy

   The dispute concerns financial issues and the applicant or another party is bankrupt.
6. The parties are in agreement and there is no dispute to mediate.
7. The whereabouts of the other party are unknown to the applicant.
8. The prospective application is for an order in relevant family proceedings which are already in existence and are continuing.
9. The prospective application is to be made without notice to the other party.
10. Urgency

    The prospective application is urgent, meaning:

    (a) there is a risk to the life, liberty or physical safety of the applicant or his or her family or his or her home; or
    (b) any delay caused by attending a Mediation Information and Assessment Meeting would cause a risk of significant harm to a child, a significant risk of a miscarriage of justice, unreasonable hardship to the applicant or irretrievable problems in dealing with the dispute (such as an irretrievable loss of significant evidence).
11. There is current social services involvement as a result of child protection concerns in respect of any child who would be the subject of the prospective application.
12. A child would be a party to the prospective application by virtue of Rule 12.3(1).
13. The applicant (or the applicant's legal representative) contacts three mediators within 15 miles of the applicant's home and none is able to conduct a Mediation Information and Assessment Meeting within 15 working days of the date of contact.

PRACTICE DIRECTION 4A – STRIKING OUT A STATEMENT OF CASE

This Practice Direction supplements FPR Part 4, rule 4.4 (Power to strike out a statement of case)

Introduction

1.1 Rule 4.4 enables the court to strike out the whole or part of a statement of case which discloses no reasonable grounds for bringing or defending the application (rule 4.4(1)(a)), or which is an abuse of the process of the court or otherwise likely to obstruct the just disposal of the proceedings (rule 4.4(1)(b)). These powers may be exercised on an application by a party or on the court's own initiative.

1.2 This practice direction sets out the procedure a party should follow to make an application for an order under rule 4.4.

Examples of cases within the rule

2.1 The following are examples of cases where the court may conclude that an application falls within rule 4.4(1)(a)–

   (a) those which set out no facts indicating what the application is about;
   (b) those which are incoherent and make no sense;
   (c) those which contain a coherent set of facts but those facts, even if true, do not disclose any legally recognisable application against the respondent.

2.2 An application may fall within rule 4.4(1)(b) where it cannot be justified, for example because it is frivolous, scurrilous or obviously ill-founded.

2.3 An answer may fall within rule 4.4(1)(a) where it consists of a bare denial or otherwise sets out no coherent statement of facts.

2.4 A party may believe that it can be shown without the need for a hearing that an opponent's case has no real prospect of success on the facts, or that the case is bound to succeed or fail, as the case may be, because of a point of law (including the construction of a document). In such a case the party concerned may make an application under rule 4.4.

2.5 The examples set out above are intended only as illustrations.

2.6 Where a rule, practice direction or order states 'shall be struck out or dismissed' or 'will be struck out or dismissed' this means that the order striking out or dismissing the proceedings will itself bring the proceedings to an end and that no further order of the court is required.

Applications which appear to fall within rule 4.4(1)(a) or (b)

3.1 A court officer who is asked to issue an application form but believes the application may fall within rule 4.4(1)(a) or (b) should issue the application form, but may then consult the court (under rule 4.2) before returning the form to the applicant or taking any other step to serve the respondent. The court may of its own initiative make an immediate order designed to ensure that the application is disposed of or (as the case may be) proceeds in a way that accords with the rules.

3.2 The court may allow the applicant a hearing before deciding whether to make such an order.

3.3 Orders the court may make include–

(a) an order that the application be stayed until further order;
(b) an order that the application form be retained by the court and not served until the stay is lifted;
(c) an order that no application by the applicant to lift the stay be heard unless the applicant files such further documents (for example a witness statement or an amended application form) as may be specified in the order.

3.4 Where the court makes any such order or, subsequently, an order lifting the stay, it may give directions about the service on the respondent of the order and any other documents on the court file.

3.5 The fact that the court allows an application referred to it by a court officer to proceed does not prejudice the right of any party to apply for any order against the applicant.

Answers which appear to fall within rule 4.4(1)(a) or (b)

4.1 A court officer may similarly consult the court about any document filed which purports to be an answer and which the officer believes may fall within rule 4.4 (1)(a) or (b).

4.2 If the court decides that the document falls within rule 4.4(1)(a) or (b) it may on its own initiative make an order striking it out. Where the court does so it may extend the time for the respondent to file a proper answer.

4.3 The court may allow the respondent a hearing before deciding whether to make such an order.

4.4 Alternatively the court may make an order requiring the respondent within a stated time to clarify the answer or to give additional information about it. The order may provide that the answer will be struck out if the respondent does not comply.

4.5 The fact that the court does not strike out an answer on its own initiative does not prejudice the right of the applicant to apply for any order against the respondent.

General provisions

5.1 The court may exercise its powers under rule 4.4(1)(a) or (b) on application by a party to the proceedings or on its own initiative at any time.

5.2 Where the court at a hearing strikes out all or part of a party's statement of case it may enter such judgment for the other party as that party appears entitled to.

Applications for orders under rule 4.4(1)

6.1 Attention is drawn to Part 18 (Procedure for Other Applications in Proceedings) and to the practice direction that supplements it. The practice direction requires all applications to be made as soon as possible.

6.2 While many applications under rule 4.4(1) can be made without evidence in support, the applicant should consider whether facts need to be proved and, if so, whether evidence in support should be filed and served.

PRACTICE DIRECTION 4B – CIVIL RESTRAINT ORDERS

This Practice Direction supplements FPR rule 4.8

Introduction

1.1 This practice direction applies where the court is considering whether to make–

    (a)   a limited civil restraint order;
    (b)   an extended civil restraint order; or
    (c)   a general civil restraint order,

against a party who has made applications which are totally without merit.

Rules 4.3(7), 4.4(5) and 18.13 provide that where a statement of case or application is struck out or dismissed and is totally without merit, the court order must specify that fact and the court must consider whether to make a civil restraint order. Rule 30.11(5) makes similar provision where the appeal court refuses an application for permission to appeal, strikes out an appellant's notice or dismisses an appeal.

The powers of the court to make civil restraint orders are separate from and do not replace the powers given to the court by section 91(14) of the Children Act 1989.

Limited civil restraint orders

2.1 A limited civil restraint order may be made by a judge of the High Court or a county court where a party has made 2 or more applications which are totally without merit.

2.2 Where the court makes a limited civil restraint order, the party against whom the order is made–

    (a)   will be restrained from making any further applications in the proceedings in which the order is made without first obtaining the permission of a judge identified in the order;
    (b)   may apply for amendment or discharge of the order, but only with the permission of a judge identified in the order; and
    (c)   may apply for permission to appeal the order and if permission is granted, may appeal the order.

2.3 Where a party who is subject to a limited civil restraint order–

    (a)   makes a further application in the proceedings in which the order is made without first obtaining the permission of a judge identified in the order, such application will automatically be dismissed–

        (i)   without the judge having to make any further order; and
        (ii)   without the need for the other party to respond to it; and

    (b)   repeatedly makes applications for permission pursuant to that order which are totally without merit, the court may direct that if the party makes any further application for permission which is totally without merit, the decision to dismiss the application will be final and there will be no right of appeal, unless the judge who refused permission grants permission to appeal.

2.4 A party who is subject to a limited civil restraint order may not make an application for permission under paragraphs 2.2(a) or (b) without first serving notice of the application on the other party in accordance with paragraph 2.5.

2.5 A notice under paragraph 2.4 must–
   (a) set out the nature and grounds of the application; and
   (b) provide the other party with at least 7 days within which to respond.

2.6 An application for permission under paragraphs 2.2(a) or (b)–
   (a) must be made in writing;
   (b) must include the other party's written response, if any, to the notice served under paragraph 2.4; and
   (c) will be determined without a hearing.

2.7 An order under paragraph 2.3(b) may only be made by a High Court judge but not a district judge.

2.8 Where a party makes an application for permission under paragraphs 2.2(a) or (b) and permission is refused, any application for permission to appeal–
   (a) must be made in writing; and
   (b) will be determined without a hearing.

2.9 A limited civil restraint order–
   (a) is limited to the particular proceedings in which it is made;
   (b) will remain in effect for the duration of the proceedings in which it is made, unless the court orders otherwise; and
   (c) must identify the judge or judges to whom an application for permission under paragraphs 2.2(a), 2.2(b) or 2.8 should be made.

Extended civil restraint orders

3.1 An extended civil restraint order may be made by a judge of the High Court but not a district judge where a party has persistently made applications which are totally without merit.

3.2 Unless the court orders otherwise, where the court makes an extended civil restraint order, the party against whom the order is made–
   (a) will be restrained from making applications in any court concerning any matter involving or relating to or touching upon or leading to the proceedings in which the order is made without first obtaining the permission of a judge identified in the order;
   (b) may apply for amendment or discharge of the order, but only with the permission of a judge identified in the order; and
   (c) may apply for permission to appeal the order and if permission is granted, may appeal the order.

3.3 Where a party who is subject to an extended civil restraint order–
   (a) makes an application in a court identified in the order concerning any matter involving or relating to or touching upon or leading to the proceedings in which the order is made without first obtaining the permission of a judge identified in the order, the application will automatically be struck out or dismissed–
      (i) without the judge having to make any further order; and
      (ii) without the need for the other party to respond to it; and
   (b) repeatedly makes applications for permission pursuant to that order which are totally without merit, the court may direct that if the party makes any further application for permission which is totally without merit, the decision to dismiss the application will be final and there will be no right of appeal, unless the judge who refused permission grants permission to appeal.

3.4 A party who is subject to an extended civil restraint order may not make an application for permission under paragraphs 3.2(a) or (b) without first serving notice of the application on the other party in accordance with paragraph 3.5.
3.5 A notice under paragraph 3.4 must–
- (a) set out the nature and grounds of the application; and
- (b) provide the other party with at least 7 days within which to respond.

3.6 An application for permission under paragraphs 3.2(a) or (b)–
- (a) must be made in writing;
- (b) must include the other party's written response, if any, to the notice served under paragraph 3.4; and
- (c) will be determined without a hearing.

3.7 An order under paragraph 3.3(b) may only be made by a High Court judge but not a district judge.

3.8 Where a party makes an application for permission under paragraphs 3.2(a) or (b) and permission is refused, any application for permission to appeal–
- (a) must be made in writing; and
- (b) will be determined without a hearing.

3.9 An extended civil restraint order–
- (a) will be made for a specified period not exceeding 2 years;
- (b) must identify the courts in which the party against whom the order is made is restrained from making applications; and
- (c) must identify the judge or judges to whom an application for permission under paragraphs 3.2(a), 3.2(b) or 3.8 should be made.

3.10 The court may extend the duration of an extended civil restraint order, if it considers it appropriate to do so, but the duration of the order must not be extended for a period greater than 2 years on any given occasion.

General civil restraint orders

4.1 A general civil restraint order may be made by a judge of the High Court but not a district judge where, the party against whom the order is made persists in making applications which are totally without merit, in circumstances where an extended civil restraint order would not be sufficient or appropriate.

4.2 Unless the court otherwise orders, where the court makes a general civil restraint order, the party against whom the order is made–
- (a) will be restrained from making any application in any court without first obtaining the permission of a judge identified in the order;
- (b) may apply for amendment or discharge of the order, but only with the permission of a judge identified in the order; and
- (c) may apply for permission to appeal the order and if permission is granted, may appeal the order.

4.3 Where a party who is subject to a general civil restraint order–
- (a) makes an application in any court without first obtaining the permission of a judge identified in the order, the application will automatically be struck out or dismissed–
  - (i) without the judge having to make any further order; and
  - (ii) without the need for the other party to respond to it; and
- (b) repeatedly makes applications for permission pursuant to that order which are totally without merit, the court may direct that if the party makes any further application for permission which is totally without merit, the decision to

dismiss that application will be final and there will be no right of appeal, unless the judge who refused permission grants permission to appeal.

4.4 A party who is subject to a general civil restraint order may not make an application for permission under paragraphs 4.2(a) or (b) without first serving notice of the application on the other party in accordance with paragraph 4.5.

4.5 A notice under paragraph 4.4 must–

    (a) set out the nature and grounds of the application; and
    (b) provide the other party with at least 7 days within which to respond.

4.6 An application for permission under paragraphs 4.2(a) or (b)–

    (a) must be made in writing;
    (b) must include the other party's written response, if any, to the notice served under paragraph 4.4; and
    (c) will be determined without a hearing.

4.7 An order under paragraph 4.3(b) may only be made by a High Court judge but not a district judge.

4.8 Where a party makes an application for permission under paragraphs 4.2(a) or (b) and permission is refused, any application for permission to appeal–

    (a) must be made in writing; and
    (b) will be determined without a hearing.

4.9 A general civil restraint order–

    (a) will be made for a specified period not exceeding 2 years;
    (b) must identify the courts in which the party against whom the order is made is restrained from making applications; and
    (c) must identify the judge or judges to whom an application for permission under paragraphs 4.2(a), 4.2(b) or 4.8 should be made.

4.10 The court may extend the duration of a general civil restraint order, if it considers it appropriate to do so, but he duration of the order must not be extended for a period greater than 2 years on any given occasion.

General

5.1 The other party or parties to the proceedings may apply for any civil restraint order.

5.2 An application under paragraph 5.1 must be made using the procedure in Part 18 unless the court otherwise directs and the application must specify which type of civil restraint order is sought.

PRACTICE DIRECTION 5A – FORMS

This Practice Direction supplements FPR Part 5, rule 5.1 (Forms).

Scope and interpretation

1.1 This Practice Direction lists the forms to be used in family proceedings on or after 6th April 2011. Table 1 lists the forms against the part of the FPR to which they are relevant, and Table 2 lists the forms individually with their description.

1.2 The forms may be–

    (a) modified as the circumstances require, provided that all essential information, especially information or guidance which the form gives to the recipient, is included;
    (b) expanded to include additional pages where that may be necessary, provided that any additional pages are also verified by a statement of truth.

1.3 Any reference in family proceedings forms to a Part, rule or Practice Direction is to be read as a reference to the equivalent Part, rule or Practice Direction in the FPR and any reference to a Practice Direction in any CPR form used in family proceedings is to be read as a reference to the equivalent Practice Direction in the FPR.

Forms for committal applications

2.1 Rule 33.1(2) applies Part 50 of, and Schedules 1 and 2 to the CPR, in so far as they are relevant and with necessary modification (including the modification referred to in rule 33.7), to an application made in the High Court and a county court to enforce an order made in family proceedings. The CPR Practice Direction 'RSC52 and CCR 29–Committal Applications' therefore applies with necessary modifications to the enforcement of such an order. The form to be used for a committal application is set out in that Practice Direction. Accordingly, where a committal application is made in existing proceedings, it must be commenced by filing an application notice under Part 18 in those proceedings (a form C2 where there are existing proceedings under the Children Act 1989, a form D11 where the existing proceedings are matrimonial or civil partnership proceedings, financial remedy proceedings and proceedings under Part 8 or otherwise a form FP2).Otherwise a committal application must be commenced by the issue of a Part 19 application notice (a form FP1).

Other Forms

3.1 Other forms may be authorised by practice directions.

Table 1 Index to forms

FPR Part	Forms
Part 3 Alternative Dispute Resolution (Family Mediation)	FM1
Part 6 Service	C9, D5, D89, FL415, FP6
Part 7 Matrimonial and Civil Partnership Proceedings	C60, D6, D8, D8 Notes, D8A, D8B, D8D, D8D Notes, D8N, D8N Notes, D11, D13B, D20, D36, D80A, D80B, D80C, D80D, D80E, D80F, D80G, D81, D84
Part 8 Miscellaneous Applications	D50, D50A, D50B, D50C, D50D, D50E, D50F, D50G, D50H, D50J, D50K
Part 8 Chapter 5 Applications for declarations	C63, C64, C65, D70
Part 9 Applications for a Financial Remedy	Form A, Form A1, Form A2, Form B, Form E, Form E Notes, Form E1, Form E2, Form F, Form I, Form P, Form P1, Form P2, Form PPF, Form PPF1, Form PPF2
Part 10 Applications under Part 4 of the Family Law Act 1996	FL401, FL403, FL407, FL415
Part 11 Applications under Part 4A of the Family Law Act 1996	FL401A, FL403A, FL407A, FL430, FL431

FPR Part	Forms
Part 12 Applications in respect of children	C1, C1A, C2, C3, C4, C5, C8, C9, C11, C12, C13, C13A, C14, C15, C16, C17, C17A, C18, C19, C20, C61, C62, C66, C67, C68, C78, C79, C100, C110, C(PRA1), C(PRA2) C(PRA3), PLO1, PLO2, PLO3, PLO4, PLO5, PLO6, PLO8, PLO9, PLP10
Part 13 Applications under section 54 of Human Fertilisation and Embryology Act 2008	C51, C52, A64A, A101A
Part 14 Adoption	A4, A5, A50, A51, A52, A53, A54, A55, A56, A57, A58, A59, A60, A61, A62, A63, A50 Notes, A51 Notes, A52 Notes, A53 Notes, A54 Notes, A55 Notes, A56 Notes, A57 Notes, A58 Notes, A59 Notes, A60 Notes, A61 Notes, A62 Notes, A63 Notes, A64, A65, A100, A101, A102, A103, A104, A105, A106, A107
Part 15 Representation of Protected Parties	FP9
Part 16 Representation of children	FP9
Part 18 Applications in proceedings	C2, D11, FP2
Part 19 Alternative Procedure for applications	FP1, FP1A, FP1B, FP3, FP5
Part 22 Evidence	N285
Part 24 Witnesses	FP25
Part 26 Notification of change of solicitor	FP8
Part 28 Costs	252, D254, D258, D258A, D258B, D258C, D259, Form H, Form H1, N260
Part 30 Appeals	N161, N161A, N161B, N162, N162A, N162, N164
Part 31 Registration of Orders under the Council Regulation, The Civil Partnership (Jurisdiction and Recognition of Judgements) Regulations 2005 and under the Hague Convention 1996	C60, C61, C62,C69, D180
Part 32 Registration and Enforcement of Orders	D151
Part 33 Enforcement	D62, N56, N323, N336, N337, N349, N379, N380
Part 34 Reciprocal Enforcement of Maintenance Orders	REMO 1, REMO 2

Table 2 List of Forms

Number	Name
A4	Application For Revocation Of An Order Freeing A Child For Adoption
A5	Application For Substitution Of One Adoption Agency For Another
A50	Application for a placement order Section 22 Adoption and Children Act 2002
A51	Application for variation of a placement order Section 23 Adoption and Children Act 2002
A52	Application for revocation of a placement order Section 24 Adoption and Children Act 2002
A53	Application for a contact order Section 26 Adoption and Children Act 2002
A54	Application for variation or revocation of a contact order Section 27(1)(b) Adoption and Children Act 2002
A55	Application for permission to change a child's surname Section 28 Adoption and Children Act 2002
A56	Application for permission to remove a child from the United Kingdom Section 28 Adoption and Children Act 2002
A57	Application for a recovery order Section 41 Adoption and Children Act 2002
A58	Application for an adoption order Section 46 Adoption and Children Act 2002
A59	Application for a Convention adoption order Section 46 Adoption and Children Act 2002
A60	Application for an adoption order (excluding a Convention adoption order) where the child is habitually resident outside the British Islands and is brought into the United Kingdom for the purposes of adoption Section 46 Adoption and Children Act 2002
A61	Application for an order for parental responsibility prior to adoption abroad Section 84 Adoption and Children Act 2002
A62	Application for a direction under section 88(1) of the Adoption and Children Act 2002
A63	Application for an order to annul a Convention adoption or Convention adoption order or for an overseas adoption or determination under section 91 to cease to be valid Section 89 Adoption and Children Act 2002
A50 Notes	Application for a placement order Section 22 Adoption and Children Act 2002 – Notes on completing the form
A51 Notes	Application for variation of a placement order Section 23 Adoption and Children Act 2002 – Notes on completing the form
A52 Notes	Application for revocation of a placement order Section 24 Adoption and Children Act 2002 – Notes on completing the form
A53 Notes	Application for a contact order Section 26 Adoption and Children Act 2002 – Notes on completing the form

Number	Name
A54 Notes	Application for variation or revocation of a contact order Section 27(1)(b) Adoption and Children Act 2002 – Notes on completing the form
A55 Notes	Application for permission to change a child's surname Section 28 Adoption and Children Act 2002 – Notes on completing the form
A56 Notes	Application for permission to remove a child from the United Kingdom Section 28 Adoption and Children Act 2002 – Notes on completing the form
A57 Notes	Application for a recovery order Section 41 Adoption and Children Act 2002 – Notes on completing the form
A58 Notes	Application for an adoption order Section 46 Adoption and Children Act 2002 – Notes on completing the form
A59 Notes	Application for a Convention adoption order Section 46 Adoption and Children Act 2002 – Notes on completing the form
A60 Notes	Application for an adoption order (excluding a Convention adoption order) where the child is habitually resident outside the British Islands and is brought into the United Kingdom for the purposes of adoption Section 46 Adoption and Children Act 2002 – Notes on completing the form
A61 Notes	Application for an order for parental responsibility prior to adoption abroad Section 84 Adoption and Children Act 2002 – Notes on completing the form
A62 Notes	Application for a direction under section 88(1) of the Adoption and Children Act 2002 – Notes on completing the form
A63 Notes	Application for an order to annul a Convention adoption or Convention adoption order or for an overseas adoption or determination under section 91 to cease to be valid Section 89 Adoption and Children Act 2002 – Notes on completing the form
A64	Application to receive information from court records Section 60(4) Adoption and Children Act 2002
A64A	Application to receive information from court records about a parental order Section 60(4) Adoption and Children Act 2002
A65	Confidential information
A100	Consent to the placement of my child for adoption with any prospective adopters chosen by the Adoption Agency Section 19 of the Adoption and Children Act 2002
A101	Consent to the placement of my child for adoption with identified prospective adopters Section 19 of the Adoption and Children Act 2002
A101A	Agreement to the making of a parental order in respect of my child Section 54 of the Human Fertilisation and Embryology Act 2008
A102	Consent to the placement of my child for adoption with identified prospective adopter(s) and, if the placement breaks down, with any prospective adopter(s) chosen by the adoption agency Section 19 of the Adoption and Children Act 2002

Number	Name
A103	Advance Consent to Adoption Section 20 of the Adoption and Children Act 2002
A104	Consent to Adoption The Adoption and Children Act 2002
A105	Consent to the making of an Order under Section 84 of the Adoption and Children Act 2002
A106	Withdrawal of Consent Sections 19 and 20 of the Adoption and Children Act 2002
A107	Consent by the child's parent to adoption by their partner The Adoption and Children Act 2002
C1	Application for an Order
C1A	Allegations of harm and domestic violence (Supplemental information form)
C2	Application For permission to start proceedings For an order or directions in existing proceedings To be joined as, or cease to be, a party in existing family proceedings under the Children Act 1989
C3	Application for an order authorising search for, taking charge of and delivery of child
C4	Application for an order for disclosure of a child's whereabouts
C5	Local Authority application concerning the registration of a child-minder or a provider of day care
C8	Confidential contact details
C9	Statement of service
C11	Supplement for an application for an Emergency Protection Order
C12	Supplement for an application for a warrant to assist a person authorised by an Emergency Protection Order
C13	Supplement for an application for a Care or Supervision Order
C13A	Supplement for an application for a Special Guardianship Order Section 14A Children Act 1989
C14	Supplement for an application for authority to refuse contact with a child in care
C15	Supplement for an application for contact with a child in care
C16	Supplement for an application for a Child Assessment Order
C17	Supplement for an application for Education Supervision Order
C17A	Supplement for an application for an extension of an Education Supervision Order
C18	Supplement for an application for a Recovery Order
C19	Application for a warrant of assistance
C20	Supplement for an application for an order to hold a child in Secure Accommodation
C51	Application for a Parental Order Section 54 Human Fertilisation and Embryology Act 2008

Number	Name
C52	Acknowledgement of an application for a Parental Order
C60	Certificate referred to in Article 39 of Council Regulation (EC) No. 2201/ 2003 of 27 November 2003 concerning judgments on parental responsibility
C61	Certificate referred to in Article 41(1) of Council Regulation (EC) No. 2201/2003 of 27 November 2003 concerning judgments on rights of access
C62	Certificate referred to in Article 42(1) of Council Regulation (EC) No. 2201/2003 of 27 November 2003 concerning the return of the child
C63	Application for declaration of parentage under section 55A of the Family Law Act 1986
C64	Application for declaration of legitimacy or legitimation under section 56 (1) (b) and (2) of the Family Law Act 1986
C65	Application for declaration as to adoption effected overseas under section 57 of the Family Law Act 1986
C66	Application for inherent jurisdiction order in relation to children
C67	Application under the Child Abduction and Custody Act 1985 or Article 11 of Council Regulation (EC) 2201/2003
C68	Application for international transfer of jurisdiction to or from England and Wales
C69	Application for registration, recognition or non recognition of a judgment under Council Regulation (EC) 2201/2003
C78	Application for attachment of a warning notice to a contact order
C79	Application related to enforcement of a contact order
C100	Application under the Children Act 1989 for a residence, contact, prohibited steps, specific issue section 8 order or to vary or discharge a section 8 order
C110	Application under the Children Act 1989 for a care or supervision order
C(PRA1)	Parental Responsibility Agreement
C(PRA2)	Step Parent Parental Responsibility Agreement
C(PRA3)	Parental Responsibility Agreement Section 4ZA Children Act 1989 (Acquisition of parental responsibility by second female parent)
D5	Notice to be indorsed on documents served in accordance with rule 6.14
D6	Statement of Reconciliation
D8	Divorce/dissolution/(judicial) separation petition
D8 Notes	Supporting notes for guidance on completing a divorce/dissolution/(judicial) separation petition
D8A	Statement of arrangements for children
D8B	Answer to a divorce/dissolution/(judicial) separation or nullity petition

Number	Name
D8D	Petition for a presumption of death decree/order and the dissolution of a marriage/civil partnership
D8D Notes	Supporting notes for guidance on completing a petition for a presumption of death decree/order and the dissolution of a marriage/civil partnership
D8N	Nullity petition
D8N Notes	Supporting notes for guidance on completing a nullity petition
D11	Application Notice
D13B	Affidavit in support of a request to dispense with service of the divorce/dissolution/nullity (judicial) separation petition on the Respondent
D20	Medical Examination: statement of parties & inspector
D36	Notice of Application for Decree Nisi to be made Absolute or Conditional Order to be made final
D50	Notice of application on ground of failure to provide maintenance or for alteration of maintenance agreement during parties' lifetime
D50A	Notice of proceedings and acknowledgement of service – maintenance/property proceedings
D50B	Application under Section 17 of the Married Women's Property Act 1882/Section 67 of the Civil Partnership Act 2004/Application to transfer a tenancy under the Family Law Act 1996 Part IV
D50C	Application on ground of failure to provide maintenance
D50D	Application for alteration of maintenance agreement after the death of one of the parties
D50E	Application for permission to apply for financial relief after overseas divorce/dissolution etc under section 13 of the Matrimonial and Family Proceedings Act 1984 / paragraph 4 of Schedule 7 to the Civil Partnership Act 2004
D50F	Application for financial relief after overseas divorce etc under section 12 of the Matrimonial and Family Proceedings Act 1984/paragraph 4 to Schedule 7 to the Civil Partnership Act 2004
D50G	Application to prevent transactions intended to defeat prospective applications for financial relief
D50H	Application for alteration of maintenance agreement during parties lifetime
D50J	Application for an order preventing avoidance under section 32L of the Child Support Act 1991
D50K	Notice of Application for Enforcement by such method of enforcement as the court may consider appropriate
D62	Request for issue of Judgment Summons
D70	Application for Declaration of Marital/Civil Partnership Status
D80A	Affidavit in Support of divorce/(judicial) separation – adultery
D80B	Affidavit in Support of divorce/dissolution (judicial) separation – unreasonable behaviour

Number	Name
D80C	Affidavit in Support of divorce/dissolution/(judicial) separation – desertion
D80D	Affidavit in Support of divorce/dissolution/(judicial) separation – 2 years consent
D80E	Affidavit in Support of divorce/dissolution/(judicial) separation – 5 years separation
D80F	Affidavit in Support of annulment – void marriage/civil partnership
D80G	Affidavit in support of annulment – voidable marriage/civil partnership
D81	Statement of information for a Consent Order in relation to a financial remedy
D84	Application for a decree nisi/conditional order or (judicial) separation decree/order
D89	Request for personal service by a court bailiff
D151	Application for registration of maintenance order in a magistrates' court
D180	Concerning judgements in matrimonial matters
D252	Notice of commencement of assessment of bill of costs
D254	Request for a default costs certificate
D258	Request for a detailed assessment of hearing
D258A	Request for detailed assessment (legal aid only)
D258B	Request for detailed assessment (Costs payable out of a fund other than the Community Legal Service Fund)
D258C	Request for detailed assessment hearing pursuant to an order under Part III of the Solicitors Act 1974
D259	Notice of appeal against a detailed assessment (divorce)
FL401	Application for a non molestation order/an occupation order
FL401A	Application for a Forced Marriage Protection Order
FL403	Application to vary, extend or discharge
FL403A	Application to vary, extend or discharge Forced Marriage Protection Orders
FL407	Applications for warrant of Arrest
FL407A	Application for warrant of arrest for a Forced Marriage Protection Order
FL415	Statement of service
FL430	Application for leave to apply for a Forced Marriage Protection Order
FL431	Application to join/cease as a party to Forced Marriage Protection Proceedings
FM1	Family Mediation Information and Assessment Form FM1
Form A	Notice of [intention to proceed with] an application for a financial order (NOTE: This form should be used whether the applicant is proceeding with an application in the petition or making a free standing application)

Practice Directions 373

Number	Name
Form A1	Notice of [intention to proceed with] an application for a financial remedy (other than a financial order) in the county or high court
Form A2	Notice of [intention to proceed with] an application for a financial remedy in the magistrates court
Form B	Notice of an application to consider the financial position of the Respondent after the divorce/dissolution
Form E	Financial Statement for a financial order or for financial relief after an overseas divorce or dissolution etc
Form E Notes	Form E (Financial Statement for a financial order or for financial relief after an overseas divorce or dissolution etc) Notes for guidance
Form E1	Financial Statement for a financial remedy (other than a financial order or financial relief after an overseas divorce/dissolution etc) in the county or high court
Form E2	Financial Statement for a financial remedy in the magistrates court
Form F	Notice of allegation in proceedings for financial remedy
Form H	Estimate of costs (financial remedy)
Form H1	Statement of Costs (financial remedy)
Form I	Notice of request for periodical payments order at the same rate as order for interim maintenance pending outcome of proceeding
Form P	Pension inquiry form
Form P1	Pension sharing annex
Form P2	Pension attachment annex
Form PPF	Pension Protection Fund Inquiry Form
Form PPF 1	Pension Protection Fund sharing annex
Form PPF 2	Pension Protection Fund attachment annex
FP1	Application under Part 19 of the Family Procedure Rules 2010
FP1A	Application under Part 19 of the Family Procedure Rules 2010 Notes for applicant on completing the application (Form FP1)
FP1B	Application under Part 19 of the Family Procedure Rules 2010 Notes for respondent
FP2	Application notice Part 18 of the Family Procedure Rules 2010
FP3	Application for injunction (General form)
FP5	Acknowledgment of service Application under Part 19 of the Family Procedure Rules 2010
FP6	Certificate of service
FP8	Notice of change of solicitor
FP9	Certificate of suitability of litigation friend
FP25	Witness Summons
N56	Form for replying to an attachment of earnings application (statement of means)

Number	Name
N161	Appellant's Notice
N161A	Guidance Notes on Completing the Appellant's Notice
N161B	Important Notes for Respondents
N162	Respondent's Notice
N162A	Guidance Notes for Completing the Respondent's Notice
N163	Skeleton Argument
N164	Appellant's Notice
N260	Statement of costs (summary assessment)
N285	General Affidavit
N323	Request for Warrant of Execution
N336	Request and result of search in the attachment of earnings index
N337	Request for attachment of earnings order
N349	Application for a third party debt order
N379	Application for a charging order on land or property
N380	Application for charging order on securities
PLO1	Application for a care order or supervision order: Supplementary form
PLO2	The local authority's case summary
PLO3	Draft case management order
PLO4	Allocation record and timetable for the child(ren)
PLO5	Directions and allocation on issue of proceedings
PLO6	Directions and allocation at first appointment
PLO8	Standard Directions on Issue
PLO9	Standard Directions at First Appointment
PLP10	Order Menu – Directions Revised Private Law Programme
REMO 1	Notice of Registration
REMO 2	Notice of Refusal of Registration.

PRACTICE DIRECTION 6A – SERVICE WITHIN THE JURISDICTION

This Practice Direction Supplements FPR Part 6, Chapters 2 and 3

Contents of this Practice Direction

General provisions

Scope of this Practice Direction	Paragraph 1
When service may be by document exchange	Paragraph 2
How service is effected by post, an alternative service provider or DX	Paragraph 3
Service by fax or other electronic means	Paragraph 4

Practice Directions 375

Service on members of the Regular Forces and United States Air Force	Paragraph 5
Application for an order for service by an alternative method or at an alternative place	Paragraph 6
Application for an order to dispense with service	Paragraph 7
Deemed service of a document other than an application for a matrimonial or civil partnership order	Paragraph 8
Service of application on children and protected parties	Paragraph 9

Provisions relating to applications for matrimonial and civil partnership orders

Acknowledgment of service	Paragraph 10
Personal service of application by bailiff	Paragraph 11
Proof of personal service by bailiff	Paragraph 12
Service by bailiff in proceedings in the Principal Registry	Paragraph 13
Service of application on children and protected parties	Paragraph 14

GENERAL PROVISIONS

Scope of this Practice Direction

1.1 This Practice Direction supplements the following provisions of Part 6–
- (a) Chapter 2 (service of the application for a matrimonial order or civil partnership order in the jurisdiction);
- (b) Chapter 3 (service of documents other than an application for a matrimonial order or civil partnership order in the United Kingdom); and
- (c) rule 6.43(2) in relation to the method of service on a party in Scotland or Northern Ireland.

(Practice Direction B supplementing Part 6 contains provisions relevant to service on a party in Scotland or Northern Ireland, including provisions about the period for responding to an application notice.)

When service may be by document exchange

2.1 Subject to the provisions of rule 6.4 (which provides when an application for a matrimonial or civil partnership order may be served by document exchange) service by document exchange (DX) may take place only where–
- (a) the address at which the party is to be served includes a numbered box at a DX; or
- (b) the writing paper of the party who is to be served or of the solicitor acting for that party sets out a DX box number; and
- (c) the party or the solicitor acting for that party has not indicated in writing that they are unwilling to accept service by DX.

How service is effected by post, an alternative service provider or DX

3.1 Service by post, DX or other service which provides for delivery on the next business day is effected by–
- (a) placing the document in a post box;
- (b) leaving the document with or delivering the document to the relevant service provider; or

(c) having the document collected by the relevant service provider.

Service by fax or other electronic means

4.1 This paragraph applies to the service of a document other than an application for a matrimonial or civil partnership order and documents in adoption proceedings and parental order proceedings.

4.2 Subject to the provisions of rule 6.26(6) and (7), where a document is to be served by fax or other electronic means–

    (a) the party who is to be served or the solicitor acting for that party must previously have indicated in writing to the party serving–

        (i) that the party to be served or the solicitor is willing to accept service by fax or other electronic means; and

        (ii) the fax number, e-mail address or other electronic identification to which it must be sent; and

    (b) the following are to be taken as sufficient written indications for the purposes of paragraph 4.2(a)–

        (i) a fax number set out on the writing paper of the solicitor acting for the party to be served;

        (ii) an e-mail address set out on the writing paper of the solicitor acting for the party to be served but only where it is stated that the e-mail address may be used for service; or

        (iii) a fax number, e-mail address or electronic identification set out on a statement of case or an answer to a claim filed with the court.

4.3 Where a party intends to serve a document by electronic means (other than by fax) that party must first ask the party who is to be served whether there are any limitations to the recipient's agreement to accept service by such means (for example, the format in which documents are to be sent and the maximum size of attachments that may be received).

4.4 Where a document is served by electronic means, the party serving the document need not in addition send or deliver a hard copy.

Service on members of the Regular Forces and United States Air Force

5.1 The provisions that apply to service on members of the regular forces (within the meaning of the Armed Forces Act 2006) and members of the United States Air Force are annexed to this practice direction.

Application for an order for service by an alternative method or at an alternative place

6.1 An application in the High Court or a county court for an order under rule 6.19 may be made without notice.

6.2 Where an application for an order under rule 6.19 is made before the document is served, the application must be supported by evidence stating–

    (a) the reason why an order is sought;

    (b) what alternative method or place is proposed; and

    (c) why the applicant believes that the document is likely to reach the person to be served by the method or at the place proposed.

6.3 Where the application for an order is made after the applicant has taken steps to bring the document to the attention of the person to be served by an alternative method or at an alternative place, the application must be supported by evidence stating–

    (a) the reason why the order is sought;

    (b) what alternative method or alternative place was used;

(c) when the alternative method or place was used; and
(d) why the applicant believes that the document is likely to have reached the person to be served by the alternative method or at the alternative place.

6.4 Examples–
(a) an application to serve by posting or delivering to an address of a person who knows the other party must be supported by evidence that if posted or delivered to that address, the document is likely to be brought to the attention of the other party;
(b) an application to serve by sending a SMS text message or leaving a voicemail message at a particular telephone number saying where the document is must be accompanied by evidence that the person serving the document has taken, or will take, appropriate steps to ensure that the party being served is using that telephone number and is likely to receive the message.

Applications for an order to dispense with service

7.1 An application in the High Court or a county court for an order under rule 6.36 (power to dispense with service) may be made without notice.

Deemed service of a document other than an application for a matrimonial or civil partnership order

8.1 Rule 6.34 contains provisions about deemed service of a document other than an application for a matrimonial or civil partnership order. Examples of how deemed service is calculated are set out below.

Example 1

8.2 Where the document is posted (by first class post) on a Monday (a business day), the day of deemed service is the following Wednesday (a business day).

Example 2

8.3 Where the document is left in a numbered box at the DX on a Friday (a business day), the day of deemed service is the following Monday (a business day).

Example 3

8.4 Where the document is sent by fax on a Saturday and the transmission of that fax is completed by 4.30p.m. on that day, the day of deemed service is the following Monday (a business day).

Example 4

8.5 Where the document is served personally before 4.30p.m. on a Sunday, the day of deemed service is the next day (Monday, a business day).

Example 5

8.6 Where the document is delivered to a permitted address after 4.30p.m. on the Thursday (a business day) before Good Friday, the day of deemed service is the following Tuesday (a business day) as the Monday is a bank holiday.

Example 6

8.7 Where the document is posted (by first class post) on a bank holiday Monday, the day of deemed service is the following Wednesday (a business day).

Service of application on children and protected parties

9.1 Rule 16.14(1) and (2) are applied to service of an application form (other than an application for a matrimonial or civil partnership order) commencing proceedings on children and protected parties by rule 6.28. Rule 6.14(7) makes provision as to how an application form must be served where the respondent is a child or protected party. A document served in accordance with rule 6.14(7) must be endorsed with the following notice which is set out in Form D5–

Important Notice

The contents or purport of this document are to be communicated to the Respondent [or as the case may be], [full name of Respondent]

if s/he is over 16 [add if the person to be served lacks capacity within the meaning of the Mental Capacity Act 2005 to conduct the proceedings] unless you are satisfied [after consultation with the responsible medical officer within the meaning of the Mental Health Act 1983 or, if s/he is not liable to be detained or subject to guardianship under that Act, his/her medical attendant] that communication will be detrimental to his/her mental condition].

PROVISIONS RELATING TO APPLICATIONS FOR MATRIMONIAL AND CIVIL PARTNERSHIP ORDERS

Acknowledgment of service to be sent to applicant

10.1 Where the court office receives an acknowledgment of service the court officer must send a photographic copy of it to the applicant.

Personal service of application by bailiff

11.1 The court will only consider a request for personal service of the application by a bailiff if the address for service is in England and Wales.

11.2 In normal circumstances, a request should only be made if postal service has been attempted. In this case, if–

(a) a signed acknowledgment of service is not returned to the court within 14 days after posting; and
(b) the applicant reasonably believes the respondent is still living at the stated address,

the applicant may make a request to the court for personal service by a bailiff.

11.3 A request for personal service by a bailiff should be made in writing to the court officer on the prescribed form and accompanied by the relevant fee. The request should also be accompanied by–

(a) evidence that postal service has been attempted and failed; or
(b) if postal service has not been attempted, an explanation as to why postal service is not considered appropriate in the circumstances of the case.

11.4 A request will rarely be granted where the applicant is legally represented and it will be necessary for the representative to show why service by bailiff is required rather than by a process server.

Proof of personal service by bailiff

12.1 Once service of the application has been effected or attempted by the bailiff he must file a certificate of service in the issuing court.

12.2 If the respondent fails to sign and return an acknowledgment of service to the court office and–

(a) the certificate contains a signature of receipt of the application by the respondent; or
(b) the identity of the respondent is to be proved by a photograph supplied by the applicant,

the applicant must prove the signature or photograph in the affidavit filed by the applicant under rule 7.19(4).

Service by bailiff in proceedings in the Principal Registry
13.1 This paragraph applies where proceedings which are pending in the Principal Registry of the Family Division are treated as pending in a divorce county court.
13.2 Where a document is to be served by a bailiff it must be sent for service to the Principal Registry for onward transmission to the court officer of the county court in whose district the document is to be served.

Service of application on children and protected parties
14.1 A document served in accordance with rule 6.14(7) must be endorsed with the notice contained in paragraph 9.1.

ANNEX – SERVICE ON MEMBERS OF THE REGULAR FORCES

1. The following information is for litigants and legal representatives who wish to serve legal documents in civil proceedings in the courts of England and Wales on parties to the proceedings who are (or who, at the material time, were) members of the regular forces (as defined in the Armed Forces Act 2006).
2. The proceedings may take place in the county court or the High Court, and the documents to be served may be claim forms, interim application notices and pre-action application notices. Proceedings for divorce or maintenance and proceedings in the Family Courts generally are subject to special rules as to service which are explained in a practice direction issued by the Senior District Judge of the Principal Registry on 26 June 1979. (now see Practice Direction 1 Maintenance Orders: Service Personnel:2 Disclosure of Addresses (1995)2FLR 813.)
3. In this Annex, the person wishing to effect service is referred to as the 'claimant' and the member of the regular forces to be served is referred to as 'the member'; the expression 'overseas' means outside the United Kingdom.

Enquiries as to address

4. As a first step, the claimant's legal representative will need to find out where the member is serving, if this is not already known. For this purpose the claimant's legal representative should write to the appropriate officer of the Ministry of Defence as specified in paragraph 10 below.
5. The letter of enquiry should in every case show that the writer is a legal representative and that the enquiry is made solely with a view to the service of legal documents in civil proceedings.
6. In all cases the letter must give the full name, service number, rank or rate, and Ship, Arm or Trade, Regiment or Corps and Unit or as much of this information as is available. Failure to quote the service number and the rank or rate may result either in failure to identify the member or in considerable delay.
7. The letter must contain an undertaking by the legal representative that, if the address is given, it will be used solely for the purpose of issuing and serving documents in the proceedings and that so far as is possible the legal representative will disclose the address only to the court and not to the claimant or to any other person or body. A legal representative in the service of a public authority or private company must undertake that the address will be used solely for the purpose of issuing and serving documents in the proceedings and that the address will not be disclosed so far as is possible to any

other part of the legal representative's employing organisation or to any other person but only to the court. Normally on receipt of the required information and undertaking the appropriate office will give the service address.

8. If the legal representative does not give the undertaking, the only information that will be given is whether the member is at that time serving in England or Wales, Scotland, Northern Ireland or overseas.

9. It should be noted that a member's address which ends with a British Forces Post Office address and reference (BFPO) will nearly always indicate that the member is serving overseas.

10. The letter of enquiry should be addressed as follows –

    (a) **Royal Navy and Royal Marine Officers, Ratings and Other Ranks**

    Director Naval Personnel
    Fleet Headquarters
    MP 3.1
    Leach Building
    Whale Island
    Portsmouth
    Hampshire
    PO2 8BY

    Army Officers and other Ranks –
    Army Personnel Centre
    Disclosures 1
    MP 520
    Kentigern House
    65 Brown Street
    Glasgow
    G2 8EX

    Royal Air Force Officers and Other Ranks –
    Manning 22E
    RAF Disclosures
    Room 221B
    Trenchard Hall
    RAF Cranwell
    Sleaford
    Lincolnshire
    NG34 8HB

Assistance in serving documents on members

11. Once the claimant's legal representative has ascertained the member's address, the legal representative may use that address as the address for service by post, in cases where this method of service is allowed by the Civil Procedure Rules. There are, however, some situations in which service of the proceedings, whether in the High Court or in the county court, must be effected personally; in these cases an appointment will have to be sought, through the Commanding Officer of the Unit, Establishment or Ship concerned, for the purpose of effecting service. The procedure for obtaining an appointment is described below, and it applies whether personal service is to be effected by the claimant's legal representative or the legal representative's agent or by a court bailiff, or, in the case of proceedings served overseas (with the leave of the court) through the British Consul or the foreign judicial authority.

12. The procedure for obtaining an appointment to effect personal service is by application to the Commanding Officer of the Unit, Establishment or Ship in which the member is serving. The Commanding Officer may grant permission for the document server to enter the Unit, Establishment or Ship but if this is not appropriate the Commanding

Officer may offer arrangements for the member to attend at a place in the vicinity of the Unit, Establishment or Ship in order that the member may be served. If suitable arrangements cannot be made the legal representative will have evidence that personal service is impracticable, which may be useful in an application for service by an alternative method or at an alternative place.

General

13. Subject to the procedure outlined in paragraphs 11 and 12, there are no special arrangements to assist in the service of legal documents when a member is outside the United Kingdom. The appropriate office will, however, give an approximate date when the member is likely to return to the United Kingdom.
14. It sometimes happens that a member has left the regular forces by the time an enquiry as to address is made. If the claimant's legal representative confirms that the proceedings result from an occurrence when the member was in the regular forces and the legal representative gives the undertaking referred to in paragraph 7, the last known private address after discharge will normally be provided. In no other case, however, will the Ministry of Defence disclose the private address of a member of the regular forces.

Service on Members of United States Air Force

15. In addition to the information contained in the memorandum of 26 July 1979, and after some doubts having been expressed as to the correct procedure to be followed by persons having civil claims against members of the United States Air Force in England and Wales, the Lord Chancellor's Office (as it was then) issued the following notes for guidance with the approval of the appropriate United States authorities.
16. Instructions have been issued by the United States authorities to the commanding officers of all their units in England and Wales that every facility is to be given for the service of documents in civil proceedings on members of the United States Air Force. The proper course to be followed by a creditor or other person having a claim against a member of the United States Air Force is for that person to communicate with the commanding officer or, where the unit concerned has a legal officer, with the legal officer of the defendant's unit requesting the provision of facilities for the service of documents on the defendant. It is not possible for the United States authorities to act as arbitrators when a civil claim is made against a member of their forces. It is, therefore, essential that the claim should either be admitted by the defendant or judgment should be obtained on it, whether in the High Court or a county court. If a claim has been admitted or judgment has been obtained and the claimant has failed to obtain satisfaction within a reasonable period, the claimant's proper course is then to write to: Office of the Staff Judge Advocate, Headquarters, Third Air Force, R.A.F. Mildenhall, Suffolk, enclosing a copy of the defendant's written admission of the claim or, as the case may be, a copy of the judgment. Steps will then be taken by the Staff Judge Advocate to ensure that the matter is brought to the defendant's attention with a view to prompt satisfaction of the claim.

PRACTICE DIRECTION 6B – SERVICE OUT OF THE JURISDICTION

This Practice Direction Supplements FPR Part 6, Chapter 4

Contents of this Practice Direction

Scope of this Practice Direction	Paragraph 1
Service in other Member States of the European Union	Paragraph 2

Documents to be filed under rule 6.46(2)(c)	Paragraph 3
Service in a Commonwealth State or British Overseas Territory	Paragraph 4
Period for responding to an application form	Paragraph 5
Service of application notices and orders	Paragraph 6
Period for responding to an application notice	Paragraph 7
Further information	Paragraph 8

Scope of this Practice Direction

1.1 This Practice Direction supplements Chapter 4 (service out of the jurisdiction) of Part 6.

(Practice Direction 6A contains relevant provisions supplementing rule 6.43(2) in relation to the method of service on a party in Scotland or Northern Ireland.)

Service in other Member States of the European Union

2.1 Where service is to be effected in another Member of State of the European Union, the Service Regulation applies.

2.2 The Service Regulation is Regulation (EC) No. 1393/2007 of the European Parliament and of the Council of 13 November 2007 on the service in the Member States of judicial and extrajudicial documents in civil or commercial matters (service of documents), and repealing Council Regulation (EC) no. 1348/2000, as amended from time to time and as applied by the Agreement made on 19 October 2005 between the European Community and the Kingdom of Denmark on the service of judicial and extrajudicial documents in civil and commercial matters.

2.3 The Service Regulation is annexed to this Practice Direction.

(Article 20(1) of the Service Regulation provides that the Regulation prevails over other provisions contained in bilateral or multilateral agreements or arrangements concluded by the Member of States and in particular Article IV of the protocol to the Brussels Convention of 1968 and the Hague Convention of 15 November 1965)

Documents to be filed under rule 6.46(2)

3.1 A duplicate of –

(a) the application form or other document to be served under rule 6.45(1) or (2);
(b) any documents accompanying the application or other document referred to in paragraph (a); and
(c) any translation required by rule 6.47;

must be provided for each party to be served out of the jurisdiction, together with forms for responding to the application.

3.2 Some countries require legalisation of the document to be served and some require a formal letter of request which must be signed by the Senior Master. Any queries on this should be addressed to the Foreign Process Section (Room E02) at the Royal Courts of Justice.

Service in a Commonwealth State or British Overseas Territory

4.1 The judicial authorities of certain Commonwealth States which are not a party to the Hague Convention require service to be in accordance with rule 6.45(1)(b)(i) and not

6.45(3). A list of such countries can be obtained from the Foreign Process Section (Room E02) at the Royal Courts of Justice.
4.2 The list of British overseas territories is contained in Schedule 6 to the British Nationality Act 1981. For ease of reference these are–

    (a)   Anguilla;
    (b)   Bermuda;
    (c)   British Antarctic Territory;
    (d)   British Indian Ocean Territory;
    (e)   Cayman Islands;
    (f)   Falkland Islands;
    (g)   Gibraltar;
    (h)   Montserrat;
    (i)   Pitcairn, Henderson, Ducie and Oeno Islands;
    (j)   St. Helena, Ascension and Tristan da Cunha;
    (k)   South Georgia and the South Sandwich Islands;
    (l)   Sovereign Base Areas of Akrotiri and Dhekelia;
    (m)   Turks and Caicos Islands;
    (n)   Virgin Islands.

Period for responding to an application form

5.1 Where rule 6.42 applies, the period within which the respondent must file an acknowledgment of service or an answer to the application is the number of days listed in the Table after service of the application.
5.2 Where an application is served out of the jurisdiction any statement as to the period for responding to the claim contained in any of the forms required by the Family Procedure Rules to accompany the application must specify the period prescribed under rule 6.42.

Service of application notices and orders

6.1 The provisions of Chapter 4 of Part 6 (special provisions about service out of the jurisdiction) also apply to service out of the jurisdiction of an application notice or order.
6.2 Where an application notice is to be served out of the jurisdiction in accordance with Chapter 4 of Part 6 the court must have regard to the country in which the application notice is to be served in setting the date for the hearing of the application and giving any direction about service of the respondent's evidence.

Period for responding to an application notice

7.1 Where an application notice or order is served out of the jurisdiction, the period for responding is 7 days less than the number of days listed in the Table.

Further information

8.1 Further information concerning service out of the jurisdiction can be obtained from the Foreign Process Section, Room E02, Royal Courts of Justice, Strand, London WC2A 2LL (telephone 020 7947 6691).

TABLE

Place or country	*Number of days*
Afghanistan	23
Albania	25

Place or country	Number of days
Algeria	22
Andorra	21
Angola	22
Anguilla	31
Antigua and Barbuda	23
Antilles (Netherlands)	31
Argentina	22
Armenia	21
Ascension Island	31
Australia	25
Austria	21
Azerbaijan	22
Azores	23
Bahamas	22
Bahrain	22
Balearic Islands	21
Bangladesh	23
Barbados	23
Belarus	21
Belgium	21
Belize	23
Benin	25
Bermuda	31
Bhutan	28
Bolivia	23
Bosnia and Herzegovina	21
Botswana	23
Brazil	22
British Virgin Islands	31
Brunei	25
Bulgaria	23
Burkina Faso	23
Burma	23
Burundi	22
Cambodia	28
Cameroon	22
Canada	22
Canary Islands	22
Cape Verde	25

Practice Directions 385

Place or country	Number of days
Caroline Islands	31
Cayman Islands	31
Central African Republic	25
Chad	25
Chile	22
China	24
China (Hong Kong)	31
China (Macau)	31
China (Taiwan)	23
China (Tibet)	34
Christmas Island	27
Cocos (Keeling) Islands	41
Colombia	22
Comoros	23
Congo (formerly Congo Brazzaville or French Congo)	25
Congo (Democratic Republic)	25
Corsica	21
Costa Rica	23
Croatia	21
Cuba	24
Cyprus	31
Czech Republic	21
Denmark	21
Djibouti	22
Dominica	23
Dominican Republic	23
East Timor	25
Ecuador	22
Egypt	22
El Salvador	25
Equatorial Guinea	23
Eritrea	22
Estonia	21
Ethiopia	22
Falkland Islands and Dependencies	31
Faroe Islands	31
Fiji	23
Finland	24
France	21

Place or country	Number of days
French Guyana	31
French Polynesia	31
French West Indies	31
Gabon	25
Gambia	22
Georgia	21
Germany	21
Ghana	22
Gibraltar	31
Greece	21
Greenland	31
Grenada	24
Guatemala	24
Guernsey	21
Guinea	22
Guinea-Bissau	22
Guyana	22
Haiti	23
Holland (Netherlands)	21
Honduras	24
Hungary	22
Iceland	22
India	23
Indonesia	22
Iran	22
Iraq	22
Ireland (Republic of)	21
Ireland (Northern)	21
Isle of Man	21
Israel	22
Italy	21
Ivory Coast	22
Jamaica	22
Japan	23
Jersey	21
Jordan	23
Kazakhstan	21
Kenya	22
Kiribati	23

Place or country	Number of days
Korea (North)	28
Korea (South)	24
Kosovo	21
Kuwait	22
Kyrgyzstan	21
Laos	30
Latvia	21
Lebanon	22
Lesotho	23
Liberia	22
Libya	21
Liechtenstein	21
Lithuania	21
Luxembourg	21
Macedonia	21
Madagascar	23
Madeira	31
Malawi	23
Malaysia	24
Maldives	26
Mali	25
Malta	21
Mariana Islands	26
Marshall Islands	32
Mauritania	23
Mauritius	22
Mexico	23
Micronesia	23
Moldova	21
Monaco	21
Mongolia	24
Montenegro	21
Montserrat	31
Morocco	22
Mozambique	23
Namibia	23
Nauru	36
Nepal	23
Netherlands	21

Place or country	Number of days
Nevis	24
New Caledonia	31
New Zealand	26
New Zealand Island Territories	50
Nicaragua	24
Niger (Republic of)	25
Nigeria	22
Norfolk Island	31
Norway	21
Oman (Sultanate of)	22
Pakistan	23
Palau	23
Panama	26
Papua New Guinea	26
Paraguay	22
Peru	22
Philippines	23
Pitcairn, Henderson, Ducie and Oeno Islands	31
Poland	21
Portugal	21
Portuguese Timor	31
Puerto Rico	23
Qatar	23
Reunion	31
Romania	22
Russia	21
Rwanda	23
Sabah	23
St. Helena	31
St. Kitts and Nevis	24
St. Lucia	24
St. Pierre and Miquelon	31
St. Vincent and the Grenadines	24
Samoa (U.S.A. Territory) (See also Western Samoa)	30
San Marino	21
Sao Tome and Principe	25
Sarawak	28
Saudi Arabia	24
Scotland	21

Place or country	Number of days
Senegal	22
Serbia	21
Seychelles	22
Sierra Leone	22
Singapore	22
Slovakia	21
Slovenia	21
Society Islands (French Polynesia)	31
Solomon Islands	29
Somalia	22
South Africa	22
South Georgia (Falkland Island Dependencies)	31
South Orkneys	21
South Shetlands	21
Spain	21
Spanish Territories of North Africa	31
Sri Lanka	23
Sudan	22
Surinam	22
Swaziland	22
Sweden	21
Switzerland	21
Syria	23
Tajikistan	21
Tanzania	22
Thailand	23
Togo	22
Tonga	30
Trinidad and Tobago	23
Tristan Da Cunha	31
Tunisia	22
Turkey	21
Turkmenistan	21
Turks & Caicos Islands	31
Tuvalu	23
Uganda	22
Ukraine	21
United Arab Emirates	22
United States of America	22

Place or country	Number of days
Uruguay	22
Uzbekistan	21
Vanuatu	29
Vatican City State	21
Venezuela	22
Vietnam	28
Virgin Islands – U.S.A	24
Wake Island	25
Western Samoa	34
Yemen (Republic of)	30
Zaire	25
Zambia	23
Zimbabwe	22

ANNEX – SERVICE REGULATION (RULE 6.44)

[Can be found at] http://www.justice.gov.uk/civil/procrules-fin/contents/form-section-images/practice- directions/pd6b-pdf-eps/pd6b-ecreg2007.pdf

PRACTICE DIRECTION 6C – DISCLOSURE OF ADDRESSES BY GOVERNMENT DEPARTMENTS (AMENDING PD OF 13 FEBRUARY 1989)

This Practice Direction supplements FPR Part 6

The arrangements set out in the Registrar's Direction of 26 April 1988 whereby the court may request the disclosure of addresses by government departments have been further extended. These arrangements will now cover:
(a) tracing the address of a person in proceedings against whom another person is seeking to obtain or enforce an order for financial provision either for himself or herself or for the children of the former marriage; and,
(b) tracing the whereabouts of a child, or the person with whom the child is said to be, in proceedings under the Child Abduction and Custody Act 1985 or in which a [Part I order] is being sought or enforced.

Requests for such information will be made officially by the [district judge]. The request, in addition to giving the information mentioned below, should certify:
1 In financial provision applications either
    (a) that a financial provision order is in existence, but cannot be enforced because the person against whom the order has been made cannot be traced; or
    (b) that the applicant has filed or issued a notice, petition or originating summons containing an application for financial provision which cannot be served because the respondent cannot be traced.

[A 'financial provision order' means any of the orders mentioned in s 21 of the Matrimonial Causes Act 1973, except an order under s 27(6) of that Act].

2 In wardship proceedings that the child is the subject of wardship proceedings and cannot be traced, and is believed to be with the person whose address is sought.
3 (deleted)

The following notes set out the information required by those departments which are likely to be of the greatest assistance to an applicant.

(1) Department of Social Security

The department most likely to be able to assist is the Department of Social Security, whose records are the most comprehensive and complete. The possibility of identifying one person amongst so many will depend on the particulars given. An address will not be supplied by the department unless it is satisfied from the particulars given that the record of the person has been reliably identified.

The applicant or his solicitor should therefore be asked to supply as much as possible of the following information about the person sought:

(i) National Insurance number;
(ii) surname;
(iii) forenames in full;
(iv) date of birth (or, if not known, approximate age);
(v) last known address, with date when living there;
(vi) any other known address(es) with dates;
(vii) if the person sought is a war pensioner, his war pension and service particulars (if known);

and in applications for financial provision:
(viii) the exact date of the marriage and the wife's forenames.

> Enquiries should be sent by the [district judge] to:
> Contribution Agency
> Special Section A, Room 101B
> Longbenton
> Newcastle upon Tyne
> NE98 1YX

The department will be prepared to search if given full particulars of the person's name and date of birth, but the chances of accurate identification are increased by the provision of more identifying information.

Second requests for records to be searched, provided that a reasonable interval has elapsed, will be met by the Department of Social Security.

Income Support [/Supplementary Benefit]

Where, in the case of applications for financial provision, the wife is or has been in receipt of [income support/supplementary benefit], it would be advisable in the first instance to make enquiries of the manager of the local Social Security office for the area in which she resides in order to avoid possible duplication of enquiries.

(2) [Office for National Statistics]

National Health Service Central Register

[The Office for National Statistics] administers the National Health Service Central Register for the Department of Health. The records held in the Central Register include individuals' names, with dates of birth and National Health Service number, against a record of the Family Practitioner Committee area where the patient is currently registered with a National Health Service doctor. The Central Register does not hold individual patients' addresses, but can advise courts of the last Family Practitioner Committee area registration. Courts can then apply for information about addresses to the appropriate Family Practitioner Committee for independent action.

When application is made for the disclosure of Family Practitioner Committee area registrations from these records the applicant or his solicitor should supply as much as possible of the following information about the person sought:

(i) National Health Service number;
(ii) surname;
(iii) forenames in full;
(iv) date of birth (or, if not known, approximate age);
(v) last known address;
(vi) mother's maiden name.

Enquiries should be sent by the [district judge] to:

[The Office for National Statistics]
National Health Service Central Register
Smedley Hydro, Trafalgar Road
Southport
Merseyside PR8 2HH

(3) **Passport Office**

If all reasonable enquiries, including the aforesaid methods, have failed to reveal an address, or if there are strong grounds for believing that the person sought may have made a recent application for a passport, enquiries may be made to the Passport Office. The applicant or his solicitor should provide as much of the following information about the person as possible:

(i) surname;
(ii) forenames in full;
(iii) date of birth (or, if not known, approximate age);
(iv) place of birth;
(v) occupation;
(vi) whether known to have travelled abroad, and, if so, the destination and dates;
(vii) last known address, with date living there;
(viii) any other known address(es), with dates.

The applicant or his solicitor must also undertake in writing that information given in response to the enquiry will be used solely for the purpose for which it was requested, i.e. to assist in tracing the husband in connection with the making or enforcement of a financial provision order or in tracing a child in connection with a [Part 1 order] or wardship proceedings, as the case may be.

Enquiries should be sent to:

The Chief Passport Officer
[UK Passport Agency]
Home Office
Clive House, Petty France
London
SW1H 9HD

(4) **Ministry of Defence**

In cases where the person sought is known to be serving or to have recently served in any branch of HM Forces, the solicitor representing the applicant may obtain the address for service of financial provision or [Part I] and wardship proceedings direct from the appropriate service department. In the case of army servicemen, the solicitor can obtain a list of regiments and of the various manning and record offices from the Officer in Charge, Central Manning Support Office, Higher Barracks, Exeter EC4 4ND.

The solicitor's request should be accompanied by a written undertaking that the address will be used for the purpose of service of process in those proceedings and that so far as is possible the solicitor will disclose the address only to the court and not to the applicant or any other person, except in the normal course of the proceedings.

Alternatively, if the solicitor wishes to serve process on the person's commanding officer under the provisions contained in s 101 of the Naval Act 1957, s 153 of the Army Act 1955 and s 153 of the Air Force Act 1955 (all of which as amended by s 62 of the Armed Forces Act 1971) he may obtain that officer's address in the same way.

Where the applicant is acting in person the appropriate service department is prepared to disclose the address of the person sought, or that of his commanding officer, to a [district judge] on receipt of an assurance that the applicant has given an undertaking that the information will be used solely for the purpose of serving process in the proceedings.

In all cases, the request should include details of the person's full name, service number, rank or rating, and his ship, arm or trade, corps, regiment or unit or as much of this information as is available. The request should also include details of his date of birth, or, if not known, his age, his date of entry into the service and, if no longer serving, the date of discharge, and any other information, such as his last known address. Failure to quote the service number and the rank or rating may result in failure to identify the serviceman or at least in considerable delay.

Enquiries should be addressed as follows:

(a)	Officers of Royal Navy and Women's Royal Naval Service	The Naval Secretary Room 161 Victory Building HM Naval Base Portsmouth Hants PO1 3LS
	Ratings in the Royal Navy WRNS Ratings QARNNS Ratings	Captain Naval Drafting Centurion Building Grange Road Gosport Hants PO13 9XA
	RN Medical and Dental Officers	The Medical Director General (Naval) Room 114 Victory Building HM Naval Base Portsmouth Hants PO1 3LS
	Naval Chaplains	Director General Naval Chaplaincy Service Room 201 Victory Building HM Naval Base Portsmouth Hants PO1 3LS
(b)	Royal Marine Officers	The Naval Secretary Room 161 Victory Building HM Naval Base Portsmouth Hants PO1 3LS

	Royal Marine Ranks	HQRM (DRORM) West Battery Whale Island Portsmouth Hants PO2 8DX
(c)	Army Officers (including WRAC and QARANC)	Army Officer Documentation Office Index Department Room F7 Government Buildings Stanmore Middlesex
	Other Ranks, Army	The Manning and Record Office which is appropriate to the Regiment or Corps
(d)	Royal Air Force Officers and Other Ranks Women's Royal Air Force Officers and Other Ranks (including PMRA FNS)	Ministry of Defence RAF Personnel Management 2b1(a) (RAF) Building 248 RAF Innsworth Gloucester GL3 1EZ

General notes

Records held by other departments are less likely to be of use, either because of their limited scope or because individual records cannot readily be identified. If, however, the circumstances suggest that the address may be known to another department, application may be made to it by the [district judge], all relevant particulars available being given.

When the department is able to supply the address of the person sought to the [district judge], it will be passed on by him to the applicant's solicitor (or, in proper cases, direct to the applicant if acting in person) on an understanding to use it only for the purpose of the proceedings.

Nothing in this practice direction affects the service in matrimonial causes of petitions which do not contain any application for financial provision, etc. The existing arrangements whereby the Department of Social Security will at the request of the solicitor forward a letter by ordinary post to a party's last known address remain in force in such cases.

The Registrar's Direction of 26 April 1988 is hereby revoked.

Issued [in its original form] with the concurrence of the Lord Chancellor.

PRACTICE DIRECTION 7A – PROCEDURE FOR APPLICATIONS IN MATRIMONIAL AND CIVIL PARTNERSHIP PROCEEDINGS

This Practice Direction supplements FPR Part 7

Applications for matrimonial and civil partnership orders: general

1.1 An application for a matrimonial or civil partnership order must be made in the form referred to in Practice Direction 5A. The application form sets out the documents which must accompany the application.

1.2 The application for a matrimonial order or a civil partnership order must be completed according to the detailed notes which accompany the form. It is especially important that the particulars provide evidence to show why the applicant is entitled to–

(a) in matrimonial proceedings, a dissolution or annulment of the marriage or a decree of judicial separation;
(b) in civil partnership proceedings, a dissolution or annulment of the civil partnership or a separation order.

The particulars should, however, be as concise as possible consistent with providing the necessary evidence.

Respondents: restrictions

2.1 Where the application refers to adultery or to an improper association with another person, that other person should not be named in the application unless the applicant believes the other party to the marriage or civil partnership in question is likely to object to the making of a matrimonial or civil partnership order on the application. Furthermore, such a person should not be a respondent if under the age of 16 or alleged to have been the victim of rape committed by the other party to the marriage or civil partnership, unless the court gives permission.

Proof of marriage or civil partnership to accompany the application

3.1 The application form for a matrimonial order or a civil partnership order sets out the documents which must accompany the application. Where the existence and validity of a marriage or civil partnership is not disputed, its validity will be proved by the application being accompanied by–

(a) one of the following–
    (i) a certificate of the marriage or civil partnership to which the application relates;
    (ii) a similar document issued under the law in force in the country where the marriage or civil partnership registration took place; or
    (iii) a certified copy of such a certificate or document obtained from the appropriate register office; and
(b) where the certificate, document or certified copy is not in English (or, where the court is in Wales, in Welsh), a translation of that document certified by a notary public or authenticated by a statement of truth.

Filing without accompanying proof of marriage or civil partnership

3.2 If–

(a) the applicant cannot produce–
    (i) the certificate, similar document or a certified copy; and
    (ii) (where necessary) an authenticated translation; at the time of filing the application; and
(b) it is urgent that the application be filed, the applicant may apply to the court without notice for permission to file the application without the certificate, document, certified copy or authenticated translation.

3.3 The applicant or the applicant's solicitor must in such a case file with the application a statement explaining why–

(a) the required document is not available; and
(b) the application is urgent.

3.4 The court may give permission to file the application without the required document if the applicant gives an undertaking to file that document at the very earliest opportunity and within any time limit set by the court.

Other methods of proof of the marriage or civil partnership

3.5 The requirements of this Practice Direction do not prevent the existence and validity of a marriage, or of an overseas relationship which is not a marriage, being proved in accordance with–

(a) the Evidence (Foreign, Dominion and Colonial Documents) Act 1933; or
(b) any other method authorised in any other Practice Direction, rule or Act.

Information required where evidence of a conviction or finding is to be relied on

4.1 An applicant for a matrimonial or civil partnership order who wishes to rely on evidence–

(a) under section 11 of the Civil Evidence Act 1968 of a conviction of an offence; or
(b) under section 12 of that Act of a finding or adjudication of adultery or paternity, must include in the application form a statement to that effect and give the following details–

   (i) the type of conviction, finding or adjudication and its date;
   (ii) the court or Court-Martial which made the conviction, finding or adjudication; and
   (iii) the issue in the proceedings to which it relates.

Amendments to applications and answers

5.1 An application for permission to amend an application for a matrimonial or civil partnership order or answer may be dealt with at a hearing.

5.2 When making an application for permission to amend an application for a matrimonial or civil partnership order or to amend an answer the applicant should file at court–

(a) the notice of application for permission; and
(b) a copy of the application for a matrimonial or civil partnership order or the answer showing the proposed amendments.

5.3 Where permission to amend has been given, the party applying to make the amendment should within 14 days of the date of the order, or within such other period as the court directs, file with the court the amended application for a matrimonial or civil partnership order or the amended answer.

Requests for further information under rule 7.15 (further information)

6.1 Before making an application under rule 7.15, the party seeking clarification or information ('the requesting party') should first serve a written request for it on the party from whom the clarification or information is sought, giving a date by which a reply should be served. The date should be such as to allow the requested party a reasonable time to respond.

6.2 A request should be made by letter or in a separate document, should contain no other subject matter, and should make clear that it is made under rule 7.15. It must be concise and confined to matters which are reasonably necessary and proportionate to enable the requesting party to prepare his or her own case or understand the case of the party to whom the request is directed.

6.3 The reply to the request must be in writing, dated and signed by the requested party or that party's legal representative.

6.4 The reply may be made by letter or in a separate document, should contain no other subject matter, and should make clear that it is a reply to the request concerned. It should repeat each request together with the reply to it. It must be served on every party to the proceedings.

6.5 A party who objects to replying to all or part of a request under rule 7.15, or who is unable to do so, must inform the requesting party promptly, and in any event within the time within which a reply has been requested, and give reasons for objecting or being unable to reply (as the case may be).

Disclosure and inspection

7.1 Where an application for a matrimonial or civil partnership order is not being dealt with as an undefended case the court may make an order for the disclosure of documents under rule 7.22(2)(c).

7.2 When an order for disclosure is made, the disclosing party must, in order to comply, make a reasonable search for the documents required to be disclosed. The extent of the search will depend upon the circumstances of the case and parties should bear in mind the overriding principle of proportionality.

7.3 Documents should be disclosed in a list which should normally list the documents in date order, numbering them consecutively and giving each a concise description. Where there are a large number of documents falling into a particular category they may be grouped together (e.g. 50 bank statements relating to x account from y date to z date).

7.4 The obligations imposed by a disclosure order continue until the proceedings come to an end. If, after the list of documents has been prepared and served, the existence of further documents to which the order applies comes to the attention of the disclosing party, that party must prepare and serve a supplemental list.

7.5 A list of documents must contain the following statement:

I, [insert name] state that I have carried out a reasonable and proportionate search to locate all the documents which I am required to disclose under the disclosure order made by the court on [insert date]. [I did not search for [insert here any limitations on search by reference to date, location, nature of documents etc]]. I understand the duty of disclosure and to the best of my knowledge I have carried out that duty. I certify that the list above is a complete list of all the documents which are or have been in my control and which I am obliged under the order to disclose.

7.6 If the disclosing party wishes to claim a right or duty to withhold inspection of a document or part of a document, that party must indicate in writing in the disclosure statement that such a right or duty is claimed, and the grounds on which it is claimed.

Decrees absolute and final orders: need for expedition

8.1 Where a party in an application for a matrimonial order has grounds for expediting the making of the decree absolute, that party should ordinarily seek directions with a view to an early hearing of the case. Where such an application has not been possible, an application should be made to the district judge making the decree nisi for the time between the decree nisi and the making absolute of that decree to be shortened.

8.2 Where the need for expedition only becomes obvious after the making of the decree nisi, or where (exceptionally) it arises in an undefended case to which the summary procedure applies, an application, on notice to the other parties to the proceedings, should be made using the procedure in Part 18 for an order shortening the time before which the decree nisi may be made absolute.

8.3 Where a party in an application for a civil partnership order has grounds for expediting the making of the final order, that party should ordinarily seek directions with a view to an early hearing of the case. Where such an application has not been possible, an application should be made to the district judge making the conditional order for the time between the conditional and final order to be shortened.

8.4 Where the need for expedition only becomes obvious after the making of the conditional order, or where (exceptionally) it arises in an undefended case to which the summary procedure applies, an application, on notice to the other parties to the proceedings, should be made using the procedure in Part 18 for an order shortening the time before which the final order may be made.

PRACTICE DIRECTION 7B – MEDICAL EXAMINATIONS ON APPLICATIONS FOR ANNULMENT OF A MARRIAGE

This Practice Direction supplements FPR Part 7, rule 7.26 (Medical examinations in proceedings for nullity of marriage)

1.1 Where an application is made for the annulment of a marriage based on the incapacity of one of the parties to consummate, it will not usually be necessary to appoint a medical inspector where the application is undefended. Where the application is defended the court should not appoint a medical inspector unless it appears necessary to do so for the proper disposal of the case.

1.2 A medical examination ordered under rule 7.26 must, if the party to be examined so requests, be conducted by a doctor of the same gender as the person to be examined. Unless both parties are to be examined, each by a doctor of their own gender, it should not normally be necessary to appoint more than one medical inspector.

1.3 The costs of any medical examination ordered under rule 7.26 will be borne, in the first instance, by the party on whose application the medical inspector is appointed. Such costs form part of the costs of the proceedings.

1.4 It is the responsibility of the party on whose application the medical inspector is appointed to address, at the case management hearing, the question of whether any medical inspector is required to attend the final hearing of the proceedings. A medical inspector who is to give evidence at the proceedings is to be treated as an expert witness and the relevant rules in Part 25 (Experts and Assessors) will apply. The relevant rules in Part 25 will also apply to the medical inspector's report.

1.5 Nothing in this Practice Direction or in rule 7.26 affects the parties' right to adduce other evidence relevant to the proper disposal of the case. Such evidence must be verified by a statement of truth.

PRACTICE DIRECTION 7C – POLYGAMOUS MARRIAGES

This Practice Direction supplements FPR Part 7 (procedure for applications in matrimonial and civil partnership proceedings), Part 9 (applications for a financial remedy) and Part 18 (procedure for other applications in proceedings)

Scope of this Practice Direction

1.1 This practice direction applies where an application is made for–

- (a) a matrimonial order;
- (b) an order under section 27 of the 1973 Act;
- (c) an order under section 35 of the 1973 Act;
- (d) an order under the 1973 Act which is made in connection with, or with proceedings for any of the above orders; or
- (e) an order under Part 3 of the 1984 Act,

and either party to the marriage is, or has during the course of the marriage, been married to more than one person (a polygamous marriage).

Polygamous marriages

2.1 Where this practice direction applies the application must state–

- (a) that the marriage is polygamous;
- (b) whether, as far as the party to the marriage is aware, any other spouse (that is, a spouse other than the spouse to whom the application relates) of that party is still living (the 'additional spouse'); and
- (c) if there is such an additional spouse–
  - (i) the additional spouse's name and address;
  - (ii) the date and place of the marriage to the additional spouse.

2.2 A respondent who believes that the marriage is polygamous must include the details referred to in paragraph 2.1 above in the acknowledgment of service if they are not included in the application.

2.3 The applicant in any proceedings to which this practice direction applies must apply to the court for directions as soon as possible after the filing of the application or the receipt of an acknowledgment of service mentioning an additional spouse.

2.4 On such an application or of its own initiative the court may–

(a) give the additional spouse notice of any of the proceedings to which this practice direction applies; and

(b) make the additional spouse a party to such proceedings.

2.5 In any case where the application or acknowledgment of service states that the marriage is polygamous (whether or not there is an additional spouse) a court officer must clearly mark the file with the words 'Polygamous Marriage'. The court officer must also check whether an application under paragraph 2.4 has been made in the case and, where no application has been made, refer the file to the court for consideration.

References in decrees to section 47 of the 1973 Act

3.1 Every decree nisi and decree absolute which is made in respect of a polygamous marriage must refer to the fact that the order is made with reference to section 47 of the 1973 Act.

PRACTICE DIRECTION 7D – GENDER RECOGNITION ACT 2004

This Practice Direction supplements FPR Part 7
Procedure: (1) Title of the Cause; (2) Evidence at Trial of Cause

1 Introduction

The Gender Recognition Act 2004 ('the Act') provides transsexual people with the opportunity to obtain legal recognition in their acquired gender. Legal recognition follows from the issue of a full gender recognition certificate by a Gender Recognition Panel. Section 4 of the Act requires that where a Panel has granted an application to a married applicant, the gender recognition certificate that it must issue shall be an interim gender recognition certificate. The interim certificate may then be used by either party to the marriage as evidence in support of an application to annul the marriage under section 12(g) of, or paragraph 11(1)(e) of Schedule 1 to, the Matrimonial Causes Act 1973 ('that an interim gender recognition certificate has, after the time of the marriage, been issued to either party to the marriage').

2 Application

2.1 This Practice Direction applies to proceedings for divorce, judicial separation and annulment of marriage commenced on or after 4 April 2005.

2.2 Where proceedings for divorce, judicial separation or annulment of marriage have been commenced prior to this date, paragraphs 3.2 to 3.5 below shall also apply to those proceedings if, but only if, the court acquires protected information (as defined by section 22 of the Act) in respect of a party to those proceedings.

3 Title of the cause

3.1 When a party to a matrimonial cause has changed his or her name since marriage, by deed poll or otherwise, the name currently being used by the party should appear first on any petition, answer and statement of arrangements followed by 'formerly known as .... (married name)'.

3.2 Subject to paragraph 3.3, when describing the parties in any Decree, Order, Notice or other document issued by the court, the parties should be described by their full current names only.

3.3 When giving details of the parties in any court list (including a special procedure cause list) they should be described by the initials and surname of their current names only. (For example, *A B Jones* v *C D Jones*).

3.4 For the sake of clarity, in any document or court list mentioned in paragraphs 3.2 and 3.3 above party titles (i.e. Mr, Mrs, Miss, etc.) should be omitted.

3.5 The Practice Note of 2 May 1940 (Title of Cause) shall cease to have effect.

4 Evidence at trial of cause

4.1 This part of the Practice Direction applies where the following conditions are met:

(a) proceedings for annulment of marriage are brought under Section 12(g) of, or paragraph 11(1)(e) of Schedule 1 to, the Matrimonial Causes Act 1973 and paragraph 11 of Schedule 1 to, that Act; and

(b) the cause is an undefended cause.

4.2 Any party requesting directions for trial may, in addition to the requirements of FPR rule 2.25(2), state in their request that they would wish to give their evidence at the trial of the cause in accordance with the provisions of this Practice Direction; and in that event, the request must be accompanied by an affidavit setting out the information required by the appendix to this Practice Direction.

4.3 Where directions for trial are given in accordance with FPR rule 2.24(5) in respect of a request to which paragraph 4.2 applies, a direction may also be given under Rule 2.28(3) that the affidavit lodged with the request for directions shall be treated as the evidence of that party at the trial of the cause (unless otherwise directed).

4.4 In the case of an undefended cause proceeding on the respondent's answer, this part of the Practice Direction and the contents of the appendix shall apply with appropriate modifications.

4.5 The appendix sets out a form of affidavit that may be used for the purposes of paragraph 4.2.

5 Issued with the approval and concurrence of the Lord Chancellor.

APPENDIX – A FORM OF AFFIDAVIT FOR THE PURPOSES OF PARAGRAPH 4.2

Affidavit by Petitioner in support of petition for annulment under Section 12(g) of the Matrimonial Causes Act 1973

In the [   ] County Court°
[Principal Registry of the Family Division°] °delete as appropriate
Between [   ] (Petitioner)
And [   ] (Respondent)
And [   ] (Co-Respondent)

Question	Answer
About the Petition	
1. Have you read the petition in this case?	
2. Do you wish to alter or to add to any statement in the petition? If so, state the alterations or additions.	

3. Subject to these alterations or additions (if any) is everything stated in your petition true? If any statement is not within your own knowledge, indicate this and say whether it is true to the best of your information and belief.	
About the interim gender recognition certificate 4. State the date on which the interim gender recognition certificate was issued: State the serial number of the interim certificate: State the name of the person to whom the certificate has been issued: State the date on which you commenced proceedings to annul your marriage: You must attach a copy of the interim gender recognition certificate to this form.	
About other proceedings 5. To the best of your knowledge and belief has been there been or is there continuing any of the following proceedings; ■ an application to amend an error in the interim certificate; ■ an appeal against a decision to amend (or not to amend) an error in the interim certificate; ■ a reference under section 8(5) of the Gender Recognition Act 2004; or ■ an appeal against a decision made following reference under section 8(5)? If so, please give details of those proceedings and any order made. (You should also attach copies of any orders made).	
About the children of the family 6. Has a Statement of Arrangements been filed in this case? If so, answer questions 7, 8 and 9.	
7. Have you read the Statement of Arrangements filed in this case?	
8. Do you wish to alter anything in the Statement of Arrangements or add to it? If so, state the alterations or additions.	

9. Subject to these alterations and additions (if any) is everything stated in the Statement of Arrangements true?

If any statement is not within your own knowledge, indicate this and say whether it is true and correct to the bet of your information and belief.

I,(full name)

Of(full residential address)

(occupation)

make oath and say as follows:-

1. I am the petitioner in this cause.
2. The answers to Question s 1 to 9 above are true.
3. [1] identify the signature..[2] appearing in the copy acknowledgement of service now produced to me and marked 'A' as the signature of my husband/wife, the respondent in this cause.
4. I exhibit marked 'B' a copy of the interim gender recognition certificate issued to myself/the respondent in this cause.
5. [3]
6. I identify the signature ....[2] appearing at Part IV of the Statement of Arrangements dated ....now produced to me and marked 'C' as the signature of the respondent.
7. I ask the court to grant a decree annulling my marriage with the respondent on the ground stated in my petition [and to order the respondent / co-respondent to pay the costs of this suit]. [4]

Sworn at:
In the County of
This day of 20

Before me, ...

A Commissioner for Oaths [5]

Officer of the Court appointed by the Judge to take Affidavits

[1] Delete if the acknowledgement is assigned by a solicitor

[2] Insert name of respondent exactly as it appears on the acknowledgement signed by him or her

[3] If you have answered 'Yes' to question 5, exhibit any document on which you wish to rely.

[4] Amend or delete as appropriate.

[5] Delete as the case may be.

PRACTICE DIRECTION 9A: APPLICATION FOR A FINANCIAL REMEDY

This Practice Direction supplements FPR Part 9

Introduction

1.1 Part 9 of the Family Procedure Rules sets out the procedure applicable to the financial proceedings that are included in the definition of a 'financial remedy'.

1.2 The procedure is applicable to a limited extent to applications for financial remedies that are heard in magistrates' courts (namely, those under section 35 of the Matrimonial Causes Act 1973, paragraph 69 of Schedule 5 to the Civil Partnership Act 2004, Part I of the Domestic Proceedings and Magistrates' Courts Act 1978, Schedule 1 to the Children Act 1989 and Schedule 6 to the Civil Partnership Act 2004). However, unless the context otherwise requires, this Practice Direction does not apply to proceedings in a magistrates' court.

1.3 Where an application for a financial remedy includes an application relating to land, details of any mortgagee must be included in the application.

Pre-application protocol

2.1 The 'pre-application protocol' annexed to this Direction outlines the steps parties should take to seek and provide information from and to each other prior to the commencement of any application for a financial remedy. The court will expect the parties to comply with the terms of the protocol.

Costs

3.1 Rule 9.27 applies in the High Court and county court. The rule requires each party to produce to the court, at every hearing or appointment, an estimate of the costs incurred by the party up to the date of that hearing or appointment.

3.2 The purpose of this rule is to enable the court to take account of the impact of each party's costs liability on their financial situations. Parties should ensure that the information contained in the estimate is as full and accurate as possible and that any sums already paid in respect of a party's financial remedy costs are clearly set out. Where relevant, any liability arising from the costs of other proceedings between the parties should continue to be referred to in the appropriate section of a party's financial statement; any such costs should not be included in the estimates under rule 9.27.

3.3 Rule 28.3 provides that the general rule in financial remedy proceedings is that the court will not make an order requiring one party to pay the costs of another party. However the court may make such an order at any stage of the proceedings where it considers it appropriate to do so because of the conduct of a party in relation to the proceedings.

3.4 Any breach of this practice direction or the pre-application protocol annexed to it will be taken into account by the court when deciding whether to depart from the general rule as to costs.

Procedure before the first appointment

4.1 In addition to the matters listed at rule 9.14(5), the parties should, if possible, with a view to identifying and narrowing any issues between the parties, exchange and file with the court–

  (a) a summary of the case agreed between the parties;
  (b) a schedule of assets agreed between the parties; and
  (c) details of any directions that they seek, including, where appropriate, the name of any expert they wish to be appointed.

4.2 Where a party is prevented from sending the details referred to in (c) above, the party should make that information available at the first appointment.

Financial Statements and other documents

5.1 Practice Direction 22A (Written Evidence) applies to any financial statement filed in accordance with rules 9.14 or 9.19 and to any exhibits to a financial statement. In preparing a bundle of documents to be exhibited to or attached to a financial statement, regard must be had in particular to paragraphs 11.1 to 11.3 and 13.1 to 13.4 of that Direction. Where on account of their bulk, it is impracticable for the exhibits to a financial statement to be retained on the court file after the First Appointment, the court may give directions as to their custody pending further hearings.

5.2 Where the court directs a party to provide information or documents by way of reply to a questionnaire or request by another party, the reply must be verified by a statement of truth. Unless otherwise directed, a reply to a questionnaire or request for information and documents shall not be filed with the court.

(Part 17 and Practice Direction 17A make further provision about statements of truth)

Financial Dispute Resolution (FDR) Appointment

6.1 A key element in the procedure is the Financial Dispute Resolution (FDR) appointment. Rule 9.17 provides that the FDR appointment is to be treated as a meeting held for the purposes of discussion and negotiation. Such meetings have been developed as a means of reducing the tension which inevitably arises in family disputes and facilitating settlement of those disputes.

6.2 In order for the FDR to be effective, parties must approach the occasion openly and without reserve. Non-disclosure of the content of such meetings is vital and is an essential prerequisite for fruitful discussion directed to the settlement of the dispute between the parties. The FDR appointment is an important part of the settlement process. As a consequence of *Re D (Minors) (Conciliation: Disclosure of Information)* [1993] Fam 231, evidence of anything said or of any admission made in the course of an FDR appointment will not be admissible in evidence, except at the trial of a person for an offence committed at the appointment or in the very exceptional circumstances indicated in *Re D*.

6.3 Courts will therefore expect–

(a) parties to make offers and proposals;
(b) recipients of offers and proposals to give them proper consideration; and
(c) (subject to paragraph 6.4), that parties, whether separately or together, will not seek to exclude from consideration at the appointment any such offer or proposal.

6.4 Paragraph 6.3(c) does not apply to an offer or proposal made during alternative dispute resolution.

6.5 In order to make the most effective use of the first appointment and the FDR appointment, the legal representatives attending those appointments will be expected to have full knowledge of the case.

6.6 The rules do not provide for FDR appointments to take place during proceedings in magistrates' courts.

(Provision relating to experts in financial remedy proceedings is contained in the Practice Direction supplementing Part 25 of the FPR relating to Experts and Assessors in Family Proceedings)

Consent orders

7.1 Rule 9.26 (1)(a) requires an application for a consent order to be accompanied by two copies of the draft order in the terms sought, one of which must be endorsed with a statement signed by the respondent to the application signifying the respondent's agreement. The rule is considered to have been properly complied with if the endorsed statement is signed by solicitors on record as acting for the respondent; but where the consent order applied for contains undertakings, it should be signed by the party giving the undertakings as well as by that party's solicitor.

(Provision relating to the enforcement of undertakings is contained in the Practice Direction 33A supplementing Part 33 of the FPR)

7.2 Rule 9.26(1)(b) requires each party to file with the court and serve on the other party a statement of information. Where this is contained in one form, both parties must sign the statement to certify that each has read the contents of the other's statement.

7.3 Rule 35.2 deals with applications for a consent order in respect of a financial remedy where the parties wish to have the content of a written mediation agreement to which the Mediation Directive applies made the subject of a consent order.

Section 10(2) of the Matrimonial Causes Act 1973 and section 48(2) of the Civil Partnership Act 2004

8.1 Where a respondent who has applied under section 10(2) of the Matrimonial Causes Act 1973, or section 48(2) of the Civil Partnership Act 2004, for the court to consider his or her financial position after a divorce or dissolution elects not to proceed with the application, a notice of withdrawal of the application signed by the respondent or by the respondent's solicitor may be filed without leave of the court. In this event a formal order dismissing or striking out the application is unnecessary. Notice of withdrawal should also be given to the applicant's solicitor.

8.2 An application under section 10(2) or section 48(2) which has been withdrawn is not a bar to making in matrimonial proceedings, the decree absolute and in civil partnership proceedings, the final order.

Maintenance Orders – registration in magistrates' courts

9.1 Where periodical payments are required to be made to a child under an order registered in a magistrates' court, section 62 of the Magistrates' Courts Act 1980 permits the payments to be made instead to the person with whom the child has his home. That person may proceed in his own name for variation, revival or revocation of the order and may enforce payment either in his own name or by requesting the designated officer of the court to do so.

9.2 The registration in a magistrates' court of an order made direct to a child entails a considerable amount of work. Accordingly, when the court is considering the form of an order where there are children, care should be taken not to make orders for payment direct where such orders would be of no benefit to the parties.

Pensions

10.1 The phrase 'party with pension rights' is used in FPR Part 9, Chapter 8. For matrimonial proceedings, this phrase has the meaning given to it by section 25D(3) of the Matrimonial Causes Act 1973 and means 'the party to the marriage who has or is likely to have benefits under a pension arrangement'. There is a definition of 'civil partner with pension rights' in paragraph 29 of Schedule 5 to the Civil Partnership Act 2004 which mirrors the definition of 'party with pension rights' in section 25D(3) of the 1973 Act. The phrase 'is likely to have benefits' in these definitions refers to accrued rights to pension benefits which are not yet in payment.

PPF Compensation

11.1 The phrase 'party with compensation rights' is used in FPR Part 9, Chapter 9. For matrimonial proceedings, the phrase has the meaning given to it by section 25G(5) of the Matrimonial Causes Act 1973 and means the party to the marriage who is or is likely to be entitled to PPF compensation. There is a definition of 'civil partner with compensation rights' in paragraph 37(1) of Schedule 5 to the Civil Partnership Act 2004 which mirrors the definition of 'party with compensation rights' in section 25G(5). The phrase 'is likely to be entitled to PPF Compensation' in those definitions refers to statutory entitlement to PPF Compensation which is not yet in payment.

ANNEX – PRE-APPLICATION PROTOCOL

Notes of guidance

SCOPE OF THE PROTOCOL

1. This protocol is intended to apply to all applications for a financial remedy as defined by rule 2.3. It is designed to cover all classes of case, ranging from a simple application for periodical payments to an application for a substantial lump sum and property adjustment order. The protocol is designed to facilitate the operation of the procedure for financial remedy applications.
2. In considering the options of pre-application disclosure and negotiation, solicitors should bear in mind the advantage of having a court timetable and court managed process. There is sometimes an advantage in preparing disclosure before proceedings are commenced. However, solicitors should bear in mind the objective of controlling costs and in particular the costs of discovery and that the option of pre-application disclosure and negotiation has risks of excessive and uncontrolled expenditure and delay. This option should only be encouraged where both parties agree to follow this route and disclosure is not likely to be an issue or has been adequately dealt with in mediation or otherwise.
3. Solicitors should consider at an early stage and keep under review whether it would be appropriate to suggest mediation and/or collaborative law to the clients as an alternative to solicitor negotiation or court based litigation.
4. Making an application to the court should not be regarded as a hostile step or a last resort, rather as a way of starting the court timetable, controlling disclosure and endeavouring to avoid the costly final hearing and the preparation for it.

FIRST LETTER

5. The circumstances of parties to an application for a financial remedy are so various that it would be difficult to prepare a specimen first letter. The request for information will be different in every case. However, the tone of the initial letter is important and the guidelines in paragraphs 14 and 15 should be followed. It should be approved in advance by the client. Solicitors writing to an unrepresented party should always recommend that he seeks independent legal advice and enclose a second copy of the letter to be passed to any solicitor instructed. A reasonable time limit for an answer may be 14 days.

NEGOTIATION AND SETTLEMENT

6. In the event of pre-application disclosure and negotiation, as envisaged in paragraph 12 an application should not be issued when a settlement is a reasonable prospect.

DISCLOSURE

7. The protocol underlines the obligation of parties to make full and frank disclosure of all material facts, documents and other information relevant to the issues. Solicitors owe their clients a duty to tell them in clear terms of this duty and of the possible consequences of breach of the duty, which may include criminal sanctions under the Fraud Act 2006. This duty of disclosure is an ongoing obligation and includes the duty to disclose any material changes after initial disclosure has been given. Solicitors are referred to the Good Practice Guide for Disclosure produced by Resolution (obtainable from the Administrative Director, 366A Crofton Road, Orpington, Kent BR2 8NN) and can also contact the Law Society's Practice Advice Service on 0870 606 2522.

The Protocol

GENERAL PRINCIPLES

8. All parties must always bear in mind the overriding objective set out at rules 1.1 to 1.4

and try to ensure that applications should be resolved and a just outcome achieved as speedily as possible without costs being unreasonably incurred. The needs of any children should be addressed and safeguarded. The procedures which it is appropriate to follow should be conducted with minimum distress to the parties and in a manner designed to promote as good a continuing relationship between the parties and any children affected as is possible in the circumstances.

9   The principle of proportionality must be borne in mind at all times. It is unacceptable for the costs of any case to be disproportionate to the financial value of the subject matter of the dispute.

10 Parties should be informed that where a court is considering whether to make an order requiring one party to pay the costs of another party, it will take into account pre-application offers to settle and conduct of disclosure.

IDENTIFYING THE ISSUES

11 Parties must seek to clarify their claims and identify the issues between them as soon as possible. So that this can be achieved, they must provide full, frank and clear disclosure of facts, information and documents, which are material and sufficiently accurate to enable proper negotiations to take place to settle their differences. Openness in all dealings is essential.

DISCLOSURE

12 If parties carry out voluntary disclosure before the issue of proceedings the parties should exchange schedules of assets, income, liabilities and other material facts, using the financial statement as a guide to the format of the disclosure. Documents should only be disclosed to the extent that they are required by the financial statement. Excessive or disproportionate costs should not be incurred.

CORRESPONDENCE

13 Any first letter and subsequent correspondence must focus on the clarification of claims and identification of issues and their resolution. Protracted and unnecessary correspondence and 'trial by correspondence' must be avoided.

14 The impact of any correspondence upon the reader and in particular the parties must always be considered. Any correspondence which raises irrelevant issues or which might cause the other party to adopt an entrenched, polarised or hostile position is to be discouraged.

SUMMARY

15 The aim of all pre-application proceedings steps must be to assist the parties to resolve their differences speedily and fairly or at least narrow the issues and, should that not be possible, to assist the court to do so.

PRACTICE DIRECTION 10A – PART 4 OF THE FAMILY LAW ACT 1996

This Practice Direction supplements FPR Part 10

Scope of this Practice Direction

1.1 Paragraphs 4.1 to 7.1 of this Practice Direction do not apply to proceedings heard in a magistrates' court. Attention is drawn to rules made under section 144 of the Magistrates' Courts Act 1980.

Applications for an occupation order or non-molestation order made by a child under the age of sixteen

2.1 If an application for an occupation order or non-molestation order is made by a child under the age of sixteen attention is drawn to section 43 of the 1996 Act. This provides that leave of the court is required for an application made by a child under the age of sixteen. Article 6(b) of the Allocation and Transfer of Proceedings Order 2008 (S.I 2008/2836) provides that such an application must be started in a county court. The application should be made in accordance with Part 18.

Privacy

3.1 If at a hearing which has been held in private–

(a) a non-molestation order is made or an occupation order is made to which a power of arrest is attached; and

(b) the person to whom it is addressed was not given notice of the hearing and was not present at the hearing, the terms of the order and the name of the person to whom it is addressed shall be announced in open court at the earliest opportunity.

3.2 This announcement may be either on the same day when the court proceeds to hear cases in open court or where there is no further business in open court on that day at the next listed sitting of the court.

3.3 When a person arrested under a power of arrest attached to an occupation order cannot conveniently be brought before the relevant judicial authority sitting in a place normally used as a courtroom within 24 hours after the arrest, that person may be brought before the relevant judicial authority at any convenient place. As the liberty of the subject is involved, the press and public should be permitted to be present, unless security needs make this impracticable.

Warrant of arrest on an application under section 47(8) of the 1996 Act

4.1 In accordance with section 47(9) of the 1996 Act, a warrant of arrest on an application under section 47(8) shall not be issued unless–

(a) the application is substantiated on oath; and

(b) the court has reasonable grounds for believing that the respondent has failed to comply with the order.

Attendance of arresting officer

5.1 Attention is drawn to section 47(7) of the 1996 Act. This provides that a person arrested under a power of arrest attached to an occupation order must be brought before a judge within the period of 24 hours beginning at the time of arrest.

5.2 When the arrested person is brought before the judge the attendance of the arresting officer will not be necessary, unless the arrest itself is in issue. A written statement from the arresting officer as to the circumstances of the arrest should normally be sufficient.

5.3 In those cases where the arresting officer was also a witness to the events leading to the arrest and his or her evidence regarding those events is required, arrangements should be made for the arresting officer to attend at a subsequent hearing to give evidence.

Application for Bail

6.1 An application for bail by a person arrested under–

(a) a power of arrest attached to an occupation order under section 47(2) or (3) of the 1996 Act; or

(b) a warrant of arrest issued on an application under section 47(8) or the 1996 Act, may be made orally or in writing.

6.2 The court will require the following information, which an application in writing should therefore contain–

(a) the full name of the person making the application;
(b) the address of the place where the person making the application is detained at the time when the application is made;
(c) the address where the person making the application would reside if granted bail;
(d) the amount of the recognizance in which the person making the application would agree to be bound; and
(e) the grounds on which the application is made and, where a previous application has been refused, full particulars of any change in circumstances which has occurred since that refusal.

6.3 An application made in writing must be signed–

(a) by the person making the application or by a person duly authorised by that person in that behalf; or
(b) where the person making the application is a child or is for any reason incapable of acting, by a children's guardian or litigation friend acting on that person's behalf.

6.4 A copy of the application must be served on the person who obtained the injunction.
6.5 A copy of the bail notice must be given to a respondent who is remanded on bail.

Remand for Medical Examination and Report

7.1 Section 48(4) of the 1996 Act provides that the judge has power to make an order under section 35 of the Mental Health Act 1983 (remand to hospital for report on accused's mental condition) in certain circumstances. If the judge does so attention is drawn to section 35(8) of that Act, which provides that a person remanded to hospital under that section may obtain at his or her own expense an independent report on his or her mental condition from a registered medical practitioner or approved clinician of his or her choice and apply to the court on the basis of it for the remand to be terminated under section 35(7).

PRACTICE DIRECTION 12A – PUBLIC LAW PROCEEDINGS GUIDE TO CASE MANAGEMENT

The Practice Direction below is made by the President of the Family Division under the powers delegated to him by the Lord Chief Justice under Schedule 2, Part 1, paragraph 2(2) of the Constitutional Reform Act 2005, and is approved by Bridget Prentice, Parliamentary Under Secretary of State, by authority of the Lord Chancellor.

Scope

1.1 This Practice Direction applies to care and supervision proceedings. In so far as practicable, it is to be applied to all other Public Law Proceedings.
1.2 This Practice Direction replaces Practice Direction Guide to Case Management in Public Law Proceedings dated April 2008.
1.3 This Practice Direction will come into effect on 6th April 2010. The new form of application for a care or supervision order (Form C110) only applies to proceedings commenced on or after 6th April 2010. Subject to this it is intended that this Practice Direction should apply in so far as practicable to applications made and not disposed of before 6th April 2010. In relation to these applications–

(1) the Practice Direction Guide to Case Management in Public Law Proceedings dated April 2008 applies where it is not practicable to apply this Practice Direction; and
(2) the court may give directions relating to the application of this Practice Direction or the April 2008 Practice Direction.

This is subject to the overriding objective below and to the proviso that such a direction will neither cause further delay nor involve repetition of steps already taken or decisions already made in the case.

1.4 This Practice Direction is to be read with the rules and is subject to them.

1.5 A Glossary of terms is at paragraph 26.

The overriding objective

2.1 This Practice Direction has the overriding objective of enabling the court to deal with cases justly, having regard to the welfare issues involved. Dealing with a case justly includes, so far as is practicable–

(1) ensuring that it is dealt with expeditiously and fairly;
(2) dealing with the case in ways which are proportionate to the nature, importance and complexity of the issues;
(3) ensuring that the parties are on an equal footing;
(4) saving expense; and
(5) allotting to it an appropriate share of the court's resources, while taking into account the need to allot resources to other cases.

Application by the court of the overriding objective

2.2 The court must seek to give effect to the overriding objective when it–

(1) exercises the case management powers referred to in this Practice Direction; or
(2) interprets any provision of this Practice Direction.

Duty of the parties

2.3 The parties are required to help the court further the overriding objective.

Court case management

The main principles

3.1 The main principles underlying court case management and the means of the court furthering the overriding objective in Public Law Proceedings are–

(1) Timetable for the Child: each case will have a timetable for the proceedings set by the court in accordance with the Timetable for the Child;
(2) judicial continuity: each case will be allocated to one or not more than two case management judges (in the case of magistrates' courts, case managers), who will be responsible for every case management stage in the proceedings through to the Final Hearing and, in relation to the High Court or county court, one of whom may be – and where possible should be – the judge who will conduct the Final Hearing;
(3) main case management tools: each case will be managed by the court by using the appropriate main case management tools;
(4) active case management: each case will be actively case managed by the court with a view at all times to furthering the overriding objective;
(5) consistency: each case will, so far as compatible with the overriding objective, be managed in a consistent way and using the standardised steps provided for in this Direction.

The main case management tools

THE TIMETABLE FOR THE CHILD

3.2 The 'Timetable for the Child' is defined by the rules as the timetable set by the court in accordance with its duties under section 1 and 32 of the 1989 Act and shall–

(1) take into account dates of the significant steps in the life of the child who is the subject of the proceedings; and
(2) be appropriate for that child.

The court will set the timetable for the proceedings in accordance with the Timetable for the Child and review this Timetable regularly. Where adjustments are made to the Timetable for the Child, the timetable for the proceedings will have to be reviewed. The Timetable for the Child is to be considered at every stage of the proceedings and whenever the court is asked to make directions whether at a hearing or otherwise.

3.3 The steps in the child's life which are to be taken into account by the court when setting the Timetable for the Child include not only legal steps but also social, care, health and education steps.

3.4 Examples of the dates the court will record and take into account when setting the Timetable for the Child are the dates of–
(1) any formal review by the Local Authority of the case of a looked after child (within the meaning of section 22(1) of the 1989 Act);
(2) the child taking up a place at a new school;
(3) any review by the Local Authority of any statement of the child's special educational needs;
(4) any assessment by a paediatrician or other specialist;
(5) the outcome of any review of Local Authority plans for the child, for example, any plans for permanence through adoption, Special Guardianship or placement with parents or relatives;
(6) any change or proposed change of the child's placement.

3.5 Due regard should be paid to the Timetable for the Child to ensure that the court remains child-focused throughout the progress of Public Law Proceedings and that any procedural steps proposed under the Public Law Outline are considered in the context of significant events in the child's life.

3.6 The applicant is required to provide the information needed about the significant steps in the child's life in the Application Form and to update this information regularly taking into account information received from others involved in the child's life such as other parties, members of the child's family, the person who is caring for the child, the children's guardian and the child's key social worker.

3.7 Before setting the timetable for the proceedings the factors which the court will consider will include the need to give effect to the overriding objective and the timescales in the Public Law Outline by which the steps in the Outline are to be taken. Where possible, the timetable for the proceedings should be in line with those timescales. However, there will be cases where the significant steps in the child's life demand that the steps in the proceedings be taken at times which are outside the timescales set out in the Outline. In those cases the timetable for the proceedings may not adhere to one or more of the timescales set out in the Outline.

3.8 Where more than one child is the subject of the proceedings, the court should consider and may set a Timetable for the Child for each child. The children may not all have the same Timetable, and the court will consider the appropriate progress of the proceedings in relation to each child.

3.9 Where there are parallel care proceedings and criminal proceedings against a person connected with the child for a serious offence against the child, linked directions hearings should where practicable take place as the case progresses. The timing of the proceedings in a linked care and criminal case should appear in the Timetable for the Child.

CASE MANAGEMENT DOCUMENTATION

3.10 Case Management Documentation includes the–
(1) Application Form and Annex Documents;

(2) Case Analysis and Recommendations provided by Cafcass or CAFCASS CYMRU;
(3) Local Authority Case Summary;
(4) Other Parties' Case Summaries.

3.11 The court will encourage the use of the Case Management Documentation which is not prescribed by the rules.

THE CASE MANAGEMENT RECORD

3.12 The court's filing system for the case will be known as the Case Management Record and will include the following main documents–

(1) the Case Management Documentation;
(2) Standard Directions on Issue and on First Appointment;
(3) Case Management Orders approved by the court.

3.13 Parties or their legal representatives will be expected to retain their own record containing copies of the documents on the court's Case Management Record.

THE FIRST APPOINTMENT

3.14 The purpose of the First Appointment is to confirm allocation of the case and give initial case management directions.

THE CASE MANAGEMENT ORDER

3.15 The Case Management Order is an order which will be made by the court at the conclusion of the Case Management Conference, the Issues Resolution Hearing and any other case management hearing. It is designed to achieve active case management as defined in paragraph 3.20 below. The parties are required to prepare and submit to the court a draft of this order in accordance with paragraphs 5.8 to 5.10 below. The order will include such of the provisions referred to in the Glossary at paragraph 26(12) as are appropriate to the proceedings.

ADVOCATES' MEETING/DISCUSSION

3.16 The court will consider directing advocates to have discussions before the Case Management Conference and the Issues Resolution Hearing. Advocates may well find that the best way to have these discussions is to meet. Such discussion is intended to facilitate agreement and to narrow the issues for the court to consider. Advocates and litigants in person may take part in the Advocates' Meeting or discussions.

THE CASE MANAGEMENT CONFERENCE

3.17 In each case there will be a Case Management Conference to enable the case management judge or case manager, with the co-operation of the parties, actively to manage the case and, at the earliest practicable opportunity to–

(1) identify the relevant and key issues; and
(2) give full case management directions including confirming the Timetable for the Child.

THE ISSUES RESOLUTION HEARING

3.18 In each case there will be an Issues Resolution Hearing before the Final Hearing to–

(1) identify any remaining key issues; and
(2) as far as possible, resolve or narrow those issues.

Active case management

3.19 The court must further the overriding objective by actively managing cases.

3.20 Active case management includes–
- (1) identifying the Timetable for the Child;
- (2) identifying the appropriate court to conduct the proceedings and transferring the proceedings as early as possible to that court;
- (3) encouraging the parties to co-operate with each other in the conduct of the proceedings;
- (4) retaining the Case Management Record;
- (5) identifying all facts and matters that are in issue at the earliest stage in the proceedings and at each hearing;
- (6) deciding promptly which issues need full investigation and hearing and which do not and whether a fact finding hearing is required;
- (7) deciding the order in which issues are to be resolved;
- (8) identifying at an early stage who should be a party to the proceedings;
- (9) considering whether the likely benefits of taking a particular step justify any delay which will result and the cost of taking it;
- (10) directing discussion between advocates and litigants in person before the Case Management Conference and Issues Resolution Hearing;
- (11) requiring the use of the Case Management Order and directing advocates and litigants in person to prepare or adjust the draft of this Order where appropriate;
- (12) standardising, simplifying and regulating–
  - (a) the use of Case Management Documentation and forms;
  - (b) the court's orders and directions;
- (13) controlling–
  - (a) the use and cost of experts;
  - (b) the nature and extent of the documents which are to be disclosed to the parties and presented to the court;
  - (c) whether and, if so, in what manner the documents disclosed are to be presented to the court;
  - (d) the progress of the case;
- (14) where it is demonstrated to be in the interests of the child, encouraging the parties to use an alternative dispute resolution procedure if the court considers such a procedure to be appropriate and facilitating the use of such procedure;
- (15) helping the parties to reach agreement in relation to the whole or part of the case;
- (16) fixing the dates for all appointments and hearings;
- (17) dealing with as many aspects of the case as it can on the same occasion;
- (18) where possible dealing with additional issues which may arise from time to time in the case without requiring the parties to attend at court;
- (19) making use of technology; and
- (20) giving directions to ensure that the case proceeds quickly and efficiently.

The Expectations

4.1 The expectations are that proceedings should be–
- (1) conducted using the Case Management Tools and Case Management Documentation referred to in this Practice Direction in accordance with the Public Law Outline;
- (2) finally determined within the timetable fixed by the court in accordance with the Timetable for the Child – the timescales in the Public Law Outline being

adhered to and being taken as the maximum permissible time for the taking of the step referred to in the Outline unless the Timetable for the Child demands otherwise.

4.2 However, there may be cases where the court considers that the child's welfare requires a different approach from the one contained in the Public Law Outline. In those cases, the court will–

(1) determine the appropriate case management directions and timetable; and
(2) record on the face of the order the reasons for departing from the approach in the Public Law Outline.

How the parties should help court case management

Main methods of helping

GOOD CASE PREPARATION

5.1 The applicant should prepare the case before proceedings are issued. In care and supervision proceedings the Local Authority should use the Pre-proceedings checklist.

THE TIMETABLE FOR THE CHILD

5.2 The applicant must state in the Application Form all information concerning significant steps in the child's life that are likely to take place during the proceedings. The applicant is to be responsible for updating this information regularly and giving it to the court. The applicant will need to obtain information about these significant steps and any variations and additions to them from others involved in the child's life such as other parties, members of the child's family, the person who is caring for the child, the children's guardian and the child's key social worker. When the other persons involved in the child's life become aware of a significant step in the child's life or a variation of an existing one, that information should be given to the applicant as soon as possible.

5.3 The information about the significant steps in the child's life will enable the court to set the Timetable for the Child and to review that Timetable in the light of new information. The Timetable for the Child will be included or referred to in the draft of a Case Management Order, the Case Management Order, Standard Directions on Issue and on First Appointment and the directions given at the Case Management Conference and Issues Resolution Hearing.

CASE MANAGEMENT DOCUMENTATION

5.4 The parties must use the Case Management Documentation.

CO-OPERATION

5.5 The parties and their representatives should co-operate with the court in case management, including the fixing of timetables to avoid unacceptable delay, and in the crystallisation and resolution of the issues on which the case turns.

DIRECTIONS

5.6 The parties will–

(1) monitor compliance with the court's directions; and
(2) tell the court or court officer about any failure to comply with a direction of the court or any other delay in the proceedings.

THE CASE MANAGEMENT RECORD

5.7 The parties are expected to retain a record containing copies of the documents on the court's Case Management Record.

DRAFTING THE CASE MANAGEMENT ORDER

5.8 Parties should start to consider the content of the draft of the Case Management Order at the earliest opportunity either before or in the course of completing applications to the court or the response to the application. They should in any event consider the drafting of a Case Management Order after the First Appointment.

5.9 Only one draft of the Case Management Order should be filed with the court for each of the Case Management Conference and the Issues Resolution Hearing. It is the responsibility of the advocate for the applicant, which in care and supervision proceedings will ordinarily be the Local Authority, to prepare those drafts and be responsible for obtaining comments from the advocates and the parties.

5.10 There should be ongoing consideration of the Case Management Orders throughout the proceedings. The Case Management Orders should serve as an aide memoire to everyone involved in the proceedings of–

(1) the Timetable for the Child;
(2) the case management decisions;
(3) the identified issues.

5.11 In paragraphs 5.4, 5.6 to 5.9 'parties' includes parties' legal representatives.

Findings of Fact Hearings

6 In a case where the court decides that a fact finding hearing is necessary, the starting point is that the proceedings leading to that hearing are to be managed in accordance with the case management steps in this Practice Direction.

Ethnicity, Language, Religion and Culture

7 At each case management stage of the proceedings, particularly at the First Appointment and Case Management Conference, the court will consider giving directions regarding the obtaining of evidence about the ethnicity, language, religion and culture of the child and other significant persons involved in the proceedings. The court will subsequently consider the implications of this evidence for the child in the context of the issues in the case.

Adults who may be protected parties

8.1 The applicant must give details in the Application Form of any referral to or assessment by the local authority's Adult Learning Disability team (or its equivalent). The Local Authority should tell the court about other referrals or assessments if known such as a referral to Community Mental Health.

8.2 The court will investigate as soon as possible any issue as to whether an adult party or intended party to the proceedings lacks capacity (within the meaning of the Mental Capacity Act 2005) to conduct the proceedings. A representative (a litigation friend, next friend or guardian ad litem) is needed to conduct the proceedings on behalf of an adult who lacks capacity to do so ('a protected party'). The expectation of the Official Solicitor is that the Official Solicitor will only be invited to act for a protected party as guardian ad litem or litigation friend if there is no other person suitable and willing to act.

8.3 Any issue as to the capacity of an adult to conduct the proceedings must be determined before the court gives any directions relevant to that adult's role within the proceedings.

8.4 Where the adult is a protected party, that party's representative should be involved in any instruction of an expert, including the instruction of an expert to assess whether the adult, although a protected party, is competent to give evidence. The instruction of an expert is a significant step in the proceedings. The representative will wish to consider (and ask the expert to consider), if the protected party is competent to give evidence, their best interests in this regard. The representative may wish to seek advice about 'special measures'. The representative may put forward an argument on behalf of the protected party that the protected party should not give evidence.

8.5 If at any time during the proceedings, there is reason to believe that a party may lack capacity to conduct the proceedings, then the court must be notified and directions sought to ensure that this issue is investigated without delay.

Child likely to lack capacity to conduct the proceedings when aged 18

9   Where it appears that a child is–
- (1) a party to the proceedings and not the subject of them;
- (2) nearing age 18; and
- (3) considered likely to lack capacity to conduct the proceedings when 18, the court will consider giving directions relating to the investigation of a child's capacity in this respect.

Outline of the process and how to use the Main Case Management Tools

10.1 The Public Law Outline set out in the Table below contains an outline of–
- (1) the order of the different stages of the process;
- (2) the purposes of the main case management hearings and matters to be considered at them;
- (3) the latest timescales within which the main stages of the process should take place.

10.2 In the Public Law Outline–
- (1) 'CMC' means the Case Management Conference;
- (2) 'FA' means the First Appointment;
- (3) 'IRH' means the Issues Resolution Hearing;
- (4) 'LA' means the Local Authority which is applying for a care or supervision order;
- (5) 'OS' means the Official Solicitor.

PUBLIC LAW OUTLINE

PRE-PROCEEDINGS	
PRE-PROCEEDINGS CHECKLIST	
Annex Documents (the documents specified in the Annex to the Application Form to be attached to that form where available): ■ Social Work Chronology ■ Initial Social Work Statement ■ Initial and Core Assessments ■ Letters Before Proceedings ■ Schedule of Proposed Findings ■ Care Plan	Other Checklist Documents which already exist on LA's files which are to be disclosed in the event of proceedings normally before the day of the FA: ■ Previous court orders & judgments/reasons ■ Any relevant assessment materials ■ Section 7 & 37 reports ■ Relatives & friends materials (e.g., a genogram) ■ Other relevant reports & records ■ Single, joint or inter-agency materials (e.g., health & education/Home Office & Immigration documents) ■ Records of discussions with the family ■ Key LA minutes & records for the child (including Strategy Discussion Record) ■ Pre-existing care plans (e.g., child in need plan, looked after child plan & child protection plan)

STAGE 1 – ISSUE AND THE FIRST APPOINTMENT	
ISSUE	FIRST APPOINTMENT
On DAY 1 and by DAY 3	By DAY 6
Objectives: To ensure compliance with preproceedings checklist; to allocate proceedings; to obtain the information necessary for initial case management at the FA	Objectives: To confirm allocation; to give initial case management directions

On Day 1:	

■ The LA files the Application Form and Annex Documents where available
■ Court officer issues application
■ Court nominates case manager(s)
■ Court gives Standard Directions on Issue including:
   – Pre-proceedings checklist compliance including preparation and service of any missing Annex Documents
   – Allocate and/or transfer
   – Appoint children's guardian
   – Appoint solicitor for the child
   – Case Analysis for FA
   – Appoint a guardian ad litem or litigation friend for a protected party or any non subject child who is a party, including the OS where appropriate
   – List FA by Day 6
   – Make arrangements for contested hearing (if necessary)
By Day 3
■ Cafcass/CAFCASS CYMRU expected to allocate case to children's guardian
■ LA serves the Application Form and Annex Documents, on parties
	■ LA normally serves Other Checklist Documents on the parties
	■ Parties notify LA & court of need for a contested hearing
	■ Court makes arrangements for a contested hearing
	■ Initial case management by court including:
	   – Confirm Timetable for the Child
	   – Confirm allocation or transfer
	   – Identify additional parties & representation (including allocation of children's guardian)
	   – Identify 'Early Final Hearing' cases
	   – Scrutinise Care Plan
	   – Court gives Standard Directions on FA including:
	   – Case Analysis and Recommendations for Stages 2 & 3
	   – Preparation and service of any missing Annex Documents
	   – What Other Checklist Documents are to be filed
	   – LA Case Summary
	   – Other Parties' Case Summaries
	   – Parties' initial witness statements
	   – For the Advocates' Meeting
	   – List CMC or (if appropriate) an Early Final Hearing
	   – Upon transfer

STAGE 2 – CASE MANAGEMENT CONFERENCE	
ADVOCATES' MEETING	CMC
No later than 2 days before CMC	No later than day 45
Objectives: To prepare a draft of the Case Management Order; to identify experts and draft questions for them	Objectives: To identify issue(s); to give full case management directions
<ul><li>Consider information on the Application Form, all Other Parties' Case Summaries and Case Analysis and Recommendations</li><li>Identify proposed experts and draft questions in accordance with Experts Practice Direction</li><li>Draft Case Management Order</li><li>Notify court of need for a contested hearing</li><li>File draft of the Case Management Order with the case manager/case management judge by 11am one working day before the CMC</li></ul>	<ul><li>Detailed case management by the court – Scrutinise compliance with directions – Review and confirm Timetable for the Child – Identify key issue(s) – Confirm allocation or transfer – Consider case management directions in the draft of the Case Management Order – Scrutinise Care Plan – Check compliance with Experts Practice Direction</li><li>Court issues Case Management Order</li><li>Court lists IRH and, where necessary, a warned period for Final Hearing</li></ul>

STAGE 3 – ISSUES RESOLUTION HEARING	
ADVOCATES' MEETING	IRH
Between 2 and 7 days before the IRH	Between 16 & 25 weeks
Objective: To prepare or update the draft of the Case Management Order	Objectives: To resolve and narrow issue(s); to identify any remaining key issues

■ Consider all Other Parties' Case Summaries and Case Analysis and Recommendations
■ Draft Case Management Order
■ Notify court of need for a contested hearing/time for oral evidence to be given
■ File draft of the Case Management Order with the case manager/case management judge by 11am one working day before the IRH
	■ Identification by the court of the key issue(s) (if any) to be determined
	■ Final case management by the court:
	  – Scrutinise compliance with directions
	  – Review and confirm the Timetable for the Child
	  – Consider case management directions in the draft of the Case Management Order
	  – Scrutinise Care Plan
	  – Give directions for Hearing documents:
	    ■ Threshold agreement or facts/issues remaining to be determined
	    ■ Final Evidence & Care Plan
	    ■ Case Analysis and Recommendations
	    ■ Witness templates
	    ■ Skeleton arguments
	    ■ Judicial reading list/reading time/judgment writing time
	    ■ Time estimate
	    ■ Bundles Practice Direction compliance
	    ■ List or confirm Hearing
	■ Court issues Case Management Order

STAGE 4 – HEARING	
Hearing set in accordance with the Timetable for the Child	
Objective: To determine remaining issues	
■ All file & serve updated Case Management Documentation & bundle ■ Draft final order(s) in approved form	■ Judgment/Reasons ■ Disclose documents as required after hearing

Starting the proceedings

Pre-proceedings checklist

11.1 The Pre-proceedings Checklist is to be used by the applicant to help prepare for the start of the proceedings.
11.2 The Pre-proceedings Checklist contains the documents which are specified in the Annex to the Application Form. The rules require those documents which are known as the 'Annex Documents' to be filed with the Application Form where available. The Annex Documents are–

(1) Social Work Chronology;
(2) Initial Social Work Statement;

(3) Initial and Core Assessments;
(4) Letters before Proceedings;
(5) Schedule of Proposed Findings; and
(6) Care Plan.

11.3 In addition, the Pre-proceedings Checklist contains examples of documents other than the Annex Documents which will normally be on the Local Authority file at the start of proceedings so that they can be served on parties in accordance with the Public Law Outline. These documents are known as the 'Other Checklist Documents' and are not to be filed with the court at the start of the proceedings but are to be disclosed to the parties normally before the day of the First Appointment or in accordance with the court's directions and to be filed with the court only as directed by the court.

Compliance with Pre-proceedings Checklist

11.4 It is recognised that in some cases the circumstances are such that the safety and welfare of the child may be jeopardised if the start of proceedings is delayed until all of the documents appropriate to the case and referred to in the Pre-proceedings Checklist are available. The safety and welfare of the child should never be put in jeopardy because of lack of documentation. (Nothing in this Practice Direction affects an application for an emergency protection order under section 44 of the 1989 Act).

11.5 The court recognises that the preparation may need to be varied to suit the circumstances of the case. In cases where any of the Annex Documents required to be attached to the Application Form are not available at the time of issue of the application, the court will consider making directions on issue about when any missing documentation is to be filed. The expectation is that there will be a good reason why one or more of the documents are not available. Further directions relating to any missing documentation are likely to be made at the First Appointment. The court also recognises that some documents on the Pre-proceedings Checklist may not exist and may never exist, for example, the Section 37 report, and that in urgent proceedings no Letter Before Proceedings may have been sent.

What the court will do at the issue of proceedings

Objectives

12.1 The objectives at this stage are for the court–

(1) to identify the Timetable for the Child;
(2) in care and supervision proceedings, to ensure compliance with the Pre-proceedings Checklist;
(3) to allocate proceedings;
(4) to obtain the information necessary to enable initial case management at the First Appointment.

12.2 The steps which the court will take once proceedings have been issued include those set out in paragraphs 12.3 to 12.5 below.

Allocation

12.3 By reference to the Allocation Order, the court will consider allocation of the case and transfer to the appropriate level of court those cases which are obviously suitable for immediate transfer.

Other steps to be taken by the court

DIRECTIONS

12.4 The court will–

(1) consider giving directions–
  (a) appropriate to the case including Standard Directions On Issue;
  (b) in care and supervision proceedings, relating to the preparation, filing and service of any missing Annex Documents and what Other Checklist Documents are to be filed and by when;
  (c) relating to the representation of any protected party or any child who is a party to, but is not the subject of, the proceedings by a guardian ad litem or litigation friend, including the Official Solicitor where appropriate;
(2) appoint a children's guardian in specified proceedings (in relation to care and supervision proceedings the court will expect that Cafcass or CAFCASS CYMRU will have received notice from the Local Authority that proceedings were going to be started);
(3) appoint a solicitor for the child under section 41(3) of the 1989 Act where appropriate;
(4) request the children's guardian or if appropriate another officer of the service or Welsh family proceedings officer to prepare a Case Analysis and Recommendations for the First Appointment;
(5) make arrangements for a contested hearing, if necessary.

(A suggested form for the drafting of Standard Directions on Issue is Form PLO 8 which is available from HMCS)

SETTING A DATE FOR THE FIRST APPOINTMENT

12.5 The court will record the Timetable for the Child and set a date for the First Appointment normally no later than 6 days from the date of issue of the proceedings and in any event in line with the Timetable for the Child.

CASE MANAGERS IN THE MAGISTRATES' COURTS

12.6 In the magistrates' courts, the justices' clerk may nominate one but not more than two case managers.

The First Appointment

Objectives

13.1 The First Appointment is the first hearing in the proceedings. The main objectives of the First Appointment are to–
  (1) confirm allocation; and
  (2) give initial case management directions having regard to the Public Law Outline.

13.2 The steps which the court will take at the First Appointment include those set out in paragraphs 13.3 to 13.6 below.

Steps to be taken by the court

13.3 The court will–
  (1) confirm the Timetable for the Child;
  (2) make arrangements for any contested interim hearing such as an application for an interim care order;
  (3) confirm in writing the allocation of the case or, if appropriate, transfer the case;
  (4) request the children's guardian or if appropriate another officer of the service or Welsh family proceedings officer to prepare a Case Analysis and Recommendations for the Case Management Conference or Issues Resolution Hearing;
  (5) scrutinise the Care Plan;

(6) consider giving directions relating to–
   (a) those matters in the Public Law Outline which remain to be considered including preparation, filing and service of any missing Annex Documents and what Other Checklist documents are to be filed and by when;
   (b) the joining of a person who would not otherwise be a respondent under the rules as a party to the proceedings;
   (c) where any person to be joined as a party may be a protected party, an investigation of that person's capacity to conduct the proceedings and the representation of that person by a guardian ad litem or litigation friend, including the Official Solicitor where appropriate;
   (d) the identification of family and friends as proposed carers and any overseas, immigration, jurisdiction and paternity issues;
   (e) any other documents to be filed with the court;
   (f) evidence to be obtained as to whether a parent who is a protected party is competent to make a statement.

(A suggested form for the drafting of Standard Directions on First Appointment is Form PLO 9 which is available from HMCS)

Early Final Hearing
13.4 Cases which are suitable for an early Final Hearing are those cases where all the evidence necessary to determine issues of fact and welfare is immediately or shortly available to be filed. Those cases are likely to include cases where the child has no parents, guardians, relatives who want to care for the child, or other carers. The court will–
   (1) identify at the First Appointment whether the case is one which is suitable for an early Final Hearing; and
   (2) set a date for that Final Hearing.

Setting a date for the Case Management Conference
13.5 The court will set a date for the Case Management Conference normally no later than 45 days from the date of issue of the proceedings and in any event in line with the Timetable for the Child.

Advocates' Meeting/discussion and the drafting of the Case Management Order
13.6 The court will consider directing a discussion between the parties' advocates and any litigant in person and the preparation of a draft of the Case Management Order as outlined below.

Experts
13.7 A party who wishes to instruct an expert should comply with the Experts Practice Direction. Where the parties are agreed on any matter relating to experts or expert evidence, the draft agreement must be submitted for the court's approval as early as possible in the proceedings.

Advocates' Meeting/discussion and the drafting of the Case Management Order
14.1 The main objective of the Advocates' Meeting or discussion is to prepare a draft of the Case Management Order for approval by the court.
14.2 Where there is a litigant in person the court will consider the most effective way in which that person can be involved in the advocates discussions and give directions as appropriate including directions relating to the part to be played by any McKenzie Friend.
14.3 Timing of the discussions is of the utmost importance. Discussions of matters 'outside the court room door', which could have taken place at an earlier time, are to be avoided.

Discussions are to take place no later than 2 days before the Case Management Conference or the Issues Resolution Hearing whichever is appropriate. The discussions may take place earlier than 2 days before those hearings, for example, up to 7 days before them.

14.4 Following discussion the advocates should prepare or adjust the draft of the Case Management Order. In practice the intention is that the advocate for the applicant, which in care and supervision proceedings will ordinarily be the Local Authority, should take the lead in preparing and adjusting the draft of the Case Management Order following discussion with the other advocates. The aim is for the advocates to agree a draft of the Case Management Order which is to be submitted for the approval of the court.

14.5 Where it is not possible for the advocates to agree the terms of the draft of the Case Management Order, the advocates should specify on the draft, or on a separate document if more practicable–

(1) those provisions on which they agree; and
(2) those provisions on which they disagree.

14.6 Unless the court directs otherwise, the draft of the Case Management Order must be filed with the court no later than 11am on the day before the Case Management Conference or the Issues Resolution Hearing whichever may be appropriate.

14.7 At the Advocates' Meeting or discussion before the Case Management Conference, the advocates should also try to agree the questions to be put to any proposed expert (whether jointly instructed or not) if not previously agreed. Under the Experts Practice Direction the questions on which the proposed expert is to give an opinion are a crucial component of the expert directions which the court is required to consider at the Case Management Conference.

Case Management Conference

Objectives

15.1 The Case Management Conference is the main hearing at which the court manages the case. The main objectives of the Conference are to–

(1) identify key issues; and
(2) give full case management directions.

15.2 The steps which the court will take at the Case Management Conference include those steps set out in paragraphs 15.3 to 15.5 below.

Steps to be taken by the court

15.3 The court will–

(1) review and confirm the Timetable for the Child;
(2) confirm the allocation or the transfer of the case;
(3) scrutinise the Care Plan;
(4) identify the key issues;
(5) identify the remaining case management issues;
(6) resolve remaining case management issues set out in the draft of the Case Management Order;
(7) identify any special measures such as the need for access for the disabled or provision for vulnerable witnesses;
(8) scrutinise the Case Management Record to check whether directions have been complied with and if not, consider making further directions as appropriate;
(9) where expert evidence is required, check whether the parties have complied with the Experts Practice Direction, in particular the section on preparation for the relevant hearing and consider giving directions as appropriate.

Case Management Order

15.4 The court will issue the approved Case Management Order. Parties or their legal representatives will be expected to submit in electronic form the final approved draft of the Case Management Order on the conclusion of, and the same day as, the Case Management Conference.

Setting a date for the Issues Resolution Hearing/Final Hearing

15.5 The court will set–

(1) a date for the Issues Resolution Hearing normally at any time between 16 and 25 weeks from the date of issue of the proceedings and in any event in line with the Timetable for the Child; and

(2) if necessary, specify a period within which the Final Hearing of the application is to take place unless a date has already been set.

The Issues Resolution Hearing

Objectives

16.1 The objectives of this hearing are to–

(1) resolve and narrow issues;
(2) identify key remaining issues requiring resolution.

16.2 The Issues Resolution Hearing is likely to be the hearing before the Final Hearing. Final case management directions and other preparations for the Final Hearing will be made at this hearing.

Steps to be taken by the court

16.3 The court will–

(1) identify the key issues (if any) to be determined;
(2) review and confirm the Timetable for the Child;
(3) consider giving case management directions relating to–

    (a) any outstanding matter contained in the draft of the Case Management Order;
    (b) the preparation and filing of final evidence including the filing of witness templates;
    (c) skeleton arguments;
    (d) preparation and filing of bundles in accordance with the Bundles Practice Direction;
    (e) any agreement relating to the satisfaction of the threshold criteria under section 31 of the 1989 Act or facts and issues remaining to be determined in relation to it or to any welfare question which arises;
    (f) time estimates;
    (g) the judicial reading list and likely reading time and judgment writing time;

(4) issue the Case Management Order.

16.4 For the avoidance of doubt the purpose of an Issues Resolution Hearing is to–

(1) identify key issues which are not agreed;
(2) examine if those key issues can be agreed; and
(3) where those issues cannot be agreed, examine the most proportionate method of resolving those issues.

16.5 The expectation is that the method of resolving the key issues which cannot be agreed will be at a hearing (ordinarily the Final hearing) where there is an opportunity for the relevant oral evidence to be heard and challenged.

Attendance at the Case Management Conference and the Issues Resolution Hearing

17 An advocate who has conduct of the Final Hearing should ordinarily attend the Case Management Conference and the Issues Resolution Hearing. Where the attendance of this advocate is not possible, then an advocate who is familiar with the issues in the proceedings should attend.

Flexible powers of the court

18.1 Attention is drawn to the flexible powers of the court either following the issue of the application in that court, the transfer of the case to that court or at any other stage in the proceedings.

18.2 The court may give directions without a hearing including setting a date for the Final Hearing or a period within which the Final Hearing will take place. The steps, which the court will ordinarily take at the various stages of the proceedings provided for in the Public Law Outline, may be taken by the court at another stage in the proceedings if the circumstances of the case merit this approach.

18.3 The flexible powers of the court include the ability for the court to cancel or repeat a particular hearing. For example, if the issue on which the case turns can with reasonable practicability be crystallised and resolved by having an early Final Hearing, then in the fulfilment of the overriding objective, such a flexible approach must be taken to secure compliance with section 1(2) of the 1989 Act.

Alternative Dispute Resolution

19.1 The court will encourage the parties to use an alternative dispute resolution procedure and facilitate the use of such a procedure where it is–

   (1)   readily available;
   (2)   demonstrated to be in the interests of the child; and
   (3)   reasonably practicable and safe.

19.2 At any stage in the proceedings, the parties can ask the court for advice about alternative dispute resolution.

19.3 At any stage in the proceedings the court itself will consider whether alternative dispute resolution is appropriate. If so, the court may direct that a hearing or proceedings be adjourned for such specified period as it considers appropriate–

   (1)   to enable the parties to obtain information and advice about alternative dispute resolution; and
   (2)   where the parties agree, to enable alternative dispute resolution to take place.

Co-operation

20.1 Throughout the proceedings the parties and their representatives should cooperate wherever reasonably practicable to help towards securing the welfare of the child as the paramount consideration.

20.2 At each court appearance the court will ask the parties and their legal representatives–

   (1)   what steps they have taken to achieve co-operation and the extent to which they have been successful;
   (2)   if appropriate the reason why co-operation could not be achieved; and
   (3)   the steps needed to resolve any issues necessary to achieve cooperation.

Agreed Directions

21.1 The parties, their advisers and the children's guardian, are encouraged to try to agree directions for the management of the proceedings.

21.2 To obtain the court's approval the agreed directions must–
- (1) set out a Timetable for the Child by reference to calendar dates for the taking of steps for the preparation of the case;
- (2) include a date when it is proposed that the next hearing will take place.

Variation of case management timetable

22 It is emphasised that a party or the children's guardian must apply to the court at the earliest opportunity if they wish to vary by extending the dates set by the court for–
- (1) a directions appointment;
- (2) a First Appointment;
- (3) a Case Management Conference;
- (4) an Issues Resolution Hearing;
- (5) the Final Hearing;
- (6) the period within which the Final Hearing of the application is to take place; or
- (7) any Meeting/discussion between advocates or for the filing of the draft of the Case Management Orders.

Who performs the functions of the court

23.1 Where this Practice Direction provides for the court to perform case management functions, then except where any rule, practice direction, any other enactment or the Family Proceedings (Allocation to Judiciary) Directions ((2009) 2 FLR 51) provides otherwise, the functions may be performed–
- (1) in relation to proceedings in the High Court or in a district registry, by any judge or district judge of that Court including a district judge of the principal registry;
- (2) in relation to proceedings in the county court, by any judge or district judge including a district judge of the principal registry when the principal registry is treated as if it were a county court; and
- (3) in relation to proceedings in a magistrates' court by–
  - (a) any family proceedings court constituted in accordance with sections 66 and 67 of the 1980 Act;
  - (b) a single justice; or
  - (c) a justices' clerk.

23.2 The case management functions to be exercised by a justices' clerk may be exercised by an assistant justices' clerk provided that person has been specifically authorised by a justices' clerk to exercise case management functions. Any reference in this Practice Direction to a justices' clerk is to be taken to include an assistant justices' clerk so authorised. The justices' clerk may in particular appoint one but not more than two assistant justices' clerks as case managers for each case.

23.3 In proceedings in a magistrates' court, where a party considers that there are likely to be issues arising at a hearing (including the First Appointment, Case Management Conference and Issues Resolution Hearing) which need to be decided by a family proceedings court, rather than a justices' clerk, then that party should give the court written notice of that need at least 2 days before the hearing.

23.4 Family proceedings courts may consider making arrangements to ensure a court constituted in accordance with s 66 of the 1980 Act is available at the same time as Issues Resolution Hearings are being heard by a justices' clerk. Any delay as a result of the justices' clerk considering for whatever reason that it is inappropriate for a justices' clerk to perform a case management function on a particular matter and the justices' clerk's referring of that matter to the court should then be minimal.

Technology

24 Where the facilities are available to the court and the parties, the court will consider

making full use of technology including electronic information exchange and video or telephone conferencing.

Other Practice Directions

25.1 This Practice Direction must be read with the Bundles Practice Direction.

25.2 The Bundles Practice Direction is applied to Public Law Proceedings in the High Court and county court with the following adjustments–

(1) add 'except the-First Appointment; Case Management Conference, and Issues Resolution Hearing referred to in the Practice Direction Public Law Proceedings Guide to Case Management: April 2010 where there are no contested applications being heard at those hearings' to paragraph 2.2;

(2) the reference to–

  (a) the 'Protocol for Judicial Case Management in Public law Children Act Cases (2003) 2 FLR 719' in paragraph 6.1;
  (b) the 'Practice Direction: Care Cases: Judicial Continuity and Judicial Case Management' in paragraph 15; and
  (c) 'the Public Law Protocol' in paragraph 15,

  shall be read as if it were a reference to this Practice Direction.

25.3 Paragraph 1.9 of the Practice Direction: Experts in Family Proceedings Relating to Children dated April 2008 should be read as if 'Practice Direction: Guide to Case Management in Public law Proceedings, paragraphs 13.7,14.3 and 25(29)' were a reference to 'Practice Direction Public Law Proceedings Guide to Case Management: April 2010, paragraphs 14.7,15.3 and 26(33)'.

Glossary

26 In this Practice Direction–

(1) 'the 1989 Act' means the Children Act 1989;
(2) 'the 1980 Act' means the Magistrates' Courts Act 1980;
(3) 'advocate' means a person exercising a right of audience as a representative of, or on behalf of, a party;
(4) 'Allocation Order' means any order made by the Lord Chancellor under Part 1 of Schedule 11 to the 1989 Act;
(5) 'alternative dispute resolution' means the methods of resolving a dispute other than through the normal court process;
(6) 'Annex Documents' means the documents specified in the Annex to the Application Form;
(7) 'Application Form' means Form C110 and Annex Documents;
(8) 'assistant justices' clerk' has the meaning assigned to it by section 27(5) of the Courts Act 2003;
(9) 'the Bundles Practice Direction' means the Practice Direction Family Proceedings: Court Bundles (Universal Practice to be Applied in all Courts other than Family Proceedings Court) of 27 July 2006;
(10) 'Case Analysis and Recommendations' means a written or oral outline of the case from the child's perspective prepared by the children's guardian or other officer of the service or Welsh family proceedings officer at different stages of the proceedings requested by the court, to provide–

  (a) an analysis of the issues that need to be resolved in the case including–
    (i)   any harm or risk of harm;
    (ii) the child's own views;
    (iii) the family context including advice relating to ethnicity, language, religion and culture of the child and other significant persons;

(iv) the Local Authority work and proposed care plan;
(v) advice about the court process including the Timetable for the Child; and
(vi) identification of work that remains to be done for the child in the short and longer term; and

(b) recommendations for outcomes, in order to safeguard and promote the best interests of the child in the proceedings;

(11) 'Case Management Documentation' includes the documents referred to in paragraph 3.10;

(12) 'Case Management Order' means an order made by the court which identifies the Timetable for the Child, any delay in the proceedings and the reason for such delay and the key issues in the proceedings and includes such of the following provisions as are appropriate to the proceedings–

(a) preliminary information:
   (i) the names and dates of birth of the children who are the subject of the proceedings;
   (ii) the names and legal representatives of the parties, and whether they attended the hearing;
   (iii) any interim orders made in respect of the children and any provisions made for the renewal of those orders;

(b) any recitals that the court considers should be recorded in the order, including those relating to:
   (i) any findings made by the court or agreed between the parties;
   (ii) any other agreements or undertakings made by the parties;

(c) orders made at the hearing by way of case management relating to:
   (i) the joinder of parties;
   (ii) the determination of parentage of the children;
   (iii) the appointment of a guardian ad litem or litigation friend (including the Official Solicitor where appropriate);
   (iv) the transfer of the proceedings to a different court;
   (v) the allocation of the proceedings to a case management judge;
   (vi) the filing and service of threshold criteria documents;
   (vii) the preparation and filing of assessments, including Core Assessments and parenting assessments;
   (viii) in accordance with the Experts' Practice Direction, the preparation and filing of other expert evidence, and experts' meetings;
   (ix) care planning and directions in any application for placement for adoption;
   (x) the filing and service of evidence/further evidence on behalf of the local authority;
   (xi) the filing and service of evidence/further evidence on behalf of the other parties;
   (xii) the filing and service of the Case Analysis and Recommendations;
   (xiii) the disclosure of documents into the proceedings held by third parties, including medical records, police records and Home Office information;
   (xiv) the disclosure of documents and information relating to the proceedings to non-parties;
   (xv) the listing of further hearings, and case management documentation to be prepared for those hearings;
   (xvi) advocates' Meetings;

(xvii) the filing of bundles and other preparatory material for future hearings;
(xviii) technology/special measures;
(xix) media attendance and reporting;
(xx) linked or other proceedings;
(xxi) non-compliance with any court orders;
(xxii) such further or other directions as may be necessary for the purposes of case management;
(xxiii) attendance at court (including child/children's guardian);

(13) 'Case Management Record' means the court's filing system for the case which includes the documents referred to at paragraph 3.12;
(14) 'Case manager' means the justices' clerk or assistant justices' clerk who manages the case in the magistrates' courts;
(15) 'Care Plan' means a 'section 31A plan' referred to in section 31A of the 1989 Act;
(16) 'Core Assessment' means the assessment undertaken by the Local Authority in accordance with The Framework for the Assessment of Children in Need and their Families (Department of Health *et al*, 2000);
(17) 'court' means the High Court, county court or the magistrates' court;
(18) 'court officer' means–

(a) in the High Court or a county court, a member of court staff ;and
(b) in a magistrates' court, the designated officer;

(19) 'Experts Practice Direction' means the Practice Direction regarding Experts in Family Proceedings relating to Children;
(20) 'genogram' means a family tree, setting out in diagrammatic form the family's background;
(21) 'hearing' includes a directions appointment;
(22) 'Initial Assessment' means the assessment undertaken by the Local Authority in accordance with The Framework for the Assessment of Children in Need and their Families (Department of Health *et al*, 2000);
(23) 'Initial Social Work Statement' means a statement prepared by the Local Authority strictly limited to the following evidence–

(a) the precipitating incident(s) and background circumstances relevant to the grounds and reasons for making the application including a brief description of any referral and assessment processes that have already occurred;
(b) any facts and matters that are within the social worker's personal knowledge limited to the findings sought by the Local Authority;
(c) any emergency steps and previous court orders that are relevant to the application;
(d) any decisions made by the Local Authority that are relevant to the application;
(e) information relevant to the ethnicity, language, religion, culture, gender and vulnerability of the child and other significant persons in the form of a 'family profile' together with a narrative description and details of the social care and other services that are relevant to the same;
(f) where the Local Authority is applying for an interim order: the Local Authority's initial proposals for the child (which are also to be set out in the Care Plan) including placement, contact with parents and other significant persons and the social care services that are proposed;
(g) the Local Authority's initial proposals for the further assessment of the parties during the proceedings including twin track /concurrent planning (where more than one permanence option for the child is being explored by the Local Authority);

(24) 'legal representative' means a–
   (a) barrister,
   (b) solicitor,
   (c) solicitor's employee,
   (d) manager of a body recognised under section 9 of the Administration of Justice Act 1985, or
   (e) person who, for the purposes of the Legal Services Act 2007, is an authorised person in relation to an activity which constitutes the conduct of litigation (within the meaning of that Act),

   who has been instructed to act for a party in relation to the proceedings;

(25) 'Letter Before Proceedings' means any letter from the Local Authority containing written notification to the parents and others with parental responsibility for the child of the Local Authority's plan to apply to court for a care or supervision order and any related subsequent correspondence confirming the Local Authority's position;

(26) 'Local Authority Case Summary' means a document prepared by the Local Authority advocate for all case management hearings including–
   (a) a recommended reading list and suggested reading time;
   (b) the key issues in the case;
   (c) any additional information relevant to the Timetable for the Child or for the conduct of the hearing or the proceedings;
   (d) a summary of updating information;
   (e) the issues and directions which the court will need to consider at the hearing in question, including any interim orders sought;
   (f) any steps which have not been taken or directions not complied with, an explanation of the reasons for non-compliance and the effect, if any, on the Timetable for the Child;
   (g) any relevant information relating to ethnicity, cultural or gender issues;

(27) 'justices' clerk' has the meaning assigned to it by section 27(1) of the Courts Act 2003;

(28) 'McKenzie Friend' means any person permitted by the court to sit beside an unrepresented litigant in court to assist the litigant by prompting, taking notes and giving advice to the litigant;

(29) 'Other Checklist Documents' means the documents listed in the Pre-proceedings Checklist which will normally be on the local authority file prior to the start of proceedings but which are not-
   (a) to be filed with the court on issue; or
   (b) Annex Documents.

(30) 'Other Parties' Case Summaries' means summaries by parties other than the Local Authority containing–
   (a) the party's proposals for the long term future of the child (to include placement and contact);
   (b) the party's reply to the Local Authority's Schedule of Proposed Findings;
   (c) any proposal for assessment / expert evidence; and
   (d) the names, addresses and contact details of any family or friends who it is suggested be approached in relation to long term care / contact or respite;

(31) 'Pre-proceedings Checklist' means the Annex Documents and the Other Checklist Documents set out in the Public Law Outline;

(32) 'Public Law Outline' means the Table contained in paragraph 10;

(33) 'Public Law Proceedings' means proceedings for–

(a) a residence order under section 8 of the 1989 Act with respect to a child who is subject of a care order;
(b) a special guardianship order relating to a child who is subject of a care order;
(c) a secure accommodation order under section 25 of the 1989 Act;
(d) a care order under section 31(1)(a) of the 1989 Act or the discharge of such an order under section 39(1) of the 1989 Act;
(e) an order giving permission to change a child's surname or remove a child from the United Kingdom under section 33(7) of the 1989 Act;
(f) a supervision order under section 31(1)(b) of the 1989 Act, the discharge or variation of such an order under section 39(2) of that Act, or the extension or further extension of such an order under paragraph 6(3) of Schedule 3 to that Act;
(g) an order making provision for contact under section 34(2) to (4) of the 1989 Act or an order varying or discharging such an order under section 34(9) of that Act;
(h) an education supervision order, the extension of an education supervision order under paragraph 15(2) of Schedule 3 to the 1989 Act, or the discharge of such an order under paragraph 17(1) of Schedule 3 to that Act;
(i) an order varying directions made with an interim care order or interim supervision order under section 38(8)(b) of the 1989 Act;
(j) an order under section 39(3) of the 1989 Act varying a supervision order in so far as it affects a person with whom the child is living but who is not entitled to apply for the order to be discharged;
(k) an order under section 39(3A) of the 1989 Act varying or discharging an interim care order in so far as it imposes an exclusion requirement on a person who is not entitled to apply for the order to be discharged;
(l) an order under section 39(3B) of the 1989 Act varying or discharging an interim care order in so far as it confers a power of arrest attached to an exclusion requirement;
(m) the substitution of a supervision order for a care order under section 39(4) of the 1989 Act;
(n) a child assessment order or the variation or discharge of such an order under section 43(12) of the 1989 Act;
(o) an order permitting the Local Authority to arrange for any child in its care to live outside England and Wales under paragraph 19(1) of Schedule 2 to the 1989 Act;
(p) a contribution order, or the variation or revocation of such an order under paragraph 23(8), of Schedule 2 to the 1989 Act;
(q) an appeal under paragraph 8(1) of Schedule 8 to the 1989 Act.

(34) 'rules' means rules of court governing the practice and procedure to be followed in Public Law Proceedings;
(35) 'Schedule of Proposed Findings' means the schedule of findings of fact prepared by the Local Authority sufficient to satisfy the threshold criteria under section 31 (2) of the 1989 Act and to inform the Care Plan;
(36) 'section 7 report' means any report under section 7 of the 1989 Act;
(37) 'section 37 report' means any report by the Local Authority to the court as a result of a direction under section 37 of the 1989 Act;
(38) 'Social Work Chronology' means a schedule containing–

(a) a succinct summary of the significant dates and events in the child's life in chronological order – a running record to be updated during the proceedings;
(b) information under the following headings–

(i) serial number;
(ii) date;
(iii) event-detail;
(iv) witness or document reference (where applicable);

(39) 'specified proceedings' has the meaning assigned to it by section 41(6) of the 1989 Act;
(40) 'Standard Directions on Issue' mean directions made by the court which will include such of the directions set out in the Public Law Outline, Stage 1, column 1 as are appropriate to the proceedings;
(41) 'Standard Directions on First Appointment' means directions made by the court which will include such of the directions set out in the Public Law Outline, Stage 1, column 2 and directions relating to the following as are appropriate to the proceedings–

(a) the Timetable for the Child;
(b) the joining of a party to the proceedings;
(c) the appointment of a guardian ad litem or litigation friend including the Official Solicitor where appropriate for a protected party or non subject child;
(d) allocation of the case to a case manager or case management judge;
(e) experts in accordance with the Experts Practice Direction;
(f) the interim care plan setting out details as to proposed placement and contact;
(g) any other evidence(such as evidence relating to vulnerability, ethnicity, culture, language, religion or gender) and disclosure of evidence between the parties;
(h) filing and service of the draft of the Case Management Order before the Case Management Conference;
(i) listing the Issues Resolution Hearing and Final Hearing;
(j) media attendance and reporting;

(42) 'Strategy Discussion Record' means a note of the strategy discussion within the meaning of 'Working Together to Safeguard Children' (2006);
(43) 'Timetable for the Child' has the meaning assigned to it by the rules. (see paragraph 3.2 of this Practice Direction)

PRACTICE DIRECTION 12B – THE REVISED PRIVATE LAW PROGRAMME

The Practice Direction below is made by the President of the Family Division under the powers delegated to him by the Lord Chief Justice under Schedule 2, Part 1, paragraph 2(2) of the Constitutional Reform Act 2005, and is approved by Bridget Prentice, Parliamentary Under Secretary of State, by authority of the Lord Chancellor.

Effective from 1st April 2010

Introduction

1.1 The Private Law Programme has achieved marked success in enabling the resolution of the majority of cases by consent at the First Hearing Dispute Resolution Appointment ('FHDRA'). It has been revised to build on the successes of the initial programme and to take account of recent developments in the law and practice associated with private family law.

1.2 In particular, there have been several legislative changes affecting private family law. The Allocation and Transfer of Proceedings Order 2008 (the 'Allocation Order'), requires the transfer of cases from the County Court to the Family Proceedings Court (FPC). Sections 1 to 5 and Schedule 1 of the Children and Adoption Act 2006 which came into force on 8th December 2008, amends the Children Act 1989 by introducing

Contact Activity Directions, Contact Activity Conditions, Contact Monitoring Requirements, Financial Compensation Orders and Enforcement Orders.

1.3 There has been growing recognition of the impact of domestic violence and abuse, drug and alcohol misuse and mental illness, on the proper consideration of the issues in private family law; this includes the acceptance that Court orders, even those made by consent, must be scrutinised to ensure that they are safe and take account of any risk factors. Coupled with this is the need to take account of the duty on Cafcass, pursuant to s16A Children Act 1989, to undertake risk assessments where an officer of the Service ('Cafcass Officer') suspects that a child is at risk of harm. (References to Cafcass include CAFCASS CYMRU and references to the Cafcass Officer include the Welsh family proceedings officer in Wales).

1.4 There is awareness of the importance of involving children where appropriate in the decision making process.

1.5 The Revised Programme incorporates these developments. It also retains the essential feature of the FHDRA as the forum for the parties to be helped to reach agreement as to, and understanding of, the issues that divide them. It recognises that having reached agreement parties may need assistance in putting it into effect in a co-operative way.

1.6 The Revised Programme is designed to provide a framework for the consistent national approach to the resolution of the issues in private family law whilst enabling local practices and initiatives to be operated in addition and within the framework.

1.7 The Revised Programme is designed to assist parties to reach safe agreements where possible, to provide a forum in which to find the best way to resolve issues in each individual case and to promote outcomes that are sustainable, that are in the best interests of children and that take account of their perspectives.

Principles

2.1 Where an application is made to a court under Part II of the Children Act 1989, the child's welfare is the court's paramount concern. The court will apply the principle of the 'Overriding Objective' to enable it to deal with a case justly, having regard to the welfare principles involved. So far as practicable the Court will–

(a) Deal expeditiously and fairly with every case;
(b) Deal with a case in ways which are proportionate to the nature, importance and complexity of the issues;
(c) Ensure that the parties are on an equal footing;
(d) Save unnecessary expense;
(e) Allot to each case an appropriate share of the court's resources, while taking account of the need to allot resources to other cases.

2.2 The court will give effect to the overriding objective when applying this programme and when exercising its powers to manage cases.

The parties are required to help the court further the overriding objective and promote the welfare of the child by the application of the welfare principle, pursuant to s1(1) of the Children Act 1989.

This Programme provides that consideration and discussion of all issues will not take place until the FHDRA when parties are on an equal footing and can hear what is said to and by each other. This excludes the safety checks and enquiries carried out by Cafcass before the first hearing that are required for that hearing and deal only with safety issues.

At the FHDRA the Court shall consider in particular–

(a) Whether and the extent to which the parties can safely resolve some or all of the issues with the assistance of the Cafcass Officer and any available mediator.
(b) Risk identification followed by active case management including risk assessment, and compliance with the Practice Direction 14th January 2009: 'Residence and Contact Orders: Domestic Violence and Harm'.

(c) Further dispute resolution.
(d) The avoidance of delay through the early identification of issues and timetabling, subject to the Allocation Order.
(e) Judicial scrutiny of the appropriateness of consent orders.
(f) Judicial consideration of the way to involve the child.
(g) Judicial continuity.

3 Practical Arrangements Before the FHDRA

3.1 Applications shall be issued on the day of receipt in accordance with the appropriate Rules of Procedure. It is important that the form C100 is fully completed, especially on pages 1, 2, 3, 10 and 11 otherwise delay may be caused by requests for information.

3.2 If possible at the time of issue, and in any event by no later than 24 hours after issue, or in courts where applications are first considered on paper, by no later than 48 hours after issue, the court shall

(i) send or hand to the Applicant
(ii) send to Cafcass

the following:
(a) a copy of the Application Form C100, (together with Supplemental Information Form C1A)(if provided)(references to form C1A are to be read as form C100A following the introduction of this replacement form),
(b) the Notice of Hearing,
(c) the Acknowledgment Form C7,
(d) a blank Form C1A,
(e) the Certificate of Service Form C9,
(f) information leaflets for the parties.

3.3 Save in urgent cases that require an earlier listing, the fully effective operation of this Practice Direction requires the FHDRA to take place within 4 weeks of the application. Where practicable, the first hearing must be listed to be heard in this period and in any event no later than within 6 weeks of the application. Where, at the time of introduction of this Programme, the Designated Family Judge/Justices' Clerk determines that it is not practicable to list the first hearing within 4 weeks, they should, in consultation with HMCS and Cafcass, formulate a timetable for revisiting the position and managing to list the FHDRA within 4 weeks.

3.4 Copies of each Application Form C100 and Notice of Hearing shall be sent by the court to Cafcass in accordance with 3.2 above.

3.5 The Respondent shall have at least 14 days notice of the hearing where practicable, but the court may abridge this time.

3.6 The Respondent should file a response on the Forms C7/C1A no later than 14 days before the hearing.

3.7 A copy of Forms C7/C1A shall be sent by the court to Cafcass on the day of receipt.

3.8 NOTE: This provision relates to cases that are placed in the FHDRA list for hearing other than by direct application in accordance with the procedure referred to in paragraph 3.1. Such listing may follow an application under the Family Law Act 1996, or a direction by the Court in other proceedings. In all such cases, or where the Court adjourns proceedings to a 'dispute resolution hearing' (sometimes called 'conciliation'), this will be treated as an adjournment to a FHDRA, and the documents referred to in para 3.2 must be filed and copied to parties and Cafcass for safety checks and enquiries, in the same way.

3.9 Before the FHDRA Cafcass shall identify any safety issues by the steps outlined below. Such steps shall be confined to matters of safety. Neither Cafcass nor a Cafcass Officer shall discuss with either party before the FHDRA any matter other than relates to safety. The Parties will not be invited to talk about other issues, for example relating to the substance of applications or replies or about issues concerning matters of welfare or the prospects of resolution. If such issues are raised by either party they will be advised that such matters will be deferred to the FHDRA when there is equality between the parties and full discussion can take place which will also be a time when any safety issues that have been identified also can be taken into account.

- (a) In order to inform the court of possible risks of harm to the child in accordance with its safeguarding framework Cafcass will carry out safeguarding enquiries, including checks of local authorities and police, and telephone risk identification interviews with parties.
- (b) If risks of harm are identified, Cafcass may invite parties to meet separately with the Cafcass Officer before the FHDRA to clarify any safety issue.
- (c) Cafcass shall record and outline any safety issues for the court.
- (d) The Cafcass Officer will not initiate contact with the child prior to the FHDRA. If contacted by a child, discussions relating to the issues in the case will be postponed to the day of the hearing or after when the Cafcass officer will have more knowledge of the issues.
- (e) At least 3 days before the hearing the Cafcass Officer shall report the outcome of risk identification work to the court by completing the Form at Schedule 2.

4   The First Hearing Dispute Resolution Appointment.

4.1 The parties and Cafcass Officer shall attend this hearing. A mediator may attend where available.

4.2 At the hearing, which is not privileged, the court should have the following documents:
- (a) C100 application, and C1A if any
- (b) Notice of Hearing
- (c) C7 response and C1A if any
- (d) Schedule 2 safeguarding information

4.3 The detailed arrangements for the participation of mediators will be arranged locally. These will include:
- (a) Arrangements for the mediator to ask the parties in a particular case to consent to the mediator seeing the papers in the case where it seems appropriate to do so.
- (b) Arrangements for the mediator to ask the parties to waive privilege for the purpose of the first hearing where it seems to the mediator appropriate to do so in order to assist the work of the mediator and the outcome of the first hearing.
- (c) In all cases it is important that such arrangements are put in place in a way that avoids any pressure being brought to bear in this connection on the parties that is inconsistent with general good mediation practice.

4.4 At the FHDRA the Court, in collaboration with the Cafcass Officer, and with the assistance of any mediator present, will seek to assist the parties in conciliation and in resolution of all or any of the issues between them. Any remaining issues will be identified, the Cafcass Officer will advise the court of any recommended means of resolving such issues and directions will be given for the future resolution of such issues. At all times the decisions of the Court and the work of the Cafcass Officer will take account of any risk or safeguarding issues that have been identified.

4.5 The Cafcass Officer shall, where practicable, speak separately to each party at court and before the hearing.

4.6 In the County Court, the Court shall have available a telephone contact to the Family Proceedings Court listing manager, diary dates for the appropriate Family Proceedings Court, or other means by which the County Court, at the time of the hearing, will be able to list subsequent hearings in the Family Proceedings Court.

5   Conduct of the Hearing. The following matters shall be considered

5.1 Safeguarding:

(a) The court shall inform the parties of the content of any screening report or other

information which has been provided by Cafcass, unless it considers that to do so would create a risk of harm to a party or the child. The court may need to consider whether and how any information contained in the checks should be disclosed to the parties if Cafcass have not disclosed it.
(b) Whether a risk assessment is required and when.
(c) Whether a fact finding hearing is needed to determine allegations whose resolution is likely to affect the decision of the court.

5.2 Dispute Resolution:

(a) There will be at every FHDRA a period in which the Cafcass Officer, with the assistance of any Mediator and in collaboration with the Court, will seek to conciliate and explore with the parties the resolution of all or some of the issues between them. The procedure to be followed in this connection at the hearing will be determined by local arrangements between the Cafcass manager, or equivalent in Wales, and the Designated Family Judge or the Justices' Clerk where appropriate.
(b) What is the result of any such meeting at Court?
(c) What other options there are for resolution e.g. may the case be suitable for further intervention by Cafcass; mediation by an external provider; collaborative law or use of a parenting plan?
(d) Would the parties be assisted by attendance at Parenting Information Programmes or other activities, whether by formal statutory provision under section 11 Children Act 1989 as amended by Children and Adoption Act 2006 or otherwise?

5.3 Consent Orders:

Where agreement is reached at any hearing or submitted in writing to the court, no order will be made without scrutiny by the court. Where safeguarding checks or risk assessment work remain outstanding, the making of a final order may be deferred for such work. In such circumstances the court shall adjourn the case for no longer than 28 days to a fixed date. A written notification of this work is to be provided by Cafcass in accordance with the timescale specified by the court. If satisfactory information is then available, the order may be made at the adjourned hearing in the agreed terms without the need for attendance by the parties. If satisfactory information is not available, the order will not be made, and the case will be adjourned for further consideration with an opportunity for the parties to make further representations.

5.4 Reports:

(a) Are there welfare issues or other specific considerations which should be addressed in a report by Cafcass or the Local Authority? Before a report is ordered, the court should consider alternative ways of working with the parties such as are referred to in paragraph 5.2 above. If a report is ordered in accordance with Section 7 of the Children Act 1989, it should be directed specifically towards and limited to those issues. General requests should be avoided and the Court should state in the Order the specific factual and other issues that are to be addressed in a focused report. In determining whether a request for a report should be directed to the relevant local authority or to Cafcass, the court should consider such information as Cafcass has provided about the extent and nature of the local authority's current or recent involvement with the subject of the application and the parties, and any relevant protocol between Cafcass and the Association of Directors of Children's Services.
(b) Is there a need for an investigation under S.37 Children Act 1989?
(c) A copy of the Order requesting the report and any relevant court documents are to be sent to Cafcass or, in the case of the Local Authority, to the Legal Adviser to the Director of the Local Authority Children's Services and, where known, to the allocated social worker by the court forthwith.

(d) Is any expert evidence required in compliance with the Experts' Practice Direction?

5.5 Wishes and feelings of the child:

(a) Is the child aware of the proceedings? How are the wishes and feelings of the child to be ascertained (if at all)?
(b) How is the child to be involved in the proceedings, if at all, and whether at or after the FHDRA?
(c) If consideration is given to the joining of the child as a party to the application, the court should consider the current Guidance from the President of the Family Division. Where the court is considering the appointment of a guardian ad litem, it should first seek to ensure that the appropriate Cafcass manager has been spoken to so as to consider any advice in connection with the prospective appointment and the timescale involved. In considering whether to make such an appointment the Court shall take account of the demands on the resources of Cafcass that such appointment would make.
(d) Who will inform the child of the outcome of the case where appropriate?

5.6 Case Management

(a) What, if any, issues are agreed and what are the key issues to be determined?
(b) Are there any interim orders which can usefully be made (e.g. indirect, supported or supervised contact) pending final hearing?
(c) What directions are required to ensure the application is ready for final hearing – statements, reports etc?
(d) List for final hearing, consider the need for judicial continuity (especially if there has been or is to be a fact finding hearing or a contested interim hearing).

5.7 Transfer to FPC

The case should be transferred to the FPC, pursuant to the Allocation and Transfer of Proceedings Order 2008 unless one of the specified exceptions applies. The date should be fixed at court and entered on the order.

6 The Order

6.1 The Order shall set out in particular:

(a) The issues about which the parties are agreed
(b) The issues that remain to be resolved
(c) The steps that are planned to resolve the issues
(d) Any interim arrangements pending such resolution, including arrangements for the involvement of children.
(e) The timetable for such steps and, where this involves further hearings, the date of such hearings.
(f) A statement as to any facts relating to risk or safety; in so far as they are resolved the result will be stated and, in so far as not resolved, the steps to be taken to resolve them will be stated.
(g) If it be the case, the fact of the transfer of the case to the Family Proceedings Court with the date and purpose of the next hearing
(h) If it be the case, the fact that the case cannot be transferred to the Family Proceedings Court and the reason for the decision.
(i) Whether in the event of an order, by consent or otherwise, or pending such an order, the parties are to be assisted by participation in mediation, Parenting Information Programmes, or other types of parenting intervention, and to detail any contact activity directions or conditions imposed by the court.

6.2 A suggested template order is available as set out in Schedule 1 below.

7 Commencement and Implementation

7.1 This Practice Direction will come into effect on April 1st 2010. So that procedural changes can be made by all agencies, the requirement for full implementation of the provisions is postponed, but in any event it should be effected by no later than October 4th 2010.

SCHEDULE 1

The suggested form of Order which courts may wish to use is PLP10 which is available from Her Majesty's Court Service.

SCHEDULE 2

Report Form on outcome of safeguarding enquiries. See version for Cafcass in England and for CAFCASS CYMRU in Wales.

PRACTICE DIRECTION 12C – SERVICE OF APPLICATION IN CERTAIN PROCEEDINGS RELATING TO CHILDREN

This Practice Direction supplements FPR Part 12 (Procedure Relating to Children except Parental Order Proceedings and Proceedings For Applications In Adoption, Placement and Related Proceedings), rule 12.8 (Service of the application).

Persons who receive copy of application form

1.1 In relation to the proceedings in column 1 of the following table, column 2 sets out the documentation which persons listed in column 3 are to receive–

Proceedings	Documentation	Who receives a copy of the documentation
1.Private law proceedings; public law proceedings; emergency proceedings (except those proceedings referred to in entries 2 and 3 of the Table below); proceedings for a declaration under rule 12.71 as to the existence, or extent, of parental responsibility under Article 16 of the 1996 Hague Convention; an order relating to the exercise of the court's inherent jurisdiction (including wardship proceedings).	Application form (including any supplementary forms); Form C6 (Notice of proceedings); and in private law proceedings, the form of answer.	All the respondents to the application.

Proceedings	Documentation	Who receives a copy of the documentation
2. An enforcement order (section 11J of the 1989 Act); a financial compensation order (section 11O of the 1989 Act).	As above	All the respondents to the application; and where the child was a party to the proceedings in which the contact order was made– (a) the person who was the children's guardian or litigation friend in those proceedings; or (b) where there was no children's guardian or litigation friend, the person who was the legal representative of the child in those proceedings.
3. A care or a supervision order (section 31 of the 1989 Act).	As above and such of the documents specified in the Annex to Form C110 as are available.	All the respondents to the application; and Cafcass or CAFCASS CYMRU.
4. Proceedings for an order for the return of a child under the 1980 Hague Convention or registration of an order under the European Convention.	As above and the documents referred to in part 2 of the Practice Direction 12F (International Child Abduction).	All the respondents to the application

(Rule 12.3 sets out who the parties to the proceedings are.)

1.2 When filing the documents referred to in column 2 of the Table in paragraph 1.1, the applicant must also file sufficient copies for one to be served on each respondent and Cafcass or CAFCASS CYMRU.

1.3 Where the application for an order in proceedings referred to in column 1 of the Table in paragraph 1.1 is made in respect of more than one child all the children must be included in the same application form.

1.4 The applicant will serve Form C6A (notice to non parties) on the persons referred to in the Table in paragraph 3.1 at the same time as serving the documents in column 2 of the Table in paragraph 1.1.

Time for serving application

2.1 In relation to the proceedings in column 1 of the following table, column 2 sets out the time period within which the application and accompanying documents must be served on each respondent–

Proceedings	Minimum number of days prior to hearing or directions appointment for service
1. Private law proceedings; and proceedings for– an order permitting the child's name to be changed or the removal of the child from the United Kingdom (33(7) of the 1989 Act); an order permitting the local authority to arrange for any child in its care to live outside England and Wales (Schedule 2, paragraph 19(1) of the 1989 Act); a contribution order (Schedule 2, paragraph 23(1) of the 1989 Act); an order revoking a contribution order (Schedule 2, paragraph 23(8) of the 1989 Act); an appeal under paragraph 8(1) of Schedule 8 to the 1989 Act; an order relating to the exercise of the court's inherent jurisdiction (including wardship proceedings); a declaration under rule 12.71 as to the existence, or extent, of parental responsibility under Article 16 of the 1996 Hague Convention.	14 days.
2. Proceedings for– a residence order under section 8 of the 1989 Act relating to a child who is the subject of a care order; a special guardianship order relating to a child who is the subject of a care order (section 14A of the 1989 Act); an education supervision order (section 36 of the 1989 Act); an order discharging a care order (section 39(1) of the 1989 Act); an order varying or discharging a supervision order (section 39(2) of the 1989 Act) or extending or further extending a supervision order under paragraph 6(3) of Schedule 3 to the 1989 Act; an order varying a supervision order in so far as it affects the person with whom the child is living (section 39(3) of the 1989 Act); an application to substitute a supervision order for a care order (section 39(4) of the 1989 Act); an order extending an education supervision order (Schedule 3, paragraph 15(2) to the 1989 Act); an order discharging an education supervision order (Schedule 3, paragraph 17(1) to the 1989 Act).	7 days.

Proceedings	Minimum number of days prior to hearing or directions appointment for service
3. Proceedings for– a care or supervision order (section 31 of the 1989 Act); an order making provision for contact under section 34(2) to (4) of the 1989 Act or an order varying or discharging such an order under section 34(9) of the 1989 Act; an order varying directions made with an interim care order or interim supervision order under section 38(8)(b) of the 1989 Act; an order under section 39(3A) of the 1989 Act varying or discharging an interim care order in so far as it imposes an exclusion requirement on a person who is not entitled to apply for the order to be discharged; an order under section 39(3B) of the 1989 Act varying or discharging an interim care order in so far as it confers a power of arrest attached to an exclusion requirement; a child assessment order (section 43(1) of the 1989 Act).	3 days.
4. Proceedings for an order for the return of a child under the 1980 Hague Convention or registration of an order under the European Convention.	4 days.
5. An order varying or discharging a child assessment order (section 43(12) of the 1989 Act).	2 days.
6. Emergency proceedings; and proceedings for a secure accommodation order (section 25 of the 1989 Act).	1 day.

2.2 The court may extend or shorten the time period referred to in column 2 of the table in paragraph 2.1 (see rule 4.1(3)(a)).

2.3 Where the application is to be served on a child, rule 6.33 provides that, in addition to the persons to be served in accordance with rules 6.28 and 6.32, the application must also be served on the persons or bodies listed in rule 6.33(3) unless the court orders otherwise.

Persons who receive a copy of Form C6A (Notice to Non-Parties)

3.1 In relation to each type of proceedings in column 1 of the following table, the persons listed in column 2 are to receive a copy of Form C6A (Notice of Proceedings/Hearing/Directions Appointment to Non-Parties)–

Proceedings	Persons to whom notice is to be given
1. All applications.	Subject to separate entries below: local authority providing accommodation for the child; persons who are caring for the child at the time when the proceedings are commenced; and in the case of proceedings brought in respect of a child who is alleged to be staying in a refuge which is certified under section 51(1) or (2) of the 1989 Act, the person who is providing the refuge.
2. An order appointing a guardian (section 5(1) of the 1989 Act).	As for all applications; and the father or parent (being a woman who is a parent by virtue of section 43 of the Human Fertilisation and Embryology Act 2008) of the child if that person does not have parental responsibility.
3. A section 8 order (section 8 of the 1989 Act).	As for all applications; and, every person whom the applicant believes– (i) to be named in a court order with respect to the same child, which has not ceased to have effect; (ii) to be party to pending proceedings in respect of the same child; or (iii) to be a person with whom the child has lived for at least 3 years prior to the application, unless, in a case to which (i) or (ii) applies, the applicant believes that the court order or pending proceedings are not relevant to the application.

4.	A special guardianship order (section 14A of the 1989 Act); variation or discharge of a special guardianship order (section 14D of the 1989 Act).	As for all applications; and every person whom the applicant believes– (i) to be named in a court order with respect to the same child, which has not ceased to have effect; (ii) to be party to pending proceedings in respect of the same child; or (iii) to be a person with whom the child has lived for at least 3 years prior to the application, unless, in a case to which (i) or (ii) applies, the applicant believes that the court order or pending proceedings are not relevant to the application; if the child is not being accommodated by the local authority, the local authority in whose area the applicant is ordinarily resident; and in the case of an application under section 14D of the 1989 Act, the local authority that prepared the report under section 14A(8) or (9) in the proceedings leading to the order which it is sought to have varied or discharged, if different from any local authority that will otherwise be notified.
5.	An order permitting the local authority to arrange for any child in its care to live outside England and Wales (Schedule 2, paragraph 19(1) of the 1989 Act).	As for all applications; and the parties to the proceedings leading to the care order.
6.	A care or supervision order (section 31 of the 1989 Act).	As for all applications; and every person whom the applicant believes to be a party to pending relevant proceedings in respect of the same child; and every person whom the applicant believes to be a parent without parental responsibility for the child.
7.	A child assessment order (section 43(1) of the 1989 Act).	As for all applications; and every person whom the applicant believes to be a parent of the child; every person whom the applicant believes to be caring for the child; every person in whose favour a contact order is in force with respect to the child; and every person who is allowed to have contact with the child by virtue of an order under section 34 of the 1989 Act.

8. An order varying or discharging a child assessment order (section 43(12) of the 1989 Act).	The persons referred to in section 43(11)(a) to (e) of the 1989 Act who were not party to the application for the order which it is sought to have varied or discharged.
9. An emergency protection order (section 44(1) of the 1989 Act).	As for all applications above; and every person whom the applicant believes to be a parent of the child.
10. An order varying a direction under section 44(6) in an emergency protection order (section 44(9)(b) of the 1989 Act).	As for all applications; and the local authority in whose area the child is living; and any person whom the applicant believes to be affected by the direction which it is sought to have varied.
11. A warrant authorising a constable to assist in the exercise of certain powers to search for children and inspect premises (section 102 of the 1989 Act).	The person referred to in section 102(1) of the 1989 Act; and any person preventing or likely to prevent such a person from exercising powers under enactments mentioned in subsection (6) of that section.
12. An enforcement order (section 11J of the 1989 Act); a financial compensation order (section 11O of the 1989 Act).	Any officer of the Service or Welsh family proceedings officer who is monitoring compliance with a contact order (in accordance with section 11H(2) of the 1989 Act).
13. An order revoking or amending an enforcement order (Schedule A1, paragraphs 4 to 7 of the 1989 Act) (rule 12.33 makes provision regarding applications under Schedule A1, paragraph 5 of the 1989 Act); an order following a breach of an enforcement order (Schedule A1, paragraph 9 of the 1989 Act).	Any officer of the Service or Welsh family proceedings officer who is monitoring compliance with the enforcement order (in accordance with section 11M(1) of the 1989 Act); the responsible officer (as defined in section 197 of the Criminal Justice Act 2003, as modified by Schedule A1 to the 1989 Act).
14. A declaration under rule 12.71 as to the existence, or extent, of parental responsibility under Article 16 of the 1996 Hague Convention.	A person who the applicant believes is a parent of the child.

PRACTICE DIRECTION 12D – INHERENT JURISDICTION (INCLUDING WARDSHIP) PROCEEDINGS

This Practice Direction supplements FPR Part 12, Chapter 5

The nature of inherent jurisdiction proceedings

1.1 It is the duty of the court under its inherent jurisdiction to ensure that a child who is the subject of proceedings is protected and properly taken care of. The court may in exercising its inherent jurisdiction make any order or determine any issue in respect of a child unless limited by case law or statute. Such proceedings should not be commenced unless it is clear that the issues concerning the child cannot be resolved under the Children Act 1989.

1.2 The court may under its inherent jurisdiction, in addition to all of the orders which can be made in family proceedings, make a wide range of injunctions for the child's protection of which the following are the most common–

(a) orders to restrain publicity;
(b) orders to prevent an undesirable association;
(c) orders relating to medical treatment;
(d) orders to protect abducted children, or children where the case has another substantial foreign element; and
(e) orders for the return of children to and from another state.

1.3 The court's wardship jurisdiction is part of and not separate from the court's inherent jurisdiction. The distinguishing characteristics of wardship are that–

(a) custody of a child who is a ward is vested in the court; and
(b) although day to day care and control of the ward is given to an individual or to a local authority, no important step can be taken in the child's life without the court's consent.

Transfer of proceedings to county court

2.1 Whilst county courts do not have jurisdiction to deal with applications that a child be made or cease to be a ward of court, consideration should be given to transferring the case in whole or in part to a county court where a direction has been given confirming the wardship and directing that the child remain a ward of court during his minority or until further order.

2.2 The county court must transfer the case back to the High Court if a decision is required as to whether the child should remain a ward of court.

2.3 The following proceedings in relation to a ward of court will be dealt with in the High Court unless the nature of the issues of fact or law makes them more suitable for hearing in the county court–

(a) those in which an officer of the Cafcass High Court Team or the Official Solicitor is or becomes the litigation friend or children's guardian of the ward or a party to the proceedings;
(b) those in which a local authority is or becomes a party;
(c) those in which an application for paternity testing is made;
(d) those in which there is a dispute about medical treatment;
(e) those in which an application is opposed on the grounds of lack of jurisdiction;
(f) those in which there is a substantial foreign element;
(g) those in which there is an opposed application for leave to take the child permanently out of the jurisdiction or where there is an application for temporary removal of a child from the jurisdiction and it is opposed on the ground that the child may not be duly returned.

Parties

3.1 Where the child has formed or is seeking to form an association, considered to be undesirable, with another person, that other person should not be made a party to the application. Such a person should be made a respondent only to an application within the proceedings for an injunction or committal. Such a person should not be added to the title of the proceedings nor allowed to see any documents other than those relating directly to the proceedings for the injunction or committal. He or she should be allowed time to obtain representation and any injunction should in the first instance extend over a few days only.

Removal from jurisdiction

4.1 A child who is a ward of court may not be removed from England and Wales without the court's permission. Practice Direction 12F (International Child Abduction) deals in detail with locating and protecting children at risk of unlawful removal.

Criminal Proceedings

5.1 Where a child has been interviewed by the police in connection with contemplated criminal proceedings and the child subsequently becomes a ward of court, the permission of the court deciding the wardship proceedings ('the wardship court') is not required for the child to be called as a witness in the criminal proceedings.

5.2 Where the police need to interview a child who is already a ward of court, an application must be made for permission for the police to do so. Where permission is given the order should, unless there is some special reason to the contrary, give permission for any number of interviews which may be required by the prosecution or the police. If a need arises to conduct any interview beyond the permission contained in the order, a further application must be made.

5.3 The above applications must be made with notice to all parties.

5.4 Where a person may become the subject of a criminal investigation and it is considered necessary for the child who is a ward of court to be interviewed without that person knowing that the police are making inquiries, the application for permission to interview the child may be made without notice to that party. Notice should, however, where practicable be given to the children's guardian.

5.5 There will be other occasions where the police need to deal with complaints, or alleged offences, concerning children who are wards of court where it is appropriate, if not essential, for action to be taken straight away without the prior permission of the wardship court, for example–

(a) serious offences against the child such as rape, where a medical examination and the collection of forensic evidence ought to be carried out promptly;

(b) where the child is suspected by the police of having committed a criminal act and the police wish to interview the child in respect of that matter;

(c) where the police wish to interview the child as a potential witness.

5.6 In such instances, the police should notify the parent or foster parent with whom the child is living or another 'appropriate adult' (within the Police and Criminal Evidence Act 1984 – Code of Practice C for the Detention, Treatment and Questioning of Persons by Police Officers) so that that adult has the opportunity of being present when the police interview the child. Additionally, if practicable the child's guardian (if one has been appointed) should be notified and invited to attend the police interview or to nominate a third party to attend on the guardian's behalf. A record of the interview or a copy of any statement made by the child should be supplied to the children's guardian. Where the child has been interviewed without the guardian's knowledge, the guardian should be informed at the earliest opportunity of this fact and (if it be the case) that the police wish to conduct further interviews. The wardship court should be informed of the situation at the earliest possible opportunity thereafter by the children's guardian, parent, foster parent (through the local authority) or other responsible adult.

Applications to the Criminal Injuries Compensation Authority

6.1 Where a child who is a ward of court has a right to make a claim for compensation to the Criminal Injuries Compensation Authority ('CICA'), an application must be made by the child's guardian, or, if no guardian has been appointed, the person with care and control of the child, for permission to apply to CICA and disclose such documents on the wardship proceedings file as are considered necessary to establish whether or not the child is eligible for an award plus, as appropriate, the amount of the award.

6.2 Any order giving permission should state that any award made by CICA should normally be paid into court immediately upon receipt and, once that payment has been made, application should made to the court as to its management and administration. If it is proposed to invest the award in any other way, the court's prior approval must be sought.

The role of the tipstaff

7.1 The tipstaff is the enforcement officer for all orders made in the High Court. The tipstaff's jurisdiction extends throughout England and Wales. Every applicable order made in the High Court is addressed to the tipstaff in children and family matters (e.g. 'The Court hereby directs the Tipstaff of the High Court of Justice, whether acting by himself or his assistants or a police officer as follows…').

7.2 The tipstaff may effect an arrest and then inform the police. Sometimes the local bailiff or police will detain a person in custody until the tipstaff arrives to collect that person or give further directions as to the disposal of the matter. The tipstaff may also make a forced entry although there will generally be a uniformed police officer standing by to make sure there is no breach of the peace.

7.3 There is only one tipstaff (with two assistants) but the tipstaff can also call on any constable or bailiff to assist in carrying out the tipstaff's duties.

7.4 The majority of the tipstaff's work involves locating children and taking them into protective custody, including cases of child abduction abroad.

PRACTICE DIRECTION 12E – URGENT BUSINESS

This Practice Direction supplements FPR Part 12

Introduction

1.1 This Practice Direction describes the procedure to be followed in respect of urgent and out of hours cases in the Family Division of the High Court. For the avoidance of doubt, it does not relate to cases in respect of adults.

1.2 Urgent or out of hours applications, particularly those which have become urgent because they have not been pursued sufficiently promptly, should be avoided. A judge who has concerns that the urgent or out of hours facilities may have been abused may require a representative of the applicant to attend at a subsequent directions hearing to provide an explanation.

1.3 Urgent applications should whenever possible be made within court hours. The earliest possible liaison is required with the Clerk of the Rules who will attempt to accommodate genuinely urgent applications (at least for initial directions) in the Family Division applications court, from which the matter may be referred to another judge.

1.4 When it is not possible to apply within court hours, contact should be made with the security office at the Royal Courts of Justice (020 7947 6000 or 020 7947 6260) who will refer the matter to the urgent business officer. The urgent business officer can contact the duty judge. The judge may agree to hold a hearing, either convened at court or elsewhere, or by telephone.

1.5 When the hearing is to take place by telephone it should, unless not practicable, be by tape-recorded conference call arranged (and paid for in the first instance) by the applicant's solicitors. Solicitors acting for potential applicants should consider having standing arrangements with their telephone service providers under which such conference calls can be arranged. All parties (especially the judge) should be informed that the call is being recorded by the service provider. The applicant's solicitors should order a transcript of the hearing from the service provider. Otherwise the applicant's legal representative should prepare a note for approval by the judge.

General Issues

2.1 Parents, carers or other necessary respondents should whenever possible be given the opportunity to have independent legal advice or at least to have access to support or counselling.

2.2 In suitable cases, application may be made for directions providing for anonymity of the parties and others involved in the matter in any order or subsequent listing of the case. Exceptionally, a reporting restriction order may be sought.
2.3 Either the Official Solicitor or Cafcass, or CAFCASS CYMRU, as the case may be, may be invited by the court to be appointed as advocate to the court.

Medical treatment and press injunction cases

3.1 It may be desirable for a child who is the subject of such proceedings to be made a party and represented through a children's guardian (usually an officer of Cafcass or a Welsh Family Proceedings Officer). Cafcass and CAFCASS CYMRU stand ready to arrange for an officer to accept appointment as a children's guardian. They should be contacted at the earliest opportunity where an urgent application is envisaged. For urgent out of hours applications, the urgent business officer will contact a representative of Cafcass. CAFCASS CYMRU is not able to deal with cases that arise out of office hours and those cases should be referred to Cafcass who will deal with the matter on behalf of CAFCASS CYMRU until the next working day. A child of sufficient understanding to instruct his or her own solicitor should be made a party and given notice of any application.
3.2 Interim declarations/orders under the wardship jurisdiction or Children Act 1989 may be made on application either by an NHS trust, a local authority, an interested adult (where necessary with the leave of the court) or by the child if he or she has sufficient understanding to make the application.

Consultation with Cafcass, CAFCASS CYMRU and Official Solicitor

4.1 Cafcass, CAFCASS CYMRU and members of the Official Solicitor's legal staff are prepared to discuss cases before proceedings are issued. In all cases in which the urgent and out of hours procedures are to be used it would be helpful if the Official Solicitor, Cafcass or CAFCASS CYMRU have had some advance notice of the application and its circumstances.
4.2 Enquiries about children cases should be directed to the duty lawyer:

Cafcass
National Office
6th Floor, Sanctuary Buildings
Great Smith Street
London SW1P 3BT
Tel: 0844 353 3350
Fax: 0844 353 3351.

Enquiries should be marked 'FAO High Court Team or FAO HCT'.
4.3 Enquiries about children cases in Wales should be directed to:

Social Care Team
Legal Services
Welsh Assembly Government
Cathays Park
Cardiff CF10 3NQ
Tel: 02920 823913
Fax: 02920 826727.

4.4 Medical and welfare cases relating to an adult lacking capacity in relation to their medical treatment or welfare are brought in the Court of Protection. Enquiries about adult medical and welfare cases should be addressed to a Court of Protection healthcare and welfare lawyer at the office of the Official Solicitor:

81 Chancery Lane
London
WC2A 1DD

Tel: 0207 911 7127
Fax: 0207 911 7105
Email: enquiries@offsol.gsi.gov.uk

Reference should also be made to Practice Direction E, accompanying Part 9 of the Court of Protection Rules 2007, and to Practice Direction B accompanying Part 10 of those Rules. Information for parties and practitioners is available on the website of the Ministry of Justice www.justice.gov.uk and general information for members of the public is available on www.direct.gov.uk.

PRACTICE DIRECTION 12F – INTERNATIONAL CHILD ABDUCTION

This Practice Direction supplements FPR Part 12, Chapters 5 and 6

Part 1 – Introduction

1.1 This Practice Direction explains what to do if a child has been brought to, or kept in, England and Wales without the permission of anyone who has rights of custody in respect of the child in the country where the child was habitually resident immediately before the removal or retention. It also explains what to do if a child has been taken out of, or kept out of, England and Wales without the permission of a parent or someone who has rights of custody in respect of the child. These cases are called 'international child abduction cases' and are dealt with in the High Court. This Practice Direction also explains what to do if you receive legal papers claiming that you have abducted a child. You can find the legal cases which are mentioned in this Practice Direction, and other legal material, on the website http://www.bailii.org (British and Irish Legal Information Institute).

1.2 If you have rights of custody in respect of a child and the child has been brought to England or Wales without your permission, or has been brought here with your permission but the person your child is staying with is refusing to return the child, then you can apply to the High Court of Justice, which covers all of England and Wales, for an order for the return of the child.

1.3 How you make an application to the High Court, what evidence you need to provide and what orders you should ask the court to make are all explained in this Practice Direction.

1.4 If your child is under 16 years of age and has been brought to England or Wales from a country which is a party (a 'State party') to the 1980 Hague Convention on the Civil Aspects of International Child Abduction ('the 1980 Hague Convention') then you can make an application to the High Court for an order under that Convention for the return of your child to the State in which he or she was habitually resident immediately before being removed or being kept away. This is explained in Part 2 below.

1.5 If your child is over 16 years of age and under 18, or has been brought to England or Wales from a country which is not a State party to the 1980 Hague Convention, then you can make an application for the return of your child under the inherent jurisdiction of the High Court with respect to children. In exercising this jurisdiction over children, the High Court will make your child's welfare its paramount consideration. How to make an application under the inherent jurisdiction of the High Court with respect to children is explained in Part 3 below.

1.6 It might be necessary for you to make an urgent application to the court if you are not sure where your child is, or you think that there is a risk that the person who is keeping your child away from you might take the child out of the United Kingdom or hide them away. Part 4 below explains how to make an urgent application to the High Court for orders to protect your child until a final decision can be made about returning the child and also how to ask for help from the police and government agencies if you think your child might be taken out of the country.

Rights of access

1.7 Rights of access to children (also called contact or visitation) may be enforced in

England and Wales. Access orders made in other Member States of the European Union can be enforced under EU law, and the 1980 Hague Convention expects State parties to comply with orders and agreements concerning access as well as rights of custody. If you have an access order and you want to enforce it in England or Wales, you should read Part 5 below.

Part 2 – Hague Convention Cases

2.1 States which are party to the 1980 Hague Convention have agreed to return children who have been either wrongfully removed from, or wrongfully retained away from, the State where they were habitually resident immediately before the wrongful removal or retention. There are very limited exceptions to this obligation.

2.2 'Wrongfully removed' or 'wrongfully retained' means removed or retained in breach of rights of custody in respect of the child attributed to a person or a body or an institution. 'Rights of custody' are interpreted very widely (see paragraph 2.16 below).

2.3 The text of the 1980 Hague Convention and a list of Contracting States (that is, State parties) can be found on the website of the Hague Conference on Private International Law at http://www.hcch.net. All Member States of the European Union are State parties to the 1980 Hague Convention, and all but Denmark are bound by an EU Regulation which supplements the operation of the 1980 Hague Convention between the Member States of the EU (Council Regulation (EC) No 2201/2003, see paragraph 2.6).

2.4 In each State party there is a body called the Central Authority whose duty is to help people use the 1980 Hague Convention.

2.5 If you think that your child has been brought to, or kept in, England or Wales, and your State is a State party to the 1980 Hague Convention, then you should get in touch with your own Central Authority who will help you to send an application for the return of your child to the Central Authority for England and Wales. However, you are not obliged to contact your own Central Authority. You may contact the Central Authority for England and Wales directly, or you may simply instruct lawyers in England or Wales to make an application for you. The advantage of making your application through the Central Authority for England and Wales if you are applying from outside the United Kingdom is that you will get public funding ('legal aid') to make your application, regardless of your financial resources.

The Central Authority for England and Wales

2.6 The Child Abduction and Custody Act 1985 brings the 1980 Hague Convention into the law of England and Wales and identifies the Lord Chancellor as the Central Authority. His duties as the Central Authority are carried out by the International Child Abduction and Contact Unit (ICACU). ICACU also carries out the duties of the Central Authority for two other international instruments. These are the European Convention on Recognition and Enforcement of Decisions concerning Custody of Children signed at Luxembourg on 20 May 1980 (called 'the European Convention' in this Practice Direction but sometimes also referred to as 'the Luxembourg Convention') and the European Union Council Regulation (EC) No 2201/2003 of 27 November 2003 on jurisdiction and the recognition and enforcement of judgments in matrimonial matters and in matters of parental responsibility ('the Council Regulation'). The Council Regulation has direct effect in the law of England and Wales.

2.7 ICACU is open Mondays to Fridays from 9.00 a.m. to 5.00 p.m. It is located in the Office of the Official Solicitor and Public Trustee and its contact details are as follows:

International Child Abduction and Contact Unit
81 Chancery Lane
London WC2A 1DD
DX 0012 London Chancery Lane
Tel: + 44 (0)20 7911 7045/7047

Fax: + 44 (0)20 7911 7248
Email: enquiries@offsol.gsi.gov.uk

In an emergency (including out of normal working hours) contact should be made with the Royal Courts of Justice on one of the following telephone numbers:
44 (0)20 7947 6000, or
44 (0) 20 7947 6260.

In addition, in an emergency or outside normal working hours advice on international child abduction can be sought from reunite International Child Abduction Centre on +44 (0)1162 556 234. Outside office hours you will be directed to the 24 hour emergency service. You can also see information on reunite's website http://www.reunite.org.

What ICACU will do

2.8 When ICACU receives your application for the return of your child, unless you already have a legal representative in England and Wales whom you want to act for you, it will send your application to a solicitor whom it knows to be experienced in international child abduction cases and ask them to take the case for you. You will then be the solicitor's client and the solicitor will make an application for public funding to meet your legal costs. The solicitor will then apply to the High Court for an order for the return of your child.

2.9 You can find out more about ICACU and about the 1980 Hague Convention and the other international instruments mentioned at paragraph 2.6 on two websites: Information for parties and practitioners is available on http://www.justice.gov.uk and general information for members of the public is available on http://www.direct.gov.uk.

Applying to the High Court – the form and content of application

2.10 An application to the High Court for an order under the 1980 Hague Convention must be made in the Principal Registry of the Family Division in Form C67. If the Council Regulation applies, then the application must be headed both 'in the matter of the Child Abduction and Custody Act 1985' and 'in the matter of Council Regulation (EC) 2201/2003'. This is to ensure that the application is handled quickly (see paragraph 2.14 below) and to draw the court's attention to its obligations under the Council Regulation.

2.11 The application must include –

(a) the names and dates of birth of the children;
(b) the names of the children's parents or guardians;
(c) the whereabouts or suspected whereabouts of the children;
(d) the interest of the applicant in the matter (e.g. mother, father, or person with whom the child lives and details of any order placing the child with that person);
(e) the reasons for the application;
(f) details of any proceedings (including proceedings not in England or Wales, and including any legal proceedings which have finished) relating to the children;
(g) where the application is for the return of a child, the identity of the person alleged to have removed or retained the child and, if different, the identity of the person with whom the child is thought to be;
(h) in an application to which the Council Regulation also applies, any details of measures of which you are aware that have been taken by courts or authorities to ensure the protection of the child after its return to the Member State of habitual residence.

2.12 The application should be accompanied by all relevant documents including (but not limited to)–

(a) an authenticated copy of any relevant decision or agreement;

(b) a certificate or an affidavit from a Central Authority, or other competent authority of the State of the child's habitual residence, or from a qualified person, concerning the relevant law of that State.

2.13 As the applicant you may also file a statement in support of the application, although usually your solicitor will make and file a statement for you on your instructions. The statement must contain and be verified by a statement of truth in the following terms:

I make this statement knowing that it will be placed before the court, and I confirm that to the best of my knowledge and belief its contents are true.

(Further provisions about statements of truth are contained in Part 17 of these Rules and in Practice Direction 17A).

The timetable for the case

2.14 Proceedings to which the Council Regulation applies must be completed in 6 weeks 'except where exceptional circumstances make this impossible'. The following procedural steps are intended to ensure that applications under the 1980 Hague Convention and the Council Regulation are handled quickly–

(a) the application must be headed both 'in the matter of the Child Abduction and Custody Act 1985' and 'in the matter of Council Regulation (EC) 2201/2003';
(b) the court file will be marked to–
  (i) draw attention to the nature of the application; and
  (ii) state the date on which the 6 week period will expire (the 'hear-by date');
(c) listing priority will, where necessary, be given to such applications;
(d) the trial judge will expedite the transcript of the judgment and its approval and ensure that it is sent to the Central Authority without delay.

(The above is taken from the judgment of the Court of Appeal, Civil Division in *Vigreux v. Michel & anor* [2006] EWCA Civ 630, [2006] 2 FLR 1180).

Applications for declarations

2.15 If a child has been taken from England and Wales to another State party, the judicial or administrative authorities of that State may ask for a declaration that the removal or retention of the child was wrongful. Or it might be thought that a declaration from the High Court that a child has been wrongfully removed or retained away from the United Kingdom would be helpful in securing his return. The High Court can make such declarations under section 8 of the Child Abduction and Custody Act 1985. An application for a declaration is made in the same way as an application for a return order, the only difference being that the details of relevant legal proceedings in respect of which the declaration is sought (if any), including a copy of any order made relating to the application, should be included in the documentation.

Rights of custody

2.16 'Rights of custody' includes rights relating to the care of the person of the child and, in particular, the right to determine the child's place of residence. Rights of custody may arise by operation of law (that is, they are conferred on someone automatically by the legal system in which they are living) or by a judicial or administrative decision or as a result of an agreement having legal effect. The rights of a person, an institution or any other body are a matter for the law of the State of the child's habitual residence, but it is for the State which is being asked to return the child to decide: if those rights amount to rights of custody for the purposes of the 1980 Hague Convention; whether at the time of the removal or retention those rights were actually being exercised; and whether there has been a breach of those rights.

2.17 In England and Wales a father who is not married to the mother of their child does not necessarily have 'rights of custody' in respect of the child. An unmarried father in England and Wales who has parental responsibility for a child has rights of custody in respect of that child. In the case of an unmarried father without parental responsibility, the concept of rights of custody may include more than strictly legal rights and where immediately before the removal or retention of the child he was exercising parental functions over a substantial period of time as the only or main carer for the child he may have rights of custody. An unmarried father can ask ICACU or his legal representative for advice on this. It is important to remember that it will be for the State which is being asked to return the child to decide if the father's circumstances meet that State's requirements for the establishment of rights of custody.

2.18 Sometimes, court orders impose restrictions on the removal of children from the country in which they are living. These can be orders under the Children Act 1989 ('section 8' orders) or orders under the inherent jurisdiction of the High Court (sometimes called 'injunctions'). Any removal of a child in breach of an order imposing such a restriction would be wrongful under the 1980 Hague Convention.

2.19 The fact that court proceedings are in progress about a child does not of itself give rise to a prohibition on the removal of the child by a mother with sole parental responsibility from the country in which the proceedings are taking place unless:

(a)   the proceedings are Wardship proceedings in England and Wales (in which case removal would breach the rights of custody attributed to the High Court and fathers with no custody rights could rely on that breach); or

(b)   the court is actually considering the custody of the child, because then the court itself would have rights of custody.

Particular provisions for European Convention applications

2.20 The European Convention provides for the mutual recognition and enforcement of decisions relating to custody and access, so if a child has been brought here or retained here in breach of a custody order, then that order can be enforced. The European Convention has now been superseded to a very great extent by the Council Regulation. If however you want to make an application under the European Convention, then you make it in the same way as is described in paragraphs 2.10 and 2.11 above, but in addition you must include a copy of the decision relating to custody (or rights of access – see paragraph 5.1 below) which you are seeking to register or enforce, or about which you are seeking a declaration by the court.

Defending abduction proceedings

2.21 If you are served with an application -whether it is under the 1980 Hague or the European Convention or the inherent jurisdiction of the High Court – you must not delay. You must obey any directions given in any order with which you have been served, and you should seek legal advice at the earliest possible opportunity, although neither you nor the child concerned will automatically be entitled to legal aid.

2.22 It is particularly important that you tell the court where the child is, because the child will not be permitted to live anywhere else without the permission of the court, or to leave England and Wales, until the proceedings are finished.

2.23 It is also particularly important that you present to the court any defence to the application which you or the child might want to make at the earliest possible opportunity, although the orders with which you will have been served are likely to tell you the time by which you will have to do this.

2.24 If the child concerned objects to any order sought in relation to them, and if the child is of an age and understanding at which the court will take account of their views, the court is likely to direct that the child is seen by an officer of the Children and Family Court Advisory and Support Service (Cafcass) or in Wales CAFCASS CYMRU. You should cooperate in this process. Children are not usually made parties to abduction cases, but in certain exceptional circumstances the court can make them parties so that they have their own separate legal representation. These are all matters about which you should seek legal advice.

(Provisions about the power of the court to join parties are contained in rule 12.3 and provisions about the joining and representation of children are contained in Part 16 of these Rules and the Practice Direction 16A (Representation of Children).)

Part 3 – Non-Convention Cases

3.1 Applications for the return of children wrongfully removed or retained away from States which are not parties to the 1980 Hague Convention or in respect of children to whom that Convention does not apply, can be made to the High Court under its inherent jurisdiction with respect to children. Such proceedings are referred to as 'non-Convention' cases. In proceedings under the inherent jurisdiction of the High Court with respect to children, the child's welfare is the court's paramount consideration. The extent of the court's enquiry into the child's welfare will depend on the circumstances of the case; in some cases the child's welfare will be best served by a summary hearing and, if necessary, a prompt return to the State from which the child has been removed or retained. In other cases a more detailed enquiry may be necessary (see *Re J (Child Returned Abroad: Convention Rights)* [2005] UKHL 40; [2005] 2 FLR 802).

3.2 Every application for the return of a child under the inherent jurisdiction must be made in the Principal Registry of the Family Division and heard in the High Court.

Provision about the inherent jurisdiction is made at Chapter 5 of Part 12 of the Rules and in Practice Direction 12D (Inherent Jurisdiction (including Wardship) Proceedings).

The form and content of the application

3.3 An application for the return of a child under the inherent jurisdiction must be made in Form C66 and must include the information in paragraph 2.11 above.

3.4 You must file a statement in support of your application, which must exhibit all the relevant documents. The statement must contain and be verified by a statement of truth in the following terms:

I make this statement knowing that it will be placed before the court, and confirm that to the best of my knowledge and belief its contents are true.

(Further provisions about statements of truth are contained in Part 17 of these Rules and Practice Direction 17A).

Timetable for non-Convention cases

3.5 While the 6 week deadline referred to in paragraph 2.14 is set out in the 1980 Hague Convention and in the Council Regulation, non-Convention child abduction cases must similarly be completed in 6 weeks except where exceptional circumstances make this impossible. Paragraph 2.14 applies to these cases as appropriate for a non-Convention case.

Part 4 – General Provisions

Urgent applications, or applications out of business hours

4.1 Guidance about urgent and out of hours applications is in Practice Direction 12E (Urgent Business).

Police assistance to prevent removal from England and Wales

4.2 The Child Abduction Act 1984 sets out the circumstances in which the removal of a child from this jurisdiction is a criminal offence. The police provide the following 24 hour service to prevent the unlawful removal of a child:

(a) they inform ports directly when there is a real and imminent threat that a child is about to be removed unlawfully from the country; and
(b) they liaise with Immigration Officers at the ports in an attempt to identify children at risk of removal.

4.3 Where the child is under 16, it is not necessary to obtain a court order before seeking police assistance. The police do not need an order to act to protect the child. If an order has already been obtained it should however be produced to the police. Where the child is between 16 and 18, an order must be obtained restricting or restraining removal before seeking police assistance.

4.4 Where the child is a ward of court (see Practice Direction 12D (Inherent Jurisdiction (including Wardship) Proceedings) the court's permission is needed to remove that child from the jurisdiction. When the court has not given that permission and police assistance is sought to prevent the removal of the ward, the applicant must produce evidence that the child is a ward such as:

(a) an order confirming wardship;
(b) an injunction; or
(c) where the matter is urgent and no order has been made, a certified copy of the wardship application.

4.5 The application for police assistance must be made by the applicant or his legal representative to the applicant's local police station except that applications may be made to any police station:

(a) in urgent cases;
(b) where the wardship application has just been issued; or
(c) where the court has just made the order relied on.

4.6 The police will, if they consider it appropriate, institute the 'port alert' system (otherwise known as 'an all ports warning') to try to prevent removal from the jurisdiction where the danger of removal is:

(a) real (i.e. not being sought merely by way of insurance); and
(b) imminent (i.e. within 24 to 48 hours).

4.7 The request for police assistance must be accompanied by as much of the following information as possible:

(a) the child: the name, sex, date of birth, physical description, nationality and passport number; if the child has more than one nationality or passport, provide details;
(b) the person likely to remove: the name, age, physical description, nationality, passport number, relationship to the child, and whether the child is likely to assist him or her; if the person has more than one nationality or passport, provide details;
(c) person applying for a port alert: the name, relationship to the child, nationality, telephone number and (if appropriate) solicitor's or other legal representative's name and contact details; if the person has more than one nationality, provide details;
(d) likely destination;
(e) likely time of travel and port of embarkation and, if known, details of travel arrangements;
(f) grounds for port alert (as appropriate)–
   (i) suspected offence under section 1 or section 2 of the Child Abduction Act 1984;
   (ii) the child is subject to a court order.
(g) details of person to whom the child should be returned if intercepted.

4.8 If the police decide that the case is one in which the port-alert system should be used, the child's name will remain on the stop list for four weeks. After that time it will be removed automatically unless a further application is made.

The Identity and Passport Service

4.9 Where the court makes an order prohibiting or otherwise restricting the removal of a child from the United Kingdom, or from any specified part of it, or from a specified dependent territory, the court may make an order under section 37 of the Family Law Act 1986 requiring any person to surrender any UK passport which has been issued to, or contains particulars of, the child.

4.10 The Identity and Passport Service ('IPS') will take action to prevent a United Kingdom passport or replacement passport being issued only where the IPS has been served with a court order expressly requiring a United Kingdom passport to be surrendered, or expressly prohibiting the issue of any further United Kingdom passport facilities to the child without the consent of the court, or the holder of such an order. Accordingly, in every case in which such an order has been made, the IPS must be served the same day if possible, or at the latest the following day, with a copy of the order. It is the responsibility of the applicant to do this. The specimen form of letter set out below should be used and a copy of the court order must be attached to the letter. Delay in sending the letter to the IPS must be kept to an absolute minimum.

'The Caveat Officer
Fraud and Intelligence Unit
Identity and Passport Service
Globe House
89 Eccleston Square
London SW1V 1PN

Dear Sir/Madam

.....................v.....................

Case no: ....

This is to inform you that the court has today made an order

°prohibiting the issue of a passport/passports to [name(s)] [date of birth (if known)] of [address] without the consent of the holder of the order.

°requiring [name(s)] [date of birth (if known)] of [address] to surrender the passport(s) issued to him/her/them/the following child[ren] / or which contain(s) particulars of the following child[ren]:

Name Date of Birth

°and has granted an injunction/°made an order restraining the removal of the child[ren] from the jurisdiction.

(°Delete as appropriate)

Please add these names to your records to prevent the issue of further passport facilities for the child[ren]. I enclose a copy of the court order.

Yours faithfully

Applicant's name / Applicant's Solicitor's name'

4.11 Following service on the IPS of an order either expressly requiring a United Kingdom passport to be surrendered by, or expressly prohibiting the issue of any further United Kingdom passport facilities to the child, the IPS will maintain a prohibition on issuing a passport, or further passport facilities until the child's 16th birthday. The order should state that a passport must not be granted/applied for without the consent of the court or the holder of the order.

Note: These requests may also be sent to any of the regional Passport Offices.

4.12 Further information on communicating with the IPS where the court has made a request of, or an order against, the IPS, may be found in the Protocol: Communicating with the Identity and Passport Service in Family Proceedings of August 2003.

4.13 Information about other circumstances, in which the IPS will agree not to issue a passport to a child if the IPS receives an application, or an order in more general terms than set out at 4.11 above, from a person who claims to have parental responsibility for the child, is available from the IPS or at www.direct.gov.uk.

The Home Office

4.14 Information about communicating with the Home Office, where a question of the immigration status of a party arises in family proceedings, may be found in the Protocol: Communicating with the Home Office in Family Proceedings (revised and re-issued October 2010).

Press Reporting

4.15 When a child has been abducted and a judge considers that publicity may help in tracing the child, the judge may adjourn the case for a short period to enable representatives of the Press to attend to give the case the widest possible publicity.

4.16 If a Child Rescue Alert has been used concerning a child, within the UK or abroad, it will give rise to media publicity. The court should be informed that this has happened. If there are already court proceedings concerning a child, it is advisable to obtain the agreement of the court before there is publicity to trace a missing child. If the court has not given its permission for a child who is the subject of children proceedings to be identified as the subject of proceedings, to do so would be contempt of court.

Other assistance

4.17 The Missing Persons Bureau will be participating for the UK in the European Union wide 116 000 hotline for missing children. Parents and children can ring this number for assistance. (It is primarily intended to deal with criminal matters, for example stranger kidnapping.)

4.18 It may also be possible to trace a child by obtaining a court order under the inherent jurisdiction or the wardship jurisdiction of the High Court addressed to certain government departments, as set out in Practice Direction 6C.

Part 5 – Applications about rights of access

5.1 Access orders made in another Member State of the European Union (except Denmark) can be enforced in England or Wales under the Council Regulation.

5.2 Chapter III of the Council Regulation sets out provision for recognition and enforcement of parental responsibility orders, which include orders for custody and access (residence and contact) between Member States. Under Article 41 of the Council Regulation you can enforce an access order in your favour from another Member State directly, provided you produce the certificate given under Article 41(2) by the court which made the order. This is a quick procedure. The unsuccessful party is not allowed to oppose recognition of the order.

5.3 The rules on recognition and enforcement of parental responsibility orders are in Part 31. You should apply to the High Court using Form C69. Rule 31.8 covers applications for Article 41 of the Council Regulation. You can make the application without notice.

5.4 If the Council Regulation does not apply, and the access order was made by a State party to the European Convention, an application can be made to enforce the order under Article 11 of the European Convention. Paragraph 2.20 above gives further information about how to make the application.

5.5 Article 21 of the 1980 Hague Convention requires the States parties to respect rights of access. However, in the case of *Re G (A Minor) (Hague Convention: Access)* [1993] 1 FLR 669, the Court of Appeal took the view that Article 21 conferred no jurisdiction to determine matters relating to access, or to recognise or enforce foreign access orders (see Practice Note of 5 March 1993: Child Abduction Unit: Lord Chancellor's Department set out in the Annex to this Practice Direction). (The Child Abduction Unit is now called ICACU see paragraph 2.6.) An access order which does not fall within the Council Regulation or the (very limited) application of the European Convention may only be enforced by applying for a 'contact order' under section 8 of the Children Act 1989.

5.6 This means that if, during the course of proceedings under the 1980 Hague Convention for a return order, the applicant decides to ask for access (contact) instead of the return of the child, but no agreement can be reached, a separate application for a contact order will have to be made, or the court invited to make a contact order without an application being made (Children Act 1989, s.10(1)(b)).

Part 6 – Child abduction cases between the United Kingdom and Pakistan

6.1 A consensus was reached in January 2003 between the President of the Family Division and the Hon. Chief Justice of Pakistan as to the principles to be applied in resolving child abduction cases between the UK and Pakistan.

The Protocol setting out that consensus can be accessed at:

http://www.fco.gov.uk/resources/en/pdf/2855621/3069133

ANNEX

See paragraph 5.5

Practice Note

5 March 1993

Citations: [1993] 1 FLR 804

Child Abduction Unit: Lord Chancellor's Department

Duties of the Central Authority for England and Wales under Article 21 of the Hague Convention on the Civil Aspects of International Child Abduction

CHILD ABDUCTION AND CUSTODY ACT 1985

In the case of *R G (A Minor) (Hague Convention: Access)* [1993] 1 FLR 669 the Court of Appeal considered the duties of the Central Authority for England and Wales on receiving an application in respect of rights of access under Art 21 of the Hague Convention.

The Court of Appeal took the view that Art 21 conferred no jurisdiction to determine matters relating to access, or to recognise or enforce foreign access orders. It provides, however, for executive co-operation in the enforcement of such recognition as national law allows.

Accordingly, the duty of the Central Authority is to make appropriate arrangements for the applicant by providing solicitors to act on his behalf in applying for legal aid and instituting proceedings in the High Court under s 8 of the Children Act 1989.

If, during the course of proceedings under Art 21 of the Convention, the applicant decides to seek access instead of the return of the child, but no agreement can be reached and the provisions of the European Convention on the Recognition and Enforcement of Decisions Concerning Custody of Children and on Restoration of Custody of Children are not available, a separate application under s 8 of the Children Act 1989 will have to be made.

Central Authority for England and Wales

460   Appendix 2

NOTE: The Child Abduction Unit is now called ICACU, see paragraph 2.6.

PRACTICE DIRECTION 12G – COMMUNICATION OF INFORMATION

This Practice Direction supplements FPR Part 12, Chapter 7

1.1 Chapter 7 deals with the communication of information (whether or not contained in a document filed with the court) relating to proceedings which relate to children.

1.2 Subject to any direction of the court, information may be communicated for the purposes of the law relating to contempt in accordance with paragraphs 2.1, 3.1 or 4.1.

Communication of information by a party etc. for other purposes

2.1 A person specified in the first column of the following table may communicate to a person listed in the second column such information as is specified in the third column for the purpose or purposes specified in the fourth column–

A party	A lay adviser, a McKenzie Friend, or a person arranging or providing pro bono legal services	Any information relating to the proceedings	To enable the party to obtain advice or assistance in relation to the proceedings
A party	A health care professional or a person or body providing counselling services for children or families		To enable the party or any child of the party to obtain health care or counselling
A party	The Child Maintenance and Enforcement Commission, a McKenzie Friend, a lay adviser or the First-tier Tribunal dealing with an appeal made under section 20 of the Child Support Act 1991		For the purposes of making or responding to an appeal under section 20 of the Child Support Act 1991 or the determination of such an appeal
A party	An adoption panel		To enable the adoption panel to discharge its functions as appropriate
A party	The European Court of Human Rights		For the purpose of making an application to the European Court of Human Rights

A party or any person lawfully in receipt of information	The Children's Commissioner or the Children's Commissioner for Wales		To refer an issue affecting the interests of children to the Children's Commissioner or the Children's Commissioner for Wales
A party, any person lawfully in receipt of information or a proper officer	A person or body conducting an approved research project		For the purpose of an approved research project
A legal representative or a professional legal adviser	A person or body responsible for investigating or determining complaints in relation to legal representatives or professional legal advisers		For the purposes of the investigation or determination of a complaint in relation to a legal representative or a professional legal adviser
A legal representative or a professional legal adviser	A person or body assessing quality assurance systems		To enable the legal representative or professional legal adviser to obtain a quality assurance assessment
A legal representative or a professional legal adviser	An accreditation body	Any information relating to the proceedings providing that it does not, or is not likely to, identify any person involved in the proceedings	To enable the legal representative or professional legal adviser to obtain accreditation
A party	A police officer	The text or summary of the whole or part of a judgment given in the proceedings	For the purpose of a criminal investigation
A party or any person lawfully in receipt of information	A member of the Crown Prosecution Service		To enable the Crown Prosecution Service to discharge its functions under any enactment

Communication for the effective functioning of Cafcass and CAFCASS CYMRU

3.1 An officer of the Service or a Welsh family proceedings officer, as appropriate, may communicate to a person listed in the second column such information as is specified in the third column for the purpose or purposes specified in the fourth column–

A Welsh family proceedings officer	A person or body exercising statutory functions relating to inspection of CAFCASS CYMRU	Any information relating to the proceedings which is required by the person or body responsible for the inspection	For the purpose of an inspection of CAFCASS CYMRU by a body or person appointed by the Welsh Ministers
An officer of the Service or a Welsh family proceedings officer	The General Social Care Council or the Care Council for Wales	Any information relating to the proceedings providing that it does not, or is not likely to, identify any person involved in the proceedings	For the purpose of initial and continuing accreditation as a social worker of a person providing services to Cafcass or CAFCASS CYMRU in accordance with section13(2) of the Criminal Justice and Courts Services Act 2000 or section 36 of the Children Act 2004 as the case may be
An officer of the Service or a Welsh family proceedings officer	A person or body providing services relating to professional development or training to Cafcass or CAFCASS CYMRU	Any information relating to the proceedings providing that it does not, or is not likely to, identify any person involved in the proceedings without that person's consent	To enable the person or body to provide the services, where the services cannot be effectively provided without such disclosure

An officer of the Service or a Welsh family proceedings officer	A person employed by or contracted to Cafcass or CAFCASS CYMRU for the purposes of carrying out the functions referred to in column 4 of this row	Any information relating to the proceedings	Engagement in processes internal to Cafcass or CAFCASS CYMRU which relate to the maintenance of necessary records concerning the proceedings, or to ensuring that Cafcass or CAFCASS CYMRU functions are carried out to a satisfactory standard

Communication to and by Ministers of the Crown and Welsh Ministers

4.1 A person specified in the first column of the following table may communicate to a person listed in the second column such information as is specified in the third column for the purpose or purposes specified in the fourth column–

A party or any person lawfully in receipt of information relating to the proceedings	A Minister of the Crown with responsibility for a government department engaged, or potentially engaged, in an application before the European Court of Human Rights relating to the proceedings	Any information relating to the proceedings of which he or she is in lawful possession	To provide the department with information relevant, or potentially relevant, to the proceedings before the European Court of Human Rights
A Minister of the Crown	The European Court of Human Rights		For the purpose of engagement in an application before the European Court of Human Rights relating to the proceedings
A Minister of the Crown	Lawyers advising or representing the United Kingdom in an application before the European Court of Human Rights relating to the proceedings		For the purpose of receiving advice or for effective representation in relation to the application before the European Court of Human Rights.

A Minister of the crown or a Welsh Minister	Another Minister, or Ministers, of the Crown or a Welsh Minister		For the purpose of notification, discussion and the giving or receiving of advice regarding issues raised by the information in which the relevant departments have, or may have, an interest

5.1 This paragraph applies to communications made in accordance with paragraphs 2.1, 3.1 and 4.1 and the reference in this paragraph to 'the table' means the table in the relevant paragraph.

5.2 A person in the second column of the table may only communicate information relating to the proceedings received from a person in the first column for the purpose or purposes–

(a) for which he or she received that information; or
(b) of professional development or training, providing that any communication does not, or is not likely to, identify any person involved in the proceedings without that person's consent.

6.1 In this Practice Direction–

'accreditation body' means–

(a) The Law Society,
(b) Resolution, or
(c) The Legal Services Commission;

'adoption panel' means a panel established in accordance with regulation 3 of the Adoption Agencies Regulations 2005 or regulation 3 of the Adoption Agencies (Wales) Regulations 2005;

'approved research project' means a project of research–

(a) approved in writing by a Secretary of State after consultation with the President of the Family Division,
(b) approved in writing by the President of the Family Division, or
(c) conducted under section 83 of the Act of 1989 or section 13 of the Criminal Justice and Court Services Act 2000;

'body assessing quality assurance systems' includes–

(a) The Law Society,
(b) The Legal Services Commission, or
(c) The General Council of the Bar;

'body or person responsible for investigating or determining complaints in relation to legal representatives or professional legal advisers' means–

(a) The Law Society,
(b) The General Council of the Bar,
(c) The Institute of Legal Executives,
(d) The Legal Services Ombudsman; or
(e) The Office of Legal Complaints.

'Cafcass' has the meaning assigned to it by section 11 of the Criminal Justice and Courts Services Act 2000;

'CAFCASS CYMRU' means the part of the Welsh Assembly Government exercising the functions of Welsh Ministers under Part 4 of the Children Act 2004;

'criminal investigation' means an investigation conducted by police officers with a view to it being ascertained–

(a) whether a person should be charged with an offence, or
(b) whether a person charged with an offence is guilty of it;

'health care professional' means–

(a) a registered medical practitioner,
(b) a registered nurse or midwife,
(c) a clinical psychologist, or
(d) a child psychotherapist;

'lay adviser' means a non-professional person who gives lay advice on behalf of an organisation in the lay advice sector;

'McKenzie Friend' means any person permitted by the court to sit beside an unrepresented litigant in court to assist that litigant by prompting, taking notes and giving him advice; and

'social worker' has the meaning assigned to it by section 55 of the Care Standards Act 2000.

PRACTICE DIRECTION 12H – CONTRIBUTION ORDERS

This Practice Direction supplements FPR Part 12

1.1 Paragraph 23(6) of Schedule 2 to the 1989 Act provides that where–

(a) a contribution order is in force;
(b) the local authority serve another contribution notice; and
(c) the contributor and the local authority reach an agreement under paragraph 22(7) in respect of that other contribution notice, the effect of the agreement shall be to discharge the order from the date on which it is agreed that the agreement shall take effect.

1.2 Where a local authority notifies the court of an agreement reached under paragraph 23(6) of Schedule 2 to the 1989 Act, the notification must be sent in writing to the designated officer of the court.

PRACTICE DIRECTION 12I – APPLICATIONS FOR REPORTING RESTRICTION ORDERS

This Practice Direction supplements FPR Part 12

1.1 This direction applies to any application in the Family Division founded on Convention rights for an order restricting publication of information about children or incapacitated adults.

Applications to be heard in the High Court

2.1 Orders can only be made in the High Court and are normally dealt with by a Judge of the Family Division. If the need for an order arises in existing proceedings in the county court, judges should either transfer the application to the High Court or consult their Family Division Liaison Judge. Where the matter is urgent, it can be heard by the Urgent Applications Judge of the Family Division (out of hours contact number 020 7947 6000).

Service of application on the national news media

3.1 Section 12(2) of the Human Rights Act 1998 means that an injunction restricting the exercise of the right to freedom of expression must not be granted where the person against whom the application is made is neither present nor represented unless the court is satisfied–

(a) that the applicant has taken all practicable steps to notify the respondent, or
(b) that there are compelling reasons why the respondent should not be notified.

3.2 Service of applications for reporting restriction orders on the national media can now be effected via the Press Association's CopyDirect service, to which national newspapers and broadcasters subscribe as a means of receiving notice of such applications.

3.3 The court will bear in mind that legal advisers to the media–

(i) are used to participating in hearings at very short notice where necessary; and
(ii) are able to differentiate between information provided for legal purposes and information for editorial use. Service of applications via the CopyDirect service should henceforth be the norm.

3.4 The court retains the power to make without notice orders, but such cases will be exceptional, and an order will always give persons affected liberty to apply to vary or discharge it at short notice.

Further guidance

4.1 The Practice Note 'Applications for Reporting Restriction Orders' dated 18 March 2005 and issued jointly by the Official Solicitor and the Deputy Director of Legal Services, provides valuable guidance and should be followed.

4.2 Issued with the concurrence and approval of the Lord Chancellor.

PRACTICE DIRECTION 12J – RESIDENCE AND CONTACT ORDERS: DOMESTIC VIOLENCE AND HARM

This Practice Direction supplements FPR Part 12

The Practice Direction issued on 9 May 2008 is re-issued in the following revised form to reflect the decision of the House of Lords in Re B *(Children)* [2008] UKHL 35, in which Baroness Hale confirmed (at [76]) that a fact-finding hearing is part of the process of trying a case and is not a separate exercise and that where the case is then adjourned for further hearing it remains part heard. This principle applies equally in private law and public law family cases. Paragraphs 15 and 23 of the Practice Direction have been amended to reinforce this principle.

1 This Practice Direction applies to any family proceedings in the High Court, a county court or a magistrates' court in which an application is made for a residence order or a contact order in respect of a child under the Children Act 1989 ('the 1989 Act') or the Adoption and Children Act 2002 ('the 2002 Act') or in which any question arises about residence or about contact between a child and a parent or other family member.

2 The practice set out in this Direction is to be followed in any case in which it is alleged, or there is otherwise reason to suppose, that the subject child or a party has experienced domestic violence perpetrated by another party or that there is a risk of such violence. For the purpose of this Direction, the term 'domestic violence' includes physical violence, threatening or intimidating behaviour and any other form of abuse which, directly or indirectly, may have caused harm to the other party or to the child or which may give rise to the risk of harm.

('Harm' in relation to a child means ill-treatment or the impairment of health or development, including, for example, impairment suffered from seeing or hearing the ill-treatment of another: Children Act 1989, ss.31(9), 105(1))

General principles

3 The court must, at all stages of the proceedings, consider whether domestic violence is raised as an issue, either by the parties or otherwise, and if so must:

(a) identify at the earliest opportunity the factual and welfare issues involved;

(b) consider the nature of any allegation or admission of domestic violence and the extent to which any domestic violence which is admitted, or which may be proved, would be relevant in deciding whether to make an order about residence or contact and, if so, in what terms;

(c) give directions to enable the relevant factual and welfare issues to be determined expeditiously and fairly.

4 In all cases it is for the court to decide whether an order for residence or contact accords with Section 1(1) of the 1989 Act or section 1(2) of the 2002 Act, as appropriate; any proposed residence or contact order, whether to be made by agreement between the parties or otherwise must be scrutinised by the court accordingly. The court shall not make a consent order for residence or contact or give permission for an application for a residence or contact order to be withdrawn, unless the parties are present in court, except where it is satisfied that there is no risk of harm to the child in so doing.

5 In considering, on an application for a consent order for residence or contact, whether there is any risk of harm to the child, the court shall consider all the evidence and information available. The court may direct a report under Section 7 of the 1989 Act either orally or in writing before it makes its determination; in such a case, the court may ask for information about any advice given by the officer preparing the report to the parties and whether they or the child have been referred to any other agency, including local authority children's services. If the report is not in writing, the court shall make a note of its substance on the court file.

Issue

6 Immediately on receipt of an application for a residence order or a contact order, or of the acknowledgement of the application, the court shall send a copy of it, together with any accompanying documents, to Cafcass or Cafcass Cymru, as appropriate, to enable Cafcass or Cafcass Cymru to undertake initial screening in accordance with their safeguarding policies.

Liaison

7 The Designated Family Judge, or in the magistrates' court the Justices' Clerk, shall take steps to ensure that arrangements are in place for:

(a) the prompt delivery of documents to Cafcass or Cafcass Cymru in accordance with paragraph 6

(b) any information obtained by Cafcass or Cafcass Cymru as a result of initial screening or otherwise and any risk assessments prepared by Cafcass or Cafcass Cymru under section 16A of the 1989 Act to be placed before the appropriate court for consideration and directions

(c) a copy of any record of admissions or findings of fact made pursuant to paragraphs 12 & 21 below to be made available as soon as possible to any Officer of Cafcass or Welsh family proceedings officer or local authority officer preparing a report under section 7 of the 1989 Act.

Response of the court on receipt of information

8 Where any information provided to the court before the first hearing, whether as a result of initial screening by Cafcass or Cafcass Cymru or otherwise, indicates that there are issues of domestic violence which may be relevant to the court's determination, the court may give directions about the conduct of the hearing and for written evidence to be filed by the parties before the hearing.

9 If at any stage the court is advised by Cafcass or Cafcass Cymru or otherwise that there is a need for special arrangements to secure the safety of any party or child attending any

hearing, the court shall ensure that appropriate arrangements are made for the hearing and for all subsequent hearings in the case, unless it considers that these are no longer necessary.

First hearing

10 At the first hearing, the court shall inform the parties of the content of any screening report or other information which has been provided by Cafcass or Cafcass Cymru, unless it considers that to do so would create a risk of harm to a party or the child.

(Specific provision about service of a risk assessment under section 16A of the 1989 Act is made by rule 12.34 of the Family Procedure Rules 2010.)

11 The court must ascertain at the earliest opportunity whether domestic violence is raised as an issue and must consider the likely impact of that issue on the conduct and outcome of the proceedings. In particular, the court should consider whether the nature and effect of the domestic violence alleged is such that, if proved, the decision of the court is likely to be affected.

Admissions

12 Where at any hearing an admission of domestic violence to another person or the child is made by a party, the admission should be recorded in writing and retained on the court file.

Directions for a fact-finding hearing

13 The court should determine as soon as possible whether it is necessary to conduct a fact-finding hearing in relation to any disputed allegation of domestic violence before it can proceed to consider any final order(s) for residence or contact. Where the court determines that a finding of fact hearing is not necessary, the order shall record the reasons for that decision.

14 Where the court considers that a fact-finding hearing is necessary, it must give directions to ensure that the matters in issue are determined expeditiously and fairly and in particular it should consider:

    (a)   directing the parties to file written statements giving particulars of the allegations made and of any response in such a way as to identify clearly the issues for determination;

    (b)   whether material is required from third parties such as the police or health services and may give directions accordingly;

    (c)   whether any other evidence is required to enable the court to make findings of fact in relation to the allegations and may give directions accordingly.

15 Where the court fixes a fact-finding hearing, it must at the same time fix a further hearing for determination of the application. The hearings should be arranged in such a way that they are conducted by the same judge or, in the magistrates' court, by at least the same chairperson of the justices.

Reports under Section 7

16 In any case where domestic violence is raised as an issue, the court should consider directing that a report on the question of contact, or any other matters relating to the welfare of the child, be prepared under section 7 of the 1989 Act by an Officer of Cafcass or a Welsh family proceedings officer (or local authority officer if appropriate), unless the court is satisfied that it is not necessary to do so in order to safeguard the child's interests. If the court so directs, it should consider the extent of any enquiries which can properly be made at this stage and whether it is appropriate to seek information on the wishes and feelings of the child before findings of fact have been made.

Representation of the child

17 Subject to the seriousness of the allegations made and the difficulty of the case, the court shall consider whether it is appropriate for the child who is the subject of the application to be made a party to the proceedings and be separately represented. If the case is proceeding in the magistrates' court and the court considers that it may be appropriate for the child to be made a party to the proceedings, it may transfer the case to the relevant county court for determination of that issue and following such transfer the county court shall give such directions for the further conduct of the case as it considers appropriate.

Interim orders before determination of relevant facts

18 Where the court gives directions for a fact-finding hearing, the court should consider whether an interim order for residence or contact is in the interests of the child; and in particular whether the safety of the child and the residential parent can be secured before, during and after any contact.
19 In deciding any question of interim residence or contact pending a full hearing the court
20 Where the court is considering whether to make an order for interim contact, it should in addition consider

    (a) the arrangements required to ensure, as far as possible, that any risk of harm to the child is minimised and that the safety of the child and the parties is secured; and in particular:

        (i) whether the contact should be supervised or supported, and if so, where and by whom; and

        (ii) the availability of appropriate facilities for that purpose

    (b) if direct contact is not appropriate, whether it is in the best interests of the child to make an order for indirect contact.

The fact-finding hearing

21 At the fact-finding hearing, the court should, wherever practicable, make findings of fact as to the nature and degree of any domestic violence which is established and its effect on the child, the child's parents and any other relevant person. The court shall record its findings in writing, and shall serve a copy on the parties. A copy of any record of findings of fact or of admissions must be sent to any officer preparing a report under Section 7 of the 1989 Act.
22 At the conclusion of any fact-finding hearing, the court shall consider, notwithstanding any earlier direction for a section 7 report, whether it is in the best interests of the child for the court to give further directions about the preparation or scope of any report under section 7; where necessary, it may adjourn the proceedings for a brief period to enable the officer to make representations about the preparation or scope of any further enquiries. The court should also consider whether it would be assisted by any social work, psychiatric, psychological or other assessment of any party or the child and if so (subject to any necessary consent) make directions for such assessment to be undertaken and for the filing of any consequent report.
23 Where the court has made findings of fact on disputed allegations, any subsequent hearing in the proceedings should be conducted by the same judge or, in the magistrates' court, by at least the same chairperson of the justices. Exceptions may be made only where observing this requirement would result in delay to the planned timetable and the judge or chairperson is satisfied, for reasons recorded in writing, that the detriment to the welfare of the child would outweigh the detriment to the fair trial of the proceedings.

In all cases where domestic violence has occurred

24 The court should take steps to obtain (or direct the parties or an Officer of Cafcass or a

Welsh family proceedings officer to obtain) information about the facilities available locally to assist any party or the child in cases where domestic violence has occurred.

25 Following any determination of the nature and extent of domestic violence, whether or not following a fact-finding hearing, the court should consider whether any party should seek advice or treatment as a precondition to an order for residence or contact being made or as a means of assisting the court in ascertaining the likely risk of harm to the child from that person, and may (with the consent of that party) give directions for such attendance and the filing of any consequent report.

Factors to be taken into account when determining whether to make residence or contact orders in all cases where domestic violence has occurred

26 When deciding the issue of residence or contact the court should, in the light of any findings of fact, apply the individual matters in the welfare checklist with reference to those findings; in particular, where relevant findings of domestic violence have been made, the court should in every case consider any harm which the child has suffered as a consequence of that violence and any harm which the child is at risk of suffering if an order for residence or contact is made and should only make an order for contact if it can be satisfied that the physical and emotional safety of the child and the parent with whom the child is living can, as far as possible, be secured before during and after contact.

27 In every case where a finding of domestic violence is made, the court should consider the conduct of both parents towards each other and towards the child; in particular, the court should consider;

(a) the effect of the domestic violence which has been established on the child and on the parent with whom the child is living;

(b) the extent to which the parent seeking residence or contact is motivated by a desire to promote the best interests of the child or may be doing so as a means of continuing a process of violence, intimidation or harassment against the other parent;

(c) the likely behaviour during contact of the parent seeking contact and its effect on the child;

(d) the capacity of the parent seeking residence or contact to appreciate the effect of past violence and the potential for future violence on the other parent and the child;

(e) the attitude of the parent seeking residence or contact to past violent conduct by that parent; and in particular whether that parent has the capacity to change and to behave appropriately.

Directions as to how contact is to proceed

28 Where the court has made findings of domestic violence but, having applied the welfare checklist, nonetheless considers that direct contact is in the best interests of the child, the court should consider what if any directions or conditions are required to enable the order to be carried into effect and in particular should consider:

(a) whether or not contact should be supervised, and if so, where and by whom;

(b) whether to impose any conditions to be complied with by the party in whose favour the order for contact has been made and if so, the nature of those conditions, for example by way of seeking advice or treatment (subject to any necessary consent);

(c) whether such contact should be for a specified period or should contain provisions which are to have effect for a specified period;

(d) whether or not the operation of the order needs to be reviewed; if so the court should set a date for the review and give directions to ensure that at the review the court has full information about the operation of the order.

29 Where the court does not consider direct contact to be appropriate, it shall consider whether it is in the best interests of the child to make an order for indirect contact.

The reasons of the court

30 In its judgment or reasons the court should always make clear how its findings on the issue of domestic violence have influenced its decision on the issue of residence or contact. In particular, where the court has found domestic violence proved but nonetheless makes an order, the court should always explain, whether by way of reference to the welfare check-list or otherwise, why it takes the view that the order which it has made is in the best interests of the child.
31 This Practice Direction is issued by the President of the Family Division, as the nominee of the Lord Chief Justice, with the agreement of the Lord Chancellor.

PRACTICE DIRECTION 12K – CHILDREN ACT 1989: EXCLUSION REQUIREMENT

This Practice Direction supplements FPR Part 12

Under s 38A(5) and s 44A(5) of the Children Act 1989 the court may attach a power of arrest to an exclusion requirement included in an interim care order or an emergency protection order. In cases where an order is made which includes an exclusion requirement, the following shall apply:
(1) If a power of arrest is attached to the order then unless the person to whom the exclusion requirement refers was given notice of the hearing and attended the hearing, the name of that person and that an order has been made including an exclusion requirement to which a power of arrest has been attached shall be announced in open court at the earliest opportunity. This may be either on the same day when the court proceeds to hear cases in open court or where there is no further business in open court on that day at the next listed sitting of the court.
(2) When a person arrested under a power of arrest cannot conveniently be brought before the relevant judicial authority sitting in a place normally used as a courtroom within 24 hours after the arrest, he may be brought before the relevant judicial authority at any convenient place but, as the liberty of the subject is involved, the press and the public should be permitted to be present, unless security needs make this impracticable.
(3) Any order of committal made otherwise than in public or in a courtroom open to the public, shall be announced in open court at the earliest opportunity. This may be either on the same day when the court proceeds to hear cases in open court or where there is no further business in open court on that day at the next listed sitting of the court. The announcement shall state (a) the name of the person committed, (b) in general terms the nature of the contempt of the court in respect of which the order of committal has been made and (c) the length of the period of committal.

Issued with the concurrence of the Lord Chancellor.

PRACTICE DIRECTION 12L – CHILDREN ACT 1989: RISK ASSESSMENTS UNDER SECTION 16A

This Practice Direction supplements FPR Part 12
1 This Practice Direction applies to any family proceedings in the High Court, a county court or a magistrates' court in which a risk assessment is made under section 16A of the Children Act 1989 ('the 1989 Act'). It has effect from 1st October 2007.
2 Section 16A(2) of the 1989 Act provides that, if in carrying out any function to which the section applies (as set out in section 16A(1)), an officer of the Service or a Welsh family proceedings officer is given cause to suspect that the child concerned is at risk of

harm, the officer must make a risk assessment in relation to the child and provide the risk assessment to the court.
3 The duty to provide the risk assessment to the court arises irrespective of the outcome of the assessment. Where an officer is given cause to suspect that the child concerned is at risk of harm and makes a risk assessment in accordance with section 16A(2), the officer must provide the assessment to the court, even if he or she reaches the conclusion that there is no risk of harm to the child.
4 The fact that a risk assessment has been carried out is a material fact that should be placed before the court, whatever the outcome of the assessment. In reporting the outcome to the court, the officer should make clear the factor or factors that triggered the decision to carry out the assessment.
5 Issued by the President of the Family Division, as the nominee of the Lord Chief Justice, with the agreement of the Lord Chancellor.

PRACTICE DIRECTION 12M – FAMILY ASSISTANCE ORDERS: CONSULTATION

This Practice Direction supplements FPR Part 12
1 This Practice Direction applies to any family proceedings in the High Court, a county court or a magistrates' court in which the court is considering whether to make a family assistance order under section 16 of the Children Act 1989, as amended ('the 1989 Act'). It has effect from 1st October 2007.
2 Before making a family assistance order the court must have obtained the opinion of the appropriate officer about whether it would be in the best interests of the child in question for a family assistance order to be made and, if so, how the family assistance order could operate and for what period.
3 The appropriate officer will be an officer of the Service, a Welsh family proceedings officer or an officer of a local authority, depending on the category of officer the court proposes to require to be made available under the family assistance order.
4 The opinion of the appropriate officer may be given orally or in writing (for example, it may form part of a report under section 7 of the 1989 Act).
5 Before making a family assistance order the court must give any person whom it proposes be named in the order an opportunity to comment upon any opinion given by the appropriate officer.
6 Issued by the President of the Family Division, as the nominee of the Lord Chief Justice, with the agreement of the Lord Chancellor

PRACTICE DIRECTION 12N – ENFORCEMENT OF CHILDREN ACT 1989 CONTACT ORDERS: DISCLOSURE OF INFORMATION TO OFFICERS OF THE NATIONAL PROBATION SERVICE (HIGH COURT AND COUNTY COURT)

This Practice Direction supplements FPR Part 12

This Practice Direction is issued by the President of the Family Division with the agreement of the Lord Chancellor.
1 This Practice Direction applies to proceedings in the High Court or a county court where:
  (a) the court is considering an application for an enforcement order or for an order following an alleged breach of an enforcement order and asks an officer of the Service or a Welsh family proceedings officer to provide information to the court in accordance with section 11L(5) of the Children Act 1989; or
  (b) the court makes an enforcement order or an order following an alleged breach of an enforcement order and asks an officer of the Service or a Welsh family

proceedings officer to monitor compliance with that order and to report to the court in accordance with section 11M of the Children Act 1989.
2   In all cases in which paragraph 1 applies, the officer of the Service or Welsh family proceedings officer will need to discuss aspects of the court case with an officer of the National Probation Service.
3   In order to ensure that the officer of the Service or Welsh family proceedings officer will not potentially be in contempt of court by virtue of such discussions, the court should, when making a request under section 11L(5) or section 11M of the Children Act 1989, give leave to that officer to disclose to the National Probation Service such information (whether or not contained in a document filed with the court) in relation to the proceedings as is necessary.
4   This Practice Direction comes into force on 8 December 2008.

PRACTICE DIRECTION 12O – ARRIVAL OF CHILD IN ENGLAND BY AIR

This Practice Direction supplements FPR Part 12

Where a person seeks an order for the return to him of children about to arrive in England by air and desires to have information to enable him to meet the aeroplane, the judge should be asked to include in his order a direction that the airline operating the flight, and, if he has the information, the immigration officer at the appropriate airport, should supply such information to that person.

To obtain such information in such circumstances in a case where a person already has an order for the return to him of children, that person should apply to a judge ex parte for such a direction.

Issued [in its original form] with the concurrence of the Lord Chancellor.

PRACTICE DIRECTION 12P – REMOVAL FROM JURISDICTION: ISSUE OF PASSPORTS

This Practice Direction supplements FPR Part 12

1   Removal from jurisdiction

The President has directed that on application for leave to remove from the jurisdiction for holiday periods a ward of court who has been placed by a local authority with foster-parents whose identity the court considers should remain confidential, for example because they are prospective adopters, it is important that such foster-parents should not be identified in the court's order. In such cases the order should be expressed as giving leave to the local authority to arrange for the child to be removed from England and Wales for the purpose of holidays.

It is also considered permissible, where care and control has been given to a local authority, or to an individual, for the court to give general leave to make such arrangements in suitable cases, thereby obviating the need to make application for leave each time it is desired to remove the child from the jurisdiction.

2   Issue of passports

It is the practice of the Passport Department of the Home Office to issue passports for wards in accordance with the court's direction. This frequently results in passports being restricted to the holiday period specified in the order giving leave. It is the President's opinion that it is more convenient for wards' passports to be issued without such restriction.

The Passport Department has agreed to issue passports on this basis unless the court otherwise directs. It will, of course, still be necessary for the leave of the court to be obtained for the child's removal.

Issued with the concurrence of the Lord Chancellor.

PRACTICE DIRECTION 14A – WHO RECEIVES A COPY OF THE APPLICATION FORM FOR ORDERS IN PROCEEDINGS

This Practice Direction supplements FPR Part 14, rule 14.6(1)(b)(ii)

Persons who receive copy of application form

1   In relation to each type of proceedings in column 1 of the following table, column 2 sets out which persons are to receive a copy of the application form:

Proceeding for	Who Receives a Copy of the Application Form
An adoption order (section 46 of the Act); or a section 84 order	Any appointed children's guardian, children and family reporter and reporting officer; the local authority to whom notice under section 44 (notice of intention to apply to adopt or apply for a section 84 order) has been given; the adoption agency which placed the child for adoption with the applicants; any other person directed by the court to receive a copy.
A placement order (section 21 of the Act); or an order varying a placement order (section 23 of the Act)	Each parent with parental responsibility for the child or guardian of the child; any appointed children's guardian, children and family reporter and reporting officer; any other person directed by the court to receive a copy.
An order revoking a placement order (section 24 of the Act)	Each parent with parental responsibility for the child or guardian of the child; any appointed children's guardian and children and family reporter; the local authority authorised by the placement order to place the child for adoption; any other person directed by the court to receive a copy.
A contact order (section 26 of the Act); an order varying or revoking a contact order (section 27 of the Act); an order permitting the child's name to be changed or the removal of the child from the United Kingdom (section 28(2) of the Act); a recovery order (section 41(2) of the Act); a section 89 order; and a section 88 direction	All the parties; any appointed children's guardian and children and family reporter; any other person directed by the court to receive a copy

PRACTICE DIRECTION 14B – THE FIRST DIRECTIONS HEARING – ADOPTIONS WITH A FOREIGN ELEMENT

This Practice Direction supplements Part 14, rule 14.8(3) of the Family Procedure Rules 2010.

1.1 Application

This Practice Direction applies to proceedings for –

(a) a Convention adoption order;
(b) a section 84 order;
(c) a section 88 direction;
(d) a section 89 order; and
(e) an adoption order where the child has been brought into the United Kingdom in the circumstances where section 83(1) of the Act applies.

2.1 The first directions hearing

At the first directions hearing the court will, in addition to any matters referred to in rule 14.8(1)–

(a) consider whether the requirements of the Act and the Adoptions with a Foreign Element Regulations 2005 (SI 2005/392) appear to have been complied with and, if not, consider whether or not it is appropriate to transfer the case to the High Court;
(b) consider whether all relevant documents are translated into English and, if not, fix a timetable for translating any outstanding documents;
(c) consider whether the applicant needs to file an affidavit setting out the full details of the circumstances in which the child was brought to the United Kingdom, of the attitude of the parents to the application and confirming compliance with the requirements of The Adoptions with A Foreign Element Regulations 2005;
(d) give directions about–
    (i) the production of the child's passport and visa;
    (ii) the need for the Official Solicitor and a representative of the Home Office to attend future hearings; and
    (iii) personal service on the parents (via the Central Authority in the case of an application for a Convention Adoption Order) including information about the role of the Official Solicitor and availability of legal aid to be represented within the proceedings; and
(e) consider fixing a further directions appointment no later than 6 weeks after the date of the first directions appointment and timetable a date by which the Official Solicitor should file an interim report in advance of that further appointment.

PRACTICE DIRECTION 14C – REPORTS BY THE ADOPTION AGENCY OR LOCAL AUTHORITY

This Practice Direction supplements FPR Part 14, rule 14.11(3)

Matters to be contained in reports

1.1 The matters to be covered in the report on the suitability of the applicant to adopt a child are set out in Annex A to this Practice Direction.
1.2 The matters to be covered in a report on the placement of the child for adoption are set out in Annex B to this Practice Direction.
1.3 Where a matter to be covered in the reports set out in Annex A and Annex B does not apply to the circumstances of a particular case, the reasons for not covering the matter should be given.

ANNEX A – REPORT TO THE COURT WHERE THERE HAS BEEN AN APPLICATION FOR AN ADOPTION ORDER OR AN APPLICATION FOR A SECTION 84 ORDER

Section A: The Report and Matters for the Proceedings
Section B: The Child and the Birth Family
Section C: The Prospective Adopter of the Child
Section D: The Placement
Section E: Recommendations
Section F: Further information for proceedings relating to Convention Adoption Orders, Convention adoptions, section 84 Orders or adoptions where section 83(1) of the 2002 Act applies.

Section A: The Report and Matters for the Proceedings

Part 1 – The report

For each of the principal author/s of the report:

(i) name;
(ii) role in relation to this case;
(iii) sections completed in this report;
(iv) qualifications and experience;
(v) name and address of the adoption agency; and
(vi) adoption agency case reference number.

Part 2 – Matters for the proceedings

(a) Whether the adoption agency considers that any other person should be made a respondent or a party to the proceedings, including the child.
(b) Whether any of the respondents is under the age of 18.
(c) Whether a respondent is a person who, by reason of mental disorder within the meaning of the Mental Health Act 1983, is incapable of managing and administering his or her property and affairs. If so, medical evidence should be provided with particular regard to the effect on that person's ability to make decisions in the proceedings.

Section B: The Child and the Birth Family

Part 1

(I) INFORMATION ABOUT THE CHILD

(a) Name, sex, date and place of birth and address including local authority area.
(b) Photograph and physical description.
(c) Nationality.
(d) Racial origin and cultural and linguistic background.
(e) Religious persuasion (including details of baptism, confirmation or equivalent ceremonies).
(f) Details of any siblings, half-siblings and step-siblings, including dates of birth.
(g) Whether the child is looked after by a local authority.
(h) Whether the child has been placed for adoption with the prospective adopter by a UK adoption agency.
(i) Whether the child was being fostered by the prospective adopter.
(j) Whether the child was brought into the UK for adoption, including date of entry and whether an adoption order was made in the child's country of origin.
(k) Personality and social development, including emotional and behavioural development and any related needs.

(l) Details of interests, likes and dislikes.
(m) A summary, written by the agency's medical adviser, of the child's health history, his current state of health and any need for health care which is anticipated, and date of the most recent medical examination.
(n) Any known learning difficulties or known general medical or mental health factors which are likely to have, or may have, genetic implications.
(o) Names, addresses and types of nurseries or schools attended, with dates.
(p) Educational attainments.
(q) Any special needs in relation to the child (whether physical, learning, behavioural or any other) and his emotional and behavioural development.
(r) Whether the child is subject to a statement under the Education Act 1996.
(s) Previous orders concerning the child:
   (i) the name of the court;
   (ii) the order made; and
   (iii) the date of the order.
(t) Inheritance rights and any claim to damages under the Fatal Accidents Act 1976 the child stands to retain or lose if adopted.
(u) Any other relevant information which might assist the court.

(II) INFORMATION ABOUT EACH PARENT OF THE CHILD

(a) Name, date and place of birth and address (date on which last address was confirmed current) including local authority area.
(b) Photograph, if available, and physical description.
(c) Nationality.
(d) Racial origin and cultural and linguistic background.
(e) Whether the mother and father were married to each other at the time of the child's birth or have subsequently married.
(f) Where the parent has been previously married or entered into a civil partnership, dates of those marriages or civil partnerships.
(g) Where the mother and father are not married, whether the father has parental responsibility and, if so, how it was acquired.
(h) If the identity or whereabouts of the father are not known, the information about him that has been ascertained and from whom, and the steps that have been taken to establish paternity.
(i) Past and present relationship with the other parent.
(j) Other information about the parent, where available:
   (i) health, including any known learning difficulties or known general medical or mental health factors which are likely to have, or may have, genetic implications;
   (ii) religious persuasion;
   (iii) educational history;
   (iv) employment history; and
   (v) personality and interests.
(k) Any other relevant information which might assist the court.

Part 2 – Relationships, contact arrangements and views.

THE CHILD

(a) If the child is in the care of a local authority or voluntary organisation, or has been, details (including dates) of any placements with foster parents, or other arrangements in respect of the care of the child, including particulars of the persons with whom the child has had his home and observations on the care provided.

(b) The child's wishes and feelings (if appropriate, having regard to the child's age and understanding) about adoption, the application and its consequences, including any wishes in respect of religious and cultural upbringing.
(c) The child's wishes and feelings in relation to contact (if appropriate, having regard to the child's age and understanding).
(d) The child's wishes and feelings recorded in any other proceedings.
(e) Date when the child's views were last ascertained.

THE CHILD'S PARENTS (OR GUARDIAN) AND RELATIVES

(a) The parents' wishes and feelings before the placement, about the placement and about adoption, the application and its consequences, including any wishes in respect of the child's religious and cultural upbringing.
(b) Each parent's (or guardian's) wishes and feelings in relation to contact.
(c) Date/s when the views of each parent or guardian were last ascertained.
(d) Arrangements concerning any siblings, including half-siblings and step-siblings, and whether any are the subject of a parallel application or have been the subject of any orders. If so, for each case give:
    (i) the name of the court;
    (ii) the order made, or (if proceedings are pending) the order applied for; and
    (iii) the date of order, or date of next hearing if proceedings are pending.
(e) Extent of contact with the child's mother and father and, in each case, the nature of the relationship enjoyed.
(f) The relationship which the child has with relatives, and with any other person considered relevant, including:
    (i) the likelihood of any such relationship continuing and the value to the child of its doing so; and
    (ii) the ability and willingness of any of the child's relatives, or of any such person, to provide the child with a secure environment in which the child can develop, and otherwise to meet the child's needs.
(g) The wishes and feelings of any of the child's relatives, or of any such person, regarding the child.
(h) Whether the parents (or members of the child's family) have met or are likely to meet the prospective adopter and, if they have met, the effect on all involved of such meeting.
(i) Dates when the views of members of the child's wider family and any other relevant person were last ascertained.

Part 3 – A summary of the actions of the adoption agency

(a) Brief account of the agency's actions in the case, with particulars and dates of all written information and notices given to the child and his parents and any person with parental responsibility.
(b) If consent has been given for the child to be placed for adoption, and also consent for the child to be adopted, the names of those who gave consent and the date such consents were given. If such consents were subsequently withdrawn, the dates of these withdrawals.
(c) If any statement has been made under section 20(4)(a) of the Adoption and Children Act 2002 (the '2002 Act') that a parent or guardian does not wish to be informed of any application for an adoption order, the names of those who have made such statements and the dates the statements were made. If such statements were subsequently withdrawn, the dates of these withdrawals.
(d) Whether an order has been made under section 21 of the 2002 Act, section 18 of the Adoption (Scotland) Act 1978 or Article 17(1) or 18(1) of the Northern Ireland Order 1987.

(e) Details of the support and advice given to the parents and any services offered or taken up.
(f) If the father does not have parental responsibility, details of the steps taken to inform him of the application for an adoption order.
(g) Brief details and dates of assessments of the child's needs, including expert opinions.
(h) Reasons for considering that adoption would be in the child's best interests (with date of relevant decision and reasons for any delay in implementing the decision).

Section C: The Prospective Adopter of the Child

Part 1 – Information about the prospective adopter, including suitability to adopt

(a) Name, date and place of birth and address (date on which last address was confirmed current) including local authority area.
(b) Photograph and physical description.
(c) Whether the prospective adopter is domiciled or habitually resident in a part of the British Islands and, if habitually resident, for how long they have been habitually resident.
(d) Racial origin and cultural and linguistic background.
(e) Marital status or civil partnership status, date and place of most recent marriage (if any) or civil partnership (if any).
(f) Details of any previous marriage, civil partnership, or relationship where the prospective adopter lived with another person as a partner in an enduring family relationship.
(g) Relationship (if any) to the child.
(h) Where adopters wish to adopt as a couple, the status of the relationship and an assessment of the stability and permanence of their relationship.
(i) If a married person or a civil partner is applying alone, the reasons for this.
(j) Description of how the prospective adopter relates to adults and children.
(k) Previous experience of caring for children (including as a step-parent, foster parent, child-minder or prospective adopter) and assessment of ability in this respect, together where appropriate with assessment of ability in bringing up the prospective adopter's own children.
(l) A summary, written by the agency's medical adviser, of the prospective adopter's health history, current state of health and any need for health care which is anticipated, and date of most recent medical examination.
(m) Assessment of ability and suitability to bring up the child throughout his childhood.
(n) Details of income and comments on the living standards of the household with particulars of the home and living conditions (and particulars of any home where the prospective adopter proposes to live with the child, if different).
(o) Details of other members of the household, including any children of the prospective adopter even if not resident in the household.
(p) Details of the parents and any siblings of the prospective adopter, with their ages or ages at death.
(q) Other information about the prospective adopter:
    (i) religious persuasion;
    (ii) educational history;
    (iii) employment history; and
    (iv) personality and interests.
(r) Confirmation that the applicants have not been convicted of, or cautioned for, a specified offence within the meaning of regulation 23(3) of the Adoption Agencies Regulations 2005 (S.I. 2005/389).
(s) Confirmation that the prospective adopter is still approved.
(t) Confirmation that any referees have been interviewed, with a report of their views and opinion of the weight to be placed thereon and whether they are still valid.

(u) Details of any previous family court proceedings in which the prospective adopter has been involved (which have not been referred to elsewhere in this report.)

Part 2 – Wishes, views and contact arrangements

PROSPECTIVE ADOPTER

(a) Whether the prospective adopter is willing to follow any wishes of the child or his parents or guardian in respect of the child's religious and cultural upbringing.
(b) The views of other members of the prospective adopter's household and wider family in relation to the proposed adoption.
(c) Reasons for the prospective adopter wishing to adopt the child and extent of understanding of the nature and effect of adoption. Whether the prospective adopter has discussed adoption with the child.
(d) Any hope and expectations the prospective adopter has for the child's future.
(e) The prospective adopter's wishes and feelings in relation to contact.

Part 3 – Actions of the adoption agency

(a) Brief account of the Agency's actions in the case, with particulars and dates of all written information and notices given to the prospective adopter.
(b) The Agency's proposals for contact, including options for facilitating or achieving any indirect contact or direct contact.
(c) The Agency's opinion on the likely effect on the prospective adopter and on the security of the placement of any proposed contact.
(d) Where the prospective adopter has been approved by an agency as suitable to be an adoptive parent, the agency's reasons for considering that the prospective adopter is suitable to be an adoptive parent for this child (with dates of relevant decisions).

Section D: The Placement

(a) Where the child was placed for adoption by an adoption agency (section 18 of the 2002 Act), the date and circumstances of the child's placement with prospective adopter.
(b) Where the child is living with persons who have applied for the adoption order to be made (section 44 of the 2002 Act), the date when notice of intention to adopt was given.
(c) Where the placement is being provided with adoption support, this should be summarised and should include the plan and timescales for continuing the support beyond the making of the adoption order.
(d) Where the placement is not being provided with adoption support, the reasons why.
(e) A summary of the information obtained from the Agency's visits and reviews of the placement, including whether the child has been seen separately to the prospective adopter and whether there has been sufficient opportunity to see the family group and the child's interaction in the home environment.
(f) An assessment of the child's integration within the family of the prospective adopter and the likelihood of the child's full integration into the family and community.
(g) Any other relevant information that might assist the court.

Section E: Recommendations

(a) The relative merits of adoption and other orders with an assessment of whether the child's long term interests would be best met by an adoption order or by other orders (such as residence and special guardianship orders).
(b) Recommendations as to whether or not the order sought should be made (and, if not, alternative proposals).
(c) Recommendations as to whether there should be future contact arrangements (or not).

Section F: **Further Information for Proceedings Relating to Convention Adoption Orders, Convention Adoptions, Section 84 Orders or an Adoption where Section 83(1) of the 2002 Act applies**
(a) The child's knowledge of their racial and cultural origin.
(b) The likelihood of the child's adaptation to living in the country he/she is to be placed.
(c) Where the UK is the State of origin, reasons for considering that, after possibilities for placement of the child within the UK have been given due consideration, intercountry adoption is in the child's best interests.
(d) Confirmation that the requirements of regulations made under sections 83(4), (5), (6) and (7) and 84(3) and (6) of the 2002 Act have been complied with.
(e) For a Convention adoption or a Convention Adoption Order where the United Kingdom is either the State of origin or the receiving State, confirmation that the Central Authorities of both States have agreed that the adoption may proceed.
(f) Where the State of origin is not the United Kingdom, the documents supplied by the Central Authority of the State of origin should be attached to the report, together with translation if necessary.
(g) Where a Convention adoption order is proposed, details of the arrangements which were made for the transfer of the child to the UK and that they were in accordance with the Adoptions with a Foreign Element Regulations 2005 (S.I. 2005/392).

ANNEX B – REPORT TO THE COURT WHERE THERE HAS BEEN AN APPLICATION FOR A PLACEMENT ORDER

Section A: The Report and Matters for the Proceedings
Section B: The Child and the Birth Family
Section C: Recommendations

Section A: The Report and Matters for the Proceedings

Part 1 – The report

For each of the principal author/s of the report:

(i) name;
(ii) role in relation to this case;
(iii) section completed in this report;
(iv) qualifications and experience;
(v) name and address of the adoption agency; and
(vi) adoption agency case reference number.

Part 2 – Matters for the proceedings

(a) Whether the adoption agency considers that any other person should be made a respondent or a party to the proceedings.
(b) Whether any of the respondents is under the age of 18.
(c) Whether a respondent is a person who, by reason of mental disorder within the meaning of the Mental Health Act 1983, is incapable of managing and administering his or her property and affairs. If so, medical evidence should be provided with particular regard to the effect on that person's ability to make decisions in the proceedings.

Section B: The child and the birth family

Part 1

(I) INFORMATION ABOUT THE CHILD

(a) Name, sex, date and place of birth and address including local authority area.

(b) Photograph and physical description.
(c) Nationality.
(d) Racial origin and cultural and linguistic background.
(e) Religious persuasion (including details of baptism, confirmation or equivalent ceremonies).
(f) Details of any siblings, half-siblings and step-siblings, including dates of birth.
(g) Whether the child is looked after by a local authority.
(h) Personality and social development, including emotional and behavioural development and any related needs.
(i) Details of interests, likes and dislikes.
(j) A summary, written by the agency's medical adviser, of the child's health history, his current state of health and any need for health care which is anticipated, and date of the most recent medical examination.
(k) Any known learning difficulties or known general medical or mental health factors which are likely to have, or may have, genetic implications.
(l) Names, addresses and types of nurseries or schools attended, with dates.
(m) Educational attainments.
(n) Any special needs in relation to the child (whether physical, learning, behavioural or any other) and his emotional and behavioural development.
(o) Whether the child is subject to a statement under the Education Act 1996.
(p) Previous orders concerning the child:

    (i) the name of the court;
    (ii) the order made; and
    (iii) the date of the order.

(q) Inheritance rights and any claim to damages under the Fatal Accidents Act 1976 the child stands to retain or lose if adopted.
(r) Any other relevant information which might assist the court.

(II) INFORMATION ABOUT EACH PARENT OF THE CHILD

(a) Name, date and place of birth and address (date on which last address was confirmed current) including local authority area.
(b) Photograph, if available, and physical description.
(c) Nationality.
(d) Racial origin and cultural and linguistic background.
(e) Whether the mother and father were married to each other at the time of the child's birth, or have subsequently married.
(f) Where the parent has been previously married or entered into a civil partnership, dates of those marriages or civil partnerships.
(g) Where the mother and father are not married, whether the father has parental responsibility and, if so, how it was acquired.
(h) If the identity or whereabouts of the father are not known, the information about him that has been ascertained and from whom, and the steps that have been taken to establish paternity.
(i) Past and present relationship with the other parent.
(j) Other information about the parent, where available:

    (i) health, including any known learning difficulties or known general medical or mental health factors which are likely to have, or may have, genetic implications;
    (ii) religious persuasion;
    (iii) educational history;
    (iv) employment history; and
    (v) personality and interests.

(k) Any other relevant information which might assist the court.

Part 2 – Relationships, contact arrangements and views

THE CHILD

(a) If the child is in the care of a local authority or voluntary organisation, or has been, details (including dates) of any placements with foster parents, or other arrangements in respect of the care of the child, including particulars of the persons with whom the child has had his home and observations on the care provided.
(b) The child's wishes and feelings (if appropriate, having regard to the child's age and understanding) about the application, its consequences, and adoption, including any wishes in respect of religious and cultural upbringing.
(c) The child's wishes and feelings in relation to contact (if appropriate, having regard to the child's age and understanding).
(d) The child's wishes and feelings recorded in any other proceedings.
(e) Date when the child's views were last ascertained.

THE CHILD'S PARENTS (OR GUARDIAN) AND RELATIVES

(a) The parents' wishes and feelings about the application, its consequences, and adoption, including any wishes in respect of the child's religious and cultural upbringing.
(b) Each parent's (or guardian's) wishes and feelings in relation to contact.
(c) Date/s when the views of each parent or guardian were last ascertained.
(d) Arrangements concerning any siblings, including half-siblings and step-siblings, and whether any are the subject of a parallel application or have been the subject of any orders. If so, for each case give:
   (i) the name of the court;
   (ii) the order made, or (if proceedings are pending) the order applied for; and
   (iii) the date of order, or date of next hearing if proceedings are pending.
(e) Extent of contact with the child's mother and father and in each case the nature of the relationship enjoyed.
(f) The relationship which the child has with relatives, and with any other person considered relevant, including:
   (i) the likelihood of any such relationship continuing and the value to the child of its doing so; and
   (ii) the ability and willingness of any of the child's relatives, or of any such person, to provide the child with a secure environment in which the child can develop, and otherwise to meet the child's needs.
(g) The wishes and feelings of any of the child's relatives, or of any such person, regarding the child.
(h) Dates when the views of members of the child's wider family and any other relevant person were last ascertained.

Part 3 – Summary of the actions of the adoption agency

(a) Brief account of the Agency's actions in the case, with particulars and dates of all written information and notices given to the child and his parents and any person with parental responsibility.
(b) If consent has been given for the child to be placed for adoption, and also consent for the child to be adopted, the names of those who gave consent and the date such consents were given. If such consents were subsequently withdrawn, the dates of these withdrawals.
(c) If any statement has been made under section 20(4)(a) of the 2002 Act that a parent or guardian does not wish to be informed of any application for an adoption order, the names of those who have made such statements and the dates the statements were made. If such statements were subsequently withdrawn, the dates of these withdrawals.

(d) Details of the support and advice given to the parents and any services offered or taken up.
(e) If the father does not have parental responsibility, details of the steps taken to inform him of the application for a placement order.
(f) Brief details and dates of assessments of the child's needs, including expert opinions.
(g) Reasons for considering that adoption would be in the child's best interests (with date of relevant decision and reasons for any delay in implementing the decision).

Section C: Recommendations

(a) The relative merits of a placement order and other orders (such as a residence or special guardianship order) with an assessment of why the child's long term interests are likely to be best met by a placement order rather than by any other order.
(b) Recommendations as to whether there should be future contact arrangements (or not), including whether a contact order under section 26 of the 2002 Act should be made.

PRACTICE DIRECTION 14D – REPORTS BY A REGISTERED MEDICAL PRACTITIONER ('HEALTH REPORTS')

This Practice Direction supplements FPR Part 14, rule 14.12(2)

Matters to be contained in health reports

1.1 Rule 14.12(1) requires that health reports must be attached to an application for an adoption order or a section 84 order except where:

    (a)   the child was placed for adoption with the applicant by an adoption agency;
    (b)   the applicant or one of the applicants is a parent of the child; or
    (c)   the applicant is the partner of a parent of the child.

1.2 The matters to be contained in the health reports are set out in the Annex to this Practice Direction.

1.3 Where a matter to be contained in the health report does not apply to the circumstances of a particular case, the reasons for not covering the matter should be given.

ANNEX – CONTENTS OF HEALTH REPORTS

This information is required for reports on the health of children and their prospective adopter(s). Its purpose is to build up a full picture of each child's health history and current state of health, including strengths and weaknesses. This will enable local authorities' medical adviser to base their advice to the court on the fullest possible information when commenting on the health implications of the proposed adoption. The reports made by the examining doctor should cover, as far as practicable, the following matters.

1 The child

Name, date of birth, sex, weight and height.

    A   A health history of each natural parent, so far as is possible, including:

        (i)   name, date of birth, sex, weight and height;
        (ii)   a family health history, covering the parents, the brothers and sisters and the other children of the natural parent, with details of any serious physical or mental illness and inherited and congenital disease;
        (iii)   past health history, including details of any serious physical or mental illness, disability, accident, hospital admission or attendance at an out-patient department, and in each case any treatment given;
        (iv)   a full obstetric history of the mother, including any problems in the ante-natal,

labour and post-natal periods, with the results of any tests carried out during or immediately after pregnancy;
- (v) details of any present illness including treatment and prognosis;
- (vi) any other relevant information which might assist the medical adviser; and
- (vii) the name and address of any doctor(s) who might be able to provide further information about any of the above matters.

B   A neo-natal report on the child, including:
- (i) details of the birth, and any complications;
- (ii) results of a physical examination and screening tests;
- (iii) details of any treatment given;
- (iv) details of any problem in management and feeding;
- (v) any other relevant information which might assist the medical adviser; and
- (vi) the name and address of any doctor(s) who might be able to provide further information about any of the above matters.

C   A full health history and examination of the child, including:
- (i) details of any serious illness, disability, accident, hospital admission or attendance at an out-patient department, and in each case any treatment given;
- (ii) details and dates of immunisations;
- (iii) a physical and developmental assessment according to age, including an assessment of vision and hearing and of neurological, speech and language development and any evidence of emotional or conduct disorder;
- (iv) details, if relevant, of the impact of any addiction or substance use on the part of the natural mother before, during or following the pregnancy, and its impact or likely future impact on the child;
- (v) the impact, if any, on the child's development and likely future development of any past exposure to physical, emotional or sexual abuse or neglectful home conditions and/or any non-organic failure to thrive;
- (vi) for a child of school age, the school health history (if available);
- (vii) any other relevant information which might assist the medical adviser; and
- (viii) the name and address of any doctor(s) who might be able to provide further information about any of the above matters.

D   The signature, name, address and qualifications of the registered medical practitioner who prepared the report, and the date of the report and of the examinations carried out.

2   The applicant

(If there is more than one applicant, a report on each applicant should be supplied covering all the matters listed below.)

A
- (i) name, date of birth, sex, weight and height;
- (ii) a family health history, covering the parents, the brothers and sisters and the children of the applicant, with details of any serious physical or mental illness and inherited and congenital disease;
- (iii) marital history, including (if applicable) reasons for inability to have children, and any history of domestic violence;
- (iv) past health history, including details of any serious physical or mental illness, disability, accident, hospital admission or attendance at an out-patient department, and in each case any treatment given;
- (v) obstetric history (if applicable);
- (vi) details of any present illness, including treatment and prognosis;
- (vii) a full medical examination;
- (viii) details of any consumption of alcohol, tobacco and habit-forming drugs;
- (ix) any other relevant information which might assist the medical adviser; and

(x) the name and address of any doctor(s) who might be able to provide further information about any of the above matters.

B The signature, name, address and qualifications of the registered medical practitioner who prepared the report, and the date of the report and of the examinations carried out.

PRACTICE DIRECTION 14E – COMMUNICATION OF INFORMATION RELATING TO PROCEEDINGS

This Practice Direction supplements FPR Part 14, rule 14.14(b)

Communication of information relating to proceedings

1.1 Rule 14.14 deals with the communication of information (whether or not it is recorded in any form) relating to proceedings.

1.2 Subject to any direction of the court, information may be communicated for the purposes of the law relating to contempt in accordance with paragraphs 1.3 or 1.4.

1.3 A person specified in the first column of the following table may communicate to a person listed in the second column such information as is specified in the third column for the purpose or purposes specified in the fourth column.

Communication of information without permission of the court

Communicated by	To	Information	Purpose
A party	A lay adviser or a McKenzie Friend	Any information relating to the proceedings	To enable the party to obtain advice or assistance in relation to the proceedings.
A party	The party's spouse, civil partner, cohabitant or close family member		For the purpose of confidential discussions enabling the party to receive support from his spouse, civil partner, cohabitant or close family member.
A party	A health care professional or a person or body providing counselling services for children or families		To enable the party or any child of the party to obtain health care or counselling.

Practice Directions 487

Communicated by	To	Information	Purpose
A party	The Secretary of State, a McKenzie Friend, a lay adviser or an appeal tribunal dealing with an appeal made under section 20 of the Child Support Act 1991		For the purposes of making or responding to an appeal under section 20 of the Child Support Act 1991 or the determination of such an appeal.
A party	An adoption panel		To enable the adoption panel to discharge its functions as appropriate.
A party or any person lawfully in receipt of information	The Children's Commissioner or the Children's Commissioner for Wales		To refer an issue affecting the interests of children to the Children's Commissioner or the Children's Commissioner for Wales.
A party or a legal representative	A mediator		For the purpose of mediation in relation to the proceedings.
A party, any person lawfully in receipt of information or a proper officer	A person or body conducting an approved research project		For the purpose of an approved research project.
A party, a legal representative or a professional legal adviser	A person or body responsible for investigating or determining complaints in relation to legal representatives or professional legal advisers		For the purposes of making a complaint or the investigation or determination of a complaint in relation to a legal representative or a professional legal adviser.
A legal representative or a professional legal adviser	A person or body assessing quality assurance systems		To enable the legal representative or professional legal adviser to obtain a quality assurance assessment.

Communicated by	To	Information	Purpose
A legal representative or a professional legal adviser	An accreditation body	Any information relating to the proceedings providing that it does not, or is not likely to, identify any person involved in the proceedings	To enable the legal representative or professional legal adviser to obtain accreditation.
A party	An elected representative or peer	The text or summary of the whole or part of a judgment given in the proceedings	To enable the elected representative or peer to give advice, investigate any complaint or raise any question of policy or procedure.
A party	The General Medical Council		For the purpose of making a complaint to the General Medical Council.
A party	A police officer		For the purpose of a criminal investigation.
A party or any person lawfully in receipt of information	A member of the Crown Prosecution Service		To enable the Crown Prosecution Service to discharge its functions under any enactment.

1.4 A person in the second column of the table in paragraph 1.3 may only communicate information relating to the proceedings received from a person in the first column for the purpose or purposes:

    (a)   for which he received that information, or

    (b)   of professional development or training, providing that any communication does not, or is not likely to, identify any person involved in the proceedings without that person's consent.

1.5 In this Practice Direction:

    (1)   'accreditation body' means:

        (a)   The Law Society,
        (b)   Resolution, or
        (c)   The Legal Services Commission;

    (1A)   'adoption panel' means a panel established in accordance with regulation 3 of the Adoption Agencies Regulations 2005[2] or regulation 3 of the Adoption Agencies (Wales) Regulations 2005[3];

    (2)   'approved research project' means a project of research:

        (a)   approved in writing by a Secretary of State after consultation with the President of the Family Division,
        (b)   approved in writing by the President of the Family Division, or

(c) conducted under section 83 of the Act of 1989 or section 13 of the Criminal Justice and Court Services Act 2000;

(3) 'body assessing quality assurance systems' includes:
  (a) The Law Society,
  (b) The Legal Services Commission, or
  (c) The General Council of the Bar;

(4) 'body or person responsible for investigating or determining complaints in relation to legal representatives or professional legal advisers' means:
  (a) The Law Society,
  (b) The General Council of the Bar,
  (c) The Institute of Legal Executives, or
  (d) The Legal Services Ombudsman;

(5) 'cohabitant' means one of two persons who are neither married to each other nor civil partners of each other but are living together as husband and wife or as if they were civil partners;

(6) 'criminal investigation' means an investigation conducted by police officers with a view to it being ascertained –
  (a) whether a person should be charged with an offence, or
  (b) whether a person charged with an offence is guilty of it;

(7) 'elected representative' means –
  (a) a member of the House of Commons,
  (b) a member of the National Assembly for Wales, or
  (c) a member of the European Parliament elected in England and Wales;

(8) 'health care professional' means –
  (a) a registered medical practitioner,
  (b) a registered nurse or midwife,
  (c) a clinical psychologist, or
  (d) a child psychotherapist;

(9) 'lay adviser' means a non-professional person who gives lay advice on behalf of an organisation in the lay advice sector;

(10) 'McKenzie Friend' means any person permitted by the court to sit beside an unrepresented litigant in court to assist that litigant by prompting, taking notes and giving him advice;

(11) 'mediator' means a family mediator who is –
  (a) undertaking, or has successfully completed, a family mediation training course approved by the United Kingdom College of Family Mediators, or
  (b) a member of the Law Society's Family Mediation Panel;

(12) 'peer' means a member of the House of Lords as defined by the House of Lords Act 1999.

PRACTICE DIRECTION 14F – DISCLOSING INFORMATION TO AN ADOPTED ADULT

This Practice Direction supplements FPR Part 14, rule 14.18(1)(d)

How to request for information

1.1 Rule 14.18 states that an adopted person who is over the age of 18 has the right to receive from the court which made the adoption order a copy of:

(a) the application form for an adoption order (but not the documents attached to that form);
(b) the adoption order and any other orders relating to the adoption proceedings; and
(c) orders allowing any person contact with the child after the adoption order was made.

1.2 An application under rule 14.18 must be made in form A64 which is contained in the practice direction supplementing rule 5 and must have attached to it a full certified copy of the entry in the Adopted Children Register relating to the applicant.

1.3 The completed application form must be taken to the court which made the adoption order along with evidence of the applicant's identity showing a photograph and signature, such as a passport or driving licence.

Additional documents that the adopted person is also entitled to receive from the court

2 The adopted adult is also entitled to receive the following documents:
(a) any transcript or written reasons of the court's decision; and
(b) a report made to the court by:
  (i) a children's guardian, reporting officer or children and family reporter;
  (ii) a local authority; or
  (iii) an adoption agency.

Before the documents are sent to the adopted adult

3 The court will remove protected information from documents before they are sent to the adopted adult.

PRACTICE DIRECTION 15A – PROTECTED PARTIES

This Practice Direction supplements FPR Part 15

General

1.1 A protected party must have a litigation friend to conduct proceedings on the protected party's behalf.

1.2 In the proceedings the protected party should be referred to in the title as 'A.B. (by C.D. his/her litigation friend).

Duties of the Litigation Friend

2.1 It is the duty of a litigation friend fairly and competently to conduct proceedings on behalf of a protected party. The litigation friend must have no interest in the proceedings adverse to that of the protected party and all steps and decisions the litigation friend takes in the proceedings must be taken for the benefit of the protected party.

Becoming a Litigation Friend without a court order

3.1 In order to become a litigation friend without a court order the person who wishes to act as litigation friend must–
(a) file an official copy of the order, declaration or other document which confers the litigation friend's authority as a deputy to conduct the proceedings in the name of a protected party or on his/her behalf; or
(b) file a certificate of suitability–
  (i) stating that the litigation friend consents to act;

(ii) stating that the litigation friend knows or believes that the [applicant][respondent] lacks capacity (within the meaning of the 2005 Act) to conduct proceedings;
(iii) stating the grounds of that belief and if the belief is based upon medical opinion attaching any relevant document to the certificate;
(iv) stating that the litigation friend can fairly and competently conduct proceedings on behalf of the protected party and has no interest adverse to that of the protected party;
(v) undertaking to pay any costs which the protected party may be ordered to pay in relation to the proceedings, subject to any right the litigation friend may have to be repaid from the assets of the protected party; and
(vi) which the litigation friend has verified by a statement of truth.

3.2 Paragraph 3.1 does not apply to the Official Solicitor.
3.3 The court officer will send the certificate of suitability to the person who is the attorney of a registered enduring power of attorney, donee of a lasting power of attorney or deputy or, if there is no such person, to the person with whom the protected party resides or in whose care the protected party is.
3.4 The court officer is not required to send the documents referred to in paragraph 3.1(b)(iii) when sending the certificate of suitability to the person to be served under paragraph 3.3.
3.5 The litigation friend must file either the certificate of suitability or the authority referred to in paragraph 3.1(a) at a time when the litigation friend first takes a step in the proceedings on behalf of the protected party.

Application for a court order appointing a litigation friend

4.1 An application for a court order appointing a litigation friend should be made in accordance with Part 18 and must be supported by evidence.
4.2 The court officer must serve the application notice–

(a) on the persons referred to in paragraph 3.3; and
(b) on the protected party unless the court directs otherwise.

4.3 The evidence in support must satisfy the court that the proposed litigation friend–

(a) consents to act;
(b) can fairly and competently conduct proceedings on behalf of the protected party;
(c) has no interest adverse to that of the protected party; and
(d) undertakes to pay any costs which the protected party may be ordered to pay in relation to the proceedings, subject to any right the litigation friend may have to be repaid from the assets of the protected party.

4.4 Paragraph 4.3(d) does not apply to the Official Solicitor.
4.5 The proposed litigation friend may be one of the persons referred to in paragraph 3.3 where appropriate, or otherwise may be the Official Solicitor. Where it is sought to appoint the Official Solicitor, provision must be made for payment of his charges.

Change of litigation friend and prevention of person acting as litigation friend.

5.1 Where an application is made for an order under rule 15.7, the application must set out the reasons for seeking it and must be supported by evidence.
5.2 Subject to paragraph 4.4, if the order sought is substitution of a new litigation friend for an existing one, the evidence must satisfy the court of the matters set out in paragraph 4.3.
5.3 The court officer will serve the application notice on–

(a) the persons referred to in paragraph 3.3; and

(b) the litigation friend or person purporting to act as litigation friend.

Procedure where the need for a litigation friend has come to an end

6.1 Where a person who was a protected party regains or acquires capacity (within the meaning of the 2005 Act) to conduct the proceedings, an application under rule 15.9(2) must be made for an order under rule 15.9(1) that the litigation friend's appointment has ceased.

6.2 The application must be supported by the following evidence–

    (a) a medical report or other suitably qualified expert's report indicating that the protected party has regained or acquired capacity (within the meaning of the 2005 Act) to conduct the proceedings; and

    (b) a copy of any relevant order or declaration of the Court of Protection.

PRACTICE DIRECTION 16A – REPRESENTATION OF CHILDREN

This Practice Direction supplements FPR Part 16

PART 1 – GENERAL

Reference in title of proceedings

1.1 Where a litigation friend represents a child in family proceedings in accordance with rule 16.5 and Chapter 5 of Part 16, the child should be referred to in the title of the proceedings as 'A.B. (a child by C.D. his/her litigation friend).'

1.2 Where a children's guardian represents a child in family proceedings in accordance with rule 16.4 and Chapter 7 of Part 16, the child should be referred to in the title as 'A.B. (a child by C.D. his/her children's guardian).

1.3 A child who is conducting proceedings on that child's own behalf should be referred to in the title as 'A.B. (a child).'

PART 2 – LITIGATION FRIEND

Duties of the Litigation Friend

2.1 It is the duty of a litigation friend fairly and competently to conduct proceedings on behalf of the child. The litigation friend must have no interest in the proceedings adverse to that of the child and all steps and decisions the litigation friend takes in the proceedings must be taken for the benefit of the child.

2.2. A litigation friend who is an officer of the Service or a Welsh family proceedings officer has, in addition, the duties set out in Part 3 of this Practice Direction and must exercise those duties as set out in that Part.

Becoming a Litigation Friend without a court order

3.1 In order to become a litigation friend without a court order the person who wishes to act as litigation friend must file a certificate of suitability–

    (a) stating that the litigation friend consents to act;

    (b) stating that the litigation friend knows or believes that the [applicant] [respondent] is a child to whom rule 16.5 and Chapter 5 of Part 16 apply;

    (c) stating that the litigation friend can fairly and competently conduct proceedings on behalf of the child and has no interest adverse to that of the child;

    (d) undertaking to pay any costs which the child may be ordered to pay in relation to the proceedings, subject to any right the litigation friend may have to be repaid from the assets of the child; and

    (e) which the litigation friend has verified by a statement of truth.

3.2 Paragraph 3.1 does not apply to the Official Solicitor, an officer of the Service or a Welsh family proceedings officer.

3.3 The court officer will send the certificate of suitability to one of the child's parents or guardians or, if there is no parent or guardian, to the person with whom the child resides or in whose care the child is.

3.4 The litigation friend must file the certificate of suitability at a time when the litigation friend first takes a step in the proceedings on behalf of the child.

Application for a court order appointing a litigation friend

4.1 An application for a court order appointing a litigation friend should be made in accordance with Part 18 and must be supported by evidence.

4.2 The court officer must serve the application notice on the persons referred to in paragraph 3.3.

4.3 The evidence in support must satisfy the court that the proposed litigation friend–

    (a) consents to act;
    (b) can fairly and competently conduct proceedings on behalf of the child;
    (c) has no interest adverse to that of the child; and
    (d) undertakes to pay any costs which the child may be ordered to pay in relation to the proceedings, subject to any right the litigation friend may have to be repaid from the assets of the child.

4.4 Paragraph 4.3(d) does not apply to the Official Solicitor, an officer of the Service of a Welsh family proceedings officer.

4.5 The proposed litigation friend may be one of the persons referred to in paragraph 3.3 where appropriate, or otherwise may be the Official Solicitor, an officer of the Service or a Welsh family proceedings officer. Where it is sought to appoint the Official Solicitor, an officer of the Service or a Welsh family proceedings officer, provision should be made for payment of that person's charges.

Change of litigation friend and prevention of person acting as litigation friend.

5.1 Where an application is made for an order under rule 16.12, the application must set out the reasons for seeking it and the application must be supported by evidence.

5.2 Subject to paragraph 4.4, if the order sought is substitution of a new litigation friend for an existing one, the evidence must satisfy the court of the matters set out in paragraph 4.3.

5.3 The court officer will serve the application notice on–

    (a) the persons referred to in paragraph 3.3; and
    (b) the litigation friend or person purporting to act as litigation friend.

PART 3 – CHILDREN'S GUARDIAN APPOINTED UNDER RULE 16.3

How the children's guardian exercises duties – investigations and appointment of solicitor

6.1 The children's guardian must make such investigations as are necessary to carry out the children's guardian's duties and must, in particular–

    (a) contact or seek to interview such persons as the children's guardian thinks appropriate or as the court directs; and
    (b) obtain such professional assistance as is available which the children's guardian thinks appropriate or which the court directs be obtained.

6.2 The children's guardian must–

    (a) appoint a solicitor for the child unless a solicitor has already been appointed;

(b) give such advice to the child as is appropriate having regard to that child's understanding; and
(c) where appropriate instruct the solicitor representing the child on all matters relevant to the interests of the child arising in the course of proceedings, including possibilities for appeal.

6.3 Where the children's guardian is authorised in the terms mentioned by and in accordance with section 15(1) of the Criminal Justice and Court Services Act 2000 or section 37(1) of the Children Act 2004 (right of officer of the Service or Welsh family proceedings officer to conduct litigation or exercise a right of audience), paragraph 6.2(a) will not apply if the children's guardian intends to have conduct of the proceedings on behalf of the child unless–

(a) the child wishes to instruct a solicitor direct; and
(b) the children's guardian or the court considers that the child is of sufficient understanding to do so.

6.4 Where rule 16.21 (Where the child instructs a solicitor or conducts proceedings on the child's own behalf) applies, the duties set out in paragraph 6.2(a) and (c) do not apply.

How the children's guardian exercises duties – attendance at court, advice to the court and reports

6.5 The children's guardian or the solicitor appointed under section 41(3) of the 1989 Act or in accordance with paragraph 6.2(a) must attend all directions hearings unless the court directs otherwise.

6.6 The children's guardian must advise the court on the following matters–

(a) whether the child is of sufficient understanding for any purpose including the child's refusal to submit to a medical or psychiatric examination or other assessment that the court has the power to require, direct or order;
(b) the wishes of the child in respect of any matter relevant to the proceedings including that child's attendance at court;
(c) the appropriate forum for the proceedings;
(d) the appropriate timing of the proceedings or any part of them;
(e) the options available to it in respect of the child and the suitability of each such option including what order should be made in determining the application; and
(f) any other matter on which the court seeks advice or on which the children's guardian considers that the court should be informed.

6.7 The advice given under paragraph 6.6 may, subject to any direction of the court, be given orally or in writing. If the advice is given orally, a note of it must be taken by the court or the court officer.

6.8 The children's guardian must–

(a) unless the court directs otherwise, file a written report advising on the interests of the child in accordance with the timetable set by the court; and
(b) in proceedings to which Part 14 applies, where practicable, notify any person the joining of whom as a party to those proceedings would be likely, in the opinion of the children's guardian, to safeguard the interests of the child, of the court's power to join that person as a party under rule 14.3 and must inform the court–

(i) of any notification;
(ii) of anyone whom the children's guardian attempted to notify under this paragraph but was unable to contact; and
(iii) of anyone whom the children's guardian believes may wish to be joined to the proceedings.

(Part 18 sets out the procedure for making an application to be joined as a party in proceedings.)

How the children's guardian exercises duties – service of documents and inspection of records

6.9 The children's guardian must serve and accept service of documents on behalf of the child in accordance with rule 6.31 and, where the child has not himself been served and has sufficient understanding, advise the child of the contents of any document so served.

6.10 Where the children's guardian inspects records of the kinds referred to in–

(a) section 42 of the 1989 Act (right to have access to local authority records); or
(b) section 103 of the 2002 Act (right to have access to adoption agency records)

the children's guardian must bring all records and documents which may, in the opinion of the children's guardian, assist in the proper determination of the proceedings to the attention of–

(i) the court; and
(ii) unless the court directs otherwise, the other parties to the proceedings.

How the children's guardian exercises duties – communication of a court's decision to the child

6.11 The children's guardian must ensure that, in relation to a decision made by the court in the proceedings–

(a) if the children's guardian considers it appropriate to the age and understanding of the child, the child is notified of that decision; and
(b) if the child is notified of the decision, it is explained to the child in a manner appropriate to that child's age and understanding.

PART 4 – APPOINTMENT OF CHILDREN'S GUARDIAN UNDER RULE 16.4

Section 1 – When a child should be made a party to proceedings

7.1 Making the child a party to the proceedings is a step that will be taken only in cases which involve an issue of significant difficulty and consequently will occur in only a minority of cases. Before taking the decision to make the child a party, consideration should be given to whether an alternative route might be preferable, such as asking an officer of the Service or a Welsh family proceedings officer to carry out further work or by making a referral to social services or, possibly, by obtaining expert evidence.

7.2 The decision to make the child a party will always be exclusively that of the court, made in the light of the facts and circumstances of the particular case. The following are offered, solely by way of guidance, as circumstances which may justify the making of such an order–

(a) where an officer of the Service or Welsh family proceedings officer has notified the court that in the opinion of that officer the child should be made a party;
(b) where the child has a standpoint or interest which is inconsistent with or incapable of being represented by any of the adult parties;
(c) where there is an intractable dispute over residence or contact, including where all contact has ceased, or where there is irrational but implacable hostility to contact or where the child may be suffering harm associated with the contact dispute;
(d) where the views and wishes of the child cannot be adequately met by a report to the court;
(e) where an older child is opposing a proposed course of action;

(f) where there are complex medical or mental health issues to be determined or there are other unusually complex issues that necessitate separate representation of the child;
(g) where there are international complications outside child abduction, in particular where it may be necessary for there to be discussions with overseas authorities or a foreign court;
(h) where there are serious allegations of physical, sexual or other abuse in relation to the child or there are allegations of domestic violence not capable of being resolved with the help of an officer of the Service or Welsh family proceedings officer;
(i) where the proceedings concern more than one child and the welfare of the children is in conflict or one child is in a particularly disadvantaged position;
(j) where there is a contested issue about scientific testing.

7.3 It must be recognised that separate representation of the child may result in a delay in the resolution of the proceedings. When deciding whether to direct that a child be made a party, the court will take into account the risk of delay or other facts adverse to the welfare of the child. The court's primary consideration will be the best interests of the child.

7.4 When a child is made a party and a children's guardian is to be appointed–

(a) consideration should first be given to appointing an officer of the Service or Welsh family proceedings officer. Before appointing an officer, the court will cause preliminary enquiries to be made of Cafcass or CAFCASS CYMRU. For the relevant procedure, reference should be made to the practice note issued by Cafcass in June 2006 and any modifications of that practice note.
(b) If Cafcass or CAFCASS CYMRU is unable to provide a children's guardian without delay, or if for some other reason the appointment of an officer of the Service of Welsh family proceedings officer is not appropriate, rule 16.24 makes further provision for the appointment of a children's guardian.

7.5 The court may, at the same time as deciding whether to join a child as a party, consider whether the proceedings should be transferred to another court taking into account the provisions of Part 3 of the Allocation and Transfer of Proceedings Order 2008.

Section 2 – Children's guardian appointed under rule 16.4

Duties of the children's guardian

7.6 It is the duty of a children's guardian fairly and competently to conduct proceedings on behalf of the child. The children's guardian must have no interest in the proceedings adverse to that of the child and all steps and decisions the children's guardian takes in the proceedings must be taken for the benefit of the child.

7.7 A children's guardian who is an officer of the Service or a Welsh family proceedings officer has, in addition, the duties set out in Part 3 of this Practice Direction and must exercise those duties as set out in that Part.

Becoming a children's guardian without a court order

7.8 In order to become a children's guardian without a court order the person who wishes to act as children's guardian must file a certificate of suitability–

(a) stating that the children's guardian consents to act;
(b) stating that the children's guardian knows or believes that the [applicant] [respondent] is a child to whom rule 16.4 and Chapter 7 of Part 16 apply;
(c) stating that the children's guardian can fairly and competently conduct proceedings on behalf of the child and has no interest adverse to that of the child;
(d) undertaking to pay any costs which the child may be ordered to pay in relation

to the proceedings, subject to any right the children's guardian may have to be repaid from the assets of the child; and
   (e) which the children's guardian has verified by a statement of truth.
7.9 Paragraph 7.8 does not apply to the Official Solicitor, an officer of the Service or a Welsh family proceedings officer.
7.10 The court officer will send the certificate of suitability to one of the child's parents or guardians or, if there is no parent or guardian, to the person with whom the child resides or in whose care the child is.
7.11 The children's guardian must file either the certificate of suitability at a time when the children's guardian first takes a step in the proceedings on behalf of the child.

Application for a court order appointing a children's guardian

7.12 An application for a court order appointing a children's guardian should be made in accordance with Part 18 and must be supported by evidence.
7.13 The court officer must serve the application notice on the persons referred to in paragraph 7.10.
7.14 The evidence in support must satisfy the court that the proposed children's guardian–
   (a) consents to act;
   (b) can fairly and competently conduct proceedings on behalf of the child;
   (c) has no interest adverse to that of the child; and
   (d) undertakes to pay any costs which the child may be ordered to pay in relation to the proceedings, subject to any right the children's guardian may have to be repaid from the assets of the child.
7.15 Paragraph 7.14 does not apply to the Official Solicitor, an officer of the Service of a Welsh family proceedings officer.
7.16 The proposed children's guardian may be one of the persons referred to in paragraph 7.10 where appropriate, or otherwise may be the Official Solicitor, an officer of the Service or a Welsh family proceedings officer. Where it is sought to appoint the Official Solicitor, an officer of the Service or a Welsh family proceedings officer, provision should be made for payment of that person's charges.

Change of children's guardian and prevention of person acting as children's guardian.

7.17 Where an application is made for an order under rule 16.25, the application must set out the reasons for seeking it and must be supported by evidence.
7.18 Subject to paragraph 7.15, if the order sought is substitution of a new children's guardian for an existing one, the evidence must satisfy the court of the matters set out in paragraph 7.14.
7.19 The court officer will serve the application notice on–
   (a) the persons referred to in paragraph 7.10; and
   (b) the children's guardian or person purporting to act as children's guardian.

PART 5 – REPORTING OFFICER

How the reporting officer exercises duties

8.1 The reporting officer must–
   (a) ensure so far as reasonably practicable that the parent or guardian is–
      (i) giving consent unconditionally to the placing of the child for adoption or to the making of an adoption order (as defined in section 46 of the Adoption and Children Act 2002) or a section 84 order; and
      (ii) with full understanding of what is involved;

(b) investigate all the circumstances relevant to a parent's or guardian's consent; and
(c) on completing the investigations the reporting officer must—
  (i) make a report in writing to the court in accordance with the timetable set by the court, drawing attention to any matters which, in the opinion of the reporting officer, may be of assistance to the court in considering the application; or
  (ii) make an interim report to the court if a parent or guardian of the child is unwilling to consent to the placing of the child for adoption or to the making of an adoption order or section 84 order.

8.2 On receipt of an interim report under paragraph 8.1(1)(c)(ii) a court officer must inform the applicant that a parent or guardian of the child is unwilling to consent to the placing of the child for adoption or to the making of an adoption order or section 84 order.

8.3 The reporting officer may at any time before the final hearing make an interim report to the court if the reporting officer considers it necessary and ask the court for directions.

8.4 The reporting officer must attend hearings as directed by the court.

PART 6 – CHILDREN AND FAMILY REPORTER AND WELFARE OFFICER

How the children and family reporter or welfare officer exercises powers and duties

9.1 In this Part, the person preparing the welfare report in accordance with rule 16.33 is called 'the officer'.

9.2 The officer must make such investigations as may be necessary to perform the officer's powers and duties and must, in particular—
  (a) contact or seek to interview such persons as appear appropriate or as the court directs; and
  (b) obtain such professional assistance as is available which the children and family reporter thinks appropriate or which the court directs be obtained.

9.3 The officer must—
  (a) notify the child of such contents of the report (if any) as the officer considers appropriate to the age and understanding of the child, including any reference to the child's own views on the application and the recommendation; and
  (b) if the child is notified of any contents of the report, explain them to the child in a manner appropriate to the child's age and understanding.

9.4 The officer must—
  (a) attend hearings as directed by the court;
  (b) advise the court of the child's wishes and feelings;
  (c) advise the court if the officer considers that the joining of a person as a party to the proceedings would be likely to safeguard the interests of the child;
  (d) consider whether it is in the best interests of the child for the child to be made a party to the proceedings, and if so, notify the court of that opinion together with the reasons for that opinion; and
  (e) where the court has directed that a written report be made—
    (i) file the report; and
    (ii) serve a copy on the other parties and on any children's guardian,
  in accordance with the timetable set by the court.

PART 7 – PARENTAL ORDER REPORTER

How the parental order reporter exercises duties – investigations and reports

10.1 The parental order reporter must make such investigations as are necessary to carry out the parental order reporter's duties and must, in particular—

(a) contact or seek to interview such persons as the parental order reporter thinks appropriate or as the court directs; and
(b) obtain such professional assistance as is available which the parental order reporter thinks appropriate or which the court directs be obtained.

How the parental order reporter exercises duties – attendance at court, advice to the court and reports

10.2 The parental order reporter must attend all directions hearings unless the court directs otherwise.

10.3 The parental order reporter must advise the court on the following matters–

(a) the appropriate forum for the proceedings;
(b) the appropriate timing of the proceedings or any part of them;
(c) the options available to it in respect of the child and the suitability of each such option including what order should be made in determining the application; and
(d) any other matter on which the court seeks advice or on which the parental order reporter considers that the court should be informed.

10.4 The advice given under paragraph 10.3 may, subject to any direction of the court, be given orally or in writing. If the advice is given orally, a note of it must be taken by the court or the court officer.

10.5 The parental order reporter must–

(a) unless the court directs otherwise, file a written report advising on the interests of the child in accordance with the timetable set by the court; and
(b) where practicable, notify any person the joining of whom as a party to those proceedings would be likely, in the opinion of the parental order reporter, to safeguard the interests of the child, of the court's power to join that person as a party under rule 13.3 and must inform the court–

   (i) of any notification;
   (ii) of anyone whom the parental order reporter attempted to notify under this paragraph but was unable to contact; and
   (iii) of anyone whom the parental order reporter believes may wish to be joined to the proceedings.

(Part 18 sets out the procedure for making an application to be joined as a party in proceedings.)

PART 8 – OFFICERS OF THE SERVICE, WELSH FAMILY PROCEEDINGS OFFICERS AND LOCAL AUTHORITY OFFICERS: FURTHER DUTIES

How officers of the Service, Welsh family proceedings officers and local authority officers exercise certain further duties

11.1 This Part applies when an officer of the Service, a Welsh family proceedings officer or a local authority officer is acting under a duty referred to in rule 16.38(1). In this Part, the person acting under a duty referred to in rule 16.38(1) is referred to as 'the officer'.

11.2 The officer must make such investigations as may be necessary to perform the officer's duties and must, in particular–

(a) contact or seek to interview such persons as the officer thinks appropriate or as the court directs; and
(b) obtain such professional assistance as the officer thinks appropriate or which the court directs.

11.3 The officer must–

(a) notify the child of such (if any) of the contents of any report or risk assessment as the officer considers appropriate to the age and understanding of the child;
(b) if the child is notified of any contents of a report or risk assessment, explain them to the child in a manner appropriate to the child's age and understanding;
(c) consider whether to recommend in any report or risk assessment that the court lists a hearing for the purposes of considering the report or risk assessment;
(d) consider whether it is in the best interests of the child for the child to be made a party to the proceedings, and, if so, notify the court of that opinion together with the reasons for that opinion.

11.4 When making a risk assessment, the officer must, if of the opinion that the court should exercise its discretion under rule 12.34(2), state in the risk assessment–

(a) the way in which the officer considers the court should exercise its discretion (including the officer's view on the length of any suggested delay in service); and
(b) the officer's reasons for that reaching that view.

11.5 The officer must file any report or risk assessment with the court–

(a) at or by the time directed by the court;
(b) in the absence of any direction, at least 14 days before a relevant hearing; or
(c) where there has been no direction from the court and there is no relevant hearing listed, as soon as possible following the completion of the report or risk assessment.

11.6 In paragraph 11.5, a hearing is relevant if the court officer has given the officer notice that a report prepared by the officer is to be considered at it.

11.7 A copy of any report prepared as a result of acting under a duty referred to in rule 16.38(1)(a)(i) to (vi) or (b) (but not any risk assessment) must, as soon as practicable, be served by the officer on the parties.

(Rule 12.34 makes provision for the service of risk assessments.)

PRACTICE DIRECTION 17A – STATEMENTS OF TRUTH

This Practice Direction supplements FPR Part 17

Documents to be verified by a statement of truth

1.1 Rule 17.2 sets out the documents which must be verified by a statement of truth.
1.2 If an applicant wishes to rely on matters set out in his application notice as evidence, the application notice must be verified by a statement of truth.
1.3 An expert's report should also be verified by a statement of truth. For the form of the statement of truth verifying an expert's report (which differs from that set out below), see the practice direction which supplements Part 25.
1.4 In addition, the following documents must be verified by a statement of truth–

(a) an application notice for–
  (i) a third party debt order (CPR Part 72 as modified by rule 33.24);
  (ii) a hardship payment order (CPR Part 72 as modified by rule 33.24); or
  (iii) a charging order (CPR Part 73 as modified by rule 33.25); and
(b) a notice of objections to an account being taken by the court, unless verified by an affidavit or witness statement.

1.5 The statement of truth may be contained in the document it verifies or it may be in a separate document served subsequently, in which case it must identify the document to which it relates.

1.6 Where the form to be used includes a jurat for the content to be verified by an affidavit, then a statement of truth is not required in addition.

1.7 In this Practice Direction, 'statement of case' has the meaning given to it by rule 17.1.

Form of the statement of truth

2.1 The form of the statement of truth verifying a statement of case or an application notice should be as follows:

'[I believe] [the (*applicant or as may be*) believes] that the facts stated in this [*name document being verified*] are true.'

2.2 The form of the statement of truth verifying a witness statement should be as follows:

'I believe that the facts stated in this witness statement are true.'

2.3 Where the statement of truth is contained in a separate document, the document containing the statement of truth must be headed with the title of and court reference for the proceedings. The document being verified should be identified in the statement of truth as follows–

- (a) application form: 'the application form issued on [*date*]';
- (b) statement of case: 'the (application or answer as may be) served on [*name of party*] on [*date*]';
- (c) application notice: 'the application notice issued on [*date*] for [*set out the remedy sought*]';
- (d) witness statement: 'the witness statement filed on [*date*] or served on [*party*] on [*date*]'.

Who may sign the statement of truth

3.1 In a statement of case or an application notice, the statement of truth must be signed by–

- (a) the party or his litigation friend; or
- (b) the legal representative of the party or litigation friend.

3.2 A statement of truth verifying a witness statement must be signed by the witness.

3.3 A statement of truth verifying a notice of objections to an account must be signed by the objecting party or his or her legal representative.

3.4 Where a document is to be verified on behalf of a company or corporation, subject to paragraph 3.7 below, the statement of truth must be signed by a person holding a senior position in the company or corporation. That person must state the office or position he or she holds.

3.5 Each of the following persons is a person holding a senior position:

- (a) in respect of a registered company or corporation, a director, the treasurer, secretary, chief executive, manager or other officer of the company or corporation; and
- (b) in respect of a corporation which is not a registered company, in addition to those persons set out in (a), the major, chairman, president, chief executive of a local authority or town clerk or other similar officer of the corporation.

3.6 Where the document is to be verified on behalf of a partnership, those who may sign the statement of truth are–

- (a) any of the partners; or
- (b) a person having the management or control of the partnership business.

3.7 Where a party is legally represented, the legal representative may sign the statement of truth on his or her behalf. The statement signed by the legal representative will refer to the client's belief, not his or her own. In signing he or she must state the capacity in which he or she signs and the name of his or her firm where appropriate.

3.8 Where a legal representative has signed a statement of truth, his or her signature will be taken by the court as his or her statement–

(a) that the client on whose behalf he or she has signed had authorised him or her to do so;
(b) that before signing he or she had explained to the client that in signing the statement of truth he or she would be confirming the client's belief that the facts stated in the document were true; and
(c) that before signing he or she had informed the client of the possible consequences to the client if it should subsequently appear that the client did not have an honest belief in the truth of those facts (see rule 17.6).

3.9 A legal representative who signs a statement of truth must print his or her full name clearly beneath his or her signature.

3.10 The individual who signs a statement of truth must sign in his or her own name and not that of his or her firm or employer.

3.11 The following are examples of the possible application of this practice direction describing who may sign a statement of truth verifying statements in documents other than a witness statement. These are only examples and not an indication of how a court might apply the practice direction to a specific situation.

Managing Agent

An agent who manages property or investments for the party cannot sign a statement of truth. It must be signed by the party or by the legal representative of the party.

Trusts

Where some or all of the trustees comprise a single party one, some or all of the trustees comprising the party may sign a statement of truth. The legal representative of the trustees may sign it.

Companies

Paragraphs 3.4 and 3.5 apply. The word 'manager' will be construed in the context of the phrase 'a person holding a senior position' which it is used to define. The court will consider the size of the company and the importance and nature of the proceedings. It would expect the manager signing the statement of truth to to have personal knowledge of the content of the document or to be responsible for those who have that knowledge of the content. A small company may not have a manager, apart from the directors, who holds a senior position. A large company will have many such managers. In a large company with specialist claims, insurance or legal departments the statement may be signed by the manager of such a department if he or she is responsible for handling the claim or managing the staff handling it.

Inability of persons to read or sign documents to be verified by a statement of truth

4.1 Where a document containing a statement of truth is to be signed by a person who is unable to read or sign the document, it must contain a certificate made by an authorised person.

4.2 An authorised person is a person able to administer oaths and take affidavits but need not be independent of the parties or their representatives.

4.3 The authorised person must certify–

(a) that the document has been read to the person signing it;
(b) that the person appeared to understand it and approved its content as accurate;
(c) that the declaration of truth has been read to that person;
(d) that that person appeared to understand the declaration and the consequences of making a false declaration; and
(e) that that person signed or made his mark in the presence of the authorised person.

4.4 The form of the certificate is set out at the Annex to this Practice Direction.

Consequences of failure to verify

5.1 If a statement of case is not verified by a statement of truth, the statement of case will remain effective unless it is struck out, but a party may not rely on the contents of a statement of case as evidence until it has been verified by a statement of truth.
5.2 Any party may apply to the court for an order that unless within such period as the court may specify the statement of case is verified by the service of a statement of truth, the statement of case will be struck out.
5.3 The usual order for the costs of an application referred to in paragraph 5.2 will be that the costs be paid by the party who had failed to verify, in any event and immediately.

Penalty

6.1 Rule 17.6 sets out the consequences of verifying a statement of case containing a false statement without an honest belief in its truth. Where a party alleges that a statement of truth is false, the party shall refer that allegation to the court dealing with the proceedings in which the statement of truth has been made.
6.2 On a reference under paragraph 6.1 the court may–
 (a) exercise any of its powers under the FPR;
 (b) initiate steps to consider if there is a contempt of court and, where there is, to punish it;

(Order 52 of the Rules of the Supreme Court and Order 29 of the County Court Rules (Schedules 1 and 2 to the CPR) make provision where committal to prison is a possibility if contempt is proved.)

 (c) direct the party making the allegation to refer the matter to the Attorney General with a request to him or her to consider whether he or she wishes to bring proceedings for contempt of court.
6.3 A request to the Attorney General must be made in writing and sent to the Attorney General's Office at 20 Victoria Street, London, SW1H 0NF. The request must be accompanied by a copy of the order directing that the matter be referred to the Attorney General and must–
 (a) identify the statement said to be false; and
 (b) explain–
  (i) why it is false; and
  (ii) why the maker knew it to be false at the time it was made; and
 (c) explain why contempt proceedings would be appropriate in the light of the overriding objective in Part 1 of the FPR.
6.4 The practice of the Attorney General is to prefer an application that comes from the court, and so has received preliminary consideration by a judge or district judge, to one made direct to him or her by a party to the proceedings in which the alleged contempt occurred without prior consideration by the court. An application to the Attorney General is not a way of appealing against, or reviewing, the decision of the judge or district judge.
6.5 Where a party makes an application to the court for permission for that party to commence proceedings for contempt of court, it must be supported by written evidence containing the information specified in paragraph 6.3 and the result of the application to the Attorney General made by the applicant.
6.6 The FPR do not change the law of contempt or introduce new categories of contempt. A person applying to commence such proceedings should consider whether the incident complained of does amount to contempt of court and whether such proceedings would further the overriding objective in Part 1 of the FPR.

ANNEX

Certificate to be used where a person is unable to read or sign a document to be verified by a statement of truth.

I certify that I [name and address of authorised person] have read the contents of this document and the declaration of truth to the person signing the document [if there are exhibits, add 'and explained the nature and effect of the exhibits referred to in it'] who appeared to understand (a) the document and approved its content as accurate and (b) the declaration of truth and the consequences of making a false declaration, and made his or her mark in my presence.

PRACTICE DIRECTION 18A – OTHER APPLICATIONS IN PROCEEDINGS

This Practice Direction supplements FPR Part 18

Application of Part 18

1.1 Part 18 makes general provision for a procedure for making applications. All applications for the court's permission should be made under this Part, with the exception of applications for permission for which specific provision is made in other Parts of the FPR, in which case the application should be made under the specific provision. Examples of where specific provision has been made in another Part of the FPR for applications for permission are rule 11.3 (Permission to apply for a forced marriage protection order) and rule 30.3 (Permission to appeal).

Reference to a judge

2.1 In the High Court or a county court a district judge may refer to a judge any matter which the district judge thinks should properly be decided by a judge, and the judge may either dispose of the matter or refer it back to the district judge.

Additional requirements in relation to application notices

3.1 In addition to the requirements set out in rule 18.7, the following requirements apply to the applications to which the respective paragraph refers.

3.2 An application notice must be signed and include–

    (a) the title of the case (if available);
    (b) the reference number of the case (if available);
    (c) the full name of the applicant;
    (d) where the applicant is not already a party, the applicant's address for service, including a postcode. Postcode information may be obtained from www.royalmail.com or the Royal Mail Address Management Guide; and
    (e) either a request for a hearing or a request that the application be dealt with without a hearing.

3.3 An application notice relating to an application under section 42(6) of the Adoption and Children Act 2002 (permission to apply for an adoption order) must include–

    (a) the child's name, sex, date of birth and nationality;
    (b) in relation to each of the child's parents or guardians, their name, address and nationality;
    (c) the length of time that the child has had his or her home with the applicant;
    (d) the reason why the child has had his or her home with the applicant;
    (e) details of any local authority or adoption agency involved in placing the child in the applicant's home; and
    (f) if there are or have been other court proceedings relating to the child, the nature of those proceedings, the name of the court in which they are being or have been dealt with, the date and type of any order made and, if the proceedings are still ongoing, the date of the next hearing.

3.4 An application notice relating to an application in the High Court by a local authority for permission under section 100(3) of the Children Act 1989 must include a draft of the application form.

3.5 Where permission is required to take any step under the Children Act 1989 (for example an application to be joined as a party to the proceedings) the application notice must include a draft of the application for the making of which permission is sought together with sufficient copies for one to be served on each respondent.

3.6 In an application for permission to bring proceedings under Schedule 1 of the Children Act 1989, the draft application for the making of which permission is sought must be accompanied by a statement setting out the financial details which the person seeking permission believes to be relevant to the request and contain a declaration that it is true to the maker's best knowledge and belief, together with sufficient copies for one to be served on each respondent.

3.7 The provisions in Schedule 1 which require an application for permission to bring proceedings are–

(a) paragraph 7(2) – permission is required to make an application for variation of a secured periodical payments order after the death of the parent liable to make the payments if a period of 6 months has passed from the date on which representation in regard to that parent's estate is first taken out; and

(b) paragraph 11(3) – permission is required to make an application to alter a maintenance agreement following the death of one of the parties if a period of 6 months has passed beginning with the day on which representation in regard to the estate of the deceased is first taken out.

Other provisions in relation to application notices.

4.1 On receipt of an application notice containing a request for a hearing, unless the court considers that the application is suitable for consideration without a hearing, the court officer will, if serving a copy of the application notice, notify the applicant of the time and date fixed for the hearing of the application.

4.2 On receipt of an application notice containing a request that the application be dealt with without a hearing, the court will decide whether the application is suitable for consideration without a hearing.

4.3 Where the court–

(a) considers that the application is suitable for consideration without a hearing; but

(b) is not satisfied that it has sufficient material to decide the application immediately,

it may give directions for the filing of evidence and will inform the applicant and the respondent(s) of its decision. (Rule 18.11 enables a party to apply for an order made without notice to be set aside or varied.)

4.4 Where the court does not consider that the application is suitable for consideration without a hearing–

(a) it may give directions as to the filing of evidence; and

(b) the court officer will notify the applicant and the respondent of the time, date and place for the hearing of the application and any directions given.

4.5 In the High Court or a county court if the application is intended to be made to a judge, the application notice should so state. In that case, paragraphs 4.2, 4.3 and 4.4 will apply as though references to the court were references to a judge.

4.6 Every application should be made as soon as it becomes apparent that it is necessary or desirable to make it.

4.7 Applications should, wherever possible, be made so that they are considered at any directions hearing or other hearing for which a date has been fixed or for which a date is about to be fixed.

4.8 The parties must anticipate that at any hearing (including any directions hearing) the court may wish to review the conduct of the case as a whole and give any necessary directions. They should be ready to assist the court in doing so and to answer questions the court may ask for this purpose.

4.9 Where a date for a hearing has been fixed, a party who wishes to make an application at that hearing but does not have sufficient time to file an application notice should as soon as possible inform the court (if possible in writing) and, if possible, the other parties of the nature of the application and the reason for it. That party should then make the application orally at the hearing.

Applications without service of application notice

5.1 An application may be made without service of an application notice only–

    (a)   where there is exceptional urgency;
    (b)   where the overriding objective is best furthered by doing so;
    (c)   by consent of all parties;
    (d)   with the permission of the court;
    (e)   where paragraph 4.9 applies; or
    (f)   where a court order, rule or practice direction permits.

Giving notice of an application

6.1 Unless the court otherwise directs or paragraph 5.1 of this practice direction applies, the application notice must be served as soon as practicable after it has been issued and, if there is to be a hearing, at least 7 days before the hearing date.

6.2 Where an application notice should be served but there is not sufficient time to do so, informal notification of the application should be given unless the circumstances of the application require no notice of the application to be given.

Pre-action applications

7.1 All applications made before proceedings are commenced should be made under this Part.

Telephone hearings

8.1 The court may direct that an application be dealt with by a telephone hearing.

8.2 The applicant should, if seeking a direction under paragraph 8.1, indicate this on the application notice. Where the applicant has not indicated such an intention but nevertheless wishes to seek a direction the request should be made as early as possible.

8.3 A direction under paragraph 8.1 will not normally be made unless every party entitled to be given notice of the application and to be heard at the hearing has consented to the direction.

8.4 No representative of a party to an application being heard by telephone may attend the court in person while the application is being heard unless the other party to the application has agreed that the representative may do so.

8.5 If an application is to be heard by telephone the following directions will apply, subject to any direction to the contrary–

    (a)   the applicant's legal representative is responsible for arranging the telephone conference for precisely the time fixed by the court. The telecommunications provider used must be one of the approved panel of service providers (see HMCS website at www.hmcourtsservice.gov.uk);

    (b)   the applicant's legal representative must tell the operator the telephone numbers of all those participating in the conference call and the sequence in which they are to be called;

    (c)   it is the responsibility of the applicant's legal representative to ascertain from all the other parties whether they have instructed counsel and, if so the identity of

counsel, and whether the legal representative and counsel will be on the same or different telephone numbers;
(d) the sequence in which those involved are to be called will be–
  (i) the applicant's legal representative and (if on a different number) his counsel;
  (ii) the legal representative (and counsel) for all other parties; and
  (iii) the judge or justices, as the case may be;
(e) each speaker is to remain on the line after being called by the operator setting up the conference call. The call may be 2 or 3 minutes before the time fixed for the application;
(f) when the judge has or justices have been connected the applicant's legal representative (or counsel) will introduce the parties in the usual way;
(g) if the use of a 'speakerphone' by any party causes the court or any other party any difficulty in hearing what is said the judge or justices may require that party to use a hand held telephone;
(h) the telephone charges debited to the account of the party initiating the conference call will be treated as part of the costs of the application.

Video conferencing

9.1 Where the parties to a matter wish to use video conferencing facilities, and those facilities are available in the relevant court, the parties should apply to the court for directions. (Practice Direction 22A provides guidance on the use of video conferencing)

Note of proceedings

10.1 The court or court officer should keep, either by way of a note or a tape recording, brief details of all proceedings before the court, including the dates of the proceedings and a short statement of the decision taken at each hearing.

Evidence

11.1 The requirement for evidence in certain types of applications is set out in some of the rules in the FPR and practice directions. Where there is no specific requirement to provide evidence it should be borne in mind that, as a practical matter, the court will often need to be satisfied by evidence of the facts that are relied on in support of or for opposing the application.
11.2 The court may give directions for the filing of evidence in support of or opposing a particular application. The court may also give directions for the filing of evidence in relation to any hearing that it fixes on its own initiative. The directions may specify the form that evidence is to take and when it is to be served.
11.3 Where it is intended to rely on evidence which is not contained in the application itself, the evidence, if it has not already been served, should be served with the application.
11.4 Where a respondent to an application wishes to rely on evidence, that evidence must be filed in accordance with any directions the court may have given and a court officer will serve the evidence on the other parties, unless the court directs otherwise.
11.5 If it is necessary for the applicant to serve any evidence in reply the court officer will serve it on the other parties unless the court directs otherwise.
11.6 Evidence must be filed with the court as well as served on the parties.
11.7 The contents of an application notice may be used as evidence provided the contents have been verified by a statement of truth.

Consent orders

12.1 The parties to an application for a consent order must ensure that they provide the court with any material it needs to be satisfied that it is appropriate to make the order. Subject to any rule in the FPR or practice direction a letter will generally be acceptable for this purpose.

12.2 Where a judgment or order has been agreed in respect of an application where a hearing date has been fixed, the parties must inform the court immediately.

Other applications considered without a hearing

13.1 Where rule 18.9(1)(b) applies the court will treat the application as if it were proposing to make an order on its own initiative.

13.2 Where the parties agree that the court should dispose of the application without a hearing they should so inform the court in writing and each should confirm that all evidence and other material on which he or she relies has been disclosed to the other parties to the application.

Miscellaneous

14.1 If the case is proceeding in the High Court and the draft order is unusually long or complex it should also be supplied in electronic form on such storage medium as shall be agreed with the judge or court staff, for use by the court office.

14.2 Where rule 18.12 applies the power to re-list the application in rule 18.12(2) is in addition to any other powers of the court with regard to the order (for example to set aside, vary, discharge or suspend the order).

Costs

15.1 Attention is drawn to the CPR costs practice direction and, in particular, to the court's power to make a summary assessment of costs.

15.2 Attention is also drawn to rule 44.13(1) of the CPR which provides that if an order makes no mention of costs, none are payable in respect of the proceedings to which it relates.

PRACTICE DIRECTION 19A – ALTERNATIVE PROCEDURE FOR APPLICATIONS

This Practice Direction supplements FPR Part 19

Types of application in which Part 19 procedure must be used

1.1 An applicant must use the Part 19 procedure if the application is for an order under–

(a) section 60(3) of the 2002 Act, to prevent disclosure of information to an adopted person;

(b) section 79(4) of the 2002 Act, to require the Registrar General to provide information; or

(c) rule 14.21 (Inherent jurisdiction and fathers without parental responsibility) in Part 14, to request directions of the High Court regarding fathers without parental responsibility.

Types of application in which Part 19 procedure may be used

1.2 An applicant may use the Part 19 procedure if Part 18 does not apply and if–

(a) there is no prescribed form in which to make the application; or

(b) the applicant seeks the court's decision on a question which is unlikely to involve a substantial dispute of fact.

1.3 An applicant may also use the Part 19 procedure if a practice direction permits or requires its use for the type of proceedings concerned.

1.4 The practice directions referred to in paragraph 1.3 may in some respects modify or disapply the Part 19 procedure and, where that is so, it is those practice directions, rather than this one, which must be complied with.
1.5 The types of application for which the Part 19 procedure may be used include an application for an order or direction which is unopposed by each respondent before the commencement of the proceedings and the sole purpose of the application is to obtain the approval of the court to the agreement.
1.6 Where it appears to a court officer that an applicant is using the Part 19 procedure inappropriately, the officer may refer the application to the court for consideration of the point.
1.7 The court may at any stage order the application to continue as if the applicant had not used the Part 19 procedure and, if it does so, the court will give such directions as it considers appropriate (see rule 19.1(3)).

The application

2.1 Where an applicant uses the Part 19 procedure, the application form referred to in Practice Direction 5A should be used and must state the matters set out in rule 19.3 and, if paragraphs 1.3 and 1.4 apply, must comply with the requirements of the practice direction in question. In particular, the application form must state that Part 19 applies. A Part 19 application form means an application form which so states.
2.2 An application–

(a) in accordance with rule 19.4, to ask the High Court for directions on the need to give a father without parental responsibility notice of the intention to place a child for adoption; or

(b) under section 60(3) of the 2002 Act for an order to prevent disclosure of information to an adopted person,

may be issued without naming a respondent.

Responding to the application

3.1 Where a respondent who wishes to respond to a Part 19 application is required to file an acknowledgement of service, that acknowledgement of service should be in form FP5 which is referred to in Practice Direction 5A but can, alternatively be given in an informal document such as a letter.
3.2 Rule 19.5 sets out provisions relating to an acknowledgement of service of a Part 19 application.
3.3 Rule 19.6 sets out the consequence of failing to file an acknowledgement of service.
3.4 A respondent who believes that the Part 19 procedure should not be used because there is a substantial dispute of fact or, as the case may be, because its use is not authorised by any rule in the FPR or any practice direction, must state the reasons for that belief in writing when filing the acknowledgement of service (see rule 19.9). If the statement of reasons includes matters of evidence, it should be verified by a statement of truth.

Managing the application

4.1 The court may give directions immediately a Part 19 application is issued either on the application of a party or of its own initiative. The directions may include fixing a hearing date where–

(a) there is no dispute; or
(b) where there may be a dispute, but a hearing date could conveniently be given.

4.2 Where the court does not fix a hearing date when the application is issued, it will give directions for the disposal of the application as soon as practicable after the respondent has acknowledged service of the application or, as the case may be, after the period for acknowledging service has expired.

4.3 Certain applications may not require a hearing.
4.4 The court may convene a directions hearing before giving directions.

Evidence

5.1 An applicant wishing to rely on written evidence should file it when the Part 19 application form is issued.
5.2 Evidence will normally be in the form of a witness statement or an affidavit but an applicant may rely on the matters set out in the application form provided it has been verified by a statement of truth. (For information about statements of truth see Part 17 and Practice Direction 17A, and about written evidence see Part 22 and Practice Direction 22A.)
5.3 A respondent wishing to rely on written evidence should file it with the acknowledgement of service (see rule 19.7(3)).
5.4 Rule 19.7 sets out the times and provisions for filing and serving written evidence.
5.5 A party may apply to the court for an extension of time to serve and file evidence under rule 19.7 or for permission to serve and file additional evidence under rule 19.8(1). (For information about applications see Part 18 and Practice Direction 18A.)
5.6 The parties may, subject to paragraphs 5.7 and 5.8, agree in writing on an extension of time for serving and filing evidence under rule 19.7(3) or rule 19.7(5).
5.7 An agreement extending time for a respondent to file evidence in reply under rule 19.7(3)–
  (a) must be filed by the respondent at the same time as the acknowledgement of service; and
  (b) must not extend time by more than 17 days after the respondent files the acknowledgement of service.
5.8 An agreement extending time for an applicant to file evidence in reply under rule 19.7(5) must not extend time to more than 28 days after service of the respondent's evidence on the applicant.

Hearing

6.1 The court may on the hearing date–
  (a) proceed to hear the case and dispose of the application;
  (b) give case management directions.

PRACTICE DIRECTION 20A – INTERIM REMEDIES

This Practice Direction supplements FPR Part 20

Scope and jurisdiction

1.1 This Practice Direction does not apply to an order under section 48 (Powers to assist in discovery of children who may be in need of emergency protection), section 50 (Recovery of abducted children, etc.) of the Children Act 1989 or section 33(Power to order disclosure of child's whereabouts) or section 34 (Power to order recovery of child) of the Family Law Act 1986.
1.2 High Court Judges and any other judge duly authorised may grant 'search orders' and 'freezing injunctions' (see rules 20.2(1)(h) and 20.2(1)(f)).
1.3 In a case in the High Court, district judges have the power to grant injunctions–
  (a) by consent;
  (b) in connection with charging orders and appointments of receivers;
  (c) in aid of execution of judgments.

1.4 In any other case any judge who has jurisdiction to conduct the hearing of the proceedings has the power to grant an injunction in those proceedings.
1.5 A district judge has the power to vary or discharge an injunction granted by any judge with the consent of all the parties.

Making an application

2.1 The application notice must state–
   (a) the order sought; and
   (b) the date, time and place of the hearing.
2.2 The application notice and evidence in support must be served as soon as practicable after issue and in any event not less than 7 days before the court is due to hear the application unless the court directs otherwise.
2.3 Where the court is to serve, sufficient copies of the application notice and evidence in support for the court and for each respondent should be filed for issue and service.
2.4 Whenever possible a draft of the order sought should be filed with the application notice and an electronic version of the draft should also be available to the court in a format compatible with the word processing software used by the court and on such storage medium as shall be agreed by the court. This will enable the court officer to arrange for any amendments to be incorporated and for the speedy preparation and sealing of the order.

Evidence

3.1 Applications for search orders and freezing injunctions must be supported by affidavit evidence.
3.2 Applications for other interim injunctions must be supported by evidence set out in either–
   (a) a witness statement; or
   (b) the application notice provided that it is verified by a statement of truth, unless the court, an Act, a rule in the FPR or a practice direction requires evidence by affidavit.
3.3 The evidence must set out the facts on which the applicant relies for the application being made against the respondent, including all material facts of which the court should be made aware.
3.4 Where an application is made without notice to the respondent, the evidence must also set out why notice was not given. (See Part 22 and the practice direction that supplements it for information about evidence.)

Urgent applications and applications without notice

4.1 These fall into two categories–
   (a) applications where an application in proceedings has already been issued; and
   (b) applications where an application in proceedings has not yet been issued, and, in both cases, where notice of the application has not been given to the respondent.
4.2 These applications are normally dealt with at a court hearing but cases of extreme urgency may be dealt with by telephone.
4.3 In relation to applications dealt with at a court hearing after issue of an application form–
   (a) the application notice, evidence in support and a draft order (as in paragraph 2.4) should be filed with the court two hours before the hearing wherever possible;

(b) if an application is made before the application notice has been issued, a draft order (as in paragraph 2.4) should be provided at the hearing, and the application notice and evidence in support must be filed with the court on the same or next working day or as ordered by the court; and

(c) except in cases where it is essential that the respondent must not be aware of the application, the applicant should take steps to notify the respondent informally of the application.

4.4 In relation to applications made before the issue of an application–

(a) in addition to the provisions set out at paragraph 4.3, unless the court orders otherwise, either the applicant must undertake to the court to issue an application notice immediately or the court will give directions for the commencement of the application (see rule 20.3(3));

(b) where possible the application should be served with the order for the injunction;

(c) an order made before the issue of an application should state in the title after the names of the applicant and respondent 'the Applicant and Respondent in Intended Proceedings'.

4.5 In relation to applications made outside normal working hours–

(a) the applicant should either–

  (i) telephone the Royal Courts of Justice on 020 7947 6000 to be put in contact with the clerk to the appropriate duty judge in the High Court (or the appropriate area Circuit Judge where known); or

  (ii) telephone the Urgent Court Business Officer of the appropriate Circuit who will contact the local duty judge;

(b) where the facility is available it is likely that the judge will require a draft order to be faxed to him;

(c) the application notice and evidence in support must be filed with the court on the same or next working day or as ordered, together with two copies of the order for sealing;

(d) injunctions will be heard by telephone only where the applicant is acting by counsel or solicitors.

Orders for injunctions

5.1 Any order for an injunction, unless the court orders otherwise, must contain–

(a) an undertaking by the applicant to the court to pay any damages which the respondent sustains which the court considers the applicant should pay;

(b) if the order is made without notice to any other party, an undertaking by the applicant to the court to serve on the respondent the application notice, evidence in support and any order made as soon as practicable;

(c) if the order is made without notice to any other party, a return date for a further hearing at which the other party can be present;

(d) if the order is made before filing the application notice, an undertaking to file and pay the appropriate fee on the same or next working day; and

(e) if the order is made before issue of an application in proceedings–

  (i) an undertaking to issue and pay the appropriate fee on the same or next working day; or

  (ii) directions for the commencement of the application.

5.2 When the court makes an order for an injunction, it should consider whether to require an undertaking by the applicant to pay any damages sustained by a person other than the respondent, including another party to the proceedings or any other person who may suffer loss as a consequence of the order.

5.3 An order for an injunction made in the presence of all parties to be bound by it or made at a hearing of which they have had notice, may state that it is effective until final hearing or further order.

5.4 Any order for an injunction must set out clearly what the respondent must do or not do.

Search orders – orders for the preservation of evidence and property

6.1 The following provisions apply to search orders in addition to those listed above.

The Supervising Solicitor

6.2 The Supervising Solicitor must be experienced in the operation of search orders. A Supervising Solicitor may be contacted either through the Law Society or, for the London area, through the London Solicitors Litigation Association.

Evidence

6.3 (1) The affidavit must state the name, firm and its address, and experience of the Supervising Solicitor, also the address of the premises and whether it is a private or business address.

(2) The affidavit must disclose very fully the reason the order is sought, including the probability that relevant material would disappear if the order were not made.

Service

6.4 (1) The order must be served personally by the Supervising Solicitor, unless the court directs otherwise, and must be accompanied by the evidence in support and any documents capable of being copied.

(2) Confidential exhibits need not be served but they must be made available for inspection by the respondent in the presence of the applicant's solicitors while the order is carried out and afterwards be retained by the respondent's solicitors on their undertaking not to permit the respondent–

  (a) to see them or copies of them except in their presence; and
  (b) to make or take away any note or record of them.

(3) The Supervising Solicitor may be accompanied only by the persons mentioned in the order.

(4) The Supervising Solicitor must explain the terms and effect of the order to the respondent in everyday language and advise the respondent–

  (a) of the respondent's right to take legal advice, and to apply to vary or discharge the order; and
  (b) that the respondent may be entitled to avail himself of–
    (i) legal professional privilege; and
    (ii) the privilege against self-incrimination.

(5) Where the Supervising Solicitor is a man and the respondent is likely to be an unaccompanied woman, at least one other person named in the order must be a woman and must accompany the Supervising Solicitor.

(6) The order may only be served between 9.30 a.m. and 5.30 p.m. Monday to Friday unless the court directs otherwise.

Search and custody of materials

6.5 (1) No material shall be removed unless clearly covered by the terms of the order.

(2) The premises must not be searched and no items shall be removed from them

except in the presence of the respondent or a person who appears to be a responsible employee of the respondent.
(3) Where copies of documents are sought, the documents should be retained for no more than 2 days before return to the owner.
(4) Where material in dispute is removed pending hearing, the applicant's solicitors should place it in the custody of the respondent's solicitors on their undertaking to retain it in safekeeping and to produce it to the court when required.
(5) In appropriate cases the applicant should insure the material retained in the respondent's solicitors' custody.
(6) The Supervising Solicitor must make a list of all material removed from the premises and supply a copy of the list to the respondent.
(7) No material shall be removed from the premises until the respondent has had reasonable time to check the list.
(8) If any of the listed items exists only in computer readable form, the respondent must immediately give the applicant's solicitors effective access to the computers, with all necessary passwords, to enable them to be searched, and cause the listed items to be printed out.
(9) The applicant must take all reasonable steps to ensure that no damage is done to any computer or data.
(10) The applicant and his representatives may not themselves search the respondent's computers unless they have sufficient expertise to do so without damaging the respondent's system;
(11) the Supervising Solicitor shall provide a report on the carrying out of the order to the applicant's solicitors.
(12) As soon as the report is received the applicant's solicitors shall–

(a) serve a copy of it on the respondent; and
(b) file a copy of it with the court.

(13) Where the Supervising Solicitor is satisfied that full compliance with paragraph 6.5(7) and (8) above is impracticable, that Solicitor may permit the search to proceed and items to be removed without compliance with the impracticable requirements.

General

6.6 The Supervising Solicitor must not be an employee or member of the applicant's firm of solicitors.
6.7 If the court orders that the order need not be served by the Supervising Solicitor, the reason for so ordering must be set out in the order.
6.8 The search order must not be carried out at the same time as a police search warrant.
6.9 There is no privilege against self incrimination in proceedings in which a court is hearing an application for an order under Part 4 or 5 of the Children Act 1989 (see section 98 of the Children Act 1989).

Delivery up orders

7.1 The following provision applies to orders, other than search orders, for delivery up or preservation of evidence or property where it is likely that such an order will be executed at the premises of the respondent or a third party.
7.2 In such cases the court will consider whether to include in the order for the benefit or protection of the parties similar provisions to those specified above in relation to injunctions and search orders.

Injunctions against third parties

8.1 The following provision applies to orders which will affect a person other than the applicant or respondent, who–

(a) did not attend the hearing at which the order was made; and
(b) is served with the order.

8.2 Where such a person served with the order requests–
(a) a copy of any materials read by the court, including material prepared after the hearing at the direction of the court or in compliance with the order; or
(b) a note of the hearing, the applicant, or the applicant's legal representative, must comply promptly with the request, unless the court directs otherwise.

PRACTICE DIRECTION 21A – DISCLOSURE AND INSPECTION

This Practice Direction supplements FPR Part 21

Chapter 1 – Orders for disclosure and inspection of documents

Interpretation

1.1 A party discloses a document by stating that the document exists or has existed. Inspection occurs when a party is permitted to inspect a document disclosed by another party.

1.2 For the purposes of disclosure and inspection in family proceedings–

'document' means anything in which information of any description is recorded and any copy of a document which contains a modification, obliteration or other marking or feature shall be treated as a separate document; and

'copy', in relation to a document, means anything on which information recorded in the document has been copied, by whatever means and whether directly or indirectly.

Types of order for disclosure in family proceedings

2.1 In family proceedings other than proceedings for a financial remedy, where the court orders disclosure, the normal order will be for disclosure by each party setting out, in a list or questionnaire, the documents material to the proceedings, of the existence of which that party is aware and which are or have been in that party's control. This process is known as 'standard disclosure'.

2.2 In proceedings for a financial remedy, the process of disclosure is staged. First, Form E (the financial statement referred to in rule 9.14(1)) is served together with the documents which are required to be attached to it. The second stage occurs by the parties requesting (further) disclosure of each other by a questionnaire served before the first appointment; the questionnaire can request both information and documents. With the court's permission, a further questionnaire can be served later in the proceedings.

2.3 In matrimonial and civil partnership proceedings, under rule 7.15, the court – either on its own initiative or on the application of the other party – may order a party to clarify any matter which is in dispute in the proceedings or give additional information in relation to any such matter, whether or not the matter is contained in or referred to in the application or in the answer.

2.4 In any family proceedings, the court may order 'specific disclosure', which is an order that a party must–
(a) disclose documents or classes of documents specified in the order;
(b) carry out a search to the extent stated in the order; or
(c) disclose any documents located as a result of that search.

PRACTICE DIRECTION 22A – WRITTEN EVIDENCE

This Practice Direction supplements FPR Part 22

Evidence in general

1.1 Rule 22.2(1) sets out the general rule as to how evidence is to be given and facts are to be proved. This is that, at the final hearing, witnesses will normally give oral evidence and, at any hearing other than the final hearing, by evidence in writing (which under rule 22.7(1) will usually be by witness statement).

1.2 Rule 22.2(2) excludes the general rule–

   (a) from proceedings under Part 12 (Children) for secure accommodation orders, interim care orders or interim supervision orders; or

   (b) where an enactment, any rule in the FPR, a practice direction or a court order provides to the contrary.

1.3 Application forms, application notices and answers except an application for a matrimonial order or a civil partnership order or an answer to such an application may also be used as evidence provided that their contents have been verified by a statement of truth (see Part 17 for information about statements of truth).

(For information regarding evidence by deposition see Part 24 and the practice direction which supplements it.)

1.4 Affidavits must be used as evidence–

   (a) where sworn evidence is required by an enactment, rule, order or practice direction; and

   (b) in any application for an order against anyone for alleged contempt of court.

1.5 If a party believes that sworn evidence is required by a court in another jurisdiction for any purpose connected with the proceedings, he may apply to the court for a direction that evidence shall be given only by affidavit on any applications to be heard before the final hearing.

1.6 The court may give a direction under rule 22.12 that evidence shall be given by affidavit instead of or in addition to a witness statement–

   (a) on its own initiative; or

   (b) after any party has applied to the court for such a direction.

1.7 An affidavit, where referred to in the FPR or a practice direction, also means an affirmation unless the context requires otherwise.

Affidavits and Witness Statements

Meaning of 'deponent' and 'witness'

2.1 For the purposes of the FPR–

a 'deponent' is a person who gives evidence by affidavit, affirmation or deposition; and

a 'witness' is a person who gives evidence by witness statement.

2.2 References in the following paragraphs to 'the maker of', or 'making', an affidavit, affirmation, deposition or witness statement are to be construed accordingly.

Heading and format

3.1 The affidavit/statement should be headed with the title of the proceedings where the proceedings are between several parties with the same status it is sufficient to identify the parties, subject to paragraph 4.2, as follows–

Number:

A.B. (and others) Applicants

C.D. (and others) Respondents

3.2 Subject to paragraph 4.2, at the top right-hand corner of the first page (and on the backsheet) there should be clearly written–

(a) the party on whose behalf it is made;
(b) the initials and surname of the maker;
(c) the number of the affidavit/statement in relation to its maker;
(d) the identifying initials and number of each exhibit referred to; and
(e) the date made.

3.3 The affidavit/statement should–

(a) be produced on durable quality A4 paper with a 3.5 cm margin;
(b) be fully legible and should normally be typed on one side of the paper only;
(c) where possible, should be bound securely in a manner which would not hamper filing or, where secure binding is not possible, each page should be endorsed with the case number and should bear the following initials–
   (i) in the case of an affidavit, of the maker and of the person before whom it is sworn; or
   (ii) in the case of a witness statement, of the maker and, where the maker is unable to read or sign the statement, of the authorised person (see paragraphs 7.3 and 7.4 below);
(d) have the pages numbered consecutively as a separate document (or as one of several documents contained in a file);
(e) be divided into numbered paragraphs;
(f) have all numbers, including dates, expressed in figures; and
(g) give the reference to any document or documents mentioned either in the margin or in bold text in the body of the affidavit/statement.

Body

4.1 Subject to paragraph 4.2 and rules 14.2 and 29.1, the affidavit/statement must, if practicable, be in the maker's own words, it should be expressed in the first person, and the maker should–

(a) commence–
   (i) in an affidavit, 'I (full name) of (residential address) state on oath .... ';
   (ii) in a statement, by giving his or her full name and residential address;
(b) if giving evidence in a professional, business or other occupational capacity, give the address at which he or she works in (a) above, the position held and the name of the firm or employer;
(c) give his or her occupation or (if none) description; and
(d) if it be the case that the maker is a party to the proceedings or is employed by a party to the proceedings, state that fact.

4.2 If, in proceedings to which Part 14 (Adoption, placement and related proceedings) applies, a serial number has been assigned under rule 14.2, the affidavit/statement must be framed so that it does not disclose the identity of the applicant.

(Rule 29.1 provides that, unless the court directs otherwise, a party to family proceedings is not required to reveal the address of his or her private residence or other contact details.)

4.3 An affidavit/statement must indicate–

(a) which of the statements in it are made from the maker's own knowledge and which are matters of information and belief; and
(b) the source for any matters of information and belief.

4.4 It is usually convenient to follow the chronological sequence of events or matters dealt with. Each paragraph should as far as possible be confined to a distinct portion of the subject.

4.5 The maker should, when referring to an exhibit or exhibits, state 'there is now shown to me marked ' ... ' the (description of exhibit)'.

Alterations to affidavits and witness statements

5.1 Any alteration to an affidavit must be initialled by both the maker and the person before whom the affidavit is sworn.
5.2 Any alteration to a witness statement must be initialled by the maker or by the authorised person where appropriate (see paragraphs 7.3 and 7.4 below).
5.3 An affidavit/statement which contains an alteration that has not been initialled in accordance with paragraphs 5.1 and 5.2 may be filed or used in evidence only with the permission of the court.

Swearing an affidavit or verifying a witness statement

6.1 An affidavit is the testimony of the person who swears it. A witness statement is the equivalent of the oral evidence which the maker would, if called, give in evidence.
6.2 The jurat of an affidavit is a statement set out at the end of the document which authenticates the affidavit. It must–
   (a) be signed by all deponents;
   (b) be completed and signed by the person before whom the affidavit was sworn whose name and qualification must be printed beneath his signature;
   (c) contain the full address of the person before whom the affidavit was sworn; and
   (d) follow immediately on from the text and not be put on a separate page.
6.3 An affidavit must be sworn before a person independent of the parties or their representatives. Only the following may administer oaths and take affidavits–
   (a) a Commissioner for Oaths (Commissioners for Oaths Acts 1889 and 1891);
   (b) other persons specified by statute (sections 12 and 18 of, and Schedules 2 and 4 to, the Legal Services Act 2007);
   (c) certain officials of the Senior Courts (section 2 of the Commissioners for Oaths Act 1889);
   (d) a circuit judge or district judge (section 58 of the County Courts Act 1984);
   (e) any justice of the peace (section 58 of the County Courts Act 1984); and
   (f) certain officials of any county court appointed by the judge of that court for the purpose (section 58 of the County Courts Act 1984).
6.4 A witness statement must include a statement of truth by the intended maker as follows:

'I believe that the facts stated in this witness statement are true.'

(Attention is drawn to rule 17.6 which sets out the consequences of verifying a witness statement containing a false statement without an honest belief in its truth.)

(For information regarding statements of truth, see Part 17 (Statements of truth) and Practice Direction 17A.)

(Paragraphs 7.1 to 7.4 below set out the procedures to be followed where the intended maker of an affidavit or witness statement is unable to read or sign the affidavit/statement.)

6.5 If, in proceedings under Part 14 (Adoption, placement and related proceedings), a serial number has been assigned under rule 14.2 or the name of the maker of the affidavit/statement is not being revealed in accordance with rule 29.1, the signature of the maker will be edited from the affidavit/statement before it is served on the other party.

Inability of maker to read or sign affidavit/statement

7.1 Where an affidavit is sworn by a deponent who is unable to read or sign it, the person before whom the affidavit is sworn must certify in the jurat that–

(a) that person read the affidavit to the deponent;
(b) the deponent appeared to understand it; and
(c) the deponent signed, or made his mark, in that person's presence.

7.2 If that certificate is not included in the jurat, the affidavit may not be used in evidence unless the court is satisfied that it was read to the deponent and that the deponent appeared to understand it. Annex 1 to this practice direction sets out forms of the jurat with the certificate for an affidavit and an affirmation respectively.

7.3 Where a witness statement is made by a person who is unable to read or sign the statement, it must contain a certificate made by an authorised person. An authorised person is a person able to administer oaths and take affidavits but need not be independent of the parties or their representatives.

7.4 The authorised person must certify–

(a) that the witness statement has been read to the witness;
(b) that the witness appeared to understand it and approved its content as accurate;
(c) that the statement of truth has been read to the witness;
(d) that the witness appeared to understand the statement of truth and the consequences of making a false witness statement; and
(e) that the witness signed or made his or her mark in the presence of the authorised person.

The form of the certificate is set out at Annex 2 to this practice direction.

Filing of affidavits and witness statements

8.1 If the court directs that an affidavit/statement is to be filed, it must be filed in the court or Division, or office or Registry of the court or Division, where the action in which it was or is to be used, is proceeding or will proceed.

8.2 Where the affidavit/statement is in a foreign language–

(a) the party wishing to rely on it must–

(i) have it translated; and
(ii) must file the foreign language affidavit/statement with the court; and

(b) the translator must sign the translation to certify that it is accurate.

Exhibits

Manner of exhibiting documents

9.1 A document used in conjunction with an affidavit/statement should be–

(a) shown to and verified by the maker, and remain separate from the affidavit/statement; and
(b) identified by a declaration of the person before whom the affidavit/statement was sworn.

9.2 The declaration should be headed with the name of the proceedings in the same way as the affidavit/statement is headed.

9.3 The first page of each exhibit should be marked–

(a) as in paragraph 3.2 above; and
(b) with the exhibit mark referred to in the affidavit/statement in accordance with paragraph 4.5 above.

9.4 Where the maker makes more than one affidavit/statement, to which there are exhibits, in the same proceedings, the numbering of the exhibits should run consecutively throughout and not start again with each affidavit/statement.

Letters

10.1 Copies of individual letters should be collected together and exhibited in a bundle or bundles. They should be arranged in chronological order with the earliest at the top, and firmly secured.

10.2 When a bundle of correspondence is exhibited, the exhibit should have a front page attached stating that the bundle consists of original letters and copies. They should be arranged and secured as above and numbered consecutively.

Other documents

11.1 Photocopies instead of original documents may be exhibited provided the originals are made available for inspection by the other parties before the hearing and by the court at the hearing.

11.2 Court documents must not be exhibited (official copies of such documents prove themselves).

11.3 Where an exhibit contains more than one document, a front page should be attached setting out a list of the documents contained in the exhibit. The list should contain the dates of the documents.

Exhibits other than documents

12.1 Items other than documents should be clearly marked with an exhibit number or letter in such a manner that the mark cannot become detached from the exhibit.

12.2 Small items may be placed in a container and the container appropriately marked.

General provisions

13.1 Where an exhibit contains more than one document–

    (a)   the bundle should not be stapled but should be securely fastened in a way that does not hinder the reading of the documents; and

    (b)   the pages should be numbered consecutively at bottom centre.

13.2 Every page of an exhibit should be clearly legible; typed copies of illegible documents should be included, paginated with 'a' numbers.

13.3 Where affidavits/statements and exhibits have become numerous, they should be put into separate bundles and the pages numbered consecutively throughout.

13.4 Where on account of their bulk the service of exhibits or copies of exhibits on the other parties would be difficult or impracticable, the directions of the court should be sought as to arrangements for bringing the exhibits to the attention of the other parties and as to their custody pending trial.

Miscellaneous

Defects in affidavits, witness statement and exhibits

14.1 Where–

    (a)   an affidavit;

    (b)   a witness statement; or

    (c)   an exhibit to either an affidavit or a witness statement,

does not comply with Part 22 or this practice direction in relation to its form, the court may refuse to admit it as evidence and may refuse to allow the costs arising from its preparation.

14.2 Permission to file a defective affidavit or witness statement or to use a defective exhibit may be obtained from the court where the case is proceeding.

Affirmations

15.1 All provisions in this or any other practice direction relating to affidavits apply to affirmations with the following exceptions–

(a) the deponent should commence 'I (full name) of (residential address) do solemnly and sincerely affirm …'; and

(b) in the jurat the word 'sworn' is replaced by the word 'affirmed'.

Certificate of court officer

16.1 In proceedings under Part 7 (Matrimonial and Civil Partnership Proceedings), where the court has ordered that a witness statement, affidavit, affirmation or deposition is not be open to inspection by the public (see rule 22.19(2) and (3)) or that words or passages in the statement etc are not to be open to inspection (see rule 22.19(5)), the court officer will so certify on the statement etc and make any deletions directed by the court under rule 22.19(3).

Video conferencing

17.1 Guidance on the use of video conferencing in the family courts is set out at Annex 3 to this practice direction.

A list of the sites which are available for video conferencing can be found on Her Majesty's Court Service's website at www.hm-courts-service.gov.uk.

ANNEX 1

Certificate to be used where a deponent to an affidavit is unable to read or sign it

Sworn at … this … day of … Before me, I having first read over the contents of this affidavit to the deponent [if there are exhibits, add 'and explained the nature and effect of the exhibits referred to in it'] who appeared to understand it and approved its content as accurate, and made his/her° mark on the affidavit in my presence. Or, (after 'Before me') the witness to the mark of the deponent having been first sworn that the witness had read over etc. (as above) and that the witness saw the deponent make his/her° mark on the affidavit. (Witness must sign.)

° delete as appropriate

Certificate to be used where a deponent to an affirmation is unable to read or sign it

Affirmed at … this … day of … Before me, I having first read over the contents of this affirmation to the deponent [if there are exhibits, add 'and explained the nature and effect of the exhibits referred to in it'] who appeared to understand it and approved its content as accurate, and made his/her° mark on the affirmation in my presence. Or, (after 'Before me') the witness to the mark of the deponent having been first sworn that the witness had read over etc. (as above) and that the witness saw the deponent make his/her° mark on the affirmation. (Witness must sign.)

° delete as appropriate

ANNEX 2

Certificate to be used where a witness is unable to read or sign a witness statement

I certify that I [name and address of authorised person] have read over the contents of this witness statement and the statement of truth to the witness [if there are exhibits, add 'and explained the nature and effect of the exhibits referred to in it'] who (a) appeared to understand the witness statement and approved its content as accurate and (b) appeared to understand the statement of truth and the consequences of making a false witness statement, and [signed the statement] [made his/her mark]° in my presence.

° delete as appropriate.

ANNEX 3

Video Conferencing Guidance

1. This guidance is for the use of video conferencing (VCF) in proceedings to which the Family Procedure Rules apply. It is in part based, with permission, upon the protocol of the Federal Court of Australia. It is intended to provide a guide to all persons involved in the use of VCF, although it does not attempt to cover all the practical questions which might arise.

   Any reference in this guide to a judge is to be taken as including a district judge or justices of the peace if the proceedings are before a magistrates' court.

Video conferencing generally

2. The guidance covers the use of VCF equipment both (a) in a courtroom, whether via equipment which is permanently placed there or via a mobile unit, and (b) in a separate studio or conference room. In either case, the location at which the judge sits is referred to as the 'local site'. The other site or sites to and from which transmission is made are referred to as 'the remote site' and in any particular case any such site may be another courtroom. The guidance applies to cases where VCF is used for the taking of evidence and also to its use for other parts of any legal proceedings.

3. VCF may be a convenient way of dealing with any part of proceedings – it can involve considerable savings in time and cost. Its use for the taking of evidence from overseas witnesses will, in particular, be likely to achieve a material saving of costs, and such savings may also be achieved by its use for taking domestic evidence. It is, however, inevitably not as ideal as having the witness physically present in court. Its convenience should not therefore be allowed to dictate its use. A judgment must be made in every case in which the use of VCF is being considered not only as to whether it will achieve an overall cost saving but as to whether its use will be likely to be beneficial to the efficient, fair and economic disposal of the litigation. In particular, it needs to be recognised that the degree of control a court can exercise over a witness at the remote site is or may be more limited than it can exercise over a witness physically before it.

4. When used for the taking of evidence, the objective should be to make the VCF session as close as possible to the usual practice in court where evidence is taken in open court. To gain the maximum benefit, several differences have to be taken into account. Some matters, which are taken for granted when evidence is taken in the conventional way, take on a different dimension when it is taken by VCF – for example, the administration of the oath, ensuring that the witness understands who is at the local site and what their various roles are, the raising of any objections to the evidence and the use of documents.

5. It should not be presumed that all foreign governments are willing to allow their nationals or others within their jurisdiction to be examined before a court in England or Wales by means of VCF. If there is any doubt about this, enquiries should be directed to the Foreign and Commonwealth Office (International Legal Matters Unit, Consular Division) with a view to ensuring that the country from which the evidence is to be taken raises no objection to it at diplomatic level. The party who is directed to be responsible for arranging the VCF (see paragraph 8) will be required to make all necessary inquiries about this well in advance of the VCF and must be able to inform the court what those inquiries were and of their outcome.

6. Time zone differences need to be considered when a witness abroad is to be examined in

England or Wales by VCF. The convenience of the witness, the parties, their representatives and the court must all be taken into account. The cost of the use of a commercial studio is usually greater outside normal business hours.
7. Those involved with VCF need to be aware that, even with the most advanced systems currently available, there are the briefest of delays between the receipt of the picture and that of the accompanying sound. If due allowance is not made for this, there will be a tendency to 'speak over' the witness, whose voice will continue to be heard for a millisecond or so after he or she appears on the screen to have finished speaking.
8. With current technology, picture quality is good, but not as good as a television picture. The quality of the picture is enhanced if those appearing on VCF monitors keep their movements to a minimum.

Preliminary arrangements

9. The court's permission is required for any part of any proceedings to be dealt with by means of VCF. Before seeking a direction, the applicant should notify the listing officer, diary manager or other appropriate court officer of the intention to seek it, and should enquire as to the availability of court VCF equipment for the day or days of the proposed VCF. If all parties consent to a direction, permission can be sought by letter, fax or e-mail, although the court may still require an oral hearing. All parties are entitled to be heard on whether or not such a direction should be given and as to its terms. If a witness at a remote site is to give evidence by an interpreter, consideration should be given at this stage as to whether the interpreter should be at the local site or the remote site. If a VCF direction is given, arrangements for the transmission will then need to be made. The court will ordinarily direct that the party seeking permission to use VCF is to be responsible for this. That party is hereafter referred to as 'the VCF arranging party'.
10. Subject to any order to the contrary, all costs of the transmission, including the costs of hiring equipment and technical personnel to operate it, will initially be the responsibility of, and must be met by, the VCF arranging party. All reasonable efforts should be made to keep the transmission to a minimum and so keep the costs down. All such costs will be considered to be part of the costs of the proceedings and the court will determine at such subsequent time as is convenient or appropriate who, as between the parties, should be responsible for them and (if appropriate) in what proportions.
11. The local site will, if practicable, be a courtroom but it may instead be an appropriate studio or conference room. The VCF arranging party must contact the listing officer, diary manager or other appropriate officer of the court which made the VCF direction and make arrangements for the VCF transmission. Details of the remote site, and of the equipment to be used both at the local site (if not being supplied by the court) and the remote site (including the number of ISDN lines and connection speed), together with all necessary contact names and telephone numbers, will have to be provided to the listing officer, diary manager or other court officer. The court will need to be satisfied that any equipment provided by the parties for use at the local site and also that at the remote site is of sufficient quality for a satisfactory transmission. The VCF arranging party must ensure that an appropriate person will be present at the local site to supervise the operation of the VCF throughout the transmission in order to deal with any technical problems. That party must also arrange for a technical assistant to be similarly present at the remote site for like purposes.
12. It is recommended that the judge, practitioners and witness should arrive at their respective VCF sites about 20 minutes prior to the scheduled commencement of the transmission.
13. If the local site is not a courtroom, but a conference room or studio, the judge will need to determine who is to sit where. The VCF arranging party must take care to ensure that the number of microphones is adequate for the speakers and that the panning of the camera for the practitioners' table encompasses all legal representatives so that the viewer can see everyone seated there.

14. If the local site is to be a studio or conference room, the VCF arranging party must ensure that it provides sufficient accommodation to enable a reasonable number of members of the public to attend if appropriate.
15. In cases where the local site is a studio or conference room, the VCF arranging party should make arrangements, if practicable, for the royal coat of arms to be placed above the judge's seat.
16. In cases in which the VCF is to be used for the taking of evidence, the VCF arranging party must arrange for recording equipment to be provided by the court which made the VCF direction so that the evidence can be recorded. An associate will normally be present to operate the recording equipment when the local site is a courtroom. The VCF arranging party should take steps to ensure that an associate is present to do likewise when it is a studio or conference room. The equipment should be set up and tested before the VCF transmission. It will often be a valuable safeguard for the VCF arranging party also to arrange for the provision of recording equipment at the remote site. This will provide a useful back-up if there is any reduction in sound quality during the transmission. A direction from the court for the making of such a back-up recording must, however, be obtained first. This is because the proceedings are court proceedings and, save as directed by the court, no other recording of them must be made. The court will direct what is to happen to the back-up recording.
17. Some countries may require that any oath or affirmation to be taken by a witness accord with local custom rather than the usual form of oath or affirmation used in England and Wales. The VCF arranging party must make all appropriate prior inquiries and put in place all arrangements necessary to enable the oath or affirmation to be taken in accordance with any local custom. That party must be in a position to inform the court what those inquiries were, what their outcome was and what arrangements have been made. If the oath or affirmation can be administered in the manner normal in England and Wales, the VCF arranging party must arrange in advance to have the appropriate holy book at the remote site. The associate will normally administer the oath.
18. Consideration will need to be given in advance to the documents to which the witness is likely to be referred. The parties should endeavour to agree on this. It will usually be most convenient for a bundle of the copy documents to be prepared in advance, which the VCF arranging party should then send to the remote site.
19. Additional documents are sometimes quite properly introduced during the course of a witness's evidence. To cater for this, the VCF arranging party should ensure that equipment is available to enable documents to be transmitted between sites during the course of the VCF transmission. Consideration should be given to whether to use a document camera. If it is decided to use one, arrangements for its use will need to be established in advance. The panel operator will need to know the number and size of documents or objects if their images are to be sent by document camera. In many cases, a simpler and sufficient alternative will be to ensure that there are fax transmission and reception facilities at the participating sites.

The hearing

20. The procedure for conducting the transmission will be determined by the judge. He will determine who is to control the cameras. In cases where the VCF is being used for an application in the course of the proceedings, the judge will ordinarily not enter the local site until both sites are on line. Similarly, at the conclusion of the hearing, he will ordinarily leave the local site while both sites are still on line. The following paragraphs apply primarily to cases where the VCF is being used for the taking of the evidence of a witness at a remote site.
21. At the beginning of the transmission, the judge will probably wish to introduce himself or herself and the advocates to the witness. He will probably want to know who is at the remote site and will invite the witness to introduce himself or herself and anyone else who is with the witness. The judge may wish to give directions as to the seating

arrangements at the remote site so that those present are visible at the local site during the taking of the evidence and to explain to the witness the method of taking the oath or of affirming, the manner in which the evidence will be taken, and who will be conducting the examination and cross-examination. The judge will probably also wish to inform the witness of the matters referred to in paragraphs 7 and 8 (coordination of picture with sound, and picture quality).

22. The examination of the witness at the remote site should follow as closely as possible the practice adopted when a witness is in the courtroom. During examination, cross-examination and re-examination, the witness must be able to see the legal representative asking the question and also any other person (whether another legal representative or the judge) making any statements in regard to the witness's evidence. It will in practice be most convenient if everyone remains seated throughout the transmission.

PRACTICE DIRECTION 24A – WITNESSES, DEPOSITIONS AND TAKING OF EVIDENCE IN MEMBER STATES OF THE EUROPEAN UNION

This Practice Direction supplements FPR Part 24

Witness summonses

Issue of witness summons

1.1 A witness summons may require a witness to–

    (a)   attend court to give evidence;
    (b)   produce documents to the court; or
    (c)   both,

on either a date fixed for the hearing or such date as the court may direct (see rule 24.2). (In relation to cases to which the Mediation Directive applies, rules 35.3 and 35.4 contain rules in relation to mediation evidence).

1.2 Two copies of the witness summons should be filed with the court for sealing, one of which will be retained on the court file.

1.3 A mistake in the name or address of a person named in a witness summons may be corrected if the summons has not been served.

1.4 The corrected summons must be re-sealed by the court and marked 'Amended and Re-Sealed'.

Magistrates' courts proceedings

2.1 An application for the issue of a summons or warrant under section 97 of the Magistrates' Courts Act 1980 may be made by the applicant in person or by his legal representative.

2.2 An application for the issue of such a summons may be made by delivering or sending the application in writing to the court officer for the magistrates' court.

Travelling expenses and compensation for loss of time

3.1 When a witness is served with a witness summons the witness must be offered a sum to cover travelling expenses to and from the court and compensation for loss of time (see rule 24.6).

3.2 If the witness summons is to be served by the court, the party issuing the summons must deposit with the court–

    (a)   a sum sufficient to pay for the witness's expenses in travelling to the court and in returning to his or her home or place of work; and
    (b)   a sum in respect of the period during which earnings or benefit are lost, or such

lesser sum as it may be proved that the witness will lose as a result of attendance at court in answer to the witness summons.

3.3 The sum referred to in paragraph 3.2(b) is to be based on the sums payable to witnesses attending the Crown Court (fixed pursuant to the Prosecution of Offences Act 1985 and Costs in Criminal Cases (General) Regulations 1986).

Depositions to be taken in England and Wales for use as evidence in proceedings in courts in England and Wales

4.1 A party may apply for an order for a person to be examined on oath before–

    (a) a judge;
    (b) an examiner of the court; or
    (c) such other person as the court may appoint (see rule 24.7(3)).

(This is subject to rules about mediation evidence in cases to which the Mediation Directive applies: see rules 35.3 and 35.4)

4.2 The party who obtains an order for the examination of a deponent (see rule 24.7(2)) before an examiner of the court must–

    (a) apply to the Foreign Process Section of the Masters' Secretary's Department at the Royal Courts of Justice for the allocation of an examiner;
    (b) when allocated, provide the examiner with copies of all documents in the proceedings necessary to inform the examiner of the issues; and
    (c) pay the deponent a sum to cover travelling expenses to and from the examination and compensation for loss of time (see rule 24.7(6)).

4.3 In ensuring that the deponent's evidence is recorded in full, the court or the examiner may permit it to be recorded on audiotape or videotape, but the deposition (see rule 24.7(2)) must always be recorded in writing by the examiner or by a competent shorthand writer or stenographer.

4.4 If the deposition is not recorded word for word, it must contain, as nearly as may be, the statement of the deponent. The examiner may record word for word any particular questions and answers which appear to have special importance.

4.5 If a deponent objects to answering any question or where any objection is taken to any question, the examiner must–

    (a) record in the deposition or a document attached to it–

        (i) the question;
        (ii) the nature of and grounds for the objection;
        (iii) any answer given; and

    (b) give the examiner's opinion as to the validity of the objection and must record it in the deposition or a document attached to it.

The court will decide as to the validity of the objection and any question of costs arising from it.

4.6 Documents and exhibits must–

    (a) have an identifying number or letter marked on them by the examiner; and
    (b) be preserved by the party or legal representative (see rule 2.3) who obtained the order for the examination, or as the court or the examiner may direct.

4.7 The examiner may put any question to the deponent as to–

    (a) the meaning of any of the deponent's answers; or
    (b) any matter arising in the course of the examination.

4.8 Where a deponent–

    (a) fails to attend the examination; or
    (b) refuses to–

            (i)   be sworn; or
            (ii)   answer any lawful question; or
            (iii)   produce any document,
    the examiner will sign a certificate (see rule 24.9) of such failure or refusal and may include in the certificate any comment as to the conduct of the deponent or of any person attending the examination.
4.9 The party who obtained the order for the examination must file the certificate with the court and may apply for an order that the deponent attend for examination or produce any document, as the case may be (see rule 24.9(2) and (3)). The application may be made without notice.
4.10 The court will make such order on the application as it thinks fit including an order for the deponent to pay any costs resulting from the failure or refusal (see rule 24.9(4)).
4.11 A deponent who wilfully refuses to obey an order of the High Court or the county court made under Part 24 may be proceeded against for contempt of court. (Where a person fails to attend before a magistrates' court in answer to a summons issued under section 97 of the Magistrates' Court Act 1980, the court may, under certain circumstances, issue a warrant for that party's arrest and to bring that party before the court at a time and place specified in the warrant: see section 97(3) of the 1980 Act.)

4.12 A deposition must–

    (a)   be signed by the examiner;
    (b)   have any amendments to it initialled by the examiner and the deponent;
    (c)   be endorsed by the examiner with–
            (i)   a statement of the time occupied by the examination; and
            (ii)   a record of any refusal by the deponent to sign the deposition and of the deponent's reasons for not doing so; and
    (d)   be sent by the examiner to the court where the proceedings are taking place for filing on the court file.

4.13 Rule 24.13 deals with the fees and expenses of an examiner.

Depositions to be taken abroad for use as evidence in proceedings before courts in England and Wales (where the Taking of Evidence Regulation does not apply)

5.1 Where a party wishes to take a deposition from a person outside the jurisdiction, the High Court may order the issue of a letter of request to the judicial authorities of the country in which the proposed deponent is (see rule 24.12). (Rule 35.4(1)(f) deals with letters of request where the Mediation Directive applies)
5.2 An application for an order referred to in paragraph 5.1 should be made by application notice in accordance with Part 18 (Procedure for other applications in proceedings).
5.3 The documents which a party applying for an order for the issue of a letter of request must file with the application notice are set out in rule 24.12(7). They are as follows–

    (a)   a draft letter of request in the form set out in Annex A to this practice direction;
    (b)   a statement of the issues relevant to the proceedings;
    (c)   a list of questions or the subject matter of questions to be put to the proposed deponent;
    (d)   a translation of the documents in (a), (b) and (c), unless the proposed deponent is in a country of which English is an official language; and
    (e)   an undertaking to be responsible for the expenses of the Secretary of State.

    In addition to the documents listed above the party applying for the order must file a draft order.
5.4 The above documents should be filed with the Masters' Secretary in Room E214, Royal Courts of Justice, Strand, London WC2A 2LL.

5.5 The application will be dealt with by the Senior Master of the Queen's Bench Division of the Senior Courts who will, if appropriate, sign the letter of request.
5.6 Attention is drawn to the provisions of rule 18.11 (Application to set aside or vary order made without notice).
5.7 If parties are in doubt as to whether a translation under paragraph 5.3(d) is required, they should seek guidance from the Foreign Process Section of the Masters' Secretary's Department.
5.8 A special examiner appointed under rule 24.12(5) may be the British Consul or the Consul-General or his deputy in the country where the evidence is to be taken if–

    (a)   there is in respect of that country a Civil Procedure Convention providing for the taking of evidence in that country for the assistance of proceedings in the High Court or other court in this country; or

    (b)   the Secretary of State has consented.

5.9 The provisions of paragraphs 4.1 to 4.12 apply to the depositions referred to in this paragraph.

Taking of evidence between EU Member States

Taking of Evidence Regulation

6.1 Where evidence is to be taken from a person in another Member State of the European Union for use as evidence in proceedings before courts in England and Wales Council Regulation (EC) No 1206/2001 of 28 May 2001 on cooperation between the courts of the Member States in the taking of evidence in civil or commercial matters ('the Taking of Evidence Regulation') applies.
6.2 The Taking of Evidence Regulation is annexed to this practice direction as Annex B.
6.3 The Taking of Evidence Regulation does not apply to Denmark. In relation to Denmark, therefore, rule 24.12 will continue to apply.

(Article 21(1) of the Taking of Evidence Regulation provides that the Regulation prevails over other provisions contained in bilateral or multilateral agreements or arrangements concluded by the Member States.)

Originally published in the official languages of the European Community in the Official Journal of the European Communities by the Office for Official Publications of the European Communities.

Meaning of 'designated court'

7.1 In accordance with the Taking of Evidence Regulation, each Regulation State has prepared a list of courts competent to take evidence in accordance with the Regulation indicating the territorial and, where appropriate, special jurisdiction of those courts.
7.2 Where Chapter 2 of this Part refers to a 'designated court' in relation to another Regulation State, the reference is to the court, referred to in the list of competent courts of that State, which is appropriate to the application in hand.
7.3 Where the reference is to the 'designated court' in England and Wales, the reference is to the appropriate competent court in the jurisdiction. The designated courts for England and Wales are listed in Annex C to this practice direction.

Central Body

8.1 The Taking of Evidence Regulation stipulates that each Regulation State must nominate a Central Body responsible for–

    (a)   supplying information to courts;

    (b)   seeking solutions to any difficulties which may arise in respect of a request; and

    (c)   forwarding, in exceptional cases, at the request of a requesting court, a request to the competent court.

8.2 The United Kingdom has nominated the Senior Master of the Queen's Bench Division, to be the Central Body for England and Wales.

8.3 The Senior Master, as Central Body, has been designated responsible for taking decisions on requests pursuant to Article 17 of the Regulation. Article 17 allows a court to submit a request to the Central Body or a designated competent authority in another Regulation State to take evidence directly in that State.

Evidence to be taken in another Regulation State for use in England and Wales

9.1 Where a person wishes to take a deposition from a person in another Regulation State, the court where the proceedings are taking place may order the issue of a request to the designated court in the Regulation State (rule 24.16 (2)). The form of request is prescribed as Form A in the Taking of Evidence Regulation.

9.2 An application to the court for an order under rule 24.16(2) should be made by application notice in accordance with Part 18 (Procedure for other applications in proceedings).

9.3 Rule 24.16(3) provides that the party applying for the order must file a draft form of request in the prescribed form. Where completion of the form requires attachments or documents to accompany the form, these must also be filed.

9.4 If the court grants an order under rule 24.16(2), it will send the form of request directly to the designated court.

9.5 Where the taking of evidence requires the use of an expert, the designated court may require a deposit in advance towards the costs of that expert. The party who obtained the order is responsible for the payment of any such deposit which should be deposited with the court for onward transmission. Under the provisions of the Taking of Evidence Regulation, the designated court is not required to execute the request until such payment is received.

9.6 Article 17 permits the court where proceedings are taking place to take evidence directly from a deponent in another Regulation State if the conditions of the article are satisfied. Direct taking of evidence can only take place if evidence is given voluntarily without the need for coercive measures. Rule 24.16(5) provides for the court to make an order for the submission of a request to take evidence directly. The form of request is Form I annexed to the Taking of Evidence Regulation and rule 24.16(6) makes provision for a draft of this form to be filed by the party seeking the order. An application for an order under rule 24.16(5) should be by application notice in accordance with Part 18.

9.7 Attention is drawn to the provisions of rule 18.11 (Application to set aside or vary order made without notice).

ANNEX A – DRAFT LETTER OF REQUEST (WHERE THE TAKING OF EVIDENCE REGULATION DOES NOT APPLY) (SEE PARAGRAPH 5.3(A) ABOVE)

1   To the Competent Judicial Authority of in the of [name] Senior Master of the Queen's Bench Division of the Senior Courts of England and Wales respectfully request the assistance of your court with regard to the following matters.

2   An application is now pending in the Division of the High Court of Justice in England and Wales entitled as follows [set out full title and case number] in which [name] of [address] is the applicant and [name] of [address] is the respondent.

3   The names and addresses of the representatives or agents of [set out names and addresses of representatives of the parties].

4   The application by the applicant is for–

   (a)   [set out the nature of the application]
   (b)   [the order sought] and
   (c)   [a summary of the facts.]

5   It is necessary for the purposes of justice between the parties that you cause the

following witnesses, who are resident within your jurisdiction, to be examined. The names and addresses of the witnesses are as follows:

6 The witnesses should be examined on oath or if that is not possible within your laws or is impossible of performance by reason of the internal practice and procedure of your court or by reason of practical difficulties, they should be examined in accordance with whatever procedure your laws provide for in these matters.

7 Either/

The witnesses should be examined in accordance with the list of questions annexed hereto. Or/

The witnesses should be examined regarding [set out full details of evidence sought]

N.B. Where the witness is required to produce documents, these should be clearly identified.

8 I would ask that you cause me, or the agents of the parties (if appointed), to be informed of the date and place where the examination is to take place.

9 Finally, I request that you will cause the evidence of the said witnesses to be reduced into writing and all documents produced on such examinations to be duly marked for identification and that you will further be pleased to authenticate such examinations by the seal of your court or in such other way as is in accordance with your procedure and return the written evidence and documents produced to me addressed as follows–

Senior Master of the Queen's Bench Division
Royal Courts of Justice
Strand
London
WC2A 2LL
England

ANNEX B – TAKING OF EVIDENCE REGULATION

[Can be found at] http://www.justice.gov.uk/civil/procrules-fin/contents/form-section-images/practice- directions/pd34-pdf-tif-gif/pd34-cr-1206-2001.pdf

ANNEX C – DESIGNATED COURTS IN ENGLAND AND WALES UNDER THE TAKING OF EVIDENCE REGULATION (SEE PARAGRAPH 7.3 ABOVE)

Area	*Designated court*
London and South Eastern Circuit	Royal Courts of Justice (Queen's Bench Division)
Midland Circuit	Birmingham Civil Justice Centre
Western Circuit	Bristol County Court
Wales and Chester Circuit	Cardiff Civil Justice Centre
Northern Circuit	Manchester County Court
North Eastern Circuit	Leeds County Court

PRACTICE DIRECTION 25 – EXPERTS AND ASSESSORS IN FAMILY PROCEEDINGS

This Practice Direction is made by the President of the Family Division under the powers delegated to him by the Lord Chief Justice under Schedule 2, Part 1, paragraph 2(2) of the

Constitutional Reform Act 2005, and is approved by the Parliamentary Under Secretary of State, by authority of the Lord Chancellor and comes into force on 6th April 2011

This Practice Direction supplements FPR Part 25

Introduction

1.1. Sections 1 to 9 of this Practice Direction deal with the use of expert evidence and the instruction of experts, and section 10 deals with the appointment of assessors, in all types of family proceedings. The guidance incorporates and supersedes the *Practice Direction on Experts in Family Proceedings relating to Children* (1 April 2008) and other relevant guidance with effect on and from 6 April 2011.

Where the guidance refers to 'an expert' or 'the expert', this includes a reference to an expert team.

1.2. For the purposes of this guidance, the phrase 'proceedings relating to children' is a convenient description. It is not a legal term of art and has no statutory force. In this guidance it means–

(a) placement and adoption proceedings; or
(b) family proceedings which–
    I.   relate to the exercise of the inherent jurisdiction of the High Court with respect to children;
    II. are brought under the Children Act 1989 in any family court; or
    III. are brought in the High Court and county courts and 'otherwise relate wholly or mainly to the maintenance or upbringing of a minor'.

Aims of the guidance on experts and expert evidence

1.3. The aim of the guidance in sections 1 to 9 is to:

(a) provide the court with early information to determine whether expert evidence or assistance will help the court;
(b) help the court and the parties to identify and narrow the issues in the case and encourage agreement where possible;
(c) enable the court and the parties to obtain an expert opinion about a question that is not within the skill and experience of the court;
(d) encourage the early identification of questions that need to be answered by an expert; and
(e) encourage disclosure of full and frank information between the parties, the court and any expert instructed.

1.4. The guidance does not aim to cover all possible eventualities. Thus it should be complied with so far as consistent in all the circumstances with the just disposal of the matter in accordance with the rules and guidance applying to the procedure in question.

Permission to instruct an expert or to use expert evidence

1.5. The general rule in family proceedings is that the court's permission is required to call an expert or to put in evidence an expert's report: see rule 25.4(1). In addition, in proceedings relating to children, the court's permission is required to instruct an expert: see rule 12.74(1).

1.6. The court and the parties must have regard in particular to the following considerations:

(a) proceedings relating to children are confidential and, in the absence of the court's permission, disclosure of information and documents relating to such proceedings may amount to a contempt of court or contravene statutory provisions protecting this confidentiality.
(b) for the purposes of the law of contempt of court, information relating to such

proceedings (whether or not contained in a document filed with the court or recorded in any form) may be communicated only to an expert whose instruction by a party has been permitted by the court (see rules 12.73 and 14.14).

(c) in proceedings to which Part 12 of the FPR applies, the court's permission is required to cause the child to be medically or psychiatrically examined or otherwise assessed for the purpose of the preparation of expert evidence for use in the proceedings; where the court's permission has not been given, no evidence arising out of such an examination or assessment may be adduced without the court's permission (see rule 12.20).

1.7. In practice, the need to have the court's permission to disclose information or documents to an expert, or to have the child examined or assessed, means that in proceedings relating to children the court strictly controls the number, fields of expertise and identity of the experts who may be first instructed and then called.

1.8. Before permission is obtained from the court to instruct an expert in proceedings relating to children, it will be necessary for the party seeking permission to make enquiries of the expert in order to provide the court with information to enable it to decide whether to give permission. In practice, enquiries may need to be made of more than one expert for this purpose. This will in turn require each expert to be given sufficient information about the case to decide whether or not he or she is in a position to accept instructions.

Such preliminary enquiries, and the disclosure of information about the case which is a necessary part of such enquiries, will not require the court's permission and will not amount to a contempt of court: see sections 4.1 and 4.2 (Preliminary Enquiries of the Expert and Expert's Response to Preliminary Enquiries).

1.9. Section 4 (Proceedings relating to children) gives guidance on applying for the court's permission to instruct an expert, and on instructing the expert, in proceedings relating to children. The court, when granting permission to instruct an expert, will also give directions about the preparation and filing of the expert's report and the attendance of the expert to give evidence: see section 4.4 (Draft Order for the relevant hearing).

1.10. In proceedings other than those relating to children, the court's permission is not required to instruct an expert. Section 5 (Proceedings other than those relating to children) gives guidance on instructing an expert, and on seeking the court's permission to use expert evidence, prior to and in such proceedings. Section 5 emphasises that the use of a single joint expert should be considered in all cases where expert evidence is required.

When should the court be asked for permission?

1.11. Any application (or proposed application) for permission to instruct an expert or to use expert evidence should be raised with the court – and, where appropriate, with the other parties – as soon as possible. This will normally mean–

(a) in public law proceedings under the Children Act 1989, by or at the Case Management Conference: see rule 12.25;

(b) in private law proceedings under the Children Act 1989, by or at the First Hearing Dispute Resolution Appointment: see rule 12.31;

(c) in placement and adoption proceedings, by or at the First Directions Hearing: see rule 14.8;

(d) in financial proceedings, by or at the First Appointment: see rule 9.15;

(e) in defended matrimonial and civil partnership proceedings, by or at the Case Management Hearing: see rules 7.20 and 7.22.

In this practice direction the 'relevant hearing' means any hearing at which the court's permission is sought to instruct an expert or to use expert evidence.

General matters

Scope of the Guidance

2.1. Sections 1 to 9 of this guidance apply to all experts who are or may be instructed to give or prepare evidence for the purpose of family proceedings in a court in England and Wales. The guidance also applies to those who instruct, or propose to instruct, an expert for such a purpose. Section 10 applies to the appointment of assessors in family proceedings in England and Wales.

2.2. This guidance does not apply to proceedings issued before 6 April 2011 but in any such proceedings the court may direct that this guidance will apply either wholly or partly. This is subject to the overriding objective for the type of proceedings, and to the proviso that such a direction will neither cause further delay nor involve repetition of steps already taken or of decisions already made in the case.

Pre-application instruction of experts

2.3. When experts' reports are commissioned before the commencement of proceedings, it should be made clear to the expert that he or she may in due course be reporting to the court and should therefore consider himself or herself bound by this guidance. A prospective party to family proceedings relating to children (for example, a local authority) should always write a letter of instruction when asking a potential witness for a report or an opinion, whether that request is within proceedings or pre-proceedings (for example, when commissioning specialist assessment materials, reports from a treating expert or other evidential materials); and the letter of instruction should conform to the principles set out in this guidance.

Emergency and urgent cases

2.4. In emergency or urgent cases – for example, where, before formal issue of proceedings, a without-notice application is made to the court during or out of business hours; or where, after proceedings have been issued, a previously unforeseen need for (further) expert evidence arises at short notice – a party may wish to call expert evidence without having complied with all or any part of this guidance. In such circumstances, the party wishing to call the expert evidence must apply forthwith to the court – where possible or appropriate, on notice to the other parties – for directions as to the future steps to be taken in respect of the expert evidence in question.

Orders

2.5. Where an order or direction requires an act to be done by an expert, or otherwise affects an expert, the party instructing that expert – or, in the case of a jointly instructed expert, the lead solicitor – must serve a copy of the order or direction on the expert forthwith upon receiving it.

Adults who may be protected parties

2.6. The court will investigate as soon as possible any issue as to whether an adult party or intended party to family proceedings lacks capacity (within the meaning of the Mental Capacity Act 2005) to conduct the proceedings. An adult who lacks capacity to act as a party to the proceedings is a protected party and must have a litigation friend to conduct the proceedings on their behalf. The expectation of the Official Solicitor is that the Official Solicitor will only be invited to act for the protected party as litigation friend if there is no other person suitable or willing to act.

2.7. Any issue as to the capacity of an adult to conduct the proceedings must be determined before the court gives any directions relevant to that adult's role in the proceedings.

2.8. Where the adult is a protected party, that party's representative should be involved in any instruction of an expert, including the instruction of an expert to assess whether the adult, although a protected party, is competent to give evidence. The instruction of an expert is a significant step in the proceedings. The representative will wish to consider (and ask the expert to consider), if the protected party is competent to give evidence, their best interests in this regard. The representative may wish to seek advice about 'special measures'. The representative may put forward an argument on behalf of the protected party that the protected party should not give evidence.

2.9. If at any time during the proceedings there is reason to believe that a party may lack capacity to conduct the proceedings, then the court must be notified and directions sought to ensure that this issue is investigated without delay.

Child likely to lack capacity to conduct the proceedings on when he or she reaches 18

2.10. Where it appears that a child is–

- (a) a party to the proceedings and not the subject of them;
- (b) nearing age 18; and
- (c) considered likely to lack capacity to conduct the proceedings when 18, the court will consider giving directions for the child's capacity in this respect to be investigated.

The Duties of Experts

Overriding Duty

3.1 An expert in family proceedings has an overriding duty to the court that takes precedence over any obligation to the person from whom the expert has received instructions or by whom the expert is paid.

Particular Duties

3.2 An expert shall have regard to the following, among other, duties:

- (a) to assist the court in accordance with the overriding duty;
- (b) to provide advice to the court that conforms to the best practice of the expert's profession;
- (c) to provide an opinion that is independent of the party or parties instructing the expert;
- (d) to confine the opinion to matters material to the issues between the parties and in relation only to questions that are within the expert's expertise (skill and experience);
- (e) where a question has been put which falls outside the expert's expertise, to state this at the earliest opportunity and to volunteer an opinion as to whether another expert is required to bring expertise not possessed by those already involved or, in the rare case, as to whether a second opinion is required on a key issue and, if possible, what questions should be asked of the second expert;
- (f) in expressing an opinion, to take into consideration all of the material facts including any relevant factors arising from ethnic, cultural, religious or linguistic contexts at the time the opinion is expressed;
- (g) to inform those instructing the expert without delay of any change in the opinion and of the reason for the change.

Content of the expert's report

3.3 The expert's report shall be addressed to the court and prepared and filed in accordance with the court's timetable and shall–

- (a) give details of the expert's qualifications and experience;
- (b) include a statement identifying the document(s) containing the material instructions and the substance of any oral instructions and, as far as necessary

	to explain any opinions or conclusions expressed in the report, summarising the facts and instructions which are material to the conclusions and opinions expressed;
(c)	state who carried out any test, examination or interview which the expert has used for the report and whether or not the test, examination or interview has been carried out under the expert's supervision;
(d)	give details of the qualifications of any person who carried out the test, examination or interview;
(e)	in expressing an opinion to the court–

take into consideration all of the material facts including any relevant factors arising from ethnic, cultural, religious or linguistic contexts at the time the opinion is expressed, identifying the facts, literature and any other material including research material that the expert has relied upon in forming an opinion;

describe their own professional risk assessment process and process of differential diagnosis, highlighting factual assumptions, deductions from the factual assumptions, and any unusual, contradictory or inconsistent features of the case;

indicate whether any proposition in the report is an hypothesis (in particular a controversial hypothesis), or an opinion deduced in accordance with peer-reviewed and tested technique, research and experience accepted as a consensus in the scientific community;

indicate whether the opinion is provisional (or qualified, as the case may be), stating the qualification and the reason for it, and identifying what further information is required to give an opinion without qualification;

(f) where there is a range of opinion on any question to be answered by the expert–

summarise the range of opinion;

identify and explain, within the range of opinions, any 'unknown cause', whether arising from the facts of the case (for example, because there is too little information to form a scientific opinion) or from limited experience or lack of research, peer review or support in the relevant field of expertise;

give reasons for any opinion expressed: the use of a balance sheet approach to the factors that support or undermine an opinion can be of great assistance to the court;

(g) contain a summary of the expert's conclusions and opinions;
(h) contain a statement that the expert–

has no conflict of interest of any kind, other than any conflict disclosed in his or her report;

does not consider that any interest disclosed affects his or her suitability as an expert witness on any issue on which he or she has given evidence;

will advise the instructing party if, between the date of the expert's report and the final hearing, there is any change in circumstances which affects the expert's answers to (i) or (ii) above;

understands their duty to the court and has complied with that duty; and

is aware of the requirements of Part 25 and this practice direction;

(i) be verified by a statement of truth in the following form–

'I confirm that I have made clear which facts and matters referred to in this report are within my own knowledge and which are not. Those that are within my own knowledge I confirm to be true. The opinions I have expressed represent my true and complete professional opinions on the matters to which they refer.'

(Part 17 deals with statements of truth. Rule 17.6 sets out the consequences of verifying a document containing a false statement without an honest belief in its truth.)

Proceedings relating to children

Preparation for the relevant hearing

PRELIMINARY ENQUIRIES OF THE EXPERT

4.1. *In good time for the information requested to be available for the relevant hearing or for the advocates' meeting or discussion where one takes place before the relevant hearing*, the solicitor for the party proposing to instruct the expert (or lead solicitor or solicitor for the child if the instruction proposed is joint) shall approach the expert with the following information–

(a) the nature of the proceedings and the issues likely to require determination by the court;
(b) the questions about which the expert is to be asked to give an opinion (including any ethnic, cultural, religious or linguistic contexts);
(c) the date when the court is to be asked to give permission for the instruction (or if – unusually – permission has already been given, the date and details of that permission);
(d) whether permission is to be asked of the court for the instruction of another expert in the same or any related field (that is, to give an opinion on the same or related questions);
(e) the volume of reading which the expert will need to undertake;
(f) whether or not permission has been applied for or given for the expert to examine the child;
(g) whether or not it will be necessary for the expert to conduct interview – and, if so, with whom;
(h) the likely timetable of legal and social work steps;
(i) in care and supervision proceedings, any dates in the Timetable for the Child which would be relevant to the proposed timetable for the assessment;
(j) when the expert's report is likely to be required;
(k) whether and, if so, what date has been fixed by the court for any hearing at which the expert may be required to give evidence (in particular the Final Hearing); and whether it may be possible for the expert to give evidence by telephone conference or video link: see section 8 (Arrangements for experts to give evidence) below;
(l) the possibility of making, through their instructing solicitors, representations to the court about being named or otherwise identified in any public judgment given by the court.

It is essential that there should be proper co-ordination between the court and the expert when drawing up the case management timetable: the needs of the court should be balanced with the needs of the expert whose forensic work is undertaken as an adjunct to his or her main professional duties.

EXPERT'S RESPONSE TO PRELIMINARY ENQUIRIES

4.2. *In good time for the relevant hearing or for the advocates' meeting or discussion where one takes place before the relevant hearing*, the solicitors intending to instruct the expert shall obtain confirmation from the expert–

(a) that acceptance of the proposed instructions will not involve the expert in any conflict of interest;
(b) that the work required is within the expert's expertise;
(c) that the expert is available to do the relevant work within the suggested time scale;
(d) when the expert is available to give evidence, of the dates and times to avoid and, where a hearing date has not been fixed, of the amount of notice the expert

will require to make arrangements to come to court (or to give evidence by telephone conference or video link) without undue disruption to his or her normal professional routines;

(e) of the cost, including hourly or other charging rates, and likely hours to be spent, attending experts' meetings, attending court and writing the report (to include any examinations and interviews);

(f) of any representations which the expert wishes to make to the court about being named or otherwise identified in any public judgment given by the court.

Where parties have not agreed on the appointment of a single joint expert before the relevant hearing, they should obtain the above confirmations in respect of all experts whom they intend to put to the court for the purposes of rule 25.7(2)(a) as candidates for the appointment.

THE PROPOSAL TO INSTRUCT AN EXPERT

4.3. Any party who proposes to ask the court for permission to instruct an expert shall, *by 11 a.m. on the business day before the relevant hearing*, file and serve a written proposal to instruct the expert, in the following detail–

(a) the name, discipline, qualifications and expertise of the expert (by way of C.V. where possible);
(b) the expert's availability to undertake the work;
(c) the relevance of the expert evidence sought to be adduced to the issues in the proceedings and the specific questions upon which it is proposed that the expert should give an opinion (including the relevance of any ethnic, cultural, religious or linguistic contexts);
(d) the timetable for the report;
(e) the responsibility for instruction;
(f) whether or not the expert evidence can properly be obtained by the joint instruction of the expert by two or more of the parties;
(g) whether the expert evidence can properly be obtained by only one party (for example, on behalf of the child);
(h) why the expert evidence proposed cannot be given by social services undertaking a core assessment or by the Children's Guardian in accordance with their respective statutory duties;
(i) the likely cost of the report on an hourly or other charging basis: where possible, the expert's terms of instruction should be made available to the court;
(j) the proposed apportionment (at least in the first instance) of any jointly instructed expert's fee; when it is to be paid; and, if applicable, whether public funding has been approved.

DRAFT ORDER FOR THE RELEVANT HEARING

4.4. Any party proposing to instruct an expert shall, *by 11 a.m. on the business day before the relevant hearing*, submit to the court a draft order for directions dealing in particular with–

(a) the party who is to be responsible for drafting the letter of instruction and providing the documents to the expert;
(b) the issues identified by the court and the questions about which the expert is to give an opinion;
(c) the timetable within which the report is to be prepared, filed and served;
(d) the disclosure of the report to the parties and to any other expert;
(e) the organisation of, preparation for and conduct of an experts' discussion;
(f) the preparation of a statement of agreement and disagreement by the experts following an experts' discussion;

- (g) making available to the court at an early opportunity the expert reports in electronic form;
- (h) the attendance of the expert at court to give oral evidence (alternatively, the expert giving his or her evidence in writing or remotely by video link), whether at or for the Final Hearing or another hearing; unless agreement about the opinions given by the expert is reached at or before the Issues Resolution Hearing ('IRH') or, if no IRH is to be held, by a specified date prior to the hearing at which the expert is to give oral evidence ('the specified date').

LETTER OF INSTRUCTION

4.5. The solicitor or party instructing the expert shall, *within 5 business days after the relevant hearing*, prepare (in agreement with the other parties where appropriate), file and serve a letter of instruction to the expert which shall–

- (a) set out the context in which the expert's opinion is sought (including any ethnic, cultural, religious or linguistic contexts);
- (b) set out the specific questions which the expert is required to answer, ensuring that they–
    - I. are within the ambit of the expert's area of expertise;
    - II. do not contain unnecessary or irrelevant detail;
    - III. are kept to a manageable number and are clear, focused and direct; and
    - IV. reflect what the expert has been requested to do by the court.

    (The Annex to this guidance sets out suggested questions in letters of instruction to (1) child mental health professionals or paediatricians, and (2) adult psychiatrists and applied psychologists, in Children Act 1989 proceedings.)
- (c) list the documentation provided, or provide for the expert an indexed and paginated bundle which shall include–

    a copy of the order (or those parts of the order) which gives permission for the instruction of the expert, immediately the order becomes available;
    an agreed list of essential reading; and
    a copy of this guidance;
- (d) identify any materials provided to the expert which have not been produced either as original medical (or other professional) records or in response to an instruction from a party, and state the source of that material (such materials may contain an assumption as to the standard of proof, the admissibility or otherwise of hearsay evidence, and other important procedural and substantive questions relating to the different purposes of other enquiries, for example, criminal or disciplinary proceedings);
- (e) identify all requests to third parties for disclosure and their responses, to avoid partial disclosure, which tends only to prove a case rather than give full and frank information;
- (f) identify the relevant people concerned with the proceedings (for example, the treating clinicians) and inform the expert of his or her right to talk to them provided that an accurate record is made of the discussions;
- (g) identify any other expert instructed in the proceedings and advise the expert of their right to talk to the other experts provided that an accurate record is made of the discussions;
- (h) subject to any public funding requirement for prior authority, define the contractual basis upon which the expert is retained and in particular the funding mechanism including how much the expert will be paid (an hourly rate and overall estimate should already have been obtained), when the expert will be paid, and what limitation there might be on the amount the expert can charge for the work which they will have to do. In cases where the parties are publicly

funded, there should also be a brief explanation of the costs and expenses excluded from public funding by Funding Code criterion 1.3 and the detailed assessment process.

ASKING THE COURT TO SETTLE THE LETTER OF INSTRUCTION TO A SINGLE JOINT EXPERT

4.6. Where possible, the written request for the court to consider the letter of instruction referred to in rule 25.8(2) should be set out in an e-mail to the court and copied by e-mail to the other instructing parties. The request should be sent to the relevant court or (by prior arrangement only) directly to the judge dealing with the proceedings; in the magistrates' court, the request should be sent to the legal adviser who will refer it to the appropriate judge or justices, if necessary. The court will settle the letter of instruction, usually without a hearing to avoid delay; and will send (where practicable, by e-mail) the settled letter to the lead solicitor for transmission forthwith to the expert, and copy it to the other instructing parties for information.

KEEPING THE EXPERT UP TO DATE WITH NEW DOCUMENTS

4.7. As often as may be necessary, the expert should be provided promptly with a copy of any new document filed at court, together with an updated document list or bundle index.

Proceedings other than those relating to children

5.1. Wherever possible, expert evidence should be obtained from a single joint expert instructed by both or all the parties ('SJE'). To that end, a party wishing to instruct an expert should first give the other party or parties a list of the names of one or more experts in the relevant speciality whom they consider suitable to be instructed.

5.2. *Within 10 days after receipt of the list of proposed experts*, the other party or parties should indicate any objection to one or more of the named experts and, if so, supply the name(s) of one or more experts whom they consider suitable.

5.3. Each party should disclose whether they have already consulted any of the proposed experts about the issue(s) in question.

5.4. Where the parties cannot agree on the identity of the expert, each party should think carefully before instructing their own expert because of the costs implications. Disagreements about the use and identity of an expert may be better managed by the court in the context of an application for directions. (see paragraphs 5.8 and 5.9 below).

AGREEMENT TO INSTRUCT SEPARATE EXPERTS

5.5. If the parties agree to instruct separate experts,–

    (a)   they should agree in advance that the reports will be disclosed; and

    (b)   the instructions to each expert should comply, so far as appropriate, with paragraphs 4.5 to 4.7 above (Letter of instruction).

AGREEMENT TO INSTRUCT AN SJE

5.6. If there is agreement to instruct an SJE, *before instructions are given* the parties should–

    (a)   so far as appropriate, comply with the guidance in paragraphs 4.1 (Preliminary inquiries of the expert) and 4.2 (Expert's confirmation in response to preliminary enquiries) above;

    (b)   have agreed in what proportion the SJE's fee is to be shared between them (at least in the first instance) and when it is to be paid; and

    (c)   if applicable, have obtained agreement for public funding.

5.7. The instructions to the SJE should comply, so far as appropriate, with paragraphs 4.5 to 4.7 above (Letter of instruction).

SEEKING THE COURT'S DIRECTIONS FOR THE USE OF AN SJE

5.8. Where the parties seek the court's directions for the use of an SJE, they should comply, so far as appropriate, with paragraphs 4.1 to 4.4 (Preparation for the relevant hearing) above.

5.9. The instructions to the SJE should comply, so far as appropriate, with paragraphs 4.5 to 4.7 above (Letter of instruction).

The Court's control of expert evidence: consequential issues

WRITTEN QUESTIONS

6.1. Where–

(a) written questions are put to an expert in accordance with rule 25.6, the court will specify the timetable according to which the expert is to answer the written questions;

(b) a party sends a written question or questions under rule 25.6 direct to an expert, a copy of the questions must, at the same time, be sent to the other party or parties.

EXPERTS' DISCUSSION OR MEETING: PURPOSE

6.2. In accordance with rule 25.12, the court may, at any stage, direct a discussion between experts for the purpose outlined in paragraph (1) of that rule. Rule 25.12(2) provides that the court may specify the issues which the experts must discuss. The expectation is that those issues will include–

(a) the reasons for disagreement on any expert question and what, if any, action needs to be taken to resolve any outstanding disagreement or question;

(b) explanation of existing evidence or additional evidence in order to assist the court to determine the issues.

One of the aims of specifing the issues for discussion is to limit, wherever possible, the need for the experts to attend court to give oral evidence.

EXPERTS' DISCUSSION OR MEETING: ARRANGEMENTS

6.3. Subject to the directions given by the court under rule 25.12, the solicitor or other professional who is given the responsibility by the court ('the nominated professional') shall – *within 15 business days after the experts' reports have been filed and copied to the other parties* – make arrangements for the experts to meet or communicate. Subject to any specification by the court of the issues which experts must discuss under rule 25.12(2), the following matters should be considered as appropriate–

(a) where permission has been given for the instruction of experts from different disciplines, a global discussion may be held relating to those questions that concern all or most of them;

(b) separate discussions may have to be held among experts from the same or related disciplines, but care should be taken to ensure that the discussions complement each other so that related questions are discussed by all relevant experts;

(c) *5 business days prior to a discussion or meeting*, the nominated professional should formulate an agenda including a list of questions for consideration. The agenda should, subject always to the provisions of rule 25.12(1), focus on those questions which are intended to clarify areas of agreement or disagreement.

Questions which repeat questions asked in the letter of instruction or which seek to rehearse cross-examination in advance of the hearing should be rejected as likely to defeat the purpose of the meeting.

The agenda may usefully take the form of a list of questions to be circulated among the other parties in advance and should comprise all questions that each party wishes the experts to consider.

The agenda and list of questions should be sent to each of the experts *not later than 2 business days before the discussion*;

(d) the nominated professional may exercise his or her discretion to accept further questions after the agenda with list of questions has been circulated to the parties. *Only in exceptional circumstances should questions be added to the agenda within the 2-day period before the meeting. Under no circumstances should any question received on the day of or during the meeting be accepted.* This does not preclude questions arising during the meeting for the purposes of clarification. Strictness in this regard is vital, for adequate notice of the questions enables the parties to identify and isolate the expert issues in the case before the meeting so that the experts' discussion at the meeting can concentrate on those issues;

(e) the discussion should be chaired by the nominated professional. A minute must be taken of the questions answered by the experts. Where the court has given a direction under rule 25.12(3) and subject to that direction, a Statement of Agreement and Disagreement must be prepared which should be agreed and signed by each of the experts who participated in the discussion. In accordance with rule 25.12(3) the statement must contain a summary of the experts' reasons for disagreeing. The statement should be served and filed *not later than 5 business days after the discussion has taken place*;

(f) in each case, whether some or all of the experts participate by telephone conference or video link to ensure that minimum disruption is caused to professional schedules and that costs are minimised.

MEETINGS OR CONFERENCES ATTENDED BY A JOINTLY INSTRUCTED EXPERT

6.4. Jointly instructed experts should not attend any meeting or conference which is not a joint one, unless all the parties have agreed in writing or the court has directed that such a meeting may be held, and it is agreed or directed who is to pay the expert's fees for the meeting or conference. Any meeting or conference attended by a jointly instructed expert should be proportionate to the case.

COURT-DIRECTED MEETINGS INVOLVING EXPERTS IN PUBLIC LAW CHILDREN ACT CASES

6.5. In public law Children Act proceedings, where the court gives a direction that a meeting shall take place between the local authority and any relevant named experts for the purpose of providing assistance to the local authority in the formulation of plans and proposals for the child, the meeting shall be arranged, chaired and minuted in accordance with the directions given by the court.

Positions of the Parties

7.1. Where a party refuses to be bound by an agreement that has been reached at an experts' discussion or meeting, that party must inform the court and the other parties in writing, *within 10 business days after the discussion or meeting or, where an IRH is to be held, not less than 5 business days before the IRH*, of his or her reasons for refusing to accept the agreement.

Arrangements for Experts to give evidence

PREPARATION

8.1. Where the court has directed the attendance of an expert witness, the party who is responsible for the instruction of the expert shall, *by the specified date or, where an IRH is to be held, by the IRH*, ensure that—

(a) a date and time (if possible, convenient to the expert) are fixed for the court to hear the expert's evidence, substantially in advance of the hearing at which the expert is to give oral evidence and no later than a specified date prior to that hearing or, where an IRH is to be held, than the IRH;
(b) if the expert's oral evidence is not required, the expert is notified as soon as possible;
(c) the witness template accurately indicates how long the expert is likely to be giving evidence, in order to avoid the inconvenience of the expert being delayed at court;
(d) consideration is given in each case to whether some or all of the experts participate by telephone conference or video link, or submit their evidence in writing, to ensure that minimum disruption is caused to professional schedules and that costs are minimised.

EXPERTS ATTENDING COURT

8.2. Where expert witnesses are to be called, all parties shall, *by the specified date or, where an IRH is to be held, by the IRH*, ensure that–
(a) the parties' advocates have identified (whether at an advocates' meeting or by other means) the issues which the experts are to address;
(b) wherever possible, a logical sequence to the evidence is arranged, with experts of the same discipline giving evidence on the same day;
(c) the court is informed of any circumstance where all experts agree but a party nevertheless does not accept the agreed opinion, so that directions can be given for the proper consideration of the experts' evidence and opinion and of the party's reasons for not accepting the agreed opinion;
(d) in the exceptional case the court is informed of the need for a witness summons.

ACTION AFTER THE FINAL HEARING

9.1. *Within 10 business days after the Final Hearing*, the solicitor instructing the expert shall inform the expert in writing of the outcome of the case, and of the use made by the court of the expert's opinion.
9.2. Where the court directs preparation of a transcript, it may also direct that the solicitor instructing the expert shall send a copy to the expert *within 10 business days after receiving the transcript*.
9.3. After a Final Hearing in the Family Proceedings Court, the (lead) solicitor instructing the expert shall send the expert a copy of the court's written reasons for its decision *within 10 business days after receiving the written reasons*.

APPOINTMENT OF ASSESSORS IN FAMILY PROCEEDINGS

10.1. The power to appoint one or more assessors to assist the court is conferred on the High Court by section 70(1) of the Senior Courts Act 1981, and on a county court by section 63(1) of the County Courts Act 1984. In practice, these powers have been used in appeals from a district judge or costs judge in costs assessment proceedings – although, in principle, the statutory powers permit one or more assessors to be appointed in any family proceedings where the High Court or a county court sees fit.
10.2. *Not less than 21 days before making any such appointment*, the court will notify each party in writing of the name of the proposed assessor, of the matter in respect of which the assistance of the assessor will be sought and of the qualifications of the assessor to give that assistance.
10.3. Any party may object to the proposed appointment, either personally or in respect of the proposed assessor's qualifications.
10.4. Any such objection must be made in writing and filed and served *within 7 business days*

of receipt of the notification from the court of the proposed appointment, and will be taken into account by the court in deciding whether or not to make the appointment.

ANNEX (DRAFTED BY THE FAMILY JUSTICE COUNCIL)

Suggested questions in letters of instruction to child mental health professional or paediatrician in Children Act 1989 proceedings

A. **The Child(ren)**

1. Please describe the child(ren)'s current health, development and functioning (according to your area of expertise), and identify the nature of any significant changes which have occurred

    - Behavioural
    - Emotional
    - Attachment organisation
    - Social/peer/sibling relationships
    - Cognitive/educational
    - Physical
        - Growth, eating, sleep
        - Non-organic physical problems (including wetting and soiling)
        - Injuries
        - Paediatric conditions

2. Please comment on the likely explanation for/aetiology of the child(ren)'s problems/difficulties/injuries

    - History/experiences (including intrauterine influences, and abuse and neglect)
    - Genetic/innate/developmental difficulties
    - Paediatric/psychiatric disorders

3. Please provide a prognosis and risk if difficulties not addressed above.
4. Please describe the child(ren)'s needs in the light of the above

    - Nature of care-giving
    - Education
    - Treatment

    in the short and long term (subject, where appropriate, to further assessment later).

B. **The parents/primary carers**

5. Please describe the factors and mechanisms which would explain the parents' (or primary carers) harmful or neglectful interactions with the child(ren) (if relevant).
6. What interventions have been tried and what has been the result?
7. Please assess the ability of the parents or primary carers to fulfil the child(ren)'s identified needs now.
8. What other assessments of the parents or primary carers are indicated?

    - Adult mental health assessment
    - Forensic risk assessment
    - Physical assessment
    - Cognitive assessment

9. What, if anything, is needed to assist the parents or primary carers now, within the child(ren)'s time scales and what is the prognosis for change?

    - Parenting work
    - Support
    - Treatment/therapy

C. **Alternatives**
10. Please consider the alternative possibilities for the fulfilment of the child(ren)'s needs
    - What sort of placement
    - Contact arrangements

    Please consider the advantages, disadvantages and implications of each for the child(ren).

Suggested questions in letters of instruction to adult psychiatrists and applied psychologists in Children Act 1989 proceedings

1. Does the parent/adult have – whether in his/her history or presentation – a mental illness/disorder (including substance abuse) or other psychological/emotional difficulty and, if so, what is the diagnosis?
2. How do any/all of the above (and their current treatment if applicable) affect his/her functioning, including interpersonal relationships?
3. If the answer to Q1 is yes, are there any features of either the mental illness or psychological/emotional difficulty or personality disorder which could be associated with risk to others, based on the available evidence base (whether published studies or evidence from clinical experience)?
4. What are the experiences/antecedents/aetiology which would explain his/her difficulties, if any, (taking into account any available evidence base or other clinical experience)?
5. What treatment is indicated, what is its nature and the likely duration?
6. What is his/her capacity to engage in/partake of the treatment/therapy?
7. Are you able to indicate the prognosis for, time scales for achieving, and likely durability of, change?
8. What other factors might indicate positive change?

(It is assumed that this opinion will be based on collateral information as well as interviewing the adult).

PRACTICE DIRECTION 26A – CHANGE OF SOLICITOR

This Practice Direction supplements FPR Part 26

Solicitor acting for a party

1.1 Rule 26.1 states that where the address for service of a party is the business address of his solicitor, the solicitor will be considered to be acting for that party until the provisions of Part 26 have been complied with.
1.2 Subject to rule 26.2(6) (where the certificate of a LSC funded client or assisted person is revoked or discharged), where a party has changed his solicitor or intends to act in person, the former solicitor will be considered to be the party's solicitor unless or until–

   (a) a notice of the change is–
       (i) served on every other party (see rule 26.2(2)(a)); and
       (ii) filed with the court (see rule 26.2(2)(b)); or
   (b) the court makes an order under rule 26.3 and the order is served on the former solicitor and every other party in accordance with directions of the court (see rule 26.2(5)).

1.3 A solicitor appointed to represent a party only as an advocate at a hearing will not be considered to be acting for that party within the meaning of Part 26.

Notice of change of solicitor

2.1 Rule 26.2(1) sets out the circumstances following which a notice of the change must be filed and served.

2.2 A notice of the change giving the last known address of the former assisted person must also be filed and served on every party where, under rule 26.2(6)–

(a) the certificate of a LSC funded client or assisted person is revoked or discharged; and

(b) the LSC funded client or the assisted person wishes either to act in person or appoint another solicitor to act on his behalf.

2.3 Where a solicitor has given notice that he or she acts for a child directly, and an officer of the Service, a Welsh family proceedings officer or the Official Solicitor continues with the permission of the court to have legal representation, notice of that legal representation must be given to the court.

2.4 In addition, where a party or solicitor changes his address for service, a notice of that change should be filed and served on every party.

2.5 A party who, having conducted an application by a solicitor, intends to act in person must give in his notice an address for service that is within the United Kingdom (see rule 6.26).

2.6 The form giving notice of any change is referred to in Practice Direction 5A. The notice should be filed in the court office in which the application is proceeding.

Application for an order that a solicitor has ceased to act

3.1 A solicitor may apply under rule 26.3 for an order declaring that he has ceased to be the solicitor acting for a party.

3.2 The application should be made in accordance with Part 18 and must be supported by evidence (see Part 18 and the Practice Direction 18A). Unless the court directs otherwise the application notice must be served on the party (see rule 26.3(2)).

3.3 An order made under rule 26.3 will be served on every party by the court officer and takes effect when it is served.

Application by another party to remove a solicitor

4.1 Rule 26.4 sets out circumstances in which any other party may apply for an order declaring that a solicitor has ceased to be the solicitor acting for another party in the proceedings.

4.2 The application should be made in accordance with Part 18 and must be supported by evidence. Unless the court directs otherwise the application notice must be served on the party to whose solicitor the application relates.

4.3 An order made under rule 26.4 will be served on every party by the court officer.

New address for service where order made under rules 26.3 or 26.4

5.1 Where the court has made an order under rule 26.3 that a solicitor has ceased to act or under rule 26.4 declaring that a solicitor has ceased to be the solicitor for a party, the party for whom the solicitor was acting must give a new address for service to comply with rule 6.26.

(Rule 6.26 provides that a party must give an address for service within the United Kingdom, or where a solicitor is acting for a party, an address for service either in the United Kingdom or any other EEA state, at which that party resides or carries on business. Where that party does not have such an address, an address within the United Kingdom must generally be given (see rule 6.26(3) and (4)).

(Until such time as a new address for service is given directions may be needed under rule 6.19.)

PRACTICE DIRECTION 27A – FAMILY PROCEEDINGS: COURT BUNDLES (UNIVERSAL PRACTICE TO BE APPLIED IN ALL COURTS OTHER THAN THE FAMILY PROCEEDINGS COURT)

1 The President of the Family Division has issued this practice direction to achieve

consistency across the country in all family courts (other than the Family Proceedings Court) in the preparation of court bundles and in respect of other related matters.

Application of the practice direction

2.1 Except as specified in paragraph 2.4, and subject to specific directions given in any particular case, the following practice applies to:
- (a) all hearings of whatever nature (including but not limited to hearings in family proceedings, CPR Part 7 and Part 8 claims and appeals) before a judge of the Family Division of the High Court wherever the court may be sitting;
- (b) all hearings in family proceedings in the Royal Courts of Justice ('RCJ');
- (c) all hearings in the Principal Registry of the Family Division ('PRFD') at First Avenue House; and
- (d) all hearings in family proceedings in all other courts except for Family Proceedings Courts.

2.2 'Hearings' includes all appearances before a judge or district judge, whether with or without notice to other parties and whether for directions or for substantive relief.

2.3 This practice direction applies whether a bundle is being lodged for the first time or is being re-lodged for a further hearing (see paragraph 9.2).

2.4 This practice direction does not apply to:
- (a) cases listed for one hour or less at a court referred to in paragraph 2.1(c) or 2.1(d); or
- (b) the hearing of any urgent application if and to the extent that it is impossible to comply with it.

2.5 The Designated Family Judge responsible for any court referred to in paragraph 2.1(c) or 2.1(d) may, after such consultation as is appropriate (but in the case of hearings in the PRFD at First Avenue House only with the agreement of the Senior District Judge), direct that in that court this practice direction shall apply to all family proceedings irrespective of the length of hearing.

Responsibility for the preparation of the bundle

3.1 A bundle for the use of the court at the hearing shall be provided by the party in the position of applicant at the hearing (or, if there are cross-applications, by the party whose application was first in time) or, if that person is a litigant in person, by the first listed respondent who is not a litigant in person.

3.2 The party preparing the bundle shall paginate it. If possible the contents of the bundle shall be agreed by all parties.

Contents of the bundle

4.1 The bundle shall contain copies of all documents relevant to the hearing, in chronological order from the front of the bundle, paginated and indexed, and divided into separate sections (each section being separately paginated) as follows:
- (a) preliminary documents (see paragraph 4.2) and any other case management documents required by any other practice direction;
- (b) applications and orders;
- (c) statements and affidavits (which must be dated in the top right corner of the front page);
- (d) care plans (where appropriate);
- (e) experts' reports and other reports (including those of a guardian, children's guardian or litigation friend); and
- (f) other documents, divided into further sections as may be appropriate.

Copies of notes of contact visits should normally not be included in the bundle unless directed by a judge.

4.2 At the commencement of the bundle there shall be inserted the following documents ('the preliminary documents'):

(i) an up to date summary of the background to the hearing confined to those matters which are relevant to the hearing and the management of the case and limited, if practicable, to one A4 page;

(ii) a statement of the issue or issues to be determined (1) at that hearing and (2) at the final hearing;

(iii) a position statement by each party including a summary of the order or directions sought by that party (1) at that hearing and (2) at the final hearing;

(iv) an up to date chronology, if it is a final hearing or if the summary under (i) is insufficient;

(v) skeleton arguments, if appropriate, with copies of all authorities relied on; and

(vi) a list of essential reading for that hearing.

4.3 Each of the preliminary documents shall state on the front page immediately below the heading the date when it was prepared and the date of the hearing for which it was prepared.

4.4 The summary of the background, statement of issues, chronology, position statement and any skeleton arguments shall be cross-referenced to the relevant pages of the bundle.

4.5 The summary of the background, statement of issues, chronology and reading list shall in the case of a final hearing, and shall so far as practicable in the case of any other hearing, each consist of a single document in a form agreed by all parties. Where the parties disagree as to the content the fact of their disagreement and their differing contentions shall be set out at the appropriate places in the document.

4.6 Where the nature of the hearing is such that a complete bundle of all documents is unnecessary, the bundle (which need not be repaginated) may comprise only those documents necessary for the hearing, but

(i) the summary (paragraph 4.2(i)) must commence with a statement that the bundle is limited or incomplete; and

(ii) the bundle shall if reasonably practicable be in a form agreed by all parties.

4.7 Where the bundle is re-lodged in accordance with paragraph 9.2, before it is re-lodged:

(a) the bundle shall be updated as appropriate; and

(b) all superseded documents (and in particular all outdated summaries, statements of issues, chronologies, skeleton arguments and similar documents) shall be removed from the bundle.

Format of the bundle

5.1 The bundle shall be contained in one or more A4 size ring binders or lever arch files (each lever arch file being limited to 350 pages).

5.2 All ring binders and lever arch files shall have clearly marked on the front and the spine:

(a) the title and number of the case;
(b) the court where the case has been listed;
(c) the hearing date and time;
(d) if known, the name of the judge hearing the case; and
(e) where there is more than one ring binder or lever arch file, a distinguishing letter (A, B, C etc).

Timetable for preparing and lodging the bundle

6.1 The party preparing the bundle shall, whether or not the bundle has been agreed, provide a paginated index to all other parties not less than 4 working days before the hearing (in relation to a case management conference to which the provisions of the Public Law Protocol [2003] 2 FLR 719 apply, not less than 5 working days before the case management conference).

6.2 Where counsel is to be instructed at any hearing, a paginated bundle shall (if not already in counsel's possession) be delivered to counsel by the person instructing that counsel not less than 3 working days before the hearing.

6.3 The bundle (with the exception of the preliminary documents if and insofar as they are not then available) shall be lodged with the court not less than 2 working days before the hearing, or at such other time as may be specified by the judge.

6.4 The preliminary documents shall be lodged with the court no later than 11 am on the day before the hearing and, where the hearing is before a judge of the High Court and the name of the judge is known, shall at the same time be sent by e-mail to the judge's clerk.

Lodging the bundle

7.1 The bundle shall be lodged at the appropriate office. If the bundle is lodged in the wrong place the judge may:

(a) treat the bundle as having not been lodged; and
(b) take the steps referred to in paragraph 12.

7.2 Unless the judge has given some other direction as to where the bundle in any particular case is to be lodged (for example a direction that the bundle is to be lodged with the judge's clerk) the bundle shall be lodged:

(a) for hearings in the RCJ, in the office of the Clerk of the Rules, Room TM 9.09, Royal Courts of Justice, Strand, London WC2A 2LL (DX 44450 Strand);
(b) for hearings in the PRFD at First Avenue House, at the List Office counter, 3rd floor, First Avenue House, 42/49 High Holborn, London, WC1V 6NP (DX 396 Chancery Lane); and
(c) for hearings at any other court, at such place as may be designated by the Designated Family Judge or other judge at that court and in default of any such designation at the court office of the court where the hearing is to take place.

7.3 Any bundle sent to the court by post, DX or courier shall be clearly addressed to the appropriate office and shall show the date and place of the hearing on the outside of any packaging as well as on the bundle itself.

Lodging the bundle – additional requirements for cases being heard at First Avenue House or at the RCJ

8.1 In the case of hearings at the RCJ or First Avenue House, parties shall:

(a) if the bundle or preliminary documents are delivered personally, ensure that they obtain a receipt from the clerk accepting it or them; and
(b) if the bundle or preliminary documents are sent by post or DX, ensure that they obtain proof of posting or despatch.

The receipt (or proof of posting or despatch, as the case may be) shall be brought to court on the day of the hearing and must be produced to the court if requested. If the receipt (or proof of posting or despatch) cannot be produced to the court the judge may (i) treat the bundle as having not been lodged and (ii) take the steps referred to in paragraph 12.

8.2 For hearings at the RCJ:

(a) bundles or preliminary documents delivered after 11 am on the day before the hearing will not be accepted by the Clerk of the Rules and shall be delivered:

(i) in a case where the hearing is before a judge of the High Court, directly to the clerk of the judge hearing the case;
(ii) in a case where the hearing is before a Circuit Judge, Deputy High Court Judge or Recorder, directly to the messenger at the Judge's entrance to the Queen's Building (with telephone notification to the personal assistant to the Designated Family Judge, 020 7947 7155, that this has been done).

(b) upon learning before which judge a hearing is to take place, the clerk to counsel, or other advocate, representing the party in the position of applicant shall no later than 3pm the day before the hearing:

(i) in a case where the hearing is before a judge of the High Court, telephone the clerk of the judge hearing the case;
(ii) in a case where the hearing is before a Circuit Judge, Deputy High Court Judge or Recorder, telephone the personal assistant to the Designated Family Judge;

to ascertain whether the judge has received the bundle (including the preliminary documents) and, if not, shall organise prompt delivery by the applicant's solicitor.

Removing and re-lodging the bundle

9.1 Following completion of the hearing the party responsible for the bundle shall retrieve it from the court immediately or, if that is not practicable, shall collect it from the court within five working days. Bundles which are not collected in due time may be destroyed.

9.2 The bundle shall be re-lodged for the next and any further hearings in accordance with the provisions of this practice direction and in a form which complies with paragraph 4.7.

Time estimates

10.1 In every case a time estimate (which shall be inserted at the front of the bundle) shall be prepared which shall so far as practicable be agreed by all parties and shall:

(a) specify separately (i) the time estimated to be required for judicial pre-reading and (ii) the time required for hearing all evidence and submissions and (iii) the time estimated to be required for preparing and delivering judgment; and

(b) be prepared on the basis that before they give evidence all witnesses will have read all relevant filed statements and reports.

10.2 Once a case has been listed, any change in time estimates shall be notified immediately by telephone (and then immediately confirmed in writing):

(a) in the case of hearings in the RCJ, to the Clerk of the Rules;
(b) in the case of hearings in the PRFD at First Avenue House, to the List Officer at First Avenue House; and
(c) in the case of hearings elsewhere, to the relevant listing officer.

Taking cases out of the list

11 As soon as it becomes known that a hearing will no longer be effective, whether as a result of the parties reaching agreement or for any other reason, the parties and their representatives shall immediately notify the court by telephone and by letter. The letter, which shall wherever possible be a joint letter sent on behalf of all parties with their signatures applied or appended, shall include:

(a) a short background summary of the case ;
(b) the written consent of each party who consents and, where a party does not

consent, details of the steps which have been taken to obtain that party's consent and, where known, an explanation of why that consent has not been given;
(c) a draft of the order being sought; and
(d) enough information to enable the court to decide (i) whether to take the case out of the list and (ii) whether to make the proposed order.

Penalties for failure to comply with the practice direction

12 Failure to comply with any part of this practice direction may result in the judge removing the case from the list or putting the case further back in the list and may also result in a 'wasted costs' order in accordance with CPR Part 48.7 or some other adverse costs order.

Commencement of the practice direction and application of other practice directions

13 This practice direction replaces President's Direction (Family Proceedings: Court Bundles) [2000] 1 FLR 536 and shall have effect from 2 October 2006.
14 Any reference in any other practice direction to President's Direction (Family Proceedings: Court Bundles) [2000] 1 FLR 536 shall be read as if substituted by a reference to this practice direction.
15 This practice direction should where appropriate be read in conjunction with President's Direction (Human Rights Act 1998) [2000] 2 FLR 429 and with Practice Direction (Care Cases: Judicial Continuity and Judicial Case Management) appended to the Public Law Protocol [2003] 2 FLR 719. In particular, nothing in this practice direction is to be read as removing or altering any obligation to comply with the requirements of the Public Law Protocol.

This Practice Direction is issued:
(i) in relation to family proceedings, by the President of the Family Division, as the nominee of the Lord Chief Justice, with the agreement of the Lord Chancellor; and
(ii) to the extent that it applies to proceedings to which section 5 of the Civil Procedure Act 1997 applies, by the Master of the Rolls as the nominee of the Lord Chief Justice, with the agreement of the Lord Chancellor.

PRACTICE DIRECTION 27B – ATTENDANCE OF MEDIA REPRESENTATIVES AT HEARINGS IN FAMILY PROCEEDINGS (HIGH COURT AND COUNTY COURTS)

This Practice Direction supplements FPR Part 27

1 Introduction

1.1 This Practice Direction supplements rule 27.11 of the Family Procedure Rules 2010 ('FPR 2010') and deals with the right of representatives of news gathering and reporting organisations ('media representatives') to attend at hearings of family proceedings which take place in private subject to the discretion of the court to exclude such representatives from the whole or part of any hearing on specified grounds. It takes effect on 27 April 2009.

2 Matters unchanged by the rule

2.1 Rule 27.11(1) contains an express exception in respect of hearings which are conducted for the purpose of judicially assisted conciliation or negotiation and media representatives do not have a right to attend these hearings. Financial Dispute Resolution hearings will come within this exception. First Hearing Dispute Resolution appointments in private law Children Act cases will also come within this exception to the extent that the judge plays an active part in the conciliation process. Where the judge plays no part in the conciliation process or where the conciliation element of a hearing is complete and the judge is adjudicating upon the issues between the parties, media representatives should be permitted to attend, subject to the discretion of the court to exclude them on the specified grounds. Conciliation meetings or negotiation conducted between the parties with the assistance of an officer of the service or a Welsh Family Proceedings officer, and without the presence of the judge, are not 'hearings' within the meaning of this rule and media representatives have no right to attend such appointments.

The exception in rule 27.11(1) does not operate to exclude media representatives from:

- Hearings to consider applications brought under Parts IV and V of the Children Act 1989, including Case Management Conferences and Issues Resolution Hearings
- Hearings relating to findings of fact
- Interim hearings
- Final hearings.

The rights of media representatives to attend such hearings are limited only by the powers of the court to exclude such attendance on the limited grounds and subject to the procedures set out in paragraphs (3)–(5) of rule 27.11.

2.2 During any hearing, courts should consider whether the exception in rule 27.11(1) becomes applicable so that media representatives should be directed to withdraw.

2.3 The provisions of the rules permitting the attendance of media representatives and the disclosure to third parties of information relating to the proceedings do not entitle a media representative to receive or peruse court documents referred to in the course of evidence, submissions or judgment without the permission of the court or otherwise in accordance with Part 12, Chapter 7 of the Family Procedure Rules 2010 and Practice Direction 12G (rules relating to disclosure to third parties). (This is in contrast to the position in civil proceedings, where the court sits in public and where members of the public are entitled to seek copies of certain documents).

2.4 The question of attendance of media representatives at hearings in family proceedings to which rule 27.11 and this guidance apply must be distinguished from statutory restrictions on publication and disclosure of information relating to proceedings, which continue to apply and are unaffected by the rule and this guidance.

2.5 The prohibition in section 97(2) of the Children Act 1989, on publishing material intended to or likely to identify a child as being involved in proceedings or the address or school of any such child, is limited to the duration of the proceedings. However, the limitations imposed by section 12 of the Administration of Justice Act 1960 on publication of information relating to certain proceedings in private apply during and after the proceedings. In addition, in proceedings to which s 97(2) of the Children Act 1989 applies the court should continue to consider at the conclusion of the proceedings whether there are any outstanding welfare issues which require a continuation of the protection afforded during the course of the proceedings by that provision.

3 **Aims of the guidance**

3.1 This Practice Direction is intended to provide guidance regarding:

- the handling of applications to exclude media representatives from the whole or part of a hearing; and
- the exercise of the court's discretion to exclude media representatives whether upon the court's own motion or any such application.

3.2 While the guidance does not aim to cover all possible eventualities, it should be complied with so far as consistent in all the circumstances with the just determination of the proceedings.

4 **Identification of media representatives as 'accredited'**

4.1 Media representatives will be expected to carry with them identification sufficient to enable court staff, or if necessary the court itself, to verify that they are 'accredited' representatives of news gathering or reporting organisations within the meaning of the rule.

4.2 By virtue of paragraph (7) of the rule, it is for the Lord Chancellor to approve a scheme which will provide for accreditation. The Lord Chancellor has decided that the scheme operated by the UK Press Card Authority provides sufficient accreditation; a card issued under that scheme will be the expected form of identification, and production of the Card will be both necessary and sufficient to demonstrate accreditation.

4.3 A media representative unable to demonstrate accreditation in accordance with the UK Press Card Authority scheme, so as to be able to attend by virtue of paragraph (2)(f) of the rule, may nevertheless be permitted to attend at the court's discretion under paragraph (2)(g).

5 Exercise of the discretion to exclude media representatives from all or part of the proceedings

5.1 The rule anticipates and should be applied on the basis that media representatives have a right to attend family proceedings throughout save and to the extent that the court exercises its discretion to exclude them from the whole or part of any proceedings on one or more of the grounds set out in paragraph (3) of the rule.

5.2 When considering the question of exclusion on any of the grounds set out in paragraph (3) of the rule the court should–

- specifically identify whether the risk to which such ground is directed arises from the mere fact of media presence at the particular hearing or hearings the subject of the application or whether the risk identified can be adequately addressed by exclusion of media representatives from a part only of such hearing or hearings;
- consider whether the reporting or disclosure restrictions which apply by operation of law, or which the court otherwise has power to order will provide sufficient protection to the party on whose behalf the application is made or any of the persons referred to in paragraph (3)(a) of the rule;
- consider the safety of the parties in cases in which the court considers there are particular physical or health risks against which reporting restrictions may be inadequate to afford protection;
- in the case of any vulnerable adult or child who is unrepresented before the court, consider the extent to which the court should of its own motion take steps to protect the welfare of that adult or child.

5.3 Paragraph (3)(a)(iii) of the rule permits exclusion where necessary 'for the orderly conduct of proceedings'. This enables the court to address practical problems presented by media attendance. In particular, it may be difficult or even impossible physically to accommodate all (or indeed any) media representatives who wish to attend a particular hearing on the grounds of the restricted size or layout of the court room in which it is being heard. Court staff will use their best efforts to identify more suitable accommodation in advance of any hearing which appears likely to attract particular media attention, and to move hearings to larger court rooms where possible. However, the court should not be required to adjourn a hearing in order for larger accommodation to be sought where this will involve significant disruption or delay in the proceedings.

5.4 Paragraph (3)(b) of the rule permits exclusion where, unless the media are excluded, justice will be impeded or prejudiced for some reason other than those set out in sub-paragraph (a). Reasons of administrative inconvenience are not sufficient. Examples of circumstances where the impact on justice of continued attendance might be sufficient to necessitate exclusion may include:

- a hearing relating to the parties' finances where the information being considered includes price sensitive information (such as confidential information which could affect the share price of a publicly quoted company); or

- any hearing at which a witness (other than a party) states for credible reasons that he or she will not give evidence in front of media representatives, or where there appears to the court to be a significant risk that a witness will not give full or frank evidence in the presence of media representatives.

5.5 In the event of a decision to exclude media representatives, the court should state brief reasons for the decision.

6 **Applications to exclude media representatives from all or part of proceedings**

6.1 The court may exclude media representatives on the permitted grounds of its own motion or after hearing representations from the interested persons listed at paragraph (5) of the rule. Where exclusion is proposed, any media representatives who are present are entitled to make representations about that proposal. There is, however, no requirement to adjourn proceedings to enable media representatives who are not present to attend in order to make such representations, and in such a case the court should not adjourn unless satisfied of the necessity to do so having regard to the additional cost and delay which would thereby be caused.

6.2 Applications to exclude media representatives should normally be dealt with as they arise and by way of oral representations, unless the court directs otherwise.

6.3 When media representatives are expected to attend a particular hearing (for example, where a party is encouraging media interest and attendance) and a party intends to apply to the court for the exclusion of the media, that party should, if practicable, give advance notice to the court, to the other parties and (where appointed) any children's guardian, officer of the service or Welsh Family Proceedings officer, NYAS or other representative of the child of any intention to seek the exclusion of media representatives from all or part of the proceedings. Equally, legal representatives and parties should ensure that witnesses are aware of the right of media representatives to attend and should notify the court at an early stage of the intention of any witness to request the exclusion of media representatives.

6.4 Prior notification by the court of a pending application for exclusion will not be given to media interests unless the court so directs. However, where such an application has been made, the applicant must where possible, notify the relevant media organisations [and should do so by means of the Press Association CopyDirect service, following the procedure set out in the Official Solicitor/CAFCASS Practice Note dated 18 March 2005].

PRACTICE DIRECTION 27C – ATTENDANCE OF MEDIA RREPRESENTATIVES AT HEARINGS IN FAMILY PROCEEDINGS (FAMILY PROCEEDINGS COURT)

This Practice Direction supplements FPR Part 27

1 **Introduction**

1.1 This Practice Direction supplements rule 27.11 of the Family Procedure Rules 2010 ('the Rules') and deals with the right of representatives of news gathering and reporting organisations ('media representatives') to attend at hearings of relevant proceedings subject to the discretion of the court to exclude such representatives from the whole or part of any hearing on specified grounds. It takes effect on 27th April 2009. References to a 'hearing' within this Practice Direction include reference to a directions appointment, whether conducted by the justices, a district judge or a justices' clerk.

2 **Matters unchanged by the rule**

2.1 Rule 27.11(1) contains an express exception in respect of hearings which are conducted for the purpose of judicially assisted conciliation or negotiation and media representatives do not have a right to attend these hearings. First Hearing Dispute Resolution appointments in private law Children Act cases will come within this exception to the extent that the justices, a district judge or a justices' clerk play an active part in the conciliation process. Where the justices, a district judge or a justices' clerk play no part in the conciliation process or where the conciliation element of a hearing is complete and the court is adjudicating upon the issues between the parties, media representatives should be permitted to attend subject to the discretion of the court to exclude them on the specified grounds. Conciliation meetings or negotiation conducted between the parties with the assistance of an officer of the service or a Welsh Family Proceedings officer, and without the presence of the justices, a district judge or a justices' clerk, are not 'hearings' within the meaning of this rule and media representatives have no right to attend such appointments.

The exception in rule 27.11(1) does not operate to exclude media representatives from:

- Hearings to consider applications brought under Parts IV and V of the Children Act 1989, including Case Management Conferences and Issues Resolution Hearings
- Hearings relating to findings of fact
- Interim hearings
- Final hearings.

The rights of media representatives to attend such hearings are limited only by the powers of the court to exclude such attendance on the limited grounds and subject to the procedures set out in paragraphs (3) to (5) of rule 27.11.

2.2 During any hearing, the court should consider whether the exception in rule 27.11(1) becomes applicable so that media representatives should be directed to withdraw.

2.3 The provisions of the rules permitting the attendance of media representatives and the disclosure to third parties of information relating to the proceedings do not entitle a media representative to receive or peruse court documents referred to in the course of evidence, submissions or decisions of the court (in particular, written reasons) without the permission of the court or otherwise in accordance with Part 12, Chapter 7 of the Family Procedure Rules 2010 and Practice Direction 12G.

2.4 The question of attendance of media representatives at hearings in family proceedings to which rule 27.11 and this guidance apply must be distinguished from statutory restrictions on publication and disclosure of information relating to proceedings, which continue to apply and are unaffected by the rule and this guidance.

2.5 The prohibition in section 97(2) of the Children Act 1989, on publishing material intended to or likely to identify a child as being involved in proceedings or the address or school of any such child, is limited to the duration of the proceedings. However, the limitations imposed by section 12 of the Administration of Justice Act 1960 on publication of information relating to certain proceedings in private apply during and after the proceedings. In addition, in the course of proceedings to which s 97(2) of the Children Act 1989 applies the court should consider whether at the conclusion of the proceedings there may be outstanding welfare issues which may require a continuation of the protection afforded during the course of the proceedings by s 97 (2) of the Children Act 1989 and which are not fully met by a direction under section 39 Children and Young Persons Act 1933, so that any party seeking such protection has an opportunity to apply to the county court or High Court for the appropriate order before the proceedings are finally concluded.

3 Aims of the guidance

3.1 This Practice Direction is intended to provide guidance regarding:

- the handling of applications to exclude media representatives from the whole or part of a hearing: and

- the exercise of the court's discretion to exclude media representatives whether upon the court's own motion or any such application.

3.2 While the guidance does not aim to cover all possible eventualities, it should be complied with so far as consistent in all the circumstances with the just determination of the proceedings.

4 Identification of media representatives as 'accredited'

4.1 Media representatives will be expected to carry with them identification sufficient to enable court staff, or if necessary the court itself, to verify that they are 'accredited' representatives of news gathering or reporting organisations within the meaning of the rule.

4.2 By virtue of paragraph (7) of the rule, it is for the Lord Chancellor to approve a scheme which will provide for accreditation. The Lord Chancellor has decided that the scheme operated by the UK Press Card Authority provides sufficient accreditation: a card issued under that scheme will be the expected form of identification, and production of the Card will be both necessary and sufficient to demonstrate accreditation.

4.3 A media representative unable to demonstrate accreditation in accordance with the UK Press Card Authority scheme so as to be able to attend by virtue of paragraph (2)(f) of the rule may nevertheless be permitted to attend at the court's discretion under paragraph (2)(g).

5 Exercise of the discretion to exclude media representatives from all or part of the proceedings

5.1 The rule anticipates and should be applied on the basis that media representatives have a right to attend family proceedings throughout save and to the extent that the court exercises its discretion to exclude them from the whole or part of any proceedings on one or more of the grounds set out in paragraph (3) of the rule.

5.2 When considering the question of exclusion on any of the grounds set out in paragraph (3) of the rule the court should–

- specifically identify whether the risk to which such ground is directed arises from the mere fact of media presence at the particular hearing or hearings the subject of the application or whether the risk identified can be adequately addressed by exclusion of media representatives from a part only of such hearing or hearings;
- consider whether the reporting or disclosure restrictions which apply by operation of law, or which the court otherwise has power to order will provide sufficient protection to the party on whose behalf the application is made or any of the persons referred to in paragraph (3)(a) of the rule;
- consider the safety of the parties in cases in which the court considers there are particular physical or health risks against which reporting restrictions may be inadequate to afford protection;
- in the case of any vulnerable adult or child who is unrepresented before the court, consider the extent to which the court should of its own motion take steps to protect the welfare of that adult or child.

5.3 Paragraph (3)(a)(iii) of the rule permits exclusion where necessary 'for the orderly conduct of proceedings'. This enables the court to address practical problems presented by media attendance. In particular, it may be difficult or even impossible physically to accommodate all (or indeed any) media representatives who wish to attend a particular hearing on the grounds of the restricted size or layout of the court room in which it is being heard. Court staff will use their best efforts to identify more suitable accommodation in advance of any hearing which appears likely to attract particular media attention, and to move hearings to larger court rooms where possible. However, the court should not be required to adjourn a hearing in order for larger accommodation to be sought where this will involve significant disruption or delay in the proceedings.

5.4 Paragraph (3)(b) of the rule permits exclusion where, unless the media are excluded, justice will be impeded or prejudiced for some reason other than those set out in sub-paragraph (a). Reasons of administrative inconvenience are not sufficient. An example of circumstances where the impact on justice of continued attendance might be sufficient to necessitate exclusion would be any hearing at which a witness (other than a party) states for credible reasons that he or she will not give evidence in front of media representatives, or where there appears to the court to be a significant risk that a witness will not give full or frank evidence in the presence of media representatives.

5.5 In the event of a decision to exclude media representatives, the court should state brief reasons for the decision.

6 Applications to exclude media representatives from all or part of proceedings.

6.1 The court may exclude media representatives on the permitted grounds of its own motion or after hearing representations from the interested persons listed at paragraph (5) of the rule. Where exclusion is proposed, any media representatives who are present are entitled to make representations about that proposal. There is, however, no requirement to adjourn proceedings to enable media representatives who are not present to attend in order to make such representations, and in such a case the court should not adjourn unless satisfied of the necessity to do so having regard to the additional cost and delay which would thereby be caused.

6.2 Applications to exclude media representatives should normally be dealt with as they arise and by way of oral representations, unless the court directs otherwise.

6.3 When media representatives are expected to attend a particular hearing (for example, where a party is encouraging media interest and attendance) and a party intends to apply to the court for the exclusion of the media, such party should, if practicable, give advance notice to the court, to the other parties and (where appointed) any children's guardian, officer of the service or Welsh Family Proceedings officer, NYAS or other representative of the child of any intention to seek the exclusion of media representatives from all or part of the proceedings. Equally, legal representatives and parties should ensure that witnesses are aware of the right of media representatives to attend and should notify the court at an early stage of the intention of any witness to request the exclusion of media representatives.

6.4 Prior notification by the court of a pending application for exclusion will not be given to media interests unless the court so directs. However, where such an application has been made, the applicant must where possible, notify the relevant media organisations [and should do so by means of the Press Association CopyDirect service, following the procedure set out in the Official Solicitor/CAFCASS Practice Note dated 18 March 2005].

PRACTICE DIRECTION 28A – COSTS

This Practice Direction is made by the President of the Family Division under the powers delegated to him by the Lord Chief Justice under Schedule 2, Part 1, paragraph 2(2) of the Constitutional Reform Act 2005, and is approved by the Parliamentary Under Secretary of State, by authority of the Lord Chancellor and comes into force on 6th April 2011

This Practice Direction supplements FPR Part 28

Application and modification of the CPR

1.1 Rule 28.2 provides that subject to rule 28.3 of the FPR and to paragraph (2) of rule 28.2, Parts 43, 44 (except rules 44.3(2) and(3), 44.9 to 44.12C, 44.13(1A) and (1B) and 44.18 to 20), 47 and 48 and rule 45.6 of the CPR apply to costs in family proceedings with the modifications listed in rule 28.2(1)(a) to (d). Rule 28.2(1)(c) refers to modifications in accordance with this Practice Direction.

1.2 In addition to the modifications to the CPR listed in rule 28.2(1), in rule 48.1(1)(b) after paragraph (ii) insert '(iii) section 68A of the Magistrates' Courts Act 1980.'.
1.3 Rule 28.2(2) provides that Part 47 and rules 44.3C and 45.6 of the CPR do not apply to proceedings in a magistrates' court.

Application and modification of the Practice Direction supplementing CPR Parts 43 to 48

2.1 For the purpose of proceedings to which these Rules apply, the Practice Direction about costs which supplements Parts 43 to 48 of the CPR ('the costs practice direction') will apply, but with the exclusions and modifications explained below to reflect the exclusions and modifications to those Parts of the CPR as they are applied by Part 28 of these Rules.
2.2 Rule 28.2(1) applies, with modifications and certain exceptions, Parts 43 to 48 of the CPR to costs in family proceedings. Paragraph 1.2 of this Practice Direction modifies rule 48.1(1)(b) when it applies to family proceedings. Rule 28.2(2), by way of exception, disapplies Part 47, rules 44.3C and 45.6 of the CPR in the case of family proceedings in a magistrates' court. Rule 28.3, again by way of exception, additionally disapplies CPR rule 44.3(1), (4) and (5) in the case of financial remedy proceedings, regardless of court.
2.3 The costs practice direction does not, therefore, apply in its entirety but with the exclusion of certain sections reflecting the non-application of certain rules of the CPR which those sections supplement.
2.4 The costs practice direction applies as follows–
- to family proceedings generally, other than in magistrates' courts, with the exception of sections 6, 15, 16, 17 and 23A;
- to family proceedings generally, in magistrates' courts only, with the exception of sections 6, 15, 16, 17, 23A and sections 28–49A;
- to financial remedy proceedings, other than in magistrates' courts, with the exception of section 6, paragraphs 8.1 to 8.4 of section 8 and sections 15, 16, 17 and 23A;
- to financial remedy proceedings in magistrates' courts only, with the exception of section 6, paragraphs 8.1 to 8.4 of section 8, sections 15, 16, 17, 23A and sections 28–49A.

2.5 All subsequent editions of the costs practice direction as and when they are published and come into effect shall in the same way extend to all family proceedings.
2.6 The costs practice direction includes provisions applicable to proceedings following changes in the manner in which legal services are funded pursuant to the Access to Justice Act 1999. It should be noted that although the cost of the premium in respect of legal costs insurance (section 29) or the cost of funding by a prescribed membership organisation (section 30) may be recoverable, family proceedings (within section 58A(2) of the Courts and Legal Services Act 1990) cannot be the subject of an enforceable conditional fee agreement.
2.7 Paragraph 1.4 of section 1 of the costs practice direction shall be modified as follows–

in the definition of 'counsel' for 'High court or in the county courts' substitute 'High Court, county courts or in a magistrates' court'.

General Interpretation of references in CPR

3.1 References in the costs practice direction to 'claimant' and 'defendant' are to be read as references to equivalent terms used in proceedings to which these Rules apply and other terms and expressions used in the costs practice direction shall be similarly treated.
3.2 References in CPR Parts 43 to 48 to other rules or Parts of the CPR shall be read, where there is an equivalent rule or Part in these Rules, to that equivalent rule or Part.

Costs in financial remedy proceedings

4.1 Rule 28.3 relates to the court's power to make costs orders in financial remedy proceedings. For the purposes of rule 28.3, 'financial remedy proceedings' are defined in accordance with rule 28.3(4)(b). That definition, which is more limited than the principal definition in rule 2.3(1), includes:

    (a)   an application for a financial order, except:

        (i)   an order for maintenance pending suit or an order for maintenance pending outcome of proceedings;

        (ii)   an interim periodical payments order or any other form of interim order for the purposes of rule 9.7(1)(a), (b), (c) and (e);

    (b)   an application for an order under Part 3 of the Matrimonial and Family Proceedings Act 1984 or Schedule 7 to the Civil Partnership Act 2004; and

    (c)   an application under section 10(2) of the Matrimonial Causes Act 1973 or section 48(2) of the Civil Partnership Act 2004.

4.2 Accordingly, it should be noted that:

    (a)   while most interim financial applications are excluded from rule 28.3, the rule does apply to an application for an interim variation order within rule 9.7(1)(d),

    (b)   rule 28.3 does not apply to an application for any of the following financial remedies:

        (i)   an order under Schedule 1 to the Children Act 1989;

        (ii)   an order under section 27 of the Matrimonial Causes Act 1973 or Part 9 of Schedule 5 to the Civil Partnership Act 2004;

        (iii)   an order under section 35 of the Matrimonial Causes Act 1973 or paragraph 69 of Schedule 5 to the Civil Partnership Act 2004; or

        (iv)   an order under Part 1 of the Domestic Proceedings and Magistrates' Courts Act 1978 or Schedule 6 to the Civil Partnership Act 2004.

4.3 Under rule 28.3 the court only has the power to make a costs order in financial remedy proceedings when this is justified by the litigation conduct of one of the parties. When determining whether and how to exercise this power the court will be required to take into account the list of factors set out in that rule. The court will not be able to take into account any offers to settle expressed to be 'without prejudice' or 'without prejudice save as to costs' in deciding what, if any, costs orders to make.

4.4 In considering the conduct of the parties for the purposes of rule 28.3(6) and (7) (including any open offers to settle), the court will have regard to the obligation of the parties to help the court to further the overriding objective (see rules 1.1 and 1.3) and will take into account the nature, importance and complexity of the issues in the case. This may be of particular significance in applications for variation orders and interim variation orders or other cases where there is a risk of the costs becoming disproportionate to the amounts in dispute.

4.5 Parties who intend to seek a costs order against another party in proceedings to which rule 28.3 applies should ordinarily make this plain in open correspondence or in skeleton arguments before the date of the hearing. In any case where summary assessment of costs awarded under rule 28.3 would be appropriate parties are under an obligation to file a statement of costs in CPR Form N260.

4.6 An interim financial order which includes an element to allow a party to deal with legal fees (see *A v A (maintenance pending suit: provision for legal fees)* [2001] 1 WLR 605; *G v G (maintenance pending suit; costs)* [2002] EWHC 306 (Fam); *McFarlane v McFarlane, Parlour v Parlour* [2004] EWCA Civ 872; *Moses-Taiga v Taiga* [2005] EWCA Civ 1013; *C v C (Maintenance Pending Suit: Legal Costs)* [2006] Fam Law 739; *Currey v Currey (No 2)* [2006] EWCA Civ 1338) is an order made pursuant to section 22 of the Matrimonial

Causes Act 1973 or an order under paragraph 38 of Schedule 5 of the 2004 Act, and is not a 'costs order' within the meaning of rule 28.3.

4.7 By virtue of rule 28.2(1), where rule 28.3 does not apply, the exercise of the court's discretion as to costs is governed by the relevant provisions of the CPR and in particular rule 44.3 (excluding r 44.3(2) and (3)).

PRACTICE DIRECTION 29A – HUMAN RIGHTS, JOINING THE CROWN

This Practice Direction supplements FPR Part 29, rule 29.5

(The Human Rights Act 1998)

Section 4 of the Human Rights Act 1998

1.1 Where a party has informed the court about–
   (a) a claim for a declaration of incompatibility in accordance with section 4 of the Human Rights Act 1998; or
   (b) an issue for the court to decide which may lead to the court considering making a declaration,

   then the court may at any time consider whether notice should be given to the Crown as required by that Act and give directions for the content and service of the notice. The rule allows a period of 21 days before the court will make the declaration but the court may vary this period of time.

1.2 The court will normally consider the issues and give the directions referred to in paragraph 1.1 at a directions hearing.

1.3 The notice must be served on the person named in the list published under section 17 of the Crown Proceedings Act 1947.

1.4 The notice will be in the form directed by the court and will normally include the directions given by the court. The notice will also be served on all the parties.

1.5 The court may require the parties to assist in the preparation of the notice.

1.6 Unless the court orders otherwise, the Minister or other person permitted by the Human Rights Act 1998 to be joined as a party must, if he or she wishes to be joined, give notice of his or her intention to be joined as a party to the court and every other party. Where the Minister has nominated a person to be joined as a party the notice must be accompanied by the written nomination.

(Section 5(2)(a) of the Human Rights Act 1998 permits a person nominated by a Minister of the Crown to be joined as a party. The nomination may be signed on behalf of the Minister.)

Section 9 of the Human Rights Act 1998

2.1 The procedure in paragraphs 1.1 to 1.6 also applies where a claim is made under sections 7(1)(a) and 9(3) of the Human Rights Act 1998 for damages in respect of a judicial act.

2.2 Notice must be given to the Lord Chancellor and should be served on the Treasury Solicitor on his behalf.

2.3 The notice will also give details of the judicial act, which is the subject of the claim for damages, and of the court that made it.

(Section 9(4) of the Human Rights Act 1998 provides that no award of damages may be made against the Crown as provided for in section 9(3) unless the appropriate person is joined in the proceedings. The appropriate person is the Minister responsible for the court concerned or a person or department nominated by him or her (section 9(5) of the Act).

PRACTICE DIRECTION 29B – HUMAN RIGHTS ACT 1998

This Practice Direction supplements FPR Part 29

1   It is directed that the following practice shall apply as from 2 October 2000 in all family proceedings:

Citation of authorities

2   When an authority referred to in s 2 of the Human Rights Act 1998 ("the Act") is to be cited at a hearing:
   (a)   the authority to be cited shall be an authoritative and complete report;
   (b)   the court must be provided with a list of authorities it is intended to cite and copies of the reports:
      (i)   in cases to which *Practice Direction (Family Proceedings: Court Bundles)* (10 March 2000) [2000] 1 FLR 536 applies, as part of the bundle;
      (ii) otherwise, not less than 2 clear days before the hearing; and
   (c)   copies of the complete original texts issued by the European Court and Commission, either paper based or from the Court's judgment database (HUDOC) which is available on the internet, may be used.

Allocation to judges

3   (1)   The hearing and determination of the following will be confined to a High Court judge:
      (a)   a claim for a declaration of incompatibility under s 4 of the Act; or
      (b)   an issue which may lead to the court considering making such a declaration.
   (2)   The hearing and determination of a claim made under the Act in respect of a judicial act shall be confined in the High Court to a High Court judge and in county courts to a circuit judge.

Issued with the concurrence and approval of the Lord Chancellor.

PRACTICE DIRECTION 30A – APPEALS

This Practice Direction supplements FPR Part 30
1   This practice direction applies to all appeals to which Part 30 applies.

Routes of appeal

2.1   The following table sets out to which court or judge an appeal is to be made (subject to obtaining any necessary permission) –

Decision of:	*Appeal made to:*
Magistrates' Court	Circuit judge
District judge of a county court	Circuit judge
District judge of the High Court	High Court judge
District judge of the principal registry of the Family Division	High Court Judge
Costs judge	High Court Judge
Circuit judge or recorder	Court of Appeal
High Court judge	Court of Appeal

(Provisions setting out routes of appeal include section 16(1) of the Senior Courts Act 1981 (as amended); section 77(1) of the County Courts Act 1984 (as amended) and the Access to Justice Act 1999 (Destination of Appeals) (Family Proceedings) Order 2009 (see paragraphs 9.1 to 9.12 below. The Family Proceedings (Allocation to Judiciary) (Appeals) Directions 2009 provide for an appeal from a magistrates' court to be heard by a Circuit judge.

The routes of appeal from an order or decision relating to contempt of court of a magistrates' court under section 63(3) of the Magistrates' Courts Act 1980 and of a county court and the High Court are set out in section 13(2) of the Administration of Justice Act 1960. Appeals under section 8(1) of the Gender Recognition Act 2004 lie to the High Court (see section 8 of the 2004 Act). The procedure for appeals to the Court of Appeal is governed by the Civil Procedure Rules 1998, in particular CPR Part 52.).

2.2 Where the decision to be appealed is a decision in a Part 19 (Alternative Procedure For Applications) application on a point of law in a case which did not involve any substantial dispute of fact, the court to which the appeal lies, where that court is the High Court or a county court and unless the appeal would lie to the Court of Appeal in any event, must consider whether to order the appeal to be transferred to the Court of Appeal under rule 30.13 (Assignment of Appeals to the Court of Appeal).

Grounds for appeal

3.1 Rule 30.12 (hearing of appeals) sets out the circumstances in which the appeal court will allow an appeal.
3.2 The grounds of appeal should–
   (a)   set out clearly the reasons why rule 30.12 (3)(a) or (b) is said to apply; and
   (b)   specify in respect of each ground, whether the ground raises an appeal on a point of law or is an appeal against a finding of fact.

Permission to appeal

4.1 Rule 30.3 (Permission) sets out the circumstances when permission to appeal is required. At present permission to appeal is required where the decision appealed against was made by a district judge or a costs judge. However, no permission is required where rule 30.3(2) (appeals against a committal order or a secure accommodation order under section 25 of the Children Act 1989) applies.

(The requirement of permission to appeal may be imposed by a practice direction – see rule 30.3(1)(b) (Permission).).

Court to which permission to appeal application should be made
4.2 An application for permission should be made orally at the hearing at which the decision to be appealed against is made.
4.3 Where–
   (a)   no application for permission to appeal is made at the hearing; or
   (b)   the lower court refuses permission to appeal, an application for permission to appeal may be made to the appeal court in accordance with rules 30.3(3) and (4) (Permission).

(Rule 30.1(3) defines 'lower court'.)
4.4 Where no application for permission to appeal has been made in accordance with rule 30.3(3)(a) (Permission) but a party requests further time to make such an application the court may adjourn the hearing to give that party an opportunity to do so.
4.5 There is no appeal from a decision of the appeal court to allow or refuse permission to appeal to that court (although where the appeal court, without a hearing, refuses permission to appeal, the person seeking permission may request that decision to be

reconsidered at a hearing-see section 54(4) of the Access to Justice Act 1999 and rule 30.3 (5) (Permission)).

Material omission from a judgment of the lower court

4.6 Where a party's advocate considers that there is a material omission from a judgment of the lower court or, in a magistrates' court, the written reasons for the decision of the lower court (including inadequate reasons for the lower court's decision), the advocate should before the drawing of the order give the lower court which made the decision the opportunity of considering whether there is an omission and should not immediately use the omission as grounds for an application to appeal.

4.7 Paragraph 4.8 below applies where there is an application to the lower court for permission to appeal on the grounds of a material omission from a judgment of the lower court. Paragraph 4.9 below applies where there is an application for permission to appeal to the appeal court on the grounds of a material omission from a judgment of the lower court. Paragraphs 4.8 and 4.9 do not apply where the lower court is a magistrates' court.

4.8 Where the application for permission to appeal is made to the lower court, the court which made the decision must –

(a) consider whether there is a material omission and adjourn for that purpose if necessary; and

(b) where the conclusion is that there has been such an omission, provide additions to the judgment.

4.9 Where the application for permission to appeal is made to the appeal court, the appeal court –

(a) must consider whether there is a material omission; and

(b) where the conclusion is that there has been such an omission, may adjourn the application and remit the case to the lower court with an invitation to provide additions to the judgment.

Consideration of Permission without a hearing

4.10 An application for permission to appeal may be considered by the appeal court without a hearing.

4.11 If permission is granted without a hearing the parties will be notified of that decision and the procedure in paragraphs 6.1 to 6.8 will then apply.

4.12 If permission is refused without a hearing the parties will be notified of that decision with the reasons for it. The decision is subject to the appellant's right to have it reconsidered at an oral hearing. This may be before the same judge.

4.13 A request for the decision to be reconsidered at an oral hearing must be filed at the appeal court within 7 days after service of the notice that permission has been refused. A copy of the request must be served by the appellant on the respondent at the same time.

Permission hearing

4.14 Where an appellant, who is represented, makes a request for a decision to be reconsidered at an oral hearing, the appellant's advocate must, at least 4 days before the hearing, in a brief written statement –

(a) inform the court and the respondent of the points which the appellant proposes to raise at the hearing;

(b) set out the reasons why permission should be granted notwithstanding the reasons given for the refusal of permission; and

(c) confirm, where applicable, that the requirements of paragraph 4.17 have been complied with (appellant in receipt of services funded by the Legal Services Commission).

4.15 The respondent will be given notice of a permission hearing, but is not required to attend unless requested by the court to do so.

4.16 If the court requests the respondent's attendance at the permission hearing, the appellant must supply the respondent with a copy of the appeal bundle (see paragraph 5.9) within 7 days of being notified of the request, or such other period as the court may direct. The costs of providing that bundle shall be borne by the appellant initially, but will form part of the costs of the permission application.

Appellants in receipt of services funded by the Legal Services Commission applying for permission to appeal

4.17 Where the appellant is in receipt of services funded by the Legal Services Commission (or legally aided) and permission to appeal has been refused by the appeal court without a hearing, the appellant must send a copy of the reasons the appeal court gave for refusing permission to the relevant office of the Legal Services Commission as soon as it has been received from the court. The court will require confirmation that this has been done if a hearing is requested to re-consider the question of permission.

Limited permission

4.18 Where a court under rule 30.3 (Permission) gives permission to appeal on some issues only, it will –

    (a)   refuse permission on any remaining issues; or

    (b)   reserve the question of permission to appeal on any remaining issues to the court hearing the appeal.

4.19 If the court reserves the question of permission under paragraph 4.18(b), the appellant must, within 14 days after service of the court's order, inform the appeal court and the respondent in writing whether the appellant intends to pursue the reserved issues. If the appellant does intend to pursue the reserved issues, the parties must include in any time estimate for the appeal hearing, their time estimate for the reserved issues.

4.20 If the appeal court refuses permission to appeal on the remaining issues without a hearing and the applicant wishes to have that decision reconsidered at an oral hearing, the time limit in rule 30.3(6) (Permission) shall apply. Any application for an extension of this time limit should be made promptly. The court hearing the appeal on the issues for which permission has been granted will not normally grant, at the appeal hearing, an application to extend the time limit in rule 30.3 (6) for the remaining issues.

4.21 If the appeal court refuses permission to appeal on remaining issues at or after an oral hearing, the application for permission to appeal on those issues cannot be renewed at the appeal hearing (see section 54(4) of the Access to Justice Act 1999).

Respondents' costs of permission applications

4.22 In most cases, applications for permission to appeal will be determined without the court requesting –

    (a)   submissions from; or

    (b)   if there is an oral hearing, attendance by, the respondent.

4.23 Where the court does not request submissions from or attendance by the respondent, costs will not normally be allowed to a respondent who volunteers submissions or attendance.

4.24 Where the court does request –

    (a)   submissions from; or

    (b)   attendance by the respondent, the court will normally allow the costs of the respondent if permission is refused.

Appellant's notice

5.1 An appellant's notice must be filed and served in all cases. Where an application for permission to appeal is made to the appeal court it must be applied for in the appellant's notice.

Human Rights

5.2 Where the appellant seeks–
   (a) to rely on any issue under the Human Rights Act 1998; or
   (b) a remedy available under that Act, for the first time in an appeal the appellant must include in the appeal notice the information required by rule 29.5(2).

5.3 Practice Direction 29A (Human Rights, Joining the Crown) will apply as if references to the directions hearing were to the application for permission to appeal.

Extension of time for filing appellant's notice

5.4 If an extension of time is required for filing the appellant's notice the application must be made in that notice. The notice should state the reason for the delay and the steps taken prior to the application being made.

5.5 Where the appellant's notice includes an application for an extension of time and permission to appeal has been given or is not required the respondent has the right to be heard on that application and must be served with a copy of the appeal bundle (see paragraph 5.9). However, a respondent who unreasonably opposes an extension of time runs the risk of being ordered to pay the appellant's costs of that application.

5.6 If an extension of time is given following such an application the procedure at paragraphs 6.1 to 6.8 applies.

Applications

5.7 Notice of an application to be made to the appeal court for a remedy incidental to the appeal (e.g. an interim injunction under rule 20.2 (Orders for interim remedies)) may be included in the appeal notice or in a Part 18 (Procedure For Other Applications in Proceedings) application notice.

(Paragraph 13 of this practice direction contains other provisions relating to applications.).

Documents

5.8 The appellant must file the following documents together with an appeal bundle (see paragraph 5.9) with his or her appellant's notice–
   (a) two additional copies of the appellant's notice for the appeal court;
   (b) one copy of the appellant's notice for each of the respondents;
   (c) one copy of the appellant's skeleton argument for each copy of the appellant's notice that is filed;
   (d) a sealed or stamped copy of the order being appealed or a copy of the notice of the making of an order;
   (e) a copy of any order giving or refusing permission to appeal, together with a copy of the court's reasons for allowing or refusing permission to appeal;
   (f) any witness statements or affidavits in support of any application included in the appellant's notice.

5.9 An appellant must include the following documents in his or her appeal bundle–
   (a) a sealed or stamped copy of the appellant's notice;
   (b) a sealed or stamped copy of the order being appealed, or a copy of the notice of the making of an order;

(c) a copy of any order giving or refusing permission to appeal, together with a copy of the court's reasons for allowing or refusing permission to appeal;
(d) any affidavit or witness statement filed in support of any application included in the appellant's notice;
(e) where the appeal is against a consent order, a statement setting out the change in circumstances since the order was agreed or other circumstances justifying a review or rehearing;
(f) a copy of the appellant's skeleton argument;
(g) a transcript or note of judgment or, in a magistrates' court, written reasons for the court's decision (see paragraph 5.23), and in cases where permission to appeal was given by the lower court or is not required those parts of any transcript of evidence which are directly relevant to any question at issue on the appeal;
(h) the application form;
(i) any application notice (or case management documentation) relevant to the subject of the appeal;
(j) any other documents which the appellant reasonably considers necessary to enable the appeal court to reach its decision on the hearing of the application or appeal; and
(k) such other documents as the court may direct.

5.10 All documents that are extraneous to the issues to be considered on the application or the appeal must be excluded. The appeal bundle may include affidavits, witness statements, summaries, experts' reports and exhibits but only where these are directly relevant to the subject matter of the appeal.

5.11 Where the appellant is represented, the appeal bundle must contain a certificate signed by the appellant's solicitor, counsel or other representative to the effect that the appellant has read and understood paragraph 5.10 and that the composition of the appeal bundle complies with it.

5.12 Where it is not possible to file all the above documents, the appellant must indicate which documents have not yet been filed and the reasons why they are not currently available. The appellant must then provide a reasonable estimate of when the missing document or documents can be filed and file them as soon as reasonably practicable.

Skeleton arguments

5.13 The appellant's notice must, subject to paragraphs 5.14 and 5.15, be accompanied by a skeleton argument. Alternatively the skeleton argument may be included in the appellant's notice. Where the skeleton argument is so included it will not form part of the notice for the purposes of rule 30.9 (Amendment of appeal notice).

5.14 Where it is impracticable for the appellant's skeleton argument to accompany the appellant's notice it must be filed and served on all respondents within 14 days of filing the notice.

5.15 An appellant who is not represented need not file a skeleton argument but is encouraged to do so since this will be helpful to the court.

5.16 A skeleton argument must contain a numbered list of the points which the party wishes to make. These should both define and confine the areas of controversy. Each point should be stated as concisely as the nature of the case allows.

5.17 A numbered point must be followed by a reference to any document on which the party wishes to rely.

5.18 A skeleton argument must state, in respect of each authority cited–
(a) the proposition of law that the authority demonstrates; and
(b) the parts of the authority (identified by page or paragraph references) that support the proposition.

5.19 If more than one authority is cited in support of a given proposition, the skeleton argument must briefly state the reason for taking that course.

5.20 The statement referred to in paragraph 5.19 should not materially add to the length of the skeleton argument but should be sufficient to demonstrate, in the context of the argument–

    (a)   the relevance of the authority or authorities to that argument; and

    (b)   that the citation is necessary for a proper presentation of that argument.

5.21 The cost of preparing a skeleton argument which–

    (a)   does not comply with the requirements set out in this paragraph; or

    (b)   was not filed within the time limits provided by this Practice Direction (or any further time granted by the court), will not be allowed on assessment except to the extent that the court otherwise directs.

5.22 The appellant should consider what other information the appeal court will need. This may include a list of persons who feature in the case or glossaries of technical terms. A chronology of relevant events will be necessary in most appeals.

Suitable record of the judgment

5.23 Where the judgment to be appealed has been officially recorded by the court, an approved transcript of that record should accompany the appellant's notice. Photocopies will not be accepted for this purpose. However, where there is no officially recorded judgment, the following documents will be acceptable–

Written judgments – Where the judgment was made in writing a copy of that judgment endorsed with the judge's signature.

Written reasons – in a magistrates' court, a copy of the written reasons for the courts decision.

Note of judgment – When judgment was not officially recorded or made in writing a note of the judgment (agreed between the appellant's and respondent's advocates) should be submitted for approval to the judge whose decision is being appealed. If the parties cannot agree on a single note of the judgment, both versions should be provided to that judge with an explanatory letter. For the purpose of an application for permission to appeal the note need not be approved by the respondent or the lower court judge.

Advocates' notes of judgments where the appellant is unrepresented – When the appellant was unrepresented in the lower court it is the duty of any advocate for the respondent to make the advocate's note of judgment promptly available, free of charge to the appellant where there is no officially recorded judgment or if the court so directs. Where the appellant was represented in the lower court it is the duty of the appellant's own former advocate to make that advocate's note available in these circumstances. The appellant should submit the note of judgment to the appeal court.

5.24 An appellant may not be able to obtain an official transcript or other suitable record of the lower court's decision within the time within which the appellant's notice must be filed. In such cases the appellant's notice must still be completed to the best of the appellant's ability on the basis of the documentation available. However it may be amended subsequently with the permission of the appeal court in accordance with rule 30.9 (Amendment of appeal notice).

Advocates' notes of judgments

5.25 Advocates' brief (or, where appropriate, refresher) fee includes –

    (a)   remuneration for taking a note of the judgment of the court;

    (b)   having the note transcribed accurately;

    (c)   attempting to agree the note with the other side if represented;

(d) submitting the note to the judge for approval where appropriate;
(e) revising it if so requested by the judge,
(f) providing any copies required for the appeal court, instructing solicitors and lay client; and
(g) providing a copy of the note to an unrepresented appellant.

Appeals from decision made by a family proceedings court under Parts 4 and 4A of the Family Law Act 1996

5.26 Where the appeal is brought against the making of a hospital order or a guardianship order under the Mental Health Act 1983, the court officer for the court from which the appeal is brought must send a copy of any written evidence considered by the magistrates under section 37(1)(a) of that Act to the appeal court.

Appeals under section 8(1) of the Gender Recognition Act 2004

5.27 Paragraph 5.28 to 5.30 apply where the appeal is brought under section 8(1) of the Gender Recognition Act 2004 to the High Court on a point of law against a decision by the Gender Recognition Panel to reject the application under sections 1(1), 5(2), 5(A)(2) or 6(1) of the 2004 Act.

5.28 The appeal notice must be –
(a) filed in the principal registry of the Family Division; and
(b) served on the Secretary of State and the President of the Gender Recognition Panels.

5.29 The Secretary of State may appear and be heard in the proceedings on the appeal.

5.30 Where the High Court issues a gender recognition certificate under section 8(3)(a) of the Gender Recognition Act 2004, the court officer must send a copy of that certificate to the Secretary of State.

Transcripts or Notes of Evidence

5.31 When the evidence is relevant to the appeal an official transcript of the relevant evidence must be obtained. Transcripts or notes of evidence are generally not needed for the purpose of determining an application for permission to appeal.

Notes of evidence

5.32 If evidence relevant to the appeal was not officially recorded, a typed version of the judge's (including a district judge (magistrates' courts) or justices' clerk's /assistant clerk's notes of evidence must be obtained.

Transcripts at public expense

5.33 Where the lower court or the appeal court is satisfied that–
(a) an unrepresented appellant; or
(b) an appellant whose legal representation is provided free of charge to the appellant and not funded by the Community Legal Service, is in such poor financial circumstances that the cost of a transcript would be an excessive burden the court may certify that the cost of obtaining one official transcript should be borne at public expense.

5.34 In the case of a request for an official transcript of evidence or proceedings to be paid for at public expense, the court must also be satisfied that there are reasonable grounds for appeal.

Whenever possible a request for a transcript at public expense should be made to the lower court when asking for permission to appeal.

Filing and service of appellant's notice

5.35 Rule 30.4 (Appellant's notice) sets out the procedure and time limits for filing and serving an appellant's notice. Subject to paragraph 5.36, the appellant must file the appellant's notice at the appeal court within such period as may be directed by the lower court, which should not normally exceed 14 days or, where the lower court directs no such period within 21 days of the date of the decision that the appellant wishes to appeal.

5.36 Rule 30.4(3) (Appellant's notice) provides that unless the appeal court orders otherwise, where the appeal is against an order under section 38(1) of the 1989 Act, the appellant must file the appellant's notice within 7 days beginning with the date of the decision of the lower court.

5.37 Where the lower court announces its decision and reserves the reasons for its judgment or order until a later date, it should, in the exercise of powers under rule 30.4 (2)(a))(Appellant's notice), fix a period for filing the appellant's notice at the appeal court that takes this into account.

5.38 Except where the appeal court orders otherwise a sealed or stamped copy of the appellant's notice, including any skeleton arguments must be served on all respondents and other persons referred to in rule 30.4(5) (Appellant's notice) in accordance with the timetable prescribed by rule 30.4(4)) (Appellant's notice) except where this requirement is modified by paragraph 5.14 in which case the skeleton argument should be served as soon as it is filed.

5.39 Where the appellant's notice is to be served on a child, then rule 6.33 (supplementary provision relating to service on children) applies and unless the appeal court orders otherwise a sealed or stamped copy of the appellant's notice, including any skeleton arguments must be served on the persons or bodies mentioned in rule 6.33(2). For example, the appeal notice must be served on any children's guardian, welfare officer or children and family reporter who is appointed in the proceedings.

5.40 Unless the court otherwise directs, a respondent need not take any action when served with an appellant's notice until such time as notification is given to the respondent that permission to appeal has been given.

5.41 The court may dispense with the requirement for service of the notice on a respondent.

5.42 Unless the appeal court directs otherwise, the appellant must serve on the respondent the appellant's notice and skeleton argument (but not the appeal bundle),where the appellant is applying for permission to appeal in the appellant's notice.

5.43 Where permission to appeal –

    (a)   has been given by the lower court; or
    (b)   is not required, the appellant must serve the appeal bundle on the respondent and the persons mentioned in paragraph 5.39 with the appellant's notice.

Amendment of Appeal Notice

5.44 An appeal notice may be amended with permission. Such an application to amend and any application in opposition will normally be dealt with at the hearing unless that course would cause unnecessary expense or delay in which case a request should be made for the application to amend to be heard in advance.

Procedure after permission is obtained

6.1 This paragraph sets out the procedure where –

    (a)   permission to appeal is given by the appeal court; or
    (b)   the appellant's notice is filed in the appeal court and–

        (i)   permission was given by the lower court; or
        (ii)   permission is not required.

6.2 If the appeal court gives permission to appeal, the appeal bundle must be served on each of the respondents within 7 days of receiving the order giving permission to appeal.
6.3 The appeal court will send the parties –
  (a) notification of the date of the hearing or the period of time (the 'listing window') during which the appeal is likely to be heard;
  (b) where permission is granted by the appeal court a copy of the order giving permission to appeal; and
  (c) any other directions given by the court.
6.4 Where the appeal court grants permission to appeal, the appellant must add the following documents to the appeal bundle –
  (a) the respondent's notice and skeleton argument (if any);
  (b) those parts of the transcripts of evidence which are directly relevant to any question at issue on the appeal;
  (c) the order granting permission to appeal and, where permission to appeal was granted at an oral hearing, the transcript (or note) of any judgment which was given; and
  (d) any document which the appellant and respondent have agreed to add to the appeal bundle in accordance with paragraph 7.16.
6.5 Where permission to appeal has been refused on a particular issue, the appellant must remove from the appeal bundle all documents that are relevant only to that issue.

Time estimates

6.6 If the appellant is legally represented, the appeal court must be notified, in writing, of the advocate's time estimate for the hearing of the appeal.
6.7 The time estimate must be that of the advocate who will argue the appeal. It should exclude the time required by the court to give judgment.
6.8 A court officer will notify the respondent of the appellant's time estimate and if the respondent disagrees with the time estimate the respondent must inform the court within 7 days of the notification. In the absence of such notification the respondent will be deemed to have accepted the estimate proposed on behalf of the appellant.

Respondent

7.1 A respondent who wishes to ask the appeal court to vary the order of the lower court in any way must appeal and permission will be required on the same basis as for an appellant.

   (Paragraph 3.2 applies to grounds of appeal by a respondent.).
7.2 A respondent who wishes to appeal or who wishes to ask the appeal court to uphold the order of the lower court for reasons different from or additional to those given by the lower court must file a respondent's notice.
7.3 A respondent who does not file a respondent's notice will not be entitled, except with the permission of the court, to rely on any reason not relied on in the lower court. This paragraph and paragraph 7.2 do not apply where the appeal is against an order under section 38(1) of the 1989 Act (see rule 30.5(7) (Respondent's notice)).
7.4 Paragraphs 5.3 (Human Rights and extension for time for filing appellant's notice) and 5.4 to 5.6 (extension of time for filing appellant's notice) of this practice direction also apply to a respondent and a respondent's notice.

Time limits

7.5 The time limits for filing a respondent's notice are set out in rule 30.5(4) and (5) (Respondent's notice).
7.6 Where an extension of time is required the extension must be requested in the

respondent's notice and the reasons why the respondent failed to act within the specified time must be included.

7.7 Except where paragraphs 7.8 and 7.10 apply, the respondent must file a skeleton argument for the court in all cases where the respondent proposes to address arguments to the court. The respondent's skeleton argument may be included within a respondent's notice. Where a skeleton argument is included within a respondent's notice it will not form part of the notice for the purposes of rule 30.9 (Amendment of appeal notice).

7.8 A respondent who–

(a) files a respondent's notice; but
(b) does not include a skeleton argument with that notice, must file the skeleton argument within 14 days of filing the notice.

7.9 A respondent who does not file a respondent's notice but who files a skeleton argument must file that skeleton argument at least 7 days before the appeal hearing.

(Rule 30.5(4) (Respondent's notice) sets out the period for filing a respondent's notice.).

7.10 A respondent who is not represented need not file a skeleton argument but is encouraged to do so in order to assist the court.

7.11 The respondent must serve the skeleton argument on –

(a) the appellant; and
(b) any other respondent; at the same time as the skeleton argument is filed at court. Where a child is an appellant or respondent the skeleton argument must also be served on the persons listed in rule 6.33(2) unless the court directs otherwise.

7.12 A respondent's skeleton argument must conform to the directions at paragraphs 5.16 to 5.22 with any necessary modifications. It should, where appropriate, answer the arguments set out in the appellant's skeleton argument.

Applications within respondent's notices

7.13 A respondent may include an application within a respondent's notice in accordance with paragraph 5.7.

Filing respondent's notices and skeleton arguments

7.14 The respondent must file the following documents with the respondent's notice in every case –

(a) two additional copies of the respondent's notice for the appeal court; and
(b) one copy each for the appellant, any other respondents and any persons referred to in paragraph 5.39.

7.15 The respondent may file a skeleton argument with the respondent's notice and –

(a) where doing so must file two copies; and
(b) where not doing so must comply with paragraph 7.8.

7.16 If the respondent considers documents in addition to those filed by the appellant to be necessary to enable the appeal court to reach its decision on the appeal and wishes to rely on those documents, any amendments to the appeal bundle should be agreed with the appellant if possible.

7.17 If the representatives for the parties are unable to reach agreement, the respondent may prepare a supplemental bundle.

7.18 The respondent must file any supplemental bundle so prepared, together with the requisite number of copies for the appeal court, at the appeal court –

(a) with the respondent's notice; or
(b) if a respondent's notice is not filed, within 21 days after the respondent is served with the appeal bundle.

7.19 The respondent must serve –
- (a) the respondent's notice;
- (b) the skeleton argument (if any); and
- (c) the supplemental bundle (if any), on –
  - (i) the appellant; and
  - (ii) any other respondent;

at the same time as those documents are filed at the court. Where a child is an appellant or respondent the documents referred to in paragraphs (a) to (c) above must also be served on the persons listed in rule 6.33(2) unless the court directs otherwise.

Appeals to the High Court

Application

8.1 The appellant's notice must be filed in –
- (a) the principal registry of the Family Division; or
- (b) the district registry which is nearest to the court from which the appeal lies.

8.2 A respondent's notice must be filed at the court where the appellant's notice was filed.

8.3 In the case of appeals from district judges of the High Court, applications for permission and any other applications in the appeal, appeals may be heard and directions in the appeal may be given by a High Court Judge or by any person authorised under section 9 of the Senior Courts Act 1981 to act as a judge of the High Court.

Appeals to a county court

Appeals to a judge of a county court from a district judge

9.1 The Designated Family Judge in consultation with the Family Division Liaison Judges has responsibility for the allocation of appeals from decisions of district judges to circuit judges.

Appeals to a county court from a magistrates' court

Appeals under section 111A of the Magistrates' Courts Act 1980 ('the 1980 Act') from a magistrates' court to a county court on the ground that the decision is wrong in law or in excess of jurisdiction

9.2 As a result of an amendment to section 111 of the 1980 Act by the Access to Justice Act 1999 (Destination of Appeals) (Family Proceedings) Order 2009 ('the Destination Order') an application to have a case stated for the opinion of the High Court under section 111 of that Act may not be made in relation to family proceedings. Family proceedings for those purposes are defined as –
- (a) proceedings which, by virtue of section 65 of the 1980 Act, are or may be treated as family proceedings for the purposes of that Act; and
- (b) proceedings under the Child Support Act 1991.

9.3 Section 111A of the 1980 Act, which is inserted by article 4(3) of the Destination Order, provides that in family proceedings as defined in paragraph 9.2 above a person may appeal to a county court on the ground that a decision is wrong in law or is in excess of jurisdiction; this appeal to a county court replaces the procedure for making an application to have a case stated. Section 111A(3)(a) provides that no appeal may be brought under section 111A if there is a right of appeal to a county court against the decision otherwise than under that section.

9.4 Subject to section 111A of the 1980 Act and any other enactment, the following rules in Part 30 apply to appeals under section 111A of the 1980 Act –

(a) 30.1 (scope and interpretation);
(b) 30.2 (parties to comply with the practice direction);
(c) 30.4 (appellant's notice);
(d) 30.6 (grounds of appeal);
(e) 30.8 (stay); and
(f) 30.9 (amendment of appeal notice).

9.5 Section 111A(4) of the 1980 Act provides that the notice of appeal must be filed within 21 days after the day on which the decision of the magistrates' court was given. The notice of appeal should also be served within this period of time. The time period for filing the appellant's notice in rule 30.4 (2) does not apply. There can be no extension of this 21 day time limit under rule 4.1(3)(a).

Other statutory rights of appeal from a magistrates court and the court at which the appellants notice is to be filed-provisions applying to those appeals and appeals under section 111A of the 1980 Act

9.6 The effect of the Destination Order is that appeals against decisions of magistrates' courts in family proceedings shall lie to a county court instead of to the High Court. In addition to replacing appeals by way of case stated by amending the 1980 Act as outlined above, the Destination Order amends the statutory provisions listed in paragraph 9.7 below to provide for the appeals under those provisions to lie to a county court instead of to the High Court Paragraph 9.7 also refers to the amendment to the 1980 Act for completeness.

9.7 Paragraph 9.8 and 9.9 below apply to appeals under –

(a) section 4(7) of the Maintenance Orders Act 1958;
(b) section 29 of the Domestic Proceedings and Magistrates' Courts Act 1978;
(c) section 60(5) of the Family Law 1986;
(d) section 94(1) to (9) of the Children Act 1989;
(e) section 61 of the Family Law Act 1996;
(f) sections 10(1)(a) to (3) and 13 (1) and (2) of the Crime and Disorder Act 1998; or
(g) section 111A of the 1980 Act.

9.8 Subject to any enactment or to any directions made by the President of the Family Division in exercise of the powers conferred on him under section 9 of the Courts and Legal Services Act 1990, a district judge may–

(a) dismiss an appeal;
  (i) for want of prosecution; or
  (ii) with the consent of the parties; or
(b) give leave for the appeal to be withdrawn,

and may deal with any question of costs arising out of the dismissal or withdrawal. Unless the court directs otherwise, any interlocutory application in an appeal under the statutory provisions listed in paragraph 9.7 may be made to a district judge.

9.9 Subject to paragraph 9.10 below, the appellant's notice and other documents required to be filed by rule 30.4 and this practice direction shall where the appeal is against the making by a magistrates' court of any order or any refusal by a magistrates' court to make such an order –

(a) in proceedings listed in Schedule 1 to this Practice Direction, be filed in a care centre within the meaning of article 2 (b) of the Allocation and Transfer of Proceedings Order 2008;
(b) in proceedings under the Adoption and Children Act 2002, be filed in an adoption centre or an intercountry adoption centre within the meaning of article 2 (c) and (d) of the Allocation and Transfer of Proceedings Order 2008; and

(c) in any other case, be filed in a family hearing centre within the meaning of article 2(a) of that Order.

9.10 Where the appeal is an appeal from a decision of a magistrates' court under section 94 of the 1989 Act or section 61 of the Family Law Act 1996, the documents required to be filed by rule 30.4 and this practice direction may be filed in the principal registry of the Family Division of the High Court.

9.11 Article 11 of the Destination Order amends article 3 of the Allocation and Transfer of Proceedings Order 2008 to provide that the principal registry of the Family Division of the High Court is treated as a county court for the purposes of appeals from decisions of a magistrates' court under section 94 of the Children Act 1989 and section 61 of the Family Law Act 1996.

9.12 This practice direction applies to appeals under the statutory provisions listed in paragraph 9.7 with the following modifications and any other necessary modifications –

(a) after paragraph 5.6 insert – "5.6A Paragraphs 5.4 to 5.6 do not apply to an appeal to a county court under section 111A of the Magistrates' Courts Act 1980."
(b) in paragraph 5.35, insert "and 5.36A" after "subject to paragraph 5.36";
(c) after paragraph 5.36 insert – "5.36A Where the appeal is to a judge of a county court under section 111A of the Magistrates' Courts Act 1980, the appellant's notice must be filed and served within 21 days after the day on which the decision of the lower court was given.".

Appeals to a county court from the Child Maintenance and Enforcement Commission ('the Commission'): Deduction order appeals

9.13 A 'deduction order appeal' is an appeal under regulation 25AB(1)(a) to (d) of the Child Support (Collection and Enforcement) Regulations 1992 (S.I. 1992/1989)('the Collection and Enforcement Regulations').A deduction order appeal is an appeal against –

(a) the making of a regular deduction order under section 32A of the Child Support Act 1991 ('the 1991 Act');
(b) a decision on an application to review a regular deduction order;
(c) a decision to withhold consent to the disapplication of sections 32G(1) and 32H(2)(b) of the 1991 Act which has the effect of unfreezing funds in the liable person's account; or
(d) the making of a final lump sum deduction order under section 32F of the 1991 Act. A deduction order appeal lies to a county court from the Commission as a result of regulation 25AB(1) of the Collection and Enforcement Regulations.

9.14 The rules in Part 30 apply to deduction order appeals with the amendments set out in paragraphs 9.15 to 9.27 and 9.29 and 9.30 below. The rules in Part 30 also apply to appeals against the decision of a district judge in proceedings relating to a deduction order appeal with the amendments set out in paragraph 9.28 below.

9.15 'The respondent' means –

(a) the Commission and any person other than the appellant who was served with an order under section 32A(1), 32E(1) or 32F(1) of the 1991 Act; and
(b) a person who is permitted by the appeal court to be a party to the appeal.

9.16 The appellant will serve the appellant's notice on the Commission and any other respondent.

9.17 The appellant shall file and serve the appellant's notice, within 21 days of –

(a) where the appellant is a deposit-taker, service of the order;
(b) where the appellant is a liable person, receipt of the order; or
(c) where the appellant is either a deposit-taker or a liable person, the date of receipt of notification of the decision.

9.18 For the purposes of paragraph 9.17 –

- (a) references to 'liable person' and 'deposit-taker' are to be interpreted in accordance with section 32E of the 1991 Act and regulation 25A(2) of the Collection and Enforcement Regulations and section 54 of the 1991 Act, respectively; and
- (b) the liable person is to be treated as having received the order or notification of the decision 2 days after it was posted by the Commission.

9.19 Rule 4.1(3)(a) (court's power to extend or shorten the time for compliance with a rule, practice direction or court order) does not apply to an appeal against the making of a lump sum deduction order under section 32F of the 1991 Act in so far as that rule gives the court power to extend the time set out in paragraph 9.17 for filing and serving an appellant's notice after the time for filing and serving the that notice set out in paragraph 9.17 has expired.

9.20 The Commission shall provide to the court and serve on all other parties to the appeal any information and evidence relevant to the making of the decision or order being appealed, within 14 days of receipt of the appellant's notice.

9.21 Subject to paragraph 9.23, a respondent who wishes to ask the appeal court to uphold the order or decision of the Commission for reasons different from or in additional to those given by the Commission must file a respondent's notice.

9.22 A respondent's notice must be filed within 14 days of receipt of the appellant's notice.

9.23 Where the Commission as a respondent, wishes to contend that its order or decision should be –

- (a) varied, either in any event or in the event of the appeal being allowed in whole or in part; or
- (b) affirmed on different grounds from those on which it relied when making the order or decision, it shall, within 14 days of receipt of the appellant's notice, file and serve on all other parties to the appeal a respondent's notice.

9.24 In so far as rule 30.7(Variation of time) may permit any application for variation of the time limit for filing an appellant's notice after the time for filing the appellant's notice has expired, that rule shall not apply to an appeal made against an order under section 32F(1) of the Act of 1991.

9.25 Rule 30.8 (stay) shall not apply to an appeal made against an order under section 32F(1) of the Act of 1991.

9.26 A district judge may hear a deduction order appeal.

9.27 Rule 30.11 (appeal court's powers) does not apply to deduction order appeals.

9.28 Rule 30.11(2)(d) (making orders for payment of interest) does not apply in the case of an appeal against a decision of a district judge in proceedings relating to a deduction order appeal.

9.29 In the case of a deduction order appeal –

- (a) the appeal court has power to –
    - (i) affirm or set aside the order or decision;
    - (ii) remit the matter to the Commission for the order or decision to be reconsidered, with appropriate directions;
    - (iii) refer any application or issue for determination by the Commission;
    - (iv) make a costs order; and
- (b) the appeal court may exercise its powers in relation to the whole or part of an order or decision of the Commission.

9.30 In rule 30.12 (Hearing of appeals) –

- (a) at the beginning of paragraph (1), for "Every" substitute "Subject to paragraph (2A), every";
- (b) at the beginning of paragraph (2), for "Unless" substitute "Subject to paragraph (2A), unless";
- (c) after paragraph (2), insert – "(2A) In the case of a deduction order appeal, the appeal will be a re-hearing, unless the appeal court orders otherwise.";

(d) in paragraph (3), after "lower court" insert "or, in a deduction order appeal, the order or decision of the Commission"; and

(e) for sub-paragraph (b) of paragraph (3), substitute – "(b) unjust because of a serious procedural or other irregularity in –

  (i) the proceedings in the lower court; or

  (ii) the making of an order or decision by the Commission."

Information about the Commission's decision

9.31 In relation to the deduction order appeals listed in column 1 of the table in Schedule 2 to this Practice Direction –

(a) the documents to be filed and served by the appellant include the documents set out in Column 3; and

(b) the relevant information to be provided by the Commission in accordance with paragraph 9.20 above includes the information set out in Column 4.

The court at which the appeal notice is to be filed

9.32 In relation to a deduction order appeal, the appellant's notice and other documents required to be filed with that notice shall be filed in a county court (the Collection and Enforcement Regulations 25AB(1)).

The Commission's address for service

9.33 For the purposes of a deduction order appeal the Commission's address for service is – Commission Legal Adviser Deduction Order Team Legal Enforcement (Civil) Antonine House Callendar Road Falkirk FK1 1XT

All notices or other documents for CMEC relating to a deduction order appeal should be sent to the above address

9.34 This practice direction applies to deduction order appeals and appeals against the decision of a district judge in proceedings relating to a deduction order appeal with the following modifications and any other necessary modifications –

(a) in paragraph 5.35, insert "and 5.36B" after "subject to paragraph 5.36A";

(b) after paragraph 5.36A insert –

"5.36A Where the appeal is a deduction order appeal, the appellant's notice must be filed and served within 21 days of –

(a) where the appellant is a deposit-taker, service of the order;

(b) where the appellant is a liable person, receipt of the order; or

(c) where the appellant is either a deposit-taker or a liable person, the date of receipt of notification of the decision the lower court was given.".

Appeal against the court's decision under rules 31.10, 31.11 or 31.14

10.1 The rules in Part 30 apply to appeals against the court's decision under rules 31.10, 31.11 or 31.14 with the amendments set out in paragraphs 10.2 to 10.5 below. Rules 31.15 and 31.16 apply to these appeals. These modifications do not apply to appeals against the decision made on appeal under rule 31.15.

10.2 Rule 30.3 (permission to appeal) does not apply.

10.3 The time for filing an appellant's notice at the appeal court in rule 30.4(2) does not apply. Rule 31.15 sets out the time within which an appeal against the court's decision under rules 31.10, 31.11 or 31.14 must be made to a judge of the High Court.

10.4 Rule 4.1(3)(a) (court's power to extend or shorten the time for compliance with a rule, practice direction or court order) does not apply to an appeal against the court's decision under rules 31.10, 31.11 or 31.14 in so far as that rule gives the court power to extend the time set out in rule 31.15 for filing an appellant's notice.

10.5 Rules 30.7 (variation), 30.8 (stay of proceedings), 30.10 (striking out appeal notices, setting aside or imposing conditions on permission to appeal) and 30.12 (hearing of appeals) do not apply.

Appeals against pension orders and pension compensation sharing orders

11.1 Paragraph 11.2 below applies to appeals against–

(a) a pension sharing order under section 24B of the Matrimonial Causes Act 1973 or the variation of such an order under section 31 of that Act;

(b) a pension sharing order under Part 4 of Schedule 5 to the Civil Partnership Act 2004 or the variation of such an order under Part 11 of Schedule 5 to that Act;

(c) a pension compensation sharing order under section 24E of the Matrimonial Causes Act 1973 or a variation of such an order under section 31 of that Act; and

(d) a pension compensation sharing order under Part 4 of Schedule 5 to the Civil Partnership Act 2004or a variation of such an order under Part 11 of Schedule 5 to that Act.

11.2 Rule 4.1(3)(a) (court's power to extend or shorten the time for compliance with a rule, practice direction or court order) does not apply to an appeal against the making of the orders referred to in paragraph 11.1 above in so far as that rule gives the court power to extend the time set out in rule 30.4 for filing and serving an appellant's notice after the time for filing and serving that notice has expired.

11.3 In so far as rule 30.7 (Variation of time) may permit any application for variation of the time limit for filing an appellant's notice after the time for filing the appellant's notice has expired, that rule shall not apply to an appeal made against the orders referred to in paragraph 11.1 above.

Appeals to a court under section 20 of the 1991 Act (appeals in respect of parentage determinations)

12.1 The rules in Chapters 1 and 5 of Part 8 will apply as appropriate to an appeal under section 20(1) of the 1991 Act where that appeal must be made to a court in accordance with the Child Support Appeals (Jurisdiction of Courts) Order 2002.

12.2 The respondent to such an appeal will be the Child Maintenance and Enforcement Commission.

12.3 Where the justices' clerk or the court is considering whether or not to transfer appeal proceedings under section 20(1) of the 1991 Act, rules 12.9 to 12.11 will apply as appropriate.

Applications

13.1 Where a party to an appeal makes an application whether in an appeal notice or by Part 18 (Procedure For Other Applications in Proceedings) application notice, the provisions of Part 18 will apply.

13.2 The applicant must file the following documents with the notice –

(a) one additional copy of the application notice for the appeal court, one copy for each of the respondents and the persons referred to in paragraph 5.39;

(b) where applicable a sealed or stamped copy of the order which is the subject of the main appeal or a copy of the notice of the making of an order;

(c) a bundle of documents in support which should include –

(i) the Part 18 application notice; and

(ii) any witness statements and affidavits filed in support of the application notice.

Appeals against consent orders

14.1 The rules in Part 30 and the provisions of this Practice Direction apply to appeals relating to orders made by consent in addition to orders which are not made by consent. An appeal is the only way in which a consent order can be challenged.

Disposing of applications or appeals by consent

15.1 An appellant who does not wish to pursue an application or an appeal may request the appeal court for an order that the application or appeal be dismissed. Such a request must state whether the appellant is a child, or a protected person.

15.2 The request must be accompanied by a consent signed by the other parties stating whether the respondent is a child, or a protected person and consents to the dismissal of the application or appeal.

Allowing unopposed appeals or applications on paper

16.1 The appeal court will not normally make an order allowing an appeal unless satisfied that the decision of the lower court was wrong, but the appeal court may set aside or vary the order of the lower court with consent and without determining the merits of the appeal, if it is satisfied that there are good and sufficient reasons for doing so. Where the appeal court is requested by all parties to allow an application or an appeal the court may consider the request on the papers. The request should state whether any of the parties is a child, or protected person and set out the relevant history of the proceedings and the matters relied on as justifying the proposed order and be accompanied by a copy of the proposed order.

Summary assessment of costs

17.1 Costs are likely to be assessed by way of summary assessment at the following hearings –

(a) contested directions hearings;
(b) applications for permission to appeal at which the respondent is present;
(c) appeals from case management decisions or decisions made at directions hearings; and
(d) appeals listed for one day or less.

(Provision for summary assessment of costs is made by section 13 of the Practice Direction supplementing CPR Part 44)

17.2 Parties attending any of the hearings referred to in paragraph 17.1 should be prepared to deal with the summary assessment.

Reopening of final appeals

18.1 This paragraph applies to applications under rule 30.14 (Reopening of final appeals) for permission to reopen a final determination of an appeal.

18.2 In this paragraph, 'appeal' includes an application for permission to appeal.

18.3 Permission must be sought from the court whose decision the applicant wishes to reopen.

18.4 The application for permission must be made by application notice and supported by written evidence, verified by a statement of truth.

18.5 A copy of the application for permission must not be served on any other party to the original appeal unless the court so directs.

18.6 Where the court directs that the application for permission is to be served on another party, that party may within 14 days of the service on him or her of the copy of the application file a written statement either supporting or opposing the application.

18.7 The application for permission, and any written statements supporting or opposing it, will be considered on paper by a single judge, and will be allowed to proceed only if the judge so directs.

SCHEDULE 1 – Description of proceedings

(1) Proceedings under section 25 of the Children Act 1989;
(2) Proceedings under Parts IV and V of the Children Act 1989;
(3) Proceedings under Schedules 2 and 3 to the Children Act 1989;
(4) Applications for leave under section 91(14),(15) or (17) of the Children Act 1989;
(5) Proceedings under section 102 of the Children Act 1989 or section 79 of the Childcare Act 2006;
(6) Proceedings for a residence order under section 8 of the Children Act 1989 or for a special guardianship order under section 14A of the Children Act 1989 with respect to a child who is the subject of a care order.
(7) Proceedings for a residence order under section 8 of the Children Act 1989 where either section 28(1)(child placed for adoption) or 29(4)(placement order in force) of the Adoption and Children Act 2002 applies;
(8) Proceedings for a special guardianship order under section 14A of the Children Act 1989 where either section 28(1)(child placed for adoption) or section 29(5)(placement order in force) of the Adoption and Children Act 2002 applies.

SCHEDULE 2

Appeal	Relevant legislation	Appellant information	Commission information
Appeal against the making of a regular deduction order (under section 32A of the 1991 Act)	■ Section 32C(4)(a) of the 1991 Act ■ The Collection and Enforcement Regulations 25AB(1)(a) (appeals)	■ A copy of the order; ■ A covering letter explaining that the order has been made and the reasons for the order namely that there are arrears of child maintenance and/or no other arrangements have been made for the payment of child maintenance, including arrears.	■ The amount of the current maintenance calculation, the period of debt and the total amount of arrears (including account breakdown if appropriate) and the reasons for the Commission's decision, details of all previous attempts to negotiate payment i.e. phone calls and letters to the non-resident parent, details of any previous enforcement action taken

Appeal	Relevant legislation	Appellant information	Commission information
Appeal against a decision on an application for a review of a regular deduction order	■ Sections 32C(4)(b) 32C(2)(k) of the 1991 Act ■ The Collection and Enforcement Regulations 25G (review of a regular deduction order) and 25AB(1)(b) (appeals).	■ A decision notification setting out whether or not the review has been agreed by the Commission and the resulting action to be taken if agreed; with an enclosure setting out the specific reasons for the Commission's decision	■ The reasons for the Commission's decision in respect of the application for review and any evidence supporting that decision
Appeal against the withholding of consent to the disapplication of sections 32G(1) and 32H(2)(b) of the 1991 Act	■ Section 32I(4) of the 1991 Act ■ The Collection and Enforcement Regulations 25N (disapplication of sections 32G(1) and 32H(2)(b) of the 1991 Act) and 25AB(1)(c) (appeals)	■ A decision notification setting out that either: (a) consent has been refused; or (b) consent has been given in relation to part of the application i.e. that only some of the funds which were requested to be released have been agreed to be released (the right of appeal will lie in respect of the part of the application which has been refused) ■ There will be an enclosure with the notification setting out the reasons for the decision on the application	■ The reasons for the Commission's decision in respect of the application for consent and any evidence supporting

Appeal	Relevant legislation	Appellant information	Commission information
Appeal against the making of a final lump sum deduction order (under section 32F of the 1991 Act)	■ Section 32J(5) of the 1991 Act ■ The Collection and Enforcement Regulations 25AB(1)(d) (appeals)	■ A copy of the order; ■ A covering letter explaining that the order has been made and the reasons for the order namely that there are arrears of child maintenance and/or no other arrangements have been made for the payment of child maintenance, including arrears	■ The amount of the current maintenance calculation (if applicable), the period of debt and the total amount of arrears (including account breakdown if appropriate) and the reasons for the Commission's decision, details of all previous attempts to negotiate payment i.e. phone calls and letters to the non-resident parent, details of any previous enforcement action taken.

PRACTICE DIRECTION 31A – REGISTRATION OF ORDERS UNDER THE COUNCIL REGULATION, THE CIVIL PARTNERSHIP (JURISDICTION AND RECOGNITION OF JUDGMENTS) REGULATIONS 2005 AND UNDER THE 1996 HAGUE CONVENTION

This Practice Direction supplements FPR Part 31

Form of application

1.1 An application under rule 31.4 must be made using the Part 19 procedure, except that the provisions of rules 31.8 to 31.14 and of this Practice Direction shall apply in place of rules 19.4 to 19.9.

1.2 Where the application is for recognition only of an order, it should be made clear that the application does not extend to registration for enforcement.

Evidence in support of all applications for registration, recognition or non-recognition

2.1 The requirements for information and evidence for applications differ according to whether the application is made under the Council Regulation, the Jurisdiction and Recognition of Judgments Regulations, or the 1996 Hague Convention.

2.2 All applications to which rule 31.4(2) applies must be supported by a statement that is sworn to be true or an affidavit, exhibiting the judgment, or a verified, certified or otherwise duly authenticated copy of the judgment. In the case of an application under the Jurisdiction and Recognition of Judgments Regulations or under the 1996 Hague Convention, a translation of the judgment should be supplied.

2.3 Where any other document required by this Practice Direction or by direction of the court under rule 31.5 is not in English, the applicant must supply a translation of that document into English certified by a notary public or a person qualified for the purpose, or accompanied by witness statement or affidavit confirming that the translation is accurate.

Evidence required in support of application for registration, recognition or non-recognition of a judgment under the Council Regulation

3.1 An application for a judgment to be registered, recognised or not recognised under the Council Regulation must be accompanied by a witness statement or an affidavit exhibiting the following documents and giving the information required by 3.2 or 3.3 below, as appropriate.

3.2 In the case of an application for recognition or registration–

   (a) the certificate in the form set out in Annex I or Annex II of the Council Regulation, issued by the Member State in which judgment was given;
   (b) in the case of a judgment given in default, the documents referred to in Article 37(2);
   (c) whether the judgment provides for the payment of a sum or sums of money;
   (d) whether interest is recoverable on the judgment or part of the judgment in accordance with the law of the State in which the judgment was given, and if that is the case, the rate of interest, the date from which interest is recoverable, and the date on which interest ceases to accrue;
   (e) an address within the jurisdiction of the court for service of process on the party making the application and stating, in so far as is known to the applicant, the name and usual or last known address or place of business of the person against whom judgment was given; and
   (f) where appropriate, whether Article 56 has been complied with, and the identity and address of the authority or authorities from whom consent has been obtained, together with evidence of that consent.

3.3 In the case of an application for an order that a judgment should not be recognised under Article 21(3)–

   (a) the certificate referred to at paragraph 3.2(a);
   (b) in relation to the documents identified at paragraph 3.2(b), those documents or a statement that no such service or acceptance occurred if that is the case;
   (c) an address within the jurisdiction of the court for service of process on the applicant and stating, in so far as is known to the applicant, the name and usual or last known address or place of business of the person in whose favour judgment was given; and
   (d) a statement of the ground or grounds under Articles 22 or 23 (as the case may be) on which it is requested that the judgment should not be recognised, the reasons why the applicant asserts that such ground or grounds is, or are, made out, and any documentary evidence on which the applicant relies.

Evidence required in support of an application for registration, recognition or non-recognition of a judgment under the 1996 Hague Convention.

4.1 An application for an order for a judgment to be registered under Article 26 or not recognised under Article 24 of the 1996 Hague Convention must be accompanied by a witness statement or affidavit exhibiting the following documents and giving the information required by 4.2, 4.3 or 4.4 below as appropriate.

4.2 In the case of an application for registration–

(a) those documents necessary to show that the judgment is enforceable according to the law of the Contracting State in which it was given;

(b) a description of the opportunities provided by the authority which gave the judgment in question for the child to be heard, except where that judgment was given in a case of urgency;

(c) where the judgment was given in a case of urgency, a statement as to the circumstances of the urgency that led to the child not having the opportunity to be heard;

(d) details of any measures taken in the non-Contracting State of the habitual residence of the child, if applicable, specifying the nature and effect of the measure, and the date on which it was taken;

(e) in as far as not apparent from the copy of the judgment provided, a statement of the grounds on which the authority which gave the judgment based its jurisdiction, together with any documentary evidence in support of that statement;

(f) where appropriate, a statement regarding whether Article 33 of the 1996 Hague Convention has been complied with, and the identity and address of the authority or authorities from which consent has been obtained, together with evidence of that consent; and

(g) the information referred to at 3.2(c) to (e) above.

4.3 In the case of an application for an order that a judgment should not be recognised–

(a) a statement of the ground or grounds under Article 23 of the 1996 Hague Convention on which it is requested that the judgment be not recognised, the reasons why the applicant asserts that such ground or grounds is or are made out, and any documentary evidence on which the Applicant relies; and

(b) an address within the jurisdiction of the court for service of process on the applicant and stating, in so far as is known to the applicant, the name and usual or last known address or place of business of the person in whose favour judgment was given.

4.4 Where is it sought to apply for recognition only of a judgment under the 1996 Hague Convention, the provisions of paragraph 4.2 apply with the exception that the applicant is not required to produce the document referred to in subparagraph 4.2(a).

Evidence required in support of an application for recognition or non-recognition of a judgment under the Jurisdiction and Recognition of Judgments Regulations

5.1 An application for recognition of a judgment under regulation 7 of the Jurisdiction and Recognition of Judgments Regulations or for non-recognition of a judgment under regulation 8 must be accompanied by a witness statement or affidavit exhibiting the following documents and giving the information at 5.2 or 5.3 below, as appropriate.

5.2 In the case of an application for recognition of a judgment–

(a) where applicable, details of any decision determining the question of the substance or validity of the civil partnership previously given by a court of civil jurisdiction in England and Wales, or by a court elsewhere;

(b) where the judgment was obtained otherwise than by means of proceedings–

(i) an official document certifying that the judgment is effective under the law of the country in which it was obtained;

(ii) where either civil partner was domiciled in another country from that in which the judgment was obtained at the relevant date, an official document certifying that the judgment is recognised as valid under the law of that country; or

    (iii) a verified, certified or otherwise duly authenticated copy of the document at (i) or (ii) above, as appropriate;

(c) in relation to a judgment obtained by means of proceedings and given in default, the original or a certified true copy of the document which establishes that the party who did not respond was served with the document instituting the proceedings or with an equivalent document, or any document indicating that the respondent has accepted the judgment unequivocally; and

(d) the information referred to at paragraph 3.2(c) to (e) above.

5.3 In the case of an application for non-recognition of a judgment–

(a) an address within the jurisdiction of the court for service of process on the applicant and stating, in so far as is known to the applicant, the name and usual or last known address or place of business of the person in whose favour judgment was given;

(b) a statement of the ground or grounds under regulation 8 of the Jurisdiction and Recognition of Judgments Regulations on which it is requested that the judgment should not be recognised together with any documentary evidence on which the applicant relies; and

(c) where the judgment was obtained by means of proceedings, the document referred to at paragraph 5.2(c) or a statement that no such service or acceptance occurred if that is the case.

Evidence in support of application for a certificate under Articles 39, 41 or 42 of the Council Regulation, or for a certified copy of a judgment

6.1 The procedure described in the following paragraphs should be used where the application for the certified copy of the judgment or relevant certificate under the Council Regulation has not been made at the conclusion of the proceedings to which it relates.

6.2 An application for a certified copy of a judgment, or for a certificate under Articles 39, 41 or 42 of the Council Regulation must be made by witness statement or affidavit, containing the information and attaching the documents required under paragraph 6.3, and paragraphs 6.4, 6.5 or 6.6 below, as appropriate.

6.3 All applications must–

(a) provide details of the proceedings in which the judgment was obtained;
(b) attach a copy of the application by which the proceedings were begun;
(c) attach a copy of all statements of case filed in the proceedings; and
(d) state–

    (i) whether the judgment provides for the payment of a sum of money; and
    (ii) whether interest is recoverable on the judgment or part of it and if so, the rate of interest, the date from which interest is recoverable, and the date on which interest ceases to accrue.

Further, where the application relates to the Council Regulation, the applicant must attach a document showing that he or she benefitted from legal aid in the proceedings to which the judgment relates, if that is the case.

6.4 An application for a certified copy of the judgment and a certificate under Article 41 or 42 of the Council Regulation must–

(a) contain a statement of whether the certificate is sought under Article 41 or Article 42;
(b) attach a document evidencing the service of the application by which the

proceedings were begun on all respondents, and if no such service occurred, details of all opportunities provided to each respondent to put their case before the court;

(c) provide information regarding the age of the child at the time of the judgment and the opportunities given during the proceedings, if any, for the child's wishes and feelings to be ascertained;

(d) state the full names, addresses and dates and places of birth (where available) of all persons holding parental responsibility in relation to the child or children to whom the judgment relates; and

(e) state the full names and dates of birth of each child to whom the judgment relates.

6.5 An application for a certified copy of the judgment and a certificate under Article 39 of the Council Regulation must–

(a) state whether the certificate sought relates to a parental responsibility matter or a matrimonial matter;

(b) in relation to a parental responsibility matter, attach evidence that the judgment has been served on the respondent;

(c) in the case of a judgment given in default, attach a document which establishes that the respondent was served with the petition or application by which the proceedings were commenced, or a document indicating that the respondent accepted the judgment unequivocally;

(d) state that the time for appealing has expired, or give the date on which it will expire, as appropriate, and state whether a notice of appeal against the judgment has been given;

(e) in relation to a matrimonial matter, give the full name, address, country and place of birth, and date of birth of each party, and the country, place and date of the marriage;

(f) in relation to a parental responsibility matter, give the full name, address, place and date of birth of each person who holds parental responsibility ;

(g) as appropriate, give the name, address, and date and place of birth of the person with access rights, or to whom the child is to be returned.

6.6 An application for a certified copy of a judgment for the purposes of recognition and enforcement of the judgment under the 1996 Hague Convention must–

(a) provide a statement of the grounds on which the court based its jurisdiction to make the orders in question;

(b) indicate the age of the child at the time of the judgment and the measures taken, if any, for the child's wishes and feelings to be ascertained; and

(c) indicate which persons were provided with notice of the proceedings and, where such persons were served with the proceedings, attach evidence of such service.

PRACTICE DIRECTION 33A – ENFORCEMENT OF UNDERTAKINGS

This Practice Direction supplements FPR Part 33

Enforcement of undertaking to do or abstain from doing any act other than the payment of money

1.1 Rule 33.1(2) provides that Part 50 of, and Schedules 1 and 2 to, the CPR (which contain the Rules of the Supreme Court (RSC) and County Court Rules (CCR) respectively) apply, as far as they are relevant and with necessary modification, to an application made in the High Court and a county court to enforce an order made in family proceedings.

1.2 Subject to the Debtors Act 1869 (which makes provision in relation to orders for the payment of money), RSC Order 45.5 and CCR Order 29.1 enable a judgment or order to be enforced by committal for contempt of court where–

(a) a person who is required by a judgment or order to do an act has refused or neglected to do that act within the specified time; or

(b) a person disobeys a judgment or order requiring him to abstain from doing an act.

1.3 These Rules apply to undertakings as they apply to orders, with necessary modifications.

1.4 The form of an undertaking to do or abstain from doing any act must be endorsed with a notice setting out the consequences of disobedience, as follows:

'You may be sent to prison for contempt of court if you break the promises that you have given to the court'.

1.5 The person giving the undertaking must make a signed statement to the effect that he or she understands the terms of the undertaking being given and the consequences of failure to comply with it, as follows:

'I understand the undertaking that I have given, and that if I break any of my promises to the court I may be sent to prison for contempt of court.'

1.6 The statement need not be given before the court in person. It may be endorsed on the court copy of the undertaking or may be filed in a separate document such as a letter.

Enforcement of undertaking for the payment of money

2.1 Any undertaking for the payment of money that has effect as if it was an order made under Part 2 of the Matrimonial Causes Act 1973 may be enforced as if it was an order and Part 33 applies accordingly.

2.2 The form of an undertaking for the payment of money that has effect as if it were an order under Part 2 of the Matrimonial Causes Act 1973 must be endorsed with a notice setting out the consequences of disobedience, as follows:

'If you fail to pay any sum of money which you have promised the court that you would pay, a person entitled to enforce the undertaking may apply to the court for an order. If it is proved that you have had the means to pay the sum but you have refused or neglected to pay that sum, you may be sent to prison.'

2.3 The person giving the undertaking must make a signed statement to the effect that he or she understands the terms of the undertaking being given and the consequences of failure to comply with it, as follows:

'I understand the undertaking that I have given, and that if I break my promise to the court to pay any sum of money, I may be sent to prison.'

2.4 The statement need not be given before the court in person. It may be endorsed on the court copy of the undertaking or may be filed in a separate document such as a letter.

PRACTICE DIRECTION 34A – RECIPROCAL ENFORCEMENTS OF MAINTENANCE ORDERS

This Practice Direction supplements FPR Part 34

Noting record of means of payment

1.1 Where a magistrates' court orders payments under a maintenance order to which Part 34 applies to be made in a particular way, the court must record that on a copy of the order.

1.2 If the court orders payment to be made to the court officer of a magistrates' court by a method referred to in section 59(6) of the Magistrates' Courts Act 1980, the court may vary the method of payment on the application of an interested party and where it does so the court must record the variation on a copy of the order.

(Section 59(6) refers to payment by standing order or other methods which require transfer between accounts of a specific amount on a specific date during the period for which the authority to make the payment is in force.)

Notification by court officer

2.1 The court officer must, as soon as practicable, notify in writing the person liable to make the payments of the method by which they must be made.

2.2 If the court orders payment to be made to the court officer of a magistrates' court by a method referred to in section 59(6) of the Magistrates' Courts Act 1980 the court officer must inform the person liable to make the payments of the number and location of the account to which the payments must be made.

2.3 If the court varies the method of payment on the application of an interested party the court officer must, as soon as practicable, notify all interested parties in writing of the result of an application (including a decision to refer it to the court).

Applications under section 2 of the 1920 Act

3.1 This paragraph refers to an application for the transmission of a maintenance order to a reciprocating country under section 2 of the 1920 Act in accordance with rule 34.10.

3.2 The applicant's written evidence must include such information as may be required by the law of the reciprocating country for the purpose of enforcement of the order.

3.3 If, in accordance with section 2 of the 1920 Act, the court sends a maintenance order to the Lord Chancellor for transmission to a reciprocating country, it shall record the fact in the court records.

Applications under section 2 of the 1972 Act (rule 34.14)

Introduction

4.1 An application for a maintenance order to be sent to a reciprocating country under section 2 of the 1972 Act is made by lodging specified documents with the court. The documents to be lodged vary according to which country it is intended that the maintenance order is be sent and the requirements are set out in this paragraph.

General provision

4.2 The general requirement is that the following documents should be lodged with the court–

 (a) an affidavit by the applicant stating–

  (i) the reason that the applicant has for believing that the payer under the maintenance order is residing in the reciprocating country; and

  (ii) the amount of any arrears due to the applicant under the order, the date to which those arrears have been calculated and the date on which the next payment under the order falls due;

 (b) a certified copy of the maintenance order;

 (c) a statement giving such information as the applicant has as to the whereabouts of the payer;

 (d) a statement giving such information as the applicant has for facilitating the identification of the payer, (including, if known to the applicant, the name and address of any employer of the payer, his occupation and the date and place of issue of any passport of the payer); and

(e) if available to the applicant, a photograph of the payer.

Republic of Ireland

4.3 If the country to which it is intended to send the maintenance order is the Republic of Ireland, then the following changes to the general requirements apply.

4.4 The applicant must lodge the following documents with the court in addition to those set out in paragraph 4.2–

    (a) a statement as to whether or not the payer appeared in the proceedings in which the maintenance order was made;

    (b) if the payer did not so appear–

        (i) the original of a document which establishes that notice of the institution of proceedings was served on the payer; or

        (ii) a copy of such a document certified by the applicant or the applicant's solicitor to be a true copy;

    (c) a document which establishes that notice of the order was sent to the payer; and

    (d) if the payee received legal aid in the proceedings in which the order was made, a copy certified by the applicant or the applicant's solicitor to be a true copy of the legal aid certificate.

Hague Convention Country

4.5 If the country to which it is intended to send the maintenance order is a Hague Convention country, then the following changes to the general requirements apply.

4.6 In addition to the matters stated in that paragraph, the affidavit referred to in paragraph 4.2(a) must also state whether the time for appealing against the maintenance order has expired and whether an appeal is pending.

4.7 The applicant must lodge the following documents with the court in addition to those set out in paragraph 4.2–

    (a) a statement as to whether or not the payer appeared in the proceedings in which the maintenance order was made;

    (b) if the payer did not so appear –

        (i) the original of a document which establishes that notice of the institution of proceedings, including notice of the substance of the claim, was served on the payer; or

        (ii) a copy of such a document certified by the applicant or the applicant's solicitor to be a true copy;

    (c) a document which establishes that notice of the order was sent to the payer;

    (d) a written statement as to whether or not the payee received legal aid in the proceedings in which the order was made, or in connection with the application under section 2 of the 1972 Act; and

    (e) if the payee did receive legal aid, a copy certified by the applicant or the applicant's solicitor to be a true copy of the legal aid certificate.

United States of America

4.8 If the country to which it is intended to send the maintenance order is a specified State of the United States of America, then the following changes to the general requirements apply.

4.9 There is no requirement to lodge a statement giving information as to the whereabouts of the payer since this information must be contained in the affidavit as mentioned in paragraph 4.10.

4.10 In addition to the matters stated in that paragraph, the affidavit referred to in paragraph 4.2(a) must also state–

(a) the address of the payee;
(b) such information as is known as to the whereabouts of the payer; and
(c) a description, so far as is known, of the nature and location of any assets of the payer available for execution.

4.11 The applicant must lodge three certified copies of the maintenance order.

Notification to the Lord Chancellor

5.1 Where, in accordance with Part 1 of the 1972 Act, a magistrates' court registers a maintenance order sent to it from a Hague Convention Country, the court officer must sent written notice of the registration to the Lord Chancellor.

Notification of means of enforcement

6.1 The court officer of a magistrates' court must take reasonable steps to notify the person to whom payments are due under a registered order of the means of enforcement available in respect of it.

6.2 Notification of the means of enforcement includes, where appropriate, notification of the possibility of registration of the order in the High Court under Part I of the Maintenance Orders Act 1958.

Certified copies of orders issued under rule 34.39

7.1 In an application under rule 34.39 by a person wishing to enforce abroad a maintenance order obtained in a magistrates' court, the certified copy of the order will be a sealed copy and will be accompanied by a certificate signed by the court officer.

7.2 In an application under the 1982 Act, the certificate signed by the court officer must state that it is a true copy of the order concerned and must give particulars of the proceedings in which it was made.

7.3 In an application under the Judgments Regulation, the certificate will be in the form of Annex V to the Regulation.

7.4 In an application under the Lugano Convention, the certificate will be in the form of Annex V to the Convention.

Countries and Territories in which Sums are Payable through Crown Agents for Overseas Governments and Territories (rule 34.23)

8.1 Gibraltar, Barbados, Bermuda, Ghana, Kenya, Fiji, Hong Kong, Singapore, Turks and Caicos Islands, United Republic of Tanzania (except Zanzibar), Anguilla, Falkland Islands and Dependencies, St Helena.

Part 1 of the 1972 Act – Modified Rules

9.1 The annexes to this Practice Direction set out rules 34.14 to 34.25 as they are modified–
(a) in relation to the Republic of Ireland, by rule 34.26 (Annex 1);
(b) in relation to the Hague Convention Countries, by rule 34.27 (Annex 2); and
(c) in relation to Specified States of the United States of America, by rule 34.28 (Annex 3).

9.2 The statutory references in the annexes are construed in accordance with rule 34.26(2), 34.27(2) or 34.28(2) as the case may be.

ANNEX 1 – APPLICATION OF SECTION 1 OF CHAPTER 2 OF PART 34 TO THE REPUBLIC OF IRELAND

34.14 Application for transmission of maintenance order to the Republic of Ireland

An application for a maintenance order to be sent to the Republic of Ireland under section 2 of the 1972 Act must be made in accordance with Practice Direction 34A.

34.15 Certification of evidence given on provisional orders

A document setting out or summarising evidence is authenticated by a court in England and Wales by a certificate signed, as appropriate, by–

(a) one of the justices; or
(b) the District Judge (Magistrates' Courts),

before whom that evidence was given.

(Section 3(5)(b) or 5(3) of the 1972 Act require a document to be authenticated by the court.)

34.16 Confirmation of a provisional order

[This rule does not apply to the Republic of Ireland]

34.17 Consideration of confirmation of a provisional order made by a magistrates' court

(1) This rule applies where–

    (a) a magistrates' court has made a provisional order by virtue of section 3 of the 1972 Act;
    (b) the payer has made representations or adduced evidence to the court; and
    (c) the court has fixed a date for the hearing at which it will consider confirmation of the order.

(2) The court officer must serve on the applicant for the provisional order–

    (a) a copy of the representations or evidence; and
    (b) written notice of the date fixed for the hearing.

34.18 Notification of variation or revocation of a maintenance order by the High Court

Where the High Court makes an order varying or revoking an order to which section 5 of the 1972 Act applies the court officer must send–

(a) a certified copy of the order of variation or revocation; and
(b) a statement as to the service on the payer of the documents mentioned in section 5(3) of the 1972 Act;

to the court in the Republic of Ireland.

(Rule 34.22 provides for the transmission of documents to a court in a reciprocating country.)

34.19 Notification of revocation of a maintenance order by a magistrates' court

Where a magistrates' court makes an order revoking an order to which section 5 of the 1972 Act applies, the court officer must send written notice of the making of the order to the Lord Chancellor.

(Section 5 of the 1972 Act applies to a maintenance order sent to the Republic of Ireland in accordance with section 2 of that Act and a provisional order made by a magistrates' court in accordance with section 3 of that Act which has been confirmed by such a court.)

(Provision in respect of notification of variation of a maintenance order by a magistrates' court under the 1972 Act is made in Rules made under section 144 of the Magistrates' Courts Act 1980.)

34.20 Taking of evidence for court in the Republic of Ireland

(1) This rule applies where a request is made by or on behalf of a court in the Republic of

Ireland for the taking of evidence for the purpose of proceedings relating to a maintenance order to which Part 1 of the 1972 Act applies.

(Section 14 of the 1972 Act makes provision for the taking of evidence needed for the purpose of certain proceedings.)

(2) The High Court has power to take the evidence where–

    (a)   the request for evidence relates to a maintenance order made by a superior court in the United Kingdom; and

    (b)   the witness resides in England and Wales.

(3) The county court has power to take the evidence where–

    (a)   the request for evidence relates to a maintenance order made by a county court; and

    (b)   the maintenance order has not been registered in a magistrates' court under the 1958 Act.

(4) The following magistrates' courts have power to take the evidence, that is–

    (a)   where the proceedings in the Republic of Ireland relate to a maintenance order made by a magistrates' court, the court which made the order;

    (b)   where the proceedings relate to an order which is registered in a magistrates' court, the court in which the order is registered; and

    (c)   a magistrates' court to which the Secretary of State sends the request to take evidence.

(5) A magistrates' court not mentioned in paragraph (4) has power to take the evidence if the magistrates' court which would otherwise have that power consents because the evidence could be taken more conveniently.

(6) The evidence is to be taken in accordance with Part 22.

34.21   Request for the taking of evidence by a court

[This rule does not apply to the Republic of Ireland]

34.22   Transmission of documents

(1) This rule applies to any document, including a notice or request, which is required to be sent to a court in the Republic of Ireland by–

    (a)   Part 1 of the 1972 Act; or

    (b)   Section 1 of Chapter 2 of this Part of these Rules.

(2) The document must be sent to the Lord Chancellor for transmission to the court in the Republic of Ireland.

34.23   Method of payment under registered orders

(1) Where an order is registered in a magistrates' court in accordance with section 6(3) of the 1972 Act, the court must order that the payment of sums due under the order be made–

    (a)   to the court officer for the registering court; and

    (b)   at such time and place as the court officer directs. (Section 6(3) of the 1972 Act makes provision for the registration of maintenance orders made in the Republic of Ireland.)

(2) Where the court orders payment to be made to the court officer, the court officer must send the payments by post–

    (a)   to the payee under the order; or

    (b)   where a public authority has been authorised by the payee to receive the payments, to that public authority.

(Practice Direction 34A contains further provisions relating to the payment of sums due under registered orders.)

34.24 Enforcement of payments under registered orders

(1) This rule applies where periodical payments under a registered order are in arrears.
(2) The court officer must, on the written request of the payee, proceed in that officer's own name for the recovery of the sums due unless of the view that it is unreasonable to do so.
(3) If the sums due are more than 4 weeks in arrears the court officer must give the payee notice in writing of that fact stating the particulars of the arrears.

34.25 Notification of registration and cancellation

The court officer must send written notice to–

- (a) the Lord Chancellor, on the due registration of an order under section 6(3) or 10(4) of the 1972 Act; and
- (b) to the payer under the order, on–
  - (i) the registration of an order under section 10(4) of the 1972 Act; or
  - (ii) the cancellation of the registration of an order under section 10(1) of that Act.

34.25A Other notices under section 6 of the 1972 Act

(1) A notice required under section 6(6) or (10) of the 1972 Act must be in the form referred to in a practice direction.
(2) Where a magistrates' court sets aside the registration of an order following an appeal under section 6(7) of the 1972 Act, the court officer must send written notice of the court's decision to the payee.

(Section 6(6) of the 1972 Act provides for notice of registration in a United Kingdom court of a maintenance order made in the Republic of Ireland, and section 6(10) of that Act for notice that a maintenance order made in the Republic of Ireland has not been registered in a United Kingdom court.)

ANNEX 2 – APPLICATION OF SECTION 1 OF CHAPTER 2 OF PART 34 TO THE HAGUE CONVENTION COUNTRIES

34.14 Application for transmission of maintenance order to a Hague Convention Country

An application for a maintenance order to be sent to a Hague Convention Country under section 2 of the 1972 Act must be made in accordance with Practice Direction 34A.

34.15 Certification of evidence given on provisional orders

[This rule does not apply to the Hague Convention Countries]

34.16 Confirmation of a provisional order made in a reciprocating country

[This rule does not apply to the Hague Convention Countries]

34.17 Consideration of revocation of a maintenance order made by a magistrates' court

(1) This rule applies where–
  - (a) an application has been made to a magistrates' court by a payee for the revocation of an order to which section 5 of the 1972 Act applies; and
  - (b) the payer resides in a Hague Convention Country.

(2) The court officer must serve on the payee, by post, a copy of any representations or evidence adduced by or on behalf of the payer.

(Provision relating to consideration of variation of a maintenance order made by a magistrates' court to which section 5 of the 1972 Act applies is made in Rules made under section 144 of the Magistrates' Courts Act 1980.)

34.18 Notification of variation or revocation of a maintenance order by the High Court or a county court

(1) This rule applies if the High Court or a county court makes an order varying or revoking a maintenance order to which section 5 of the 1972 Act applies.

(2) If the time for appealing has expired without an appeal having been entered, the court officer will send to the Lord Chancellor–

    (a)   the documents required by section 5(8) of the 1972 Act; and

    (b)   a certificate signed by the district judge stating that the order of variation or revocation is enforceable and no longer subject to the ordinary forms of review.

(3) A party who enters an appeal against the order of variation or revocation must, at the same time, give written notice to the court officer.

34.19 Notification of confirmation or revocation of a maintenance order by a magistrates' court

[This rule does not apply to the Hague Convention Countries]

34.20 Taking of evidence for court in a Hague Convention Country

(1) This rule applies where a request is made by or on behalf of a court in a Hague Convention Country for the taking of evidence for the purpose of proceedings relating to a maintenance order to which Part 1 of the 1972 Act applies.

(Section 14 of the 1972 Act makes provision for the taking of evidence needed for the purpose of certain proceedings.)

(2) The High court has power to take the evidence where–

    (a)   the request for evidence relates to a maintenance order made by a superior court in the United Kingdom: and

    (b)   the witness resides in England and Wales.

(3) The county court has power to take the evidence where–

    (a)   the request for evidence relates to a maintenance order made by a county court; and

    (b)   the maintenance order has not been registered in a magistrates' court under the 1958 Act.

(4) The following magistrates' courts have power to take the evidence, that is–

    (a)   where the proceedings in the Hague Convention Country relate to a maintenance order made by a magistrates' court, the court which made the order;

    (b)   where the proceedings relate to an order which is registered in a magistrates' court, the court in which the order is registered; and

    (c)   a magistrates' court to which the Secretary of State sends the request to take evidence.

(5) A magistrates' court not mentioned in paragraph (4) has power to take the evidence if the magistrates' court which would otherwise have that power consents because the evidence could be taken more conveniently.

(6) The evidence is to be taken in accordance with Part 22.

34.21 Request for the taking of evidence by a court in a Hague Convention country

[This rule does not apply to the Hague Convention countries.]

34.22 Transmission of documents

(1) This rule applies to any document, including a notice or request, which is required to be sent to a court in a Hague Convention country by–

    (a) Part 1 of the 1972 Act; or

    (b) Section1 of Chapter 2 of this Part of these Rules.

(2) The document must be sent to the Lord Chancellor for transmission to the court in the Hague Convention country.

34.23 Method of payment under registered orders

(1) Where an order is registered in a magistrates' court in accordance with section 6(3) of the 1972 Act, the court must order that the payment of sums due under the order be made–

    (a) to the court officer for the registering court; and

    (b) at such time and place as the court officer directs.

(Section 6(3) of the 1972 Act makes provision for the registration of maintenance orders made in a Hague Convention country.)

(2) Where the court orders payment to be made to the court officer, the court officer must send the payments by post to the payee under the order.

(Practice Direction 34A contains further provision relating to the payment of sums due under registered orders.)

34.24 Enforcement of payments under registered orders

(1) This rule applies where a court has ordered periodical payments under a registered maintenance order to be made to the court officer.

(2) The court officer must take reasonable steps to notify the payee of the means of enforcement available.

(3) Paragraph (4) applies where periodical payments due under a registered order are in arrears.

(4) The court officer, on that officer's own initiative–

    (a) may; or

    (b) if the sums due are more than 4 weeks in arrears, must,

proceed in that officer's own name for the recovery of the sums due unless of the view that it is unreasonable to do so.

34.25 Notification of registration and cancellation

The court officer must send written notice to–

    (a) the Lord Chancellor, on the due registration of an order under section 10(4) of the 1972 Act; and

    (b) the payer under the order, on–

        (i) the registration of an order under section 10(4) of the 1972 Act; or

        (ii) the cancellation of the registration of an order under section 10(1) of the 1972 Act.

34.25A General provisions as to notices

(1) A notice to a payer of the registration of an order in a magistrates' court in accordance with section 6(3) of the 1972 Act must be in the form referred to in a practice direction.

(Section 6(8) of the 1972 Act requires notice of registration to be given to the payer.)

(2) If the court sets aside the registration of a maintenance order following an appeal under section 6(9) of the 1972 Act, the court officer must send written notice of the decision to the Lord Chancellor.

(3) A notice to a payee that the court officer has refused to register an order must be in the form referred to in a practice direction.

(Section 6(11) of the 1972 Act requires notice of refusal of registration to be given to the payee.)

(4) Where, under any provision of Part 1 of the 1972 Act, a court officer serves a notice on a payer who resides in a Hague Convention Country, the court officer must send to the Lord Chancellor a certificate of service.

ANNEX 3 – APPLICATION OF SECTION 1 OF CHAPTER 2 OF PART 34 TO THE UNITED STATES OF AMERICA

34.14 Application for transmission of maintenance order to the United States of America

An application for a maintenance order to be sent to the United States of America under section 2 of the 1972 Act must be made in accordance with Practice Direction 34A.

34.15 Certification of evidence given on provisional orders

[This rule does not apply to the United States of America]

34.16 Confirmation of a provisional order made in a reciprocating country

[This rule does not apply to the United States of America]

34.17 Consideration of revocation of a maintenance order made by a magistrates' court

(1) This rule applies where–
  (a) an application has been made to a magistrates' court by a payee for the revocation of an order to which section 5 of the 1972 Act applies; and
  (b) the payer resides in the United States of America.

(2) The court officer must serve on the payee by post a copy of any representations or evidence adduced by or on behalf of the payer.

(Provision relating to consideration of variation of a maintenance order made by a magistrates' court to which section 5 of the 1972 Act applies is made in rules made under section 144 of the Magistrates' Courts Act 1980.)

34.18 Notification of variation or revocation

If the High Court or a county court makes an order varying or revoking a maintenance order to which section 5 of the 1972 Act applies, the court officer will send to the Lord Chancellor the documents required by section 5(7) of that Act.

34.19 Notification of confirmation or revocation of a maintenance order by a magistrates' court

[This rule does not apply to the United States of America]

34.20 Taking of evidence for court in United States of America

(1) This rule applies where a request is made by or on behalf of a court in the United States of

America for the taking of evidence for the purpose of proceedings relating to a maintenance order to which Part 1 of the 1972 Act applies.

(Section 14 of the 1972 Act makes provision for the taking of evidence needed for the purpose of certain proceedings.)

(2) The High Court has power to take the evidence where–
- (a) the request for evidence relates to a maintenance order made by a superior court in the United Kingdom; and
- (b) the witness resides in England and Wales.

(3) The county court has power to take the evidence where–
- (a) the request for evidence relates to a maintenance order made by a county court; and
- (b) the maintenance order has not been registered in a magistrates' court under the 1958 Act.

(4) The following magistrates' courts have power to take the evidence, that is–
- (a) where the proceedings in the United States of America relate to a maintenance order made by a magistrates' court, the court which made the order;
- (b) where the proceedings relate to an order which is registered in a magistrates' court, the court in which the order is registered; and
- (c) a magistrates' court to which the Secretary of State sends the request to take evidence.

(5) A magistrates' court not mentioned in paragraph (4) has power to take the evidence if the magistrates' court which would otherwise have that power consents because the evidence could be taken more conveniently.

(6) The evidence is to be taken in accordance with Part 22.

34.21 Request for the taking of evidence by a court in a reciprocating country

[This rule does not apply to the United States of America]

34.22 Transmission of documents

(1) This rule applies to any document, including a notice or request, which is required to be sent to a court in the United States of America by–
- (a) Part 1 of the 1972 Act; or
- (b) Section 1 of Chapter 2 of this Part of these Rules.

(2) The document must be sent to the Lord Chancellor for transmission to the court in the United States of America.

34.23 Method of payment under registered orders

(1) Where an order is registered in a magistrates' court in accordance with section 6(3) of the 1972 Act, the court must order that the payment of sums due under the order be made–
- (a) to the court officer for the registering court; and
- (b) at such time and place as the court officer directs.

(Section 6(3) of the 1972 Act makes provision for the registration of maintenance orders made in the United States of America.)

(2) Where the court orders payment to be made to the court officer, the court officer must send the payments by post to the payee under the order.

(Practice Direction 34A contains further provisions relating to the payment of sums due under registered orders.)

34.24 Enforcement of payments under registered orders

(1) This rule applies where a court has ordered periodical payments under a registered maintenance order to be made to the court officer.
(2) The court officer must take reasonable steps to notify the payee of the means of enforcement available.
(3) Paragraph (4) applies where periodical payments due under a registered order are in arrears.
(4) The court officer, on that officer's own initiative–
   (a) may; or
   (b) if the sums due are more than 4 weeks in arrears, must,

proceed in that officer's own name for the recovery of the sums due unless of the view that it is unreasonable to do so.

34.25 Notification of registration and cancellation

The court officer must send written notice to–
(a) the Lord Chancellor, on the due registration of an order under section 10(4) of the 1972 Act; or
(b) the payer under the order, on–
   (i) the registration of an order under section 10(4) of the 1972 Act; or
   (ii) the cancellation of the registration of an order under section 10(1) of that Act.

PRACTICE DIRECTION 34B – PRACTICE NOTE (TRACING PAYERS OVERSEAS)

This Practice Direction supplements FPR Part 34

Difficulties can arise where a person in this country wishes to take proceedings under the Maintenance Orders (Facilities for Enforcement) Act 1920 or Part I of the Maintenance Orders (Reciprocal Enforcement) Act 1972 to obtain or enforce a maintenance order against a payer living overseas whose address is unknown to the applicant.

To mitigate these difficulties, arrangements have now been made with the appropriate authorities in Australia, Canada, New Zealand and South Africa, whereby the court may on request ask the authorities in those countries to make enquiries with a view to tracing the whereabouts of the payer. The following procedure should be followed.

On or before an application is made for a provisional maintenance order, or for transmission of an absolute maintenance order under the above Acts by an applicant who does not know the payer's actual address in either Australia, Canada, New Zealand or South Africa, there should be completed and lodged with the [district judge] a questionnaire, in duplicate, ([Principal] Registry Form D312 or county court Form D85 as appropriate) obtainable from the registry or court office, together with a written undertaking from the solicitor (or from the applicant if acting in person) that any address of the payer received in response to the enquiries will not be disclosed or used except for the purpose of the proceedings.

This Note is issued [in its original form] with the concurrence of the Lord Chancellor.

PRACTICE DIRECTION 35A – MEDIATION DIRECTIVE

This Practice Direction supplements FPR rule 35.2 (Relevant disputes: applications for consent orders in respect of financial remedies)

1.1 An application for an order to which rule 35.2 applies must be completed in English or accompanied by a translation into English.
1.2. Where the application is supported by evidence of explicit consent to the application by a party, the evidence must also be in English or accompanied by a translation into English.

1.3. Where a party chooses to write to the court consenting to the making of the order the correspondence must be in English or accompanied by a translation into English.

PRACTICE DIRECTION 36A – TRANSITIONAL ARRANGEMENTS

This Practice Direction supplements FPR Part 36

Content of this Practice Direction

1.1 This Practice Direction deals with the application of the FPR to proceedings started before 6th April 2011 ('existing proceedings').

1.2 In this Practice Direction 'the previous rules' means, as appropriate, the Rules of the Supreme Court 1965 and County Court Rules 1981 as in force immediately before 26 April 1999, and–

the Maintenance Orders (Facilities for Enforcement) Rules 1922;

the Magistrates' Courts (Guardianship of Minors) Rules 1974;

the Magistrates' Courts (Reciprocal Enforcement of Maintenance Orders) Rules 1974;

the Magistrates' Courts (Reciprocal Enforcement of Maintenance Orders) (Republic of Ireland) Rules 1976;

the Magistrates' Courts (Child Abduction and Custody) Rules 1986;

the Magistrates' Courts (Civil Jurisdiction and Judgments Act 1982) Rules 1986;

the Magistrates' Courts (Reciprocal Enforcement of Maintenance Orders) (Hague Convention Countries) Rules 1986;

the Family Proceedings Courts (Children Act 1989) Rules 1991;

the Family Proceedings Courts (Matrimonial Proceedings etc.) Rules 1991 (in so far as those rules do not relate to enforcement or variation of orders);

the Magistrates' Courts (Costs Against Legal Representatives in Civil Proceedings) Rules 1991 (in so far as those rules relate to family proceedings);

the Family Proceedings Rules 1991;

the Family Proceedings Courts (Child Support Act 1991) Rules 1993;

the Magistrates' Courts (Reciprocal Enforcement of Maintenance Orders) (United States of America) Rules 1995 (subject to the saving in paragraph 3.6 of this Practice Direction);

the Magistrates' Courts (Hearsay Evidence in Civil Proceedings) Rules 1999 (in so far as those rules relate to family proceedings); and the Family Procedure (Adoption) Rules 2005,

as in force immediately before 6th April 2011.

General scheme of transitional arrangements

2.1 The general scheme is–
   (a)   to apply the FPR to existing proceedings so far as is practicable; but
   (b)   where this is not practicable, to apply the previous rules to such proceedings.

Where the previous rules will normally apply

General principle

3.1 Where an initiating step has been taken in a case before 6th April 2011, in particular a step using forms or other documentation required by the previous rules, the case will proceed in the first instance under the previous rules. Where a party must take a step in response to something done by another party in accordance with the previous rules, that step must also be in accordance with those rules.

Responding to old process

3.2 A party who is served with an old type of originating process (for example, an originating summons) on or after 6th April 2011 must respond in accordance with the previous rules and the instructions on any forms received.

Filing and service of pleadings where old process served

3.3 Where a case has been begun by an old type of originating process (whether served before or after 6th April 2011), filing and service of pleadings will continue according to the previous rules.

Pre-commencement order inconsistent with FPR

3.4 Where a court order has been made before 6th April 2011, that order must still be complied with on or after that date.

Steps taken before commencement

3.5 Where a party has, before 6th April 2011, taken any step in the proceedings in accordance with the previous rules, that step will remain valid on or after that date, and a party will not normally be required to take any action that would amount to taking such a step again under the FPR.

Saving – Reciprocal enforcement of maintenance orders (United States of America)

3.6 Where, by virtue of article 6(2) of the Reciprocal Enforcement of Maintenance Orders (United States of America) Order 2007, the Reciprocal Enforcement of Maintenance (United States of America) Order 1995 continues in full force and effect, the Magistrates' Courts (Reciprocal Enforcement of Maintenance Orders) (United States of America) Rules 1995 shall, notwithstanding any provision in the FPR, continue to apply as if they had not been amended by the Magistrates' Courts (Reciprocal Enforcement of Maintenance Orders) (Miscellaneous Amendment) Rules 1995.

Where the FPR will normally apply

General principle

4.1 Where a new step is to be taken in any existing proceedings on or after 6th April 2011, it is to be taken under the FPR.

Part 1 (Overriding objective) to apply

4.2 Part 1 of the FPR (Overriding objective) will apply to all existing proceedings from 6th April 2011 onwards.

Issuing of application forms after the FPR come into force

4.3 (1)   The general rule is that–
    (a)   only application forms under the FPR will be issued by the court on or after 6th April 2011; and
    (b)   if a request to issue an old type of form or originating process (summons, etc.) is received at the court on or after 6th April 2011, it will be returned unissued.

(2) By way of exception to the general rule, the court may in cases of urgency direct that the form or process is to be issued as if the request to issue it had been a request to issue an application form under the FPR and, if it does so, the court may make such supplementary directions as it considers appropriate.

First time before a court on or after 6th April 2011

4.4 (1) When proceedings come before a court (whether at a hearing or on paper) for the first time on or after 6th April 2011, the court may direct how the FPR are to apply to the proceedings and may disapply certain provisions of the FPR. The court may also give case management directions.
(2) The general presumption will be that the FPR will apply to the proceedings from then on unless the court directs or this practice direction provides otherwise.
(3) If an application has been issued before 6th April 2011 and the hearing of the application has been set on or after that date, the general presumption is that the application will be decided having regard to the FPR.
(4) When the first occasion on which existing proceedings are before a court on or after 6th April 2011 is a hearing of a substantive issue, the general presumption is that the hearing will be conducted according to the FPR.

Costs

4.5 (1) Any assessment of costs that takes place on or after 6th April 2011 will be in accordance with FPR Part 28 and the provisions of the Civil Procedure Rules as applied by that Part.
(2) However, the general presumption is that no costs for work undertaken before 6th April 2011 will be disallowed if those costs would have been allowed on detailed assessment before that date.
(3) The decision as to whether to allow costs for work undertaken on or after 6th April 2011 will generally be taken in accordance with FPR Part 28 and the provisions of the Civil Procedure Rules as applied by that Part.